THE NEW
FUNK & WAGNALLS
ENCYCLOPEDIA

PAINTINGS BY
LEONARDO DA VINCI
Above: "Mona Lisa."
Right: "Madonna of the Rocks."

As a boy James Watt became interested in steam pressure by observing a boiling teakettle.

George Washington, first President of the United States (painting by Gilbert Stuart)

In the early days of whale fishery men harpooned the giant sea mammals from small boats.

PAINTINGS BY
JAMES WHISTLER
At right: "The Little White Girl." Below: "The Artist's Mother."

THE NEW
FUNK & WAGNALLS
ENCYCLOPEDIA

VOLUME 35

VESSELS—WHITE SLAVE TRAFFIC

Prepared Under the Editorial Direction of
JOSEPH LAFFAN MORSE, Sc. B., LL. B.

With an Editorial Staff of Experts and with the Help of Leading Scholars, Scientists, and Educators, United States and Foreign Government Agencies, Museums, Libraries, Research Laboratories, and Industrial Organizations

Based on the Funk & Wagnalls New Standard Encyclopedia compiled under the editorship of the late FRANK H. VIZETELLY

UNICORN PUBLISHERS, INC., NEW YORK

☆

Copyright 1950 And 1951,
FUNK & WAGNALLS COMPANY

★

Funk & Wagnalls New Standard Encyclopedia
Copyright 1931, 1934, 1935, 1937, 1942, 1943, 1944,
1945, 1946, 1947, 1948 And 1949
By Funk & Wagnalls Company

Printed in the United States of America
ALL RIGHTS RESERVED

★

Copyright Under the Articles of the Copyright Convention
of the Pan-American Republics and the United States

CEA

THE NEW
FUNK & WAGNALLS
ENCYCLOPEDIA

LIST OF ABBREVIATIONS USED

abbr., abbreviated
A.D., Anno Domini
alt., altitude
A.M., ante meridiem
anc., ancient
approx., approximately
Ar., Arabic
AS., Anglo-Saxon
A.S.S.R., Autonomous Soviet Socialist Republic
at.no., atomic number
at.wt., atomic weight
b., born
B.C., before Christ
b.p., boiling point
B.T.U., British Thermal Unit
Bulg., Bulgarian
C., centigrade, syn. Celsius
cap., capital
cent., century
Chin., Chinese
cm., centimeter
Co., County
colloq., colloquial
cu., cubic
Czech., Czechoslovakian
d., died
Dan., Danish
Du., Dutch
E., east, easterly, eastern
ed., edition
e.g., for example
Egypt., Egyptian
Eng., English
est., estimated
et seq., and following
F., Fahrenheit
fl., flourished
fr., from

Fr., French
ft., foot
Gael., Gaelic
Gen., General
Ger., German
Gr., Greek
Heb., Hebrew
Hind., Hindustani
Hon., Honorable
h.p., horsepower
hr., hour
Hung., Hungarian
I., Island
i.e., that is
in., inch
Ind., Indian
Ir., Irish
It., Italian
Jr., junior
kg., kilogram
km., kilometer
lat., latitude
Lat., Latin
lb., pound
lit., literally
long., longitude
m., mile
M., Middle
min., minute
M.L., Medieval Latin
mm., millimeter
mod., modern
m.p., melting point
M.P., Member of Parliament
m.p.h., miles per hour
Mt., Mount, Mountain
N., north, northerly, northern
N.T., New Testament
OE., Old English

OF., Old French
OHG., Old High German
ON., Old Norse
ONF., Old Norman French
O.T., Old Testament
oz., ounce
P.M., post meridiem
Pol., Polish
pop., population
Port., Portuguese
pron., pronounced
q.v., which see
R., River
Rev., Reverend
Rom., Romanian
Russ., Russian
S., south, southerly, southern
sec., second
Skr., Sanskrit
Sp., Spanish
sp.gr., specific gravity
sq., square
S.S.R., Soviet Socialist Republic
Sum., Sumerian
Sw., Swedish
syn., synonym
temp., temperature
trans., translation, translated
U.K., United Kingdom
U.N., United Nations
U.S., United States
U.S.A., United States of America
U.S.S.R., Union of Soviet Socialist Republics
var., variety
vol., volume
W., west, westerly, western
yd., yard

Note.—The official abbreviations for the States of the Union are used throughout. For academic degrees, see article DEGREE, ACADEMIC. Other abbreviations or contractions are self-explanatory.

THE NEW FUNK & WAGNALLS ENCYCLOPEDIA

VESSELS, NAVAL. Naval vessels fall into the following principal classes (AIRCRAFT CARRIERS and SUBMARINES are dealt with in separate articles).

Battle Cruiser. The battle cruiser differs from a battleship only in having a much higher speed and much thinner armor. The guns of the main battery are of the same or about the same caliber and power as those on contemporary battleships, but may be fewer in number.

Battleship. A battleship is a war vessel possessing the greatest offensive and the greatest defensive power, especially the former, which can be given to a ship without rendering inadequate such other necessary attributes as speed (up to 30 knots, but battleships are the slowest ships in the fleet), habitability, and seaworthiness. Battleships, like other surface and submarine vessels, are now called on to meet bombing attack from the air; they must have armored upper decks and strong batteries of anti-aircraft guns and must be defended in the air by accompanying aircraft as they are defended on the water by cruisers and destroyers. A ship of premier force, capable of taking its place in the line of battle in a fleet action, is known as a capital ship.

Cruisers. Cruisers, a lighter type of naval vessel, are built to develop high speed. Some have waterline belts of thin armor, 3 to 5 inches thick, and some have part or all of the main battery guns in lightly armored turrets or gun houses.

Destroyer. Vessels of this type were originally designed to drive off or destroy torpedo boats, hence the name. The destroyer has become the greatest protector of large vessels against submarine attack. These boats are equipped with torpedoes, depth charges, and 5-inch guns. Destroyers may attack every type of ship. They have high speed and a considerable cruising radius, which makes them valuable in convoy duty.

Destroyer Escort. A destroyer much larger in size than those of World War I, displacing 1300 tons and with an over-all length of 300 feet. It is designed primarily to combat U-boats.

Flotilla Leader or *Destroyer Leader.* A destroyer designed to act as flagboat for the commanding officer of a destroyer flotilla.

Mine Layer. Mine layers are of all sizes and kinds, from small launches to vessels of 5000 tons or more. The main operating deck is fitted with fore and aft tracks or trolleys on which the mines are placed when hoisted from below and from which they are dropped after being carried to the stern.

Mine Sweeper. As mines are usually anchored so as to be held 12 feet or more below the surface, it is highly desirable that mine sweepers should draw less than 12 feet of water; 3 or 4 feet less is practicable. British steam trawlers, used normally in the fisheries, proved efficient sweepers in World War I when fitted with proper appliances. The boats specially built for sweeping were of 750 to 800 tons with a draft of 7 feet and had about 16 knots speed; one third were paddle steamers and the others had twin screws.

Monitors. The monitors built and used during World War I were shallow-draft armored vessels of moderate speed, used chiefly on the Belgian coast. Most of them had a single turret with guns of 6- to 15-inch caliber.

Patrol Boats. Probably 2000 of these were used in World War I by the Allies alone. They were of every conceivable type of small craft, yachts, motor boats, old torpedo boats, small destroyers, and boats built for the service. Of the latter were the P boats of Great Britain and the Ford boats built in the United States. Both types were about 600 tons. None of the Ford boats were completed in time for active service abroad.

Patrol Torpedo Boats. See TORPEDO BOATS, MOTOR.

Q Ships. These were decoy ships used by the Allies in World War I against submarines. Old merchant steamers and sailing vessels were changed into inoffensive-looking craft.

Submarine Chasers and *Convoy Escort Vessels.* Small, fast craft, similar to Britain's corvettes. Submarine chasers average about 165 feet in length, have little protection, but are heavily armed with depth charges and machine guns. Other escort vessels may be converted yachts or gun boats. All are aided in their protective duties by aircraft.

Transports. Vessels fitted for the transportation of troops, animals, or supplies.

Landing Craft. Vessels of all types and sizes, designed for specific purposes in amphibious warfare, from the 36-foot Higgins boat (similar to a speedboat with a bow which drops down to land the men) to the 327-foot L.S.T. (Landing-Ship-Tank), which has a displace-

Official Navy Photo; U.S. Army

TYPES OF VESSELS OF THE U.S. NAVY. *Top: The DE 13, a destroyer escort.* Bottom: Tanks emerging from the hold of the U.S. 77, a Landing-Ship-Tank (L.S.T.).

Official Navy Photos
TYPES OF VESSELS OF THE U.S. NAVY.
Above: The battleship Indiana.
Right: The destroyer Nicholas.
Below: The Chicago, a battle cruiser.

ment of 5500 tons and is best described as a "low-lying, shallow draft, seagoing craft".

VESTA, one of the planetoids (q.v.), the fourth to be discovered, first observed by the German astronomer H.W.M. Olbers (q.v.) in 1807. It revolves about the sun in 1325 days.

VESTA, in Roman mythology, the goddess of the hearth and the hearth fire, identified with the Greek Hestia. She was custodian of the sacred fire brought by Æneas with the Penates from Troy. This fire, kindled anew every year on the first of March, was watched day and night by the vestal virgins. To let it die out of itself was regarded as a national calamity.

VESTAL VIRGINS, in Roman antiquity, the priestesses of Vesta. There were originally four vestals, selected by the king, and later six selected by the Pontifex Maximus. They were vowed to 30 years of service as virgins (10 of learning, 10 of performance, and 10 of teaching). A vestal who broke her vow of chastity was buried alive. To be eligible a girl had to be over six and under ten years of age; her father and mother both had to be living; she had to be without mental or physical defects; and, finally, she had to be a daughter of a free-born citizen resident in Italy. They were busy with exacting duties, chief among which were the guarding and annual renewing of the sacred fire. In return they enjoyed many privileges.

VESTED RIGHT, in the law of property in England and the United States, a phrase designating a presently held, settled, and absolute right or interest in property, as opposed to a contingent or prospective right subject to be defeated by a condition precedent or otherwise. Originally, the term had application only to real property, but is applied today also to rights in personal property. A vested right may be held in both an estate in possession or an estate in expectancy (an estate in possession is one which entitles the owner to immediate possession of the property, whereas an estate in expectancy is one in which the right of possession is postponed to a future time). Full ownership of property or of a life estate in property are examples of vested rights in estates in possession. Examples of vested rights in estates in expectancy are those held in a vested remainder or reversion (qq.v.), or in a future estate dependent on a precedent estate when a person in being would have an immediate right to the possession of the property on termination of the precedent estate.

For the security of property interests and the general welfare, the law jealously protects vested rights, and does not permit their destruction or their holders to be hindered in the full enjoyment of them, except for the public good, and then only upon just compensation. The Fifth Amendment of the United States Constitution provides that no person shall be deprived of property without due process of law, but as this clause was construed to be a restraint upon the Federal government only, it became necessary to incorporate in the Fourteenth Amendment a prohibition against such action by any State. These constitutional provisions make vested rights secure from unwarranted attack by legislation. However, the determination of what constitutes a vested right is often a matter requiring interpretation by the courts, and in a number of instances it has been held that even such rights may be divested by reason of public necessity or welfare. See DUE PROCESS OF LAW.

VESTERVIK, town of Kalmar County, Sweden, situated about 125 miles s.s.w. of Stockholm. It has iron, metal, and electrical industries. Pop., about 12,500.

VESTIBULE, a term designating either an entrance lobby preceding a more important interior space for general circulation and communication, or a lobby or small antechamber in the interior of a building. In dwellings and small buildings it is the space between the outer or storm door and the inner entrance door. Its function is, first, to provide an intermediate space between the outdoor air and the interior of the building, so that the wind, rain, heat, or cold from out of doors may not penetrate the building with every entrance or exit of one or more persons; secondly, to form an approach or gradual transition from the exterior architecture to that of the interior; thirdly (this especially in ancient Roman buildings), to provide a waiting place sheltered and enclosed for persons awaiting admission to the house or hall. In this sense the term is also often applied to an anteroom between a public hall and an important office or suite, and to the lobby between the public hall of an apartment house and the private hall or corridor of any of the apartments. The narthex of a church or basilica is also called the vestibule.

VESTIGIAL STRUCTURES, rudimentary, functionless organs which are homologous with fully developed, functional organs in related organisms. Biologists believe that vestigial structures were, at some time in the evolutionary development of a species, essential functioning parts which lost their utility during the ensuing period but are nevertheless

Italian National Tourist Office
Mount Vesuvius on the shore of the Bay of Naples, Italy

transmitted to new generations by the mechanism of heredity. Most of the recognizable vestigial structures, such as the vermiform appendix, are animal organs, but plants also possess unimportant vestiges, such as sterile stamens or pistils.

VESTMENTS, SACRED. See COSTUME, ECCLESIASTICAL.

VESTRIS, MADAME LUCIA ELIZABETH MATHEWS, *nee* BARTOLOZZI (1797–1856), English actress, born in London. She was married at the age of sixteen to Armand Vestris, a ballet master, and made her debut in Winter's *Il Ratto di Proserpina* in 1815 at the King's Theatre, London. In Paris she played Camille in *Les Horaces* with the celebrated Talma as *Horace*. Her greatest English success was as Tilla in the *Siege of Belgrade* (London, 1820). She became manager in turn of the Olympic, Covent Garden, and Lyceum theaters. Her husband deserted her in 1817. She married in 1838 Charles Mathews the younger, and with him produced at Drury Lane operas and musical productions.

VESTRY, originally, the room in which church vestments were kept, and where the clergy robed. Since meetings for parish business were sometimes held there, it came to mean also the representative and administrative body in parishes of the Church of England and of the Episcopal Church in the United States. In England vestries are either general or common, i.e., composed of all the parishioners who are ratepayers, or select, i.e., composed of representative parishioners.

The vestry in American parishes is a much more highly developed body with wider powers. They, together with two wardens, are elected by the members of the congregation at the annual parish meeting to serve for one year. The rector is ex officio a member of the vestry, and is entitled to preside, if present, at all its meetings. The function of the vestry is to represent the congregation in law, to have charge and care of its property, and to collect and disperse its revenues. The vestry choose and call a rector and make provision for his support. If the rector proves unworthy or incompetent, they may make complaint to the bishop of the diocese, but they may not themselves remove him. In some dioceses the vestry, instead of the body of parishioners, elect the lay deputies to represent the parish in the convention or council of the diocese.

VESUVIANITE or **IDOCRASE,** a crystalline, subtransparent to translucent mineral composed mainly of calcium aluminum silicate, $Ca_{10}Al_4Si_9O_{34}(OH)$, and crystallizing in the tetragonal system. It has a hardness of 6.5, a specific gravity of 3.35 to 3.45, and shines with a vitreous to resinous luster. The color ranges from green or brown to yellow, blue, and red; when colored blue by the action of copper, the mineral is known as *cyprine*. Vesuvianite was first discovered in the lava flows of Mount Vesuvius. It is also found in crystalline limestones, in association with such minerals as garnet, wollastonite, diopside, and tourmaline, and contains varying amounts of magnesium, iron, boron, or fluorine. Important deposits of vesuvianite occur in Switzerland, Norway, N. Italy, and Mexico, and in the vicinity of the Ural Mountains and the Vilyuy River in central Siberia. Lesser deposits are found in E. Canada. In the United States, the mineral is found in metamorphic deposits in California, Maine, New York, and New Jersey. A compact, green variety, known as *californite,* occurs in Siskiyou, Fresno, and Tulare counties of California. The mineral is used chiefly as a semiprecious stone in jewelry.

VESUVIUS, a volcano near the eastern shore of the Bay of Naples, about 10 m. from the city of Naples. It is a solitary mountain rising from the plain of Campania, with a base about 30 m. in circumference, and surmounted by two summits, of which the higher is the cone known as Vesuvius proper. On August 24, 79 A.D., a great eruption of Vesuvius began, the top of the mountain being blown off by an explosion and the cities of Herculaneum, Pompeii, and Stabiae being overwhelmed by a rain of ashes, lapilli, and mud. No lava was ejected in this eruption, nor in any subsequent eruption until 1066. In 1794 a violent outbreak destroyed the town of Torre del Greco. Following numerous smaller outbreaks, a violent eruption took place in April, 1906, lasting ten days and causing great destruction of property and the loss of 2000 lives. Smaller outbreaks occurred in 1913 and in each year from 1926 to 1929.

The present height of Vesuvius is a little over 4000 feet, while that of Somma, the lesser summit, is 3730 feet. A funicular railroad has been built from the base of the cinder cone to the summit near the edge of the crater, while an observatory is maintained near the crater. See POMPEII.

VESZPREM, administrative center of the county of the same name, Hungary, situated about 25 m. by rail s.w. of Stuhlweissenburg. The town lies in a coal-mining and agricultural region. Iron making and the manufacture of cement, brick, soap, and wool textiles are important industries. The chief articles of trade are wine, fruit, and timber. Among points of interest in the town is a cathedral dating from the 14th century. Area of county, 1527 sq.m.; pop., about 243,000. Pop. of town, about 18,000.

VETĀLAPAÑCAVIMŚATI, a collection of Sanskrit novelettes. According to the framework of the tales, King Vikrama is bidden by an ascetic to carry a corpse which hangs on a certain tree to a graveyard where certain magic rites are to be performed which will give the monarch supernatural powers. While bearing this corpse, complete silence is enjoined on the king. As Vikrama carries the body, a Vetāla, or demon, which enters corpses, tells him a story, which ends in a problem that he asks the king to solve. Vikrama inadvertently answers, and the corpse returns immediately to the tree. This continues until the Vetāla has told twenty-five stories. The tales are of much interest, and the entire work bears a marked resemblance to the two other principal Sanskrit collections of like genre, the *Siṁhāsanadvātriṁśikā,* or *Thirty-two Stories of the Lion-Throne* and the *Sukasaptati,* or *Seventy Stories of a Parrot.*

VETCH, common name applied to annual, biennial, or perennial, herbs of the genus *Vicia* belonging to the Pea family. The genus, which contains approximately 30 species, is native to the Northern Hemisphere and South America, and is cultivated throughout the world. The blue, violet, yellow, or white axillary flowers have a five-parted calyx, a five-lobed corolla, one solitary and nine united stamens, and a solitary pistil. The fruit is a dehiscent pod, containing flat or globular seeds. Vetches are important in soil management; when plowed under the plants add both nitrogen and humus to the soil. Common or spring vetch, *V. sativa,* also called tare, is an annual or biennial prostrate herb native to Eurasia and cultivated in Europe and s.e. and w. United States as an important forage crop. It bears showy, purple and rose-colored flowers, and produces seeds which are used in making flour. Hairy, sand, or Russian vetch, *V. villosa,* is an annual, biennial, or perennial herb native to Eurasia. It bears violet-blue and white flowers, and is planted for fodder in dry, open soils of the U.S. The bitter vetch, *V. ervilia,* is an annual herb native to Europe. It bears rose-colored flowers, and serves as a winter green-manure crop in California; see GREEN MANURING. The smooth, reddish-brown seeds are used in many countries as feed for livestock. The broad bean, horse bean, or Windsor bean, *V. faba,* also known as the English dwarf bean, is an erect annual found in N. Africa and s.w. Asia, and grows to a height of

4 feet. It bears dull-white, blue, and black-spotted flowers, and is used in the U.S. as a winter-vegetable or green-manure crop, and for feeding cattle. The large, flat seeds are used in Europe for human consumption. The American vetch, *V. americana,* is a trailing or climbing perennial native to moist areas of northern U.S. It bears purplish flowers and reaches a height of 3 feet.

VETCH, SAMUEL (1668–1732), the first British governor of Nova Scotia, born near Edinburgh, Scotland. He was educated at Utrecht, and returned to England in 1688 with Prince William of Orange. A plan for the capture of Canada proposed by him in 1708 was accepted by the British government, but was never carried out. Subsequently, as the representative of the colonists, he induced the government to undertake an expedition against Port Royal (now Annapolis, Nova Scotia). Vetch was one of the commanders of this expedition, and after the capture of Port Royal in October, 1710, he became governor of the conquered territory, part of which was now renamed Nova Scotia. In 1711 he was besieged in Port Royal by the French, but was relieved by the approach of a British squadron. He was again governor in 1715–17.

VETERANS' ADMINISTRATION, an independent agency of the U.S. government, established by Congressional enactment in July, 1930. The "V.A.", as the Administration is popularly called, is authorized to administer all Federal laws relating to the various benefits established by Congress for former members of the armed forces, and for the dependents and beneficiaries of deceased former members of the armed forces. The most important veterans' benefits administered by the V.A. include vocational rehabilitation and education; pensions; the guaranty of loans for the purchase or construction of homes, farms, and business property; readjustment allowances for unemployed veterans; National Service and U.S. Government life-insurance benefits; death benefits; emergency and certain other officers' retirement pay; and physical examinations, hospital and outpatient treatment, and domiciliary care. The V.A. also administers that section of the Soldiers' and Sailors' Civil Relief Act relating to private insurance policies held by persons on active duty in the armed forces.

At the head of the V.A. is the administrator of veterans' affairs, an official appointed by the President with the approval of the Senate. Under the supervision of the administrator, the specific tasks of the V.A. are carried out by a number of assistant administrators and other subordinate officials. The assistant administrator for claims is charged with the administration of laws relating to disability compensation and pension claims; emergency officers' retirement claims; reserve officers' retirement pay; death compensation and pension claims; insurance and adjusted compention claims filed by beneficiaries of deceased veterans; and various other types of claims. In a recent year, the V.A. was paying monthly compensation and pensions to more than 2,260,000 veterans and to more than 955,000 dependents of deceased veterans; the monthly disability payments ranged from $13.80 to $360 per month. Appeals concerning claims for benefits filed by veterans and veterans' dependents are adjudicated by the Board of Veterans' Appeals. Plans and policies relating to the acquisition, construction, utilization, and maintenance of real property required by the V.A. including supplies and equipment, are formulated by the assistant administrator for construction, supply, and real estate. The assistant administrator for finance directs all financial activities of the V.A., the most important of which are the payment of benefits and of administrative expenses incurred in connection therewith. The administration of insurance laws affecting veterans is the responsibility of the assistant administrator for insurance, under whose supervision broad studies are conducted of insurance experience and practice throughout the field of commercial life insurance as well as within the Federal government. Almost 7,000,000 National Service Life Insurance policies were in force, and were administered by the V.A. in a recent year.

The assistant administrator for legislation is charged with the handling of all matters pertaining to proposed legislation, executive orders, and proclamations affecting the V.A.; he also supervises the preparation of compilations of Federal enactments relating to veterans' affairs, and the preparation of relevant pamphlets, résumés, press releases, and other documents. The assistant administrator for vocational rehabilitation and education is responsible for the determination of the eligibility and the extent of entitlement of veterans to the educational and vocational-training benefits provided by law; for the advisement and guidance of veterans seeking education and vocational rehabilitation; for the preparation of a roster of training facilities; for the prescription of vocational-rehabilitation courses designed to restore employability lost by reason of service-incurred disabilities; and for supervising the training and education of disabled and other

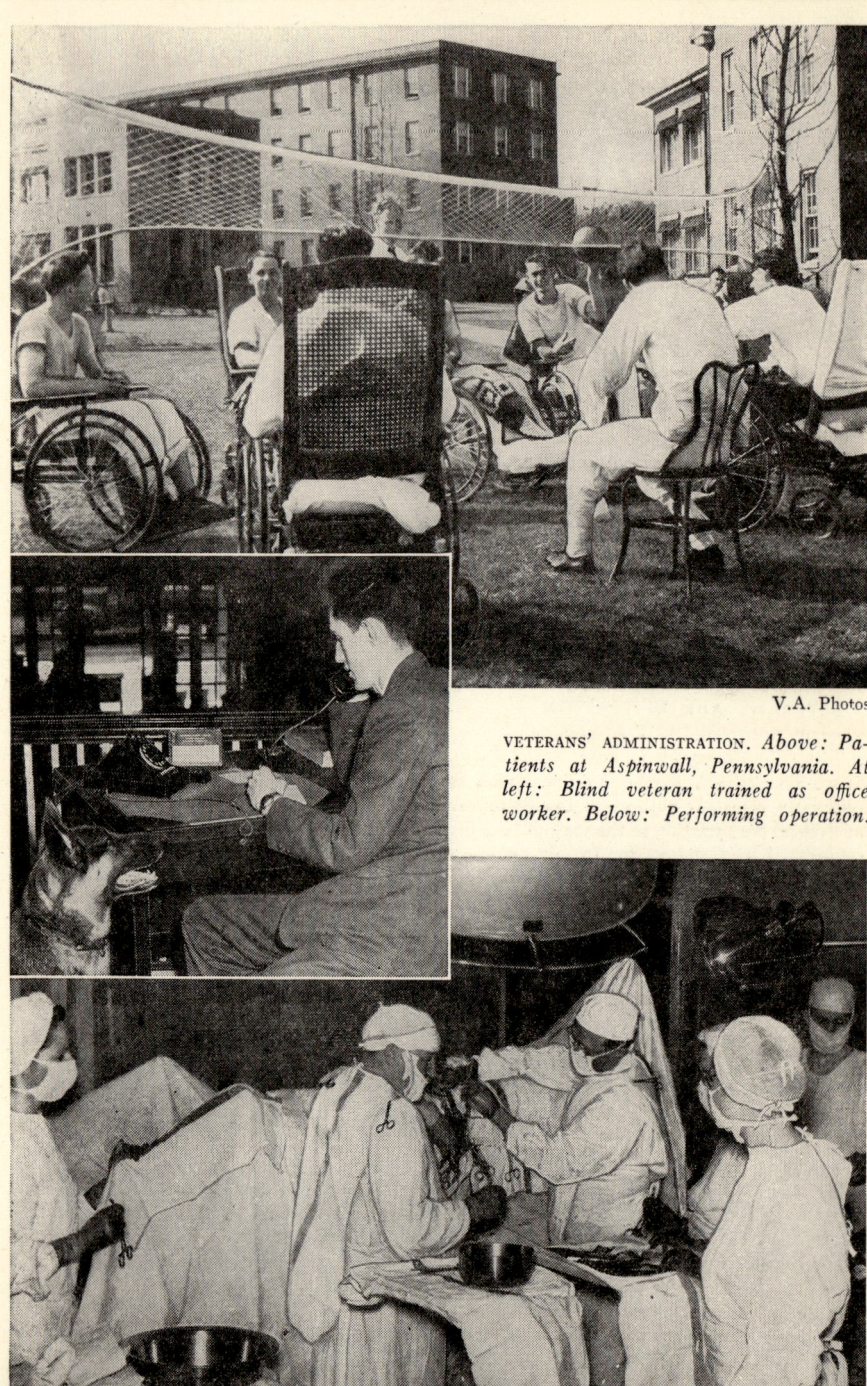

V.A. Photos

VETERANS' ADMINISTRATION. *Above: Patients at Aspinwall, Pennsylvania. At left: Blind veteran trained as office worker. Below: Performing operation.*

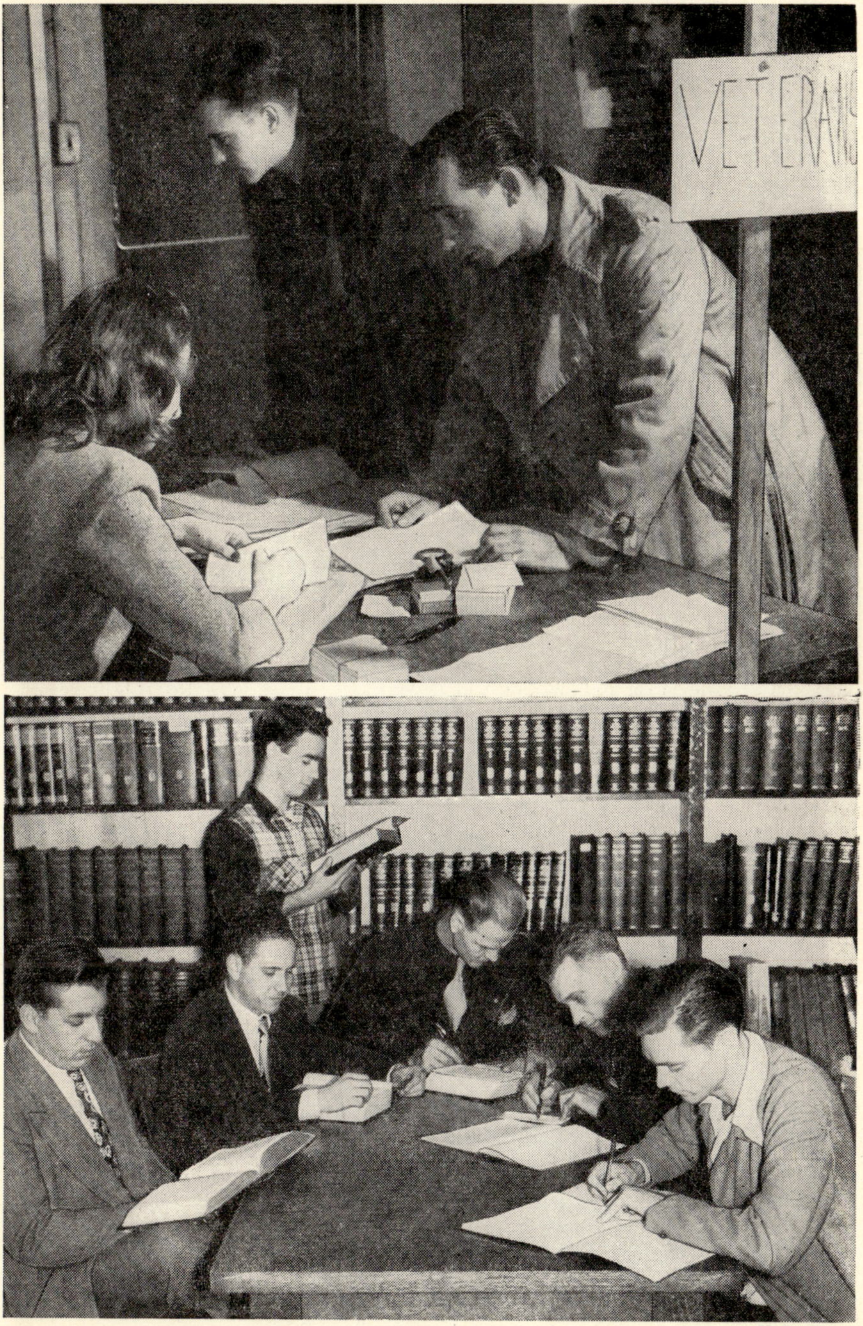

VETERANS' ADMINISTRATION. *Top: Veterans enrolling at George Washington University under the G.I. Bill of Rights. Bottom: Veterans studying at the same university.*

veterans. The terms under which veterans are accepted for education and vocational training are set forth principally in the Servicemen's Readjustment Act of 1944, popularly known as the "G.I. Bill of Rights" (q.v.). Veterans are permitted to select their places of study or job-training establishments, subject to the approval of the selected institution by appropriate agencies of the respective State governments. Education or training may be carried on for one year plus a period equal to the time served in the armed forces between September 16, 1940, and July 25, 1947; the maximum allowable period is forty-eight months. An exception is made in the case of veterans with service-connected disabilities, who are permitted to remain in training for as long as is necessary to restore their ability to work, up to a maximum of four years. Veteran-students and job-trainees are eligible for the following maximum subsistence allowances: for full-time students, $75 per month to those without dependents, $105 with one dependent, and $120 with more than one dependent; for job-trainees, $65 without dependents and $90 with one or more dependents.

The Department of Medicine and Surgery, headed by the chief medical director, is responsible for providing complete medical and hospital services for veterans. The Department formulates policies governing the professional and physical standards and training of its personnel; the standards of medical, surgical, and dental examinations and care, and of nursing care; and the use of prosthetic appliances and sensory aids. Within the purview of the Department are the supervision and co-ordination of the hospital, domiciliary, and outpatient services of the V.A., and of its pharmaceutical, dietetic, and social-service facilities. It also develops policies relating to medical research, including clinical and laboratory research. In co-operation with the Department of Medicine and Surgery, the assistant administrator for special services plans and carries out a program designed primarily to help the hospitalized veteran-patient to recover, chiefly by furnishing recreational and welfare services and facilities.

The plans, policies, and procedures formulated by the foregoing officials and agencies of the V.A. are implemented by regional and district offices, hospital V.A. centers, and V.A. domiciliary centers situated in various parts of the United States, Alaska, the Territory of Hawaii, the Philippines, and Puerto Rico. The district and regional offices comprise organizational elements of the V.A. concerned with granting the benefits and services provided by law for veterans and their dependents and beneficiaries residing within specific areas. The district offices are normally responsible for large areas, often covering several States, while the regional offices are local in scope. In a recent year, thirteen district and seventy regional offices were in operation. V.A. hospitals are of three general types: general medical and surgical (designated G.M.&S.), neuropsychiatric (N.P.), and tuberculosis (T.B.). These designations indicate merely the major type of treatment afforded by the individual hospitals; usually, the hospitals are equipped to render more than one type of treatment, and some hospitals have facilities for highly specialized services such as those for tumors, chest surgery, neurosurgery, and paraplegia. The V.A. operated a total of 130 hospitals in a recent year. Veterans are admitted to the hospitals under the following priority system: first, emergency cases; second, veterans with illnesses or disabilities incurred in or aggravated by military service; and third, those who state under oath that they are unable to pay hospital charges for the treatment of non-service-connected ailments. About 95,000 beds were occupied in the V.A. hospitals in a recent year, and an additional 12,000 beds in non-V.A. hospitals were used by the V.A. for eligible veterans.

The function of the V.A. domiciliary centers is to provide a home, domiciliary care, and medical treatment to those veterans who, while unable because of their disabilities to care for themselves, do not require the nursing service, constant medical supervision, and medical treatment furnished by hospitals. Of the sixteen domiciliary centers operated by the V.A. in a recent year, all but three were functioning in conjunction with V.A. hospitals. The organizational element comprising a jointly operated hospital and domiciliary center is designated a V.A. center, as are the organizational elements comprising a hospital and a regional office. In addition to the thirteen V.A. centers consisting of hospitals and domiciliary centers, eleven V.A. centers composed of hospitals and regional offices were in operation in a recent year.

VETERANS OF FOREIGN WARS OF THE UNITED STATES. Founded in 1899, the association served (1945) the welfare of more than 1,200,000 members through about 4500 posts in the United States and territories as well as in the Far East, on Midway Island, and in occupied France. Eligibility requirements include service on foreign soil or in hostile waters in a

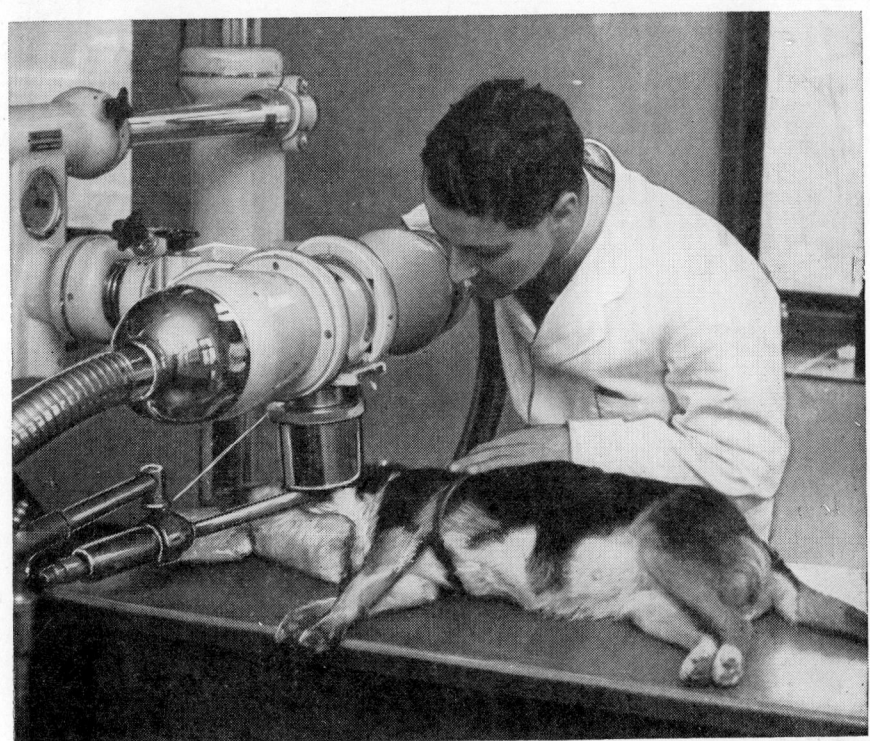

VETERINARY MEDICINE. *Dog being given X-ray treatment for a tumor in its neck.*

campaign for which the U.S. government has authorized a medal. All oversea veterans of World War II are eligible (since Dec. 6, 1941). Headquarters are in Kansas City, Mo. A National Home for widows and orphans is located in Eton Rapids, Mich.

VETERANS' PENSIONS. Under a series of enactments passed by Congress at various periods in United States history, provision was made for the financial compensation of veterans disabled while in military service, and of the dependents of persons killed while on active duty in the military services. The compensation and pension systems are administered by the Veterans' Administration (q.v.). In a recent year, pensions and disability compensation payments were being paid to disabled veterans and dependents of deceased veterans of the Mexican War, Indian Wars, Civil War, Spanish-American War, World War I, and World War II. The number of individuals receiving payment ranges from a few dependents of deceased veterans of the Mexican War to nearly two million persons receiving payment in connection with World War II. In addition, pensions were paid to almost 57,000 former members of the regular military establishment. The monthly disability payments ranged from $13.80 to $360. The total amount disbursed by the Veterans' Administration for pensions and disability compensation payments by a recent year was in excess of two billion dollars.

VETERINARY MEDICINE. The first systematic book on the diseases of animals was written by Vegetius, *De Arte Veterinaria,* in the 4th century, a work which became the oracle of succeeding ages. The first step toward the establishment of the art as a science was taken in 1761, by the founding of a veterinary college in Lyons. Later schools were established at Alfort (1766), Copenhagen (1773), Vienna (1777), Marburg (1789), Berlin (1790), London (1792), Madrid (1793), St. Petersburg (1808), Stockholm (1820), Edinburgh (1825), and New York City (1857).

In the United States the best veterinary schools are now connected with State universities or other institutions of learning. Among the more important of these are the universi-

VETERINARY MEDICINE. *Professor demonstrating method of examining the throat of a cow.*

ties of Pennsylvania, Cornell, and Ohio. In connection with a number of the agricultural colleges, courses in veterinary science are given and veterinary degrees are granted.

The American Veterinary Medical Association, founded in 1863, has headquarters in Detroit, Mich.

Modern veterinary medicine has been placed upon the same basis as human medicine and similar methods of investigation are employed. The veterinary investigator has found a most fruitful field in the pathology of organic, constitutional, functional, and infectious diseases of animals, as well as in bacteriology, methods of vaccination and immunization, and animal hygiene and methods of disinfection. Systematic investigations have been made in veterinary pharmacology and toxicology (including mineral and plant poisons). The field now includes meat and milk inspection, and establishment of quarantine, regulating traffic in livestock, and stamping out animal plagues, as well as general practice. While in the past there was most demand for the practitioner's services in connection with the horse, the raising of more improved stock and the increased value of livestock in general have caused greater attention to be given to their ailments and to providing proper conditions of hygiene for them. In large cities there are specialists in the diseases of dogs, cats, and other pets. The establishment of veterinary schools has done much to promote the science.

Great changes have taken place in veterinary practice. In place of the indiscriminate use of firing iron, purgation, and bloodletting, we have a more rational system of treatment on a humane basis. Moreover, the excessive use of drugs has been abandoned and more attention given to the proper care and diet of animals and to preventive medicine. The course and severity of most diseases may be greatly modified by the use of pure water and wholesome food in reasonable quantities. Careful attention to the temperature and ventilation of stables is also important, especially in the treatment of diseases of the respiratory organs. It is along the line of preventive medicine, however, that the greatest progress has been made. Successful methods of vaccination and immunization have been devised for the prevention of such diseases as anthrax, blackleg, hydrophobia, Texas fever, rinderpest, hog cholera, and tetanus, and much use is made of serodiagnosis—especially complement fixation, which is employed in glanders, dourine, contagious abortion, Malta fever, and hemorrhagic septicemia. The period of incubation of various diseases has been definitely determined and upon the data thus obtained quarantine regulations for dealing with infectious diseases have been formulated. The importance of isolating diseased animals and thoroughly disinfecting the premises after the occurrence of animal plagues is well understood. The adoption of such measures tends to restrict the spread of any epizootic. Sometimes great losses to the animal industry of a country have been avoided apparently by the application of very drastic methods of eradication, including the destruction and disposal of all affected animals. Such measures are usually accompanied with the payment of an indemnity by the government. Great advances have been made in methods of disinfection by means of corrosive sublimate, formalin, live steam, lime, copper sulphate, lysol, carbolic acid, and other antiseptics. The development of antisepsis has yielded as important results in veterinary practice as in human surgery. In ordinary veterinary practice, however, the observance of strict antiseptic precautions is an exceedingly difficult matter.

In veterinary surgery a much larger proportion of operations are made without anesthesia than in human surgery. It is generally believed that minor operations cause less pain and inconvenience to the animal than the struggles during administration of anesthetics. Ether or chloroform is used for the larger animals, and ether alone for cats and dogs. In minor operations and in determining the location of lameness cocaine is satisfactory. In veterinary practice drugs are ordinarily administered in the allopathic form. Medicines are administered by way of the mouth in the form of balls, boluses, pills, capsules, and drenches; by hypodermic, intratracheal, intravenous, intra-abdominal, or intragastric injections; or in the form of an enema.

Drug doses are usually larger than for man and vary according to the size of the animal.

As a rule veterinary dentistry is merely one branch of the ordinary practitioner's work. There are but few locations where there is demand for specialists to devote the whole of their time to this work.

VETO, in American government, the power of the executive to negate legislative acts. In spite of the tripartite division (following Montesquieu) of the functions of government in the Federal constitution of 1787 and of the determined effort of its framers to keep these functions separate, the constitution gives this (negative) legislative power to the executive.

Art. 1, Section 7, provides that every bill after passing the two legislative bodies shall, before it becomes a law, be presented to the President for his approval and signature, which make it a law, or for his disapproval (or veto) and his return of the measure to the house in which it originated; it can then become a law only if passed by a two-thirds vote in each house. But if the President does not return it within ten days (excepting Sundays) it becomes a law, unless the adjournment of Congress in the interval prevents its return, when it does not become a law—this is called a "pocket" veto.

The veto was patterned on a similar power granted to the governors of South Carolina and Massachusetts by the State constitutions of 1776 and 1780 respectively. The principle of the veto has been incorporated in all the State constitutions except that of North Carolina, where the legislative authority is vested in the legislature alone.

VETTER LAKE. See WETTER LAKE.

VEVEY (Ger. *Vivis*), a town of the canton of Vaud, Switzerland, on the Veveyse, near its influx into Lake Geneva, 11 miles E.S.E. of Lausanne. It is a tourist resort, with a magnificent view of the Valais Alps. Pop., about 13,000.

VÉZELAY, town in the department of Yonne, France. It contains the basilica of the Madeleine, dating back to an abbey founded in 864. Here St. Bernard preached the Second Crusade in 1147. Pop., about 500.

VEZIN, HERMANN (1829–1911), American actor, born in Philadelphia, Pa. He studied for the stage in England under Charles Kean, made his debut at the Theatre Royal, York, in 1850, and appeared as Pembroke in *King John* at the Princess Theatre, London, in 1852.

Ancient Roman tomb on the Via Appia

He visited the United States in 1857, but in the following year returned to England, where he settled. While chiefly known for Shakespearian roles, Vezin was also successful in modern plays.

VIA, a Roman highway, especially the military roads that served as means of communication between Rome and its provinces. As Rome was the central point of all roads, numerous branches converged there and thus even the most remote of the provinces was made easily accessible by one *via* or another. The building of these highways was entrusted, in the early years of the republic, to the censors. Augustus was particularly strict in his supervision of their construction. To him the Romans owed the employment of couriers and messengers. The roads were built in a straight line and curves avoided by lowering elevations, filling valleys, building bridges, and tunneling. To indicate the breadth of a road *sulci,* or trenches, were dug; the soil between these was removed down to solid ground, and there a bedding of road metal was used to build the highway up to the height required. The main Roman roads were from 13 feet to 15 feet wide. The road surface itself was in three parts—the middle was paved and slightly arched so that water might easily flow from it. The space on either side of the center was bedded in gravel through which the water percolated easily. Some of the roads were narrower and only eight feet wide. The footpaths (*margines*) at each side were raised and protected by a gravel covering. Frequently triumphal arches, temples, villas, and memorials to the illustrious dead were built abutting the highways.

Among the chief of the military roads were the following. *Via Appia,* called also *Regina Viarum,* was begun 312 B.C. by Appius Claudius Caecus, the censor. Its course ran from Porta Capena where it began, through Aricia, Tres Tabernæ, Apii Forum, Terracina, Fundi, Formiæ, Minturnæ, Sinuessa, Casilinum, and it ended at Capua. Later it was extended by Trajan to Beneventum and thence through Venusia, Tarentum, and Uria to Brundusium. This road was the main highway to southern Italy, to Greece, and thence to more remote eastern possessions of Rome. Brundusium (modern Brindisi) was developed into a great port and thence the Romans sailed for Greek ports.

Via Latina started from Porta Capena and had Beneventum as its ultimate point. There it joined Via Appia after passing through Anagnia, Frusino, Aquinum, Casinum, and Venafrum.

Via Labicana led from Porta Esquilina through Labicum, meeting Via Latina at Bivium, about 30 miles from Rome. *Via Prænestina,* once known as Via Gabina, beginning at Porta Esquilina, passed through Gabii and Præneste, then merged with Via Latina below Anagnia.

Via Tiburtina led to Tibur or Tivoli. It started from Porta Tiburtina and ran through the country of the Sabines, where it became *Via Valeria,* to Adria.

Via Nomentana, which derived its name from the fact that it led to the Sabine town of Nomentum, began originally at Porta Collina and later from Porta Nomentana. Crossing the Anio three miles from Rome it met the Via Salaria at Eretum. This highway bore another name, Ficulnensis, from Ficulnea, another Sabine town seven miles from Porta Nomentana.

Via Salaria ran from Porta Salaria, so named because it was used by the Sabines when they came to Rome for salt, crossed the Sabine country and Picenum leading to Reate and Asculum Picenum. Thence it led to the coast, which it threaded until it merged with Via Flaminia at Ancona.

Via Flaminia started from Porta Flaminia, and was built during the censorship of C. Flaminius and L. Æmilius Papus 220 B.C. It passed by Ocriculum (Otricoli), Interamna (Terni), Fanum Fortunae (Fano), and led to Ariminum (Rimini). There Via Æmilia began. This was built during the consulship of M. Æmilius Lepidus. It skirted Bononia (Bologna), Parma, Placentia, Mediolanum (Milan), Brixia (Brescia), Verona, Patavium (Padua), and led to Aguileia.

Via Cassia branched off Via Flaminia near Pons Milvius (Ponte Molle), passed near Veii, and crossed Etruria, until it joined Via Aurelia at Luna.

Via Aurelia started from Porta Aurelia and approached the sea at Alsium (Palo), and thence followed the coast of Etruria and Liguria. This road led to Gaul. *Via Vitellia,* another highway, started also from Porta Aurelia.

Via Ostiensis started from Porta Ostiensis and, following the left bank of the Tiber, it led to Ostia, near its mouth. From this highway branched, at a short distance from Rome, *Via Ardeatina* and *Via Laurentina*—the first leading to Ardea; the second to Laurentum.

Via Portuensis led from Porta Portuensis to Portus Trajani, near the mouth of the Tiber. One of its branch roads is *Via Campana.*

Via Severiana was a continuation of Via Ostiensis and followed the coast through Laurentum Antium and Circeii, to Terracina.

The Romans built roads over almost all of the world known to them to give employment to the people and to enable their cohorts to march in direct line toward their objective. Sometimes malefactors were condemned to work on the highways.

VIADANA, LODOVICO (1564–1645), Italian composer, credited with being the inventor (1602) of the *basso continuo,* born in Viadana, near Mantua. Little is known of his life, except for his birthplace and the facts that he became a monk, and held successive posts as organist and choirmaster in Mantua, Venice, and elsewhere. Among his numerous works may be mentioned the famous *Cento Concerti Ecclesiastici a Una, a Due, Tre e Quattro Voci, con il Basso Continuo per Sonar Nell' Organo* (1602, 1603, 1609, 1611, and 1612) and *Sinfonie Musicali a Otto Voci* (1617).

VIA DOLOROSA, the name, probably given during the Middle Ages, applied to a narrow street in Jerusalem, indicated by a doubtful tradition as the street through which Jesus carried his cross from the Hall of Judgment to Mount Calvary. The fourteen stations are marked by tablets. The locations of the tablets have varied at different times.

VIADUCT, a bridgelike structure, especially a large one of arched masonry, to carry a roadway or the like over a valley or ravine, or across another roadway. They are of every kind of construction—of wood, iron, or steel, stone, brickwork, and in recent practice reinforced concrete. In recent years, and more particularly in America, the term "viaduct" has come to mean more specifically a structure composed of a number of comparatively short spans carried by towerlike piers of steel framework. These piers usually consist of four columnlike legs spread wide apart at the base, converging toward the top, and braced together in all directions.

This construction was best typified for a great many years by a viaduct crossing Kinzua Creek in Northwestern Pennsylvania, on the Erie Railroad, which is familiarly known as the Kinzua Viaduct. The Lethbridge Viaduct on the Crow's Nest branch of the Canadian Pacific Railway in southern Alberta, a steel structure of this type, is 1 mile, 47 feet

Philip Gendreau, N.Y.
The Pulaski Skyway in northern New Jersey, a viaduct constructed of steel and concrete

in length, and 307 feet above water level. This structure is carried on thirty-three rigidly braced steel towers rising from concrete pedestals supported on concrete piles.

Two notable viaducts of a quite different type were completed (1914-15) west of Scranton, Pa., on the Lackawanna Railroad, to cross the valleys of Tunkhannock Creek and Martins Creek. The former, or Nicholson Viaduct, is one of the largest concrete bridges in the world, 2375 feet in length, comprised of 10 spans of 180 feet each and two spans of 100 feet each. It is 242 feet high.

The Pulaski Skyway, a 3-mile motor highway built over the meadows between Newark and Jersey City, New Jersey, and spanning the Passaic and Hackensack rivers, was opened to traffic on November 24, 1932.

Several smaller works of the viaduct type, such as the west Garfield Street viaduct in Seattle, Washington, indicate that the problem of relieving traffic congestion stimulates this type of construction. See BRIDGE.

VIA-MALA, a road running through a gorge in the Swiss canton of Grisons, on the course of the Rhine R. It was completed in 1824 and is carried for nearly 2 m., partly in half-open galleries, partly in a tunnel, the rock walls on either hand rising to 1600 ft.

VIARDOT-GARCÍA, MICHELLE PAULINE (1821-1910), celebrated French vocalist, born in Paris. She was the daughter of the tenor Manuel Garcia, sister of Madame Malibran, and one of Liszt's most accomplished pupils. Her concert debut was in Brussels in 1837, and her first London appearance was at the Opera House, in 1839, as Desdemona in Rossini's *Otello*. She then appeared in Italian opera at the Paris Odéon with equal success. In 1840 she married the director of the Paris Italian Opera, Louis Viardot. After her marriage she made numerous European tours, until her retirement in 1863. Her name is associated with the first performances of Meyerbeer's *Les Huguenots* and *Le Prophète,* and Gounod's *Sapho*. She sang the title roles in the revivals in Paris of Gluck's *Orphée* (1859) and *Alceste* (1861). In 1871 she settled in Paris as a teacher of singing. Her compositions include several operas, sixty popular vocal melodies, instrumental pieces, and an *École Classique de Chant.*

VIAREGGIO, Italian town and resort on the Mediterranean coast, 15 m. by rail N.W. of Pisa. There is a monument to Shelley, who was drowned near Viareggio. Pop., about 22,000.

VIATICUM (Lat., "provision for a journey"), Holy Communion administered to persons in danger of death. It may be received without fasting (as is required in all other cases) from the midnight previous, and it may be given frequently during the same sickness.

VIATKA. See VYATKA.

VIAUD, LOUIS MARIE JULIEN. See LOTI, PIERRE.

VIBERT, JEAN GEORGES (1840–1902), French genre painter, born in Paris. He first exhibited in 1863, and, after turning to genre paintings, produced "Roll Call after the Pillage", and a succession of subjects mainly drawn from the clerical life. These included, "The Cardinal's Menu", "The Missionary's Story", "The Convent under Arms", "The Wonderful Sauce", "The Antechamber of Monseigneur", and "The Startled Confessor". In 1867 Vibert was one of the five founders of the Society of French Aquarellists.

VIBORG, capital of the government of Viborg, in Jutland, Denmark, about 140 miles N.W. of Copenhagen. The foundation dates back into antiquity, when it was the main sacrificial place for N. Jutland. The cathedral, built in Romanesque style in 1130–69, rebuilt in 1864–76, is the most important granite church in the country. Pop. of government, about 140,000; of town, about 15,000.

VIBORG (Finn. *Viipuri*), a department and a fortified seaport in S.E. Karelo-Finnish S.S.R., at the mouth of the Saima Canal. The harbor is not sufficiently deep for large vessels, which anchor at Transund, about 8 miles distant. An extensive trade in lumber, dairy products, and paper is carried on. After the recognition of the independence of Finland, in January, 1918, war broke out between "White Guards" and "Red Guards", the former capturing Viborg on April 29, 1918. Pop. of department, about 663,000; of town, about 56,000.

VIBRATION, or OSCILLATION, a rapid and repeated motion back and forth past a central position called the *neutral position* or *position of equilibrium*. A single motion from one extreme position to the other and back (passing through the neutral position twice) is called a *cycle,* and the number of cycles per second is called the *frequency* of the vibration. The vibrations which are of importance in engineering generally have frequencies of from two to several hundred cycles per second; the vibrations important in physics and chemistry have frequencies up to billions of billions; see FREQUENCY. The swinging of a pendulum is a simple form of vibration, usually having a frequency of less than one per second.

Any vibrating object possesses energy of vibration; this energy is alternately in the form of kinetic energy (energy of motion) and potential energy (energy of position). When an object passes through the neutral position, it is moving rapidly and the energy is entirely kinetic; when an object reaches one of the extreme positions, it is momentarily without motion as it reverses direction and the energy is entirely potential. In the case of the pendulum, the potential energy at the extreme positions is due to the gravitational force on the body. In the case of a vibrating string (as on a violin) the potential energy is due to the elasticity of the stretched string. Many other forms of potential energy may be involved; kinetic energy, however, always involves simple motion.

The swinging pendulum or the plucked violin string eventually comes to rest if no further forces are impressed on them. The force which causes them to stop vibrating is called *damping,* and is a factor entering into every vibrating system. In these examples the damping forces are all frictional, but other damping forces, such as electrical or magnetic forces, may enter into vibrational systems.

Every object which is capable of vibrating has a *natural frequency*. For example, the natural frequency of a pendulum 39 inches long is $\frac{1}{2}$. One of the essentials of a vibration system is an impressed force causing the vibration. If swinging is initiated in a 39-inch pendulum, it swings back and forth once every 2 seconds. However, it will not swing without impetus. If the 39-inch pendulum is struck lightly once every $2\frac{1}{2}$ seconds, or every $1\frac{1}{2}$ seconds, it will move very little; but if it is struck lightly exactly once every 2 seconds, it will swing slightly more with each strike, until eventually it is swinging widely, or, in technical terms, until the *amplitude* of vibration is large. In general, vibrations of large amplitude can be caused only by a large impressed force, or by a small force impressed repeatedly with the same frequency as the natural frequency. Most of the serious vibration problems in engineering are due to the latter cause. Such problems can often be solved by changing one of the two frequencies. For example, the natural frequency of vibration of an automobile body may be the same as the frequency of explosions

European viburnum (Viburnum tinus)

in the engine when the automobile is traveling 40 miles per hour; in such a case, the body may vibrate objectionably at 40 miles per hour. Such vibration can be avoided by traveling below 35 or above 45 miles per hour, and by accelerating through this speed as rapidly as possible. It is preferable, of course, for the designing engineer to use other means of avoiding such vibration. He may, for example, adjust the body so that its natural period of vibration will correspond to a very high speed. If possible, he makes the body so stiff that its amplitude of vibration is so small as to be unobjectionable. However, the best means of solving this particular vibration problem is by *isolation*; by preventing the vibratory forces of the engine from being impressed on the body. Such isolation can be accomplished by mounting the engine on soft rubber; the rubber fails to carry the vibrations to the body, and so vibrations are kept within the engine and thus do comparatively little harm.

An exactly opposite solution has been applied to the vibration caused by certain washing machines. In this case, the vibration of the machine is likely to damage the machine itself. Therefore the machine is mounted to the floor by very stiff anchorages, so that as much as possible of the vibration is transmitted out of the machine, and into the building, and thence to the ground. In a large building such vibration is not likely to be objectionable, but an object in a far corner of the building may start vibrating violently if its natural frequency happens to be almost identical to the frequency of the washing machine.

When a vibration is damped, some of the vibration energy degenerates into heat. For example, a violin string plucked in a vacuum would eventually stop vibrating through damping due to the internal friction of the string and sounding board. When the string is plucked in air, however, the damping is much more rapid, and some of the vibration energy is transmitted to the air. It is then carried through the air in the form of a sound wave When vibration is carried from one object to another, it is always carried in the form of vibrational waves. See WAVE.

VIBRATO (It., "vibrated"), a term denoting an effect somewhat similar to tremolo. On stringed instruments it is produced by the quick oscillation of the finger on the string which it is stopping. The result is a pulsating, wavering tone. In vocal music it is a partial suppression and reinforcement of a note, producing an apparent reiteration.

VIBURNUM, a genus of plants of the Caprifoliaceae family, having a five-toothed calyx, a five-lobed, wheel-shaped, bell-shaped, or tubular corolla, five stamens, three sessile stigmas, and a one-seeded berry. The species are shrubs with simple leaves, natives chiefly of the northern parts of the world. *V. lantana,* sometimes called the wayfaring tree, is a native of the warmer temperate parts of Europe and Asia. Two North American species, *V. edule* and *V. oxycoccus,* nearly allied to the guelder-rose, produce berries of an agreeable taste, which are used like cranberries.

VICAR (Lat., "delegate"), in England, a parson of a parish where the tithes are impropriate (see IMPROPRIATION). In ecclesiastical usage the title is given to those who hold authority as the delegates or substitutes of others. Thus in the Roman Catholic Church the pope is called the Vicar of Christ. A *vicar apostolic* (formerly one to whom the pope delegated some remote portion of his jurisdiction) is now usually a titular bishop appointed to a country where either no sees have been formed or the episcopal succession has been broken. *Vicars forane* are ecclesiastics to whom a bishop gives a limited jurisdiction in a town or district of his diocese—in effect, rural deans. *Vicars-general* in the Roman Catholic Church perform the work of archdeacons. They must be clerks, not laymen, but need not be in holy orders. *Vicars choral* are assistants, cleric or lay, of the canons and prebendaries in the public services and music.

VICAR-GENERAL, the title of an ecclesiastical functionary in the Roman Catholic Church and in the Church of England. In the former a vicar-general is an ecclesiastic who is appointed to exercise, in a general way, episcopal jurisdiction in the bishop's stead, and in such manner that his acts are considered the acts of the bishop himself. In the United States a vicar-general can (unless the bishop disposes otherwise) give priests faculties, together with the cure of souls, and revoke them for just reasons. He cannot, however, erect, unite, or divide benefices or parishes, nor can he give another bishop permission to exercise pontifical functions in the diocese.

In the Church of England a vicar-general is a lay legal officer of some diocese, whose duties are practically the same as those of a chancellor.

VICE-CHANCELLOR, in England, a judge of the court of equity who is appointed by the crown under letters patent as an associate to the lord chancellor. The office was created in the reign of Henry II and later fell into disuse, but was revived by the Statute of George III, appointing one vice-chancellor, and the Act of Victoria by which two vice-chancellors were appointed, because of the increase of business on the abolition of the equitable jurisdiction of the court of exchequer. The vice-chancellor presides over a branch of the court of equity, and is authorized to perform the duties of the lord chancellor in the latter's absence or illness. The term is employed in a few of the States in the U.S., as New Jersey, to designate an associate of a chancellor of a court of equity.

The vice-chancellor of a university is an officer with authority to discharge certain duties of a chancellor, generally those connected with granting degrees in the absence of the latter. See CHANCELLOR.

VICE-CONSUL, a subordinate officer, to whom consular functions are delegated in some part of a district already under the supervision of a consul. The vice-consul acts under the supervision of the consul. See CONSUL.

VICENTE, GIL (1470–1540), founder of the Portuguese drama, born probably in Lisbon. His first production was a pastoral monologue in Spanish, which celebrated in 1502 the birth of the prince who became John III. Other pieces followed, a number of them being the religious mysteries called *autos,* and also various comedies.

VICENZA, capital of the department of Vicenza, Italy, situated at the confluence of the Bacchiglione and Retrone rivers, 42 m. by rail w. of Venice. It is surrounded by a moat, and walls half in ruins, and contains many palaces and churches. Manufactures of silk, straw hats, woolen goods, leather, machinery, and musical instruments are carried on. The department contains on the north the *Sette Communi,* seven village communes, which, formerly German, for a time formed a kind of republic under Venetian protection. Area of department, 1051 sq.m.; pop., about 528,000. Pop. of city, about 65,000.

VICE-PRESIDENT, the second officer of the government of the United States in rank and chosen for the same term and in the same manner as the President, except that in case no candidate for the Vice-Presidency receives a majority of the electoral votes, the election is thrown into the Senate, which then chooses by a majority vote one of the two leading candidates. Although described as an executive officer, the Vice-President performs no executive functions whatever, his only duty being to preside over the deliberations of the Senate, except when it is sitting as a court of impeachment for the trial of the President, when the Chief Justice presides. He has a casting vote in the Senate in case of a tie, and he presides at the joint meeting of the two Houses when the electoral votes are counted.

The chief importance of the office consists

Building designed by Palladio in Vicenza

Vice-Presidents of the United States

Name	Birthplace	Year	State	Qualified	Politics	Died Year	Age
John Adams	Quincy, Mass.	1735	Mass.	1789	Fed.	1826	90
Thomas Jefferson	Shadwell, Va.	1743	Va.	1797	Rep.	1826	83
Aaron Burr	Newark, N.J.	1756	N.Y.	1801	Rep.	1836	80
George Clinton	Ulster Co., N.Y.	1739	N.Y.	1805	Rep.	1812	73
Elbridge Gerry	Marblehead, Mass.	1744	Mass.	1813	Rep.	1814	70
Daniel D. Tompkins	Scarsdale, N.Y.	1774	N.Y.	1817	Rep.	1825	51
John C. Calhoun (resigned 1832)	Abbeville, S.C.	1782	S.C.	1825	Rep.	1850	68
Martin Van Buren	Kinderhook, N.Y.	1782	N.Y.	1833	Dem.	1862	79
Richard M. Johnson	Louisville, Ky.	1780	Ky.	1837	Dem.	1850	70
John Tyler	Greenway, Va.	1790	Va.	1841	Dem.	1862	72
George M. Dallas	Philadelphia, Pa.	1792	Pa.	1845	Dem.	1864	72
Millard Fillmore	Summerhill, N.Y.	1800	N.Y.	1849	Whig	1874	74
William R. King	Sampson Co., N.C.	1786	Ala.	1853	Dem.	1853	67
John C. Breckenridge	Lexington, Ky.	1821	Ky.	1857	Dem.	1875	54
Hannibal Hamlin	Paris, Me.	1809	Me.	1861	Rep.	1891	81
Andrew Johnson	Raleigh, N.C.	1808	Tenn.	1865	Rep.	1875	66
Schuyler Colfax	New York, N.Y.	1823	Ind.	1869	Rep.	1885	62
Henry Wilson	Farmington, N.H.	1812	Mass.	1873	Rep.	1875	63
William A. Wheeler	Malone, N.Y.	1819	N.Y.	1877	Rep.	1887	68
Chester A. Arthur	Fairfield, Vt.	1830	N.Y.	1881	Rep.	1886	56
Thomas A. Hendricks	Muskingum Co., O.	1819	Ind.	1885	Dem.	1885	66
Levi P. Morton	Shoreham, Vt.	1824	N.Y.	1889	Rep.	1920	96
Adlai E. Stevenson	Christian Co., Ky.	1835	Ill.	1893	Dem.	1914	78
Garret A. Hobart	Long Beach, N.J.	1844	N.J.	1897	Rep.	1899	55
Theodore Roosevelt	New York, N.Y.	1858	N.Y.	1901	Rep.	1919	60
Charles W. Fairbanks	Unionville Center, O.	1852	Ind.	1905	Rep.	1918	66
James S. Sherman	Utica, N.Y.	1855	N.Y.	1909	Rep.	1912	57
Thomas R. Marshall	N. Manchester, Ind.	1854	Ind.	1913	Dem.	1925	71
Calvin Coolidge	Plymouth, Vt.	1872	Mass.	1921	Rep.	1933	60
Charles G. Dawes	Marietta, O.	1865	Ill.	1925	Rep.		
Charles Curtis	Topeka, Kans.	1860	Kans.	1929	Rep.	1936	76
John N. Garner	Red River Co., Tex.	1869	Tex.	1933	Dem.		
Henry Agard Wallace	Adair County, Ia.	1888	Ia.	1941	Dem.		
Harry S. Truman	Lamar, Mo.	1884	Mo.	1945	Dem.		
Alben W. Barkley	Graves Co., Ky.	1877	Ky.	1949	Dem.		

in the fact that the Vice-President is made by the Constitution the successor of the President in case of the latter's removal from office or of his death, resignation, or inability to discharge the powers and duties of the office. The qualifications required of the Vice-President are the same as those of the President (see PRESIDENT). His salary is $30,000 a year.

The deaths of Presidents Harrison in 1841, Taylor in 1850, Lincoln in 1865, Garfield in 1881, McKinley in 1901, Harding in 1923, and Roosevelt in 1945 caused the succession to devolve upon the Vice-President.

The Constitution originally provided that the Presidential candidate receiving the second largest number of electoral votes be declared Vice-President; this method of selection was superseded by the Twelfth Amendment (1804).

VICEROY, common name applied to a butterfly, *Basilarchia archippus,* native to the Western Hemisphere from southern Canada to southern United States. The viceroy is bright orange red in color with a wide black band running along the outer margins of the wings. The band is punctuated with a uniform row of white spots. The insect bears a remarkable color resemblance to the monarch butterfly, *Danaïs plexippus.* The viceroy lacks the acrid secretions of the monarch which render the latter repugnant in taste and odor, but are avoided carefully by insectivorous animals because of the superficial resemblance. The eggs of the viceroy are laid at the tips of oak, willow, birch, or linden leaves and are spherical in shape. The surface of the egg is covered with bristles and pitted with six-sided cells. The larva, or caterpillar, is cylindrical in shape and divided into a series of segments. The young caterpillar feeds upon the leaf tip on which it was hatched and attaches bits of partially chewed leaf to the leaf midrib by strands of silk. This reinforcement stiffens the midrib and prevents it from curling or breaking as it dries. When winter approaches the caterpillar detaches the uneaten portions of the leaf from the midrib, glues the rib of the leaf to the stem with a stout silk thread, rolls itself up in the detached leaf to form a hibernaculum, or winter quarters, and re-attaches the leaf to the rib. Before emerging from the hibernaculum the caterpillar pupates. The adult butterfly emerges from the pupa in late spring or early summer.

VICEROY, a ruler acting with royal authority in place of the sovereign.

VICH, or VIQUE, city of the province of Barcelona, Spain, 38 miles N. of Barcelona. It has agricultural interests, and manufactures include hats and paper and cotton goods. Pop., about 13,000.

VICHY-LES-BAINS, town of the department of Allier, France, on the Allier R., 30 miles S.S.E. of Moulins by rail. It has springs of the alkaline class, somewhat acidulous, and the most efficacious of the kind known. Vichy water is exported in large quantities. After the defeat of France (q.v.) by Germany in World War II, Vichy-les-Bains was made the seat of the government under Marshal Pétain and Pierre Laval. Pop., about 22,000.

VICKSBURG, county seat of Warren Co., Miss., situated at the confluence of the Mississippi and Yazoo rivers, about 221 m. by rail s. of Memphis, Tenn., and about 236 m. by rail N. of New Orleans, La. It is served by two railroads and by river steamers and barges, and maintains a municipal airport. A railroad, vehicular, and pedestrian bridge crosses the Mississippi at Vicksburg, and the city is an important railroad division point, with extensive railroad shops and yards, and an important terminal of the Federal Barge Line. A concrete sea wall protects the water front of the city, which rises from the river to high bluffs reaching 300 ft. above river level. Vicksburg is the third-largest city in population in the State, a leading distribution point and manufacturing center, and one of the principal cotton and hardwood-lumber markets in the South. The chief products of the surrounding area are cotton, corn, hay, soybeans, garden truck, clover seed, pecans, fruits, livestock, poultry, timber, oil, limestone, clays, and sand and gravel. Industrial establishments in the city include large lumber mills, sawmills, oil refineries, cottonseed-oil mills, cotton gins, machine shops, and factories manufacturing heavy earth-moving machinery, boxes, wood veneer, barrels, hoops, staves, boat oars, tool handles, other lumber and hardwood products, house trailers, textiles, and work garments. Various Federal agencies located in the city furnish a large part of the employment. Vicksburg is the site of the U.S. Waterways Experiment Station, largest hydraulic experiment station in the world, built in 1929 for flood control, and of the U.S. District Engineers, organized in 1883 for the purpose of improving facilities for navigation on the Mississippi R. The city is also the headquarters of the Mississippi River Commission, created by Congress in 1879.

Among the educational institutions in Vicksburg are several vocational schools and All Saints' College (Episcopal), a junior college for women established in 1908. Surrounding the city on the N., E., and S., is the famous Vicksburg National Military Park (see VICKSBURG, CAMPAIGN OF) established in 1899. The park covers 1323 acres and is traversed by 32 miles of driveways; it contains nearly 1600 memorials, monuments, and markers, and extensive remains of the fortified battle lines of the Union and Confederate armies. North of the park is the Vicksburg National Cemetery, one of the most beautiful of the national cemeteries. It was established in 1866 and contains about 120 acres, in which are the graves of 17,519 soldiers, 12,912 of which are marked "unknown."

The region of the present city was held successively by the French, British, Spanish, and Americans in the 18th century. Fort Nogales, occupied by U.S. troops in 1798, was built by the Spanish on the site of Vicksburg in 1791, and the first permanent settlement was established in 1812 by the Rev. Newitt Vick, a Methodist preacher, for whom the city is named. Vicksburg was incorporated as a town in 1825 and chartered as a city in 1836. The Vicksburg campaign of the Civil War, because of the strategic location of the city and its almost impregnable position, was one of the most decisive of Union victories. Pop. (1950) 27,344.

VICKSBURG, CAMPAIGN OF. Vicksburg, perched on a steep bluff, 235 ft. high, on the eastern bank of the Mississippi R., was after the fall of Fort Donelson (February, 1862) during the Civil War the one serious obstacle to complete command of the Mississippi by the Federal forces. The Confederates strengthened their land defenses the following May. On June 27 Farragut's fleet appeared below the town, and the following day two frigates and six gunboats ran the blockade. The attack, however, proved unsuccessful, and Farragut abandoned it on July 20, sailing downstream for New Orleans.

A second attack was made in December, 1862. General Grant proposed moving from Holly Springs on Granada with a view to cutting the Confederate line of communications and drawing General Pemberton, the Confederate commander of Vicksburg, from his stronghold. Meanwhile General Sherman, with 40,000 troops, was to be convoyed down river by Admiral Porter's fleet, and to seize the city in the absence of the major part of the defenders. These plans were, however, upset by a Confederate raid on Holly Springs, the Federal base, which hindered Grant's advance. Sherman, after a successful landing, found the country virtually impassable. He had just reached firm ground when Pemberton's return made a further attack useless, and the Union army had to retreat to its transports.

Grant now assumed full command, and made two attempts to dig ship canals which would give uninterrupted passage to Federal navigation, but both were unsuccessful. Landing his army on the west bank of the river he marched to Bruinsburg, where he safely crossed (April 30, 1863), Porter meantime running the blockade downstream with forage and supplies, losing one steamer in the action. Marching eastward, Grant dispersed a Confederate force under General Bowen near Port Gibson, and was joined by Sherman, who had crossed the river at Grand Gulf. General J.E. Johnston was advancing to the relief of the beleaguered town, but Grant thrust his army between the city and his force. Turning on Johnston, Grant defeated him at Champion's Hill (May 16) and then attacked the city. Two assaults on the fortress failed, and regular siege operations were begun which lasted for six weeks. On July 4 the defenders capitulated. The total casualties in the campaign were: Union army, 10,142; Confederates, 9091. In addition, the Confederates lost 31,000 prisoners of war.

VICO, GIOVANNI BATTISTA (1668–1744), Italian philosopher and jurist, born in Naples. He studied law, history, and philosophy, and in 1697 became professor of rhetoric at the University of Naples. In 1734 he was appointed historiographer to Charles III, King of Naples. The great work which has made his name illustrious, the *Principi di una Scienza Nuova d'Intorno alla Comune Natura delle Nazioni,* first appeared in Naples in 1725. Due in part to its obscure and enigmatical style, the work was not immediately appreciated. The *Scienza Nuovo* was virtually unknown outside of Italy until 1822, when a German translation appeared in Leipzig. It was five years later translated into French by Michelet, and the author has since that time found his proper rank among the most profound of modern thinkers. His other writings include *De Ratione Studiorum* (1708), *De Antiquissima Italorum Sapientia* (1710), *De Universi Juris Uno Principio et Fine Uno* (1720), and *De Constantia Jurisprudentis* (1721).

Vico proposed to himself the task of distinguishing amid social phenomena the regular from the accidental; of discovering the laws which govern the formation, the growth, and the decay of all societies; briefly, of tracing the outlines of the history of peoples—the idea of which he himself believed to have existed from eternity in the mind of God.

VICOL or **BICOL,** a Christianized Malay people living on southern Luzon, Philippines, and on Catanduanes and Masbate islands. Their dialect is composed of part Tagalog and part Visayan, while in general appearance and culture they differ little from the people of the latter group. See PHILIPPINE ISLANDS.

VICTOR, the name of three popes. **1.** VICTOR I, SAINT, Pope from 189 to 198. He is designated by St. Jerome the first Latin ecclesiastical author. See POPE. **2.** VICTOR II, real name GEBHARD (1018–57), Pope from 1055 to 1057, born in Swabia. He was a firm ally of the Imperial house, and on the death of Henry III secured the succession of Henry IV under the regency of his mother. **3.** VICTOR III, real name

Dauferius (1027–87), Pope from 1086 to 1087. He assumed the dignity with reluctance, was forced to leave Rome by the Imperial party, but was enthroned in St. Peter's the following year, displacing the Antipope Guibert. The name of Victor IV was assumed by two antipopes: Cardinal Gregorio Conti, who opposed Innocent II in 1138; and Cardinal Octavian, whom Frederick Barbarossa supported against Alexander III in 1159–64.

VICTOR or **VICTOR-PERRIN**, Claude, Duc de Bellune, real name Claude Victor Perrin (1766–1841), French soldier, born in La Marche in the Vosges. He enlisted in the army in 1781, gained the attention of Napoleon I by his conduct at the siege of Toulon (1793), and was promoted at the close of that year to the rank of brigadier general. He became general of division in 1797. In the Italian campaigns of 1796–97 and 1799–1800 Victor commanded the vanguard. He did brilliant service at Marengo. In 1806 he fought against Prussia, was captured in 1807, was exchanged for Blücher, and at Friedland won the baton of a marshal of France and the title of Duc de Bellune. He was governor of Berlin after the Treaty of Tilsit. In 1808 he commanded a corps in Spain, and gained several victories, but was defeated by Wellington at Talavera (July 27–28). In 1812 he commanded the Ninth Corps in the Russian campaign, and shared in the defense of the passage of the Berezina. He then went over to the Bourbons, from whom he received a peerage; he was president of the military commission appointed to try those officers who deserted to Napoleon after the emperor's return from Elba. He was minister of war, 1821–23, and second in command on the Spanish Peninsula in 1823, but was recalled on suspicion of complicity in fraudulent contracts.

VICTOR EMMANUEL I (1759–1824), King of Sardinia from 1802 to 1821, born in Turin. At first the French occupied his continental dominions, but after the fall of Napoleon I in 1814 he returned to Turin, and by his reactionary government provoked the revolution of 1821 which caused his abdication in favor of his brother, Charles Albert.

VICTOR EMMANUEL II (1820–78), King of Italy from 1861 to 1878, son of Charles Albert, King of Sardinia, born in Turin. He was the first king of a united Italy, ascending the throne after the defeat of the Piedmontese army by the Austrians at Novara. Aided by Garibaldi he created a new Italian kingdom. Venice entered it in 1866, and Rome in 1871.

Claude Victor (painting by A. J. Gros)

VICTOR EMMANUEL III (1869–   ), King of Italy from 1900 to 1946, born in Naples. He succeeded to the throne on the assassination of his father, King Humbert I. In 1896 he married Princess Elena, daughter of King Nicholas of Montenegro. After Rome's fall in World War II (1944), the king withdrew from public life and abdicated in favor of his son Crown Prince Humbert.

VICTORIA, in botany, genus of giant, perennial, herbaceous waterlilies belonging to the family Nymphacaceae, and often called the royal or Victoria waterlily in honor of the English queen. The genus, which contains two distinct species, is native to standing waters throughout South America, and is cultivated in many parts of the world for use in aquaria and informal gardens. It bears enormous, deep-green, circularly arranged leaves which sometimes attain a diameter of 7 feet and which curl upward at the circumference to a height of 8 inches, giving the leaf the appearance of a floating basin. The undersides of the leaves are covered with thick, spiny veins which are equipped with numerous air pockets and air canals to buoy up the mass. The

N.Y. Botanical Garden
The underside of a Victoria waterlily leaf

upper surfaces of the leaves are perforated with minute holes, or "stomatodes", which serve to drain off rain or water collected from other sources. A very thick, tuberous rhizome and numerous spongy roots anchor the plant to the bottom of the pond or river.

Victoria bears conspicuous flowers which grow from 12 to 18 inches in diameter and emit a fragrance similar to that of the pineapple. They open during the evening on two successive days, and do not close until the middle of the following mornings. On the first day they are pure white in color, but turn to deep rose or red by the second day. After the second closing the flower sinks below the surface of the water, where the seeds develop. The flowers have 4 sepals, 50 to 70 delicate petals, 150 to 200 stamens, and a solitary pistil. The fruit is a large, prickly, green or brown-seeded berry. *V. regia*, native to waters of British Guiana, bears dull-crimson flowers. Its principal variety, *V. regia* var. *randii,* is found along the main body and tributaries of the Amazon River, and is the waterlily most commonly cultivated in the United States. *V. cruziana,* a larger species, is found throughout Paraguay and along the Paraná River of Argentina and Brazil, and bears reddish-pink flowers. The variety *V. cruziana* var. *mattogrossensis* is characterized by a low leaf rim, and is common throughout Brazil.

VICTORIA, county seat of Victoria Co., Tex., situated at the head of navigation on the Guadalupe R., about 115 miles S.E. of San Antonio. Transportation facilities include two railroads. Oil and natural gas are produced in abundance in the area, and the principal agricultural products are beef cattle, cotton, corn, feed crops, small grains, peanuts, and pecans. In addition to numerous oil-well supply houses and oil refineries, which are a major source of the city's wealth, Victoria contains railroad repair shops, cottonseed-oil mills, cotton compresses, cotton gins, meat-packing plants, pecan-shelling plants, food-processing plants, a foundry, a machine shop, sand and gravel plants, and a cheese factory. On the outskirts of the city are two large U.S. Air Force fields and nearby are the ruins of a Spanish fort and mission, built in 1721. Victoria is the site of Victoria Junior College, a municipal institution established in 1925. The city was founded in 1824 by the Spanish and incorporated as a city of Texas in 1837. Pop. (1950) 16,102.

VICTORIA, a State of the Australian Commonwealth, occupying the southeastern part of the island continent, with an area of 87,884 sq.m. In 1949 the population was estimated at 2,139,124. Melbourne, the capital and largest city, including its suburbs, had approximately 1,259,000 inhabitants in 1948.

The S.E. coast of Australia was sighted by Captain Cook in 1770, the harbor of Port Philip was discovered in 1801, and an unsuccessful attempt to form a settlement on its shores was made by Lieutenant Colonel Collins in 1804. From 1836 till 1851 Port Phillip was administered by the government of Sydney, but in the latter year the district was constituted into the colony of Victoria, with a separate executive and legislature. Melbourne was created a city in 1847. Gold was discovered in 1851, and attracted a large number of immigrants.

Victoria is traversed from west to east by an irregular range of mountains, an extension of the Great Dividing Range. The mountains are low in the west, but rise toward the east into the rugged Australian Alps, whose highest peak in Victoria, Mount Bogong, has an altitude of 6508 feet. The coast is lined with broken ranges of hills, and is irregular, with granitic headlands and landlocked bays, such as Port Phillip, the harbor of Melbourne. There are several navigable rivers. Those on the northern watersheds are tributaries of the Murray R., which forms most of the boundary on the side of New South Wales. Over eighty extinct volcanic peaks occur just west of Port Phillip and basaltic flows mark some of the plains. The mountains and drift deposits are rich in minerals, of which gold is the most important. About two thirds of the enormous gold production of Australia has been obtained in Victoria. Coal, silver, tin, lead, and copper are also found. Farming continues to occupy a leading place in the activities of the

| VICTORIA | 12,799 | VICTORIA |

Aus. News & Info. Bur.

IN VICTORIA, AUSTRALIA

Above: Pasture land near Lilydale, 26 miles from Melbourne. Right: Sandstone precipice in the mountains. Below: Aerial view of harbor of Melbourne.

State. The chief crops are wheat, oats, potatoes, hay, and wine. Horses, cattle, sheep, and pigs are raised. Trapping, forestry, fishing, and poultry and bee raising also constitute major industries. Wool, wheat and flour, skins, fruits, butter, milk and cream, and meats are the leading exports. Primary education is free, secular, and compulsory.

Executive power is vested in a governor, acting through a responsible ministry, and legislative power in a parliament of two houses —the Legislative Council of 34 members elected for six years and subject to property qualifications, and the Legislative Assembly of 65 members, elected for three years by male and female suffrage.

VICTORIA, seaport and capital of the State of Espirito Santo, Brazil, on the island of Espirito Santo, 75 miles N.E. of Rio de Janeiro. It is the principal commercial center of the State and exports sugar, coffee, rice, and manioc. The town was founded in 1535. Pop., about 21,000.

VICTORIA, capital of British Columbia, Canada, and of the Victoria district, at the southeast extremity of Vancouver Island. The city was incorporated in 1862. Victoria has regular steamship communication with all points on the northwest coast. There are extensive sawmills, shipbuilding yards, brickyards, ironworks, and furniture factories. Pop. (1941) 44,068.

VICTORIA. See Ciudad Victoria.

VICTORIA. See Cameroons.

VICTORIA. See Seychelles Islands.

VICTORIA, town of the State of Aragua, Venezuela, on the Aragua River, 45 miles S.W. of Carácas. It has a trade in coffee, cacao, and sugar. Pop., about 15,000.

VICTORIA, the Roman goddess of victory, the counterpart of the Greek goddess Nike (q.v.). A temple was erected to Victoria on the Palatine Hill in 294 B.C., and her name was specifically associated with certain Roman legions.

VICTORIA, in full Alexandrina Victoria (1819–1901), Queen of the United Kingdom of Great Britain and Ireland from 1837 to 1901, and Empress of India from 1876 to 1901, born in Kensington Palace, London. She ascended the throne on the death of her uncle, William IV, June 20, 1837; her uncle, the Duke of Cumberland, becoming king of Hanover, in virtue of the law which excluded females from that throne. Victoria was proclaimed queen on June 21, 1837, and crowned at Westminster, June 28, 1838. Lord Melbourne was then prime minister, and Victoria's early political course was largely influenced by him. Melbourne's administration lasted until 1841. Victoria's reign included the administrations of Peel (1841–46), Russell (1846–52, 1865–66), Derby (1852, 1858–59, 1866–68), Aberdeen (1852–55), Palmerston (1855–58, 1859–65), Disraeli (1868, and as Earl of Beaconsfield, 1874–80), Gladstone (1868–74, 1880–85, 1886, 1892–94), Salisbury (1885–86, 1886–92, 1895–1901), and Roseberry (1894–95).

Victoria was married at St. James's Palace (February 10, 1840) to Albert, Prince of Saxe-Coburg and Gotha, and second son of the then reigning duke. Although the union was not at the time greatly approved of by the queen's advisers and subjects, it proved a most felicitous one, marked by a degree of mutual affection rarely found in marriages of state. To them were born four sons and five daughters: the Princess Royal, Victoria, born Nov. 21, 1840, married Jan. 25, 1858, Frederick William, who in 1888 became Frederick III, Emperor of Germany (died 1901); Albert Edward, King of Great Britain, 1901–10, born Nov. 9, 1841, married March 10, 1863, Princess Alexandra Caroline, eldest daughter of Christian IX, King of Denmark; Princess Alice, born April 25, 1843, married July 1, 1862, Prince Frederick William of Hesse (died 1878); Prince Alfred, born Aug. 6, 1844, created Duke of Edinburgh, 1866, married Jan. 23, 1874, Marie, only daughter of the emperor of Russia (died 1901); Princess Helena, born May 25, 1846, married in 1866 to Prince Christian of Denmark; Princess Louise, born March 18, 1848, married in 1871 to the Marquis of Lorne; Prince Arthur, born May 1, 1850, created Duke of Connaught, 1874, married in 1879 Princess Louise Marguerite of Prussia; Prince Leopold, born April 7, 1853, created Duke of Albany, 1881, married Princess Helena of Waldeck in 1882 (died 1884); Princess Beatrice, born April 14, 1857, married, 1885, Prince Henry of Battenberg.

The legislative record of Victoria's reign includes many important acts which may be traced in the articles on England, Great Britain, Ireland, the several colonies, and India. The most important were the establishment of penny postage (1840), amendment of the poor laws of Scotland (1845) and Ireland (1847), repeal of the corn laws (1846), the Irish encumbered estates act (1848), repeal of the navigation laws (1849), the removal of the disabilities of the Jews (1858), the reform act of 1867, the disestablishment of the Irish church (1869), elementary education act (1870) and abolition of religious tests in the universities (1871), Irish land acts (1870, 1881), abolition of purchase in the army (1871), Scotch educational act (1872), and the franchise bill of 1884.

Events of national and international importance were numerous in her long reign; they include the rebellion in Canada (1837–38), Afghan War (1838–42), Opium War in China (1840–42), the establishment of a Catholic hierarchy in England (1850), Crimean War (1854–56), transfer of India from the East India Company to the crown (1858), complicated relations with the United States during the Civil War (1861–65), Abyssinian War (1867–68), the assumption by Victoria of the title of Empress of India (1876), Zulu War (1879), Transvaal War (1880), the virtual establishment of British domination in Egypt (1882), the conquest of Burma (1885), South African War (1899–1902), and Australian federation (1900–01). For many years the agitation for home rule in Ireland was the main feature of internal politics. The death of the prince consort in 1861 led his widow to live mainly in seclusion for several years, but she never neglected any of her essential duties as queen.

The reign of Victoria, the longest in English history, witnessed an extraordinary development of Imperial Britain as shown in the growth and political organization of the Canadian, Australian, and African colonies. Victoria was pre-eminent among sovereigns by her personal character. She "for many years ... exerted an almost unbounded moral control over the larger policies of the British Empire. She was industrious and methodical, patient and tactful, with a memory that was a great storehouse of knowledge of things past and present." The leading feature of the Victorian epoch was "the new conception of the British monarchy which sprang from the development of the colonies and dependencies of Great Britain, and the sudden strengthening of the sense of unity between them and the mother country. The crown after 1880 became the living symbol of Imperial unity, and every year events deepened the impression that the Queen in her own person typified the common interest and the common sympathy which spread a feeling of brotherhood through the continents that formed the British Empire." Her jubilee (1887) and diamond jubilee (1897) emphasized the loyalty of the colonies to the mother country. Her *Letters,* edited by A.C. Benson (3 vols., London, 1907) illustrated her self-devotion and her high idea of the importance of her office.

British Information Services
Queen Victoria

VICTORIA, ADELAIDE MARY LOUISE (1840–1901), Princess Royal of England and later known as Empress Frederick. She was the oldest daughter of Prince Albert and Queen Victoria, and in 1858 married Crown Prince Frederick William of Prussia, subsequently the German emperor, Frederick III. She strove to introduce English manners and ideas at her court, but was opposed by the dislike of Bismarck.

VICTORIA, GUADALUPE, real name MANUEL FÉLIX FERNÁNDEZ (1789–1843), President of Mexico from 1824 to 1829, born in Durango. After joining the patriotic ranks he changed his name to Victoria in honor of the Virgin of Guadalupe. He took part in the siege of Oaxaca (1812), and (1814) became the leader of the revolution in Vera Cruz. He assisted Santa Anna in overthrowing Iturbide and establishing the republic. In 1824 he was elected the first president of Mexico. During his administration he secured the recognition of the republic by England and the abolition of slavery.

VICTORIA, TOMÁS LUIS DE (1540?–1611), Spanish composer of the Roman school, born in Avila Castile. He is perhaps even better known by the Italianized form of his name,

The Victoria Cross

Tommaso Ludovico da Vittoria. In 1573 he became maestro di cappella at the Collegium Germanicum, and two years later at Sant' Apollinare. From 1589 till his death he lived in Madrid. As a composer Victoria is classed with the masters of the Roman school because his style resembles that of Palestrina, an intimate friend. His greatest work is the *Requiem*, written in 1605.

VICTORIA AND ALBERT MUSEUM, an important museum of decorative and applied art under the control of the national Board of Education, located in London. It was opened in 1857 at South Kensington (London) in the temporary structure which now houses the Bethnal Green Museum, with funds derived from the International Exhibition of 1851. The present extensive buildings were begun in 1899 and opened in 1909. The museum's collections of applied and decorative art, derived largely from private gifts and legacies, are among the finest in the world. The museum contains a collection of paintings, including Raphael's world-famous cartoons for the tapestries of the Sistine Chapel, a historical collection of British water colors, and many modern British and French paintings. Besides these collections it possesses an Art Library of about 120,000 volumes and 200,000 photographs; an important art school, known as the Royal College of Art; and the collections of the former India Museum. The museum has issued a series of important catalogues of its collections, many of them of high critical and scholastic value.

VICTORIA CROSS, an award first given at the end of the Crimean War in 1856, and conferred on members of the British naval and military services, of the mercantile marine if subject to enemy action, and of the staffs of the nursing and hospital services, and on others, both men and women, serving under orders of the armed forces. In 1912 the right to receive the award was extended to native soldiers in the Indian army. The Victoria Cross is in the form of a Maltese cross, and is made of bronze. In the center is the royal crown, surmounted by the lion, and below, on a scroll, the words "For Valour".

It is the most highly prized decoration of the British military and naval services. Non-commissioned officers and men, and such commissioned officers as may have risen from the ranks, who have been awarded the Victoria Cross receive an annuity of £10, which, under special circumstances, may be increased to £50. Civilians acting under military orders are eligible for the medal. Prior to World War I the ribbon was red for the army and blue for the navy, but now it is red for both branches of the service.

VICTORIA EMBANKMENT, an embankment in London, England, extending along the north bank of the Thames River, from Westminster Bridge to Blackfriars Bridge. It was constructed between 1864 and 1870. The embankment is 100 ft. wide and about 2300 yds. long.

VICTORIA FALLS, a magnificent cataract on the middle Zambezi in s. Rhodesia, British South Africa, a few miles below the Kwando confluence. The river, here nearly 1 mile wide, suddenly plunges to a depth of 400 feet. Below the falls, spanning the gorge, a railroad bridge was completed in 1905. The name Victoria was given to the falls by Livingstone, who discovered them in 1855.

VICTORIA LAND, or SOUTH VICTORIA LAND, the name given to that part of the

Victoria Falls on the Zambesi River in southern Rhodesia — British Information Services

Antarctic continent s. of New Zealand, having Ross Sea to the w. The volcanoes Erebus and Terror, discovered by Ross in 1841, are in Victoria Land.

VICTORIAN GOTHIC, the general name commonly applied to those phases of the Gothic Revival in England which developed during the reign of Queen Victoria (1837-1901). It was characterized at first by the effort to attain archeological correctness of detail, to which the extensive restorations of medieval buildings greatly contributed. Later, in its adaptations to secular architecture, its leaders developed an increasingly free eclecticism. The most noted of these leaders were Sir G. Gilbert Scott, George Edmund Street, Alfred Waterhouse, and William Burges. Among the most noted Victorian Gothic productions are the Houses of Parliament (by Barry), the Manchester Town Hall and Courts, Exeter College Chapel at Oxford University, and the New Law Courts, London.

VICTORIA NYANZA, or UKEREWE, a great lake in E. central Africa. It has an area of about 26,000 sq.m., and lies 3775 ft. above sea level. The lake is drained by the Nile, and its chief feeder is the Kagera. The lake was discovered by Speke in 1858, circumnavigated by Stanley (1875), and subsequently explored at various times by him and others. During World War I the lake was the scene of military operations between the British and German forces in 1915-16, both sides arming little steamers for raiding purposes. Belgian columns arrived at Kagera, in German territory, in April, 1916, and Ukerewe Island was captured by British forces in June. With the fall to the British of Mwanza, the following month, all hostilities ended on Victoria Nyanza.

VICTORIAVILLE, a town in Arthabaska County, Quebec, Canada. Pop., about 6000.

The vicuña

N.Y. Zoological Society

VICTORS, JAN (about 1620–about 82), Dutch genre and Biblical painter, pupil, and follower of the Dutch painter Rembrandt van Rijn. His work is represented in Amsterdam, Brunswick, Copenhagen, and Prague.

VICTORY LOAN, the fifth and last of the Liberty bonds issued by the United States government, through popular subscription, to finance World War I. See LIBERTY LOANS.

VICUDA, a barracuda, *Sphyraenia ensis,* about 2 feet long. It is a food fish of some importance on the Pacific coast of Mexico and Central America.

VICUÑA, common name applied to a ruminant mammal, *Lama vicugna,* belonging to the Camel family. The animal is native to the Andes mountains, in Ecuador, Peru, and Bolivia, and is a close relative of the domesticated llama. Vicuñas are slender small animals with orange-red fur, and generally roam in small herds. The animals have never been successfully domesticated, and are much hunted for their hides and for their wool, which is valued for weaving. The term "vicuña" is also applied to the fabrics manufactured from the wool of the animal, and also to textile fabrics made from the wool of the Merino sheep in imitation of natural vicuña. Such fabrics generally resemble serge in weave, but are fuller, softer, and have a distinct nap.

VICUÑA-MACKENNA, BENJAMIN (1831–86), Chilean historian and politician, born in Santiago. He took part in the revolt of 1851 and, being captured, was sentenced to death, but was able to escape. Returning to his native country (1856), he founded a newspaper in opposition to the government, and suffered in consequence a short term of imprisonment. He was editor of numerous periodicals and wrote many works on the history of Chile. He sat for some years in the Chilean congress.

VIDAL, PEIRE (fl. 1175–1215), Provençal poet. He was the son of a furrier of Toulouse and became a favorite in the courts of southern France and of Spain, being on terms of special intimacy with Barral, Viscount of Marseilles, whose wife he celebrated under the name of Vierna. Vidal lived for a time in the East, in later life visited the Marquis of Montferrat and the king of Hungary, and probably went on a crusade with the former. Among his poems are to be found some of the best specimens of Provençal literature.

VIDAURRI, SANTIAGO (1803–67), Mexican general and statesman, born in the State of Nuevo León. He abandoned the profession of law for the career of a soldier, and in 1852 was elected governor of Nuevo León. In 1854 he assisted in the campaign against General Antonio Santa Anna. Defeated (1855) by Juan Alvarez in the election for the presidency, Vidaurri set up an independent government in the northern States. When Maximilian was proclaimed (1864) emperor, Vidaurri was elected a member of the Imperial Council. In 1867 he was appointed president of the ministry and lieutenant of the empire. After the capture of the city of Mexico by the patriot forces (1867) he was arrested and shot as a traitor.

VIDIN, a town in the district of Vratza, Bulgaria, situated on the Danube R., about 70 miles N.W. of the city of Vratza. The town is a shipping point for the surrounding agricultural region and an industrial center, with breweries, distilleries, and tobacco factories. Fishing and the manufacture of filigreed gold and silver ornaments are also important. Among points of interest in Vidin are a cathedral, a number of mosques, and an old clock tower. Pop. (1947 est.) 18,580.

VIDOCQ, FRANÇOIS EUGÈNE (1775–1857), French criminal and detective, born in Arras. When a boy he stole from his father, a baker, and was imprisoned, but on release appropriated a sum of money. He was later an

The opera house in the city of Vienna, Austria
Austrian State Tourist Department

acrobat, and then entered the army. Returning home, he lived a disreputable life, and in 1796 went to the galleys for forgery. Escaping, he joined a band of highwaymen, afterward turned them over to the police, and soon acquired some note as a spy upon criminals. In 1812 Vidocq was made chief of a small detective force, the *brigade de sûreté,* which developed great efficiency in detecting crime and in creating crime to detect. His *Mémoires* (1829) are of doubtful authenticity and, if authentic, are unreliable.

VIEDMA, formerly EL MERCED, capital of the territory of Rio Negro, Argentina. Pop., about 3,000.

VIELÉ, EGBERT LUDOVICKUS (1825–1902), American soldier and civil engineer, born in Waterford, N.Y., and educated at the U.S. Military Academy. In 1861, following the outbreak of the Civil War, he became a brigadier general of volunteers. He commanded the land forces in the capture of Fort Pulaski; was engaged in the advance on Norfolk, Va., and was military governor of Norfolk from August, 1862, until October, 1863, when he resigned from active service. In 1883 he was elected to Congress.

VIELÉ, HERMAN KNICKERBOCKER (1856–1908), American author, painter, and engineer, born in New York City. Though his paintings found some favor, he was more widely known as a novelist. His writings include *The Inn of the Silver Moon* (1900), *The Last of the Knickerbockers* (1901), *Myra of the Pines* (1902), *Random Verse* (1903), *Heartbreak Hill* (1908), and *On the Lightship* (1909).

VIEN, COUNT JOSEPH MARIE (1716–1809), French historical painter, born in Montpellier. In 1743 he won the Prix de Rome. He became the head of an influential school, in which were trained the French painter Jacques Louis David and the principal leaders of classicism in France. Vien's masterpiece, "St. Denis Preaching to the Gauls", is in the church of St. Roch; "A Sleeping Hermit" and "St. Germain and St. Vincent" are in the Louvre, and his work is also represented in many French provincial museums.

VIENNA, (Ger. *Wien*; anc. *Vindobona*), capital, largest city, and a province of Austria, located in the eastern portion of the country, about 25 miles W. of Bratislava, Czechoslovakia, and 380 miles S.S.E. of Berlin, Germany. The city lies on both banks of the Danube (Donau) River and the Donaukanal, a canalized arm of the Danube. In addition to its favorable situation on the Danube, Vienna is a major European railroad center. The principal industries of Vienna include the manufacture of jewelry, leather goods, textiles,

A young couple and a musician at a "Heurige" (May-wine festival) in Vienna, Austria

clothing, hats, optical and scientific instruments, chemicals, beer, furniture, porcelain, hardware, musical instruments, heavy steel and iron machinery, gold, silver, bronze, and tin products, tools, and paper. The city also possesses a publishing and a motion-picture industry, and is a major commercial center.

Although Vienna contains buildings of the 13th and 14th centuries, it is essentially a modern city. The Ringstrasse, a boulevard 2 miles long and 150 feet wide, which is lined with trees and impressive monuments and buildings, circles the old Inner City, the hub of the city's 21 districts. The boulevard was constructed after the removal of the Inner City's fortifications between 1858 and 1860. Situated in the Inner City are the cathedral of St. Stephen, a Gothic structure dating from 1300 to 1510, and possessing a tower 450 ft. high; the Hofburg, a collection of buildings dating from the 13th century to modern times, which was formerly the imperial palace, and now contains State offices and the National Library, in which are more than 1,400,000 volumes, manuscripts, maps, and papyri; the Augustine church, a 14th-century Gothic structure; and the Minorite church, also a 14th-century Gothic structure, containing a splendid mosaic of Leonardo da Vinci's "Last Supper" done by the painter Jean François Raffaeli at the command of Napoleon Bonaparte. Bordering the Ringstrasse are numerous important buildings and impressive parks, the palace of justice, the museums of art and natural history, the houses of parliament, and the opera house. The principal public park of Vienna, the Prater, is situated on the island formed by the Danube river and canal, and is about 4 miles long and 2 miles wide. The outstanding cultural institution of the city is the University of Vienna (see VIENNA, UNIVERSITY OF), which was founded in the 14th century and is renowned for its medical school.

Prior to the Roman occupation in the 1st century A.D., the town was a Celtic settlement. The emperor Marcus Aurelius is supposed to have died there in 180 A.D. Vienna declined in importance during the later Roman Empire, and in 450 Attila and his Huns pillaged the city. It was later taken by the Avars (q.v.), but at the close of the 8th century the Frankish king Charlemagne subdued the Avars and captured the city. In the 12th century Vienna became the residence of the Babenberg dukes of Austria. The traffic across Europe during the period of the Crusades caused Vienna to prosper. The city was enlarged in the 13th century and soon afterward became the capital of the Hapsburg emperors. In 1477 the city resisted a siege by the Hungarians, but in 1485 it fell to the Hungarian king Matthius Corvinus. The Turks twice besieged Vienna without success, in 1529 and 1683. Polish and German forces assisted in defeating the Turks during the second siege. In 1735 and 1738 treaties were concluded at Vienna in connection with the War of the Polish Succession. In 1805 and 1809 Vienna was, for a brief period, occupied by Napoleon Bonaparte, and the battles of Aspern and Wagram were fought in its environs. The famous Congress of Vienna, which followed the Napoleonic Wars, was held in the city during 1814 and 1815.

The composers Ludwig van Beethoven, Franz Joseph Haydn, Johann Georg Leopold Mozart, Franz Peter Schubert, and Johann Strauss lived and worked in Vienna during various periods in their careers. During the reign of Austria-Hungary's last great emperor, Francis Joseph I, Vienna emerged as one of the most architecturally imposing capitals of the world, and also during this period Vienna became known as a city of gaiety, and music, particularly in the light-opera field. In 1921 the city received the status of a province. During the period between the two world wars, Vienna, capital of the new Austrian republic, was often the site of riots and strikes occasioning bloodshed. In 1926, during a general strike, the Palace of Justice was burned by a mob. The Karl Marx Hoff, a Socialist housing settlement, was bombarded by government forces in 1934 (see DOLLFUSS, ENGELBERT). In the same year the city was the site of an uprising by Austrian Nazis which, though quickly suppressed, resulted in the murder of Dollfuss, the Austrian chancellor. Following World War II and the liberation of Austria, which had been made a part of Germany in March, 1938, Vienna was divided into four zones which were controlled by the occupying powers, the United States, France, Great Britain, and the Soviet Union, and the city was established as the seat of the Allied Council, the supreme governing body of occupied Austria. For additional information on Vienna, see AUSTRIA; AUSTRIA-HUNGARY. The city and province of Vienna covers an area of 469 sq.m. The population (1948 est.) is 1,730,613.

VIENNA, CONGRESS OF, a European conference held in Vienna from September, 1814, to June, 1815, to discuss the European situation upon the downfall of Napoleon I. All the European powers, except Turkey, assembled at the Congress. The main results, interrupted by the escape of Napoleon, are as follows: Russia received the larger part of the duchy of Warsaw as the kingdom of Poland; Prussia received West Prussia, Posen, the northern half of Saxony, and the bulk of the provinces of the Rhine and Westphalia; Hanover received additions, and became a kingdom; Austria was given back most of the territory she had recently lost, and was compensated in Germany, Italy, and Illyria for the loss of Belgium; Britain kept Cape Colony, Ceylon, Mauritius, Heligoland, and Malta; the king of Sardinia received Genoa; and a Bourbon received the kingdom of Naples. A territorial commission was established at Frankfort, and by 1819 had reorganized Germany as a confederation of thirty-nine States. The history of modern Europe springs from this Congress.

The Congress was one of the most brilliant assemblages of crowned heads and prominent diplomats and statesmen that had ever gathered in the history of Europe. Of the sovereigns of Europe there were in attendance the czar of Russia, the emperor of Austria, and the kings of Prussia, Denmark, Bavaria, and Württemberg, besides a large number of the princes of the smaller German states. Among these royal visitors Czar Alexander I was the most conspicuous; he was one of the few liberal-minded men at the Congress. He had interested himself in the democratic development of Swiss institutions. He sympathized with Stein's schemes for unifying the German states and set his heart on the restoration of the Polish nation under a liberal constitutional government.

Of the diplomats, Prince Metternich, the Austrian minister of state, who acted as president of the Congress, played perhaps the most prominent part in the work of the Congress. Undoubtedly the most astute of the representatives was the French diplomat, Prince Talleyrand. When he arrived at the Congress he found that the representatives of the four principal powers—Great Britain, Russia, Prussia, and Austria—had agreed that neither France nor Spain, nor any of the smaller powers, should take part in the deliberations, but that all decisions should be made by the four "Great Powers". Talleyrand soon showed that this arrangement was contrary to the agreement for calling the Congress and succeeded in securing for France a share in the deliberations on an equal footing with the other powers. Among the other prominent diplomats and statesmen in attendance were Castlereagh and Wellington from Great Brit-

Representatives of the European powers at the Congress of Vienna

ain, Hardenberg and Humboldt from Prussia, and Nesselrode from Russia.

Certain questions had been decided in principle in the first Treaty of Paris, immediately after the overthrow of Napoleon, and the Congress of Vienna simply arranged the details of this settlement. France was deprived of all of the territory conquered by Napoleon. Holland and Belgium were united into a single kingdom under the house of Orange in order to provide a stronger buffer state to the north of France. Norway and Sweden were joined under a single ruler, one of Napoleon's generals, Bernadotte. The independence and neutrality of Switzerland were guaranteed, and the union of the cantons was reconstituted as a loose confederation.

While the Congress is chargeable with many shortcomings, and some of its decisions were certain not to remain permanent, it did achieve much important work. It re-established a real balance of power among the states of Europe, and it paved the way for a concert of the "Great Powers" which succeeded in maintaining the peace of Europe practically undisturbed for forty years. The Congress, moreover, took a noteworthy step forward in condemning the slave trade and in providing for the freedom of navigation of rivers traversing several states or which formed the boundaries between states.

VIENNA, UNIVERSITY OF, one of the oldest and most famous universities of Europe, founded by Duke Rudolph IV in 1365. The magnificent new university building designed by the famous architect Ferstel was dedicated in 1884. The university consists of the faculties of law and political science, theology, medicine, and philosophy. The university departments include, besides a large number of seminaries, museums, and laboratories in art and sciences, three medical clinics, two surgical clinics, two lying-in clinics, two for psychiatry, and one each for such purposes as the treatment of diseases of women, skin diseases, and children's diseases. These clinics have attained a world-wide reputation, due to the eminent specialists conducting them. Notable also are the observatory, botanical garden, and Central Institute for experimenting in meteorology and terrestrial magnetism. See VIENNA.

VIENNE, a department in the w. of France, constituted mainly of the old province of Poitou, and situated south of the Loire. Principal crops include wheat, oats, barley, potatoes, and beets. Large numbers of sheep are raised. Vineyards occupy about 72,000 acres, with an annual productive value of about $3,500,000. The chief manufactures are cutlery, paper, and alcohol. The capital is Poitiers. Area, 2711 sq.m.; pop. (1946) 313,932.

VIENNE, the capital of an arrondissement in the department of Isère, France, on the left bank of the Rhone R., 20 miles s. of Lyons. There are many relics of Roman antiquity. In 1312 a council was held here in which Pope Clement V pronounced the suppression of the order of the Templars. The value of the annual production of textiles is about $4,000,000. Gloves, cutlery, glass, paper, woolen caps, bricks, and leather are manufactured and there are foundries and brass works. The trade by rail and river is important, especially in wine, and there are iron and silver mines in the area. The Rhone, spanned at Vienne by a suspension bridge, is joined by the Gère, which flows through the town. The remarkable Corinthian temple of Augustus and Livia, rebuilt in the 2nd century, is 88 feet long and adorned with columns. The town has also some immense arches, now thought to belong to a Roman edifice. The Plan d'Aiguille, a pyramidal structure resting on arches, was formerly pointed out as Pilate's tomb, but is now recognized as a probable goal of an ancient circus. The Gothic cathedral of St. Maurice (12th to 16th century), with its two towers, façade, and balustrade, produces an attractive effect. The ruins of the Château de la Bâtie are picturesque. Pop., about 25,000.

VIENNE, HAUTE. See HAUTE-VIENNE.

VIEQUES, ISLA DE, or CRAB ISLAND, a small island belonging to Puerto Rico, geographically one of the Virgin Islands. It lies 7 m. from the east extremity of Puerto Rico, and is 21 m. long, with a breadth of 6 m. The island is fertile, and sugar growing and cattle raising are the chief occupations. Pop., about 11,000.

VIERECK, GEORGE SYLVESTER (1884–   ), German-American editor and poet, born in Munich, Germany. He went to America in 1895. He became editor of a periodical, *The International,* and associate editor of *Current Opinion.* After the outbreak of World War I he assumed the editorship of the *Fatherland,* a paper devoted to pro-German propaganda, and discontinued in 1917. Viereck lectured at the University of Berlin on American poetry in 1911. His publications include *America— A Litany of Nations* (1906); *Roosevelt, A Study in Ambivalence* (1920); *An Empress in Exile* (with Empress Hermine, 1928); *Salome, the Wandering Jewess* (with Paul Eldridge, 1930); and *The Temptation of Jonathan* (1938). Viereck was imprisoned in 1942, during World War II, for failure to register with the U.S. State Department as a German agent; he was released in 1947.

VIERGE, DANIEL (1851–1904), Spanish illustrator, born in Madrid, and trained by his father and at the Madrid Academy. In 1867 he went to Paris, where he first became known by his drawings of events of the Commune. Vierge worked principally for the *Monde Illustrée* and *La Vie Moderne,* supplying these and other journals with a great number of sketches. He also illustrated works of Victor Hugo, Émile Zola, Edgar Allan Poe, and Jules Michelet's *Histoire de France* and Francisco Gómez de Quevedo's *Pablo de Segovia* (1882). The last two works are masterpieces of illustration and remarkable, as is all his work, for the drawing of scenery and architecture. Vierge's last and perhaps most noteworthy achievement is a set of 260 illustrations for *Don Quixote* by the Spanish novelist Miguel de Cervantes; an edition of the novel containing these illustrations was published in London in 1907. After his right side became completely paralyzed, when he was thirty years old, Vierge learned to draw equally well with his left hand. The art of illustration owes much to Vierge, his influence being particularly strong on American draftsmen. He worked chiefly in pen and ink, of which he made a new art, but he also essayed pastel, water color, and etching.

VIERNE, LOUIS VICTOR JULES (1870–1937), French organist and composer, born in Poitiers. In 1900 he became organist at Notre Dame in Paris and professor of organ at the Schola Cantorum. Numerous recitals in Paris and tours throughout Europe established his reputation as one of the greatest masters of the organ of his time. He wrote, in addition to other compositions, a string quartet, a violin sonata, and a cello sonata; five symphonies; and numerous other works for organ.

VIERORDT, KARL VON (1818–84), German physiologist, born in Lahr, Baden. After holding several posts at the University of Tübingen, he became professor of physiology in 1855. Through his *Lehre vom Arterienpuls* (1855) he became the founder of sphygmography.

VIERSEN, a town in the State of North Rhine-Wesphalia, West Germany, situated about 18 miles w. of Düsseldorf. Pop., about 33,000.

VIET NAM, a republic in Indo-China, recognized by France on Mar. 6, 1946, as a free state within the framework of the Federation of Indo-China and the French Union (q.v.). Viet Nam consists of the former French protectorates of Annam and Tonkin, and claims the French colony of Cochin China as an integral part of its territory. For physical features, production, and statistical data, see INDO-CHINA, FEDERATION OF, and articles on the component territories.

In theory, "Viet Nam" connotes the geographic area in which Annamites and the Annamite language predominate. The republic of Viet Nam was first proclaimed in Aug., 1945, while Indo-China was occupied by Japan. French forces re-occupied the territory in Sept., 1945, and France signed an accord with Ho Chi-Minh, president of the Viet Nam republic, on Mar. 6, 1946. However, the claims of Viet Nam to Cochin China on the basis of the Annamite predominance in that colony were not allowed by France. Civil war between the Viet Nam republic and France began on Dec. 19, 1946. In June, 1948, the French sponsored a central government in Viet Nam in opposition to that of Ho Chi-Minh. In April, 1949, Cochin China joined the French-recognized Viet Nam Republic. Area, about 124,000 sq.m.; pop., about 21,000,000.

VIEUSSENS, RAYMOND (1641–1716), French anatomist, born in Rouergue, and educated at Montpellier, where he became professor of neurology in 1671. He was well known for his anatomical studies of the brain, practical anatomy being then in its infancy, and it was stated that he had made over 500 dissections. His *Neurographia Universalis* (1685), with an account of his important researches on the anatomy of the brain and of the spinal column, won him membership in the French Academy of Sciences and in the Royal Society of London. The "valve of Vieussens" is a name still applied to the superior medullary velum, which he discovered.

VIEUXTEMPS, HENRI (1820–81), Belgian violinist and composer, born in Verviers. Before he was five years of age he began to study the violin. Two years later, accompanied by his master, he made a tour of the principal towns of Belgium, and in Brussels met De Bériot, who gave him instruction for several months. In 1833 he made a tour of Germany, and in Vienna became a pupil of Simon Sechter, the court organist. Later he was received with great enthusiasm in Moscow and St. Petersburg (now Leningrad). Other successful tours followed, notably those of America (1844–45, 1856, and 1870). In 1846 he was appointed solo violinist to the emperor of Russia, and in 1871 was made first professor of the violin, in the place of De Bériot, at the Brussels Conservatory. In 1873, after he sustained a stroke of paralysis, he devoted himself to composition entirely. He died in Algeria. Vieuxtemps ranks with the greatest violin virtuosi of the world. As a composer for the violin he holds a high place. His compositions include six violin concertos, solos, duets, études, variations, fantasies, transcriptions, and caprices.

VIGAN, the capital of the province of Ilocos Sur, Luzon, Philippine Islands, 210 miles N.W. of Manila, near the right bank of the Abra River. The surrounding country produces rice, indigo, cotton, sugar cane, and livestock. In the town there are fisheries, brick and tile kilns, and yards for the construction of small coasting vessels. Pop., about 19,000.

VIGÉE-LEBRUN, MARIE ANNE ÉLISABETH (1755–1842), French portrait painter, born in Paris. In 1775 she was elected a member of the Academy of St. Luke, in Rome. She became a great favorite of society, and was appointed painter in ordinary to Marie Antoinette, of whom she painted about thirty portraits. At the time of the Revolution (1789) she fled to Italy, where she remained three years, then visited Vienna, Prague, Dresden, and St. Petersburg (now Leningrad). She was everywhere received with high honor, and she was admitted to membership in the principal academies. In 1802–05 she lived in England. Later she visited Holland, Belgium, and Switzerland, making her home alternately in Paris and Louveciennes.

Among the best of her portraits are two of the artist and her daughter (Louvre); self-portraits in the Uffizi, Florence, the National Academy, London, and St. Luke's Academy, Rome; Jean Paesiello; the painter Hubert Robert; Joseph Vernet (Louvre); Madame Molé-Raymond; Lord Byron; Marie Antoinette and her three children (Versailles Museum); and Marquise de Lorabde, Morgan Collection, Metropolitan Museum of Art, New York City.

VIGER, DENIS BENJAMIN (1774–1861), Canadian statesman, born in Montreal. In 1808 he was elected a member of the Lower Canada (Quebec) Legislative Assembly. Viger became a leader of the French Canadians in the province, and twice (1828 and 1831) went as a delegate to London to state their views and grievances to the British government. During the rebellion of 1837 he was arrested for sedition, but was shortly afterward set free. After the union of Upper and Lower Canada in 1841 he sat in the Canadian parliament.

VIGFÚSSON, GUTHBRANDUR (1827–89), Icelandic philologist and author, born in Litli Galtardalur. In 1864 he was called to England to complete and publish the Icelandic-English dictionary, left unfinished by the English philologist Richard Cleasby at his death. This was published in 1869–74. Vigfússon became in 1884 professor of the Old Norse-Icelandic language and literature at Oxford University. He published numerous works.

VIGIL, originally the watch kept, with public prayer, on the night before a feast; it is traceable in the earliest centuries. The observance survives in the Roman Church now only in the Matins and Lauds and the midnight mass before Christmas, and the term is applied to the day and night preceding a feast, on certain of which fasting is obligatory. In the English *Book of Common Prayer* the vigils or evens of the chief festivals are retained in the calendar as days of fasting, but they have no special observance appointed for them.

VIGILANCE COMMITTEE, in the United States, an unauthorized organization of citizens for the purpose of administering summary justice in the absence of a regular judiciary or when the courts are prevented from exercising their accustomed functions. During and immediately preceding the American Revolution, vigilance committees were formed in many communities to enforce the nonimportation agreements and to ferret out Tories. Associations of "regulators", such as the Ku Klux Klan, are also generally described as vigilance societies. The most notable instance of the employment of the vigilance committee as a governmental improvisation occurred in California during the years 1848 and 1849. Thousands of adventurous persons had immigrated to this region on account of the discovery of gold, and, as no legal government had yet been organized, the law-abiding citizens supplied the deficiency by the organization of vigilance committees, which undertook the task of administering justice and punishing criminals.

VIGNALI, JACOPO (1592–1664), Italian painter, born in Prato, and trained in Florence. He belonged to the school of painters known as the Florentine Mannerists. A large number of Vignali's works, both oil and fresco, survive, principally in Florentine churches. He appears to greatest advantage in the frescoes of the Capella Buonarotti, Florence.

VIGNAUD, (JEAN) HENRY (1830–1923), American diplomat and writer, born of Creole parentage in New Orleans. During the first year of the Civil War (1861–62) he served as a captain in the 6th Louisiana regiment. In 1863 he became connected with the Confederate agency in Paris, and in 1872 was connected with the Alabama Claims Commission in Geneva. He was second secretary (1875–82) and first secretary (1882–1909) to the American Legation at Paris. Among his writings are *Toscanelli and Columbus* (1902), *Études Critiques sur la Vie de Colomb* (1905), and *Henry Harrisse: Étude Biographique et Morale, avec la Bibliographie de ses Écrits* (1912).

VIGNETTE, properly an ornament such as vine twigs and leaves with grapes; the name is now given to any small engraving (as on the title page of a book), design, or photograph which is not circumscribed by a definite border.

VIGNOLA, GIACOMO BAROZZIO DA (1507–73), Italian architect, born in Vignola, near Modena. In 1550 he was made papal architect by Pope Julius III. His masterpiece is the famous Caprarola palace and villa near Viterbo. He became the architect of St. Peter's in Rome after the death of Michelangelo, and designed the two lateral cupolas. His treatise on the orders has been translated into nearly all modern languages and is still considered a classical standard.

VIGNOLES, CHARLES BLACKER (1793–1875), British engineer, born in Woodbrook County, Wexford, Ireland. The Vignoles, or flat-based, rail, was introduced by him into Europe from the United States. He built the Dublin and Kingstown (1832–34), the Sheffield and Manchester (1835–40), and the London, Chatham, and Dover (1855–64) railways, and carried out important works in Russia, including the great suspension bridge across the Dnieper R. at Kiev.

VIGNY, COMTE ALFRED VICTOR DE (1797–1863), French author, born in Loches, Indre-et-Loire. Before the July Revolution he published his collected *Poèmes Antiques et Modernes* (1822), which were among the first attempts to treat philosophic subjects in epic form. He also published a translation of *Othello* (1829); and a drama, *La Maréchale d'Ancre* (1830). After that he published only works in prose. His *Cinq Mars* was a romance based on the most tragic of the crimes of Richelieu.

VIGO, a town of the province of Pontevedra, Spain, 72 miles N. of Oporto, on Vigo Bay. The tunny and sardine fisheries give employment to a large element of its population. There are iron foundries, machine shops, paper, flour, and saw mills, petroleum and sugar refineries, chocolate, soap, leather, and pasta factories, and cognac and alcohol distilleries. The building of small steamers and the manufacture of cordage are also important industries. The town of Vigo was attacked by Drake in 1585 and 1589, by a combined Anglo-Dutch fleet in 1702, and by Lord Cobham in 1719. Pop. (1948) 131,645.

VIGOREUX, a woolen textile fabric in which the color is applied to the yarn, before weaving, by a printing process, as contrasted with the usual methods of wool dyeing, yarn dyeing, or piece dyeing.

VIGOUROUX, FULCRAN GRÉGOIRE (1837–1915), French Biblical scholar, born in Nantes. After he was made secretary of the commission created by Pope Leo XIII in 1902 to settle moot Biblical questions, Vigouroux lived in Rome. Conservative in exposition, his most important work is *Dictionnaire de la Bible* (5 vols., 1890–1912).

VIHĀRA, a designation for a pleasure garden in early India, and more especially of the temple precincts and monastic grounds of the Buddhist and Jain religions. Originally the word designated the hall or halls where Buddha and the priests by whom he was accompanied used to meet. Adjoining the sanctum there is usually a narrow room, in which are images and paintings; opposite the entrance there is another door, protected by a screen. When this screen is withdrawn, a very large image of Buddha is seen with a table or altar before it, upon which flowers are placed. In front of the temple stands a sacred bo-tree, regarded as the descendant of the original bo-tree (q.v.). The best examples of the old Vihāra are still to be seen in Ceylon, but the finest specimens in India itself are those at Ajunta, Ellora, Salsette, and Junir.

VIIPURI. See VIBORG.

VIJANAGARA, or BIJAYANAGAR, a ruined city in Madras Province, India, about 40 miles N.W. of Bellary. After having been for two centuries the metropolis of a powerful Hindu kingdom, Vijanagara was sacked and ruined by the Mohammedans of the Deccan in 1565. The modern village on its site is called Hampi.

VIKINGS, the piratical Northmen who infested the coasts of the British Islands and of France in the 8th, 9th, and 10th centuries. The word "viking" is unconnected with "king", and is derived from the Scandinavian *vik,* "a bay". See NORTHMEN.

VIKOVÁ-KUNETICKA, BOZENA (1862–1934), Czech novelist and advocate of woman's rights, the first woman to be elected a deputy to the Bohemian Diet. Her best-known novels are *Revolt* (1900–01) and *The Lord* (1906). She also wrote several dramas and, under the pseudonym Ignota, *Má Lásko* ("My Love", 1909).

VIKRAMADITYA, or VIKRAMA, the name of a famous king or kings of India, after whom the Vikrama, or Samvat, Era is called. Tradition ascribes it to 57 B.C., but recent researches have shown that the Vikrama Era was previously called the Malava Era, and the coins and inscriptions of Chandragupta II, named Vikramaditya, belong to a period of about 400 A.D. The present tendency, therefore, is to date the reign of Vikramaditya in the beginning of the 5th instead of in the middle of the 6th century.

VILAS, WILLIAM FREEMAN (1840–1908), American lawyer, soldier, and political leader, born in Chelsea, Vt. He began to practice law in Madison, Wis. In 1862 he entered the Federal army as lieutenant colonel, and served during the siege of Vicksburg. From 1868 to 1885 he was a professor in the law school of the University of Wisconsin. He was United States postmaster general from 1885 to 1888, was secretary of the interior from January, 1888, to March, 1889, and United States senator from 1891 to 1897. When the American statesman William Jennings Bryan was nominated for the Presidency, on a free-silver platform, by the Democratic Party in 1896, Vilas was one of those who helped to organize the National (gold) Democrats.

VILAYET, formerly the name of the provinces of the Turkish Republic.

VILKOMIR, a city of Lithuania, U.S.S.R., situated about 130 miles S.E. of Riga. Pottery is manufactured. Pop., about 15,000.

VILLA, a somewhat extensive country estate, occupied for rest and pleasure for a part of the year; the house and grounds together are generally indicated. It is not used of farms, nor of rural or suburban estates occupied the whole year. The villa originated with the ancient Romans, and received its highest development in Italy in the 16th and 17th centuries. The Italian villas of the Renaissance were due in large measure to the splendor of the papal court. They were intended as places for brief sojourn and recreation. Villas of more modern date in Europe and the United States borrow from the Italian many suggestions as to landscape architecture and detail, but, being intended for a season's residence, the dwelling presents a more permanent character than the casino of the Italian villas, and is accompanied by dependencies, as stables, lodges, tennis courts, and kitchen gardens, which are foreign to the purposes of the Italian villa.

VILLA, FRANCISCO, known as PANCHO, real name DOROTEO ARANGO (1877–1923), Mexican revolutionary general, born in Las Nieves. He took the name of Villa after joining the Madero revolt. An outlaw, a price was put on his head by the Díaz administration. Upon the outbreak of the revolution in 1910 Villa offered his services to Madero in return for pardon. During Madero's administration he served under Huerta against Orozco, in 1914 joined Carranza in the revolution against Huerta, and later in the same year himself headed a revolt against Carranza. In response to President Wilson's note of June 2, 1915, Villa agreed to treat with Carranza to settle the difficulties of the country, but the latter refused. On March 9, 1916, he crossed the border and attacked the town of Columbus, New Mexico, killing a number of citizens and destroying a portion of the town. The United States immediately dispatched a punitive expedition to Mexico to capture Villa and disperse his forces. (See UNITED STATES: *History*.)

VILLACH, a district city in Carinthia, Austria, 24 miles w. of Klagenfurt, on the Drave. Manufactures include colors and other chemical products. To the southwest are the Villacher Alps (Dobratsch, 7110 feet). Pop., about 22,000.

VILLA D'ESTE, one of the most important of Italian villas, situated on a steep slope at the edge of the town of Tivoli, 18 miles from Rome. It was laid out in 1549 for Cardinal Ippolito d'Este, and is remarkable for the skill with which the steep slope and the more level lower portion were treated, and for the extent and variety of its water works, cascades, grottoes, and fountains. These consist in part of later additions. The casino, really a vast palace decorated with paintings, was never completed externally. It became the property of the Austrian crown prince, but was requisitioned in 1915, during World War I, by the Italian government for use as a barracks.

VILLAFRANCA DI VERONA, a town in the province of Verona, Italy, on the Tione, 14 miles N. of Mantua. The preliminary treaty of peace between France and Austria, which ended the War of 1859, was signed here on July 11, 1859. Pop., about 12,000.

VILLAGE COMMUNITY, the name given to the organized agricultural community of primitive times. Fustel de Coulanges and Seebohm (qq.v.) held that the village communities of Germany and England were not free communistic organizations, as the mark theory would have them, but that the villages were inhabited by serfs.

VILLA GIULIA, a palace near Rome, built by Pope Julius III (1550–55). It forms part of a complex of buildings, the *Vigna di Papa Giulio,* just to the north of Rome, near the Via Flaminia, and is one of the best examples of the High Renaissance in Rome. After the death of Julius III the building sank into decay, but it has been restored, and is now a museum of Etruscan antiquities found outside of Rome, chiefly at Falerii.

VILLAGRAN, or VILLAGRA, FRANCISCO DE (1507?–63), Spanish colonial administrator, born in Astorga, León. He served conspicuously with Pedro de Valdivia during the conquest of Chile (1540–45), and succeeded him as governor when Valdivia was killed in the Araucanian revolt (1553–54). In 1557 he was superseded by Antonio de Mendoza, but replaced him in turn in 1561.

VILLA-LOBOS, HEITOR (1881–   ), Brazilian composer, born in Rio de Janeiro, and mainly self-trained. In 1912 he accompanied a scientific expedition to the interior of the country to study the music of Indian tribes, later an important influence on his own music. Other native influences upon his work include that of the Negroes of Africa and South America. On the other hand, Villa-Lobos was exposed to contemporary European music, particularly that of the Impressionists (see IMPRESSIONISM, in music); he first encountered this music through personal association with the French composer Darius Milhaud, who was attached to the French legation in Brazil from 1917 to 1919. In 1922 the Brazilian government awarded Villa-Lobos a fellowship for study in Paris, where he remained until 1926. After 1931 he held the post of Supervisor and Director of Musical Education in the public schools of Rio de Janeiro. In this position he exerted a profound influence on public musical education throughout Brazil; among his notable achievements were the organization of the Orfeao de Professores, a training school for teachers of music based mainly on Villa-Lobos' theories of music education, and the systematic accumulation under his direction of a large collection of Brazilian folk and popular music, which served to focus nationwide attention on this rich source of musical material. In 1936 he represented Brazil at the International Congress for Musical Education, held in Prague. Villa-Lobos visited the United States in 1945, appearing as a guest conductor with many major symphony orchestras.

Villa-Lobos was one of the most prolific of 20th-century composers; over 1300 of his works were published. Among his best-known compositions are the *chôros* ("Serenades"), scored for a variety of instrumental and vocal combinations, which represent, in the words of the composer, "a synthesis . . . of different types of Brazilian music, Indian and popular, reflecting . . . the rhythm and characteristic melodies of the people"; and the *Bachianas*

Brasileiras, a group of five suites, also varied in their instrumentation, in which the musical idiom of the German composer Johann Sebastian Bach is ingeniously blended with the powerful rhythms and melodic turns of the folk music of northeastern Brazil. All of Villa-Lobos' music is characterized by brilliant orchestration, often marked by the use of original technical effects, and by a prevailing pictorial and literary interest. His other works include five operas; concertos for cello, violin, and piano with orchestra; a large amount of chamber music; and piano pieces and songs.

VILLANELLA, a rustic Italian part song without accompaniment. It was originally a country dance accompanied by singing, but the singing gradually displaced the dance and became a separate art form. The villanella and the villotte, a rustic composition in counterpoint, were the precursors of the madrigal.

VILLANI, GIOVANNI (1280?–1348) Italian historian. He held many offices in Florence and wrote a history of that city, in the vernacular, consisting of twelve books, extending to 1348. His work included the history of other countries, and is sometimes called *Chronicon Universale.* For the history of Villani's own time in Italy it is of great value. A continuation to 1363 in eleven books was written by his brother Matteo. The eleventh book was continued by Matteo's son Filippo, to 1364. Giovanni's work is noteworthy for its excellent style.

VILLA-NOVA or **VILLANOVA,** the name given by archeologists to a cemetery discovered near Bologna in which were found, in great quantity, important remains of the earliest Iron Age of Italy. These remains, and similar relics discovered widely elsewhere over northern Italy in cemeteries at Este, Golasecca, Rivoli, Trezzo, and Oppiano, show a marked advance in the power to work metals over the civilization represented by the Terramare. In one view, the Terramare civilization was Ligurian, the Villa-nova, Umbrian. The Villa-nova remains include cist graves, whose four sides are often of flat, unhewn stones; in each grave was an urn, containing the ashes of the dead. The urns show incised linear ornament. Articles of many kinds, in bronze and iron, especially many varieties of brooches, appear. So do figures of animals, which may have been votive offerings; these bear repoussé work in geometric designs.

VILLANOVANUS, ARNALDUS, or (Fr.) ARNAUD DE VILLENEUVE (1235?–1312?), Spanish-Italian alchemist, born in Villanova, Aragon. In his numerous writings, as, for example, the *Tractatus Chemicus,* he calls attention for the first time to the potency of the philosopher's stone and the potion known as *Aurum Potabile.* His chief work is the *Rosarius Philosophorum.*

VILLANUEVA, JOAQUÍN LORENZO DE (1757–1837), Spanish author and patriot, born in Játiva, near Valencia. He went into the Church and rose to be court preacher and royal confessor. He was elected to the Cortes in 1813, and was imprisoned for six years after the restoration of 1814. In 1820 he re-entered the Cortes, was sent in 1822 by the Constitutional Party on a mission to the pope and upon the second return of Ferdinand VII in 1823 fled to Ireland where he died. Villanueva's works include *El Año Cristiano de España* (1791–1803); *Las Angélicas Fuentes, ó el Tomista en las Cortes* (1811–13); and *Viaje Literario á las Iglesias de España* (1803–52).

VILLARD, HENRY, originally, FERDINAND HEINRICH GUSTAV HILGARD (1835–1900), American journalist and financier, born in Speyer, Rhenish Bavaria. He emigrated to the United States in 1853. During the Civil War he won distinction as a war correspondent with the Federal armies. He was correspondent for the New York *Tribune* in the brief Austro-Prussian war of 1866. After the financial panic of 1873 he was made the representative of several committees of German bondholders in connection with the Pacific Coast railroads. Going to the Pacific Northwest, he bought the interests of certain European investors and organized the Oregon Railroad and Navigation Company, and obtained control of the Northern Pacific Railroad. In 1881 he became president of this company, but owing to financial difficulties retired from the presidency. In 1881 he bought a controlling interest in the New York *Evening Post,* and his interest in Edison's inventions caused him to organize the Edison General Electric Company, of which he became president.

VILLARD, OSWALD GARRISON (1872–1949), American journalist, son of Henry Villard and grandson of William Lloyd Garrison. He was born in Wiesbaden, Germany, and educated at Harvard University, where he was an assistant in United States history (1894–96). After working as a reporter on the Philadelphia *Press* (1896–97), he became an editorial writer for the New York *Evening Post* and its publisher, and was owner and editor of *The Nation* (1918–32). In 1916 he was elected president of the Symphony Society of New

York. He wrote *John Brown—A Biography Fifty Years After* (1910); *Germany Embattled* (1915); *The German Phœnix* (1933); monographs on the early history of Wall Street and on the German imperial court; and *Fighting Years: Memoirs of a Liberal Editor* (1939).

VILLARI, PASQUALE (1827–1914), Italian scholar, born in Naples. Exiled in 1848, he long resided in Florence. He was elected to the Chamber in 1867; was appointed senator in 1884, and was minister of education in 1891–92. Villari wrote biographies of Savonarola (1888) and Machiavelli (1895).

VILLA RICA, city of Paraguay, 85 miles S.E. of Asuncion, in a rich agricultural district, with fine timber forests and a trade in tobacco. Pop., about 26,000.

VILLA RICA. See OURO PRETO.

VILLA ROSA, town of Sicily, in the province of Caltanissetta and 10 miles N.E. of the city of Caltanissetta. There are sulfur mines in the area. Pop., about 12,000.

VILLARREAL, a Spanish town of 7020 inhabitants, 40 miles N.E. of Valencia. The town has distilleries and woolen and paper factories. The district of Villarreal has an area of 1650 sq.m. and a population of about 250,000.

VILLARS, DUC CLAUDE LOUIS HECTOR DE (1653–1734), French marshal, born in Moulins, department of Allier. He became a court page, and entered the army in Holland as a volunteer in 1672. He served in many important campaigns under Turenne, Condé, and Luxembourg, and in 1686, and again from 1698 to 1701, represented France at the Austrian court. In 1702, after the outbreak of the War of the Spanish Succession, he was given an independent command and sent to aid the elector of Bavaria, who had taken up arms on the side of France. He defeated the Imperialists at Friedlingen and in the following year gained the victory of Höchstädt (Sept. 20, 1703). In 1704 he suppressed the insurrection of the Camisards (q.v.). He opposed the Duke of Marlborough and entering Germany, outgeneraled the Imperialists under the margrave of Baden. In 1708 with a comparatively small force he foiled the attempts of Prince Eugène to penetrate France from Italy. In 1709 he commanded in Flanders and was defeated by Marlborough and Prince Eugène at Malplaquet. He was severely wounded at the beginning of the battle, and the reopening of his wound in the autumn of 1710 forced him again to resign the command. In 1711 he returned to his post, defeated the English and Dutch at Denain, on July 24, 1712, and gained a success over Prince Eugène near Landrecy. These victories hastened the conclusion of the Peace of Rastatt, which Villars signed as plenipotentiary, in 1714. He then became chief adviser of the court on military and foreign affairs. In 1733 as marshal general he took command of the French forces in Italy, but later resigned. Villars was the last of the great military leaders of the French monarchy. His *Mémoires* (1884–91) were published by the Société de l'Histoire de France.

VILLARSIA, or FLOATING HEART, a genus of plants of the family Gentianaceae. *Villarsia,* or *Limnanthemum, peltatum,* or *Nymphoides peltatum* as it is now called, is a native of Europe, from Denmark to the Mediterranean, and is very abundant in Holland. There are two indigenous species in the United States, *N. lacunosum* and *N. aquaticum.*

VILLASIS, a town of Pangasinan Province, Luzon, Philippines, situated near the Rio Agno Grande and 26 miles S.E. of Lingayen. Pop., about 13,000.

VILLA-URRUTIA, WENCESLAO RAMÍREZ, MARQUÉS DE (1850–1933), Spanish diplomat, statesman, and scholar, born in Havana, Cuba. He studied law at the University of Madrid and entered the diplomatic service at the age of eighteen. After serving as attaché and secretary of various legations and embassies, he was minister resident in Carácas and then in The Hague, and minister plenipotentiary in Constantinople (now Istanbul) and in Brussels. At the time of the negotiation of the Peace Treaty at Paris between Spain and the United States (1898), he was Spain's plenipotentiary. He was also a delegate for Spain at The Hague peace conferences of 1899 and 1907. Afterward he served as ambassador in Vienna, as minister of foreign affairs, and as ambassador in London (1906–13) and in Paris (1913–14).

VILLEFRANCHE-DE-ROUERGUE, the capital of an arrondissement in the department of Aveyron, France, 27 miles w. of Rodez. Among its interesting features are the 13th-century bridge across the Aveyron, the medieval church of Notre Dame, and the old Carthusian convent. The industrial establishments include foundries, oil mills, and tanneries, and a trade is carried on in flour, linen, truffles, wine, and liquors. Lead and phosphates are found in the vicinity. Pop., about 8000.

VILLEFRANCHE-SUR-SAÔNE, the capital of an arrondissement in the department of Rhône, France, on the left bank of the Saône. The church of Notre Dame des Marais (14th to 16th century) and the Renaissance Hôtel de Ville are noteworthy. There is a large trade in Beaujolais wine, and in cotton and thread. Pop. (1946) 20,017.

VILLEGAIGNON or **VILLEGAGNON,** NICOLAS DURAND DE (1510–71), French naval officer, born in Provence. He became a member of the Order of St. John, fought in the disastrous expedition of Charles V to Algiers in 1541, transported to Scotland the French force destined to assist the regency, and carried Mary Stuart from Dumbarton to France. He then fought against the Turks, and was afterward vice-admiral of Brittany. With the approbation of Coligny he attempted to found in South America a colony for French Protestants, but it was not successful. For having sided with the Catholics in the disputes, Villegaignon was called the "Cain of America". Among his published works are *Caroli V. Imperatoris Expeditio in Africam ad Arginam* (1542) and the controversial work, *Ad Articulos Calvinianæ de Sacramento Eucharistæ Traditionis Responsiones* (1560).

VILLEGAS, JOSÉ (1848–1921), Spanish genre painter, born in Seville, and trained there at the Academy, in Madrid, and in Rome. His paintings, which display great versatility and dexterity, include "Columbus at La Rabida"; "Palm Sunday in Venice"; "A Spanish Christening", "Examining Arms", and "A Dream of the Arabian Nights" (all three in the Metropolitan Museum of Art, New York City); and "A Cairo Slipper Market" (1872; Walters Gallery, Baltimore, Md.). Villegas was awarded the grand gold medal at the Berlin Exhibition of 1875, and in 1895 was elected to the Academy of that city. He also became a member of the Academy of St. Luke, Rome, and director of the Prado Museum, Madrid.

VILLEHARDOUIN, GEOFFROI DE (1150?– 1218?), French nobleman and historian, born in Villehardouin in Aube. He took part in the so-called Fourth Crusade, became marshal of "Romanie", and seigneur of Messinople in Thrace in 1207. His *Conquête de Constantinople* relates the course of events from the preaching of the crusade in 1198 down to the death of the Marquis de Montferrat in 1207. He took Argos, Nauplia, and Corinth (1210– 12).

VILLEIN. See VILLEINAGE.

VILLEINAGE, in the English feudal system of land tenure (q.v.), the status of tenants who held land as villeins or serfs and not as freeholders. A villein was bound to the soil; he was, however, allowed to hold and cultivate some land for himself on condition of assisting the lord of the manor in his farming operations. A villein could not leave the manor, but he could not be turned out so long as he discharged his obligations to his lord. By the middle of the 15th century the custom developed of money payment by the villeins to the lord of the manor as rent for the use of their lands in lieu of performing services on their lord's lands. See COPYHOLD; MANORIAL SYSTEM.

VILLÈLE, COMTE JEAN BAPTISTE SÉRAPHIN JOSEPH DE (1773–1854), French statesman, born in Toulouse. In 1814 he wrote a pamphlet, *Observations sur le Projet de Constitution,* in which he opposed the *Charte* issued by Louis XVIII. He became mayor of Toulouse, was elected to the Chamber of Deputies in 1815, and soon became the most influential among the leaders of the Royalist Party. He entered the Richelieu ministry in 1820, and a year later became minister of finance. Villèle's extreme Royalist policy was satisfactory to Charles X, but it tended to bring on the revolution which finally overthrew the Bourbons.

VILLEMAIN, ABEL FRANÇOIS (1790–1867), French scholar and critic, born in Paris. At the age of twenty he became professor of rhetoric at the Lycée Charlemagne, and shortly afterward at the École Normale. He filled the chair of eloquence at the Sorbonne (1816–26), held government offices under Louis XVIII, was made a peer in 1831, and served as minister of public instruction under Soult and Guizot, retiring in 1840. His principal works are the invaluable *Cours de Littérature Française* (1828–30), *Essais sur le Génie de Pindare et sur la Poésie Lyrique* (1859), and *Histoire de Cromwell* (1819).

VILLENA, a city of Alicante Province, Spain, 25 miles N.W. of Alicante. It has manufactures of linen, silk, brandies, flour, and soap. Pop., about 16,500.

VILLENA, DON ENRIQUE DE (1384–1434), Spanish author and scholar. He was connected by blood with the royal houses of Castile and Aragon. Villena was an enthusiastic student of the sciences, and because of his knowledge was suspected of sorcery. Among his works were *Arte de Trovar, Tractado del Arte del Cortar del Cuchillo* (usually called *Arte Cisoria,* a treatise on carving); *Libro del Dojamiento ó Fascinologia* (a treatise on the "evil eye"); and *Doce Trabajos de Hércules* (original in Catalan).

VILLENEUVE, PIERRE CHARLES JEAN BAPTISTE SYLVESTRE DE (1763–1806), French vice-admiral, born in Valensoles, Provence. He entered the navy at the age of fifteen. He became a rear admiral (1796), and commanded the rear division at the Battle of the Nile (1798). At the Azores he encountered a British squadron under Sir Robert Calder, and an indecisive battle ensued (July 22, 1805). The failure of Villeneuve's movement broke up Napoleon's plan for invading England, and the admiral, blamed unjustly and about to be superseded, sailed out and engaged Nelson in the great sea fight of Trafalgar (see NELSON, HORATIO). Villeneuve's vessel, the *Bucentaure,* was dismasted; he struck his flag, was made prisoner, and conveyed to England. He returned to France in April, 1806, but, learning at Rennes of the emperor's disfavor, committed suicide.

VILLENEUVE-SUR-LOT, the capital of an arrondissement, in the department of Lot-et-Garonne, France. The river Lot is spanned by a remarkably bold 13th-century bridge with a single arch. There are manufactures of paper, cloth, table linen, and copper wares. Pop. (1946) 17,055.

VILLEROI, FRANÇOIS DE NEUVILLE, DUC DE (1644–1730), French marshal, educated at court with Louis XIV. He was, however, banished to Lyons for a love affair. In 1680 he returned, and in 1693 became marshal. Sent to Italy in 1701, he was taken prisoner by Prince Eugene. Again he commanded in the Netherlands, but was defeated by Marlborough at Ramillies. Madame de Maintenon had him made guardian to Louis XV, and he was subsequently governor of Lyons.

VILLERS, CHARLES DE (1765–1815), French soldier and author, born in Boulay, Lorraine. In 1782 he entered the army as an artillery officer, but was compelled to emigrate in 1793. After a few months in the army of Condé he lived in various cities of Germany until 1797, when he settled in Lübeck. There he took up German literature and philosophy, with which he subsequently endeavored to familiarize his countrymen, and published *La Philosophie de Kant ou Principes Fondamentaux de la Philosophie Transcendentale* (1802), the first introduction of Frenchmen to the works of the German philosopher. It was followed by *Essai sur l'Esprit et l'Influence de la Réformation de Luther* (1804) and *Coup d'Œil sur les Universités de l'Allemagne Protestante* (1808). His sympathy for Germany was not, however, confined to its literature. In 1806 he wrote *Lettre à Madame la Comtesse Fanny de Beauharnais sur Lubeck,* in which he related the outrages committed by the French when they took that city. As a result, when the Hanseatic towns were incorporated in the French Empire, De Villers was exiled from Lübeck. He then secured a professorship at Göttingen, but was deprived of his post after the restoration of the Hanoverian dynasty by the French.

VILLERS-COTTERETS, a town in Aisne Department, France, situated about 50 miles N.E. of Paris, and 14 miles S.W. of Soissons. The town possesses a variety of industrial plants, including biscuit factories. In World War I, during the retreat from Mons of the British army, an action to delay the German advance was fought in the town by the British Guards Brigade, on Sept. 1, 1914. A surprise attack upon the German line near Villers-Cotterets was made, July 17, 1918, by the American 1st and 2nd divisions, aided by the French 1st Moroccan Division, of which the Foreign Legion formed a part. The commanding heights s. of Soissons were captured, and the Soissons-Paris railroad and the Soissons-Château Thierry road, the German lines of communication, were so seriously threatened as to cause the immediate withdrawal of all German forces in the Marne salient. Pop., about 5600.

VILLEURBANNE, French city in Rhône Department, 3 miles E. of Lyons. Manufactures include chemicals, bronzes, and liqueurs. Pop. (1946) 82,399.

VILLIERS, the family name of two English noblemen.

1. GEORGE VILLIERS, DUKE OF BUCKINGHAM (1592–1628), English courtier, born in Brooksby, Leicestershire. The possessor of great personal beauty, he supplanted Somerset as court favorite in 1614. He was knighted, raised to the peerage, and, in 1618, created Marquis of Buckingham. During his absence in Spain, where he tried to arrange the marriage of Prince Charles (afterward Charles I) to the Spanish infanta, he was made a duke, with other honors, but the result of his disastrous military expedition to Cádiz was his impeachment by the House of Commons. In 1627 he appeared with an armament before Rochelle but was defeated. He undertook a second expedition to Rochelle but was assassinated at Portsmouth.

2. GEORGE VILLIERS, 2nd DUKE OF BUCKINGHAM (1628–87), English politician. He was brought up with the royal princes and educated at Trinity College, Cambridge. In the Civil War he served in the royal army, and as a result his estates were confiscated. In 1650 Villiers was given an important command in the projected invasion of Scotland, and fought with Charles II at Worcester. Later, however, he sought to make his peace with the Protector by returning secretly to England and marrying the daughter of Fairfax, the parliamentary general. He was arrested, and not released until after the abdication of Richard Cromwell. When Charles II was placed on the throne Villiers received various minor offices. After the downfall in 1667 of Clarendon, who had been his enemy, Villiers became one of the chief advisers of Charles, though he held no official position. Later his influence rapidly declined, and in 1673 he came to an open rupture with Arlington, who had the support of the king. The result was that he soon retired to private life. Villiers was a patron of authors, and also wrote himself. His drama, *The Rehearsal* (1671), enjoyed some popularity.

VILLIERS, BARBARA, COUNTESS OF CASTLEMAINE and DUCHESS OF CLEVELAND (1641–1709), famous as the mistress of Charles II after the Restoration. She used her influence principally against the Earl of Clarendon, who fell from power as the result of court intrigue.

VILLIERS, CHARLES PELHAM (1802–98), English statesman, born in London. In 1834 he was returned to the House of Commons for Wolverhampton. In 1838 he introduced in Parliament the first of his famous annual motions for the repeal of the Corn Laws. This was before the formation of the Anti-Corn Law Association (afterward transformed into the Anti-Corn Law League) and before either Cobden or Bright had become interested in the subject, hence to Villiers belongs the honor of being the pioneer in the movement. He continued to be one of the leaders in the agitation until the repeal was effected in 1846.

VILLIERS, FREDERIC (1852–1922), English war artist and correspondent, born in London. In 1876 he was war artist for the *Graphic* in Serbia, and two years later was with the Russians in the war with Turkey. Subsequent assignments took him to all parts of the world. He was correspondent for the *Illustrated London News* during the Boer War (1899), the Russo-Japanese War (1905), and the Balkan War (1912–13). Villiers wrote *Pictures of Many Wars* (1902), *Port Arthur* (1905), *Peaceful Personalities and Warriors Bold* (1907), all illustrated by himself; and *Five Decades of Adventure* (1921).

VILLIERS DE L'ISLE ADAM, COMTE PHILIPPE AUGUSTE MATHIAS DE (1838–89), French author, born in Saint-Brieuc, Brittany. He is perhaps to be considered the originator of the symbolistic movement in French literature. He died in poverty in the care of the Frères Saint-Jean-de-Dieu. His first publication was a volume entitled *Premières Poésies* (1856–58). Among his other works are *Contes Cruels* (1883), *L'Eve Future* (1886), *L'Amour Suprême* (1886), *Tribulat Bonhomet* (1887), and *Secret de l'Echafaud* (1888).

VILLOISON, JEAN BAPTISTE GASPARD D'ANSSE DE (1750–1805), French classical scholar, born in Corbeil-sur-Seine. In 1778 he was commissioned by the French government to examine the manuscripts of the library of St. Mark in Venice. The results of his study there were published in his *Anecdota Græca* (1781). The most important of these results was the discovery of the famous *Codex Venetus* of Homer with the scholia. His other works are the *Homeric Lexicon* of Apollonius (1773); *Longi Pastoralium Libri IV* (1788); and his most famous work, the *Iliad,* edited on the basis of the *Codex Venetus* (1788).

VILLON, FRANÇOIS (b. 1431), French lyric poet, born near Paris, and educated at the Sorbonne. His real name is thought to have been François de Montcorbier; he assumed the name Villon, however, out of gratitude to his patron Guillaume de Villon, a professor of canon law, who adopted and befriended the fatherless boy. At the university, Villon was well liked by his fellow students, and participated fully in the roistering academic life of the time. In 1455 he killed a priest in a street brawl, and was sentenced to banishment. The sentence was eventually rescinded on the ground that Villon had acted in self-defense. A year later he participated in the theft of five hundred crowns from the chapel of the Collège de Navarre in Paris. He fled to Angers in western France, and was tried *in absentia* and again sentenced to banishment.

Thereafter, for a period of four years, Villon wandered about France, visiting the splendid court of Charles of Orleans (see ORLEANS, CHARLES, DUKE OF) at Blois and that of John II of Bourbon. In 1461 he was arrested by order of the Bishop of Orleans and imprisoned in the town of Meung on the Loire River. After several months of detention, however, Villon was set free in consequence of an amnesty proclaimed by the French king Louis in honor of his recent accession to the throne. Before the end of 1462 Villon returned to Paris with the intention of settling down to a sober and industrious life. This resolution, however, was not kept; in November, 1462, he was imprisoned in the Châtelet (q.v.) on a charge of theft, and in the same month, shortly after his release, he was again arrested, this time for engaging in a serious fracas, and condemned to death. Villon was jailed for more than a year; at the end of this time his sentence was commuted to banishment from

Paris. Thenceforth nothing more is known of his life.

His writings comprise *Le Petit Testament* ("The Little Testament", 1456), a poem in 40 stanzas; *Le Grand Testament* ("The Great Testament", 1461), a poem in 173 stanzas, in which approximately a score of rondeaux or ballads are introduced; a *Codicile*, consisting mainly of ballads; *Le Jargon,* a group of ballads in Parisian argot; a *Dialogue* between the seigneurs Mallepaye ("Pinchpenny") and Baillavent ("Wastrel"); and a monologue titled *Le Franc Archier* ("The Free Archier"). Villon's great merit resides in the intense subjectivity of his verse. He dissimulates nothing that he feels, whether good or bad. His frankness about himself led him to believe that he was justified in being equally frank about others, with the result that his writings present a colorful and generally reliable picture of the times in which he lived.

VILNA (Pol. *Wilno*), city and district of Poland. In World War I, the German forces, under Eichhorn, closing in on Vilna, engaged the Russians before Meiszagola and defeated them in a ten days' battle in September, 1915. The city was closely invested and was captured by the Germans at the end of the month, the Russians retreating eastward. The Bolshevik government obtained possession of Vilna following the Treaty of Brest-Litovsk in 1918 and, on July 12, 1920, they ceded it to Lithuania after evicting Polish forces earlier in the year. A long dispute for sovereignty ensued between Lithuania and Poland. General Zeligowski entered the city, Oct. 9, 1920, and claimed it for Poland. By the Treaty of Riga, Oct. 12, 1920, the Soviet Union recognized Polish claims to sovereignty and following a favorable plebiscite, the Council of Ambassadors legalized the Polish occupation in 1923. Vilna formed a part of the Polish territory which Russia occupied (Sept., 1939), transferring it soon afterward to Lithuania. Pop. of district, about 1,273,000; of city, about 197,000.

VILVORDE, town of Belgium, in Brabant Province, 7 miles N.N.E. of Brussels. Manufactures include lace, starch, and soap, and there are oil and chemical factories. Pop., about 21,000.

VIMY, village N. of the river Scarpe, and 10 miles N. of Arras, France. In World War I the ridge dominating Vimy was captured by French forces in 1915, Hill 140 being secured on September 29. Successive German counterattacks drove the French from the ridge and back nearly 2 miles to Neuville-St. Vaast. The following year Vimy was taken and lost again, by the British, in February and, though they recaptured it in May, the Germans once more wrested it from them.

Possession of Vimy Ridge was of supreme importance to the Allies for, from its crest, Lens and Douai lay open to view, together with open country as far as Lille and the Low Countries. In the course of the third battle of Arras, in April, 1917, the Ridge was stormed once more, this time by Canadian troops. The general attack was launched at 5.30 A.M., April 9, and under cover of an artillery barrage the infantry overwhelmed the German defenses, securing their whole frontline system within forty minutes. By noon Canadian divisions had completed the capture of the ridge from Commandant's House to Hill 145 and, early in the afternoon, the final objectives in this area had been gained. A week before the battle the United States had declared war on Germany and, at Vimy Ridge, the Stars and Stripes went into action for the first time in World War I, being carried by William Clancy, of Texas, who was serving in a British infantry regiment.

VINA, the principal musical instrument of the ancient Hindus. It consists of a cylindrical pipe of bamboo 3½ feet long with a finger board about 2 feet long. At the ends of the pipe are two hollow gourds for resonators, each 15 inches in diameter. Behind one of these resonators are four pegs on which metal strings are fastened, tuned as follows: dominant, leading tone, tonic, and subdominant. On the bamboo pipe are eighteen movable bridges, somewhat lower than the principal bridge. These bridges can be adjusted so that the instrument can be tuned in any of the Hindu scales. Along the finger board run three sympathetic strings acting as bourdons. The vina has a range of two octaves with all chromatic intervals. The player knelt, so that one resonator rested upon the left shoulder, the other upon the right knee. The strings were struck be means of the first and second fingers of the right hand, each having a kind of thimble with a flexible point.

VINCENNES, county seat of Knox Co., Ind., situated on the Wabash R., 53 miles N. of Evansville. It is a railroad junction point, with service by four major railroads. The Lincoln Memorial Bridge connects the city with Illinois on the opposite bank of the river. Vincennes is the trading center and distributing and shipping point of a rich agricultural and mineral-producing region. The surrounding area ranks first in the State in the cultivation of wheat, sweet potatoes, peaches, apples, cantaloupes, and watermelons, and first in beekeeping. Other important agricultural products are corn, soybeans, tomatoes, strawberries, hogs, mules, poultry, and dairy products. Coal, natural gas, oil, and sand and gravel are the chief mineral products of the region. Industrial establishments in the city include creameries, chick hatcheries, flour and feed mills, bottling works, cold-storage plants and frozen-food lockers, commercial greenhouses and nurseries, fruit and vegetable canneries, packing plants, distilleries, bakeries, paper mills, lumber mills, foundries, coal mines, plants processing dairy products, and factories manufacturing candy, shoes, electrical devices, neon signs, automobile supplies and parts, baskets and crates, corrugated paper and boxes, sand and gravel products, structural steel, glass products, and foundry supplies. Vincennes has a wholesale and retail trading area with an estimated population of 145,000.

The city is the site of Vincennes University, a junior college established in 1806, the first institution of higher learning established in Indiana Territory. Vincennes, oldest city in Indiana, contains many historical landmarks, notably the George Rogers Clark Memorial, occupying part of the site of an old fort and commemorating the role played by Clark and his followers in the winning of the Northwest and in the American Revolution. Other interesting structures in the city are the old Cathedral, erected in 1826 on the site of the first log church, built about 1702; the Cathedral library, oldest in Indiana, containing a collection of 5000 volumes, many printed before 1700; Territorial Hall, built about 1800 and the first capitol of Indiana Territory; and the mansion of William Henry Harrison (1804), first governor of Indiana Territory and later President of the U.S. On the outskirts of the city are several ancient Indian burial mounds.

The first settlement on the present site was established by the French explorer Jean Baptiste Bissot, Sieur de Vincennes, in 1732. The fort built by Vincennes was captured by the British in 1777 and named Fort Sackville. On Feb. 25, 1779, Fort Sackville was captured by a small force of Americans under George Rogers Clark. From 1800 to 1813 Vincennes was the capital of Indiana Territory. It was incorporated as a city in 1856. Pop. (1950) 18,798.

VINCENNES, a town of the department of Seine, France. There are immense barracks, a great fortress famous for its arsenal and its school of marksmanship, and depots of military supplies. The château to which the town owes its historical importance is built in the form of a parallelogram. The building was begun by Louis VII in 1164, and was used as a royal residence until 1740. In 1832 Louis Philippe fortified it and turned it into a military depot. Among its famous prisoners were Henry IV, the great Condé, Cardinal de Retz, Mirabeau, and the unfortunate Duc d'Enghien, who was executed here in 1804. During World War I many notorious spies were executed here, including Mata Hari. Chemicals, rubber goods, and hardware are manufactured. Pop. (1946) 49,226.

VINCENNES, JEAN BAPTISTE BISSOT, SIEUR DE (1688–1736), Canadian explorer. He became an ensign in 1701 and in 1704 he served in the Miami country. There he rescued a number of Iroquois who had been taken prisoners by the Ottawas contrary to treaty stipulations, and thus prevented a general war. About 1725 he built a fort and trading post on the site of the city in Indiana that now bears his name. In 1736 he participated in an expedition against the Chickasaws, but was taken prisoner and burned at the stake.

VINCENT, SAINT (d. 304), Spanish deacon and martyr, born in Hulsea. He was under Diocletian's persecution imprisoned and tortured at Valencia. His feast day is January 22.

VINCENT, SIR CHARLES EDWARD HOWARD (1849–1908), English author and soldier, born in Slinfold, Sussex. After serving with other regiments he became colonel commandant of the Queen's Westminster Volunteers (1884–1904). From 1885 until his death he represented Sheffield in Parliament; he founded the United Empire Trade League in 1891, and was chairman of the National Union Conservative Associations in 1895. He wrote *Law of Extradition* (1880) and *Police Code and Manual of Criminal Law* (1904).

VINCENT, EDGAR, 1st VISCOUNT D'ABERNON (1857–1941), British financier and diplomatist, born in Sussex. In 1883 he was president of the council of the Ottoman public debt, held in Constantinople (now Istanbul), and then until 1889 was financial adviser to the Egyptian government. While in that post he reformed the Egyptian currency, and later, as governor of the Imperial Ottoman Bank (1889–97), freed Turkey from financial embarrassment. From 1899 to 1906 he was a Conservative member of Parliament for Exeter. In 1915 he was appointed chairman of the Central Control Board, which had control of the liquor traffic in Great Britain during World War I. From 1920 to 1926 he was ambassador in Berlin. In 1929 he headed the British Economic Mission to Argentina and Brazil. Vincent wrote *A Grammar of Modern Greek* (1881), *An Ambassador of Peace* (1929), *Alcohol—Its Action on the Human Organism* (1930), and *The Economic Crisis—Its Causes and the Cure* (1931).

VINCENT, FRANK (1848–1916), American traveler and author, born in Brooklyn, N.Y. He spent many years in traveling in almost all parts of the world, and in 1884 he presented to the New York Metropolitan Museum of Art a valuable collection of Indo-Chinese antiquities and art and industrial objects. Among his writings are *Around and About South America* (1895), *In and Out of Central America* (1896), and *Actual Africa* (1895).

VINCENT, GEORGE EDGAR (1864–1941), American educator, born in Rockford, Ill., and educated at Yale University. In 1888 he became associated with the Chautauqua system as vice-principal, and after 1907 was president of the Chautauqua Institution. From 1894 to 1904 he was a member of the faculty of the University of Chicago; from 1900 to 1907 he was dean of the junior colleges at that institution, and from 1907 to 1911 dean of the faculties of arts, literature, and science. In 1911 Vincent became president of the University of Minnesota. He served as president of the Rockefeller Foundation, New York, from 1917 to 1929, and was a member of the General Education Board and of the Commission for Relief in Belgium. In 1940, he was appointed first James Humphrey Hoyt Memorial lecturer at Yale University.

VINCENT, JEAN HYACINTH (1862–1950), French physician, born in Bordeaux, and educated at the University of Bordeaux. He served as professor of epidemiology at the Collège de France and founded and became director of the Laboratory of Antityphoid Vaccination at Val-de-Grâce in 1911. After 1925 he was director of the epidemiological laboratory at the Collège de France. His research was done on medical, clinical, and bacteriological problems. He developed a vaccine against typhoid and paratyphoid fevers and discovered the bacterium and the spirochete which cause the lesions of "Vincent's angina" or "trench mouth".

VINCENT, JOHN HEYL (1832–1920), American Methodist Episcopal bishop, born in Tuscaloosa, Ala. He entered the New Jersey Conference (1853), and was transferred to the Rock River Conference (1857). He was pastor of churches in Chicago and established the *Northwest Sunday-School Quarterly* (1865) and the *Sunday-School Teacher* (1866). In 1888 he was elected bishop and was appointed resident bishop in Europe in 1900, stationed in Zurich, Switzerland; in 1904 he retired from the active episcopate. Vincent was the chief founder of the Chautauqua Assembly (1874), and chancellor of Chautauqua University from its organization (1878). He wrote *A Study in Pedagogy* (1890) and *Family Worship for Every Day in the Year* (1905).

VINCENT, MARVIN RICHARDSON (1834–1922), American Presbyterian scholar, born in Poughkeepsie, N.Y., and educated at Columbia University. He became the first classical instructor in a grammar school connected with the college. Subsequently, he was professor of Latin at Troy University from 1858 to 1860, and held two Presbyterian pastorates, in Troy and New York, from 1863 to 1888. In 1888 he became professor of New Testament exegesis and criticism at the Union Theological Seminary. Among his works are *History of the Textual Criticism of the New Testament* (1899) and a translation of Dante's *Inferno* (1904).

VINCENT DE BEAUVAIS (d. about 1260), French Dominican monk. He compiled a large Latin encyclopedia and wrote several religious works. His vast summary of the knowledge of the times is divided into four parts: *Speculum Naturale, Doctrinale, Historiale,* and *Morale.* This last, however, is considered by most scholars to be an addition by a different hand. The *Speculum Naturale* contains all that was known at that time of natural history. The *Speculum Doctrinale* is a compendium of the scholastic learning of the day. The *Speculum Historiale* begins with the creation and gives the history of the world down to 1244.

VINCENT DE PAUL, SAINT (1581?–1660), a distinguished French priest, founder of the missionary Order of the Lazarists, born in Ranquines, near Pouy, in Gascony. On a voyage which he was making from Marseilles to Narbonne his ship was captured by corsairs, and he was sold into slavery in Tunis, but some months later escaped to France. In Châtillon-les-Dombes, where he was curé, he founded the order of Mission Priests, which later was established in St. Lazare, Paris, and became known as the Lazarist Fathers. His life was devoted to the organization of works of charity and benevolence. To him Paris owes the establishment of the foundling hospital. The Sisters of Charity were founded under his direction, and he was intrusted by St. Francis of Sales with the direction of the newly founded Order of Sisters of the Visitation. He left nothing behind him but the *Constitutions*

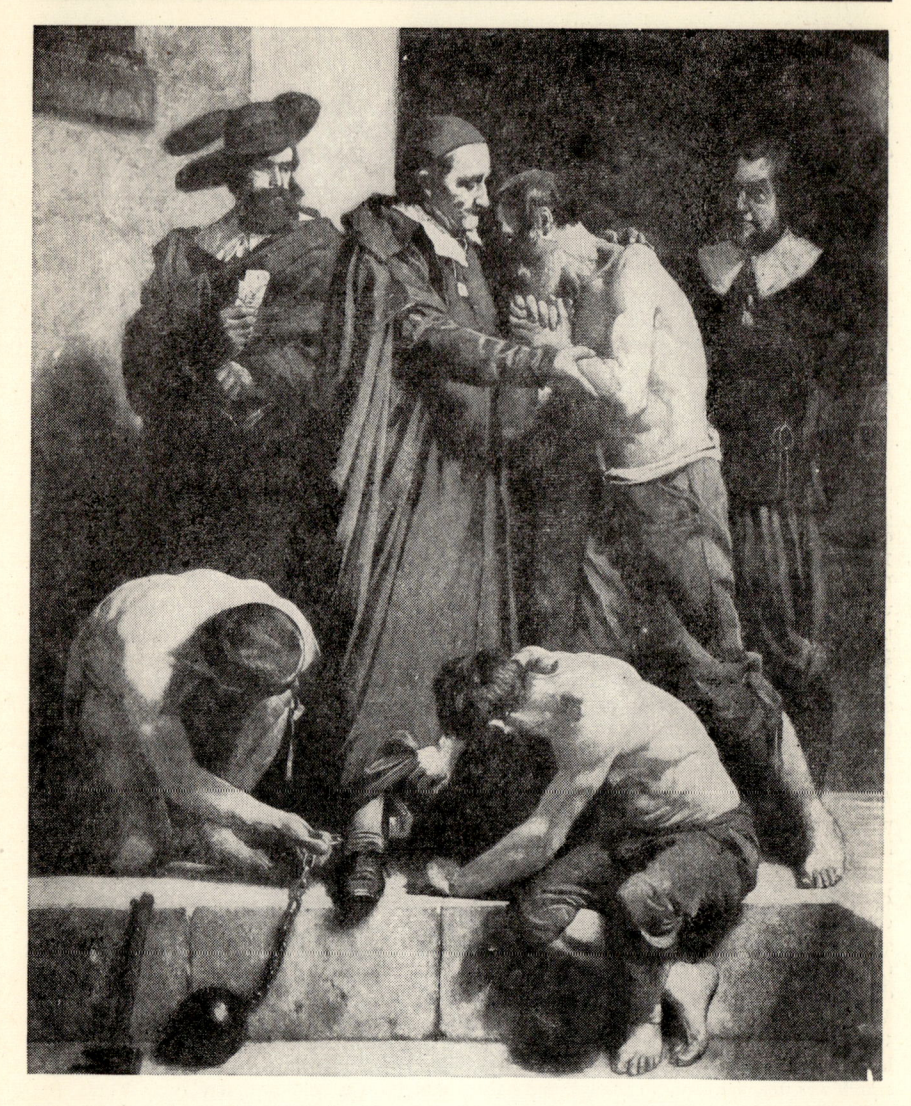

Saint Vincent de Paul, famous for his benevolent acts, assumes the chains of an exhausted galley slave while chaplain in a French prison.

of the Congregation of the Mission, *Conferences* on these constitutions, and a considerable number of letters, chiefly on spiritual subjects. He was canonized by Clement XII in 1737. His festival is July 19, the day of his canonization.

VINCENT'S ANGINA. See TRENCH MOUTH.

VINCI, LEONARDO DA (1452–1519), Florentine painter, one of the greatest masters of the High Renaissance, also celebrated as a sculptor, architect, engineer, and scientist. He was born in Vinci, a Tuscan mountain town near Empoli, the illegitimate son of Ser Piero d'Antonio, a Florentine notary, and Catarina, a peasant woman. His boyhood was spent in the paternal home in Vinci. By 1469 the family settled in Florence, where his father's wealth enabled him to enjoy the very best education which Florence, at that time the intellectual

THE WORKS OF LEONARDO DA VINCI

Above: "The Virgin, Jesus, and Saint Anne," a painting. Right: Study drawing for head of the Magdalen.

and artistic center of Italy, could afford, and he speedily became the embodiment of every social and intellectual charm. He was singularly handsome in person, powerful in physique, persuasive in conversation, a fine musician and improvisator; his mind was possessed of a profound and insatiable love of knowledge and research, which proved the controlling factor of his life. Before taking up painting he began the studies in mechanics and in the natural sciences which went hand in hand with his artistic activities throughout life.

About 1466–69 he became the pupil of his father's friend Andrea del Verrocchio. In 1472 he was entered into the painters' guild of Florence, and in 1476 he is still mentioned as Verrocchio's assistant, but in 1478 he was working as an independent master.

In 1478 he was commissioned by the Signoria of Florence to paint a picture of the Chapel of St. Bernard in the Palazzo Publico. His first masterpiece, the "Adoration of the Kings", which in an unfinished state survives in the Uffizi, was ordered in 1481 for San Donato a Scopello, Florence. Of the other works ascribed to this youthful period, none seem genuine except his unfinished "St. Jerome" (Vatican).

Da Vinci first visited Milan about 1482–83 as the bearer of a present from Lorenzo de' Medici to Lodovico il Moro, the reigning duke. This present was a strange musical instrument sounding like a lute, and invented by Da Vinci himself, who thus sang his way into the duke's favor. He remained there until his patron was driven from the city by the French in 1499. This was the most fruitful period of Da Vinci's activity.

His work in Milan was important and varied. As a sort of general factotum for the ruler, he was principal engineer in his numerous military enterprises, constructed the Martesana Canal, and directed great festivities, as when Lodovico married his niece to Emperor Maximilian. He was also active as an architect, being one of those employed upon the cathedral of Milan, and he probably designed other public buildings. He found time to prosecute his studies in anatomy, especially of animals, with Marco della Torre, and to assist Luca Pacioli in one of his mathematical works. At the same time he was at the head of a large and important band of pupils, whether or not they then constituted the supposed Milanese Academy; for them he probably wrote his *Treatise on Painting,* and it is certain he designed paintings which they carried out. The artistic task in which Da Vinci took chief interest, and indeed the dearest plan of his life, was a colossal bronze monument to Francesco Sforza, the father of Lodovico. On it he labored constantly till his departure from Milan in 1499, without having brought it to completion.

Of his paintings during the early Milan period, the most important panel is the well-known "Virgin of the Grotto", in the Louvre, executed for the Confraternità della Concezione (1482–90). From 1494 to 1497 Da Vinci labored on his masterpiece of painting, the "Last Supper", a wall decoration in the refectory in the monastery of Santa Maria delle Grazie, Milan.

In December, 1499, after the expulsion of Duke Lodovico, Da Vinci left Milan for Venice. He remained in Venice until about 1500, when he returned to Florence and assiduously devoted himself to the study of mathematics.

In 1502 Da Vinci entered the service of Cesare Borgia as a military engineer, rendering important services in different parts of central Italy. In January, 1503, he was again in Florence, where he served on the commission of artists to decide upon the proper location for Michelangelo's "David", and served as an engineer in the war against Pisa. Toward the end of the year he entered upon his famous contest with Michelangelo in a design for the decoration of the great hall of the Palazzo Vecchio.

During this second Florentine period (1503–06) Da Vinci painted several portraits, but the only one which survives is the world-famous "Mona Lisa", the pride of the Louvre, perhaps the most celebrated portrait in the world. The subject was the third wife of the Florentine Francesco del Giocondo, whence the name "La Gioconda", by which the portrait is known in France. The face has sadly suffered at the restorer's hand, but the eyes still have their dewy shimmer, as in life, a subtle smile plays about the mouth, and the wonderful hands are almost unspoiled. After four years' labor on the work, he pronounced it unfinished; but to other eyes it seems one of the most highly finished works in modern art.

In 1506 Da Vinci went to Milan on a three months' leave of absence from Florence.

In the art of painting Da Vinci wielded great influence. He was the pioneer of the High Renaissance, the first to achieve that complete mastery of form and technique which admitted of a new freedom of handling, a new truth to nature and life. He was the first to attain a sound and complete mastery of anatomy and to introduce color, in the higher sense, into Florentine painting. By the use of sfumato—a smoky, hazy quality—he achieved a remarkable melting tone and blending of color; he was the first great master of light and shade, which he made witching and lovely. His drawings reveal the consummate draftsman seeking rather after finesse than general effect; they may be found in the principal

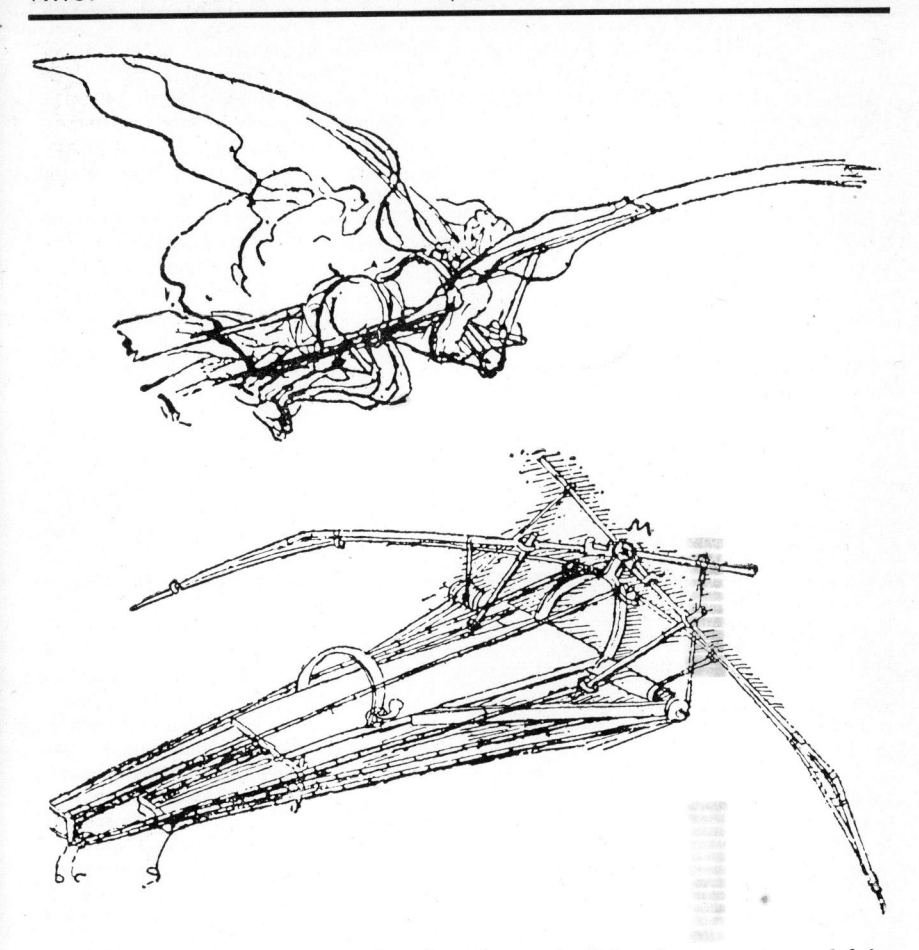

WORKS OF LEONARDO DA VINCI. *Top: Drawing of a man in flight using a man-powered flying machine. Bottom: Diagram of another type of man-powered flying machine.*

European collections, especially at Windsor. Among the principal are the studies for his principal paintings, such as the "Kneeling Leda" (Chatsworth, and Ducal Palace, Weimar), "Neptune Driving His Team", "The Battle of the Standard", "The Last Supper", the magnificent head of Da Vinci in old age (Royal Library, Turin), and the large series of caricatures in which he displays a remarkable sense of humor. The beautiful beardless head of Christ in the Ambrosiana is now generally ascribed to Luini. Especially characteristic of Da Vinci's art are his landscape backgrounds, into which he was among the first to introduce atmospheric perspective, that mysterious quality which heightens most admirably the effect of the picture, and the subtle mysterious smile, which Vasari has characterized as more than human. The influence which he wielded over Italian art was profound and wholesome. The chief masters of the High Renaissance in Florence, including Raphael, Andrea del Sarto, and Fra Bartolommeo, all learned from him; he completely transformed the school of Milan (see RENAISSANCE ART AND ARCHITECTURE), and at Parma Correggio carried his art to its logical development.

Da Vinci was named court painter to King Louis XII, and for the next few years he divided his time between the two cities. In Milan he continued his engineering projects, and he had studios both there and in Florence.

Da Vinci was the most extraordinarily ver-

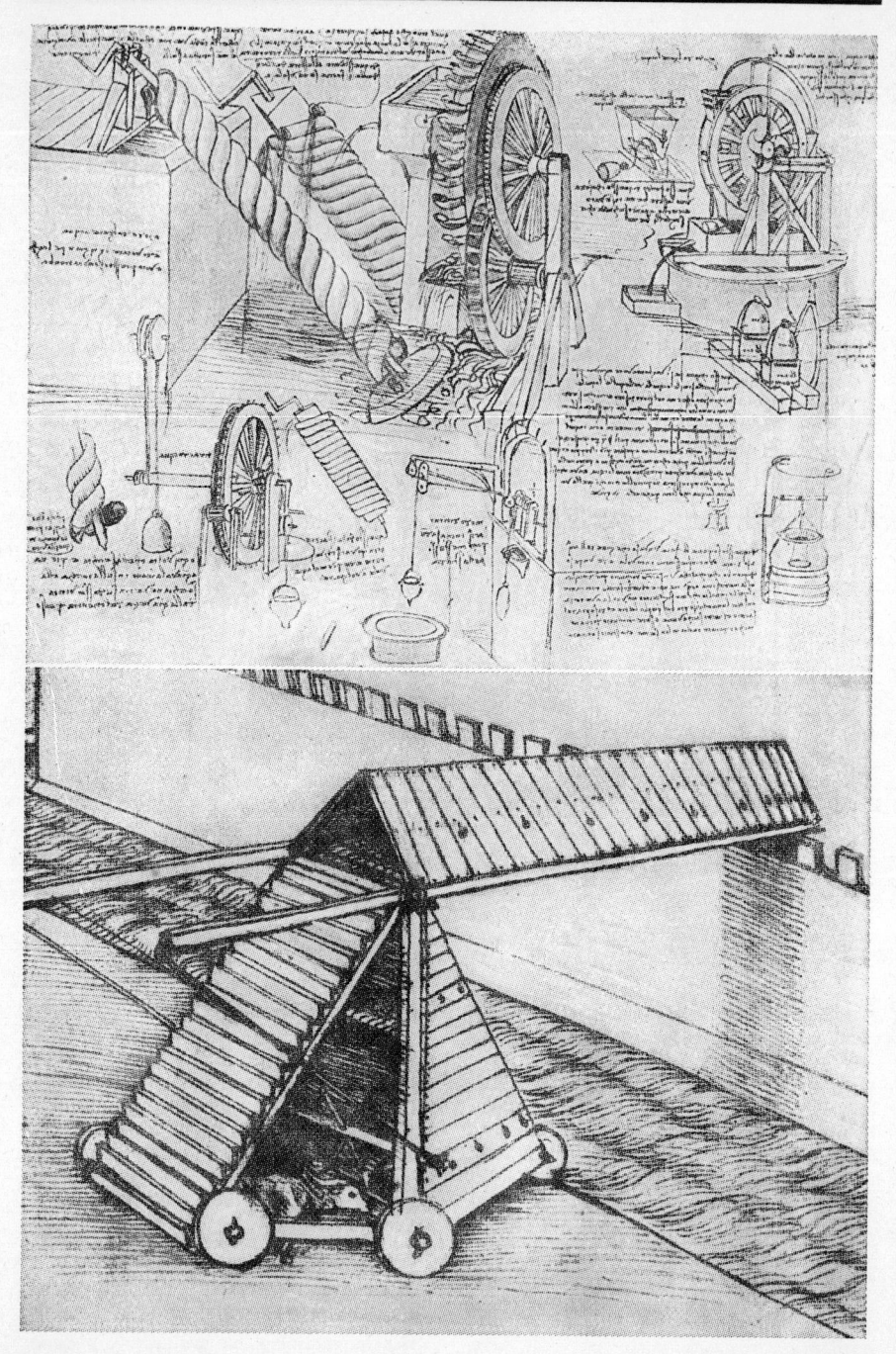

WORKS OF LEONARDO DA VINCI. *Top: Portion of a page on which various devices for raising water from wells are shown. Bottom: Drawing of a movable bridge for spanning a moat.*

satile genius of that age of geniuses, the Renaissance. As a man of science he towered above all contemporaries, and had his views been known and generally published, they must have revolutionized the science of his day. That they were not known is perhaps due to the fact that his manuscripts were almost undecipherable, being written with the left hand, back-handed, and from right to left. With an almost inspired glance he divined the secrets of nature, making discoveries which it has been reserved for our own time to perfect. A consummate master of anatomy, he even divined the circulation of the blood and the action of the eye in vision. He made astounding observations in meteorology and aeronautics, knew the earth's annual motion and the effect of the moon upon the tides, foreshadowed the hypothesis of the elevation of continents, and discovered the nature of fossil shells. He originated the science of hydraulics, and probably invented the hydrometer; his scheme for the canalization of rivers is still of practical value. He invented a large number of labor-saving machines, very remarkable for his day, and as a mathematician he takes high rank, especially for his study of spirals.

VINDELICIA, in ancient geography, a country bounded on the N. by the Danube River, on the E. by the Œnus (modern Inn) River, on the s. by Rhætia, and on the w. by the land of the Helvetians. It was subdued in 15 B.C. by Tiberius Claudius Nero Cæsar, later the emperor Tiberius, and was made a part of the province of Rhætia late in the 1st century A.D. Its chief city was Augusta Vindelicorum (modern Augsburg).

VINDHYA HILLS, a range of mountains in India. In its widest sense the name is applied to the whole northern escarpment of the great triangular plateau of the Dekkan, stretching in an east and west direction from the mouth of the Ganges to the head of the Gulf of Cambay. The range consists chiefly of Mesozoic sandstone, and has an average altitude of 2000 feet, with a maximum of 5500 feet.

VINDOBONA, the Roman name of Vienna (q.v.), which originally had a Celtic population. From the early 2nd to the end of the 4th century A.D. Vindobona was an important fortress of the Roman legions.

VINE. See GRAPE.

VINEGAR, a sour liquid obtained by acetic fermentation of alcoholic products, usually wine, cider, or malt, used chiefly for culinary purposes and for preserving. The active principle of vinegar is acetic acid, which varies in amount from 2 percent to 10 percent and even more; the distinctive flavor and aroma are derived from the materials from which it is made or, in artificial products, from added substances. Cider vinegar contains traces of malic acid, the acid of the apple. Formerly some mineral acid, usually sulfuric, was added to vinegar as a preservative and to reinforce it, but this practice is now regarded as an adulteration. In Europe wine and spirit vinegars are most commonly used, that from white wine being most highly esteemed; in Great Britain malt vinegar is extensively used; and in the United States cider vinegar is preferred.

There are two methods of making vinegar —the slow or natural fermentation and the quick process. The liquor in the slow process is exposed in casks and takes five to six months to complete.

In the quick process the original liquor is allowed to trickle through casks, containing clean shavings soaked in hot vinegar. The casks are in three horizontal sections; the top contains the alcoholic liquor, the center one the shavings, and in the bottom one the vinegar is collected.

In pharmacy a solution of a drug in dilute acetic acid is known as a vinegar. Two such preparations are official in the pharmacopœia, *acetum scillae,* or vinegar of squill, and *acetum opii* or vinegar of opium, popularly known as black drop, and used as a sedative. Vinegar of squill is employed for its expectorant properties. *Acetum aromaticum,* aromatic vinegar, is a solution of the volatile oils of cinnamon, cloves, juniper, lavender, lemon, peppermint, and rosemary in alcohol, vinegar, and water, and is used as a cooling lotion in headaches and fever.

VINEGAR EEL, or PASTE EEL. See EEL WORM.

VINEGAR FLY. See DROSOPHILA.

VINELAND, a borough of Cumberland Co., N.J., situated 35 miles s. of Philadelphia, Pa. It is the trading center of an agricultural area, is noted as one of the principal poultry-raising centers in the U.S., and is also an important manufacturing center. The principal industries in the borough are the packing and canning of fruits and vegetables, and the manufacture of glassware, chemicals, paper boxes, sash and doors, Venetian blinds, thermometers, curtains, clothing, shoes, and pearl buttons. Vineland is the site of the State home for the care and training of feeble-minded women, of the State training school for backward children, and of the State home for disabled soldiers, sailors, and marines. The borough is served by two railroads. It was founded in 1861 by Charles K. Landis (1835–1900), and incorporated in 1880. Pop. (1940) 7914.

VINER, CHARLES (1678–1756), English jurist, born in Salisbury, Wiltshire. His great work was *A General Abridgment of Law and Equity* (1742–53). To the compilation of this work he devoted half a century of toil. At his death Viner left about £12,000 to the University of Oxford for the establishment of the Vinerian chair of common law and for fellowships and scholarships. The first incumbent of the chair was Sir William Blackstone.

VINES, ELLSWORTH (1911–   ), American tennis and golf player, born in Los Angeles, Calif. In tennis, Vines won the United States Amateur Singles Championship in 1931 and 1932, and the British Amateur Men's Singles (Wimbledon) Championship in 1932; in 1932 he won the United States Doubles Championship (with Keith Gledhill). Vines became a professional tennis player in 1934, playing a series of matches on tour that year against William T. Tilden; in 1937 and 1938 he played on tour against Frederick J. Perry, and in 1939 against J. Donald Budge. Vines won the Professional Singles Championship in 1939. In 1941 he won a number of amateur golf tournaments and in 1942 turned golf professional. As a professional golf player he won the Rocky Mountain Open Championship in 1944, the Southern California Open in 1945, and the Massachusetts Open in 1946.

VINES, RICHARD (d. 1651), English merchant adventurer in the employ of Sir Ferdinando Gorges, born near Biddeford. He arrived at the mouth of the Saco River, Me., in the autumn of 1616 and passed the following winter there, whence the local name of Winter Harbor for the spot. He established the first permanent settlements within the limits of Saco and Biddeford, but was not the first to enter the Saco River, Martin Pring having done so in 1603 and Captain John Smith in 1614.

VINES, SYDNEY HOWARD (1849–1934), English botanist, born in London. In 1888 he was made Sherardian professor of botany at Oxford University. He served as president of the Linnean Society of London from 1900 to 1904. He was one of the founders of the *Annals of Botany,* and became its editor. His works include *Lectures on the Physiology of Plants* (1886), *Student's Text-Book of Botany* (1895), and *An Account of the Morisonian Herbarium* (1914).

VINET, ALEXANDER RODOLPHE (1797–1847), Swiss theologian and literary historian, born in Ouchy, canton of Vaud. At the age of twenty he became professor of the French language and literature in the Gymnasium in Basel. He was professor of theology at the University of Lausanne from 1837 to 1845. Vinet's numerous writings include *Études sur la Littérature Française au XIXème Siècle* (1849–51), *Histoire de la Littérature Française au XVIIIème Siècle* (1853), *Moralistes des XVIème et XVIIème Siècles* (1859), and *Poètes du Siècle de Louis XIV* (1862).

VINEYARD SOUND, a passage 20 miles long and 3½ to 7 miles wide between the Elizabeth Islands, off the southeast coast of Massachusetts, and the island of Martha's Vineyard.

VINGT-ET-UN, a game of cards, the aim in which is to get as near as possible to the value of twenty one (hence the name) without exceeding it. The game is played with the whole pack, the ordinary cards being reckoned according to the number of pips on them. The court cards are ten, and the ace is one or eleven, as the holder may elect.

VINITA, county seat of Craig Co., Okla., situated about 60 miles N.E. of Tulsa. It is served by two railroads, and is the shipping point and trading center of an extensive agricultural area. Vinita is the site of the headquarters of the Grand River Dam Authority, and of the Eastern Oklahoma Hospital for the Insane. An annual event in the city is the Will Rogers Memorial Rodeo. Vinita was founded in 1870 and chartered as a city in 1898. Pop. (1945 est.) 7600.

VINJE, AASMUND OLAFSSON (1818–70), Norwegian journalist and author, born in Vinje, Telemarken. With Henrik Ibsen and others he founded *Andhrimner,* a satirical weekly. Accepting Ivar Aasen's *Landsmaal,* he founded (1858) the weekly *Dolen,* which he conducted to his death. In 1861 appeared his notable *Ferdaminni fraa Sumaren 1860, Diktsamling* (1863) and *A Norseman's Views of Britain and the British* (1873).

VINLAND or **WINELAND,** the name given to that part of the continent of America visited in 986 by Bjarni Herjulfson; the land was not explored and named until 1000, when it was visited by Lief Ericson, who sailed along the coast from Labrador southward and gave the name of Wineland to one portion of the country because of the number of grapes he found growing there. Rafn, in his *Antiquitates Americanæ* (1837), sets forth such evidence as exists respecting colonization in America by the Norsemen. To this work may be traced the extended popular belief in the statements that

N.Y. Philharmonic-Symphony

Musician with a viola. He is not playing instrument but picking out notes of a score.

the Old Mill at Newport, the Dighton Rock, and other supposed remains can actually be ascribed to the Viking settlements.

VINNITZA, capital of the region of the same name, Ukrainian Soviet Socialist Republic, situated on the Bug R., about 120 miles s.w. of Kiev. The city is an important industrial center, with sugar refineries and plants engaged in the manufacture of lumber, iron castings, and phosphates, and serves as the shipping point of the region. Sugar beets, grain, and timber are the region's principal products. Area of region, 18,259 sq.m.; pop., about 4,875,000. Pop. of city, about 93,000.

VINOGRADOFF, SIR PAUL GAVRILOVITCH (1854–1925), British social and legal historian, born in Kostroma, Russia. He became a professor at Moscow, but his educational activities brought him into conflict with the bureaucracy. Settling in England, he made a special study of the village community in England, and showed that the early Anglo-Saxon village was a free community and not a manor. His important works, dealing with this subject, include *Villainage in England* (1892), an essay on Folkland in the *English Historical Review* (1893), *The Growth of the Manor* (1905), and *English Society in the Eleventh Century* (1908). He wrote also *Common Sense in Law* (1914) and *The Russian Problem* (1915).

VINOGRADSKY, ALEXANDER NIKOLAIEVITCH (1854–1912), Russian musical conductor. He studied piano under Rubinstein in Moscow and theory under Soloviev in St. Petersburg (now Leningrad). From 1884 to 1886 he was director of the music school in Saratov, and in 1889 he became director of the Kiev branch of the Imperial Russian Musical Society and conductor of its symphony

Bird's-foot violets

concerts. He conducted orchestras also in various foreign capitals, where he did much to arouse appreciation of Russian music by Western audiences. Among his compositions the more important are a violin sonata; two string quartets; a set of variations for orchestra; a symphonic poem, *La Nonne*; and *Air Finnois* for violin and orchestra.

VINSAUF, GEOFFREY DE (fl. about 1200), Norman poet and rhetorician, who lived in England. The name De Vino Salvo, by which he is sometimes known, seems to have been derived from a work on the vine preserved at Cambridge University, once attributed to him. He was the author of a poem, variously known as *Poetria Novella, Nova Poetria,* and *Ars Poetica.* It is written in Latin hexameters.

VINTON, county seat of Benton Co., Iowa, situated on the Cedar R., 25 miles N.W. of Cedar Rapids. The city is served by rail and is the center of a fertile agricultural area. The principal industrial establishments are a vegetable cannery and a poultry and egg-packing plant. The city was settled in 1845 and incorporated in 1869. It is the site of the Iowa State School for the Blind. Pop. (1948 est.) 5000.

VIOL, a musical instrument played with a bow; it was the immediate precursor of the violin. The back was flat; there were larger bends in the sides than in the violin; and frets, like those of the guitar, were placed on the neck of the instrument, to show where the fingers of the left hand should be put to produce the desired notes. There was great variety in the number of strings, which were tuned by fourths and thirds. There were four sizes of viol in use, *treble* or *discant, tenor* or *viola da braccio, bass* or *viola da gamba,* and *double bass* or *violone,* and they were often played together in concerted music.

VIOLA, the tenor violin. An instrument in size and compass midway between the violin and the violoncello. It has four gut strings, the lower two covered with silvered copper wire. The *viola d'amore* is an obsolete stringed instrument popular during the early 18th century. It had from five to seven strings of catgut, and below them, passing under the bridge, were an equal number of wire strings, which were tuned in unison and vibrated sympathetically with them. In the orchestra and string quartet the viola is a fixture, but, in spite of its clear, mellow tone, very little use has been made of it as a solo instrument.

VIOLET, a genus of herbaceous plants, mostly perennial, of the Violaceae family. They have a short stem, or are stemless, having in the latter case a short rootstock (rhizome); the leaves are alternate, and have long stalks; the flowers have five petals, different in form and size, the lowest having a spur behind. Several species are much cultivated in gardens, some, as *V. tricolor,* on account of their beautiful flowers; others, as *V. odorata,* on account of their fragrance. The *V. tricolor,* or pansy, is a very variable plant, its flowers differing much in size and color. North America has a number of native species, two of which, *V. blanda* and *V. lanceolata,* are of swampy places and are sweet-scented. The Canada violet, *V. canadensis,* is a tall, leafy-stemmed species, with starlike white flowers; *V. pedata* is the exquisite bird's foot, and has pedately parted leaves and broad flowers, tinted with every imaginable color. Other common species are the early *V. palmata* and *V. sagittata,* the latter of which has enormously broad leaves after flowering; *V. rostrata* grows in moist rocky woods; *V. rotundifolia* is yellow; and *V. pubescens* has broad, pale-green foliage. The dog-tooth violet, *Erythronium denscanis,* has no connection with this genus, but is of the Liliaceae family.

Violets are of easy cultivation on various soils, best in cool, shady positions, with rich, moist, sandy loam and good drainage. They are propagated chiefly by cuttings or divisions.

Jascha Heifetz playing the violin

N.B.C. Photo

Cuttings are made from vigorous shoots in the spring and set in fine sandy soil in a cool greenhouse or frame, and the resulting plants are transplanted to permanent quarters in the fall. Propagation by division consists in dividing the plants after the flowering period and replanting them immediately. Such plants flower the following spring.

VIOLET SNAIL, common name for small pelagic pectinibranch gastropod mollusks of the genus *Janthina*. Several species are known, all inhabitants of the open sea, where they cling to floating seaweeds and the like. Their shells are fragile, purple in color, and shaped like small turban shells (q.v.). They are especially interesting from the curious float which they construct to support their egg capsules. This is a gelatinous raft secreted by the foot in which a cluster of eggs is entangled with air bubbles, buoying them up; thus the collection is dragged about by the mollusk until the young hatch. They occur in shoals and feed upon jellyfishes.

VIOLIN, the most popular of stringed instruments played with the bow. In its primitive form it is a development of the lyre and monochord, the strings from the former, and the elongated resonant box with its sound holes, finger board, and movable bridge, from the latter. The history of the violin begins with the invention of the bow, which was first applied to the crwth, or crowd, some time before the 13th century, when the viole, or vielle, of the troubadours appeared. The rebec, the geige, the fidel, and many kinds of viols and violas underwent changes until toward the middle of the 16th century the true violin model appeared, and superseded other instruments of its class, except the viola, violoncello, and double bass. The primitive violins had no contour, and it was not until the 13th century that the body of the vielle was scooped out at the ribs, forming a kind of waist. The corner blocks were added about the 15th century, and it is supposed that they originated in Germany. The foundation on which violinmaking was to rest was the viol with the double corners. These produced a new constructive feature, the bouts, the ribs which curve inward between the two corner blocks.

N.Y. Philharmonic-Symphony
Playing the violoncello

These bouts rendered it possible for the first time for a player to get at the strings. At first they were of large size, but were tapered down later. For nearly a century the sound holes were shifted all over the violin, sometimes crowding with the bridge near the tailpiece. It was not until the violin model had been some time in use that they were cut in their proper place and the bridge fixed between them. The bridge was the last point perfected, and that by Stradivari. Violins may be divided into two classes: those made on the high and those on the flat model. The former is characteristic of the Stainer pattern, the latter of the Stradivari. The violin consists of seventy different parts, all of which, except the strings and loop, are made of wood.

In playing the violin eleven positions are recognized. By means of shifting, the compass of the violin is extended to almost four octaves, g to c^4. Skillful players can go beyond this compass. A peculiar, veiled tone is obtained by placing a mute (sordino) upon the bridge to check the vibrations. The quality of tone depends chiefly upon the method of bowing. In many compositions the bowing is specially marked. A peculiar effect is obtained by plucking the strings with the finger (see PIZZICATO). By playing with the bow close to the bridge the tone becomes very hard and metallic. This effect is called for by the words "sul ponticello". Harmonics are tones of a very ethereal character and are produced not by pressing the string against the finger board, but by touching it lightly at certain points. (See HARMONICS.) Chords can be played when the different tones are produced on different strings. This is called double stopping. In the orchestra the violins are the principal instruments, being divided into first and second. See ORCHESTRA.

The art of violinmaking was at its height in Italy during the 18th century. One of the greatest of violinmakers was Stradivari of Cremona, whose violins today bring immense prices.

VIOLLET, PAUL MARIE (1840–1914), French historian, born in Tours. His work deals principally with the history of the old French law. Among his writings are *Histoire du Droit Civil Français avec Notions du Droit Canonique en Notes Bibliographiques* (1905), *Les Communes Françaises au Moyen Âge* (1906), and *Le Roi et Ses Ministres pendant les Trois Derniers Siècles de la Monarchie* (1912).

VIOLLET-LE-DUC, EUGÈNE EMMANUEL (1814–79), the most prominent architect of the Gothic revival in France, equally well known as an author on architectural subjects, born in Paris, and educated at the Collège Bourbon. He was especially skilled in the restoration of works of medieval architecture, and did more than any other man to arouse an intelligent interest in its monuments. He wrote a number of important books. Among them are *Dictionnaire Raisonné de l'Architecture Française* (1854–68), *Dictionnaire Raisonné du Mobilier Français* (1858–75), *Histoire d'une Forteresse* (1874), and *Histoire d'un Hôtel de Ville et d'une Cathédrale* (1878).

VIOLONCELLO, a large instrument of the violin class, held by the performer between his knees. It has four gut strings, the lowest of them covered with silvered copper wire, and is tuned in fifths: C, G, d, a. Its compass extends from C to a^2, and even higher. In its present form the instrument dates from the latter half of the 16th century. Up to the 18th century its quality was little known, but since the time of Haydn the instrument has steadily gained in favor. It soon superseded the viola da gamba.

VIONVILLE, BATTLE OF, the most desperately contested battle of the Franco-Prussian War, fought on the plateau of Vionville, 12 miles w. of Metz, between about 130,000 French under Marshal Bazaine and a German force of 67,000 under Prince Frederick Charles, on Aug. 16, 1870. The battle was also known as the battle of Mars-la-Tour. The battle was one of the series of conflicts that prevented the retreat of the French army on Chalons, being preceded by the battle of Colombey-Nouilly on the 14th and succeeded by that of Gravelotte on the 16th. The battle began at 10 A.M. with an attack by the Third Prussian Corps on the French under Frossard at Vionville. It lasted for nearly twelve hours and was marked by great cavalry charges on the part of the Germans and desperate fighting on both sides. Bazaine overestimated the German strength and held himself on the defensive until the enemy had been reinforced sufficiently to repel all French attempts to break through their lines. The Germans lost 711 officers and 15,079 men; the French, 879 officers and 16,128 men.

VIOTTI, GIOVANNI BATTISTA (1753–1824), Italian violin player, born in Fontanetto, Piedmont, and chiefly educated under Pugnani in Turin. After holding for a short time the appointment of first violinist in the royal chapel in Turin, he relinquished that office (1780) in order to travel in Europe with Pugnani. In Berlin, St. Petersburg (now Leningrad), Paris, and London his playing created a furore. He first visited London in 1782. An attempt to found an Italian opera was frustrated by the Revolution of 1791, and Viotti again went to London as a soloist. A groundless charge against him of being a revolutionary agent drove him from England; but after living a while in retirement in Hamburg he returned to London, where he became manager of the Italian opera, and in 1795 director of the opera concerts. Ill success caused his return to Paris, where he was director of the opera (1819–22). His compositions include violin concertos and quartets for violin, tenor, and violoncello, violin duets and solos, and a few pianoforte compositions. His playing was characterized by vigor and brilliancy.

VIPER, a genus of venomous snakes, representative of the family Viperidae. This family includes many important forms, e.g., the common adder; the asp, extending as far N. as Sweden; the African horned viper and puff adder; the Indian daboia or Russell's viper; and the Indian *Echis carinata.* The head is relatively broad, somewhat triangular, and generally covered with scales; the eye has a vertical pupil, and there is no pit between it and the nostril; the maxilla bears on each side one functional fang, usually with several reserve fangs beside it; the poison is virulent. The vipers are widely distributed through the Old World and in Australia; the majority are African. As far as is known they are viviparous.

VIPER'S BUGLOSS, common name applied to plants of the genus *Echium,* belonging to the Borage family. The flowers have a calyx with five deep segments, an almost bell-shaped corolla, with dilated throat, and irregular limb, very long unequal filaments, and a bifid style. The species are large herbaceous plants or shrubs, rough with tubercles and hairs. The flowers are at first reddish, and afterward blue. It is a native of Europe, western Siberia and northern Africa.

VIPSANIUS. See AGRIPPA, M. VIPSANIUS.

VIQUE. See VICH.

VIRACOCHA, a man with superhuman attributes in the traditions of Peruvian Indians. While accounts from various early sources vary greatly, he is generally represented as being much lighter in color than the Indians and as wearing a long beard. The Indians of today speak of all white men as viracochas. One account of this tradition runs that Viracocha appeared in the province of Collasuyu in very ancient times when the land was in darkness, having neither light nor day. He went to a village called Tiaguanaco, where, being moved by the condition of the people, he created the sun and caused it to move in its course, after which he made the stars and the moon. According to another version there had been two successive creations by Viracocha. On his first appearance he had created the earth, the sky, and the people, and disappeared, leaving darkness everywhere. Later he had come out of Lake Titicaca and created the sun, the stars, and the moon and regulated their course in the heavens.

Still another version relates that at a time long before the Incas had ever been heard of, the Indians were a long time without seeing the sun, and in their distress offered up many prayers and vows to their gods. Presently the sun, shining very brightly, came forth from the island of Titicaca, at which every one rejoiced. Then appeared a white man of great stature who, by his aspect and presence, called forth great veneration and obedience. This man had the power to change plains into mountains, and great hills into valleys, and to

The red-eyed vireo

make water flow out of stones. The Indians say he performed other wonders, giving life to men and animals, and that through him marvelous benefits were conferred on the people. It is stated by the early Spanish chroniclers Francisco López de Gomara and Agustín de Zárate that Viracocha signifies froth or grease of the sea.

VIRBIUS, ancient Roman deity of childbirth, whose worship was associated with that of Diana (q.v.) in the grove of Aricia. In traditional mythology, Virbius is the mortal Hippolytus (q.v.), revived after his death by Diana.

VIRCHOW, RUDOLF (1821–1902), Prussian pathologist and publicist, born in Schivelbein, Pomerania, and educated in Berlin. In 1843 he became prosector at the Charité there, and in 1847 a university lecturer. In 1849 he was invited to Würzburg as professor; in 1856 he returned to Berlin as professor and director of the pathological institute. He founded and edited important medical journals, took part in commissions, and became one of the foremost pathologists in Europe. Of his works on medical and anthropological science *Cellular Pathology as Based on Histology* (1850; Eng. trans., 1860) is the most famous. Others are *Famine Fever* (trans. 1868), *Freedom of Science* (trans. 1878), and *Post-mortem Examinations* (trans. 1878).

Virchow was also distinguished as an archeologist. Archeological anthropology gained much from his description of the Neanderthal skull and of the bones found in the graves at Koban. He contributed more than one hundred articles on anthropology, especially well known being his *Crania Ethnica Americana* (1892).

Perhaps Virchow's greatest material monument is the Pathological Institute and Museum in Berlin, erected by the government in accordance with his desires. It contained 23,000 specimens at the time of his death, and by far surpasses all similar collections in the world. He also wrote on political and social questions and on a variety of other topics —the gorilla, prehistoric syphilis, medieval leprosy, plague in its relations to public health, Goethe, Morgagni, Schoenlein, Johannes Müller, and the relation between lupus and tuberculosis and between spedalskhed (a Scandinavian disease) and leprosy.

VIRDEN, a city of Macoupin Co., Ill., situated 22 miles s.w. of Springfield. It lies in a farming and coal-mining area, and is served by three railroads. Coal mining and soybean processing are the principal occupations of the inhabitants of the city. Virden was incorporated in 1873. Pop. (1940) 3041.

VIREO, common name applied to oscine birds belonging to the family Vireonidae. The family comprises about seventy-five species, only twelve of which are found in the United States, the rest being native to tropical America. Vireos are small birds with head, wings, back, and tail ranging in color from olive-green to grayish-yellow, and with breast and abdomen predominantly white. The bill is slightly hooked at the tip. The birds are largely arboreal in habit. They subsist on insect larvae, which they find under dead leaves and in the crevices of tree bark. Vireos build small, deep, cup-shaped nests of bits of bark, grasses, weeds, mosses, roots, and other soft materials, suspending them in the forks of tree branches. The nests are built 4 to 50 feet above the ground, and are usually set well away from the main trunk of the tree. Three to five white or cream-colored eggs with clearly defined reddish and brownish markings are laid in a clutch. The red-eyed vireo, *Vireo olivaceus,* the white-eyed vireo, *V. noveboracensis,* the yellow-throated vireo, *V. flavifrons,* and the warbling vireo, *V. gilvus,* are four of the species commonly found in the United States.

VIRGIL. See VERGIL.

VIRGINAL, a keyed instrument, one of the precursors of the pianoforte. It resembled in form a small pianoforte, with a compass of four octaves, furnished with a quill and jack like those of the spinet, and a single string to each note. Generally the case was elaborately ornamented. See HARPSICHORD.

VIRGIN BIRTH, in Christian theology, a term signifying the virginity of Mary (q.v.), the mother of Jesus, at the time of His birth. The dogma of the Virgin Birth is not to be confused with that of the Immaculate Conception (q.v.), according to which the soul of the Virgin Mary, from the first instant of its creation, was altogether free from original sin (q.v.). The claim of Mary's virginity is made in the accounts of Jesus' birth contained in Matthew 1:25 and in Luke 1:35, but nowhere

Virginia State Capitol in the city of Richmond — Virginia Conservation Commission

else in the New Testament. The belief was apparently not essential in the creed (see CREEDS) of the early Christian Church. In the 2nd century A.D. the acceptance of the Virgin Birth is attested by the Church fathers Ignatius, Irenæus, and Justin (qq.v.). The belief was rejected only by the Ebionites and the Gnostics (qq.v.). After the passing of these sects, however, the doctrine became universally accepted throughout the Church and was incorporated into the creeds. It subsequently acquired great prominence as a result of the high esteem in which virginity was held by the Church.

In modern times the doctrine of the Virgin Birth has been attacked by liberal theologians and scientific scholars of the Bible as being, according to the New Testament itself, not a necessary doctrine; as being based on Biblical narratives the accuracy of which is not above suspicion; as having its natural explanation in pagan and Old Testament stories of miraculous birth; as tending to degrade the institution of marriage; and as being needless to the divinity of Christ. In both the Orthodox Church and the Roman Catholic Church (qq.v.), however, the doctrine of the Virgin Birth remains a cardinal tenet of faith.

VIRGINIA, one of the South Atlantic States of the United States, bounded on the N.W. and N. by West Virginia, on the N.E. by the Potomac R., which separates the State from Maryland and the District of Columbia, on the E. by the Atlantic Ocean, on the S. by North Carolina and Tennessee, and on the W. by Kentucky. A small portion of Virginia is separated from the remainder of the State by Chesapeake Bay; it occupies the southern tip of the peninsula on which both Maryland and Delaware are also located. Virginia ranks as the 35th State in the Union in area, 15th in the order of population (1950), and 10th in the order of admission to the Union; it was one of the original thirteen colonies and entered on June 25, 1788. The state's capital and largest city is Richmond (q.v.). Other leading cities in the order of population (1950) are Norfolk, Roanoke, Portsmouth, Alexandria, Lynchburg, Newport News, and Petersburg (qq.v.). From E. to W. the extreme length of the State is 440 m., and from N. to S. the extreme width is 196 m. Area, 40,815 sq.m., including 916 sq.m. of inland water surface. Pop. (1950) 3,318,680.

Virginia is divided into three topographical regions: the coastal plain or Tidewater region, the Piedmont Plateau, and the Appalachian Mountains. The coastal plain, the easternmost province, comprises the area between the Atlantic Ocean and the Piedmont Plateau. It is more than 100 m. wide and includes approximately 11,000 sq.m., or about one fourth of the total area of the State. It is a low-lying, level area, gradually increasing in elevation from sea level at the coastal border to a few hundred feet at its western edge. Parts of the plain are marshy. In the S.E. corner of the State is the great Dismal Swamp (q.v.), which covers about 750 sq.m. Although the general coast line of Virginia is only 112 m., the overall coast line, measured around bays, inlets, and estuaries reached by tidal water, is 3206 m. The Piedmont Plateau is bordered by the coastal plain on the E. and extends to and along the S.E. base of the Appalachian Mts. Its width increases from about 40 m. in the northern portion of the State along the Potomac R. to nearly 175 m. along the Virginia-North Carolina boundary. The surface of the Piedmont Plateau is broadly undulating; it slopes from an altitude of 1000 ft. at the western edge to nearly sea level along the eastern margin. The third topographical province, the Appalachian Mts., is sometimes subdivided into the Blue Ridge and Allegheny ranges and the Great Valley. The Blue Ridge, from 3 to 20 m. wide, traverses the State in a southwesterly direction. The lowest elevation is 1460 ft. above sea level, and the highest elevation is 5719 ft., also the highest point in Virginia, at Mt. Rogers in Grayson and Smyth counties. The average elevation of the State is 950 ft. The Great Valley, which is from 25 to 30 m. in width, separates the Blue Ridge and the Allegheny ranges and extends diagonally across the State. It is subdivided by five separate valleys through which flow the rivers which drain the area. The elevation of the Allegheny range to the W. of the Great Valley varies between 1500 and 4000 ft.

The drainage of much of the greater part of the State is directly into the Atlantic Ocean or its arm, Chesapeake Bay, through the Potomac, Rappahannock, York, James, and Roanoke rivers, and their tributaries. These streams flow across the Piedmont Plateau and coastal plain provinces in parallel southeastward courses. The Blue Ridge forms the principal watershed in the State. The New and Holston rivers in the southern portion of the Great Valley, and their tributaries, flow N.W. and S.W. out of the State. The climate of Virginia is variable, and differences in temperature and precipitation exist among the three major topographic divisions of the State. Temperatures over the coastal plain are more equable than over the more elevated Piedmont Plateau to the W., and sudden changes to warmer or colder weather are comparatively rare. In the mountain province, where varying elevations produce marked effects, greater daily and monthly changes of temperature are shown. The average annual temperature is 57° F. on the coastal plain, 55° F. on the Piedmont Plateau, and 53° F. in the Appalachian Mts. Rainfall is well distributed and averages more than 40 inches annually.

Virginia is noted as a vacation State, with many mountain and seashore resorts. The Shenandoah National Park, the George Washington Birthplace National Monument (qq.v.), and a number of national military parks, battlefields, historical monuments, sites, and cemeteries are located in the State. State parks cover about 25,000 acres. National forests in the State comprise more than 4,120,000 acres.

Va. Cons. Comm.; Va. State Chamb.

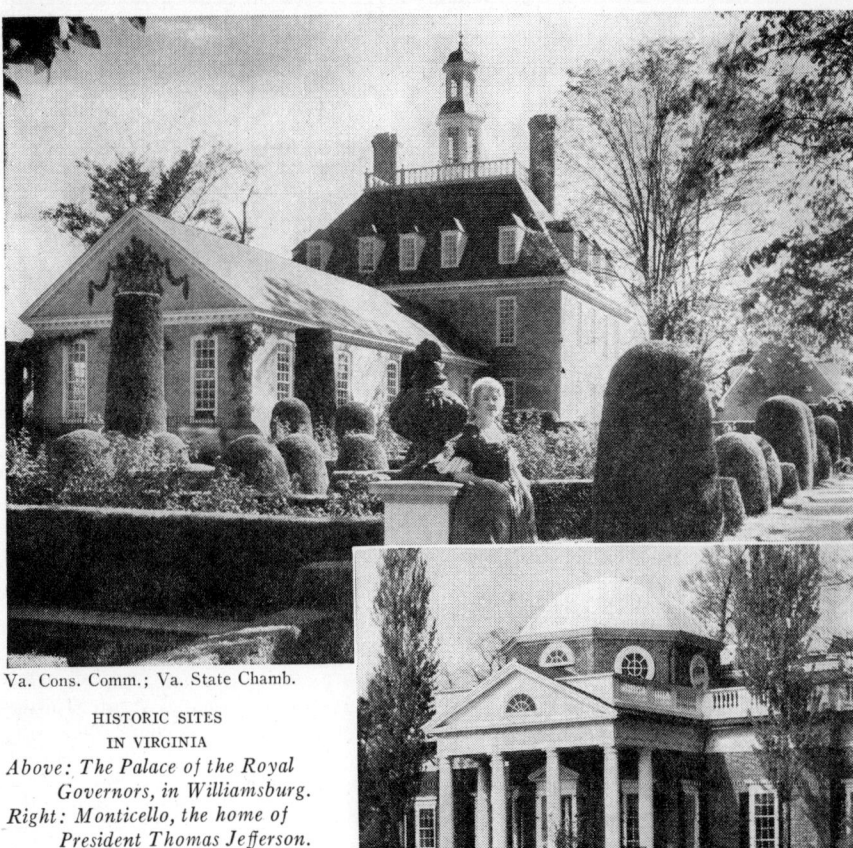

HISTORIC SITES IN VIRGINIA

Above: The Palace of the Royal Governors, in Williamsburg.
Right: Monticello, the home of President Thomas Jefferson.
Below: Mount Vernon, the home of President George Washington.

Va. Cons. Comm.; Nat. Pk. Ser.

HISTORIC SITES IN VIRGINIA

Above: Wren Building at William and Mary College, the oldest academic building in U.S. Left: Gun emplacements on battlefield at Yorktown.

Although the economic return from manufacturing industries in Virginia is almost three times higher than that of agriculture, the latter industry employs approximately 50% of the population. In a recent year the cash income from the sale of crops and livestock was approximately $360,600,000; this total was supplemented by more than $10,000,000 in Federal subsidies. Virginia is a leading tobacco-producing State. The annual tobacco crop exceeds 161,000,000 pounds. Among other important crops are apples, cotton, peanuts, corn, winter wheat, oats, potatoes, sweet potatoes, and barley. Almost 70% of the State's total area is under cultivation, and recently there were more than 173,000 farms possessing a total area of more than 16,358,000 acres and valued at (land and buildings) more than $868,806,000. The State is also noted for its Smithfield hams and thoroughbred horses. In a recent year livestock numbered 1,066,000 cattle (including 469,000 milch cows), 790,000 swine, 290,000 sheep, 148,000 horses, and 73,000 mules. The recent wool clip from 279,000 sheep was about 1,451,000 pounds.

The most important manufactured or processed products are cigarettes (more are manufactured in Richmond than in any other city in the world), cigars, cotton and rayon textiles, chemicals, furniture, packaged meats and other food products, flour, leather, paper and pulp, and ships. The State possesses more than 2500 industrial establishments, employing about 146,000 people, paying annual salaries and wages exceeding $142,880,000, and with an annual output valued at about $988,000,000. Lumbering and fishing are also important in the economy of the State. The annual production of lumber averages more than 511,000,000 board feet, and the State ranks 14th in the U.S. for lumber production. The principal trees include oak, chestnut, poplar, cedar, pine, ash, and gum. Oysters and crabs are the chief products of the fisheries.

The State is rich in mineral resources. Coal

is the most important mineral produced; a recent annual output was approximately 20,368,000 short tons. Manganese ores, sheet mica, titanium, lead, gypsum, feldspar, cement, clay, gravel, sand, pyrites, limestone, zinc, barite, and black marble are other minerals produced. In a recent year the output of minerals was valued at over $92,000,000.

Transportation in Virginia is provided by more than 4200 m. of steam railway and more than 47,000 m. of State-maintained highways. Recently there were more than 115 airports in the State, of which 19 were municipal and 24 equipped for night flying. Of interest is the Blue Ridge Parkway, a scenic road which extends for 485 m. along the crest of the Blue Ridge range from the Shenandoah National Park in Virginia to the Great Smoky Mountains National Park in North Carolina and Tennessee.

Attendance at the elementary and secondary schools of Virginia is free and compulsory during the full school year for all children between the ages of seven and sixteen. Separate institutions are maintained for white and Negro students. In a recent year there were more than 3500 public elementary and secondary schools, attended by more than 565,000 students and staffed by more than 15,500 teachers. State-supported institutions of higher learning in Virginia include the University of Virginia at Charlottesville, William and Mary College at Williamsburg, Virginia Military Institute at Lexington, Virginia Polytechnic Institute at Blacksburg, four teachers colleges (at Fredericksburg, Farmville, Radford, and Harrisonburg), and a Negro teachers normal school at Petersburg. Private institutions of higher learning include Washington and Lee University at Lexington, the University of Richmond at Richmond, Randolph-Macon Woman's College at Lynchburg, Sweet Briar College at Sweet Briar, Hollins College at Hollins, Hampden-Sydney College at Hampden-Sydney, and Virginia Union University at Richmond. In all, the State contains nineteen universities and colleges, thirteen junior colleges, four teachers colleges, and seven professional schools. Six of these institutions are for Negroes.

Virginia is governed according to the terms of the constitution of 1902, the sixth State constitution in Virginia's history. Executive authority is vested in a governor, lieutenant governor, and an attorney general, all elected for four-year terms; and a secretary of the commonwealth, controller, commissioner of agriculture, superintendent of public buildings, and other officials, all appointed by the governor. Legislative authority is vested in a general assembly, which consists of a senate of 40 members elected for four-year terms, and a house of delegates of 100 members elected for two-year terms. Judicial authority is in a supreme court of appeals, circuit courts, city courts, and justices of the peace. The supreme court consists of justices who are elected by the general assembly for twelve-year terms. Electors are all United States citizens who have passed the age of twenty-one, resided in the State one year, the county six months, and the election district one month. In addition, the prospective elector must pay a State poll tax and pass a literacy test. Disenfranchisement, chiefly because of the last-mentioned qualifications, is great. In the 1948 Presidential election, less than 25% of Virginia's 1,772,000 potential voters cast ballots. The State is divided into 100 counties and 24 independent cities, and is represented in the Congress of the U.S. by 2 senators and 9 representatives.

History. The name of Virginia was given by Queen Elizabeth to the country explored by an expedition under the auspices of Sir Walter Raleigh (q.v.) in 1584. The actual history of the region begins with the grant by James I, on April 10, 1606, of the territory 200 miles wide, between lat. 34° and 45°N., to two companies, usually called the London and Plymouth companies. By this charter, the London Company (q.v.) could colonize between 34° and 41° and the Plymouth between 38° and 45°, provided the colonies were 100 miles apart. The government was vested in a Royal Council of Virginia in London. It was provided that there would be a local constitution and an annual president for the colony. The land was to be held in free and common socage, and the settlers and their children were "forever to enjoy all liberties, franchises, and immunities enjoyed by Englishmen in England". The London Company, holding the southern grant, was organized under Sir Thomas Smith, the treasurer. Christopher Newport (q.v.) sailed for America with the first English colonists and reached Cape Henry on April 26, 1607. Having explored Chesapeake Bay, Newport entered the James R. and on May 14, 1607, founded Jamestown (q.v.), the first permanent English settlement in America. Newport returned to England, but the colony did not fare well. Malaria, Indian hostility, insufficient provisions, and unaccustomed labor reduced the number of Jamestown settlers, one of whom was John

Aerial view of Newport News, Virginia

Smith (q.v.), to half in less than four months. When Captain Newport returned on Jan. 12, 1608, only 38 men were left.

John Smith was elected president of the colony in 1608. In 1609 a new charter incorporated the London Company, enlarged its territory, and vested the colony's government in the company's treasurer and council in London. More ships and colonists were sent to Virginia and new towns were founded. John Rolfe (q.v.) established the tobacco-growing industry which was to insure the success of the colonial venture, and in 1614 married Pocahontas (q.v.), daughter of the powerful Indian sachem, Powhatan, thus improving relations between the colonists and the Indians. On July 30, 1619, the first representative assembly in America (a council elected by the company and a house of burgesses chosen by the free colonists) met. In the same year, the first Negro slaves (see SLAVERY) were introduced into the country. By 1620 the population of the colony had reached 4000, including apprentices, indentured servants, and some petty convicts sent over by the king, who was becoming bitterly hostile to the company. In 1624 the king revoked the charter and Virginia became a royal colony. Although Indian massacres occurred in 1622 and 1644, the colony prospered with the growth of the tobacco industry, and the population in 1648 reached 15,000. In 1632 Charles I granted a portion of the territory to Lord Baltimore (see MARYLAND: *History*).

Virginia resisted briefly the Cromwellian government which replaced the government of Charles I (q.v.) following the Great Rebellion in England (see ENGLAND: *History*), but in 1652 the colony surrendered when Parliament sent a fleet to Virginia. Upon the collapse of the Commonwealth in England, the colony elected Sir William Berkeley (q.v.) governor. Following his coronation, Charles II encouraged the slave trade, economically burdened the colony with the Navigation Acts, and granted vast tracts of land to court favorites. These acts, control of the government by a small privileged class consisting of the older families, and Governor Berkeley's refusal to send soldiers to protect the frontier from Indians precipitated a popular uprising led by Nathaniel Bacon (see BACON'S REBELLION). When Bacon died in 1676, his rebellion, which had been successful up until that point, collapsed. Berkeley regained power and took severe measures against his opponents, of whom 23 were executed, eliciting from Charles II the remark, "That old fool has hanged more men in that naked country than I have done for the murder of my father." Berkeley was censured by Charles, and the governor returned to England to defend himself, but died before seeing the king. The rebellion is now regarded to have been

Virginia State Chamber

FARMING IN VIRGINIA. *Above: Harvesting peanuts near Suffolk. Right: Boy in a peanut field, on farm in southeastern Virginia. Below: Milk cattle grazing in the Shenandoah Valley.*

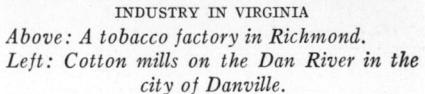

INDUSTRY IN VIRGINIA
Above: A tobacco factory in Richmond.
Left: Cotton mills on the Dan River in the city of Danville.

the forerunner of the American Revolution.

The charter of 1609 had fixed the limits of Virginia at 200 miles north and 200 miles south of Point Comfort, and west and northwest from sea to sea. Maryland and Pennsylvania also claimed western lands claimed by Virginia, but the colony's title to a large part of the Northwest Territory (q.v.) was undisputed until the French, moving s. from Canada, settled in the region, which had been explored by Jacques Marquette (q.v.). The Ohio Company, comprised chiefly of Marylanders and Virginians, was formed in 1749 for the exploitation of the Northwest Territory. During the French and Indian War (q.v.), Virginians saved the British army under Gen. Edward Braddock from complete annihilation, and the Virginians organized by George Washington successfully held the Virginia frontier against the Indians and the French. In 1776 Kentucky, a part of the western territory of Virginia, was organized as a separate county.

During the pre-Revolutionary period, Virginia was a leader of the colonies in their resistance to England. Patrick Henry's famous speech in opposition to the Stamp Act (q.v.), delivered in 1765 before the House of Burgesses, was quoted everywhere throughout the colonies, and three of his five resolutions against taxation without representation were adopted. The British general Thomas Gage later said that "Virginia gave the signal to the continent." Although dissolved by the royal governor for a second time, the House of Burgesses met in revolutionary convention at Raleigh Tavern in 1774 and proposed a Virginia convention and a general congress of the thirteen American colonies. Committees of safety were organized and forces raised in every county. In June, 1775, the royal governor attempted to quell the threatening revolution, but he was driven to refuge aboard a ship by a mob. George Washington was elected commander in chief of the Continental armies, and Patrick Henry was elected to head the Virginia forces (see REVOLUTION, THE AMERICAN). In addition to Washington and Henry, the Colony furnished other great Revolutionary leaders, including Thomas Jefferson, Richard Henry Lee, George Mason, and Edmund Pendleton (qq.v.).

Following the Revolution, the conflicting land claims of other States and the refusal

Scene along the shore at Virginia Beach, Virginia

of Maryland to sign the Articles of Confederation (q.v.) unless these conflicts were resolved, led Virginia to cede its portion of the Northwest Territory to the Union, reserving only a small part for the State's veterans. The transfer was conditioned on the erection therein of new States, and was formally executed in March, 1784. Later, Kentucky also was relinquished to become a separate State. Virginia was prominent in advocating a general convention to make necessary changes in the Articles of Confederation. When the Constitutional Convention produced the Constitution of the U.S., many able patriots, including Henry, Lee, and Mason of Virginia, bitterly opposed its ratification as destructive to States' rights. After long debate, Virginia finally ratified the document by a small majority (see CONSTITUTION). During the first 36 years of the Nation, Virginians held the Presidency for 32 years and the proportion of Virginia citizens in other high Federal offices was very large. During the War of 1812, Norfolk was saved from the British in a battle at Craney Islands.

Slavery had been recognized by a statute in 1661, but Virginia's first assembly had prohibited the slave trade in 1778, and Thomas Jefferson, in the revision of the Virginia Code in 1779, proposed emancipation and colonization of the slaves. During the years leading up to the Civil War, Virginia acted as a moderator between the deep South and the North on the slavery question. In spite of the capture of Harper's Ferry, Va., in 1859 by John Brown (q.v.), and his plan to raise a general slave insurrection, Virginia opposed secession. Virginia suggested a peace convention of the States and sent commissioners to Washington in an endeavor to prevent hostilities. The State convention met on Feb. 13, 1861, to decide the question, and as late as April 1, it voted (89 to 45) against secession. However, President Abraham Lincoln's call for troops decided Virginia, as it decided other southern States (see CIVIL WAR), to abandon the Union and on April 17 an ordinance of secession was voted by the convention. Robert Edward Lee (q.v.), a Virginian then an officer in the U.S. Army and a former superintendent of the U.S. Military Academy at West Point, resigned his commission, eventually becoming commander in chief of the Confederate Army. Richmond became the strategic capital and Virginia a great battleground of the Confederacy. The region in the western portion of the State had little sympathy for secession and during the war the Federal government recognized West Virginia (q.v.) as a separate State.

Following the Civil War, the Reconstruction (q.v.) Acts gave Negroes the right to vote for State convention delegates, and a new constitution was adopted in 1868 embodying Negro suffrage; but so great was the popular feeling against it that the constitution was not submitted to the people until July, 1869, when it was then adopted. Virginia was readmitted into the Union on Jan. 26, 1870. A new constitution in 1902 suppressed the

Negro vote by stipulations with regard to property and literacy.

In Presidential elections the voters of Virginia have consistently cast a majority of their ballots for the Democratic candidate in all national election years since the State's readmission to the Union, except in 1872, when the Republican candidate, Ulysses S. Grant, defeated Horace Greeley, an Abolitionist, and 1928, when Herbert Hoover defeated Alfred E. Smith. In the 1948 Presidential election the Democratic incumbent Harry S. Truman received 202,808 votes, and Thomas E. Dewey, the Republican candidate, received 173,093 votes. The States' Rights candidate, J. Strom Thurmond, received 42,840 votes.

VIRGINIA, a city of St. Louis Co., Minn., situated about 65 miles N.W. of Duluth. It is served by three railroads. The city lies in the Mesabi iron-mining area and is surrounded by the vacation region known as the "Arrowhead country", with numerous lakes and resorts. In the city and vicinity are large iron mines, and the city also contains lumber mills, a sawmill, and plants processing dairy products. Virginia was settled in 1892 and chartered as a city in 1895. It is the site of Virginia Junior College, established in 1921. Pop. (1940) 12,264.

VIRGINIA BLUEBELL, or VIRGINIA COWSLIP. See MERTENSIA.

VIRGINIA CITY, county seat of Storey Co., Nev., situated about 23 miles S.E. of Reno. Transportation facilities include a railroad. The city lies on the E. slope of Mount Davidson, at an altitude of about 6500 ft. above sea level. Virginia City was at one time a famous mining town. The celebrated Comstock Lode, one of the richest deposits of gold and silver ever discovered, was found nearby in 1859 and the city was settled in the same year, developing rapidly into a boom mining town. Numerous mines were opened along the lode, including the Consolidated Virginia Mine which has yielded ore valued at about $234,000,000. Although some mining operations are still carried on, the lode is no longer the source of wealth it once was and the many buildings which lined the streets in the old days are deserted. Several of the old buildings are maintained as museums for tourists who are attracted to Virginia City as the most famous of the so-called "ghost towns". Places of interest include Piper's Opera House, where many of the greatest actors and actresses of the period appeared, including Edwin Booth and Sarah Bernhardt. The first newspaper in Nevada, *The Territorial Enterprise,* was published at Virginia City with a reportorial staff which included the authors Mark Twain and Bret Harte. From 1880 to 1930 the population of Virginia City, which was chartered as a city in 1864, decreased from 10,900 to 550. Pop. (1940) 1009.

VIRGINIA CREEPER. See IVY.

VIRGINIA, or **WHITE-TAILED, DEER,** a common deer, *Odocoileus virginianus,* native to eastern United States. In summer the deer have red-brown fur which changes to gray brown in winter. The tail is characteristically long and white. The Virginia deer is one of the largest American deer, the buck reaching about 6 feet in length, 3 feet in height at the shoulder, and weighing close to 300 pounds. It is one of the most popular targets of American big-game hunters, but because of strict conservation laws regulating deer hunting, the total number of these deer remains almost constant. The full-grown antlers of the male are arched forward and have five or six points. The animals are very swift, and canter with their heads and tails erect. Two fauns, born during the spring months, comprise a typical brood; the young have red-brown fur flecked with white spots which disappear during the first winter. See DEER.

VIRGINIA MILITARY INSTITUTE, a State-controlled institution of higher education for men, situated in Lexington, Va., and established in 1839. Students at the institute are known as cadets, and are organized in battalions according to a military discipline based upon that of the U.S. Military Academy (see MILITARY ACADEMY, UNITED STATES); by State law, the faculty and officers of the institution hold commissions in the State militia. The school was prominent during the Civil War as an arm of the army of the Confederate States of America. From 1864 to 1865 the entire student body saw active service with the Confederate army as a military corps of cadets, and in June, 1864, the entire plant of the school was destroyed by Federal troops. The institute was reopened in October, 1865, and has offered courses continuously since that time. Courses in chemistry, premedicine, and civil and electrical engineering are offered leading to the degree of B.S.; students may also elect a course in the liberal arts leading to the degree of B.A., and graduate courses leading to the M.S. degree are available. A group of cadets numbering no less than fifty and known as "State cadets" is enrolled each year, by special appointment of the State legislature, without charge for tuition or board. In a recent year about 800 students were enrolled and the faculty numbered about 70.

VIRGINIA POLYTECHNIC INSTITUTE, a partly coeducational, State-controlled, land-grant institution of higher education, situated in Blacksburg, Va. It was founded as the Virginia Agricultural and Mechanical College in 1872, and the present name was adopted in 1896. Since 1921, a limited number of women have been regularly enrolled. Radford College (established 1913), a women's college formally affiliated with the institute, maintains a campus at Radford, Va. The divisions of the institute comprise agriculture, applied science, business administration, engineering, and home economics; courses are offered leading to the degrees of B.S., M.S., and PH.D. Radford College offers courses in the liberal arts and teacher training, leading to the degrees of B.A., B.S., and B.S. in education. At Blacksburg are located the State Agricultural Experiment Station and the centers of State entomological work and livestock sanitary work, all conducted by the institute; an extension division is also maintained by the institute. In a recent year about 5500 students were enrolled at the Virginia Polytechnic Institute, and the faculty numbered about 230; in the same year Radford College had a student body of about 800 women and a faculty of about 50.

VIRGINIA REEL. See SIR ROGER DE COVERLEY.

VIRGINIA RESOLUTIONS, THE, eight resolutions drawn up in December, 1798, by James Madison, and submitted to the legislature of Virginia. Their object was to protest against the liberal interpretations the Federal Party was placing on the United States Constitution, and claiming "that in a case of a deliberate, palpable, and dangerous exercise of other powers not granted by the said compact, the states which are parties thereto have the right, and are in duty bound to interpose, for arresting the progress of the evil". These resolutions were transmitted to the other States, and met with a mixed reception. They were remitted to a legislative committee with Madison as chairman, and an exhaustive report on the subject was submitted in 1800.

VIRGINIA, UNIVERSITY OF, a partly coeducational, State-controlled institution of higher education, situated in Charlottesville, Va. It was founded and organized in 1819 by the American statesman Thomas Jefferson, and opened for instruction in 1825; Jefferson also designed the campus and the eight original buildings of the university, and is generally

Virginia State Chamber
On campus of the University of Virginia

known as the father of the institution. The co-ordinate women's college of the university, the Mary Washington College of the University of Virginia, with its campus at Fredericksburg, Va., was founded in 1908 as the State Normal and Industrial School for Women. Its name was changed in 1924 to State Teachers College, and the present name was adopted in 1938. Mary Washington College was formally affiliated with the University of Virginia in 1940. The degrees offered by the university are the B.A., B.S. in commerce, architecture, chemistry, education, and engineering, LL.B., M.D., M.S., M.A., and PH.D.; women enrolled at Mary Washington College are eligible for B.A. and B.S. degrees, and other women are admitted to graduate and professional divisions of the university. Among the special schools maintained by the university is the Woodrow Wilson School of Foreign Affairs, which offers seminars and classes conducted by visiting lecturers. In a recent year over 5100 students were enrolled at the university, and the faculty numbered over 350; in the same year Mary Washington College had a student body of about 1550 women and a faculty of about 80.

VIRGINIA, WEST. See WEST VIRGINIA.

VIRGIN ISLANDS, BRITISH, a group of thirty-six islands forming part of the Lesser Antilles in the West Indies, and comprising one of the four presidencies of the British Leeward Islands. The principal islands of the eleven that are inhabited are Tortola, Virgin

Gorda, Anegada, Jost Van Dykes, Peter's Island, and Salt Island. The capital and only town in the group is Road Town (pop., about 700), which is situated on the s.e. coast of Tortola and is a port of entry. Tortola, the largest island of the group, has an area of about 24 sq.m. and a population (1946) of 5423. The islands are generally rocky, or arid and sandy. The principal industries include fishing, the raising of livestock and poultry, the cultivation of fruits and vegetables, and the production of charcoal. The islands were discovered by Christopher Columbus on his second voyage to America in 1493. Tortola was occupied by the British in 1666. The island and its neighbors have been under British jurisdiction since that date. During the 17th century, the Virgin Islands were often frequented by buccaneers. Total area, about 67 sq.m.; pop. (1946) 6508.

VIRGIN ISLANDS OF THE UNITED STATES, formerly the DANISH WEST INDIES, a group of three islands and about 50 islets, chiefly uninhabited, in the Lesser Antilles chain of the West Indies, e. of Puerto Rico and lying between the Caribbean Sea and the Atlantic Ocean. The three islands are Saint Thomas (32 sq.m.), Saint John (19 sq.m.), and Saint Croix (82 sq.m.). The populations (1946 est.) are 13,000, 800, and 16,200 respectively. About 69% of the people are Negroes, 9% are whites, and 22% are of mixed blood. The capital is Charlotte Amalie (pop., about 9800), the only town on Saint Thomas. There are only two other towns in the group, Christiansted (pop., about 4500) and Frederiksted (pop., about 500), both on Saint Croix.

The chief industries of Saint Thomas, which is the leading port of the group, include fueling and servicing ships, manufacturing rum and bay rum, fishing, cattle raising, and truck gardening. There is also a large tourist industry. The chief industries of Saint Croix are the cultivation of sugar cane and vegetables, the raising of cattle, and the manufacture of rum. Saint John's industries include the production of charcoal, the raising of cattle, and farming.

The Virgin Islands form the most eastern outpost of the U.S. and are so situated as to furnish protection to U.S. holdings in the Caribbean Sea and the Panama Canal. There is a fine harbor at Charlotte Amalie, which can provide shelter for as many as 23 warships at one time. Defenses in the group include a permanent U.S. Marine Corps air base on St. Thomas, a large submarine base at Charlotte Amalie, and additional airfields on St. Thomas and St. Croix.

Education is compulsory for all children between the ages of five and a half and fifteen, and free schooling is provided by the local government in elementary and secondary schools. In a recent year more than 6000 students attended the 22 public and 9 private of parochial schools on the islands.

From 1917, when the U.S. acquired the Virgin Islands, to 1931, the islands were under U.S. naval government. In 1931 jurisdiction was transferred from the Navy Department to the Department of the Interior, and a civil governor was appointed by the President. Congress passed an Organic Act for the islands in 1936 which effected little change in the government although it did allow for a greater measure of political freedom. According to the terms of this act local legislative authority is vested in two municipal councils, one of which represents both Saint Thomas and Saint John, and the other, Saint Croix. The former consists of 7 members and the latter of 9 members, and all are elected for two-year terms. The councils serve a dual role; together they comprise the legislative assembly for the entire Virgin Islands of the United States, and separately they serve as municipal councils which are limited to local legislation. The executive and judiciary departments are appointed by the President, and include a governor, district judge, U.S. attorney, government secretary, and a commissioner of finance.

History. Christopher Columbus discovered the Virgin Islands in 1493, on his second voyage to America. Denmark colonized Saint Thomas in 1666. Until 1755 the Danish West Indies Company controlled the group, but in the latter year, Frederick V of Denmark bought the islands. Saint Thomas was declared a free port in 1764. In 1800, during the Napoleonic Wars, England blockaded St. Thomas and in 1801 occupied the island. In 1802 Saint Thomas was returned to Denmark, but again from 1807 to 1815, England occupied the Danish West Indies. The islands were restored to Denmark a second time in the latter year. In 1917, after negotiations which had begun prior to 1867, the United States purchased the Danish West Indies for $25,000,000. In 1946 President Harry S. Truman asked Congress to give the people of the U.S. Virgin Islands more self-government. In the same year Judge William Henry Hastie was appointed governor of the group, the first Negro to hold that office. In 1948 the

Alcoa SS. Co.

VIRGIN ISLANDS OF THE U.S. *Above: The town of Charlotte Amalie, capital of the islands. Right: Donkey carrying a load of fish, St. Thomas Island. Below: Bluebeard's Castle on St. Thomas.*

islands celebrated the 100th anniversary of the abolition of slavery in the Virgin Islands.

VIRGINIUS, LUCIUS, a Roman centurion who killed his daughter to prevent her falling into the hands of the decemvir Appius Claudius Crassus. The story has been a favorite theme. It was the subject of tragedies by the French authors Mairet, Leclerc, and Campistron in the 17th century. Lessing in 1772 cast it in a modern Italian setting, and it was treated also by Alfieri in Italy (1773), by Miss Brooke in England (1760), and in France by La Beaumelle (1760), Chabanon (1769), Laharpe (1786), Guiraud (1827), and Latour Saint-Ybars (1845).

VIRGINIUS AFFAIR, THE, an incident originating in the capture (October 31, 1873) of the United States steamer *Virginius,* commanded by Captain Fry, off Jamaica by the Spanish warship *Tornado,* while carrying supplies to the Cuban insurgents. The ship was taken to the port of Santiago de Cuba, and four Cuban leaders were summarily executed. Thereafter fifty-two of the passengers and crew were court-martialed and executed. The opportune arrival of the British sloop *Niobe* arrested further executions. The affair created a great sensation because of widespread sympathy felt for the Cubans in their fight for independence. The action of the local officials was disowned by the Spanish authorities, and the vessel and survivors were forthwith restored. The *Virginius* foundered in a storm on its return journey.

VIRGIN MARY. See MARY.

VIRGIN'S BOWER, the name of several species of clematis, especially the American climber, *C. virginiana,* and the traveler's joy, *C. vitalba,* of English roadsides.

VIRGO, in astronomy, a constellation denoted by the symbol ♍. It is the sixth sign of the zodiac (q.v.), and was known to the ancients as a symbol of the harvest. Virgo is situated south of the handle of Ursa Major (q.v.) on the celestial equator, and contains the first-magnitude star Spica or α Virginis, and a large number of variable stars; see STARS. It is famous for its many nebulae, of which more than 500 have been identified.

VIROQUA, county seat of Vernon Co., Wis., situated about 85 miles N.W. of Madison. It is served by rail, and is the center of an agricultural area noted for dairy products and leaf tobacco. Among the industrial establishments in the city are creameries and tobacco warehouses. Pop. (1940) 3549.

VIRUS (Lat., "slime", "poison"), specially, the contagium of an infectious disease. See CONTAGION; INFECTION; DISEASE; GERM; POISON; SNAKES; and the articles on the infectious diseases.

VISA or VISE (from Lat. *visa,* past participle of *videre,* "to see"), the formal endorsement placed by governmental authorities on a passport (q.v.), indicating that the passport has been examined and found valid, and that the bearer may legally proceed to his destination. The most common type of visa is the *entry* visa, which signifies that the bearer of the passport to which the visa has been affixed has received official permission to enter a country of which he is not a citizen. The entry visa serves the general purpose of enabling a government to limit and control the entry of aliens into a country. Entry visas are of two general types: the *passport* entry visa, which is issued to persons desiring to enter a country for a visit of stated duration; and the *immigration* entry visa, which is issued to persons desiring to enter and settle permanently in the country.

Some countries require that any of their own citizens desiring to travel or settle abroad obtain *exit* visas, i.e., governmental authorization to leave the country. The exit visa is frequently employed by countries in which the development of unfavorable political, social, or economic conditions has resulted in a marked rise in the amount of emigration; by restricting the issuance of exit visas, such countries check or may even halt the flow of emigrants. Almost all modern countries require aliens to obtain entry visas; notable among the governments which have instituted the use of exit visas as well as entry visas at various periods in the 20th century are the Fascist regime in Italy (1922-43), the National Socialist regime in Germany (1933-45), and the government of the Soviet Union, which has continued this practice to the present.

In the United States, the governmental regulations pertaining to visas were relatively lenient up to 1918. Prior to that year, aliens were permitted under certain conditions to enter the country without an entry visa. The visa regulations were changed by Congressional enactment after the entry of the United States into World War I, at a time when strict control over the entry of aliens was deemed an essential aid to the curtailment of enemy espionage and sabotage. Several enactments passed since 1918 have fully defined the visa requirements and have rendered them increasingly stringent. Under the Federal visa laws, American consular officials may refuse entry visas to aliens whose presence in the United

States is deemed inimical to the public interest and safety. Among the categories of aliens to whom entry visas may be refused are aliens coming to the United States for the purpose of carrying on operations or engaging in activities involving a willful violation of the laws of the United States; aliens engaged in the white-slave or in illicit liquor or narcotic traffic; aliens afflicted with a loathsome or dangerous contagious disease; and aliens deemed undesirable for political reasons. In common with most other governments, the U.S. government takes legal measures to discover, penalize, and expel persons entering U.S. territory without an entry visa, or with a visa obtained by fraudulent means.

Aliens applying to U.S. consular officials abroad for immigration entry visas are normally required to present documentary evidence of their status as responsible and law-abiding citizens of their own country. They must also prove to the satisfaction of the consular official that they will either be able to support themselves financially in the United States, or that they will be supported by persons residing in the United States. Both quota and nonquota immigrants are required to obtain immigration visas; see IMMIGRATION.

VISALIA, county seat of Tulare Co., Calif., situated in the heart of the rich San Joaquin Valley, 160 miles N. of Los Angeles. It is served by two railroads and maintains a municipal airport. The city is the trading center and shipping point of a fertile agricultural area yielding citrus and other fruits, vegetables, olives, walnuts, cotton, and dairy and poultry products. The principal industries in Visalia are the processing, canning, and packing of the products of the region. Sequoia National Park, with its groves of giant redwoods, is 30 miles E. of the city. Visalia was founded in 1852, became the county seat in 1853, and was incorporated in 1874. Pop. (1948) 10,363.

VISAYAS, or BISAYAS, one of the four main insular groups of the Philippine Archipelago, lying between Mindanao and Luzon in the Otón or Visayan Sea. The chief islands are Cebú, Panay, Negros, Leyte, Samar, Bohol, Masbate, and Romblon. The islands are mainly inhabited by Visavas, a Malay people.

VISCACHA or **VIZCACHA,** common name for a large, burrowing rodent, *Lagostomus maximus*, belonging to the Chinchilla family. The animal inhabits the pampas of South America, and grows to a length of 18 inches. Its long, very soft fur is mottled gray above and white or yellowish white below; the muzzle and cheeks are covered with white and dark bands, respectively. Viscachas assemble on the pampas in colonies called *viscacheras,* and always post a sentry to warn the colony in case of danger. They feed mainly on vegetable matter, which they drag to their burrows before eating. Viscacha burrows are so numerous and so deep that they constitute a danger to horseback riders.

VISCHER, FRIEDRICH THEODOR VON (1807–87), German critic, born in Ludwigsburg, Württemberg, and educated at the University of Tübingen. He spent the years 1832 and 1833 in developing his esthetic taste in the art centers of Germany and Austria. He was successively *Privatdocent* (1836–37) and assistant professor (1837–44) at the University of Tübingen, and in 1844 was appointed professor of esthetics. The too independent tone of his inaugural lecture, however, caused his suspension for two years. In 1848 he was elected to the National Assembly of Frankfort, where he voted with the Left. In 1855 he was called to the polytechnic institute of Zurich, and in 1866 to that of Stuttgart. He resumed at the same time the professorship of esthetics and German literature at Tübingen, but from 1869 taught only at Stuttgart. As a literary critic and student of esthetics, Vischer was one of the most distinguished members of the Hegelian school. Among his numerous and valuable publications are *Kritische Gänge* (1844; new series, 1860–75); *Aesthetik oder Wissenschaft des Schönen* (1847–58); *Faust, der Tragödie dritter Teil* (1862), a satire on the second part of the tragedy; *Epigramme aus Baden-Baden* (1867); *Der Deutsche Krieg 1870–71* (1874); *Goethes Faust: Neue Beiträge zur Kritik des Gedichts* (1875); *Auch Einer* (1878), a novel; *Mode und Cynicismus* (1878); *Altes und Neues* (1881–82; new series, 1889); *Lyrische Gänge* (1882); *Allotria* (1892); and *Shakespeare-Vorträge* (posthumously published, 1898–1905).

VISCHER, PETER, THE ELDER (about 1455–1529), German sculptor and bronze founder, born in Nuremberg, and trained by his father, the brazier Hermann Vischer the Elder (d. 1487). He was admitted to the guild as a master in 1489. His productions increased the reputation of the foundry to such a degree that for half a century it was practically without competition in Germany, and also received important orders from other countries. Five sons assisted Peter in his extensive productions. While there are scarcely any records of his life, the master's artistic development may be followed in his numerous works, all marked with his monogram and dated, with the excep-

Detail of carving on the "Shrine of Saint Sebaldus," by Peter Vischer the Elder

tion of his earliest known work, the statue of "Count Otto von Henneberg" in the church in Römhild (about 1487). To his early period also belong several sepulchral slabs in the cathedrals of Bamberg, Würzburg, Meissen, and Breslau, among which that of Bishop John IV (1496) in Breslau is remarkable for its powerful realism. The most important monument of his early period is the stately memorial to Archbishop Ernst (1495) in Magdeburg Cathedral, with the majestic reclining figure of the archbishop, and a rich base decorated with statues of the twelve apostles and two other saints. During the following years the transition from the Gothic to the Renaissance appears in Vischer's work. His treatment becomes freer, the design more elaborate, and the forms more refined and truer to nature. This is seen in a series of grave slabs designed for the churches of Cracow, of which that of Cardinal Frederick Casimir in the cathedral, completed in 1510, is the most important. It is seen also in the fine monument of Count Herman VIII of Henneberg and his wife in the church of Römhild (1508), and especially in his master creation, the "Shrine of St. Sebaldus" (1508–19), in the church of that saint, in Nuremberg, the most important monument of German plastic art during this period. It consists of an elaborate Gothic canopy inclosing the silver sarcophagus of the saint, adorned with reliefs, many portrait statuettes (including one of Peter Vischer himself), and an astonishing wealth of Renaissance decoration. The execution of these works shows a difference of style that can be explained only by supposing the special assistance of Peter's sons. While engaged on the shrine he modeled also the powerful statues of King Theodoric and King Arthur (1513), and the monument of Emperor Maximilian at Innsbruck. The statue of King Theodoric shows medieval reminiscences, but that of Arthur, conceived in the spirit of the freedom of the Renaissance, is one of the finest works of its kind produced by German sculpture.

A number of other bronzes, unquestionably the product of Vischer's foundry, are so purely Renaissance in spirit and conception that they are now attributed to his talented son, Peter the Younger (about 1487–1528), who visited Italy about 1507. They include the grave relief of Margaretha Tucher (1521, Regensburg Cathedral), representing the meeting of Christ with the sisters of Lazarus; and the monuments of Cardinal Albrecht of Brandenburg (1525, Stiftskirche, Aschaffenburg), and of the elector Frederick the Wise (1527, Schlosskirche, Wittenberg). Peter the Younger also designed a number of small bronzes, inkstands, and the like, and two reliefs of Orpheus and Eurydice, the better of which is in the Berlin Museum. The beautiful wooden statue of the Virgin in the Germanic Museum, Nuremberg, claimed by some as his design, is more properly ascribed to the Vischer atelier.

VISCONTI, a Lombard family who for nearly four hundred years exercised supreme sway over Milan, from the 11th to the 15th century. The more prominent members of the family were Ottone, Viscount of Milan (1078), Gian Galeazzo (1347–1402), and Filippo Maria (1391–1447), last of the family.

VISCONTI, LOUIS TULLIUS JOACHIM (1791–1853), French architect, born in Rome, and trained in Paris at the École des Beaux-Arts and in the atelier of the French architect Charles Percier. Among his varied works in Paris were the architectural designs of the Molière, Louvois, and St. Sulpice fountains, plans for a Bibliothèque Royale, and the transformation of the Dome des Invalides into a mausoleum for the remains of Napoleon Bonaparte (completed 1853). To him is also due the masterly design for the union of the Louvre and the Tuileries, a problem which his master Percier, in collaboration with the French architect Pierre François Léonard Fontaine, had earlier endeavored to solve. This colossal enterprise was begun in 1852 under Napoleon III, and carried out during the following thirty years, chiefly under Visconti's associate, Hector Lefuel (1810–81), who succeeded him on his death. While the exterior detail of the new wings is largely Lefuel's, the general disposition of the plan was Visconti's.

VISCOSITY, the internal friction or resistance to motion of a fluid which causes it to have the property commonly but incorrectly called "consistency", "thickness", or "heaviness". "Heaviness" is a particularly misleading term; "heavy cream", for example, is lighter than "light cream", and will float on the latter just as cream floats on milk. It is, of course, more viscous than "light cream". The very heavy liquid mercury is only slightly more viscous than water, at most temperatures, and at 0°C. (32°F.) is actually less viscous. The resistance to motion of small drops of mercury is due not to viscosity, but to surface tension. Only fluids show true viscosity. Some apparently solid substances, such as rosin, flow viscously if enough pressure is applied to them; however, such substances are probably more truly liquids than solids (see CRYSTAL).

Theoretical analysis of viscosity is very complex. In theory, the force required to move a plate of known area past another plate with a uniform, measured velocity is measurable. If the plates are immersed in a suitable liquid, the resultant force gives a measure of the viscosity, and the units of force (in dynes) per square centimeter of area, per centimeter-per-second of velocity, per centimeter of separation between the plates. This unit is called the poise (see ABSOLUTE UNITS), and is a convenient measurement of viscosity. Experiments of this kind are difficult to perform, but comparable experiments have been carried out in the laboratory. The viscosity of water, for example, is one hundredth of a poise at room temperature; it is 80% greater at the freezing point, and 70% less at the boiling point. By comparison, the viscosity of glycerine at room temperature is fifteen poise, and the viscosity of rosin is six thousand million million poise. The viscosity of gasoline is half as great as that of water, while ether is only half as viscous as gasoline.

A simpler method of measuring viscosity is ordinarily used. If a vessel is filled with water, and the water is then allowed to escape through an orifice, the time which the escape requires depends only on the density and viscosity of the liquid, and on the shape and size of the vessel and orifice. If such a vessel, called a viscometer, is calibrated by allowing some liquid such as water to flow out of it, the viscosity-divided-by-density (called the *kinematic viscosity*) of any other liquid can then be measured by observing its time of escape. Viscosity of liquids is often specified by the time required for them to escape from a standard viscometer. For example, the S.A.E. number of an automotive lubricating oil is the number of seconds required for it to escape from a standardized Society of Automotive Engineers viscometer, at standard temperature.

The viscosity of all liquids decreases when the temperature is increased, but some liquids change viscosity more rapidly than others. For lubricating oils, this property is measured by *viscosity index*, determined by comparing the oil in question to a standard. A low rate of change with temperature is desirable for all-weather use. Some of the new synthetic lubricants, notably the silicones (q.v.), have extremely low rates of change.

Gases have appreciable viscosities. That of air at 0°C. (32°F.) is about 0.00017 poise, about one hundredth as great as the viscosity of water at the same temperature. The viscosity of gases increases slightly as the temperature is increased, but remains essentially unchanged when the pressure is greatly increased or decreased.

VISCOUNT (OF. *viconte, viscount*; Lat. *vice,* "in place of"; *comes,* "earl"), the acting deputy to the earl, the *vice-comes,* who ultimately became the sheriff. The hereditary title of viscount was first granted in England to John Beaumont in 1440. A viscount is now the fourth degree of nobility in the United Kingdom, intermediate between earl and baron, and has not been very largely conferred. A viscount is styled "Right Honorable"; his wife is a viscountess; and all his sons and daughters are styled "Honorable".

VISHINSKY or **VYSHINSKY,** ANDREI YA-NARIEVICH (1883–   ), Soviet jurist and diplomat, born in Odessa, and educated at the University of Kiev. In 1902 he joined the Russian Social Democratic Labor Party; after the division in the party in 1903, he was a member of the Menshevik group, which opposed the Bolsheviks led by Nikolai Lenin (q.v.); see BOLSHEVISM. During the unsuccessful revolution of 1905, Vishinsky was secretary of the soviet ("council") established by the revolutionists in the Caucasian city of Baku. He was subsequently imprisoned several times for his anticzarist activities. In the revolution of 1917 he was an opponent of the Bolsheviks; he joined the Soviet Communist Party in 1920.

He was the attorney general of the Russian Soviet Federated Socialist Republic from 1923 to 1925. In the latter year he became professor of jurisprudence at the University of Moscow; subsequently, he served as dean for a number of years. With the Soviet leaders Joseph Stalin, Nikolai Bukharin, and Karl Radek (qq.v.) Vishinsky was a member of the commission which drafted the present constitution of the U.S.S.R., officially styled the Stalin Constitution. Following his appointment in 1935 as procurator general of the U.S.S.R. (see UNION OF SOVIET SOCIALIST REPUBLICS: *The Political Structure*), Vishinsky was the prosecutor in the celebrated trials (1936–38) of old Bolsheviks, as a result of which almost all the revolutionists who had built the Bolshevik Party and led it in the revolution of 1917 were executed as fascist spies and traitors.

In 1938 Vishinsky was made vice-chairman of the council of ministers of the Soviet government. During World War II, in 1940, he became deputy minister of foreign affairs and was sent to Latvia, where he directed the political campaign leading to the incorporation of Latvia into the U.S.S.R. He was a member of the Soviet delegations to the Potsdam Conference (q.v.) in 1945, the Paris peace conference in 1946, and the London conference of Allied foreign ministers in 1947. He attracted world-wide attention, following his appointment in 1946 as head of the Soviet delegation to the General Assembly of the United Nations, by his blunt attacks on the foreign policy of the United States and his truculent defense of Soviet policy. He became minister of foreign affairs of the U.S.S.R. in 1948 and thereafter also played a prominent role in international affairs as the head of the Soviet delegations to various conferences. Vishinsky was the author of many works, including notably *The Law of the Soviet State* (1948).

VISHNU, "the Preserver", the second god of the Hindu triad, now the most worshiped of all Hindu gods. His chief incarnations were the seventh as Ráma, hero of the *Rámáyana,* and the eighth as Krishna, the more human hero of the *Mahábhárata.* The Vishnuite doctrines were gathered into one body in the

11th century as the Vishnu-Purána. See BRAHMANISM.

VISIGOTHS. See GOTHS.

VISION, the act of seeing, that faculty of the mind by means of which, through its appropriate material organ, the eye, we perceive (see PERCEPTION) the visible appearances of the external world. Vision is mainly concerned with the color, form, distance, and tridimensional extension of objects. It is caused by impact of ether waves on the retina of the eye (see EYE); but if these waves are longer or shorter than a certain limit (see COLOR) there is no visual impression produced by them. The apparent color of an object depends partly on the wave length or wave lengths of the incident light waves, single or mixed, and partly upon the state of the eye itself, as in color blindness, or after taking santonine, which makes external objects look yellow, or in jaundice. The apparent brightness of an object depends upon the amplitude of the light waves which pass from it to the eye; and the smallest perceptible difference of brightness always bears a nearly constant ratio to the full intensity of the bright objects (Fechner's psychophysical law).

On ordinary optical principles a point above the direct line of vision comes to a focus at a point of the retina below its center and vice versa. If the retina could be looked at by another person it would be found that an image of the object is formed on the retina, and that this image is inverted. Any increase in the magnitude of the retinal image is generally associated with approach of the object, and in the exceptional cases in which this result can be brought about by means of lenses, even where the real distance is increased, the object seems to approach; this seeming to approach is the result of an unconscious process of reasoning. The mind, on the basis of tactile experience, interprets any given object as being of a known or ascertained size; if it comes to look larger, it is inferred that it has come nearer.

As to single vision with two eyes, the figure shows that if L and R represent the two eyes and SS a line (the "horopter") drawn through the point A where the optic axes LA and RA intersect, and parallel to a line joining the two eyes L and R, the point A is seen in corresponding points of the two eyes, axially situated; but two points r and l may be so placed, either in the plane of the horopter or outside it, that the two eyes together perceive them as one point B. This point is in Fig. 1 nearer to the eye and in Fig. 2 farther from the eye than

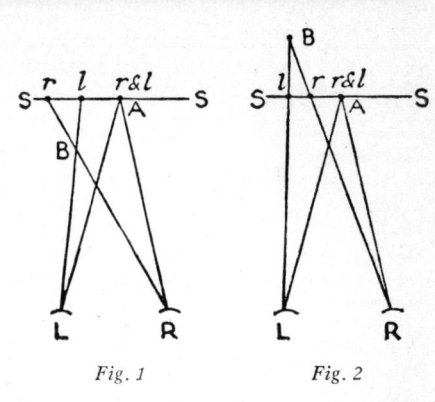

Fig. 1   *Fig. 2*

the horopter SS itself. If now, in Fig. 1, a diagram be made representing l and A and another representing r and A; and if the former be laid before the left eye and the latter before the right eye, the two optic axes being made to converge so that the image of A is formed in corresponding points in the two eyes, the points l and r will appear to blend into one, situated nearer the eye than A or farther from it; this explains the action of the stereoscope, and also the "pseudoscopic" effect produced when the pictures are reversed (see STEREOSCOPE).

VISIONS, mental representations of external objects or scenes, as in sleep or trance. Hence the term denotes dreams, fantasies, or apparitions, and specifically, inspired and prophetic revelations. See APPARITIONS.

VISITATION. The Festival of the Visitation, to commemorate the visit of the Virgin Mary to her cousin Elizabeth, is observed by Roman Catholics on July 2. Visitations are among the duties of archbishops, bishops, and archdeacons. The festival is also observed in the Greek Church.

VISTULA, a river of central Europe, rising in s.w. Poland, 50 miles s. of Kraków, among the outliers of the Carpathians, and flowing N., describing a curve to the E., then another to the W. It enters the Baltic lagoon of the Frisches Haff. The Vistula is 650 m. in entire length. Area of its basin, 73,400 sq.m. It becomes navigable at Kraków for small vessels.

VISUAL EDUCATION, the term applied to the use of school journeys, objects, maps and charts, still pictures, slides and filmstrips, and motion pictures as an integral part of the school experience. It implies the use of these materials in a manner similar to that in which textual material has been used, that is, as materials of instruction. Pictures, maps, and charts have long been used in the classroom

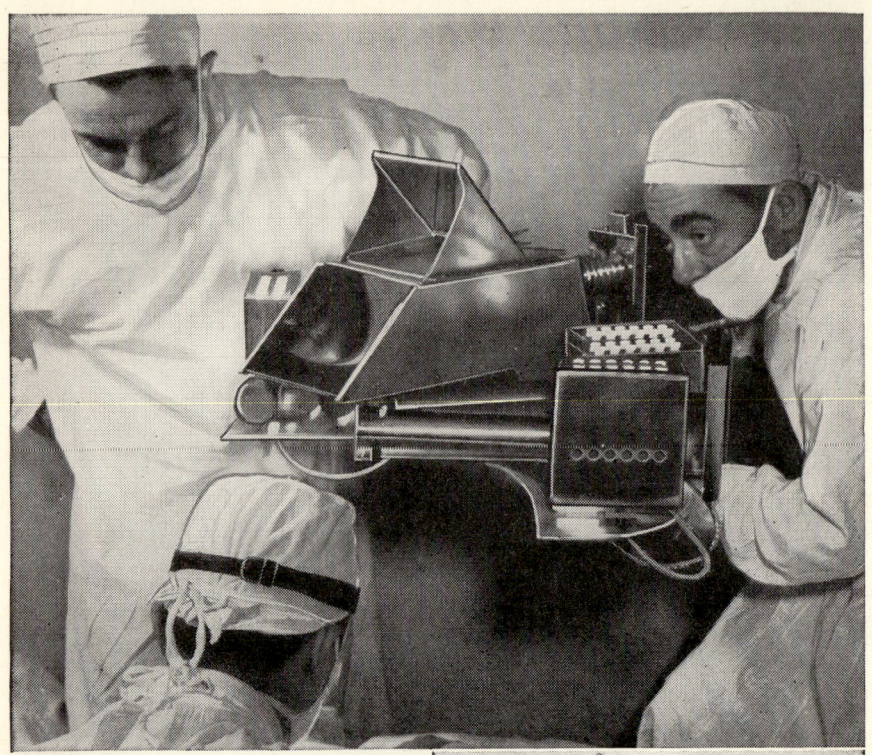

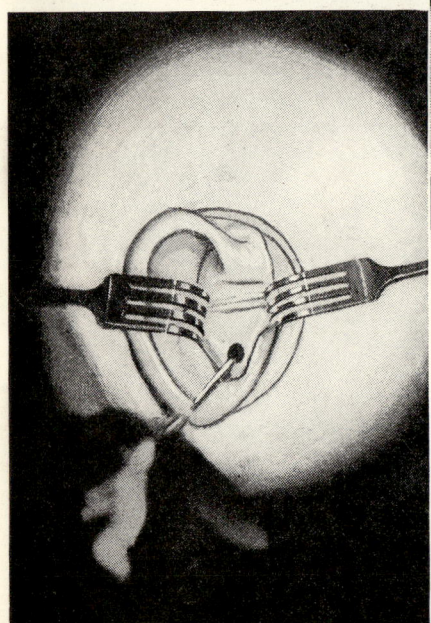

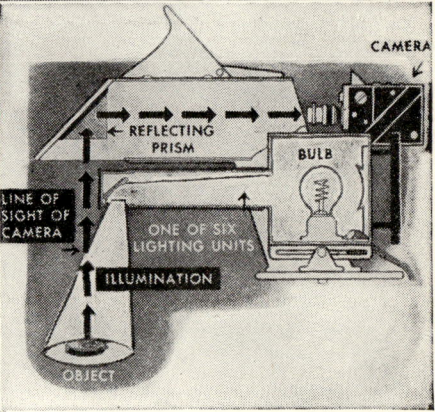

Science Pictures
VISUAL EDUCATION FOR SURGEONS

Top: Lempertscope in use during a surgical operation. This machine, invented by the American physician Julius A. Lempert, enables a motion-picture camera to photograph an entire operation as it is being performed. Above: Diagram showing how Lempertscope works. Left: Lempertscope picture taken as surgeons performed an ear operation.

but use of others of the above-mentioned methods is more recent.

VITALIAN or (Lat.) **VITALIANUS,** SAINT (657–72), Pope, born in Campania. He came to the papal throne when the Greek emperor Constans II (q.v.) was persecuting those who opposed monothelitism (q.v.). Tactfully he ignored this opposition and cultivated friendly relations with the emperor, with such success that the latter visited him in Rome in 663. He also put Constans' successor Constantine IV under obligation to the papal see by helping him in his campaign against a rival. Vitalian is also remembered as the sender of the distinguished Theodore (see THEODORE OF TARSUS) to the see of Canterbury.

VITALIS, ORDERICUS (1075–about 1143), Norman historian, born in Atcham, near Shrewsbury, England. He entered the monastery of St. Evroult in Normandy in 1085, and with the exception of short intervals spent the remainder of his life there. At the suggestion of his superiors he began to compose the annals of St. Evroult, and afterward expanded his work into a general history of thirteen books, bearing the title *Historia Ecclesiastica.* The work, which begins with the apostolic era, is of value chiefly for the period in which Vitalis himself lived. The original manuscript is now in the Bibliothèque Nationale in Paris.

VITAL STATISTICS, that branch of statistics which deals with the growth and changes of population. The figures are taken from census and registration reports. The average of births or deaths for a unit of one thousand population over a calendar year is taken and this figure is called a rate. The general rates are called crude rates. When these are subdivided into sex, color, occupation, and age they are known as refined rates. Death rates are higher for men than women and the highest rate is before the age of one and after the age of fifty. The lowest death rate for both sexes is between the ages of eleven and thirteen. The advance of medical science and social welfare work in recent years has increased the expectation of life but has not increased the span of life. For the elucidation of this statement sixty-five years is considered to be the average span of life. A greater number of people reaches that age today than did in 1900, but no appreciably greater number survives it.

The difference between the birth rate and the death rate of a country gives the proportionate increase in population of that country. The figure for the proportionate increase of the world's population is necessarily speculative as there are large areas where no record of births and deaths are kept.

VITAMIN, any one of a number of organic chemical compounds widely distributed in natural foods, and required in minute amounts for proper nutrition. Vitamins are required for healthy living by humans and all other higher animals, and probably also by lower animals and microorganisms. Different animal species require different vitamins; for example, guinea pigs and humans require vitamin C, and die in a comparatively short time if it is withheld from their diets, but rats, which are closely related to guinea pigs, do not require this vitamin, and are not benefited by its administration. Cattle require certain vitamins, not necessary to humans, which occur in forage grasses (q.v.).

The word "vitamine" was coined in 1912 by the Polish chemist Casimir Funk, and applied by him to the substance now called vitamin B_1, or thiamine. This vitamin belongs to the group of chemical compounds called amines (q.v.), and the term "vitamine" was applied to the group of chemicals which supposedly were "amines of life" (Lat. *vita,* "life"). The reformed spelling vitamin indicates that most of these compounds are not amines.

The absence of any one of several vitamins leads to specific symptoms of one or another deficiency disease (q.v.). Vitamins were used for the prevention and cure of such deficiency diseases long before their cause was known. Thus, scurvy (q.v.) is a serious and often fatal disease which invariably appears in human beings who have not had vitamin C for several months. Vitamin C occurs in a large number of fresh fruits and vegetables, but is destroyed by most preservation processes. Sailors and others who had no fresh foods over a long period of time were for centuries accustomed to "epidemics" of scurvy. Long before the discovery of vitamins, practical seamen discovered that limes acted as a preventative and as a cure for scurvy. Nutritionists now know that limes are a concentrated source of vitamin C., and are able to preserve this vitamin even for some years after the fruits are picked. Similarly, cod-liver oil (q.v.) was used as a therapeutic substance before the 20th century, and not until this century was the reason for its therapeutic value realized: it contains an extremely high concentration of vitamins A and D. Even in the middle 1920's, when the value of calf's liver as a cure for anemia was discovered, the true nature of the reason was not understood; more than twenty years elapsed before vitamin B_{12} was isolated from liver and shown to be the potent antianemia factor.

The "discovery" of vitamins was thus a gradual process. Shortly before 1900, the Dutch physician Christiaan Eijkman showed that the disease beriberi (q.v.) was caused by deficiency of a minute amount of a substance found in rice polishings. This substance was later called vitamin B; when scientists discovered that several different substances were present in vitamin B, Eijkman's "antineuritic factor" was called vitamin B_1. But not until 1925, when the American physician Joseph Goldberger demonstrated that pellagra (q.v.) is a deficiency disease, preventable and curable by a vitamin of the B complex, was the importance of these substances realized by most nutritionists.

When scientists first discovered that several different vitamins were important in human nutrition, they designated them by letters, such as vitamin A, vitamin B, and vitamin C. This system of nomenclature soon became chaotic, because of the discovery that "vitamin B" was actually a complex of many different vitamins, and because numerous scientists discovered and named "vitamins" which later turned out to be nonexistent. Beginning in the late 1920's, many vitamins were prepared synthetically in chemical laboratories, and given chemical names, and although the letter nomenclature is still widely applied, the chemical names are generally more precise.

The quantitative determination of vitamins is equally chaotic. The only method originally available for measuring the amounts of a particular vitamin in a particular food was biological assay (see ANALYSIS, MEDICAL). For example, a group of guinea pigs are placed on a diet deficient in vitamin C, and fed varying amounts of some additional food containing vitamin C. The amount of the vitamin in the additional food is measured by determining the minimum amount of that food required to keep the animal healthy; this amount might be expressed in "International Units" or "U.S.P. (United States Pharmacopeia) Units", or some other units, based on the amount required per guinea pig per day, or per kilogram body weight of guinea pig per day, or on some other basis. Since pure synthetic vitamins have been available, scientists have generally specified the actual weights of pure vitamins, or have defined the units in terms of such weights. Thus, 1 International Unit of vitamin A equals $3/5$ microgram of β-carotene (a microgram is one millionth of a gram, and a gram is about one thirtieth of an ounce); 1 International Unit of vitamin B_1 equals 3 micrograms of thiamine chloride; 1 International Unit of vitamin C equals 50 micrograms of ascorbic acid; and 1 International Unit of vitamin D equals 1/40 microgram of calciferol.

Exact human daily requirements for the various vitamins cannot be stated. Scientists are not certain that some of the vitamins are necessary for healthy humans, although these same vitamins are useful in curing certain conditions which may or may not have been caused by vitamin deficiency. Average requirements can be stated for certain other vitamins, and are given below. In cases of deficiency, however, doses far larger than the daily average requirement are necessary. Moreover, diets may contain unknown antivitamins, substances which destroy the vitamins, or inhibit their assimilation in the body. A substance found in live yeast destroys vitamin B_1, and other B-vitamin destroyers occur in corn and egg white. Even vitamins may be antivitamins; excessively large doses of vitamin A interfere with the use of vitamin C by the body, and can cause scurvy. No important human diseases are known to be due to antivitamins, but cattle often die from eating dicumarol in spoiled clover hay, which acts as an antivitamin K. Certain forms of infection in the body may require greatly increased doses of particular vitamins. Changes in metabolism, normal or pathological, affect vitamin requirements; thus pregnant women, and people with overactive thyroid glands, have abnormal vitamin requirements.

Vitamins are generally classified as fat-soluble and water-soluble. Vitamins A, D, E, and K are fat-soluble; vitamin C and the vitamins of the B complex are water-soluble.

Vitamin A. Vitamin A or axerophthol, $C_{20}H_{29}OH$, is a rare vitamin found in butter fat, fish-liver oils, and to some extent in the livers of higher animals. It never occurs in plants, but some plants are rich sources of chemicals called provitamins which can be converted into vitamin A in the body. The most common of these provitamins is β-carotene, $C_{40}H_{56}$, a yellow pigment which constitutes the chief coloring matter of carrots, and is also present in many other yellow vegetables, such as squash, apricots, and sweet potatoes, and some green vegetables, such as spinach. One molecule of β-carotene is converted into two molecules of vitamin A in the body. See CAROTIN. **The daily requirement for**

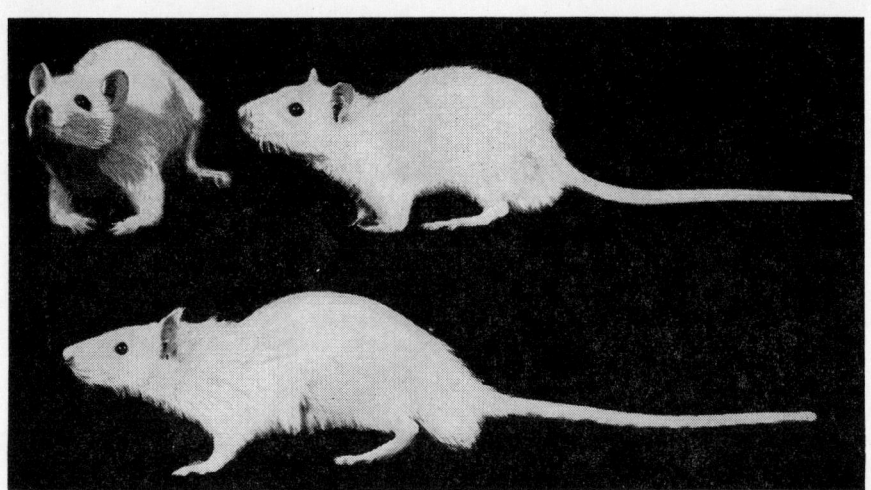

EFFECTS OF VITAMIN DEFICIENCY IN DIET

Top: Rat with rickets, caused by the lack of vitamin D in its diet. Above: Rat which has been fed sufficient amounts of foods containing vitamin D. Right: Rat on a diet notably lacking in thiamine has lost ability to co-ordinate muscles. Right, bottom: Same rat 24 hours later, after receiving thiamine.

U.S. Bur. of Human Nutrit. & Home Econ.

humans is about 2.4 milligrams. Vitamin A extracts were formerly obtained from fish livers, including cod, halibut, and soupfin shark. By the end of World War II, U.S. factories were producing 40 tons of vitamin A per year from 8000 tons of fish livers. Since that time, demand for vitamin A has increased, but much of this demand has been met by synthetic vitamin A, which does not have the fishy odor and taste characteristic of the fish-liver product. Vitamin A deteriorates rapidly when heated or exposed to air; provitamins are more stable.

Lack of vitamin A interferes with growth and with the functioning of epithelial tissue. In particular, it causes mucous membranes to become hard or horny, and prevents the formation of *visual purple* in the retina of the eye. The latter is necessary for vision under conditions of low illumination, and so one of the common early symptoms of vitamin-A deficiency is "night blindness". Because mucous membranes form a barrier against infection, vitamin-A deficient individuals are probably susceptible to infections, particularly to colds. Long continued vitamin-A deficiency may lead to blindness, urinary calculi, or other serious conditions. However, excessive dosage of Vitamin A to normal individuals will not cure colds or give remarkable visual acuity during darkness.

Vitamin D, the antirachitic vitamin. The name "vitamin D" is applied to several rare chemicals, some synthetic and some found in fish-liver oils and other animal products, all of which are closely related chemically, and belong to the chemical family called sterols (q.v.). Calciferol, also called vitamin D_2, has the formula $C_{28}H_{43}OH$. A number of common sterols, found in both plants and animals, are converted to vitamin D when irradiated with (i.e., exposed to) ultraviolet light. For example, ergosterol, $C_{28}H_{44}O$, which occurs in yeast and various oils, is converted into viosterol, $C_{28}H_{43}OH$, a vitamin D, when irradiated. A

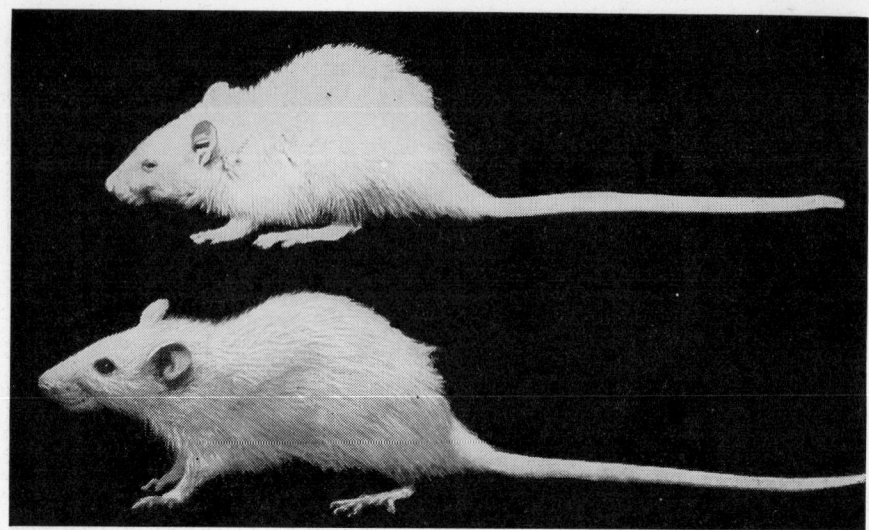

EFFECTS OF VITAMIN DEFICIENCY IN DIET. *Top: Rat whose diet lacks vitamin A. Eyes are sore and fur is rough. Bottom: Rat given vitamin A. Its eyes are clear and its fur is smooth.*

sterol which occurs in human skin is converted to vitamin D_3 when the skin is exposed to ultraviolet radiation. Thus, a human can obtain vitamin D in three different ways: by ingesting any form of vitamin D; by ingesting irradiated, sterol-containing foods; or by ingesting sterol-containing foods, which supply sterol to the skin, and then being irradiated. Sterols exist in many different foods, and so vitamin-D deficiency is rare in tropical countries, where ultraviolet radiation from the sun is plentiful through most of the year. However, very little ultraviolet radiation of the proper wave length is present in sunlight in temperate regions during winter, and ultraviolet light is cut off by ordinary glass windows. Hence vitamin-D deficiency may be common in temperate and frigid climates, particularly in cities, where people are little exposed to sunlight. The daily requirement of vitamin D in humans is about 10 micrograms. This vitamin is now produced in large quantities by irradiation of common foods, such as milk.

Vitamin D plays an important part in the metabolism of the elements calcium and phosphorus in the body, and hence is necessary for the formation of bones and teeth. Vitamin-D deficiency in growing children causes the disease known as rickets (q.v.), characterized by by insufficient calcification of the bones; an obvious symptom is bowleggedness.. The deficiency can always be prevented by regular intake of milk, vitamin-D concentrates, or irradiated foods; this prophylactic measure is especially necessary for pregnant and lactating mothers and for growing children. However, overdosage of vitamin D is harmful.

Vitamin E, the antisterility vitamin. Alpha-tocopherol, $C_{29}H_{50}O_2$, is the principal natural product which has vitamin-E activity. Deficiency of this vitamin in experimental animals results in muscular dystrophy and paralysis of the hind quarters. Vitamin E has been called the "sex vitamin", because its lack causes sterility in both male and female rats. The lack of it probably has a similar result in humans, but the vitamin is so widespread, and required in such minute amounts, that deficiency in a human being is extremely rare. The vitamin does not, however, increase sexual potency in normal human beings. The richest source of vitamin E is wheat-germ oil, but is also found in many other vegetable oils, in which it apparently inhibits formation of rancidity.

Vitamin K, the antihemorragic vitamin. A number of naphthoquinone derivatives have vitamin-K activity. Among these are vitamin K, $C_{11}H_8O_2$, and vitamin K, $C_{31}H_{46}O_2$. Such substances are present in egg yolk, liver, fish oils, and a wide variety of vegetables. Deficiencies in the diet are extremely rare, but digestive disturbances may lead to insufficient absorption of vitamin K. Synthetic water-

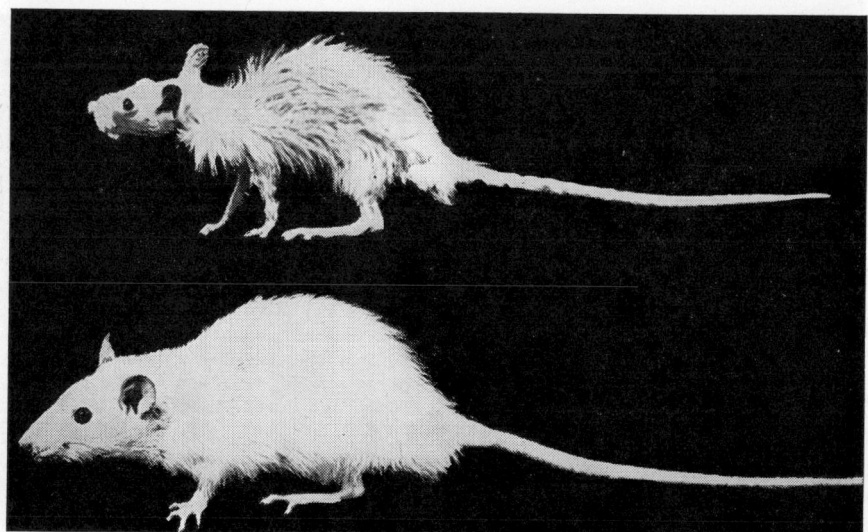

EFFECTS OF VITAMIN DEFICIENCY IN DIET
Top: Rat whose diet lacks riboflavin, which promotes health by helping body cells to use oxygen. Above: Same rat 6 weeks later, after receiving foods rich in riboflavin. Right: Guinea pig with scurvy, caused by lack of vitamin C. Right, bottom: Healthy guinea pig which has had plenty of vitamin C.

soluble compounds with vitamin-K activity may then be injected. Vitamin K is necessary in the formation of prothrombin, without which blood cannot clot (see BLEEDING). Vitamin K is sometimes administered by physicians to prevent anticipated hemorrhages, particularly in patients suffering from liver damage and jaundice.

Vitamin C, the antiscorbutic vitamin. Ascorbic acid (sometimes called cevitamic acid), $C_6H_8O_6$, is the only known chemical which has vitamin-C activity. Chemically, it is closely related to the sugars, but is a true acid. It is destroyed by alkalies, heat, and exposure to air, and is thus destroyed in most cooking and preservation processes. Richest natural sources are fresh fruits and vegetables. Citrus fruits, which are naturally acidic, and are protected by their skins from access to air, are very rich sources of vitamin C, and retain their vitamin-C content over long periods of time. New processes of canning and quick freezing preserve vitamin C. The daily requirement is about 30 milligrams. Vitamin C is probably the only important nutritive element absent from milk; for this reason, orange juice or synthetic vitamin C is usually the first food, after milk or milk "formula", added to the diet of babies (see INFANTS, FEEDING OF).

The exact biochemical function of vitamin C is not known. It is apparently necessary in virtually every cell in the body, as a catalyst in the oxidation of the hydrogen of food, the principal source of bodily energy. Vitamin C, unlike some other vitamins, cannot be stored in the body; excessive quantities are rapidly excreted. A minor deficiency can therefore occur within a single day if the diet is deficient in this substance. Severe deficiency leads to scurvy (q.v.), of which the first symptom is often bleeding and blackened gums. Almost all fresh vegetables contain some vitamin C, so that scurvy is generally confined to persons subsisting on dried and preserved foods.

The Vitamin-B Complex. Many of the water-soluble vitamins occur together in plants, and were confused with one another during the early period of vitamin research. Yeast and liver are rich sources of many of them. When the complex nature of "vitamin B" was discovered, different numbers were given to the various substances by different scientists. Only vitamins B_1, B_2, B_6, and B_{12} have any standard numerical nomenclature today, and even these are generally identified by chemical names. The modern tendency is to include in the term "vitamin B" all water-soluble vitamins except vitamin C.

Thiamine or Vitamin B_1, the antineuritic vitamin. Thiamine, $C_{12}H_{17}ON_4SCl$, is an alkaline organic chemical, containing nitrogen, sulfur, chlorine, and alcohol and amine groups. It is usually supplied synthetically in the form of its hydrochloride. Average daily requirement is about one milligram. It is common in a large number of vegetable products, especially yeast and the embryos of cereal-grass seeds. Cereal-grass embryos are often removed from the cereals in processing, to improve the appearance and palatability of the cereals, and to aid in their preservation. For example, the thiamine-containing portions of rice are removed by polishing the rice, and people in the Orient, who remained comparatively healthy on a diet consisting principally of rice, developed the disease beriberi (q.v.), due entirely to thiamine deficiency, when fed on polished rice. Thiamine is necessary in the metabolism of carbohydrates in the body; an intermediate product in this metabolism, called pyruvic acid, cannot be further metabolized without thiamine as a catalyst. Minor deficiencies of thiamine may cause nervous disorders, loss of appetite, and gastric disorders.

Riboflavin, Vitamin B_2, or Vitamin G, the growth vitamin. Riboflavin, $C_{17}H_{20}N_4O_6$, is widely distributed in vegetable products, and deficiency of this vitamin alone is rare, although it may occur in conjunction with deficiencies of other B vitamins. Milk, eggs, fruits, legumes and many other vegetables, yeast, and liver are all good sources. Average daily riboflavin requirement in humans is about 2 milligrams. The vitamin is necessary for growth, and for "respiration" of cells, acting as a catalyst in metabolism of carbohydrates, amino acids, or both. Deficiencies of riboflavin causes dermatitis, particularly around the mouth and nose, and certain eye abnormalities.

Riboflavin fluoresces with greenish-yellow light when exposed to ultraviolet light; its presence in natural foods or synthetic products may be determined, and its quantity estimated, by means of this property.

Pyridoxine or Vitamin B_6. Pyridoxine, $C_8H_{11}NO_3$, is a pyridine derivative and an alcohol. Several other pyridine derivatives appear to have lesser vitamin-B_6 activity. This vitamin is found in the same foods in which vitamins B_1 and B_2 are found. Average daily requirement is about one milligram, and deficiency of this vitamin alone is so rare that the symptoms in humans are not known; in animals, deficiency produces various kinds of anemia, skin diseases, and organic nerve disorders. Massive doses (such as 20 milligrams per day) have been found helpful in treating certain human nervous and muscular disorders, and in alleviating nausea of pregnancy, although these disorders are probably not due to vitamin deficiency.

Vitamin B_{12}. The efficacy of liver extracts in curing pernicious anemia is due to the presence of vitamin B_{12}, a complex organic cobalt compound which is effective in amounts so small as to be "minute" even in comparison with other vitamins. No other source of this vitamin is known. The chemical structure of this vitamin has not yet been elaborated. See ANEMIA.

Niacin, Nicotinamide, or Vitamin P–P. Nicotinic acid, $C_6H_5NO_2$, or nicotinic acid amide (niacin) $C_6H_6N_2O$, is one of the important vitamins of the B complex. Dairy products, fresh meats, and most fresh vegetables are rich sources, but corn is not a source, and persons subsisting on a diet primarily of corn and preserved meat develop a deficiency, producing the disease called pellagra (q.v.); niacin is sometimes called the pellagra-preventive vitamin. Average daily niacin requirement in humans is about 10 milligrams. This vitamin functions in the metabolism of carbohydrates, acting in the oxidation of the derivatives formed by the breakdown of glucose. Niacin is now made synthetically on a large scale. Although it can be made from nicotine, other methods of niacin synthesis are simpler.

Pantothenic Acid. Pantothenic acid, $C_9H_{17}NO_5$, occurs with most of the other B vitamins. Although average daily human requirement is probably about 10 milligrams, no human deficiency disease due to lack of this vitamin is known. Deficiency diseases may be caused in animals by withholding this vitamin, and may then be cured by administration of the synthetic vitamin. Of the many symptoms produced by pantothenic-acid deficiency, grayness of hair is perhaps most interesting. It is possible that deficiency of this vitamin may be connected with senile graying of hair in humans, but no connection has thus far been demonstrated.

Biotin or Vitamin H. Fifty micrograms of biotin, $C_{10}H_{16}N_2O_3S$, is probably the daily human requirement. A substance in egg white acts as an antivitamin for biotin, thus greatly increasing the daily requirement if much egg white is ingested. Although deficiency of this vitamin is extremely rare in humans, it was through the antivitamin effect of egg white that biotin was discovered. See separate article, BIOTIN.

Folic Acid. Daily human requirement is about 1 milligram. Deficiency is extremely rare. This vitamin, in natural extract or synthetic form, has been useful in treating certain types of anemia, and a deficiency of it may have something to do with premature grayness of hair.

Para-aminobenzoic Acid. This substance is not definitely a vitamin for humans, but is a vitamin for certain lower forms of life. It is related chemically to folic acid. See AMINOBENZOIC ACID.

Choline. Choline, $C_5H_{15}NO_2$, is found in a variety of animal products, particularly liver and other internal organs, egg yolk, and milk, and in yeast. It is required in comparatively large amounts, larger than any other vitamin, and so large that some biochemists do not consider that choline is a vitamin. It is necessary in fat metabolism, and deficiency of choline leads to degeneration of the liver and kidneys. See CHOLINE; ACETYLCHOLINE.

Inositol. Like choline, the classification of meso-inositol, $C_6H_{12}O_6$, as a vitamin, is doubtful. It is needed by yeast and by some lower animals in very large amounts. Its requirement by humans is uncertain. It plays a part in fat metabolism. Chemically it is an alicyclic (see AROMATIC COMPOUNDS) sugar. See INOSITOL.

VITEBSK, a city in the republic of White Russia, U.S.S.R., on the Dvina R., 380 miles s. of Leningrad. It trades in grain, flax, sugar, and timber with Riga. Pop., (1939) 167,424.

VITELLIUS, AULUS (15–69 A.D.), Roman Emperor. He was put in command of the legions in lower Germany by the emperor Galba in 68 A.D. Vitellius was proclaimed emperor by his soldiers in January, 69 A.D. Marching into Italy, he secured the throne by the overthrow of Otho, Galba's successor, and ruled until December, when his forces were defeated by the legions supporting Titus Flavius Vespasianus (see VESPASIAN); soon afterward Vitellius himself was killed by Vespasian's troops.

VITERBO, city of Italy, in the province of Rome and 50 miles N.N.W. of the city of Rome, with an ancient cathedral and papal palace. It has manufactures of soap, paper, leather, and matches. Pop. (1943) 36,123.

VITET, LUDOVIC (1802–73), French author and political leader, born in Paris, and educated at the École Normale. After spending some time in travel, he gave up the profession of teaching for that of letters. In 1824 he began contributing literary and artistic criticisms to the *Globe*. In his first books, *Les Barricades* (1826), *Les États de Blois* (1827), and *La Mort d'Henri III à St. Cloud* (1829), Vitet opened a romantic vein new to French literature by presenting historical occurrences in vivid dramatic form. After the Revolution of 1830 the French statesman François Pierre Guizot created for the young writer the post of inspector of historic monuments. He was a member of the Chamber of Deputies from 1834 to 1848, of the Legislative Assembly in 1849, and of the Constituent Assembly in 1871. In 1845 he became a member of the French Academy. Among Vitet's other works are *Histoire des Anciennes Villes de France* (1833), *Histoire de Dieppe* (1833), *Fragments et Mélanges* (1846), *Histoire Financière du Gouvernement de Juillet* (1848), *Les États d'Orléans* (1849), *Le Louvre* (1852), *Essais Historiques et Littéraires* (1862), *Études sur l'Histoire de l'Art* (1863–64), *La Science et la Foi* (1865), *Lettres sur le Siège de Paris* (1870–71), and *Études Philosophiques et Littéraires* (posthumously published, 1874).

VITEX, a genus of trees or shrubs of the Verbenaceae family. *V. agnus castus,* the chaste tree, a native of the countries around the Mediterranean, is downy, with digitate leaves white on the back, and has an acrid fruit, the seeds of which have been used as an external application in cases of colic.

VITI ISLANDS. See FIJI.

VITORIA, capital of the province of Álava, Spain, 121 miles N.E. of Valladolid. It has manufactures of paper, mirrors, woolens, and hardware. Wellington here defeated the French under Joseph Bonaparte and Jourdain in 1813. Pop. (1941 est.) 51,162.

VITRIOL, a name given by early chemists to certain glasslike salts, especially sulfates, including chiefly blue vitriol or copper sulfate, green vitriol or ferrous sulfate, red vitriol or cobalt sulfate, and white vitriol or zinc sul-

Antonio Vivaldi (from early engraving)

fate. Oil of vitriol or vitriolic acid, the old name given to sulfuric acid, and still retained in manufacturing parlance, refers to the primitive method of production from ferrous sulfate.

VITRUVIUS POLLIO, MARCUS (fl. 1st century B.C.), Roman architect and engineer, author of the earliest extant work on architecture. He was born probably in Formiæ and died during the reign of Augustus (27 B.C.–14 A.D.) The work *De Architectura Libri Decem,* by which he is chiefly known, was composed in the later years of his life, and consists of dissertations upon a wide variety of subjects relating to architecture, engineering and sanitation, practical hydraulics, acoustic vases, and the like. It has been studied for the past four centuries as a thesaurus of the practice and theory of building in the Augustan age.

VITTORIA, FRANCISCO DI (about 1480–1549), Spanish theologian, born in Vittoria, Navarre, and educated in Burgos, Valledolid, and Paris. He joined the Dominican Order, was appointed a teacher at the University of Paris (1516), became professor at Valladolid (1522), and (1524–44) held a chair at Salamanco. Through his teaching and his disciples Vittoria exercised a profound influence. In dealing with the law of nations he was one of the forerunners of the Dutch student of international law, Hugo Grotius. Vittoria maintained that the pope's authority was limited to religious matters, that the right to life, liberty, and property could not be denied to the pagans beyond the Atlantic Ocean because of their unbelief, that noncombatants—women, children, farmers, strangers, and clergy—should not be slaughtered in war, that slavery was not a legitimate consequence of war, that hostages could not rightfully be put to death on a breach of faith by an enemy, and that looting was illegitimate. Among his works, all published after his death, are *Relectiones XII Theologicæ* (1557), *Summa Sacramentorum Ecclesiæ* (1561), *Instrucción y Refugio del Alma* (1552), and *Confessionario* (1562).

VITTORIO VENETO, a town of the province of Treviso, Italy, 23 miles N. of the city of Treviso. It was formed in 1879 by the union of Ceneda and Serravalle. There is a masterly altarpiece by Titian in the cathedral of Serravalle. Vittorio has saline and sulfur springs and is a pleasant summer resort. The breeding of silkworms is extensively carried on, and woolens, paper, cement, and lime are manufactured. Pop. (1943) 23,475.

VITUS, SAINT, a martyr of the time of the Roman emperor Diocletian. He is supposed to have been put to death in Lucania or in Rome, and his feast day is June 15. Relics purporting to be of him are preserved in Corvei and in Prague. His name is commonly applied to the peculiar nervous disorder scientifically known as chorea. See CHOREA.

VIVALDI, ANTONIO (1680?–1743), Italian violinist and composer, born in Venice, and trained by his father, a violinist at the church of San Marco. He entered the priesthood at an early age, and is known to have lived for some years in Darmstadt, Germany. In 1713 he returned to Venice, and was appointed director of the Conservatorio della Pietà; he held this position until his death. Vivaldi was known in his time both as a composer and as one of the earliest violin virtuosos. His most famous contemporary, Johann Sebastian Bach, who was somewhat younger than Vivaldi, took the older composer's music as a model during his formative years, and some of Vivaldi's works for violin and orchestra and for violin solo have come down to us only through transcriptions, usually for solo harpsichord, which Bach made for purposes of study. Of Vivaldi's extant works, the most notable are *concerti grossi* for stringed instruments and sonatas for violin; in both categories, but particularly in that of the *concerto grosso,* forgotten or lost works have come to light in recent years. His extant work also includes about forty operas and a large amount of music for various instrumental combinations.

VIVERRIDAE, a family of small carnivorous mammals comprising the civet, mongoose, binturong (qq.v.), and foussa (see CRYPTOPROCTA). The family also includes fossil forms that range back to Eocene times. The early members are interesting in that they show points of resemblance to animals of other families, such as cats, weasels, bears, and hyenas, and thus present a very generalized type of early carnivore. The principal fossil genera are *Amphictis, Ictitherium,* and *Palaeoprionodon,* all from the Tertiary deposits of Europe.

VIVES, JUAN LUIS (1492–1540), Spanish philosopher, born in Valencia. He studied at Valencia, Paris, and Louvain, and taught at the latter university. He was invited to England by Henry VIII, who made him tutor of Princess Mary in 1523. He was imprisoned for opposing the divorce of Queen Catharine of Aragon. His principal works are *De Disciplinis, De Causis Corruptorum Artium,* and *De Anima et Vita;* in addition to these and several other metaphysical works, he wrote commentaries on Augustine's *City of God* (Eng. trans., 1620).

VIVIAN, VIVIANE, or **VIVIEN,** an enchantress in Arthurian romance, the nymph who brought up Lancelot in her fairy palace in the lake, whence she was called the Lady of the Lake, also the mistress of Merlin.

VIVIANI, RENÉ (1863–1925), French statesman, born in Sidi Bel Abbès, in French North Africa. At an early age he associated himself with the Socialist Party, soon becoming one of its most brilliant orators and prominent leaders. When the party was reorganized in 1904 into the United Socialist Party, Viviani, like Briand, stayed outside, and thenceforth called himself an Independent Socialist. His parliamentary career began in 1893, when he was elected deputy of the fifth ward in Paris. He retained this office until 1902, when he failed to be re-elected, but four years later he was elected deputy of the department of Creuse. In the same year he entered the cabinet of Clémenceau with the portfolio of the department of labor. Subsequently, in the ministry of Doumergue, he was minister of public instruction. In 1914 President Poincaré appointed Viviani premier of France. Shortly afterward the war with Germany commenced, and in August, 1914, Viviani reorganized his cabinet on a war basis. He retained the premiership for over a year, but resigned on Oct. 27, 1915, being succeeded by Briand. Viviani remained in Briand's cabinet, however, as minister of justice, later holding the same office under Ribot. He visited the United States in 1917 as the head of the French Commission sent for the purpose of influencing the American people to help in the war, and again in 1921, when he was a delegate to the Disarmament Conference in Washington. In 1920 he was appointed French delegate to the first meeting of the League of Nations.

VIVIEN DE SAINT-MARTIN, LOUIS (1802–97), French geographer, born in Caen, Normandy. After completing his education, he devoted his life to the writing of works on geography. Among his works are two volumes of a *Histoire Universelle des Découvertes Géographiques* (1845–47) ; *Études de Géographie Ancienne et d'Ethnographie Asiatique* (1850–54) ; *Étude sur la Géographie et les Populations Primitives du Nord-Ouest de l'Inde d'après les Hymnes Védiques* (1860) ; *Étude sur la Géographie Grecque et Latine de l'Inde* (1858–60) ; *Le Nord de l'Afrique dans l'Antiquité Grecque et Romaine* (1863) ; *Histoire de la Géographie et des Découvertes Géographiques* (1873) ; and *L'Atlas Universel* (1877–85), finished by Franz Schrader. He also issued the first two volumes of the monumental work, *Nouveau Dictionnaire de Géographie Universelle,* and the next two with the assistance of Louis Rousselet, who completed the work (7 vols., with two supplements, 1879–99).

VIVIPAROUS ANIMALS, those animals which bring forth living young, as opposed to those producing their young from eggs. See OVIPAROUS ANIMALS.

VIVISECTION, a term originally employed to designate cutting operations upon living animals for experimentation, but now including experimentation of any kind upon living creatures, to demonstrate or discover physiological facts or theories. This comprises inoculation with disease, subjection to different temperatures, atmospheric pressure, food changes, or the action of various drugs and medicines, as well as to cutting operations involving ligature of arteries, exposure of nerves, or removal of vital organs. An active propaganda for the total suppression of vivisection has been steadily maintained in Great Britain and in the United States. The chief argument against vivisection (based mainly on the undoubtedly cruel experiments carried on before the days of anesthetics) is that the practice is unnecessary and cruel. The whole weight of scientific opinion is in favor of vivisection conducted in a humane manner. The benefits to mankind derived from animal experimentation are incalculable. Practically all our knowledge of physiology, of the effect of medicines, and

VIZCACHA. See VISCACHA.

VIZCAÍNO, SEBASTIÁN (1550–1615), Spanish explorer, born in Huelva. He became chief pilot of New Spain, and in 1596–97 attempted unsuccessfully to explore Lower California. In 1602–03 he explored and carefully surveyed the coast north of Cape Mendocino, discovered a bay, which he named Monterey in honor of the viceroy, and dispatched northward from Cape Orford a vessel which sailed to 46° N. lat., and reached the mouth of a large river, probably the Columbia. The observations made by him on the California coast were used by Enrico Martínez in constructing thirty-two charts, which are still preserved in the archives of the Council of the Indies. His reports on his two voyages to California were published by Juan de Torquemada in *Monarquía Indiana* (3 vols., Madrid, 1615), and the greater part of them can be found in James Burney's *Collection of Voyages to the South Sea* (London, 1811).

VIZCAYA. See BISCAY.

VIZETELLY, an English family name of Italian origin—a corruption of Italian *visiatello,* long or far-sighted—traced to Ravenna, Italy, in the 14th century. Thence the family removed to Venice where its members engaged in the manufacture of glass. From Venice they migrated to England, where Jacopo Vizzetelli settled in Cheshire in the middle of the 16th century; from glass-blowing the members of the family turned to printing and engraving.

VIZETELLY, EDWARD HENRY (1847–1903), English war correspondent and author, born in Chiswick. During the Franco-Prussian War he was war correspondent for the New York *Times* and the London *Daily News,* and as aide took part in the Vosges campaign on the staff of the Italian patriot Garibaldi in 1870. As war correspondent Vizetelly reported other campaigns in various parts of Europe, Asia, and Africa. He served in the Turkish army as colonel of a regiment of bashi-bazouks during the Russo-Turkish War (1877) and was present at the fall of Kars but escaped capture. He founded the Cyprus *Times* in 1881 and the *Times of Egypt* in Alexandria in 1882, at which time he witnessed the bombardment of that city. Vizetelly was commander of the expedition sent by James Gordon Bennett of the New York *Herald* in 1889 to meet Stanley in "darkest Africa". He wrote *Reminiscences of a Bashi-Bazouk* (1897), *The Warrior Woman* (1899), and *From Cyprus to Zanzibar* (1901).

VIZETELLY, ERNEST ALFRED (1853–1922), English journalist, artist, and author, born in London. He served as a newspaper correspondent and artist during the Franco-Prussian War. In addition to his translations of many of Zola's novels he wrote *With Zola in England* (1899); *Émile Zola, Novelist and Reformer* (1904); *The Anarchists* (1911); the novels *The Scorpion* (1894), *A Path of Thorns* (1901), *The Lover's Progress* (1902), and *Loves of the Poets* (1915); *Republican France, 1870–1928* (1912); *My Days of Adventure* (1914); and *My Adventures in the Commune, Paris, 1871* (1914). Under his pseudonym, "Le Petit Homme Rouge", he wrote *The Court of the Tuileries* (1907), *The Favorites of Henry of Navarre* (1910), and *The Favorites of Louis XIV* (1912).

VIZETELLY, FRANK (1830–83), English war correspondent and artist, born in London. He received his newspaper training from Henry Vizetelly, and began his career in 1843 with the *Illustrated London Times.* In 1856 he went to Paris where he served as first editor of *Le Monde Illustré.* When the war between Sardinia and Austria began he was sent to Italy, where he reported and sketched the great battle of Solferino. In 1860 he was sent by the *Illustrated London News* to Sicily when Garibaldi set out on his expedition with the "One Thousand", and accompanied the Italian patriot throughout his entire campaign. At the beginning of the American Civil War he was sent to America by his paper and reached the Confederate capital by the "underground route", just as the advance of the Federals was repulsed in 1862. He accompanied generals Longstreet, Johnston, and Stuart in many of their engagements, and was present throughout the bombardment of the city of Charleston. During this time he was sending sketches and portraits to his journal, but many of them failed to reach London. Running the blockade of Charleston, he returned to London in 1865, and there followed a period of comparative quiet, broken only by a visit to Vienna in 1866 for the *London News* during the Seven Weeks' War. At the outbreak of the Don Carlos insurrection in Spain he was sent as correspondent for *The Times,* and at the end of the insurrection he went to France and lived a year or two at Hendaye in the Pyrenees. From there he went to Paris, Tunis, and Egypt, and arrived in Alexandria at the time of its bombardment in 1882. He arranged with the London *Graphic* to accompany Hicks Pasha in 1883 in an expedition against the Mahdi, but the expedition was betrayed by the guides and fell into an ambush at Kashgil on November 3, 1883. After severe fighting the entire expedition was practically annihilated. The body of Frank Vizetelly was never found. His name is engraved upon the memorial tablet to war correspondents and special artists now in the crypt of St. Paul's Cathedral, in London.

VIZETELLY, FRANK (FRANCIS) HORACE (1864–1938), American lexicographer, editor, radiologist, and author, son of Henry Richard Vizetelly, born in London. From 1883 to 1891 he was junior member of the publishing house of Vizetelly & Company. Coming to New York in 1891 he joined the Funk & Wagnalls Company as a member of its editorial staff and as assistant editor of the *Standard Dictionary,* of which he became managing editor in 1908 and editor in 1912. He was the editor of *The Mental Efficiency Series* (1916), *A Practical Standard Dictionary* (1922, rev., 1933), and also of the *New Standard Encyclopedia.*

VIZETELLY, HENRY RICHARD (1820–94), English engraver, printer, publisher, and author, born in London. As a wood engraver he cut Birket Foster's choice vignettes for Longfellow's *Evangeline.* In 1841 he was joint founder with Herbert Ingram of *The Illustrated London News.* In 1843 he founded the *Pictorial Times* and in 1855 the *Illustrated Times,* the latter of which he sold in 1860. In 1865 he became Paris correspondent of *The Illustrated London News,* later embodying his experiences in his *Paris in Peril* (1882). Subsequently in London he established a publishing business, making a specialty of translations of French, Russian, German, and Spanish authors. He wrote many books, monographs on wine, and an autobiography, *Glances Back Through Seventy Years* (1893).

VIZETELLY, MONTAGUE (1846–97), English war correspondent and journalist, born in London. He served as war correspondent for the *Morning Advertiser* during the Franco-Prussian War. During the Italian campaign in Ethiopia, he acted as correspondent for the London *Times.* Then he was sent by the *Manchester Courier* to Newfoundland to investigate the fisheries problem and the condition of the projected Panama Canal when under French control. Later he was connected with the staffs of the *Daily Chronicle* and the *Morning Advertiser* as a specialist on military subjects, and was also the "Captious Critic" of the *Illustrated Sporting and Dramatic News.*

VIZIER (Arabic, *wazīr*, "bearer of a burden"), the title of the chief political officer of the early caliphs. It was adopted in 1328 by the Ottomans, and until 1878 was assigned to the highest official in other Mohammedan states. The title was afterward changed into *vezīrazam,* "grand vizier".

V-J DAY, Sept. 2, 1945, the day of formal surrender by Japan, ending **World War II.** It was proclaimed by President Harry S. Truman.

VLAARDINGEN, a town of the province of South Holland, Netherlands. Pop., about 31,000.

VLADIVOSTOK, administrative center of the Maritime Province of the Far Eastern Region of Soviet Russia, and the chief Soviet port and naval station on the Pacific Ocean. The city is situated on the northern shore of the Golden Horn harbor, a part of Amur, or Petra Velikogo, Bay, which is an extension of the Sea of Japan. Vladivostok is the center of a farming and industrial area, and its principal industries include shipbuilding, the refining of soybean oil, zinc and copper smelting, fishing and fish canning, and sawmilling. The harbor, 4 miles long and a mile wide, is ice-free for nine months of the year, and is kept open during winter months by ice breakers. Vladivostok was founded as a military post in 1862. It contains the first electric-power station in the Far Eastern Region, and is the site of a university. The city is the eastern terminus of the Trans-Siberian railway and of the Moscow-Vladivostok air route. Pop., about 206,000.

VLISSINGEN. See FLUSHING.

VLONA, or VALONA (anc. *Aulon*), seaport of Albania. It stands upon an inlet of the Adriatic Sea, protected by an island. Hides, cattle, grain, oil, wool, and tortoise shells are exported, as well as valonia, which is the pericarp of an acorn used for tanning leather. From 1464 until the Balkan War of 1912–13, Vlona was held by the Turks. The formation of Albania, at the Conference of London (1913), with Vlona as the seat of government, resulted from conflicting rivalries on the part of the Great Powers, none being willing that any of the others should profit by getting a hold on this key territory. Italy occupied Vlona three months after World War I began and seven months before declaring war against

Austria. After the war the city was restored to Albania. Pop., about 9000.

VLTAVA. See MOLDAU.

VOCAL CORD. See LARYNX.

VOCATIONAL EDUCATION AND GUIDANCE. The basic principle of vocational guidance is that an individual should be able to make his occupational plans after (1) learning about his own characteristics; (2) examining the requirements of various occupations; and (3) matching the two sets of facts under the guidance of a skilled counselor. The founding of the vocational movement in America is credited to Frank Parsons, who founded a "Vocation Bureau" in Boston in 1908.

Since individual analysis and occupational research provide the two sets of data basic to guidance work, many elaborate techniques have been developed in these fields. In the first, psychologists have provided the standardized test, forms of which have been developed to measure native intelligence, knowledge of subject matter, specific skills, aptitudes, interests, and other abilities and traits. In the second field, various methods, such as community surveys, utilization of census material, and job analysis, have been elaborated.

The more advanced program of guidance in schools usually involves (1) cumulative records for all pupils providing factual evidence as to their physical, mental, and personality characteristics; (2) the gathering and disseminating of comprehensive occupational information, especially that relevant to school enrollment; (3) provision for individual counseling of every pupil; (4) means for adapting the curriculum, and utilizing extracurricular and community resources, to supply the individual needs of pupils both as to rate and type of learning, and as to occupational tryout experiences; (5) provisions for job placement, or adjustment in further educational experiences, for all pupils; and (6) research procedure to determine the outcomes of schooling through follow-up studies of school-leavers. The vocational guidance program uses freely many referral aids and has close relationships with medical, psychological, social, and economic services and draws upon their supporting sciences.

Vocational guidance in public schools is officially promoted by the U.S. Office of Education through its Occupational Information and Guidance Service. Thirty States provide supervision in the guidance field. The professional organization of the movement is the National Vocational Guidance Association, which publishes the magazine *Occupations*.

VODENA. See EDESSA.

VODKA, Russian brandy, a strong spirituous beverage. Originally vodka was made almost exclusively of rye, but later it was also obtained from barley and oats mixed with rye, as well as from potatoes and maize. Vodka, as manufactured, contains about 90 percent of alcohol, but is diluted to 60 and 40 percent.

VOEGTLIN, CARL (1879–   ), American pharmacologist and biochemist, born in Switzerland, and educated at the universities of Basel, Munich, Geneva, and Freiburg. He came to the United States in 1904 and after serving as instructor in chemistry at the University of Wisconsin in 1904–05, he was associate professor of chemistry at the Johns Hopkins Medical School from 1906 to 1913. From the latter year until 1939 he was chief of the Division of Pharmacology in the U.S. Public Health Service and chief of the National Cancer Institute of the National Institute of Health.

VOËTIUS, GISBERT (1588–1676), Dutch theologian, born in Heusden. He became a minister in Blymen in 1611, and in 1634 was made professor of theology and Oriental languages at the University of Utrecht. He was engaged in numerous bitter religious controversies; at the synod of Dordrecht he combated Arminianism with great violence, and he afterward attacked the works of the French philosopher René Descartes and the German theologian Johannes Cocceius. Voëtius exercised great influence upon the theology of his time. His works were published under the title of *Selectæ Disputationes Theologicæ* (1648–69), and again as *Politica Ecclesiastica* (1663–76).

VOGEL, EDUARD (1829–56), German explorer, born in Crefeld. He was educated at Leipzig, at Berlin, and at Bishop's Observatory in London. In 1853 he was commissioned by the British government to assist Adolf Overweg and Heinrich Barth in explorations of western Sudan. He reached Murzuk in August, 1853, Kuka in January of 1854, and in December met Barth near Bundi. Returning with the latter to Kuka and Lake Chad, he went southward alone to Yakuba, the first white man ever seen in that region. The remainder of 1855 he spent in the vicinity of Yakuba and the Benue River. In November he went back to Bornu and Kuka. Early in 1856 he started eastward for the Nile, reaching Wadai. In Wara he was apprehended by the sultan and killed, probably about February 8. Several expeditions were undertaken in search of him. It was not until 1873 that his fate was finally ascertained by Gustav Nachtigal. His sister Elise Polko published his notes in her *Erinnerungen an einem Verschollenen* (1863).

VOGEL, HERMANN KARL (1841–1907), German astronomer, born in Leipzig, and educated at the universities of Dresden and Leipzig. He became assistant and later second observer in the Leipzig observatory. In 1870 he became astronomer in the private observatory of Von Bülow at Bothkamp near Kiel, and here he devoted himself with great success to astrophysics. In 1874 he became observer in the new astrophysical observatory at Potsdam and in 1882 director of this institution. In 1892 he was elected member of the Berlin Academy. The first spectroscopic star catalogue ever published was that by Vogel in 1883. His works also include *Beobachtungen und Positionsbestimmungen von Nebelflecken und Sternhaufen* (1867–76), *Bothkamper Beobachtungen* (2 vols., 1872–73), *Untersuchungen über die Spektra der Planeten* (1874), *Der Sternhaufen χ Persei* (1878), *Sternspektraltafel* (1888), and *Über der Neuen Stern im Fuhrmann* (1893).

VOGEL, HERMANN WILHELM (1834–98), German photochemist, born in Dobrilugk, Lower Lusatia, and educated at the Royal School of Technology in Berlin. To that institution he was called in 1864 as instructor of photochemistry and later became full professor. He carried on researches in photography, devised a photometer in 1864, and in 1878 he discovered the ultraviolet rays in the spectrum of hydrogen and contributed greatly to the knowledge of spectral photography. His publications include *Lehrbuch* (4th ed., as *Handbuch*) *der Photographie* (1867–70), *Die Chemischen Wirkungen des Lichts und die Photographie* (1874), *Praktische Spektralanalyse Irdischer Stoffe* (1877), *Lichtbilder nach der Natur* (1879), and *Das Photographische Pigmentverfahren* (5th ed., 1905).

VOGELSANG, HERMANN (1838–74), German mineralogist, born in Minden, and educated at the University of Bonn. In 1865 he was appointed professor at the Polytechnic School of Delft. He is remembered for his pioneer work in the use of the microscope for geological purposes, for his demonstration of the presence of liquid carbonic acid in many minerals, for his researches in the formation of crystals, and for his beginning of a new classification of rocks. Among his works are *Über die Mikroskopische Struktur der Schlacken und Beziehungen zur Genesis der Kristallinischen Gesteine* (1864), *Über die Systematik der Gesteinslehre* (1871), *Über die Natürlichen Ultramarinverbindungen* (1873), and *Die Kristalliten* (1875).

VOGEL VON FALCKENSTEIN, EDUARD (1797–1885), Prussian general, born in Breslau. In 1813 he entered the army and distinguished himself at Montmirail in 1814. He became a lieutenant general and commander of the Fifth Division in 1858, and was chief of staff in the Schleswig-Holstein War of 1864. On the outbreak of the Seven Weeks' War in 1866, he was put in charge of the army in western Germany that was to act against the allies of Austria. He defeated the Hanoverians in the battle of Langensalza on June 28th, and forced them to capitulate. On July 2nd he set out for Frankfort by way of Fulda and Hanau, defeated the Bavarians at Kissingen on the 10th, and the troops of Hesse-Darmstadt on the 13th. On the 14th of July he drove back a reinforcement of Austrian and Hessian troops; and on the 16th entered Frankfort. A few days afterward he was appointed commander. After the war he was made commander of the First Army Corps, and in 1867 he was elected to the North German Reichstag. In 1870 he commanded the forces upon the Baltic, and in 1873 was retired.

VOGL, HEINRICH (1845–1900), German tenor, born in Munich. His debut occurred in *Der Freischütz,* by the German composer Karl Maria von Weber, at the Munich Court Opera, in 1865, in which he achieved immediate success. Afterward he succeeded the German tenor Ludwig Schnorr von Carolsfeld as the model Tristan in the music drama *Tristan und Isolde* by the German composer Richard Wagner, and became famous as a Wagnerian singer.

VOGLER, GEORG JOSEPH, better known as ABBÉ or ABT VOGLER (1749–1814), German organist, theorist, and composer, born in Würzburg. He went to Rome and took holy orders. From 1786 to 1799 he was court conductor in Stockholm, where he founded a music school. In 1807 he was appointed court Kapellmeister in Darmstadt and founded a *Tonschule* where both Weber and Meyerbeer received instruction. Among his works are the operas *Der Kaufmann von Smyrna* (1780), *Albert III von Bayern* (1781), *Castor und Pollux* (1784), *Gustavus Adolphus* (1791), *Samori* (1804), and *Der Admiral* (1810), besides much church music.

VOGT, KARL (1817–95), Swiss naturalist and philosopher, born in Giessen, and educated at the University of Bern. He assisted the naturalist Louis Agassiz in the preparation of Agassiz' famous work on fishes. In 1847 Vogt became professor of zoology in Giessen, but a year later was dismissed because of his political opinions. He became professor of natural history in Geneva in 1852, remaining there till his death. He was elected a member of the Swiss Federal Council in 1878. Vogt was an exponent of Darwinism and materialistic philosophy. His works include *Physiologische Briefe* (1845-56), *Ocean und Mittelmeer* (1848), and *Die Säugethiere in Wort und Bild* (1883).

VOGÜE, EUGÈNE MARIE MELCHIOR, VI-COMTE DE (1848-1910), French critic and historian, born in Nice. During the Franco-Prussian War he served as a volunteer and was wounded at Sedan. After 1871 he was attaché to the French embassies in Constantinople (now Istanbul), Cairo, and St. Petersburg (now Leningrad), successively. At the last-named court he spent seven years, but in 1882 gave up the diplomatic service to devote himself to literature. In 1888 he was made a member of the French Academy. It was through Vicomte de Vogüé that Russian novelists first became widely known in France and afterward throughout the English-speaking world. His more important publications include *Syrie, Palestine, Mont Athos* (1876); *Histoires Orientales* (1879); *Le Roman Russe* (1886); *Regards Historiques et Littéraires* (1892); *Heures d'Histoire* (1893); *Cœurs Russes* (1894); *Le Rappel des Ombres* (1900); *Pages d'Histoire* (1902); *Le Maitre de la Mer* (1903); *Maxime Gorky* (1905); *Les Routes* (1910); *Trois Drames de l'Histoire de Russie* (1911); *Pages Choisies* (1912); and *Les Morts Qui Parlent* (1899).

VOGULS, Finno-Ugrian tribe living in the northern Ural Mountains of the Soviet Union. They are of short stature and robust, dolichocephalic, with blue or gray eyes, flat concave nose, long blond or brown hair, and light skin inclined to yellow. In their natural state they live by hunting, using as weapons the bow and arrow, the flintlock gun, and traps. Their domestic animals are the dog and cattle. Their tents and domestic utensils are made from birch bark; their birch canoes are made watertight with resin. They are nominally Christians, but worship idols and make sacrifices of animals. They practice totemic tattooing; polygamy is common.

VOICE AND SPEECH. Voice can be defined as the audible sounds which are produced by forcing air out of the lungs through the larynx and through the cavities of the pharynx, mouth, and nose. The expired air reaches the larynx with varying pressures, causing the larynx to vibrate. Simple vocal sound produced in this manner can be changed in pitch and quality by altering the positions of the various parts of the vocal apparatus and can also be "articulated" by the use of the tongue, the lips, and the teeth. Such altered and articulated voice sounds are the sounds used in speech. The various parts of the vocal mechanism are discussed in the articles on the individual organs: LARYNX; MOUTH; NOSE; RESPIRATORY SYSTEM.

The variation between individual voices depends almost entirely upon differences in the structure of the vocal apparatus. Thus the voices of men are generally lower in pitch than those of women and children because men's vocal cords are usually longer. Individuals with long vocal cords may have high-pitched voices, however, when the cords are sufficiently thin and flexible to have a high rate of vibration. The "change of voice" which appears at puberty is the result of unequal growth of the various parts of the larynx and a consequent loss of muscular control.

In the same larynx different portions of the musical scale are produced by different laryngeal mechanisms, and portions produced by the same mechanism are said to be in the same *register*. Since the timbre or tone quality of the different registers differ perceptibly, trained vocalists must learn to control the mechanisms of the larynx so that the same note can be sung in different registers.

The fundamental range of the human voice varies greatly with individuals. The average range of the bass male voice is generally between 80 to 320 cycles per second (the note E below the bass clef to the low E in the treble clef), and women's soprano voices have a compass of approximately 256 cycles to 853 cycles (from middle C to A above the treble clef). Many trained singers can sing well above and well below the limits indicated, and at least one case is known of an individual who had a singing range of five full octaves.

Speech Sounds. The various vowel sounds used in speech are formed by the acoustical resonance of various portions of the vocal passage above the vocal cords. Oral sounds such as *a, e,* and *o* are produced by two separate resonating cavities: one in the mouth from the lips to the back of the tongue, and one at the back of the tongue between the tongue and the vocal cords. These two cavities resonate at different frequencies and the combination of the two frequencies produces the vowel sound. The resonant fre-

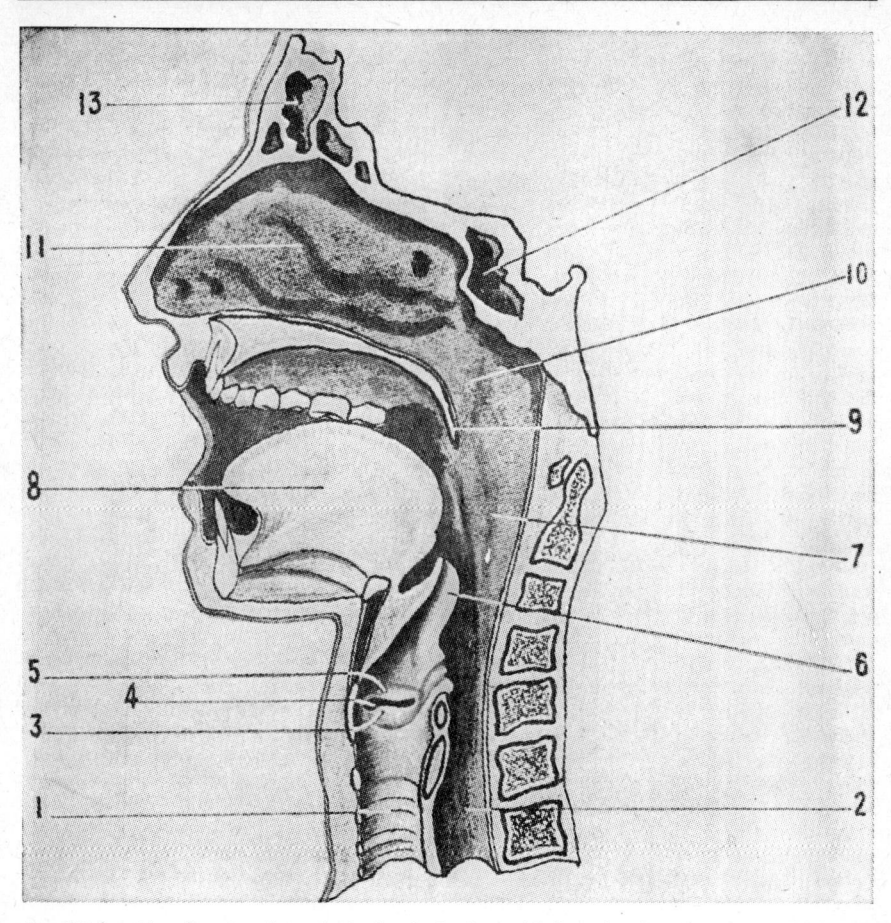

A sagittal-section drawing through the head of a human being, showing the organs which produce voice and speech. 1, trachea; 2, esophagus; 3, vocal cord; 4, Morgagni's ventricle; 5, false vocal cords; 6, epiglottis; 7, pharynx; 8, tongue; 9, soft palate; 10, nasal pharynx; 11, nasal cavity; 12, ethmoid sinus; 13, frontal sinus.

quency of each cavity is determined by two factors: the volume of the cavity and the size of its opening.

The nasal sounds *m*, *n*, and *ng* are produced by resonance in the nasal cavity with the mouth cavity closed off. The sound of *m* is produced by forming a closed resonator of the maximum size in the front of the mouth with the lips closed.

The various articulative sounds which correspond to most of the consonants of the alphabet are formed with the lips only, the tongue and the teeth, or the tongue and the roof of the mouth. These sounds are known respectively as *labial*, such as the sounds of *p* and *b*; *dental*, such as the sounds of *t* and *d*; and the *linguals* such as *l*. In addition certain consonants are articulated voicelessly without any sound from the larynx. Among these consonants are *s* and *f*.

Various devices have been constructed which can produce voice and speech sounds by mechanical or electrical means. Mechanical devices include those based on vibrating air columns and acoustical resonating chambers. Electrical devices are based on oscillating circuits and amplifiers. One such electrical mechanism is capable of producing entire sentences of normal speech by the manipulation of a keyboard.

VOICING, a term applied to regulating the quality of tone in organ pipes. Tuning has to do only with correctness of pitch, but in voicing a certain quality is aimed at. The first requirement is that all the pipes must be made uniform. This is done by carefully regulating the amount of wind admitted and the angle at which it strikes the upper lip, and also by slightly changing the edge of the lip.

VOIT, KARL VON (1831–1908), German physiologist, born in Amberg, Bavaria, and educated at the universities of Munich, Würzburg, and Göttingen. He entered the Physiological Institute of the University of Munich in 1856 as assistant, and was professor of physiology there from 1863 till his death. In 1865 he founded, with Buhl and Pettenkofer, the *Zeitschrift für Biologie,* in which most of his important writings on the subject of nutrition and metabolism appeared. His works include *Physiologisch-chemische Untersuchungen* (1857), *Ueber die Theorien der Ernährung der Tierischen Organismen* (1868), *Ueber die Kost in Öffentlichen Anstalten* (1876), *Untersuchung der Kost in einigen Öffentlichen Anstalten* (1877), and *Physiologie des Allgemeinen Stoffwechsels und der Ernährung.*

VOITURE, VINCENT (1597–1648), French poet and courtier, born in Amiens, and educated at the Collège de Calvé et Boncour and at the University of Orleans. He was introduced to the fashionable life of Paris and soon became a favorite at the Hôtel de Rambouillet among such men as the French writers Pierre Corneille and Jean Louis Guez de Balzac. Voiture's wit was redoubtable. On the formation of the French Academy in 1635 he was one of the first members admitted, but took no active part in its proceedings. Voiture's brilliant verse delighted the salons during his lifetime, but remained unpublished till 1650, when his *Œuvres* appeared.

VOKES, ROSINA (1858–94), English actress, the youngest of a celebrated family of actors which comprised her brother Frederick (1846–88) and her sisters Jessie (1851–84) and Victoria (1853–94). In 1885 the family toured the United States, where they played in *A Pantomime Rehearsal, Wig and Gown,* and *The Circus Rider.*

VOLAPÜK (*vol,* fr. Eng. "world"; *puk,* for "speak"), the name for a universal language invented in 1879 by Johann Martin Schleyer, a Swabian pastor in Constance. Volapük has been almost completely superseded by Esperanto.

VOLATILITY, the property possessed by certain liquids of passing rapidly into the vapor state from an exposed surface under ordinary conditions of temperature and pressure. The cooling effect of this evaporation (q.v.) makes such volatile substances as alcohol useful in rubbing lotions, and is the basis for the use of refrigerants such as dichloro-difluoromethane; see FREON. The extreme volatility of certain inflammable liquids such as ether can create serious fire hazards if an appreciable surface of the liquid is exposed to the air in a closed space in which a flame or spark may be generated; under these conditions an explosive mixture of ether vapor and air may be formed in a relatively short time. Glycerine and mercury are examples of extremely nonvolatile substances, the vapor over the surface of the latter liquid at room temperature (20°C.; 68°F.) having a pressure of less than 1/600,000 of an atmosphere; by comparison, the vapor pressure of ether under similar conditions is more than .5 atmospheres. In general, the lower the boiling point of a liquid the greater its volatility. Relatively small differences in the volatility of the component liquids in a mixture enable the separation of the various constituents to be effected by the process of distillation (q.v.). See also BOILING; BOILING POINT; VAPOR PRESSURE.

VOLCANIC ROCKS. See IGNEOUS ROCKS.

VOLCANISM, in geology and geophysics, the process of change in the crust of the earth caused by movements of molten material beneath or through the solid surface of the earth. The term is also applied to the geological theory that the principal changes in the surface of the earth are due to such movements (see GEOLOGY; DIASTROPHISM), rather than cataclysms (q.v.) affecting the lithosphere. Several theories are current concerning the fluidity of the magma underlying the earth's crust. Some geologists regard it as the result of heat persisting from a time when the entire earth was a molten mass; others believe that heat generated by the shearing and crushing of deep rock masses in the course of geological change and the relief of pressure by the arching of solid surface strata in the formation of folds and mountains is sufficient to account for the fluidity of the material. Such fluid material, forcing a passage along faults or melting its way through rocky strata, manifests itself at the surface of the earth in the formation of volcanoes (q.v.).

Volcanism is regarded by most geologists as the process by which the ores and like mineral resources of the world have been deposited. Magnetite and nickel deposits show signs of having been formed at the same time as the inclosing igneous rock; copper ores, from deposition by limestone metamorphosed by intrusions of magma; and other ores by precipitation from hot magmatic waters upon cooling. The term "volcanism" is also applied to the theory of *Plutonism*, which was opposed to the equally obsolete theory of Neptunism; the former held that all terrestrial rocks were deposited by cooling of igneous material, and the latter, that all rocky strata were formed by deposition from primitive oceans.

VOLCANO, a vent in the crust of the earth, from which gaseous, liquid, or solid material is ejected. The ejected material accumulates around the vent, and builds up a *cone* having at the top a bowl-shaped depression called a *crater*.

During successive eruptions the heavier portions of the solid materials fall back within and around the vent, while lava streams issue from the crater. Thus the cone is built up of rudely alternate sheets of fragmental materials and lenticular flows of lava, which are all inclined outward from the orifice of eruption. By far the great majority of volcanoes are composite in character; that is, they are built up partly of lava and partly of fragmental materials. Etna and Vesuvius are examples of composite cones.

Many volcanoes have commenced their eruptions upon the bed of the sea. Etna and Vesuvius were in their earlier days submarine volcanoes, and the same is the case with the vast cones of the Hawaiian Islands.

Some volcanoes are much more active than others. A few may be said to be in a state of permanent eruption, such for example as Stromboli, which has been constantly active since the time of Homer; Izalco (in El Salvador, Central America), which had no existence before 1770, has continued active ever since. Other examples of constantly active volcanoes are those of Masaya and Amatitlan in Nicaragua, Sangay and Cotopaxi in the Andes of Ecuador, Sion in the Moluccas, and Tofoa in the Friendly Islands. Many volcanoes, such as Vesuvius, continue in a state of moderate activity for longer or shorter periods, and then become quiescent or dormant for months or years. The eruption that succeeds prolonged repose is usually correspondingly violent or paroxysmal.

In a paroxysmal eruption the lava in the pipe is highly charged with steam or other gases such as hydrogen, carbon oxides, and sulfur, and these continually escape from its surface with violent explosions and rise in a dark turbid cloud. From this cloud showers of rain are frequently discharged. Large and small portions of the lava are shot upward, forming a fiery fountain of incandescent drops and fragments (*bombs, slags, cinders*), which fall back in showers upon the external slopes of the cone or into the crater, from which they are again and again ejected. Lightning often plays through the cloud, especially if the cloud is heavily charged with dust particles. The lava rises in the vent, and finally oozes, as a pasty mass, through a fissure in the side of the crater. This marks the crisis of the eruption, and after a final ejection of stones and dust the volcano relapses into a quiescent state. Such paroxysmal eruptions often result in great changes in the appearance of a volcano. The upper part of the cone disappears, and a vast yawning cauldron takes its place. The cone of Vesuvius has frequently been modified in this way. Thus in 1822 the summit was reduced by 800 ft. Again the entire summit of Papandayang in Java was blown off during a great eruption in 1772. The same appears to have been the case with Bandaisan in Japan—one of the principal peaks of which (Kobandai) was greatly reduced in height by the terrible eruption of 1888. It is estimated that 1,587,000,000 cubic yards of rock were blown from the top of the mountain and scattered over an area of 27 square miles. The great eruption of Tarawera in New Zealand (1886) showed that both ejection and engulfment accompany paroxysmal action. One of the most remarkable eviscerated volcanoes of the kind is the island of Palma, one of the Canaries, from 3 to 4 geographical miles in diameter. In not a few cases the enormous craters, or *calderas* of eviscerated volcanoes are occupied by deep lakes, such as the lake of Gustavila in Mexico, and Crater Lake in Oregon.

A time comes in the life of all volcanoes when they cease to erupt either lava or fragmental materials. But for a long period they continue to give out acid gases and vapor. This is called the *solfatara stage*. After this stage hot springs arise and eventually the last traces of volcanic heat disappear, and springs of cold water, often impregnated with mineral matter, may issue from the mountain and the ground in its vicinity.

In prehistoric times lava seems in many cases to have issued from long vertical fissures, and deluged wide regions. Some of these inundations of lava are well seen in western North America, as in the great basalt plain of Snake River, Idaho. As a rule the volcanoes

VOLCANOES. *Top: Mount Pelée erupting, French West Indies (painting by the American artist Charles R. Knight). Bottom: Kilauea, Hawaii, during the eruption of May 17, 1924.*

which emit lava in greatest volume are comparatively quiet in their action. This is the case with the volcanoes of Hawaii. The paroxysmal eruptions of such volcanoes as Etna and Vesuvius are unknown in Hawaii. The enormous energy displayed during an explosive eruption is shown by the heights to which stones and ashes are projected. The fine ashes of Krakatoa are said to have been carried by the uprush of gas and vapors to the height of 17 miles. The clouds of vapor, mingled with smoke and dust, which emanate from violent volcanic eruptions, sometimes cause days of darkness in places some distance away.

Active volcanoes are limited to particular regions of the earth. The Pacific Ocean is bounded by an almost unbroken line of active volcanoes—the "belt of fire". The Caribbean Sea and the Mediterranean Sea wash the shores of lands which show active and recently extinct volcanoes in considerable numbers.

Some writers have maintained that the chief cause of volcanic action is the introduction of water to the highly heated interior of the earth. The most probable view is that volcanoes are closely related to those earth movements which have resulted in the flexing and fracturing of strata. The crust yields to the enormous tangential pressure by cracking across and wrinkling up, in various linear directions, and it is along these lines of fracture and flexure that molten matter (*magma*) and heated gases are enabled to escape from reservoirs formed by earthquakes about 20 miles below the surface of the earth. Several theories are held by vulcanologists to explain the action of the volcanic gases in producing an eruption. The simplest theory holds that the action is similar to that of the gas in producing a fountain of soda water from a warm, shaken bottle of a carbonated beverage.

It is significant that all the great volcanoes are situated within or along the margins of what are believed to be sinking areas. There is reason to believe that all the notable volcanoes and volcanic islets of the great ocean basins rise from the backs of ridges and swellings of the crust.

The birth of a volcano and the building of its cone and crater were observed in 1943 when the volcano of Paracutin erupted from a cornfield in Mexico. On February 5, 1943, the district was shaken by earthquakes, which continued for two weeks. On February 20, a vent was observed to open and emit first smoke, then hot fragments of rock, and later molten rock. The eruption proceeded almost continuously, and in eight months had built up a cone about 1500 feet high, the accompanying lava flow burying the village of Paracutin and nearby towns.

Mud volcanoes, salses, air volcanoes, or maccalubas, are conical hills of mud, from which material is ejected, generally cold, by and with various gases. The usual quiet emissions are interrupted at times by violent discharges, sometimes with columns of flame. Puys are conical hills of volcanic origin, especially those in Auvergne, France.

The following tabulation gives altitudes (in feet) of the principal volcanic peaks.

Peak and Country	Altitude
Cotopaxi, Ecuador	19,635
San Pedro y Pablo, Bolivia	19,423
Orizaba, Mexico	18,701
Popocatepetl, Mexico	17,887
Sangay, Ecuador	17,464
Carahuairazo, Ecuador	16,515
Pichincha, Ecuador	15,918
Karissimbi, Africa	14,683
Clarence Peak, Fernando Po.	14,683
Cameroon, Africa	13,370
Erebus, Antarctic	13,300
Mauna Loa, Hawaii	12,675
Colima, Mexico	12,661
Fuji, Japan	12,395
Semeru, Java	12,044
Luse, Sumatra	12,000
Santa Maria, Guatemala	11,480
Slamar, Java	11,250
Irazu, Costa Rica	11,200
Abong-Abong, Sumatra	11,000
Raun, Java	10,820
Etna, Sicily	10,740
Marababu, Java	10,670
Lassen, U.S.	10,570
Dempo, Sumatra	10,562
Cerro Quemado, Guatemala	10,436
Tjirmaj, Java	10,075
Pico de Cano, Cape Verde	9,744
Gede, Java	9,720
Merapi, Sumatra	9,488
Merapi, Java	9,432
Ruapehu, New Zealand	9,175
Shishaldin, Alaska	8,952
Papandayang, Java	8,611

VOLCANO ISLANDS or **MAGELLAN ARCHIPELAGO**, a chain of three small islands in the western Pacific Ocean, situated s. of the Bonin Islands and about midway between the Marianas Islands and the Japanese home island of Honshu. The islands are Iwo Jima, the largest, possessing an area of 8 sq.m.; and Kita and Minami, Kita, the most northerly of the archipelago, rises to an elevation of 2520 ft. above sea level, and Minami, the most southerly, possesses an extreme elevation of 3021 ft. The highest point on Iwo Jima is Surabachi, 546 ft. above sea level. The islands were annexed by Japan in 1891, and under Japanese rule Iwo Jima (q.v.) became a fortified air base and played an important role in World War II. Total area, 10 sq.m.; pop. (1940 est.) 1151.

VOLDEMARAS, AUGUSTINAS (1883–   ), Lithuanian statesman. He was virtual dictator of Lithuania from November, 1926, until September, 1929. During this period, he held both the premiership and the portfolio for foreign affairs. He dealt severely with the Communists. His attitude toward Poland alienated a section of the army and in November, 1927, he met Pilsudski and Zalewski of Poland, ending the technical state of war which had existed between Poland and Lithuania since 1920. An attempt was made to assassinate him in the spring of 1929. Forced to resign the following September, he took part in an unsuccessful attempt to seize the government and was jailed (1934–38).

VOLE (*Arvicola*), a genus of rodents typical of the subfamily Arvicolinae, which also includes the lemmings (*Myodes*), the muskrats (*Fiber*), and several related genera. North America has many species, but the term "vole" is seldom heard in the United States. The most common varieties are the water vole, *A. amphibius,* the field vole, *A. agrestis,* and the bank vole, *A. glareolus.*

VOLGA, the greatest river in Russia and the longest in Europe, with a length of 2400 m. from its source in a small lake among the Valdai Hills to its mouths in the Caspian Sea. It has a drainage area of 590,000 sq.m. By means of artificial cuttings it communicates with the White Sea, the Euxine, the Baltic, and the Gulf of Finland, as well as with the Don, the Dniester, the Dnieper, the Dwina, and other rivers. Traffic almost entirely ceases in winter, when the waters are frozen. The fisheries of the Volga are of great importance, sturgeon, carp, and pike being captured in immense numbers. Seal hunting, near the shores of the Caspian, also employs a number of persons.

VOLGA GERMAN REPUBLIC, formerly an autonomous republic within the Russian Soviet Federated Socialist Republic—one of the constituent republics of the Union of Socialist Soviet Republics. Situated on the lower Volga, the republic had an area of 24,400 sq.m. and a population of about 570,000. Catherine II, in 1762, invited settlers to occupy the lower Volga to provide a barrier against Tatar invasion. Between 1764 and 1773 about 8000 families, principally Germans, settled here, and founded 106 colonies. A special department of government administered the area with its own code of laws until 1876, when it was merged with the general administration. The capital was transferred from Markstadt to Pokrovsk when the republic was proclaimed. In 1941 the republic was abolished and its territory was divided between the Regions of Saratov and Stalingrad.

VOLHYNIA, formerly a county of Poland, before that a part of the Soviet Republic of Ukraine and, before that, of the Russian Empire. It now forms the Volyn Region of the Ukraine. Rye, wheat, oats, sugar beets, tobacco, and hops are produced. Stock raising is also important. The chief manufactures are beet sugar, spirits, and leather. The region of Volhynia was inhabited by Slavs and belonged to Russia at the very beginning of Russian history. In the 14th century it passed to Lithuania and was united with Poland in 1569. With the annexation of Poland (1793–95) it passed to Russia. During World War I the Russians and Germans were fighting in Volhynia from 1915 to 1917, the Germans securing possession of the greater part of the territory.

VOLK, DOUGLAS (1856–1935), American figure painter, born in Pittsfield, Mass., and trained in Paris under the French painter Jean Léon Gérôme. After his return to America he organized and became director of the Minneapolis School of Fine Arts (1893) and afterward taught at the Cooper Union art school, the Art Students League, and the National Academy of Design, New York City. Good examples of Volk's work are to be found in most American public collections. Among his mural decorations are those in the Minnesota capitol at St. Paul and the Des Moines (Iowa) courthouse. He was elected a member of the National Academy in 1899, and of the Architectural League in 1912 and received many prizes, including gold medals at Charleston (1907), the National Academy of Design (1910), National Arts Club, New York (1915), and the Panama-Pacific Exposition, San Francisco (1915). He painted several war portraits, including those of General John Joseph Pershing, King Albert of Belgium, and the British statesman David Lloyd George, in the National Gallery, Washington (1921). In 1915–16 he received the Beck Gold Medal of the Pennsylvania Academy and a gold medal from the National Arts Club, New York City. His powerful portrait of Lincoln (1923) was acquired by the Albright Art Gallery, Buffalo, N.Y.

VOLK, LEONARD WELLS (1828–95), American sculptor, born in Wellstown, N.Y. After working as a marble cutter and modeling by himself in St. Louis he studied for two years in Rome. On his return in 1857 he settled in Chicago, where he assisted in founding the Academy of Design, of which he was president eight years. He modeled the monument to the American political leader Stephen Arnold Douglas in Chicago and various soldiers' monuments, but is at his best in his faithful and dignified portrayals of prominent Americans. These include the statues of Abraham Lincoln and Douglas (Illinois State House), General James Shields (Capitol, Washington), and a bust of Lincoln. For his son, see VOLK, DOUGLAS.

VOLKMANN, ROBERT (1815–83), German instrumental composer, born in Lommatzsch. From 1839 to 1842 he taught music in Prague and finally settled in Pesth, where he remained, except for four years in Vienna (1854–58). He was professor of harmony and counterpoint at the National Academy of Music for several years. Among his works are two symphonies (D minor and B flat), three *Serenades* for string orchestra, two concert overtures, a cello concerto, a *Concertstück* for piano and orchestra, six string quartets, two trios, and numerous works for piano (two and four hands). Among his vocal works are two masses, offertories, sacred songs, and a Christmas carol of the 12th century.

VOLLMAR, GEORG HEINRICH VON (1850–1922), German Socialist leader, born in Munich. He entered the Bavarian army at an early age and served as lieutenant in the war with Prussia in 1866. He then enlisted in the papal army and later entered the Bavarian railway service. He left to take part in the Franco-German War, in which he served as an officer until badly wounded at Blois. Having become interested in social studies, he embraced socialism and (in 1878–86) was imprisoned several times for activity in propagating socialistic ideas and organizing secret societies. Vollmar became prominent in the German Reichstag, in which he served continuously after 1881, except during the period 1887–90, until 1918. He became a leader of the conservative wing of the Social Democrats. He showed himself ready to make concessions to the principle of private ownership in the case of the small landowners or peasants. His publications include *Der Isolierte Socialistische Staat* (1880), *Ueber die Näehsten Aufgaben der Socialdemokratie* (1891), and *Ueber Staatssocialismus* (1892).

VOLLON, ANTOINE (1833–1900), French still-life, landscape, and figure painter, born in Lyons, and trained at the Lyons School of Fine Arts and under the French painter Théodule Augustin Ribot (1823–91). Vollon was one of the finest still-life painters of the 19th century. His coloring is rich and harmonious, and in the rendering of metals, the color and bloom of flowers, and in the painting of fish he has few equals. He also painted figure subjects. His works include "Sea Fish", "Curiosities", "The Port of Antwerp", and the portrait of the artist, all in the Luxembourg Gallery, Paris; and "The Kettle" (1872, Lyons Museum).

VOLNEY, CONSTANTIN FRANÇOIS CHASSEBŒUF, COMTE DE (1757–1820), French philosophic writer and politician, born in Craon. He studied medicine and Eastern languages, spent some years in Egypt and Syria, wrote *Voyage en Égypte et en Syrie* (2 vols., 1787), was elected to the States-General (1789), and joined the Republican movement and contributed to its anti-Christian "philosophy" the famous *Les Ruines ou Méditations sur les Révolutions des Empires* (1791) and to its pedagogy *La Loi Naturelle, ou le Catéchisme du Citoyen Français* (1793), in spite of which he fell under suspicion of Royalist leanings and was saved from execution only by the fall of Robespierre. Soon afterward (1794) he was made professor in the École Normale, traveled in the United States (1795–1808), was made senator (1799), academician, and commander of the Legion of Honor. He was created count by Napoleon (1808) and a peer by Louis XVIII (1814). His later works are *Tableau du Climat et du Sol des États-Unis* (1803) and *Recherches Nouvelles sur l'Histoire Ancienne* (1814–15).

VOLOGDA, a former government of the Russian empire in N.E. Russia, now included in the Russian Soviet Federated Socialist Republic. Area, 155,500 square miles. It is a flat region, marshy and wooded in the north, and with some offshoots of the Ural Mountains in the east, reaching an altitude of nearly 5000 feet. This mountainous region is barren and almost uninhabited. The agricultural area is very restricted, and the larger part of the inhabitants find a source of livelihood in fishing, hunting, and lumbering. In the southern part the crops are abundant, and some products, especially flax, are even exported.

The forests cover over three-fourths of the entire surface.

VOLOGDA, a city of Russia, situated on both banks of the river Vologda, 289 miles N.N.E. of Moscow. It trades extensively with Archangel and Leningrad in agricultural and forest products, spirits, and leather. Lace making is an important industry. The town was founded in the 12th century and attained considerable commercial importance in the 16th century, when Archangel carried on an extensive trade with England and Holland. The foundation of St. Petersburg (now Leningrad) removed the center of the foreign trade of Russia to the west, and Vologda lost its former importance. Pop., about 95,000.

VOLOS, the capital of the nomarchy of Magnesia, Greece, 37 miles S.E. of Larissa, on the Gulf of Volo. It is situated near the sites of the three ancient cities of Demetrias, Pagasæ, and Iolcus and has interesting remains of the early Greek and Roman periods. It is an important exporting center of the products of Thessaly. Pop., about 42,000.

VOLPE, ARNOLD (1869–1940), Russian-American orchestral conductor, born in Kovno, and trained under the Hungarian violinist and teacher Leopold Auer at the Imperial Conservatory in St. Petersburg (now Leningrad). In 1898 he went to the United States, settling in New York, where he became conductor of several orchestral societies. In 1902 he established the Young Men's Symphony Orchestra for the purpose of training orchestral players. The more advanced players he formed in 1904 into the Volpe Symphony Orchestra, which was constantly strengthened by the addition of new members from the older organization. In 1910–14 he was conductor of the municipal concerts in New York City. In 1918 he founded and was first conductor of the Stadium Symphony Orchestra in New York City.

VOLSCI, a people of ancient Italy, closely related to the Umbrians. To the south of them lay the sea, to the east the Samnites, to the north the Æqui and the Hernici, and to the west the Latini. The Volsci were hardy mountaineers and fine warriors; they were incessantly at war with the Romans, but about 383 B.C. they were finally subdued by Rome, and their territory incorporated into Latium.

VOLSK, a town in Russia, situated on the right bank of the Volga, 91 miles N.E. of Saratov. It has extensive ironworks and tanneries. Pop., about 55,000.

VOLSTEAD, ANDREW J. (1860–1947), American public official, born in Goodhue County, Minn. In 1884 he was admitted to the bar and practiced law in Granite Falls, Minn. He was for fourteen years county attorney of Yellow Medicine County. In 1903 he was elected to Congress and was successively re-elected until 1922. He was the author of the Volstead Act for the enforcement of the Federal Prohibition Amendment (see PROHIBITION) and also of the Farmers' Coöperative Marketing Act.

VOLSUNGA SAGA, a 13th-century saga recounting the history of the legendary family of the Volsungs. Though the saga was composed in Iceland, its characters are drawn from Germanic legend. The founder of the family, Volsung, or Walsung, is represented in the saga as the grandson of the Norse god Odin. His son Siegmund, or Sigmund, is the hero of a large part of the saga; Siegmund's son Sigurd, or Siegfried, the most notable hero of the family, is the main character of a somewhat later saga, the *Niebelungenlied* (q.v.). The stories of both Siegmund and Sigurd were adapted by the German composer Richard Wagner for his cycle of operas collectively entitled *Der Ring des Nibelungen* (1848–74); the Sigurd legend was retold in English verse by the English poet William Morris in *The Story of Sigurd the Volsung* (1876). See also SAGA; SCANDINAVIAN MYTHOLOGY.

VOLSUNGS, a famous heroic race in Old Germanic legend, its founder Volsung or Walsung, the grandson of Odin, and its brightest ornament Volsung's son, Siegmund. Sigfried or Sigurd, hero of the *Nibelungenlied*, is of the same stock. The tale is enshrined in the Old Icelandic Volsunga saga, and has been followed in Richard Wagner's trilogy, *Der Ring des Nibelungen*.

VOLT, the practical unit of electrical pressure or *electromotive force* (abbreviated E.M.F.). A *millivolt* is one thousandth of a volt; a *microvolt* is one millionth of a volt. See ELECTRICAL UNITS. If one volt is applied across the ends of a resistance of one ohm, a current of one ampere will flow. See ELECTRIC CIRCUIT; *Ohm's Law*. As, in the mechanical analogy, water is forced through a pipe by the "head" of water overcoming the resistance of friction in the pipe, so electrically the current is forced through the circuit by the E.M.F. overcoming the resistance of the wire.

VOLTA, a river of west Africa, formed in the northern part of the British Gold Coast Colony by the confluence of the Black and the White Volta. It flows in a southerly course, and empties into the Gulf of Guinea, 400 miles w. of the mouths of the Niger. Its total length, including the Black Volta, is about 900 miles.

VOLTA, Count Alessandro (1745–1827), Italian physicist, born in Como, and educated at the public schools of his native town. His first important essay, with the Leyden jar, was followed in 1771 by a discussion of the phenomena of frictional electricity. In 1774 he became professor of physics at the Royal School in Como and in the following year devised the electrophorus. In 1776–77 he applied himself to chemistry, studied atmospheric electricity and devised many experiments, such as igniting gases by the electric spark in closed vessels. In 1779 he became professor of physics at the University of Pavia, a chair he occupied for twenty-five years. By 1800 he had developed his electric pile of dissimilar metals in contact and separated from a corresponding pair by a piece of moistened cloth or paper. Then came the crown of cups, or first voltaic battery, in which strips of metal were placed in cups containing brine or weak acid. In 1801 Volta was called to Paris and was received by Napoleon, who made him count and senator and gave him a gold medal. See Voltaic Cell.

VOLTAIC CELL, name applied to any device which generates electric current by means of an irreversible chemical reaction. Such cells, which are often called primary cells, take their name from the Italian physicist Alessandro Volta (q.v.) who first devised a current-generating device of this kind. Voltaic or primary cells differ from secondary cells in that the chemical reactions in the latter type of cell are reversible. For this reason secondary cells are often called storage cells because they are able to store energy in chemical form when an electric current is passed through them. Volta's original device was not a single cell, but a battery or series of cells. It consisted of a pile of strips of zinc, copper, and cloth moistened with salt solution. A single cell of Volta's battery would consist of a strip of copper and a strip of zinc immersed in a salt solution.

A number of different types of voltaic cells have been produced, of which the most common is the modified Leclanché cell, invented by the French chemist Georges Leclanché, and known as a dry cell or dry battery. Cells of this design are used as sources of electric current for a variety of purposes, ranging from powering radio sets and hearing aids to providing ignition current for internal-combustion engines; see Dry Cell.

The voltage of various types of voltaic cells

Voltaire (pastel by Maurice de La Tour)

varies with the materials used for electrodes and electrolytes. The voltage of the ordinary Leclanché type of dry cell is 1.5 volts for a new cell, diminishing with use. See Electrolysis; Storage Battery.

VOLTAIRE, assumed name of François Marie Arouet (1694–1778), French author and philosopher, born in Paris, and educated at the Collège Louis-le-Grand, a Jesuit institution. Soon after graduation he traveled to The Hague as secretary of the French ambassador to Holland. Upon his return to Paris Voltaire became known as a brilliant and sarcastic wit. A number of his writings, particularly a lampoon accusing the French regent Philippe II, Duc d'Orléans (see Orleans, Philippe, Duke of) of heinous crimes, resulted in his imprisonment in the Bastille (q.v.). During his eleven-month detention, Voltaire completed his first tragedy, Œdipe, based upon the Œdipus Tyrannus of the ancient Greek dramatist Sophocles, and commenced an epic poem on Henry IV of France. Œdipe was given its initial performance at the Théâtre-Français in 1718, and received with great enthusiasm. The work on Henry IV was printed anonymously in Geneva, Switzerland, under the title of Poème de *la Ligue* ("Poem of the League", 1723). In his first philosophical poem, *Le Pour et le Contre* ("For and Against"), Voltaire gave eloquent expression to both his anti-Christian views and his deistic (see DEISM) creed.

A quarrel with a member of an illustrious French family, the Chevalier de Rohan, resulted in Voltaire's second incarceration in the Bastille, from which he was released within a few days on his promise to quit France and proceed to England. He accordingly crossed the Channel in 1726, remaining in England for a period of twenty-six months. Voltaire soon mastered the English language, and in order to prepare the British public for an enlarged edition of his *Poème de la Ligue,* wrote in English two remarkable essays, one on epic poetry and the other on the history of civil wars in France. The poem itself, under its altered title of *La Henriade* ("The Henriad"), presently followed. Although the Catholic and autocratic French government attempted to prevent the introduction of this work, an eloquent defense of religious toleration, into France, its success elsewhere on the continent of Europe, and in Great Britain, was almost unprecedented.

In 1728 Voltaire was granted permission to return to France. During the next four years he resided in Paris, and devoted most of his time to literary composition. The chief work of this period is the *Lettres Anglaises ou Philosophiques* ("English or Philosophical Letters," 1734), probably based upon actual letters sent by Voltaire to a friend during the author's sojourn in England. These epistles treat of such subjects as the system of religious toleration then operative in the British Isles; the guarantees of personal freedom enjoyed by British subjects; liberty of speech and of the press; the operation of the free British Parliament; the practice in England of inoculating against smallpox; and the philosophical and scientific theories of John Locke and Sir Isaac Newton. The work, containing a covert attack upon the political and ecclesiastical institutions of France, brought Voltaire into conflict with the authorities, and he was once more forced to quit Paris. He found refuge at the Château de Cirey in the independent duchy of Lorraine. There he contracted an intimate relationship with the aristocratic and learned Gabrielle Émilie Le Tonnelier de Breteuil, Marquise du Châtelet (q.v.), who exerted a strong intellectual influence upon him.

Voltaire's sojourn at Cirey in companionship with the Marquise du Châtelet comprised a period of intense literary activity. In addition to an imposing number of plays (most of which were performed at Paris with notable success), he wrote the *Élements de la Philosophie de Newton* ("Elements of the Philosophy of Newton"), designed to acquaint French readers more thoroughly with the Newtonian system; began work on a universal history extending from the death of Charlemagne to the accession of Louis XIV; and produced a multitude of lighter compositions, including novels, tales, satires, and light verses. The poem *Le Mondain* ("The Man of the World", 1736), containing a defense of refined and luxurious living, brought upon Voltaire the charge of having ridiculed religion through his irreverent references to Adam and Eve. To the aforementioned period likewise belongs the composition of a portion of *La Pucelle* ("The Maid", 1739), the mock heroine of which is Joan of Arc. From references to the Maid of Orleans interspersed throughout Voltaire's historical writings, it would appear that he had no intention of aspersing the historical figure of Joan in *La Pucelle;* his satire is directed rather at the high-flown mystical conception of her career presented in *La Pucelle* (1656) of the French poet Jean Chapelain (q.v.).

Voltaire's stay at Cirey was not continuous. He often traveled thence to Paris, and to Versailles, where, through the influence of Jeanne Antoinette Poisson, Marquise de Pompadour (q.v.), the famous mistress of Louis XV, he became a court favorite. He was first appointed historiographer of France, and then a gentleman of the king's bedchamber; finally, he was elected to the French Academy (1746). His *Poème de Fontenoy* (1745), describing a battle won by the French over the English during the War of the Austrian Succession (see SUCCESSION WARS), and his *Précis du Siècle de Louis XV* ("Epitome of the Age of Louis XV"), in addition to his dramas *La Princesse de Navarre* and *Le Triomphe de Trajan,* were the outcome of Voltaire's connection with the court of Louis XV.

Following the death of Madame du Châtelet in 1749, Voltaire finally accepted a long-standing invitation of Frederick II of Prussia to become a permanent resident at the Prussian court. The French writer's relationship with the Prussian king had begun in 1736, when Frederick had asked Voltaire to become one of his regular correspondents. Both as prince royal and, later, as king, Frederick had employed all manner of persuasion to induce Voltaire to make his home in Prussia. With the death of Madame du Châtelet the only impor-

"Descent from the Cross," by Daniele Ricciarelli da Volterra

tant obstacle which had kept Voltaire from accepting Frederick's invitation was removed. Accordingly, in 1750, he journeyed from Paris to Berlin, where he was received by the king with demonstrations of the deepest affection. The difference in the temperaments of the two men soon manifested itself, however, in frequent altercations, due equally to Frederick's autocratic temper and to Voltaire's acidulous and irreverent wit. Within two years Voltaire left Berlin, never to return. During his stay at the Prussian court he had completed his *Siècle de Louis XIV,* the success of which was greater than that of any other history previously published. For some years he led a migratory existence but finally settled in 1758 at Ferney in eastern France, where he spent the remaining twenty years of his life. In the interval between his return from Berlin and his establishment at Fernay, he had issued his most ambitious work, the *Essai sur l'Histoire Générale et sur les Moeurs et l'Esprit des Nations* ("Essay on General History and on the Customs and the Character of Nations", 1756).

When Voltaire settled in Ferney, all his major productions, with the exception of his *Dictionnaire Philosophique* (1764), had been published; his polemical work, however, was not yet done. Feeling that he enjoyed a measure of security in his sequestered retreat, he sent forth hundreds of short squibs and broadsides exposing and satirizing the abuses he desired to destroy. All men who suffered because of their beliefs found in Voltaire an eloquent and powerful defender. His mordant wit was directed principally against religious intolerance and fanaticism and against belief in miracles. The satirical romance *Candide* (q.v.) appeared in 1759 and the tragedy *Tancrede* in 1760. In 1778, following the death of Louis XV, Voltaire, at the advanced age of eighty, once more visited Paris after an absence of thirty-four years. He was received in all quarters with demonstrations of the greatest enthusiasm and respect.

As a writer, Voltaire produced, perhaps, not a single great masterpiece; every one of his works, however, contains memorable passages distinguished by elegance, perspicuity, and wit. His other writings include the tragedies *Brutus* (1730), *Zaïre* (1732), *Alzire* (1736), *Mahomet* (1741), and *Mérope* (1743); the philosophical romance *Zadig* (1747); the philosophical poems *Discours sur l'Homme* ("Discourse on Man", 1738) and *Le Désastre de Lisbonne* ("The Lisbon Disaster", 1756); and the historical study *Charles XII* (1730).

VOLTAMETER, an instrument for determining the quantity or rate of flow of electric current by measurement of the electrolysis (q.v.) it effects over a given period of time in passing between two electrodes immersed in a chemical solution. See ELECTROCHEMISTRY). Each unit of electrical charge, or coulomb (q.v.), produces a definite quantitative chemical change in each of the various reactions employed, for details of which see ELECTRIC METERS. The rate of flow of current in amperes (q.v.) is found by dividing the number of coulombs, indicated in the quantitative determination of the electrolytic reaction, by the number of seconds the apparatus has been allowed to operate. The voltameter differs in purpose and construction from the *voltammeter,* also called the wattmeter (q.v.), and from the *voltmeter* (see ELECTRIC METERS).

VOLTERRA, a town of the province of Pisa, Italy, 39 miles S.E. of Pisa. It is surrounded by a high, massive wall, 4½ miles in circumference. Outside this wall is the ancient Etruscan necropolis. The notable cathedral, consecrated in 1120, was enlarged and embellished by Niccola Pisano. The leading industries are alabaster working, for which the town is famous; and the manufacture of salt from the brine springs at Leopoldo, 5 miles s. of the town. The salt industry supplies all Tuscany. Pop., about 16,000.

Volterra, the Etruscan *Velathri* (Roman *Volaterræ*), was one of the twelve league cities of Etruria. It was destroyed during the 10th century. It came under the rule of Florence in 1361.

VOLTERRA, DANIELE RICCIARELLI DA (1509–66), Italian painter of the late Renaissance, born in Volterra, Tuscany. He was a pupil first of Sodoma, and later became a follower of Michelangelo, occupying himself with painting after his designs. A more ungrateful task was the clothing of the nude figures in Michelangelo's "Last Judgment". His best picture, "Descent from the Cross", after Michelangelo, in Trinità de' Monti, in Rome, is a great composition, full of emotional power; in the same church are his frescoes of the "Life of the Virgin". Other well-known paintings are "Baptism of Christ", in San Pietro in Montorio (Rome), "David Killing Goliath" (Louvre), and "Massacre of the Innocents" (Uffizi, Florence).

VOLTMETER. See ELECTRIC METERS.

VOLTUMNA, goddess of the Etruscans. The deputies from twelve divisions of the Etruscans met at her temple in the territory of Volsinii. She can scarcely be separated from the Roman god Vortumnus, or Vertumnus, whose temple on the Aventine seems to have been built in 264 B.C., at the time of a war with Volsinii. The god is expressly called the chief god of that city, and his temple seems to have been vowed to induce him to desert to the Romans.

VOLTURNO, river of south Italy, flowing southeastward, then westward past Capua, and emptying, after a course of 115 miles, into the Tyrrhenian Sea. On its banks Garibaldi defeated the Neapolitan army in 1860.

VOLUNTARISM, a metaphysical theory which holds that reality is basically will; it is thus a form of idealism, differing from intellectualistic idealism in making will more fundamental than sensation and idea. In modern times Schopenhauer is the best-known voluntarist; but perhaps the philosophy of Wilhelm

Wundt is the most thoroughly developed voluntarism of recent times. Münsterberg and Royce are also voluntaristic.

VOLUNTARY ASSOCIATION, in law in the United States, an unincorporated organization of individuals for moral, benevolent, social, political, or other noncommercial or nonprofit purposes. A voluntary association differs from a membership corporation in that it is not a legal entity and cannot be sued as a person in the courts. A voluntary association does not have the legal status or incidents of a partnership; the associate members do not incur personal and unlimited liability for obligations of the association. No individual member of the association is therefore responsible for debts and liabilities incurred by another member or by a committee of the association. The members of a voluntary association are liable for the association's debts only when they have authorized or ratified the contract upon which the liability may be incurred. A member of a voluntary association may, however, be authorized to act as agent for the association; one who is not authorized to act as an agent for the association becomes personally responsible for debts contracted for the association's benefit.

VOLUNTARY CONVEYANCE. See GIFT.

VOLUNTARYISM, the principle or system which advocates the complete separation of church and state, and the support of the church by voluntary contributions. The term "voluntaryism" first came into use in the early part of the 19th century in connection with discussions between churchmen and dissenters in Scotland, although there had been advocates of the principle long before this, notably the Baptists, Congregationalists, and Friends. The principle is held to be based on the express law of Christ respecting the church, as well as on conscience, the nature of civil government, and considerations of general equity and policy. It is the principle embodied in the relation of the United States government to churches. See CIVIL CHURCH LAW, AMERICAN; ESTABLISHMENTS, ECCLESIASTICAL; NONCONFORMISTS.

VOLUNTEER, MILITARY. See ENLISTMENT.

VOLUNTEERS OF AMERICA, a nonsectarian philanthropic organization with headquarters in New York City, founded by General and Mrs. Ballington Booth in 1896, and incorporated under the laws of the State of New York. The society works in harmony with the evangelical churches. No pledge of life membership is required of its members; it promotes its officers on a merit system; its funds are audited at stated periods and balance sheets are issued. The society has over sixty homes or institutions throughout the United States. There are fourteen summer camps, and the society owns the property and equipment of most of these. The winter activities of the society embrace all branches of relief work in a number of cities, in conjunction with the gospel mission work. The official organ of the society is the *Volunteers' Gazette*.

VOLUTE, in architecture, the spiral ornaments of the Ionic and Corinthian capitals, probably derived from Assyrian architecture.

VOLVOX, a genus of simple organisms which some authorities regard as animals and others as plants. They consist of green flagellate cells, united by protoplasmic bridges in a hollow spherical colony, and occur in ponds, canals, and clear fresh-water pools.

VOLVULUS, form of intestinal obstruction due to twisting of the gut upon itself. This usually occurs in the vicinity of the cecum and especially in cases where the bowel has a long mesenteric attachment. These knots and twists occur, as a rule, in individuals over the age of thirty and give rise to the same symptoms that characterize intestinal obstruction of whatever variety—pain, vomiting, complete constipation, abdominal distention, and syncope. Vomiting occurs early and consists at first of the contents of the stomach, and later of the intestine. The only safe treatment is prompt operation.

VOMITING, the emptying of the stomach by way of the mouth through its own spasmodic contractions. At first the stomach contents are vomited, consisting of food, mucus, and thin serous fluid. If persistent and violent, the vomiting causes the ejection of bile, which has regurgitated from the duodenum into the stomach under the pressure of the diaphragm, and, rarely, of feces from the intestine.

VONDEL, JOOST VAN DEN (1587–1679). Dutch dramatist, born in Cologne. He kept a hosier's shop in Amsterdam. His literary work begins with a drama, *The Pasha* (1612), and some lyrics, aided by study of the classical drama and the *Poetics* of Aristotle. Some of the lyrics from his dramas are among the finest in the Dutch language. His classical imitations or adaptations (*Hecuba,* 1625; *Hippolytus,* 1628; *Electra,* 1638; *King Œdipus,* 1660; *Hercules in Trachis,* 1663; *Iphigenia in Taurus,* 1666; *The Phœnician Iphigenia,* 1668; and others) were accompanied by a parallel series of original tragedies (*Jerusalem Laid Waste,* 1620; *Lucifer,* 1654; *Jephtha,* 1659; and *Adam* *in Banishment,* 1664). Of his thirty-three plays, the most interesting is *Lucifer* (1654). Lennep edited his complete works (12 vols., 1850–69).

VON EMMICH, OTTO. See EMMICH, OTTO VON.

VONNOH, BESSIE POTTER (1872–), American sculptor, born in St. Louis, and trained at the Art Institute of Chicago under the American sculptor Lorado Taft. She assisted Taft in his work on the Agricultural Building at the World's Fair of 1893. Afterward she studied in Paris and in Italy. In 1899 she married Robert Vonnoh. Her subjects are portrait and ideal statuette groups of children and young women. Among her works, which have a wide popular appeal, are "Mother and Child" (1905), "A Modern Madonna" (1905), "Beatrice" (1906), and "The Young Mother" (Metropolitan Museum of Art, New York City). Bessie Vonnoh was elected an associate of the National Academy of Design in 1906 and a member in 1921.

VONNOH, ROBERT WILLIAM (1858–1933), American painter, born in Hartford, Conn. He taught art at the Cowles Art School, Boston (1884–85), at the Boston Museum of Fine Art Schools (1885–87), and at the schools of the Pennsylvania Academy of the Fine Arts, Philadelphia (1891–96). He was made a member of the National Academy of Design, New York (1906). Vonnoh's work was exhibited in the Paris Salon, in London and Munich, and at various expositions at home and abroad. After 1918–19 he was instructor in the Composition Class, Pennsylvania Academy of Fine Arts.

VOODOO, the name given to the superstitions (collectively) prevalent among West Indian and southern United States creoles, mulattoes, and Negroes. It deals with charms, conjuring, snake worship, and witchcraft. The *voodoo doctor* or *priest* is a conjurer supposed to have power or skill in such practices; if prominent in a locality, such a person is sometimes also known as *king* or *queen,* or *papa* or *mamma,* and is held in great veneration by the devotees. The worship is always at night, is secret, and characterized by prayer to the snake, who is exhibited during the rite, by hysterical manifestations by the priest and priestess, by a dance for the initiation of novices said to be marked by wild debauchery and indecency, and by cannibalism and human sacrifice. Careful examination of apparently circumstantial accounts of the voodoo rites and orgies has eliminated the more horrible phases in practically every instance. If cannibalism ever occurred, it probably was merely sporadic. Other features are nothing more than shamanistic and magic practices common the world over. The word is derived from Dahomeyan *rodu.*

VOORHEES, DANIEL WOLSEY (1827–97), American politician, born in Butler Co., Ohio, of Dutch and Irish extraction. He was admitted to the bar (1850), and began to practice in Covington, Ind. After being United States district attorney for Indiana (1858–60), he sat in Congress as a Democrat (1861–66 and 1877–79), and was a United States senator (1877–97). As a senator he was a member of the committee on finance, and his first speech in the Senate was a defense of free silver and a plea for the preservation of the full legal tender of the greenback issue.

VOORHEES, EDWARD BURNETT (1856–1911), American agricultural chemist, born in Mine Brook, N.J. From 1882 he was associated with the New Jersey Agricultural Experiment Station, of which he became director in 1893. After 1890 he was also professor of agriculture at Rutgers College. Voorhees received the Nichols research medal in 1902. Among his works are *First Principles of Agriculture* (1896), *Fertilizers* (1898), and *Forage Crops* (1907).

VOORHEES, FOSTER MACGOWAN (1856–1927), American politician. He began law practice in Elizabeth, N.J., in 1880, was a member of the Elizabeth Board of Education in 1884, and was elected to the Assembly for a three-year term, 1888–90. When Governor John William Griggs resigned to become attorney general of the United States the duties of governor devolved upon the president of the senate and on February 1, 1898, Mr. Voorhees became acting governor. A year later he was elected governor in his own right, serving a three-year term.

VORARLBERG, formerly the most westerly province of Austria. The Arlberg chain lies on the east of this mountainous territory. In the south, on the boundary, tower the Rhætian Alps, crowned by the Silvretta mass, the highest point in the crownland (about 11,300 feet). The Ill valley crosses the southwest portion. In the north part are the Bregenzerwald and Lechthal Alps, with the Bregenzer Ach valley in the extreme north. The Rhine valley from the Ill to Lake Constance is the feature on the west. About one third of the area is in Alpine meadow and over one fourth in productive forests, the tilled land being small. In 1938 Vorarlberg united with Tirol, forming the province of Tirol-Vorarlberg.

VORONEZH, capital of the Region of the same name, in Russia, on the right bank of the river Voronezh, 5 miles above its confluence with the Don, 332 miles S.S.E. of Moscow. It has large industrial establishments. The city was founded in 1586. It was the site of heavy Russo-German fighting in July and September, 1942, and in January, 1943. Pop., about 327,000.

VOROSHILOV, KLEMENT EFREMOVICH (1881–), Russian soldier and politician, born in Ukraine, and educated in a country school. A revolutionary in his youth, he was frequently imprisoned by the imperial authorities. He saw service in the Civil War, was cofounder of the Red Cavalry, and commissar for defense, 1925–40. He was later appointed assistant chairman of the Council of People's Commissars, but went to the front lines when Germany invaded Russia (June, 1941) and organized the defense of Leningrad. Thereafter he was a member of the war cabinet of the Soviet Union.

VOROSHILOVGRAD, formerly LUGANSK, a city in the Ukrainian S.S.R., situated on the Lugan R., 10 m. from its confluence with the Donets R. and about 240 miles E. of Dnepropetrovsk. The city, which is located in a coal-mining region, is noted as being the oldest iron-and-steel center in southern Russia. An iron foundry was established there in 1795, and in 1797 the first experiments in Russia in the smelting of iron with coke took place there. The principal present-day industries include smelting and the manufacture of locomotives, alcoholic beverages, timber saws, enamel, ball bearings, munitions and ordnance equipment, agricultural machinery, tallow candles, beet sugar, leather, bricks, and flour. The city is the site of a meteorological station and a mineralogical museum and library. Pop., about 213,000.

VÖRÖSMARTY, MIHÁLY (1800–55), Hungarian poet, born in Nyék. Of his epic poems, *Zalán Futása* ("The Flight of Zalán", 1825) and *Eger* (1827) are the best. At the time of his death he was translating the works of William Shakespeare into Hungarian.

VORPARLAMENT, a preliminary parliament which met at Frankfort on the Main from March 31 to April 4, 1848, to devise ways and means for calling a national German parliament to deal with the widespread demand for reorganization of the Germanic political system on the basis of a closer national unity.

VORSE, MARY HEATON (MRS. ROBERT MINOR) (?–), American author, born in New York City. Her works include, *The Prestons* (1918), *The Heart's Country* (1913), *Growing Up* (1920), *Man and Steel* (1921), *Strike—A Novel of Gastonia* (1930), *Labor's New Millions* (1938), and *Time and the Town* (1942).

VORSPIEL, the German word for introduction or prelude (qq.v.). Beginning with his opera *Lohengrin* (1848), the German composer Richard Wagner, in order to obtain an elastic form for the unhampered expression of the dramatic ideas, abandoned the form of the overture for his dramatic works and designated the orchestral introductions, both to the entire drama and the separate acts, as *Vorspiel*. Several later operatic composers have also adopted this term. The earlier German composer Johann Sebastian Bach wrote a series of preludes for organ which he called *Choral-Vorspiele*. These are intended as free introductions sometimes canonic or fugal in form, to a chorale, which is made the basis of these *Vorspiele*. The same treatment is found in the *Choral-Vorspiele* of the German composer Johannes Brahms.

VORSTERMANS or **VORSTERMAN,** LUCAS (1595–1675), Flemish engraver, born in Bommel (Gelderland). He became a member of the Antwerp Guild in 1618, and was already trained as an engraver when he entered the studio of Rubens. Reforming his style, he became the greatest interpreter of that master's works, rendering in a wonderful manner the line, color, and spirit of the originals. Among his best plates are "Adoration of the Magi", "Descent from the Cross", and "Susannah and the Elders". After quarreling with Rubens he went to England, where he worked for Charles I and the Earl of Arundel (1624–30).

VORTEX, a mass of fluid rotating about a closed curve as an axis. Vortices are usually circular and have, as an essential condition of their existence, an axis or filament around which they turn and which must be either a closed curve or a curve of infinite length. Familiar examples of vortices are smoke rings and the whirlpools formed by water running out of a tub or basin. An elaborate mathematical analysis of vortices in frictionless fluids was made by the German physicist Hermann von Helmholtz and his analysis plays an important part in the study of aerodynamics. The British physicist James Clerk Maxwell applied the theory of vortex motion to the theory of magnetism (q.v.), assuming that magnetic tubes of force moved like vortices.

VORTICELLA, or BELL ANIMALCULE, a genus of ciliated infusorians belonging to the

A forest in the Vosges Mountains, France

order Peritricha, in which the cilia are restricted to a fringe around the mouth. During most of their life the little animals are attached to the stems and leaves of plants in fresh-water pools, a group being just visible to the unaided eye as a whitish fringe.

VOS, CORNELIS DE (1585–1651), Flemish portrait and historical painter, born in Hulst. He is represented in the Antwerp Gallery, with the "Meerbecker Epitaph"; "St. Norbert with the Schnoeck Family"; and the portrait of "Abraham Grapheus", servant of the guild. Other works include "The Hutten Family" (Munich) and a portrait and group in the Metropolitan Museum of Art, New York City.

VOSE, GEORGE LEONARD (1831–1910), American engineer, born in Augusta, Me. After being engaged as an engineer in railroad construction for a number of years, he was associate editor of *The American Railroad Times* (1859–63). He was appointed professor of civil engineering at Bowdoin College, Maine, in 1872, and during 1881–86 filled a similar chair in the Massachusetts Institute of Technology. His works include *Handbook of Railroad Construction* (1857), *Manual for Railroad Engineers* (1873), *Memoir of George W. Whistler* (1887), and *Bridge Disasters in America* (1887).

VOSGES, a range of mountains in the N.E. of France and the W. of Germany, running from S. to N., on the W. bank of the Rhine, and from the borders of Switzerland to Mainz. Large forests exist in the mountains. The highest summits, which are in the southern portion of the range, are between 4100 and 4700 ft. in height.

VOSGES, a department in the N.E. of France, bounded on the E. by Alsace. The surface is mountainous, the hills being well wooded, while the western plain is very fertile. There are iron, silver, lead, copper, cobalt, zinc, manganese, and antimony mines. The capital is Epinal. During World War I, fighting between the Germans and French in the Vosges continued intermittently from 1914 to 1918. Area, 2303 sq.m.; pop. (1945) 342,315.

VOSS, RICHARD (1851–1918), German author, born in Neugrape, in Pomerania. He studied in Jena and Munich, traveled in Italy, and in 1884 became librarian of the Wartburg. His works are very numerous. His best-known dramas, many with a psychological-pathological bent, are *Pater Modestus* (1882), dealing with religion; *Alexandra* (1886); *Brigitta* (1887); *Eva* (1889), patterned after Ibsen's "Nora"; *Schuldig* (1890); *Zwischen Zwei Herzen* (1896); *Die Patrizierin*, a classical drama; and *Jürg Jenatsch*, written in 1893, produced in 1906. His novels include *Die Sabinerin* (1890), *Villa Falconieri* (1896), *Amata* (1901), *Römisches Fieber* (1902), *Die Leute von Valdaré* (1903), *Die Schuldige* (1906), *Narcissuszauber* (1909), *Zwei Menschen* (1911), *Kundry* (1913), *Aus einem Phantastischen Leben* (1920), and *Ausgewählte Werke* (1922).

VOTER, one entitled to a vote or voice in the determination of a question before a number of individuals. The term implies some qualification. There are certain general requirements in all States, which may be summarized as follows: (1) citizenship; (2) residence for a certain time in the State, county, and election district; (3) that the voter shall have attained his majority (21 years); (4) that the voter shall be of sound mind; and (5) that he shall not be a convicted felon under sentence. Registration is also required in many States. Some of the States have established either property or educational qualifications. This has been done in most of the southern States in order to exclude the Negro vote.

VOTING, the act of recording a vote, or giving formal expression of will or opinion in regard to some question submitted for decision, as in electing, sanctioning laws, and passing resolutions. It is commonly signified by the voice, by a show of hands, by rising to one's feet, or by ballot. Voting by ballot is in general practice in the United States, and is also used in the parliamentary elections of Canada and the United Kingdom. In elections bribery, treating, undue influence, personation, and false declarations as to election expenses, are universally regarded as corrupt and illegal practices. See BALLOT; ELECTORAL COLLEGE; ELECTORAL REFORM IN THE UNITED STATES; PARLIAMENT; REGISTRATION.

VOTING, ABSENTEE, the practice of voting by absentee ballot if a voter is absent from, or physically unable to appear in person at, the voting center. In wartime, voting by absentee ballot becomes of importance to men in the armed forces. All States except Delaware, Kentucky, and New Mexico permit absentee voting. In five States, however, servicemen alone may vote absentee. These are Louisiana, Maryland, Mississippi, New Jersey, and Pennsylvania.

VOTING MACHINE, a mechanical device which automatically records and counts votes. Besides preventing repeating and other fraud, an ideal voting machine has the additional advantages over the paper ballot system of greater secrecy, simplicity, rapidity, and cheapness, The first State law authorizing the use of automatic machines was passed by New York in 1892.

VOTING TRUST, in corporation law in the United States, a device by which the shares in a corporation owned by a number of stockholders are placed in the hands of one or more persons who are authorized as trustees (see TRUSTS) to vote the stock at corporate elections. The stockholders indorse their certificates to the trustees, who in turn issue voting trust certificates to the participating stockholders. As the voting trust constitutes a pooling of the votes of a group of stockholders, the formation of a voting trust often results in placing control of the policy of the corporation in the hands of the group forming the trust. Voting trusts are declared to be against public policy in some States; in others voting-trust agreements have been held to be valid if the agreement is for the advantage of the corporation and its stockholders and is not in fraud of the rights of the other stockholders. Voting-trust agreements that are monopolistic or in restraint of trade are illegal, since they violate both Federal and State antitrust laws.

VOTYAKS, Finno-Ugrian tribe, neighbors of the Permiaks, living between the Vetluga and Kama rivers, tributaries of the Volga, in northeastern Russia. They number about 360,000, and are skillful husbandmen, stock breeders, and apiarists. Their height is 1.619 meters and their cephalic index 82.0 meters. They have high cheek bones, straight nose, small lips, blue or gray eyes, blond or red

VOTING MACHINE. *Top, left:* Curtain of machine is closed during voting to insure privacy. *Top, right:* After voting a lever is pulled, simultaneously opening curtain and recording votes. *Bottom:* Votes are cast by pulling small levers down over the choices on the ballot.

hair, and a slender physique. They are mentally undeveloped. Polygamy is practiced, and, though nominal Christians, they secretly continue their pagan cult. Their speech is allied to that of the Zyrians, and they have a little Russian admixture.

VOUCHER, in law, a book, document, or other instrument, which may be used in evidence to prove essential facts pertaining to an account (q.v.) between the parties. The voucher may take the place of oral testimony or merely corroborate such testimony, and may be a receipt or other paper showing payment or release of part or all of the debt claimed. In the old common law of conveyancing by fine and recovery (see RECOVERY OR COMMON RECOVERY), the term "voucher" designated the person called into court by a tenant to defend the latter's title.

VOUET, SIMON (1590–1649), French decorative and historical painter, born in Paris. In 1627 he was called to Paris by Louis XIII, who made him first painter to the crown, and commissioned him to decorate the royal palaces of the Louvre, the Luxembourg, Fontainebleau, and Versailles. He also painted decorations in the Palais-Royal and the Château de Rueil for Cardinal Richelieu. His "Susanna and the Elders" and eight other canvases are in the Louvre, and he is represented in all French provincial museums.

VOUGHT, CHANCE MILTON (1888–1930), American aeronautical engineer, born in New York City. He designed and constructed such planes as the PLV biplane, Mayo biplane, Simplex 3-place flying boat, Wright model-V military biplane, and the Wright Hispano flying boat. For the U.S. Navy he designed the VO-catapult-observation convertible airplane for scout-cruisers and battleships and the famous Corsair or OU, a convertible land and seaplane for observation and fighting. At the time of his death he was president of the Chance Vought Corporation, manufacturers of military and naval airplanes.

VOUSSOIRS, the individual stones or bricks forming an arch, of which the central one is called the keystone. They are generally of a truncated wedge form. See ARCH.

VOW, in religion, a promise of a future gift to a god, or of some action supposed to be pleasing to the god. In primitive religion, gifts or worship of any kind could commonly be made to the god only by the entire tribe; between the times of sacrifice, the favor of the god could be secured by promising a gift on the next proper occasion. Every religion has used vows, but they are most prominent in religions with forms of sacrifice, or with a strong sense of personal relation between God and man. With the growth of monasticism, vows became of more importance, and began to receive more attention. Catholic theology discriminated between real and personal vows, dealing respectively with property and personal life; and between simple and solemn vows. The last are irrevocable and absolute, when accepted by competent authority. Vows of abstinence, pilgrimages, and individual acts of charity or piety are simple. So are the first vows of monastic orders. Vows can be dispensed only by ecclesiastical authority. Certain vows, including the vows of chastity, are reserved for the pope; other vows may be dispensed by a bishop or prelate. Protestantism, laying aside authority of the church over individual Christian life, denied the perpetual binding power of vows, and left promises to God and the methods of their fulfillment with the individual conscience.

VOWEL. See LETTERS; PHONETICS.

VOYSEY, CHARLES (1828–1912), English clergyman, founder of the Theistic Church, born in London, and educated at Oxford University. He was curate of Hessle, Yorkshire (1852–59); of Craighton, Jamaica (1860–61); and of St. Mark's, Whitechapel, London (1861–63). From this last charge he was removed on account of a sermon against endless punishment. He was vicar of Healaugh, Yorkshire (1864–71). In 1866 he published, in *The Sling and the Stone,* sermons preached at Healaugh, which were deemed at variance with the Bible and the Thirty-nine Articles (q.v.). The secretary of the archbishop of York prosecuted him in the Chancery Court of the diocese. From the sentence of condemnation he appealed to the judicial committee of the Privy Council, which confirmed the sentence (1871). He afterward preached and lectured in St. George's Hall, London, a fund having been raised called the Voysey establishment fund, the outcome of which was the Theistic church (1885). Voysey wrote *Religion for All Mankind* (1903) and *Testimony of the Four Gospels Concerning Jesus Christ* (1907).

VOZNESENK, a town of the Ukrainian Soviet Socialist Republic, situated on the Bug R., about 100 miles N.W. of Kherson. Industrial establishments in the town include warehouses for the storage of grain and salt and brick and iron-products factories. Pop., about 21,000.

VRANJE, a city in Yugoslavia, on the Morava River. It is an important railway and commercial center, and is noted for the manu-

"The Forge of Vulcan," painting by Velázquez

facture of rope. Hemp and flax are the principal products of the vicinity. There are numerous sulphur springs. Vranje was captured by the Bulgarians in 1915. Pop., about 10,000.

VRATTSA or **VRACA**, the capital of a department in Bulgaria, 59 miles N. by E. of Sofia. It manufactures leather, wine, and jewelry and carries on an important trade. There is a school of sericulture. Pop., about 16,200.

VRAZ, STANKO (1810–51), Serbo-Croatian poet, born in Zerovec, in Lower Styria. He was educated at Gratz and, as editor of the periodical *Kolo* (1842–50), joined the movement to fuse the Slovene and Serbo-Croatian languages under the name of Illyrian. This attempt was not successful. Vraz wrote many graceful lyrics and made collections of national songs which are of great value. He ranks as one of the most important Serbo-Croatian poets. His collected works, *Djela*, were published in Agram in four volumes (1863–64), and a fifth volume containing his letters was added in 1877.

VRIES or **FRIES,** ADRIAEN DE (1560–1603), Dutch sculptor, born in The Hague. Many of his original works were done for Holy Roman Emperor Rudolf II, who invited the sculptor to Prague. They include busts and reliefs of the emperor (Vienna Museum); bronze statues and groups, such as "Mercury and Psyche" (Louvre); and reliefs in wax. Numerous later statues, executed for the Austrian general Albrecht Eusebius von Wallenstein, are now in Drottningholm Park, near Stockholm, Sweden. A "Triton" is in the Metropolitan Museum of Art, New York City (Altman collection).

VULCAN (Lat. *Volcanus*), in Roman mythology, the god of fire. Originally an old Italian deity who seems to have been associated with volcanic fire, he was as early as the 3rd century B.C. identified with the Greek god Hephæstus (q.v.). At Rome the Vulcanalia was celebrated in his honor every August 23, and he was worshiped especially at Ostia, where the grain from Sicily, Africa, and Egypt was stored and where fire in midsummer was particularly feared.

VULCANIZATION. See RUBBER.

VULCANO. See LIPARI ISLANDS.

VULGATE, the edition of the Latin Bible which was pronounced "authentic" by the Council of Trent. The name was originally given to the "common edition" of the Septuagint used by the Greek Fathers, and thence transferred to the "Itala" or the "Old Latin" version of both Old Testament and New Testament current during the first centuries in the Western Church. It finally passed to the present composite work, which gradually took the place of the "Old Latin", sometimes unwarrantably called the Itala, which probably came into existence at Carthage. In this, the Old Testament translation, embracing also the Apocrypha, was made from the Septuagint, while the New Testament omitted three Epistles (Hebrews, James, 2 Peter). Jerome, at the request of Damascus in 382 A.D., undertook a revision of the New Testament. He corrected the Gospels thoroughly, and the rest more cursorily, with the aid of Greek codices which were then reputed trustworthy. Next, he took in hand the Old Testament. Of the Psalms he made two revisions, called the Roman and Gallican respectively, the latter of which is now read in the Vulgate.

VULPECULA (Lat., "the little fox"), a small northern constellation, situated directly s. of Cygnus. It was first described by Hevelius in 1690. Its chief objects of interest are the variable star τ Vulpeculae, with a period of 4.4 days, and the Dumbbell nebula, M 27. In 1670 a nova was discovered in this constellation by Anthelmus, a Carthusian monk of Dijon.

VULTURE, common name given to raptorial, carrion-eating birds belonging to the families Vulturidae, or Old World vultures, and Cathartidae, or American vultures. Old World vultures, or true vultures, are very closely related to the Hawk family. All the members of the family are large birds, having a naked head and neck and a long, downward-curving beak. The toes are long and curved, the third toe being the longest, and are adapted to seizing prey. Vultures are restricted in their range to the warm and tropical regions of Eurasia and Africa. The cinereous or black vulture, *Vultur monachus,* native to southeastern Asia, is typical of the true vultures. The feathers of this bird are black with dark-brown stripes. The head and neck are flesh colored, the beak is black, and the claws yellow. The bird averages 3½ feet in length. Black vultures live in forests, nesting generally in trees; the nest consists of a structure of boughs, lined with small twigs. Each spring one to two large white eggs with red markings are laid in a clutch. Black vultures are extremely valuable in tropical countries with inadequate sanitary facilities because they feed entirely on carrion and other refuse. Ungainly as they are on the

American Museum of Natural History

Museum model of a turkey vulture in its natural surroundings

ground, these vultures are graceful and agile in flight, flying in groups at high altitudes seeking food. They have remarkable vision and hunt by sight rather than smell. The griffon vulture, *Gyps fulvus,* frequents rocky regions and builds its immense nest of sticks on rocks in inaccessible places. Griffon vultures are capable of going without food for long periods, but when they obtain food they frequently gorge themselves until they are temporarily incapable of flight.

The American vultures closely resemble the Old World species both in appearance and in habits. They differ from European species by the absence of any partition between the nostrils, and by the lack of a syrinx in the lower windpipe, so that the only noise these birds can make is a hissing sound. About nine species are included in the family Cathartidae, most of which are South American, although the family is represented as far north as southern Canada. The condor of the Andes region, *Sarcorhampus gryphus,* is a large, black bird with a conspicuous ruff of white feathers around the neck, and a white bill. The king vulture, *Cathartes papa,* is black above and creamy white below, with head and neck colored red, orange, yellow, and blue; it has a range from Brazil to Florida. The American black vulture, *Coragyps atratus,* is found northward as far as the Carolinas, and is about 2 feet in length. The turkey vulture, or turkey buzzard, *Cathartes aura,* resembles the black vulture and is found as far north as New York and British Columbia. The California vulture, *Gymnogyps californianus,* is a large, brown-black bird restricted in range to the Pacific Coast regions of the United States.

VYĀSA, a legendary Hindu sage to whom is ascribed the authorship, or compilation, of a large body of ancient Sanskrit literature. The redaction of the Vedic hymns and the authorship of the *Mahābhārata* (q.v.) are attributed to him, while his name is attached to the *Purānas* (q.v.), to a *Brahmasūtra* (see VEDANTA), and to several other works. According to tradition his father was Paraśara and his sons were Pandu and Dhritarashtra, the kings of the *Mahābhārata.* His full name is given as Krishna Dvāipāyana Vyāsa, and legend accounts for the title *Krishna* (Skr., "black") by his dark complexion, and for the attribute *dvāipāyana* by his birth on an island in the Yamuna or River Jumna. The immense mass of literature ascribed to him is so varied in character and so different in point of age, that Vyāsa is not regarded as an individual but is understood to typify the literary activity which brought order into the heterogenerous mass of Sanskrit literature.

W, the twenty-third letter and eighteenth consonant in the English alphabet. The character is a ligature rather than a letter, as is implied by the name, *double u.* In the earliest known West Saxon manuscripts the sound is represented by *uu,* a digraph for which the Northumbrian rune **P,** called *wen,* was substituted. This was used until the 13th century, except in Anglo-Norman manuscripts, such as the Domesday Book, in which the French scribes used *uu* for medials, and for initials the capital form VV, which, when ligatured, became the present English W.

In uttering its sound, as in *wit,* the vocal cords are set in vibration with the lips in position for the *oo* of *pool,* but without the formation of the resonance chamber necessary for a distinct vowel. The sound is thus really a half ū, instead of a double yū; whence the technical name for the sound: "labial semivowel". W stands in the same relation to ū as y to ī.

If the lip movement of *w* is made without vibration of the vocal cords, the result is a voiceless or whispered *w.* This is the sound usually substituted by Englishmen for the initial wh of *white* and *whet,* which in the United States is generally pronounced *hw.* The voiceless *w* occurs also in other words after voiceless consonants, as in *quart, sweet, twin.*

In the old combination *wr* the symbol *w* has been preserved, but its sound has been lost, as in the words *wright, wrench, wrong, wrist.* The combination *cw* has become *qu,* as in "quoth" from *cwæth.* The *w* is occasionally intrusive, as in "whole" from *hál.* The intrusive *w* is probably due to analogy, and is useful as distinguishing the words from the homophone *hole.* A final *w* is vocalic, as in "few" and "new", in which the spellings are survivals from the Anglo Saxon *feáwa* and *niwe,* in which *w* was a consonant. In these cases the consonantal sound has been lost.

As an abbreviation, the letter W stands for Week, Wales, Washington, Wednesday, West, Worshipful, and for Walter, Wilhelmina, and other personal names beginning with W. It also is used in nautical log books for *wet dew,* and constitutes a word in wigwagging. The drygoods trade employs it to denote wide or width. As a symbol, it denotes tungsten (Wolfram); the component of the velocity parallel to the axis of Z in hydrodynamics; a watt in electricity; the twenty-second or twenty-third in a class, group, or series; twenty-two or twenty-three as a number or numeral; the perforation in a paper roll for machine-cast composition representing this symbol; and the letter in the international code of signals for ships.

WAAL, the southernmost and largest arm of the Rhine delta. It flows westward through the Dutch province of Gelderland, and is joined by the Meuse or Maas near Gorinchem.

WAALS, Johannes Diderik van der (1837–1923), Dutch physicist, born in Leiden. He taught in secondary schools in Deventer and The Hague, and after 1877 was professor of physics at the University of Amsterdam. In 1910 he was awarded the Nobel Prize in Physics.

WABASH, county seat of Wabash Co., Ind., situated on the Wabash R., 83 miles N.N.E. of Indianapolis. It is served by two railroads, and is the trading center of a fertile agricultural area. The city is also a manufacturing center, with machine shops, rock-wool plants, and factories which make furniture, paper containers, rubber tires and tubes, radio cabinets, filing supplies, meter boxes, thermostats, and electrical supplies. A county museum in the city contains collections on local history. Wabash was settled about 1835 and chartered as a city in 1866. It was one of the first cities in the world to have its streets lighted by electricity (1880). Pop. (1949 est.) 12,000.

WABASHA, county seat of Wabasha County, Minn., situated on the Mississippi R., about 65 m. from St. Paul. Industrial establishments include flour mills, brick yards, and furniture and machine shops. The town is also the shipping point of the surrounding agricultural region. Pop. (1940) 2368.

WABASH COLLEGE, an institution of higher education, founded in 1832 in Crawfordsville, Ind. It has no organic connection with any ecclesiastical body, but is closely affiliated with the Presbyterian Church. The student enrollment averages about 400 annually and faculty members number about 30.

WABASH RIVER, river rising in w. Ohio, flowing southwest across Indiana, and then turning south and separating Indiana for 200 m. from Illinois; it flows into the Ohio River after a course of 550 m. The river has a drainage area of 33,725 sq.m. At high water it is navigable as far as Lafayette. Its chief tributaries are the White River and the Tippecanoe River.

WAC. See WOMEN'S ARMY CORPS.

WACE (about 1100–75), Anglo-Norman poet, born in Guernsey. He enjoyed the patronage of the Norman kings of England, and was given by Henry II a prebend at Bayeux. His two romances, the *Geste des Bretons* or *Brut,* a history of the British kings, and the *Roman de Rou,* a poetical history of the Norman dukes, are among the best examples of Norman French.

WACHT AM RHEIN, DIE (Ger., "The Watch on the Rhine"), a German national air and patriotic song, the words of which were written by Max Schneckenburger (1819–49) and the music by Karl Wilhelm (1815–73). The words were written in 1840, when the left bank of the Rhine seemed threatened by France. The music, which is a part song for men's voices, was composed and first played in 1854, but the air did not become a national song until the Franco-Prussian War. In 1871 the composer was granted a pension of 3000 marks.

WACHUSETT MOUNTAIN, an isolated monadnock in Worcester County, Mass., situated about 8 miles s.w. of Fitchburg. Its summit is 2108 ft. above sea level.

WACKENRODER, WILHELM HEINRICH (1773–98), German Romantic author, born in Berlin, and educated at the universities of Erlangen and Göttingen. While a schoolboy he became the friend of the better-known German Romanticist Johann Ludwig Tieck (q.v.); Wackenroder subsequently communicated to Tieck his enthusiasm for the art and literature of the Middle Ages, and the two men remained closely associated until Wackenroder's early death. In 1794 they went together to Berlin, and in 1796 to Dresden, where they lived thereafter. Tieck contributed an introduction and other material to Wackenroder's only completed work, *Herzensergiessungen eines Kunstliebenden Klosterbruders* (1797), a group of studies of medieval art and religion. After the younger man's death, Tieck completed two works of their joint authorship: *Franz Sternbalds Wanderungen* (1798) and *Phantasien über die Kunst* (1799). In these books Wackenroder and Tieck expressed for the first time the esthetic principles which were to govern the Romantic movement in Germany. See ROMANTICISM.

WACO, name of a North American Indian tribe of Cadoan stock. Located near the site of the present city of Waco, Tex., they were nearly exterminated by the Cherokees in 1830. The remnant was removed to a reservation in 1855, and in 1859 became incorporated with the Wichita.

WACO, county seat of McLennan Co., Tex., situated on both banks of the Brazos R., about 88 miles S.E. of Fort Worth. It is served by four railroads and maintains a municipal airport. The city is the commercial and manufacturing center of a rich agricultural area. Oats, corn, cotton, wheat, grain sorghums, barley, fruits, garden truck, livestock, poultry, and dairy products are the chief agricultural products. Mineral resources of the area include limestone, clays, sand, and gravel. Waco ships vast quantities of farm products and is an important cotton market. Among the industrial establishments in the city are railroad repair shops, machine shops, paper mills, cottonseed-oil mills, bottling works, a tire-manufacturing plant, plants processing dairy products, and factories manufacturing textiles, canvas goods, garments, work clothing, patent medicines, food products, furniture, saddles, cement, and glass. Waco has many wholesale and retail houses, and offices of large life insurance companies, including the oldest legal reserve life insurance company in the Southwest.

The city is the site of Baylor University (Baptist), founded in 1845, the oldest institution of its kind in Texas. The university is especially noted for its Browning library, said to contain the world's largest collection of works by the poet Robert Browning. In addition, the city is the site of the Paul Quinn College for Negroes, founded in 1872 by the African Methodist Church, of a U.S. veterans hospital, and of the Methodist Home and the Waco State Home orphanages. The city's park system includes Cameron Park, along the Brazos R., which covers 560 acres, and is said to be one of the largest municipal parks in the U.S.

The region of the present city was inhabited until about 1830 by the Huaco Indians, who were almost completely annihilated in that year by the Cherokee Indians. The town of Waco was founded in 1849. The first suspension bridge to span the Brazos R. was built there in 1870, and is still in use, together with several modern bridges. The development of the city as a commercial center dates from the arrival of the first railroad, in 1881. Pop. (1950) 84,300.

WADAI, former State of central Sudan, but in 1920 made part of the independent Chad Territory in French Congo, Africa, between Bagirmi and Darfur. Ivory and feathers are exported, and except in the north the country is fertile. It has been under French protection since 1903. The area is estimated at 170,000 sq.m. and the semicivilized population at 1,-000,000 of whom the greater part are Mabas.

The Wadai kingdom was founded in 1635, and paid tribute to both Bornu and Darfur. The country has had powerful rulers. The sultan Ali conquered, after about 1860, the territory of Runga, the east half of Kanem, and also Borku. The Sudanese Rabaj conquered Wadai during 1892–93, and extended his rule to surrounding states. The present native conditions of political rule are not definitely known. In 1901 a revolution occurred owing to local political feuds, and a new sultan was enthroned. Eduard Vogel was the first European to enter the land, about the middle of the 19th century. Nachtigal explored it in 1873 and Matteuci and Massari in 1879. By the Anglo-French agreement of 1898–99 the region passed to the French, who extended their colonial system to it in 1903.

WADDELL, GEORGE EDWARD, popularly known as "RUBE" WADDELL (1876–1914), American professional baseball player, born in Bradford, Pa. Waddell was one of the most gifted left-hand pitchers in baseball history, especially noted for his speed and for his strikeout records; during the first decade of the 20th century he made 343 strikeouts in a season, a record which stood until Robert Feller, the noted Cleveland pitcher, in 1946 established the record of 349 strikeouts. During his career Waddell pitched for a number of minor league teams and for the Louisville, Chicago, and Pittsburgh teams of the National League and the St. Louis and Philadelphia teams of the American League. He did his most outstanding work for the Philadelphia team, for which he pitched 250 games between 1902 to 1907, winning 131 and losing 81 for a percentage of .618. In his lifetime he pitched 406 games, winning 193 and losing 140, for a percentage of .580. Waddell was appointed to the Baseball Hall of Fame (q.v.) in 1946.

WADDELL, JAMES IREDELL (1824–86), American naval officer, born in Pittsboro, N.C. After serving in the Mexican War, he was appointed assistant professor of navigation at the Naval Academy (1859). Soon after the outbreak of the Civil War he resigned from the United States Navy and entered the Confederate Navy. In 1864 he was placed in command of the *Shenandoah* off Madeira, and before reaching Melbourne captured nine vessels. In the Arctic he captured many United States whalers, most of which he destroyed. He continued his destructive operations until August 2, 1865, when he learned from the captain of a British vessel that the war had been over for three months. He then sailed for Liverpool, where he surrendered the *Shenandoah* to the British government.

WADDING, LUKE (1588–1657), Irish Franciscan friar and historian of the order, born in Waterford. He taught theology at Salamanca, and went to Rome in 1618. He founded the college of St. Isidore and another at Capranica for the members of his order, and was influential in founding the Irish College in Rome.

WADDINGTON, WILLIAM HENRY (1826–94), French statesman, born in Paris, of English parentage. In February, 1871, he was returned by Aisne to the National Assembly. From 1876 till 1885 he sat as senator for Aisne. He served in 1876–77 as minister of foreign affairs, and subsequently as plenipotentiary at the Berlin Congress (1878), president of the Council (1879), and ambassador at London from 1883 to 1892.

WADE, BENJAMIN FRANKLIN (1800–78), American politician, born near Springfield, Mass. He was a member of the State senate (1837–39 and 1841–43) and of the United States Senate (1851–1869). As chairman of the Senate Committee on Territories he secured (1862) emancipation in the Federal territories. In 1864, with Henry Winter Davis, he drew up the Wade-Davis Bill, its principle being that reconstruction was a legislative and not an executive problem. It passed Congress, but was vetoed by Lincoln, which led to the Wade-Davis Manifesto, in which the pair attacked his leadership. In 1871 he was a member of President Grant's Santo Domingo Commission.

WADE, FESTUS JOHN (1859–1927), American financier, born in Limerick, Ireland. He was brought to America in 1860. In 1899 the Mercantile Trust Company of St. Louis was organized with Wade as president. The total deposits at that time were $17,000, as compared with approximately $60,000,000 in 1927. In 1918 during World War I he was appointed a member of the advisory committee of the Division of Finance and Purchases of the U.S. Railway Administration. In 1920 Wade was chairman of the American Bankers' Association committee at the International Chamber of Commerce meeting in Paris.

WADE, HERBERT WINDSOR (1886–   ), American leprologist, born in Haddonfield, N.J. After teaching at Tulane University he became pathologist and bacteriologist of the Bureau of Science, Manila, Philippine Islands, and also taught at the university there. He was chief pathologist of the Culion Leper Colony in the Philippines, 1922–31. With J. Rodriques he wrote *A Description of Leprosy*.

WADE, JAMES FRANKLIN (1843–1921), American soldier, born in Jefferson, Ohio. He was appointed first lieutenant in the 6th United States Cavalry in 1861 and rose through the various grades to the brevet rank of brigadier general in 1865, when he was mustered out of the service. Re-entering the army as captain in 1866, he was promoted to brigadier general in 1897. During the Spanish-American War he was major general of volunteers and (1898) head of the Cuban Evacuation Commission. Sent to the Philippines in 1901, he was made major general of the regular army two years later. In 1903–04 he commanded the Division of the Philippines. He was afterward in command of the Atlantic Division until 1907, when he was retired.

WADE, JOSEPH SANFORD (1880–   ), American entomologist, born in Cumberland County, Ky. From 1913 to 1917 he conducted cereal and forage insect investigations with the United States Department of Agriculture. He subsequently did administrative and research work with the department in Washington, D.C. He wrote many of the bulletins on these subjects for the department.

WADE, MARY HAZELTON (1860–1936), American author, born in Charlestown, Mass. At first a teacher, she later became a prolific writer of books for children, her work emphasizing geography and history. Among her works are *The Boy Who Found Out* (*Henri Fabre*) (1928), *The Boy Who Dared* (*Story of William Penn*) (1929), and *New Pioneers* (1931).

WADE, THOMAS (1805–75), English writer, born in Woodbridge, Suffolk. He went to London and began to publish verse under the inspiration of the English poets Percy Bysshe Shelley and John Keats. Wade also wrote several dramas and became editor and part proprietor of *Bell's Weekly Messenger*. Later he retired to the Isle of Jersey, where he edited the *British Press,* and continued to write verse until his death.

WADE, SIR THOMAS FRANCIS (1818–95), British diplomat, born in London. In 1853 he became chief of the commission that established the customs administration which developed into the Imperial Maritime Customs Service of China. In 1861 he assisted in establishing the British legation in Peking (now Peiping). He retired in 1883. In 1888 he was appointed the first professor of Chinese at Cambridge University. He bequeathed his large Chinese library to Cambridge.

WADESBORO, county seat of Anson Co., N.C., situated 52 miles S.E. of Charlotte. It is served by three railroads, and is the trading center of an area producing cotton and tobacco. The principal industries in Wadesboro are the manufacture of textiles, hosiery, underwear, lumber, flour and feeds, fertilizers, brooms, concrete products, and surgical forms and braces. Pop. (1940) 3857.

WADHAM COLLEGE, a constituent college of Oxford University, England, founded in 1610 by Dorothy Wadham under the terms of the will of her husband Sir Nicholas Wadham (d. 1609) of Mayfield, Sussex. The college was chartered by letters patent from King James I in 1612. The original foundation provided for the maintenance of a warden, fifteen fellows, fifteen scholars, two chaplains, and two clerks; in 1882 the college was reorganized to maintain a warden, a body of college officers, eight fellows, several honorary fellows, eighteen scholars, two chaplains, lecturers, and an undergraduate student body of about one hundred. For an account of the curricula and degrees offered, see the article on OXFORD UNIVERSITY. Among the best-known graduates of

Wadham College are the architect Sir Christopher Wren and the writer Frederic Harrison.

WADI, or WADY, Arabic word signifying a river, a river course, a ravine, or a valley.

WADING BIRDS, popular name for a group of birds characterized by long, naked legs, partly webbed feet, long and capacious neck, and long, strong, pointed bill. They are found along the seashores or in swamps and shallow waters, where they walk about in the shallows, catching fish, frogs, and crayfish by a dart of the bill. The group includes families representative of three orders. In the order Charadriiformes, the family Recurvirostridae includes the avocets and stilts, and the family Scolopocidae includes sandpipers and snipe. The order Gruiformes includes the Rallidae, the rails, and Gruidae, the cranes. The largest part of the group is in the order Ciconiiformes, including the families Ardeidae, the herons; Ciconiidae, the storks; Phoenicopteridae, the flamingoes; and Threskiornithidae, the ibises and spoonbills. For complete scientific classification, see BIRD, and separate articles on each order; for specific descriptions and habits, see articles under the common name of each species.

WADLIN, HORACE GREELEY (1851–1925), American librarian and statistician, born in Wakefield, Mass. From 1888 to 1903 he was chief of the Massachusetts Bureau of Statistics and Labor; subsequently, he was librarian of the Boston Public Library. He also served as a member of the Massachusetts house of representatives (1884–88), and as a supervisor of the United States census (1899–1900). Besides editing *The Decennial Census of Massachusetts for 1895* (7 vols.) and other statistical works, Wadlin wrote *Carroll Davidson Wright, a Memorial* (1911) and *The Public Library of the City of Boston: A History* (1911).

WADSWORTH, a city of Medina Co., Ohio, situated about 15 m. by rail s.w. of Akron. It is surrounded by an agricultural area, and is a manufacturing center, with factories producing metal castings, valves, matches, and lubricators. Wadsworth was settled in 1814, incorporated as a village in 1866, and chartered as a city in 1930. Pop. (1940) 6495.

WADSWORTH, AUGUSTUS BALDWIN (1872–   ), American biologist, born in Brooklyn, N.Y. At first instructor in hygiene and bacteriology, he was later assistant professor in these subjects from 1909 to 1913 at the College of Physicians and Surgeons in New York. He became director of the division of laboratories and research of the New York State department of health in 1914, and served until his retirement in 1945.

WADSWORTH, ELIOT (1876–   ), American financier, born in Boston, Mass., and educated at Harvard University. He was vice-chairman of the central committee of the American Red Cross from 1916 to 1919, and member of the executive committee and national treasurer of the organization from 1921 to 1926. Wadsworth was assistant secretary of the treasury from 1921 to 1925.

WADSWORTH, FRANK LAWTON OLCOTT (1867–1936), American engineer, born in Wellington, Ohio. In 1892–94 he was senior assistant in charge of the Astrophysical Observatory, Washington, D.C., was assistant professor of physics in the University of Chicago (1894–96), assistant professor of astrophysics in the Yerkes Observatory (1896–98), and was director of the Allegheny Observatory (1900–04). After 1908 he acted as a consulting engineer. He invented more than 250 devices.

WADSWORTH, JAMES SAMUEL (1807–64), American soldier born in Geneseo, N.Y. At the outbreak of the Civil War he joined the Union Army as a volunteer; was promoted to brigadier general of volunteers; commanded a division in the army of the Potomac under General Burnside; and fought with great gallantry at the battles of Gettysburg and of the Wilderness, dying two days after the latter.

WAGER, in law in England and the United States, a contract or agreement, frequently verbal, whereby money or other consideration of value is gambled on the outcome of a future event; see GAMBLING. Wagers are most commonly placed on sports events, such as horse racing, prize fighting, wrestling, and baseball and football games; on card games and other games of chance or skill; and on various types of raffles and lotteries; see LOTTERY. In England and in many States of the United States, wagering on horse races is carried on through legal, government-supervised, parimutuel facilities. Wagering or placing bets of any kind with private agents, known as "bookmakers", is illegal in almost all States of the United States. Despite the multiplicity of State and Federal laws designed to suppress the various forms of wagering in the United States, the practice of wagering has continued to enjoy wide popularity, although generally conducted surreptitiously.

Many types of commercial contracts are technically wagers; notable examples include contracts of insurance and contracts dealing in commodity futures. By statute both in England and the United States, wagering agreements which are declared to be against public policy are illegal, and no action at law can be instituted to enforce such agreements. The types of wagering contracts considered inimical to public policy are defined differently in various jurisdictions. In general, insurance contracts, options, and contracts for trading in stocks and bonds are valid. An insurance contract may, however, be declared invalid when a party taking out insurance on the life or property of another does not have an insurable interest (q.v.) in the life or property of the insured. An agreement involving a transaction on a stock or commodity exchange is also invalid if it does not explicitly empower one of the parties to demand delivery of the security or commodity mentioned in the contract; thus, an agreement made for the sole purpose of speculating on the rise or fall of prices is illegal.

WAGES, reward of economic labor, i.e., exertion systematically directed toward the creation of goods or utilities. Economic writers make no distinction between the rewards for the different classes of services.

A law of wages formulated by Ricardo was one of many theoretical explanations of the economic basis of wages and was interpreted to mean that the tendency of economic conditions is to reduce wages to the minimum necessary to support life. Adam Smith urged that in societies in which wealth is increasing wages may exceed the minimum of subsistence. To a considerable extent later economists adopted the so-called productivity theory, one of the earlier exponents being Francis A. Walker. According to this, wages are not paid out of capital at all; the product of labor is the natural reward of labor, and the money wage represents not an advance, but a price paid for a product already created. The same idea was brought out by Henry George. Recent discussions of the wages question have largely turned upon the significance of the term "productivity of labor". Von Thünen demonstrated that it is the product of the laborer who is in the least advantageous situation that really determines wages. This theory has been still further developed by Professor J.B. Clark, whose work makes it clear that under free competition it is possible to discover units of labor which are virtually unaided by capital or land, and that the pure product of such units sets the standard for all units of labor.

Adherents of the productivity theory are under no necessity of believing that the wages of labor are incapable of substantial and indefinite rise. An increase in wages naturally increases the efficiency of labor, and hence its natural reward. High wages may thus be more economical from every point of view than low wages.

A revival of the old idea that wages depend on the cost of subsistence of the laborer appears in the modern theory of the dependence of wages upon the standard of living. As expounded by Gunton, this theory teaches that wages tend toward a standard which just covers the needs of labor; to raise wages, it is essential that needs should be increased. Labor of women and children is regarded as having a depressing influence on the wages of men, since the needs of the husband and father are reduced through the possibility of an income earned by other members of the family. Savings of laborers, resulting in an income through interest, result in a proportional decline of wages. If laborers eschew comforts and luxuries, with the hope of having a surplus of income above needs, the only result in the long run will be a fall in wages until they cover necessaries only. Critics of this theory point out that it would be true only if the Malthusian doctrine that population tends to outrun subsistence were correct; and at present no one would hold to that doctrine in its unqualified form. Employment of women and children may, indeed, depress wages of men; but that fact is due partly to the decline in efficiency of the population, and partly to the fact that an increase in labor supply renders necessary the resort to poorer opportunities of employment, and a consequent lowered standard of wages.

The wage level depends, not on the minimum for subsistence nor mainly on the standard of living, but chiefly on the specific productivity of each group. An increase in the quantity of land available for cultivation through improvements in transportation will make it possible for labor to abandon employments which produce little, and devote itself to the cultivation of new lands of unimpaired fertility. The product of the laborer in the least advantageous position rises, and with it wages. On the other hand, an increase in population, attended by no other change, must force labor to poorer and poorer positions, with a universal lowering of wages. An increase in capital, again, will give each laborer a more complete outfit of tools, etc., and thus increase his productivity, raising wages. Labor-saving inventions, it is generally believed, while they lower wages of certain classes of labor, increase in the long run the productivity of labor. But while productivity determines what the laborer will, in the long run, secure, it is far from true that the laborer is always able to secure his whole product. The laborer may be able to sell his labor to only one employer, who thereby is enabled to fix his own price. Only if competition among employers were active or if capital and labor could meet on equal terms would the laborer be sure of getting exactly what he produces.

A trade union, by preventing an employer from taking advantage of the weakness in bargaining of the individual workman, may raise the rate of wages to the level of productivity. Where wages fail to keep up with productivity of labor, strikes can secure the amount withheld, but strikes cannot permanently hold wages ahead of productivity. By excluding labor from a certain occupation, a union may artificially raise productivity therein, and so gain at the expense of the public. On the other hand, by putting pressure on the employer to increase efficiency, a union has power, not only to raise wages, but to benefit the public.

Many laborers believe that wages would be increased if the hours of labor could be reduced in number, or if laborers would systematically endeavor to produce as little as possible. Prices, they believe, would rise, and with them wages. The view is fallacious, since it fails to take into account the fact that rise in prices would force the laborer to pay more for everything which he buys so that the apparent rise in wages would represent no net gain. Restriction of output in some one industry, however, may raise wages there, if other labor can be excluded from the industry. Such a raising of wages is largely at the expense of the excluded labor, the disadvantage to laborers as a class exceeding the advantages to special groups.

Time wages represent the price for a certain number of hours of the workers' time; piece wages, a payment for a task accomplished. When labor consists in a series of definite operations, as in the making of certain portions of shoes, the efficiency of labor can be accurately tested by quantity of product. Payment in proportion to product is likely to stimulate the workers to greater effort than payment in proportion to time. The plan is, however, unpopular with most laborers, because they believe that it results in a degree of strain which is injurious to the physical health of the worker; and, moreover, because of a tendency of employers to reduce wages whenever the increased energy of the workers affords them much more than the average rate of pay. From the point of view of society, it is probable that every increase in the efficiency of labor increases the sum of wealth obtained by the working class as a whole; and, therefore, so far as the piece-wage system increases time efficiency, it is advantageous to labor.

So far as the theory of wages rests upon the assumption of free and decisive competition, it is subject at every point to qualifications made necessary by failure to realize the competitive norm. Labor is not completely fluid. Inertia, poverty, and ignorance prevent free movement from place to place and from trade to trade, and nullifies the theoretical bargaining power of labor; therefore the custom of the locality or of the industry plays a larger part in fixing wage levels than pure theory supposes.

Nominal wages increased markedly in all countries after 1914, whether comparison is based on wage rates or actual earnings. In the postwar decade, the principle of high wages became one of the keystones of the American economic system. Several of the States of the United States have established a minimum wage law. So far as can be determined from available statistical data, the relative increase has been especially great in the case of wages of unskilled workers and has made their remuneration in most countries more nearly like that of skilled workers than before World War I. Among skilled workers, there has been considerable variation in the rate and amount of increase in wages; the increase was at first most noticeable in the wage of war workers, and not until later in the wages of those in the building and other trades where production was not actively stimulated until the postwar period.

Foreign observers were amazed at the high standards of living of the American working class and reported that American working populations were earning anywhere from twice to four times as much, in buying power, as were European workers. Undoubtedly, one of the stabilizing effects in the system of installment selling was the ability of the American consuming public to absorb the extraordinary amount of luxury and semiluxury commodities being placed on the market. The earnest efforts, following the stock-market collapse of October, 1929, of industrialists to assure a high level of wages, was one of the most salutary expressions of faith in our modern economic order. President Hoover made the maintenance of wage levels almost his first

Cosima Wagner

concern in the series of industrial conferences he called following the stock break; the response he received from all industry proved the acceptance of the principle. Henry Ford was the first to take action in December, 1929, when he announced a general leveling of wages upward, the minimum wage in his American and Canadian plants being raised from $6 to $7 a day. Edsel Ford estimated that on the basis of the October pay roll of 144,990 employees, the increase would amount to $19,-500,000 a year.

Studies in real wages show that the American manufacturing wage earner was receiving more for his labor in the period following World War I than at any time before in American history. The size of his earned income also demonstrates how pitifully small these earnings are. Even if an additional 10 percent should be added to his wage to include the earnings of members of his family and income from rent, still the total would be a long way from the hypothetical $2000 needed by the average American family to provide the ordinary comforts of life. One of the ironies of the situation is to be found in the fact that this $2000 standard budget is employed by welfare societies in their ministrations of dependent families; economically independent families, not dependent upon charity, are expected to live on much less, and the average wage for the country as a whole was $1280. The industrialists, who support the family welfare societies and therefore give tacit consent at least to the use of the standard budgets for dependents, are the very ones who expect their workers to subsist on smaller budgets.

Interesting in this connection are the various estimates made in regard to the distribution of wealth in this country. The *Conference Board Bulletin* (April 10, 1935) of the National Industrial Conference Board, Inc. stated that the statement that 2% of the people own 60% of the wealth probably was based on a study made by Dr. W.I. King in *The Wealth and Income of the People of the United States* (1915). The Federal Trade Commission in its *National Wealth and Income* (1926), examining data regarding 43,512 estates from county probate court records in a dozen States, computed that about 1% of the deceased owned 59% of the estimated wealth. In 1927, Dr King, reporting on a study made in 1921, concludes that among living gainful workers and recipients of income 2% owned 40% of the nation's wealth.

WAGNALLS, ADAM WILLIS (1843–1924), American minister, lawyer, and publisher, born in Lithopolis, Ohio. After studying for the ministry at Wittenberg College, Springfield, Ohio, he was called as pastor of the first English-speaking Lutheran Church in Kansas City in 1867. He remained there for two years, and then took up the study of law. In 1870 he moved to Atchison, Kansas, serving as city clerk until 1873. In 1876 he moved to New York, resuming his acquaintance with his college classmate, Isaac Funk, who was a publisher and in 1878 joined him in the partnership, I.K. Funk & Co., later organized as a corporation, Funk & Wagnalls Co. He assisted in founding *The Literary Digest* and in projecting *The Standard Dictionary* and *The Jewish Encyclopedia*.

WAGNER, COSIMA (1837–1930), wife of Richard Wagner, the German composer. She was born in Bellagio on Lake Como, Italy, daughter of Franz Liszt, the Hungarian pianist, and the Comtesse Marie d'Agoult. In 1857 she married her father's pupil Hans von Bülow, the orchestra conductor, from whom she was divorced in 1869. A year later she married Wagner, by whom she had three children, Isolde, Eva, and Siegfried. In 1872 she and her husband moved to Bayreuth where, through the patronage of Ludwig II of Bavaria, an opera house was erected for the production of the composer's operas. So profoundly had she penetrated into and assimilated Wagner's ideals that after his death in 1883 she became the leading spirit of Bayreuth, developing the annual festival into a world-famous institution.

WAGNER, HEINRICH LEOPOLD (1747–79), German poet, born in Strasbourg. He made the acquaintance of Goethe while both were students. The friendship was continued at Frankfort. Wagner published two tragedies, *Die Reue nach der That* (1775) and his best work, *Die Kindesmörderin* (1776), both of which discuss social problems. His talent is seen to better advantage in *Prometheus, Deukalion, und seine Rezensenten* (against Goethe's critics) and *Voltaire am Abend Seiner Apotheose*, dramatic satires. Wagner was among the oldest of Goethe's followers, and a typical poet of the so-called storm and stress period.

WAGNER, JOHANNA (1828–94), German dramatic soprano and actress, niece of the German composer Richard Wagner, born in Hanover. Her talent showed itself very early, and she virtually grew up on the stage. At the age of seventeen she created the role of Elisabeth in Wagner's opera *Tannhäuser*. From 1850 to 1861 she was one of the chief artists at the Royal Opera in Berlin. The sudden loss of her voice necessitated her retirement from opera; she appeared with great success as a tragedienne in the spoken drama until her final retirement in 1872.

WAGNER, JOHANN MARTIN VON (1777–1858), German sculptor, born in Würzburg, and trained in sculpture by his father, a sculptor, and in painting in Vienna under the German painter Heinrich Friedrich Füger. In 1840 King Louis I of Bavaria made him director of the gallery in Munich. The bas-relief "An Eleusinian Festival" (1819), the great frieze in the Valhalla (1827–37) in Regensburg, and the classic reliefs and "Triumphal Chariot" on the Siegesthor in Munich are among Wagner's best works.

WAGNER, JOHN PETER HONUS (1874–), popularly known as "Hans" Wagner and by the sobriquet "The Flying Dutchman", American professional baseball player, born in Mansfield (now Carnegie), Pa. In 1896, after playing on a number of minor-league professional teams, Wagner became a member of the Louisville team of the National League, and in 1899 of the Pittsburgh team of the same league. He played shortstop for the Pittsburgh team until retirement from baseball in 1918; in 1933 he became a coach for the Pittsburgh team. Wagner is generally considered the best

Richard Wagner

shortstop in the history of baseball. He was an unerring fielder, led the National League in batting eight times, and led the league in stolen bases five times. During his major-league career he played in 2785 games and had a lifetime batting average of .329. He was elected to the Baseball Hall of Fame in 1936.

WAGNER, RICHARD, in full, WILHELM RICHARD WAGNER (1813–83), German composer, musical theorist, and originator of the music drama, born in Leipzig, and educated at the University of Leipzig. Although Wagner's father is generally considered to have been Friedrich Wilhelm Wagner, a clerk in the Leipzig police court, the eminent Wagnerian scholar Ernest Newman, after exhaustive examination of original documentary material, has advanced the hypothesis that Richard may actually have been Frau Wagner's son by Ludwig Geyer, an itinerant actor whom the composer's mother married soon after the death of her husband. In 1833 Wagner became the conductor of the chorus at the opera house in Würzburg, in northeastern Bavaria. Thereafter, he was successively conductor for brief periods at the opera houses of Magdeburg (1834–36), Königsberg (1836), and Riga (1837–39). During this period, he composed the operas *Die Feen* ("The Fairies", 1833) and *Das Liebesverbot* ("The Forbidden Love", 1836); the overtures *König Enzio* ("King

Enzio", 1832), *Christopher Columbus* (1835), *Rule Brittania* (1836), and *Polonia* (1836); seven songs for the drama *Faust*, by the German poet Johann Wolfgang von Goethe (q.v.); and a *Symphony* in C major (1832). In 1836, while at Königsberg, Wagner married the actress Wilhelmina Planer. At Riga he completed the libretto and the first two acts of his first important opera *Rienzi*, based on the novel of the same name by the English writer Edward George Earle Lytton Bulwer-Lytton (q.v.).

Accompanied by his wife, Wagner sailed in 1839 from Pillau, East Prussia, to London, England. During the tempestuous voyage across the North Sea, he conceived the idea for his second major opera, *Der Fliegende Holländer* ("The Flying Dutchman", completed in 1841). After eight days in London, he traveled to Boulogne, France, whence he finally made his way to Paris. There he remained until April, 1842, at times reduced to the direst poverty. The first version of *Eine Faust Ouvertüre* ("A Faust Overture") was finished in 1840 (revised 1855). Somewhat later, Wagner submitted the score of *Rienzi* to the Court Theater at Dresden, Germany, at which it was produced on October 20, 1842. The success of this work led to the production of *Der Fliegende Holländer* at Dresden on January 2, 1843. In the same month Wagner moved to Dresden, where he became one of the conductors at the Court Theater.

Wagner's music drama *Tannhäuser*, the theme of which was suggested to the composer by his reading of the medieval poem *Der Wartburgkrieg* ("The Wartburg Contest") and *Der Sängerkrieg* ("The Song Contest"), a story by the German romantic writer Ernst Theodor Wilhelm Hoffman, was produced at Dresden on October 19, 1845. This work, with its many experimental innovations in structure and technique, perplexed audiences accustomed to the conventional opera of the day, and elicited a storm of adverse criticism. Nevertheless, *Tannhäuser* was produced at Weimar three years later by the Hungarian composer Franz Liszt, who thenceforth became an enthusiastic proponent of Wagnerian music drama. The meeting of Liszt and Wagner in 1848 resulted in a lifelong friendship. In the same year *Lohengrin* was completed, but the management of the Court Theater at Dresden, apprehensive of public and critical reaction to another work by the composer of *Tannhäuser*, declined to produce it. Liszt once more came to the rescue, and produced *Lohengrin* at Weimar on August 28, 1850.

Throughout the 1840's Wagner was an extreme radical in politics; he participated in the abortive German revolutionary uprising of 1848–49, and, in consequence, was obliged to flee from his homeland, first to Paris, and then to Zurich, Switzerland. There he amplified the sketches, previously begun, for his famous tetralogy of music dramas, known collectively as the *Ring des Nibelungen,* and based upon the 12th-century Middle High German epic poem of the *Nibelungenlied* (q.v.). The texts of the *Nibelung* dramas were written in reverse order. Finding that certain narrative episodes in *Götterdämmerung* ("The Twilight of the Gods"), the final work of the tetralogy, required elaboration and dramatic exposition to make the story altogether comprehensible, Wagner wrote the third part, *Siegfried*. Still not satisfied, however, he wrote *Die Walküre* ("The Valkyries") and, as a further explanatory prelude, *Das Rheingold* ("The Rheingold"). Wagner began work on the score of *Das Rheingold* in November, 1853, completing it in May of the following year. By the end of December, 1854, the score of *Die Walküre* was finished.

Meanwhile, in 1852, Wagner had made the acquaintance of the wealthy merchant Otto Wesendonk and his wife Mathilde. The former placed at the disposal of Wagner and Wilhelmina a small cottage, the *Asyl* (Ger. "Asylum"), on the Wesendonk estate near Zurich; the latter furnished the composer with the inspiration for some of his finest music. Close association between Wagner and Mathilde soon developed into love, the fulfillment of which was thwarted, however, by the jealous vigilance of Wilhelmina, who communicated her suspicions to Otto. Although Wagner and Mathilde were forced to renounce their love, it eventually found transfigured expression in the passionate score of *Tristan und Isolde* (1857–59).

By the summer of 1857 Wagner had virtually completed the second act of *Seigfried*. At this time, however, two circumstances supervened which caused the composer to suspend work on his tetralogy for a period of eleven years. One was the composition of *Tristan und Isolde*; the other was the refusal of the Leipzig music publishers Breitkopf and Härtel to accept the *Ring des Nibelungen* on the ground that the work would be virtually impossible to stage because of its extraordinary length and technical requirements. They expressed their willingness, however, to undertake publication of a less ambitious work, which could be performed in one evening. At the same time Dom Pedro II, Emperor of Brazil, an enthusiastic admirer of *Tannhäuser* and *Lohengrin,* urged Wagner to write an opera for the opera house at Rio de Janeiro. Thus the text of *Tristan und Isolde* was written in August and September of 1857, and two years later the orchestral score was finished. *Tristan* was intended to satisfy the requirement of Breitkopf and Härtel for a work at once shorter and simpler than the *Ring des Nibelungen*; actually, it is, with the exception of *Parsifal,* the longest of all the Wagnerian music dramas and the most difficult to interpret. In Vienna, in 1861, it was pronounced "impossible" to stage after fifty-four rehearsals; and its production could not be effected until June 10, 1865, at Munich, and then only under the auspices of Louis II, King of Bavaria, who had become Wagner's patron.

In 1861 the political ban against Wagner was lifted, largely through the exertions of his admirer, the wife of the Austrian statesman Prince Klemens von Metternich. Upon his return to Germany, the composer settled at Biebrich in southwestern Prussia, where he began work on his only comic opera *Die Meistersinger von Nürnberg* ("The Mastersingers of Nuremberg", completed 1867). In 1863, Wagner wrote a preface to his *Nibelung* dramas, expressing the hope that some German ruler would subsidize the production of the work. The answer to this appeal came in the following year from King Louis of Bavaria. Intrigues at the royal court and in musical circles subsequently made it expedient for the composer to leave Munich, whence he traveled to Lucerne, Switzerland; nevertheless, Louis remained his steadfast patron. *Die Meistersinger von Nürnberg* was produced on June 21, 1868, at Munich, where in 1869 and 1870 *Das Rheingold* and *Die Walküre* also were given by command of the king.

Immediately after the production of *Die Meistersinger* Wagner resumed work on the score of *Siegfried,* completing it in February, 1871. At the same time he began the composition of *Götterdämmerung*. Meanwhile, on August 25, 1870, the composer, who had been separated from his first wife for nine years, married Cosima von Bülow (1837–1930), the divorced wife of the pianist and conductor Hans Guido von Bülow (q.v.) and the daughter of Liszt. When, in the spring of 1872, Wagner took possession of his villa "Wahnfried" at Bayreuth, in Bavaria, the actual composition of the last part of the *Ring des Nibelungen* was finished. The completion of the instrumentation was delayed, however, by many details connected with the erection at Bayreuth of the Festspielhaus ("Festival Theater"), the cornerstone of which was laid on May 22, 1872, the anniversary of Wagner's birth. This theater, designed and constructed especially for the presentation of the Wagnerian music dramas, was financed by contributions from admirers of Wagner's art all over the world, and represented the fulfillment of the composer's most cherished dream. In November, 1874, the orchestration of *Götterdämmerung* was finally completed. The next summer rehearsals began, and on August 13, 14, 15, and 17, 1876, the premier performance of the whole tetralogy took place at the Festspielhaus under the direction of the German conductor Hans Richter (q.v.). In 1877 Wagner began work on his religious festival play *Parsifal*. This work, based upon the legends of the Holy Grail contained in the metrical romance *Parzival* by the Middle High German poet Wolfram von Eschenbach (q.v.), was not completed until January, 1882. Under the direction of the German conductor Hermann Levi (1839–1900), the last of the Wagnerian music dramas was given its first performance on July 26, 1882.

Toward the close of 1882 the composer's health began to fail. Thinking to benefit from a change of climate, he rented the Palazzo Vendramin on the Grand Canal in Venice; he died there suddenly on February 13th of the following year. Five days later his body was interred in the mausoleum of his Bayreuth villa. In addition to the works already mentioned, Wagner also composed the song cycle, *Fünf Gedichte von Mathilde Wesendonk* ("Five Poems by Mathilde Wesendonk", 1857–58), consisting of *Der Engel* ("The Angel"), *Träume* ("Dreams"), *Schmerzen* ("Sorrows"), *Stehe Still* ("Rest Tranquil"), and *Im Treibhaus* ("In the Greenhouse"); and the orchestral work *Siegfried Idyll* (1870), composed for his wife Cosima. His theoretical and critical writings include *On German Music* (1840), *The Art Work of the Future* (1849), *Judaism in Music* (1850), *Opera and Drama* (1850–51), *The Music of the Future* (1860), *Religion and Art* (1880), *On Conducting* (1869), *On the Application of Music to the Drama* (1879), and *A Communication to My Friends* (1851). Wagner also wrote an autobiography, *Mein Leben* ("My Life", 1865–80).

Wagner's reputation is based not only upon his musical creations, which represent the highest expression of romanticism (q.v.) in European music, but also upon the revolution he effected in both the theory and practice of operatic composition. He began his career as a composer of operas in the conventional manner, but by the time he started work on the *Ring des Nibelungen* he was creating an entirely new musico-dramatic form. The true line of development of the Wagnerian music drama is from Greek drama through the dramas of William Shakespeare and Johann Christoph Friedrich von Schiller (qq.v.). On the purely musical side its lineal evolution is from Johann Sebastian Bach through Ludwig van Beethoven (qq.v.). The fundamental principle of the music drama is the leitmotiv, or leading motive (see MOTIVE), by means of which a continuous thematic development is achieved. This thematic development is absent from the pre-Wagnerian opera, which, lacking the dynamic and unifying principle of the leitmotiv, is little more than a static succession of stereotyped arias, recitatives, duets, interludes, and finales, each formally complete in itself. The reform effected in traditional opera is not due to any direct, intentional effort on the part of Wagner, but rather to the tremendous influence of his art on every form of music. For a detailed discussion of Wagner's work and its historical significance, see MUSIC; OPERA.

WAGNER, ROBERT FERDINAND (1877–), American lawyer and legislator, born in Germany. He came to the United States in childhood. A member of the New York assembly, 1905–08 and of the State senate, 1909–18, he was a justice of the N.Y. Supreme Court, 1919–26. He resigned from the bench to take a U.S. Senate seat. Wagner introduced a series of social and economic laws in the Senate, among them the National Labor Relations Act, Social Security Act, U.S. Housing Act of 1937, and "from the cradle to the grave" social insurance (q.v.) plan, 1943. In 1933 he was chairman of the National Industrial Recovery Adjustment Board. He resigned from the Senate in 1949 because of ill-health.

WAGNER, RUDOLF (1805–64), German physiologist, born in Bayreuth, and educated at the universities of Erlangen and Würzburg. He went to Erlangen in 1829, and became professor of zoölogy there in 1833. From 1840 till his death he occupied a chair at Göttingen. Wagner discovered the germinal spot in the human ovum. In his later years he became a defender of Christianity and an opponent of materialism, his writings in this field leading to a controversy with Karl Vogt.

Wagner was also known as an anthropologist and archeologist. Among his writings are *Lehrbuch der Vergleichenden Anatomie* (1834–35), republished under the title *Lekrbuch der Zoötomie* (1843–47); *Lehrbuch der Physiologie* (1839); *Handwörterbuch der Physiologie* (1842–55); and *Neurologische Untersuchungen* (1854).

WAGNER, SIEGFRIED (1869–1930), German composer and orchestra conductor, son of Richard and Cosima Wagner, born in Triebschen, near Lucerne, Switzerland. Although destined by his father for an architect's career, he early determined to become a musician, studying under Kniese and Humperdinck. In 1893 he entered upon his career as an orchestra conductor, touring through Germany, Austria, Italy, and England, where he met with marked success as an interpreter of the works of his father.

In 1896 he became codirector, with his mother, of the Wagnerian Festival Playhouse in Bayreuth, and in that year won general favor by his work as conductor of *Der Ring des Nibelungen.* In 1914, Mme. Schumann-Heink had just completed a solo in *Parsifal* at the annual Bayreuth festival when news came that war had been declared. The production was dramatically stopped, and the festivals discontinued until 1924. In 1924 Siegfried Wagner assumed general direction of the Bayreuth festival and the playhouse, due to the advanced age and precarious health of his mother. His principal works are the operas *Der Bärenhäuter* (1899), *Herzog Wildfang* (1901), *Der Kobold* (1904), *Bruder Lustig* (1905), *Das Sternengebot* (1908), *Banadietrich* (1910), *An Allem Ist Hütchen Schuld* (1917), *Schwarzschwanenreich* (1918), *Sonnenflammen* (1918), *Der Schmied von Marienburg* (1920), and *Der Friedensengel* (1926). In 1922 he published his memoirs under the title *Erinnerungen.*

WAGNER VON JAUREGG, JULIUS (1857– 1940), Austrian psychiatrist. He was professor of psychiatry and neurology at Graz University, 1889–93, and at Vienna University, 1893–1938. His malarial inoculation treatment of paresis, introduced in 1917, cured about 30 percent of all patients treated. The disease was previously fatal. For this he was awarded the Nobel Prize in medicine in 1927. He introduced the treating of cretinism with thyroid gland preparations and goiter with iodine.

WAGONER, county seat of Wagoner Co., Okla., situated 15 miles N. of Muskogee. It is served by three railroads. The city is surrounded by an agricultural area, which also contains fields of oil and natural gas. Among the industrial establishments in the city are chick hatcheries, feed mills, cotton gins, a cottonseed-oil mill, and factories producing brick and clay products. Pop. (1940) 3535.

WAGRAM, a village of Lower Austria, 11 miles N.E. of Vienna. On Jnly 5–6, 1809, the Austrians were defeated by Napoleon at Wagram.

WAGTAIL, family (Motacillidae) and genus (*Motacilla*) of Passerine birds. The genus *Motacilla,* the true wagtails, includes about thirty species, of which eight are European. They frequent open and well-cultivated districts, where they are found on banks of streams and ponds and in pastures. They are almost exclusively terrestrial in habits. The pied wagtail *M. yarrelli* or *lugubris,* is from 7 to 8 in. long, and has beautifully marked white and black plumage. A variety of *M. alba* occurring in Alaska is the only true wagtail found in the New World.

WAHABIS, a Moslem sect, named after its founder, Mohammed Abd al Wahhab. He seems to have been born in 1704 (1116 A.H.), probably in Ayane in the District of Arid, Nejd, central Arabia, and died in Deriye in 1792 (1206 A.H.). He became a staunch supporter of the Koran and Sunna, and an opponent of the Ijma', or consensus of opinion, and the Bida', or novelty. His stern preaching and ascetic life were not calculated to win for him a ready adherence in Nejd where people cared little for religion, and he was forced to leave both Ayane and Horeimle. In Deriye, however, he made a convert of the ruler, Mohammed ibn Sa'ud, in 1746. Before his death in 1765 this emir of Deriye had extended his power and the influence of Abd al Wahhab through the neighboring towns. But Riad was not finally captured until 1772 by his successor Abd al Aziz (1765–1803). Mohammed Abd al Wahhab himself never sought political power; he remained to the end a warner and a spiritual guide, faithful to the Koran and tradition as interpreted by the Hanbalite school, and fighting all innovations, such as the mention of Mohammed and other men in prayer, and the veneration of local saints, as well as all luxury, the use of tobacco, music, dancing, and gambling.

Abd al Aziz spread the power of the Wahabite state beyond the boundaries of Nejd. In 1801 he sent his son Sa'ud to Kerbelah, the greatest shrine of the Shiites, and he destroyed the sanctuary, killed the priests, and brought back enormous booty. Mecca was plundered in 1803; but in that year Abd al Aziz was murdered at Deriye by a Shiite in revenge for the destruction of Husain's shrine. Sa'ud (1803–14) captured Medina in 1804 and in 1810 opened Mohammed's grave and carried away its treasures; at Mecca he cut the black stone of the Ka'bah to pieces. In 1811 Damascus was held for ransom, and the territory east of Jordan paid tribute. Then Mahmud II directed Mehemet Ali, Viceroy of Egypt, to restore Turkish authority in Arabia. He first sent his son Tusun, who after an initial defeat captured Jidda, Mecca, and Medina in 1812; then Mehemet Ali came himself and defeated the Wahabis at Bessel in 1815; finally Ibrahim Pasha was sent, and he destroyed Deriye after a long siege in 1818. The brave defender, Abdallah ibn Sa'ud, was put to death in Constantinople (now Istanbul). About 1820 the Egyptian governor was overthrown, and Turki made himself independent emir in Riad. He was succeeded by his son Faizal (1830–36), and he by his brother Abdallah (about 1866–92). See also ABDUL AZIZ IBN SAUD; ARABIA.

WAHOO. See SPINDLE TREE.

WAHOO, county seat of Saunders Co., Nebr., situated on Cottonwood Creek, 35 miles w. of Omaha. It is served by three railroads, and is the center and shipping point of a rich agricultural area yielding corn, wheat, and livestock. Industrial establishments in the city include stockyards, bottling works, and factories producing cement blocks and other cement products. Wahoo is the site of Luther College, a junior college established in 1883. Pop. (1940) 2648.

WAHPETON, county seat of Richland Co., N.Dak., situated on the Red River of the North, 45 miles s. of Fargo. It is served by three railroads and maintains a municipal airport. The city is the trading center of a rich agricultural area, noted for the production of grain, poultry, dairy products, and cattle. The principal industries in Wahpeton are printing and binding, the processing of agricultural products, and the manufacture of foundry and machine-shop products, culvert pipes, and pottery. Wahpeton is the site of the North Dakota State School of Science and of a U.S. Indian School. Recreational facilities are provided by Chahinkapa Park. Wahpeton was settled about 1865 and was known as Chahinkapa until 1893. It was incorporated as a city in 1885. Pop. (1948 est.) 5020.

WAIKATO, the principal river of the North Island of New Zealand. It flows first into Lake Taupo, and then northward to Port Waikato,

25 miles s. of Manakau Harbor. The river is 220 miles in length.

WAILING WALL. See PLACE OF WAILING.

WAINSCOT, a wooden lining or covering of an interior wall, usually paneled. The term originally was applied in Great Britain to oak of superior quality imported and used for panels. Eventually any wooden covering or facing of a wall of an apartment, especially when of elaborate workmanship, came to be known as a wainscot or wainscoting. See DADO.

WAINWRIGHT, JONATHAN MAYHEW (1793–1854), American clergyman, born of American parentage in Liverpool, England. From 1819 to 1834 he had charge of churches in New York City, and was assistant in charge of St. John's Chapel, Trinity Parish, from 1838 to 1852, when he was consecrated provisional bishop of New York City.

WAINWRIGHT, JONATHAN MAYHEW (1864–   ), American congressman, born in New York City. He was a member of the New York assembly from 1902 to 1908, of the senate from 1909 to 1913, and was assistant secretary of war from 1921 to 1923. He represented the 25th District of New York in Congress from 1923 to 1931.

WAINWRIGHT, JONATHAN MAYHEW (1883–   ), U.S. Army officer, born in Walla Walla, Wash., and educated at the U.S. Military Academy at West Point, New York. He was promoted through the ranks, becoming major general in 1941. He received the Distinguished Service Cross early in 1942. Succeeding to the Philippine command in March, 1942, he was captured by the Japanese at the end of this campaign. Wainwright remained a prisoner of war until 1945, when he was rescued in Manchuria. He was made a general in 1945, and became commander of the 4th Army in 1946.

WAINWRIGHT, RICHARD (1849–1926), American naval officer, born in Washington, D.C. He attained the rank of rear admiral in 1908. He was executive officer of the *Maine* from 1897 until it was blown up in Havana Harbor in 1898. During the Spanish-American War he commanded the *Gloucester,* and won distinction for the services he rendered in the destruction of Cervera's squadron off Santiago. In 1900–02 he was superintendent of the Naval Academy, was commander of the second division of the Atlantic fleet in its voyage to the Pacific and back (1908–9), and was commander of the third division (1909–10). He retired in 1911.

WAITS, name originally applied in England to watchmen who sounded horns and afterward to bands of musicians and carol singers at Christmas time.

WAITZ, GEORG (1813–86), German historian, born in Flensburg, and educated at the universities of Kiel and Berlin. He became professor at Kiel in 1842, member of the German National Assembly in 1848, and professor at Göttingen in 1849. In 1875 he became member of the Academy in Berlin, and director of the reorganized *Monumenta Germaniæ Historica.*

WAKAMATSU, a town of Fukushima prefecture, Japan, situated on Honshu Island, about 75 m. from Sendai. Its chief industry is the manufacture of lacquer ware. Pop., about 50,000.

WAKASHAN, name applied to an Indian tribal group, of Vancouver Island.

WAKAYAMA, town and port of Honshu Island, Japan, 35 miles s.s.w. of Osaka. It is an important trade center. Pop. (1945) 147,523.

WAKE, the English equivalent of the ecclesiastical vigil; a name for English festival celebrations, preceded by a night vigil. The saint's-day festivals are still kept in many English parishes under the name of country wakes. A lykewake or lichwake is a watching of a dead body all night by the friends and neighbors of the deceased. This watching, called simply a wake, still persists as a common custom among the humbler Irish. It no doubt originated in superstitious fear either of passing the night alone with a dead body, or of its being interfered with by evil spirits. See FUNERAL RITES.

WAKEFIELD, a town of Middlesex Co., Mass., situated about 10 m. by rail N. of Boston. The principal industries are the manufacture of shoes, knit goods, clock and indicator hands, and iron pipe. Notable buildings in the town include the Hartshorne House, built in 1663, and the town hall, presented by Cyrus Wakefield (1811–73), who established a rattan furniture factory at Wakefield. The site of the present town was first settled in 1639. Until 1812 it was part of Reading; in that year it was separately incorporated as South Reading, and in 1868 it received its present name in honor of Cyrus Wakefield. Pop. (1950) 19,600.

WAKEFIELD, capital of the West Riding of Yorkshire, England, situated on the Calder R., 10 miles s. of Leeds. It has manufactures of woolens, worsteds, and hosiery, as also of agricultural implements, and machinery.

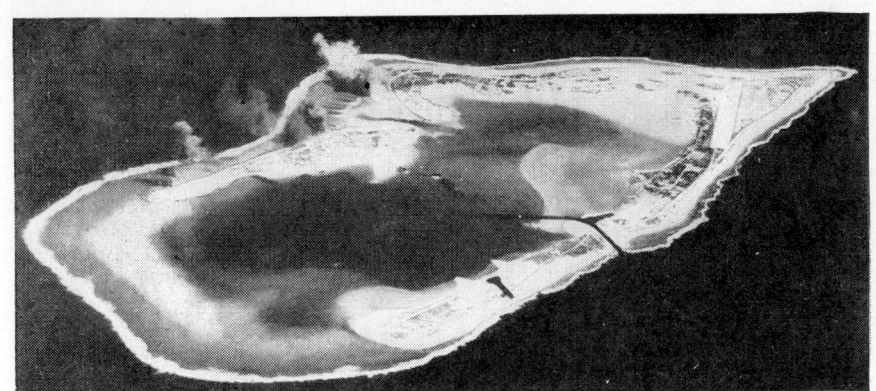

Aerial view of Wake Island during an attack by U.S. bombers in World War II

The chief event in the history of Wakefield is the Yorkist defeat in the Wars of the Roses on December 30, 1460. Pop., about 59,000.

WAKEFIELD, EDWARD GIBBON (1796–1862), British colonial statesman, born in London. In 1834 he assisted in the colonization of South Australia. He was private secretary to Lord Durham in Canada in 1838, and from 1839 to 1849 was manager of the New Zealand Land Company, which colonized New Zealand. He was founder of the Church of England colony at Canterbury.

WAKEFIELD, GILBERT (1756–1801), English classical scholar, born in Nottingham, and educated at Jesus College, Cambridge University. In 1778 he was ordained a deacon in the Church of England, but after holding for a brief time two curacies, he gave up his profession owing to his inability to subscribe to the doctrine of the Trinity. He turned to teaching for support, becoming classical tutor in Warrington Academy (1779–83) and in the dissenting college at Hackley (1790–91). Resigning this position on account of his objection to public worship (elaborated in *An Enquiry into the Expediency and Propriety of Public or Social Worship,* 1791), he devoted the rest of his life to study and controversy. He wrote a reply to the American deist Thomas Paine's *Age of Reason* (1795), and was imprisoned for two years (1799–1801) in Dorchester jail for seditious libel contained in a violent *Reply* to Bishop Richard Watson's *Address to the People of Great Britain.* Wakefield's scholarship is well represented by a critical edition of *Lucretius* (3 vols., 1796–99), and *Silva Critica* (1789–95), an attempt to illustrate the Scriptures "by light borrowed from the philology of Greece and Rome". Among his other works are a translation of the New Testament (1792); a group of Greek tragedies edited under the title of *Tragœdiarum Delectus* (1794); editions of the works of ancient Roman poets, including Vergil's *Georgica* (1788), of Horace (1794), Moschus (1795); and a treatise on Greek meters called *Noctes Carcerariæ* (1801).

WAKE FOREST COLLEGE, a partly coeducational, privately maintained institution of higher education under the control of the Baptist Church, situated in Wake Forest, N.C. It was chartered in 1833 as the Wake Forest Institute, and opened for instruction in 1834; the present name was adopted in 1838. The institute consists of a group of fifteen independent schools, devoted to Latin, Greek, English, modern languages, mathematics, astronomy, chemistry, biology, physics, moral philosophy, history and political science, the Bible, pedagogy, law, and medicine; courses are offered leading to the degrees of B.A., B.S., B.S. in business administration, LL.B., M.D., and M.A. The medical course is given at the affiliated Bowman Gray School of Medicine, situated in Winston Salem, N.C., 110 miles from the main campus. An accelerated course permits students to earn undergraduate degrees in three instead of the normal four years. Women are admitted to the professional schools of the institute. In a recent year over 2000 students were enrolled, and the faculty numbered about 125.

WAKE ISLAND, a coral atoll in the central Pacific Ocean, situated 2004 miles w. of Hawaii and 1334 miles N.E. of Port Apra, Guam. It comprises a group of three islets (Wake, Peale, and Wilkes) which enclose a

Selman Abraham Waksman
John Wiley & Sons

shallow lagoon. The total land area is 2600 acres. A thick growth of umbrella hardwood covers the higher portions of the atoll and the shores consist of sand beaches and coral rocks. The atoll was discovered in 1796 and formally occupied by the U.S. in 1898. In 1934 Wake was placed under the jurisdiction of the U.S. Navy Department, and in 1935 Pan American Airways established a base on the atoll to serve its clipper planes on their flights between the U.S. and the Orient. During 1939 the U.S. Congress appropriated special funds for the construction of a naval air base and a submarine base on Wake. Other measures were taken to fortify the island in the event of war in the Pacific

On Dec. 9, 1941, immediately after the Japanese surprise attack on Pearl Harbor, Japanese air and naval forces attacked Wake Island. For a period of two weeks the island garrison, consisting of 377 U.S. Marines equipped with light armament and a few planes, and aided by about 1000 civilians employed in strengthening the atoll's defenses, fought off a combined air and naval attack and succeeded in sinking a cruiser, three destroyers, and a submarine, destroying approximately 12 planes, and damaging other warships. The defense of Wake Island against overwhelming odds is one of the most heroic achievements in American military history. The garrison's commander, Major James P.S. Devereux, was in constant radio communication with Washington, D.C. On the day of the successful Japanese landing on Wake, the message, "The issue is in doubt," was heard. On Dec. 24th the epic resistance of the Marines ended with the capture of Wake. The U.S. flag was again raised over Wake Island on Sept. 4, 1945, following the Japanese surrender in World War II. Devereux and the survivors were freed after the close of the war.

WAKEMAN, HENRY OFFLEY (1852–99), English historical writer, educated at Christ Church, Oxford University. His life was passed at Oxford. He became a tutor in Keble College, and afterward fellow and bursar of All Souls. His *Introduction to the History of the Church of England* (1896) is regarded as the standard work from the Anglican point of view. Next to this comes *The Church and the Puritans, 1570–1660* (1887). Among his other works are *History of Religion in England* (1885); *Europe, 1598–1715* (1894); and *Life of Charles James Fox* (1890).

WAKE ROBIN. See TRILLIUM.

WAKIDI (747–823), one of the first biographers of Mohammed. Unsuccessful as a merchant, he finally gained patronage in Bagdad, and found opportunity for his literary labors. His chief work is the *Kitāb al maghāzi*, or "Book of the Campaigns of Mohammed".

WAKLEY, THOMAS (1795–1862), English surgeon and reformer, born in Membury, Devonshire. In 1823 he founded the *Lancet*, a weekly medical journal which became famous, and through which he made many bitter enemies, but accomplished much good. He attacked abuses in his profession and especially in the College of Surgeons. From 1835 till 1852, while a member of the House of Commons, he carried through many humanitarian reforms. In 1851 he began in the *Lancet* a crusade against adulterated foods which resulted in legislation to correct the evil.

WAKONDA, a Sioux Indian term now found in general literature and expressing a native religious concept of the essential supernatural element in the universe. It appears in various forms, as *wakonda, wakanda,* and *wakan,* according to the dialects of the various Siouan tribes. Such a concept is not peculiar to the Sioux, for there are the almost parallel terms *orenda* (Iroquois), *manitou* (Algonquian), *tirawa* (Pawnee), *natosiwa* (Blackfoot).

WAKSMAN, SELMAN ABRAHAM (1888–), Russian-American microbiologist, born

Two peasant women of Walcheren Island wearing their native headgear

in Priluki, Kiev, Russia. He emigrated to the U.S. in 1910, and was educated at Rutgers University and the University of California. Following graduation he served as biologist at the Takamine biochemical laboratories in Clifton, N.J., and in addition was appointed lecturer in soil microbiology at Rutgers, at which he became associate professor in 1924 and professor in 1930. He also held the posts of microbiologist at the New Jersey Agricultural Experiment Station after 1921, and of marine bacteriologist at Woods Hole Oceanographic Institution after 1930. Waksman is noted for his discovery of the drug streptomycin (q.v.), and for the discovery and development of several other antibiotic agents, which he isolated from microorganisms. He has also done important research in the biology of soil microorganisms. He served as president of the International Congress of Microbiologists in 1947, and was elected a member of the National Academy of Sciences, the National Research Council, the Swedish Academy of Agriculture, and the French Academy of Sciences. His works include *Principles of Soil Microbiology* (1932), *Humus* (1938), and *Microbial Antagonisms and Antibiotic Substances* (1945).

WALACHIA, or WALLACHIA. See ROMANIA.

WALAFRID STRABO (about 808–49), medieval German monk and scholar. At an early age he went to the famous cloister of Reichenau for his education, and entered the Benedictine Order at the age of fifteen. He spent about three years at Fulda under Rabanus Maurus and then returned to the imperial court as instructor of the young son of Louis the Pious. As a reward, the emperor bestowed on him the Abbey of Reichenau (838). In the contest that followed the death of Louis, Walafrid, like Rabanus, took the side of German unity as represented by Lothair; he was obliged to leave his abbey, but recovered it in 842. Little is known of his life after this. He was of a poetical nature, and left some notable verse, distinguished by elevation of thought. His name is even better known for his *Glossa Ordinaria,* partly a compilation, but the most popular commentary on Scripture throughout the Middle Ages.

WALAPAI or **HUALAPAI,** tribe of Yuman stock originally residing about the Great Bend of the Colorado and extending eastward into Arizona.

WALCHEREN, an island belonging to the province of Zeeland, the Netherlands, and situated at the mouth of the Scheldt R. The Sloe, which is bridged, passes between it and the island of South Beveland on the east. The island, about 12 m. in diameter, is protected from the sea by dunes and dikes, and is very fertile. Middelburg, Vlissingen, and Flushing are the chief towns. Walcheren was the scene of a British military disaster during the Napoleonic Wars. In July, 1809, a British fleet comprising nearly 250 vessels of war and 400 transports carrying some 40,000 men, set sail for Holland with the intention of seizing Antwerp and obtaining command of the Scheldt. Criminal negligence was displayed in the preparations for the expedition, and both Sir Richard Strachan, the naval commander, and the Earl of Chatham, who was placed at the head of the land forces, were markedly incapable. Valuable time was wasted in the reduction of Flushing, and not until late in August was Chatham prepared to march on Antwerp. By that time, however, the French forces in Holland had been greatly strengthened, and the British commander deemed it inexpedient to pursue the campaign. The French assumed the offensive and in the first days of September the British abandoned Flushing. Chatham, with part of the forces, returned to England, leaving 15,000 men on the island of Walcheren. There the swamp fever played havoc with the men, and the medical authorities were utterly incompetent to combat the ravages of the disease. The island was finally abandoned in the latter part of December, the results of the expedition being a loss of 7000 dead and the permanent disablement of half of the remainder. Area, about 82 sq.m.; pop., about 66,000.

WALCOTT, CHARLES DOOLITTLE (1850–1927), American geologist and paleontologist, born in New York Mills, N.Y. In 1876 he became one of the assistants in the Geological Survey of the State of New York, and three years afterward entered the service of the United States Geological Survey, of which he was the director from 1894 to 1907. In 1897–98 he was at the head of the National Museum, and in 1905–07 served also as director of the United States Reclamation Service. He was secretary of the Carnegie Institution in 1902–05, and secretary of the Smithsonian Institution after 1907. He became president of the Geological Society of America in 1901.

WALCOTT, HENRY PICKERING (1838–1932), American surgeon and officer of public health, born in Salem, Mass., and educated at Harvard and Bowdoin colleges. He served as surgeon in the Civil War, and was health officer of Massachusetts, serving on the State Board of Health, Lunacy, and Charity until 1885. He was chairman of the State Board of Health until 1914.

WALD, LILLIAN D. (1867–1940), American social worker, born in Ohio. In 1893 she became president and head worker of the Henry Street Settlement, New York (also known as the Nurses' Settlement). The National Institute of Social Sciences awarded her its gold medal. She published *The House on Henry Street* (1915).

WALDECK, COUNT GEORG FRIEDRICH (1620–92), German soldier and statesman, born in Arolsen. In 1656 he was active in bringing about the League of Marienburg with Sweden against Poland. In 1664, as a field marshal, he distinguished himself at St. Gotthard against the Turks; in 1682 for services against the French he received the title of prince; and in 1683 he helped to drive the Turkish army from before Vienna. In 1689 he was put in command of the allied forces in the Netherlands. In the same year he gained a success at Walcourt over the French under Marshal d'Humières, but in 1690 he was badly defeated by Marshal Luxembourg at Fleurus.

WALDECK-PYRMONT, or WALDECK, a small State of Germany, absorbed by Prussia in 1929.

WALDECK-ROUSSEAU, PIERRE MARIE RENÉ (1846–1904), French statesman, born in Nantes. For ten years (1879–89) he represented Rennes in the Chamber of Deputies, became minister of the interior in Gambetta's cabinet (1881), and during 1883–85 held the same office in Jules Ferry's cabinet, when he showed himself the possessor of great administrative abilities. In 1894 he was elected senator for the department of the Loire, became the recognized leader of the Moderate Republicans, and on the fall of the Dupuy cabinet (1899) formed a coalition cabinet. He permitted the Dreyfus case to be reopened, and was chiefly instrumental in securing the passage of the Amnesty Bill (1900), but the most important measure passed during his administration was the Associations Bill (1901). He resigned in June, 1902, with the prestige of having held office longer than any other premier since the establishment of the Third Republic.

WALDEN, a small lake in Massachusetts made famous by Thoreau. See THOREAU, HENRY DAVID.

WALDEN, a village of Orange Co., N.Y., situated on the Wallkill R., about 55 m. by rail N.W. of New York City. It is in a fertile farming area, and is a manufacturing center. The principal industries are the manufacture of engines, cutlery, paper bags, hats, and underwear. The site of the present village was settled before 1768. Walden was incorporated as a village in 1855. Pop. (1940) 4262.

WALDENBURG or (Pol.) **WALBRZYCH**, a city of the department of Wroclaw, s.w. Poland, 42 miles s.w. of Wroclaw. Waldenburg was a part of Germany until 1945, when the Potsdam Conference (q.v.) assigned the city to Poland. It has porcelain, pottery, and glass works, and coal mines. Pop. (1946) 66,372.

WALDENSES, VALDENSES, or VAUDOIS, a Christian community which grew out of an antisacerdotal movement originated by Peter Waldo, a rich merchant of Lyons, in the second half of the 12th century. His followers were known as the "poor men of Lyons". The archbishop of Lyons vainly forbade them to preach; Pope Alexander III gave them a modified approval, but Lucius III and Innocent III anathematized them. In southern France they became involved in the destruction of the Albigenses. Their principal seats were the vastnesses of the Cottian Alps. After the Cathari were crushed they became the victims of the Inquisition in France. Persecutions continued in 1432 and later years. In 1488 Innocent VIII organized a crusade against them in both Dauphiné and Savoy. Louis XII stopped the proceedings, with consent of Pope Alexander VI. Their remnants continued more or less under disguise of Catholicism, until they finally merged with the Calvinists after the Reformation.

In 1740 they secured some indulgence, but there was little change in their position, although there was also little persecution, up to the time of the French Revolution. In 1799 liberty of conscience was proclaimed. After the fall of Napoleon in 1814 there was a reaction under Victor Emmanuel I. Finally, in 1848, under Charles Albert, the Waldenses acquired civil and religious liberty. In 1855 they founded a school of theology in Torre Pellice, which was removed to Florence in 1860. The Waldenses have about sixty organized churches throughout Italy and several settlements associated with their church in the United States. They are also found in Uruguay and Argentina.

WALDERSEE, COUNT ALFRED VON (1832–1904), German soldier, born in Potsdam. He entered the army in 1850 and at the beginning of the Franco-Prussian War was an aide-de-camp to the king of Prussia. He was at the battle of Gravelotte, and became chief of the staff to the grand duke of Mecklenburg. When peace came he was appointed chargé d'affaires in Paris, in 1882 became quartermaster general of the Prussian staff, and in 1888 succeeded Moltke as chief of staff. In 1900 he became field marshal. In August of that year he took command of the German forces in China, and was made commander in chief of the allied forces engaged in suppressing the Boxer uprising in that country.

WALDIS, BURKARD (1490–1556?), German fabulist, born in Allendorf, Hesse. He became a monk, but afterward turned Protestant, and suffered persecution. After many vicissitudes he became pastor in Abterode (1544). His first important literary production, the drama *Die Parabel vom Verlornen Sohn,* was performed in Riga in 1527. He is remembered for his *Esopus Ganz Neu Gemacht und in Reimen Gefasst* (1548). Among other works was a paraphrase of the Psalter in verse, composed in prison, and published in 1553.

WALDMÜLLER, FERDINAND GEORG (1793–1865), Austrian landscape, portrait, and genre painter, born in Vienna, and trained at the Academy there. After traveling in Italy and Germany, Waldmüller settled in his native city, where he became professor at the Academy. He owed his popularity during his lifetime to his genre scenes of peasant life in Lower Austria, such as "Soup Day at the Convent" (Vienna Museum) and "After School" (Kaiser Friedrich Museum). His "Ruins at Schönbrunn" is in the Vienna Gallery, which also contains fine examples of his portraiture.

WALDO, PETER. See WALDENSES.

WALDO, SAMUEL LOVETT (1783–1861), American portrait painter, born in Windham, Conn. After painting portraits in Charleston, S.C., he went to London in 1806 to become a pupil of Benjamin West. On his return in 1809 he opened a studio in New York, and rapidly acquired popularity as a portrait painter. His sitters included Peter Remsen and David Grim (both in New York Historical Society), and Andrew Jackson (Metropolitan Museum of Art, New York City). About 1812 he formed a partnership with his pupil William Jewett, which lasted eighteen years. Among the numerous portraits which they painted jointly is that of Rev. Dr. Gardner Spring (Metropolitan Museum).

WALDOBORO, a town of Lincoln County, Me., situated on Muscongus Bay, about 19 miles w. of Rockland. The population is largely engaged in granite quarrying and canning. Pop. (1940) 2497.

Public building in the city of Cardiff, Wales
British Information Services

WALDSEEMÜLLER, or WALTZEMÜLLER, MARTIN (1470?–1518?), German geographer and the most distinguished cartographer of his time, born in Freiburg. In 1506 he and some compatriots matured a plan for a new edition of the work of Ptolemy, revised and amended so as to include the results of recent discovery. In the following year Waldseemüller published a large map of the world in twelve sheets and finished a small treatise, published under the title of *Cosmographiæ Introductio* on the college press in the same year. The work is famous because in it Waldseemüller said: "But now the parts have been more extensively explored and another fourth part has been discovered by Americus Vespucius (as will appear from what follows); wherefore I do not see what is rightly to hinder us from calling it Amerige or America, i.e., the land of Americus, after its discoverer Americus."

WALDSTEIN, SIR CHARLES (1856–1927), British-American archeologist, born in New York City. From 1880 he was identified with Cambridge University, being reader in classical archeology (1883–1907), director of the Fitzwilliam Museum (1883–89), Slade professor of fine art (1895–1901; 1904–11), and lecturer at King's College. In addition he served as director of the American School of Classical Studies in Athens (1889–93). While in this office he discovered that the so-called "Apollos" are simply statues of athletes. In 1883 he lectured before the Royal Institution and in 1886 at Columbia University. In 1912 he was knighted. Among his works are *Essays on the Art of Phidias* (1885), *Excavations at the Heraion of Argos* (1892), and *Greek Sculpture and Modern Art* (1914).

WALDTEUFEL, ÉMILE (1837–1915), French composer, trained at the Paris Conservatoire. Because of the immediate success of his dance forms (waltzes), he continued to produce several hundred.

WALES, historical division of the United Kingdom of Great Britain and Ireland, administratively a part of England. Wales extends 136 m. from N. to S. and has a breadth varying from 36 to 96 m. Area, 7446 sq.m. The northwestern corner is cut off by Menai Strait to form the island of Anglesey. Snowdon, the highest point of Wales, is 3590 ft. Pop., about 2,063,000. The mineral deposits are extensive and valuable, including coal, iron, copper, zinc, tin, lead, and gold. Of these the most important by far is coal, amounting in value to about 85 percent of the mineral output of Wales and in quantity to about 20 percent of the coal supply of the United Kingdom. There are two coal fields, the north, in Denbigh and Flint, and the south, more than

British Info. Ser.; Black Star
Top: Typical Welsh mining village. Bottom: Welsh miners at Windsor Colliery, Senghenydd.

British Info. Ser.; Black Star
Top: Harlech Castle in Wales. Bottom: Happy Valley, on Menai Strait, Caernarvon, Wales.

Country scene in the county of Merionethshire, Wales
British Information Services

half in Glamorgan and the rest in Carmarthen, Pembroke, Brecknock, and the English county Monmouth. Cardiff has become the largest coal-exporting port in the world. See UNITED KINGDOM.

History. The earliest inhabitants of Wales, as of the rest of Britain, are supposed to have been of non-Caucasic origin. These were succeeded by Celts, possibly first of the Gaelic division, although in the earliest historic times Wales, like Britain, was occupied by Cymric or Brythonic Celts. At the time of the coming of the Romans, 55 B.C., the tribes of Wales represented a mixture of the primitive Iberians with the later invading Celts. They bore the general name of Cymry.

After a long struggle the subjugation of these tribes was accomplished under Vespasian. The Celtic inhabitants of Britain, fleeing before the wave of Anglo-Saxon invasion, took refuge in the Welsh mountains, where, in time, they were merged with their native kinsmen and maintained their independence against the Teuton conquerors. The country was divided into several states, of which Gwynedd, Gwent, Dyved, and Powys were the most important.

In 1062–64 Harold, the son of Godwin, overran Wales with an English army after a struggle with Llewellyn ap Griffith, King of Gwynedd. William the Conqueror succeeded in forcing the recognition of his sovereignty from the Welsh princes, but this did not prevent them from raiding the English border, for protection of which the early Norman kings erected a number of feudal lordships with very extensive powers, the so-called lords of the marchers. The marchers were a turbulent class and a source of trouble to the kings, but they served their purpose in holding the Welsh back. In 1136 the Welsh won a victory over Henry I, but were again reduced to homage by Henry II. Llewellyn, Prince of North Wales, sided with Simon de Montfort against Henry III, but later submitted to the king. In 1273, however, he refused to pay homage to the new king, Edward I, who in 1276 invaded Wales and at Rhuddian compelled Llewellyn to submit to humiliating terms, including the surrender of the eastern portion of his lands and the annual acknowledgment of fealty. Llewellyn rose in rebellion in 1282, but perished, and his brother David, who carried on the struggle, was captured in the following year and beheaded. By 1284 the English conquest of the country was complete, and the process of introducing English law and administration was begun.

In 1301 Edward I conferred on his second son, Edward, born in Caernarvon, Wales, the title of Prince of Wales (see WALES, PRINCE OF), and this sufficiently satisfied the pride of the Welsh to keep them loyal for a hundred years. The national spirit did not die out, however, and was nourished by the songs of the bards, whom the English government regarded with great disfavor. Upon the seizure of the English throne by Henry IV a revolt broke out in Wales, which, under the leadership of Owen Glendower, assumed, in 1402, formidable proportions. Henry IV repeatedly invaded the country, but the revolt was not suppressed till the death of Glendower, about 1415. The Welsh submitted to Henry IV, whom they regarded as their countryman. Glendower's was the last national uprising. In 1536 Wales was incorporated with England, its inhabitants receiving all the rights and privileges of English subjects. A national revival of recent years has taken the form of a patriotic cultivation of the ancient Cymric tongue and literature. See WELSH LANGUAGE AND LITERATURE.

WALES, PRINCE OF, the title borne by the eldest son of the sovereign of Great Britain and Ireland. It was first conferred on Prince Edward, afterward Edward II, in 1301. The idea of making Wales an appanage for the heir apparent seems due to Edward III, who in 1343 invested his son, the Black Prince, with the principality, and from that time the title has been borne by the eldest son of the reigning king. The principality of Wales has usually been bestowed by patent investiture, though in a few instances the heir to the throne has become Prince of Wales simply by being so declared. The Earldom of Chester was made a principality for the king's eldest son in 1393, and has since the accession of Henry IV been annexed to the principality of Wales. On the death of a Prince of Wales in his father's lifetime, the title has been conferred on the heir apparent. As heir of the crown of Scotland, the eldest son of the sovereign is Prince and High Steward of Scotland, Duke of Rothesay, Earl of Carrick, Baron of Renfrew, and Lord of the Isles. As heir to the crown of Ireland, the Prince of Wales bears the title of Earl of Dublin, created in 1849.

WALES, UNIVERSITY OF, an institution of higher education, established in 1893 by the union of four colleges of Aberystwyth, Bangor, Cardiff, and Swansea. These colleges had been founded, originally, in 1872, 1883, and 1885, and previous to their unification gave no degrees, although their work was accepted as partially equivalent to the degrees in English, Scotch, and Irish universities. Aberystwyth was founded and is largely patronized by the dissenting churches. The others are free and give no theological work. Instruction for women is provided. The administration of the university is in the hands of a council composed of representatives from various county political and educational boards of Wales, and of a senate consisting of members of the instructing staff.

WALEWSKI, COMTE ALEXANDRE FLORIAN JOSEPH COLONNA (1810–68), French statesman, son of Napoleon I and the Polish countess Walewska. When the revolt of 1830 broke out in Poland he joined the Polish army, and after the capitulation of Warsaw he went to France. He went to Egypt on a diplomatic mission; held appointments under the Guizot Ministry; was chargé d'affairs in Argentina in 1848; and then was envoy in Florence and in Naples, and in 1854 in London. He became minister of foreign affairs in 1855, and as French plenipotentiary presided over the Congress of Paris in 1856. He served as minister of state from 1860 to 1863. He was created a duke in 1866, and served as president of the legislative assembly in 1866–67. His writings include *Un Mot sur la Question d'Afrique* (1837), *L'Alliance Anglaise* (1838), and a drama, *L'École du Monde* (1840).

WALFISH, or **WALVIS, BAY,** a harbor on the coast of s.w. Africa. It belongs to Great Britain.

WALKE, HENRY (1808–96), American naval officer, born in Princess Anne County, Va. He entered the navy as a midshipman in 1827, was commissioned a lieutenant in 1839, and served on the bomb-brig *Vesuvius* in the Mexican War. When the Civil War broke out he was placed in command of the *Mount Vernon,* and subsequently held various important commands in the United States Navy. He participated in the capture of Fort Henry and Fort Donelson, and in the battles of Fort Pillow and Grand Gulf. In 1863, in command of the *Sacramento,* he blockaded the steamer *Rappahannock* in Calais until the close of the war. He attained the rank of rear admiral in 1870, and retired in the following year. He wrote *Naval Scenes in the Civil War* (1877).

WALKEM, GEORGE ANTHONY (1834–1908), Canadian political leader and jurist, born in Newry, Ireland. He came to Canada in his youth, and was educated at McGill University. He was a member of the Legislative Council, 1864–70, took an active part in effecting the entrance of British Columbia into the Dominion of Canada as a province in 1870, and was elected a member of the provincial legislature. Later he was a member of the

Cabinet (1872–74), premier (1874–76), leader of the opposition (1876–78), again premier (1878–82), and in the latter year was appointed a puisne judge of the Supreme Court. During his second premiership he did much to further the construction of the Canadian Pacific Railway in British Columbia.

WALKER, AMASA (1799–1875), American economist, born in Woodstock, Conn. In 1842–48 he lectured on political economy at Oberlin College; in 1853–60 was examiner on political economy at Harvard; and in 1859–69 lecturer on political economy at Amherst. In 1843 he was delegate to the First International Peace Congress in London, and in 1849 delegate to the Peace Congress in Paris. He was elected to several political offices, among them that of secretary of state of Massachusettes (1851–53), and representative in Congress (1862–63). He was a frequent contributor to periodical literature, especially on financial subjects, on which he was regarded as an authority. His principal work was *Science of Wealth* (1866).

WALKER, SIR BYRON EDMUND (1848–1924), Canadian financier, born in Ontario. Entering the Canadian Bank of Commerce in 1868, he was appointed general manager in 1886, a director in 1906, and president in 1907. He was elected president of the Canadian Bankers' Association, president of the Canadian Institute (1898–99), and chairman of the board of governors of Toronto University in 1910. In the last-named year he was knighted. Among Walker's writings are *The Canadian System of Banking* (1890), *Banking in Canada* (1893), *A Canadian View of the Financial Situation in the United States* (1895), *Why Canada Is against Bi-metallism* (1897), and *Canadian Surveys and Museums* (1900).

WALKER, CHARLES HOWARD (1857–1936), American architect, born in Boston, and educated at the Massachusetts Institute of Technology. He was a member of the Archæological Institute of America expedition to Assos in Asia Minor in 1881. After two years of travel in Europe he established himself in the practice of architecture in Boston and from 1889 to 1900 was a member of the firm of Walker and Kimball. From 1902 to 1913 he was director of the department of design in the Museum of Fine Arts, Boston; he served on the National Fine Arts Commission appointed by President Theodore Roosevelt in 1909; was president of the Metropolitan Improvement League of Boston (1909–13); and from 1887 was instructor and professor of the history of ornament in the Massachusetts Institute of Technology. He became editor of the (Boston) *Architectural Review,* and published *Parish Churches of England* (1915). He was appointed director of the School of Fine Arts in Boston in 1913 and lecturer in the history of architecture at Harvard University in 1917. In 1922 he became lecturer in the philosophy of architecture at Harvard and in European civilization and art the following year.

WALKER, FRANCIS AMASA (1840–97), American economist, son of Amasa Walker, born in Boston, and educated at Amherst College. He served throughout the Civil War, and at its close was breveted brigadier general of volunteers. In 1869 he became chief of the Bureau of Statistics of the United States Treasury, and was supervisor of the ninth and tenth United States censuses in 1870–72 and 1879–81. He was United States commissioner of Indian affairs in 1871–72, and in 1878 represented the United States at the International Monetary Conference in Paris, France. During 1872–80 he was professor of economics at Yale University, and from 1881 until his death was president of the Massachusetts Institute of Technology. His works include *Money, Trade, and Industry* (1879); *Political Economy* (1883); and *History of the Second Army Corps* (1886).

WALKER, FREDERICK (1840–75), English figure and landscape painter and illustrator. His earliest studies consisted in drawing the Elgin marbles in the British Museum, the influence of which may be seen in all of his works. In 1858 he joined the Royal Academy schools and later was employed by Whymper, a line engraver, with whom he remained two years. He soon became well known as an illustrator, especially for the works of Thackeray, whose friendship he formed at this time, but he finally relinquished engraving in 1865. His few oil paintings include "The Wayfarers" (1866), "Vagrants" (1868, National Gallery), and "Harbor of Refuge" (1872, Tate Gallery). But it is in his water colors, few in number and highly prized, that the full charm of his painting appears—the sureness and delicacy of drawing, bloom of color, and poetic grace of form and movement. "Philip in Church" (1863), "A Rainy Day at Bisham", "The Violet Field", and a version of "The Harbor of Refuge", are good examples. Walker was an associate of the Royal Academy (1871). He is supposed to be the prototype of Little Billee in Du Maurier's *Trilby.*

WALKER, GEORGE (1618–90), Irish clergyman, born of English parents in County Tyrone, Ireland. He is chiefly remembered as the inspirer of the defense of Londonderry. The siege began in April, and lasted till August 12, 1689. When the siege was raised Walker went to London, was received at court, and thanked by the House of Commons. He headed the men of Derry at the battle of the Boyne, and there perished. A lofty Doric column bearing a colossal statue of Walker stands on the walls at Londonderry.

WALKER, HENRY OLIVER (1843–1929), American figure and mural painter, born in Boston, Mass., and trained in Paris under Bonnat. He settled in New York, exhibiting ideal figure compositions of poetic beauty and refined feeling. Good examples are "Eros et Musa" and "Musa Regina" (National Gallery, Washington, D.C.) and "Morning Vision" (Metropolitan Museum of Art, New York City). But he is chiefly known for mural decorations, the most important including a series of lunettes in the Library of Congress, Washington; "Wisdom Attended by Learning" (Appellate Court, New York); and panels in the Massachusetts State House, Boston, and the Essex County Courthouse, Newark, N.J. He was elected a member of the National Academy of Design in 1902 and of the National Institute of Arts and Letters, and received a gold medal in Charleston in 1902.

WALKER, HORATIO (1858–1938), Canadian artist, born in Listowel, Ontario, Canada. He came, some years afterward, with his family to Rochester, N.Y. Although Walker was a self-taught painter, he showed in his pictures of animals, figures, and landscapes a fine taste in choice of theme, and a feeling for largeness of composition, which recalls the art of his recognized masters, the American painter Dwight William Tryon and the French painter Jean François Millet. His numerous awards include gold medals in New York (1887), Chicago (1893), Buffalo (1901), Charleston (1902), St. Louis (1904), at the Pennsylvania Academy of Fine Arts, Philadelphia (1906), and the Panama-Pacific Exposition, San Francisco (1915).

WALKER, JAMES (1794–1874), American educator, educated at Harvard College. He studied divinity, and was settled over the Unitarian Church in Charlestown (1818–39). He was professor of moral and intellectual philosophy at Harvard College (1839–53), and its president (1853–60). In 1831–39 he served as editor of the *Christian Examiner.* Walker wrote *Sermons* (1861), *Memoir of Daniel Appleton White* (1863), and *Memoir of Josiah Quincy* (1867).

WALKER, JAMES JOHN (1881–1946), American politician, born in New York City. He was admitted to the New York bar in 1912. Elected to the New York senate, he became the Democratic majority leader. He was elected mayor of New York City for two terms (1926–30 and 1930–34), but resigned in 1932 when he was charged with irregularities in municipal affairs and summoned before the State governor Franklin Delano Roosevelt.

WALKER, JOHN (1732–1807), English lexicographer and actor, born in Colney Hatch, Middlesex. He played under the management of David Garrick at the Drury Lane Theatre. In 1758 he joined the company of Barry and Woodward to open the Crow Street Theatre, Dublin. His chief roles were tragic, especially noteworthy being his Cato and Brutus. In 1768 he left the stage, and the following year he opened a school at Kensington Gravel-pits. The school failed after two years, and Walker then began to lecture on elocution, and made several tours. His most permanent work was his *Critical Pronouncing Dictionary and Expositor of the English Language* (1791).

WALKER, JOHN BRISBEN (1847–1931), American editor, born near Pittsburgh. As a young man he served in the Chinese army. Returning to America, he began the manufacture of iron but lost a fortune in the panic of 1873. After doing newspaper work for some time he turned to the West and became a successful alfalfa grower. In 1907, having acquired another fortune, he gave a 15-acre park to Denver. In 1889 he came to New York City, where he bought the *Cosmopolitan Magazine.* This he made the most successful periodical of its day, and he was responsible for many innovations in the magazine publishing field. In his long and varied career he was an automobile manufacturer, one of the earliest enthusiasts of aviation, a Western rancher, educator, peace advocate, and a crusader for good dirt roads throughout the country. He fought Richard Croker and Tammany Hall in New York, and campaigned for the parcel-post legislation.

WALKER, JOHN GRIMES (1835–1907), American naval officer, born in Hillsboro, N.H. He served throughout the Civil War, participated in the capture of New Orleans and Vicksburg, and as commander of the *Shawmut* assisted in the capture of Wilmington. He was commissioned rear admiral in 1894, and retired in 1897. During 1897–99 he was chairman of the Nicaragua Canal Commission, and in 1899 became president of the Isthmian Canal Commission.

WALKER, LEROY POPE (1817–84), Confederate secretary of war, born near Huntsville, Ala. Early in life he began to take an active interest in politics, became a member of the State legislature in 1843, was speaker of the house, 1847–49, and from 1850 to 1853 was judge of the State Circuit Court. He was a strenuous advocate of secession, was appointed secretary of war in the Confederate cabinet (1861), and as such directed the order to Beauregard for the attack on Fort Sumter. In 1861 he resigned and subsequently was commissioned brigadier general. In 1862 he retired.

WALKER, MARY EDWARDS (1832–1919), American physician and dress reformer, born in Oswego, N.Y., and educated at the Syracuse Medical College in 1855. She practiced in Columbus, Ohio, and later in Rome, N.Y. When the Civil War broke out she became an assistant army surgeon, being the first woman to hold such a commission. For her bravery and services on the field a medal of honor was awarded to her by Congress. She did much to advance the cause of woman suffrage in the United States and in England and claimed to have been the first woman to attempt to vote at the polls. Mary Walker zealously urged dress reform for women, and during her later life wore male attire habitually. She finally retired to her estate near Oswego, where she founded a hospital for consumptives.

WALKER, ROBERT JAMES (1801–69), American political leader and financier, born in Northumberland, Pa. After settling in Mississippi he became an opponent of slavery and freed his own slaves (1838). As a politician he became prominent for his opposition to nullification, and his support of the independence and, afterward, of the annexation of Texas. As secretary of the treasury in the Polk administration (1845–49), he was the most influential member of the cabinet. Besides financing the Mexican War (1847), he prepared his famous treasury report of December, 1845, which is often compared with Hamilton's *Report on Manufactures* and which attacked the protectionist system. This was followed by the Walker Tariff (1846). Stephen A. Douglas won him over to his compromise proposals and President Buchanan appointed him governor of Kansas Territory (1857). In November, 1857, however, he resigned, over the Lecompton Constitution. During the Civil War he supported the Union and as financial agent of the United States secured a loan of $250,000,000 in Germany, and did much to create confidence in Europe concerning the financial stability of the United States.

WALKER, SEARS COOK (1805–53), American astronomer, born in Wilmington, Massachusetts, and educated at Harvard College. After teaching school for some time he became assistant at the Naval Observatory in Washington, D.C. In 1847 he was placed in charge of the longitude department of the United States Coast Survey, and in this capacity introduced the use of the electric telegraph for determining the difference of longitude between two stations. He was also the first to register transit observations electrically by means of the chronograph.

WALKER, STUART (1888–1941), American playwright, born in Augusta, Ky. He was play reader, actor, and stage manager for the American producer David Belasco (1909–14) and in 1914 became stage director for the producer Jessie Bonstelle. Walker became an independent producer in 1915 and directed the Repertory Company in Indianapolis from 1917 to 1923 and the Repertory Theater in Cincinatti in 1922–23. He was the originator of the Portmanteau Theater and wrote *Portmanteau Plays (The Trimplet, Nevertheless, The Medicine Show, Six Who Pass While the Lentils Boil,* 1917) and *More Portmanteau Plays (The Lady of the Weeping Willow Tree, The Very Naked Boy, Jonathan Makes a Wish,* 1919); his other plays include *Five Flights Up* (1922) and *The King's Great Aunt Sits on the Floor* (1923).

WALKER, TIMOTHY (1806–56), American lawyer, educated at Harvard University. He taught mathematics for three years and then entered the Harvard Law School. In association with Judge John C. Wright he established the Cincinatti Law School, in which he was a professor of law until 1844. He was presiding judge of the Hamilton County Court of Common Pleas (1842–43). He edited the *Western Law Journal* for several years. His lectures on law and his chief work, *An Introduction to American Law,* have always been popular with law students.

WALKER, WILLIAM (1824–60), American adventurer and filibuster, born in Nashville, Tenn. In the summer of 1853 he organized an expedition for the conquest of the Mexican State of Sonora. It failed and he surrendered to United States officials in San Diego. He next planned an expedition to Nicaragua, then in a state of civil war. He landed at Realejo on June 11, 1855, and succeeded in capturing

Granada and making an arrangement with General Corral, the president, by which Walker was appointed secretary of war and commander in chief. The two leaders soon quarreled and Walker had Corral tried for conspiracy and shot. Walker was then in complete control of Nicaragua, of which, after a short and successful war with Costa Rica, he had himself proclaimed president. His rule soon became arbitrary, however, and provoked an insurrection, resulting in his expulsion from Granada. To save himself he surrendered, May 1, 1857, to Commander C. H. Davis of the United States sloop *St. Mary's,* by whom he was conveyed to New Orleans, and put under bonds there to keep the peace. In November, 1857, he was again in Nicaragua with a strong force of Americans and natives, but was again driven from the country. Later in 1858 he started with a force of adventurers for Honduras, but a shipwreck caused him to abandon the expedition. In June, 1860, he made a second attempt, landed at Ruatan on August 15, and captured Truxillo (Trujillo), but was compelled to flee, and subsequently surrendered himself to the captain of the British sloop of war *Icarus,* by whom he was handed over to the Honduran government. He was condemned by court-martial at Truxillo and shot there. He wrote *The War in Nicaragua* (1860).

WALKER, WILLIAM DAVID (1839–1917), American Protestant Episcopal bishop, educated at Columbia University and at the General Theological Seminary. He was vicar of Calvary Chapel, New York City, in 1862–83. Thenceforth he served as Missionary bishop of North Dakota until 1896, when he was appointed Bishop of Western New York. While in North Dakota he originated the Cathedral car, by means of which it was possible to conduct the services of the church at places that could not otherwise be reached. In 1887 he was appointed by the President a member of the United States Board of Indian Commissioners. He served as select preacher to the University of Cambridge and received honorary degrees from Oxford and Columbia universities.

WALKER, WILLIAM HULTZ (1869–1934), American chemist, born in Pittsburgh, Pa., and educated at Pennsylvania State College and the University of Göttingen. In 1894 he accepted the chair of industrial chemistry at the Massachusetts Institute of Technology, where from 1908 he was also director of the research laboratory of applied chemistry. Walker was a vice-president of the International Congress of Applied Chemistry in 1893 and president of the American Electrochemical Society in 1910. The New York Section of the American Chemical Society conferred on him its Nichols medal in 1908. During World War I, he served as colonel in charge of the Gas Offensive Division. He wrote *Principles of Chemical Engineering* (1923).

WALKER, WILLIAM SIDNEY (1795–1846), British Shakespearean critic, educated at Trinity College, Cambridge University. He was a fellow of Trinity College from 1820 to 1829. During his later years he was at times insane. He published numerous poems and other literary productions, but his great work consisted in his studies of Shakespeare's plays. Part of the results of these studies were published posthumously under the title *Shakespeare's Versification* (1854). There followed *A Critical Examination of the Text of Shakespeare* (3 vols., 1860). The works are poorly arranged, but they have been invaluable to later commentators, especially as regards points of prosody and syntax.

WALKERVILLE, formerly a town in Essex County, Ontario, Canada, on Detroit River, opposite Detroit, Mich. Walkerville was annexed to Windsor in 1935.

WALKING FERN, a tufted evergreen fern, *Camptosorus rhizophyllus,* whose simple fronds end in a long, tapering tip which bends over backward, takes root, and thus gives rise to new plants. It grows on shaded rocks from New England to Minnesota and southward.

WALKING FISH, one of the curious eellike fishes of the Snakehead family, Ophiocephalidae, numerously represented in the fresh waters of the East Indies and China. They are elongated, reaching in some cases a length of 4 feet, and have a snakelike head covered with shieldlike scales. Their respiratory apparatus is double, as they must be able to breathe air direct, and their habit of occasionally going out upon land has given them the name "walking fish" in India. They are common in tanks and ponds, where they lie at the margin with the head out of water. They breed twice a year, preparing a nest for the eggs, which the male guards, and survive droughts by burying themselves in the mud.

WALKING LEAF. See LEAF INSECT.

WALKING STICK, the popular name of many Orthopterous insects of the family Phasmidae. The body is long and slender, the legs are also twiglike, and the wings are sometimes absent, sometimes rudimentary, and sometimes leaflike. Sluggish in their habits, herbiv-

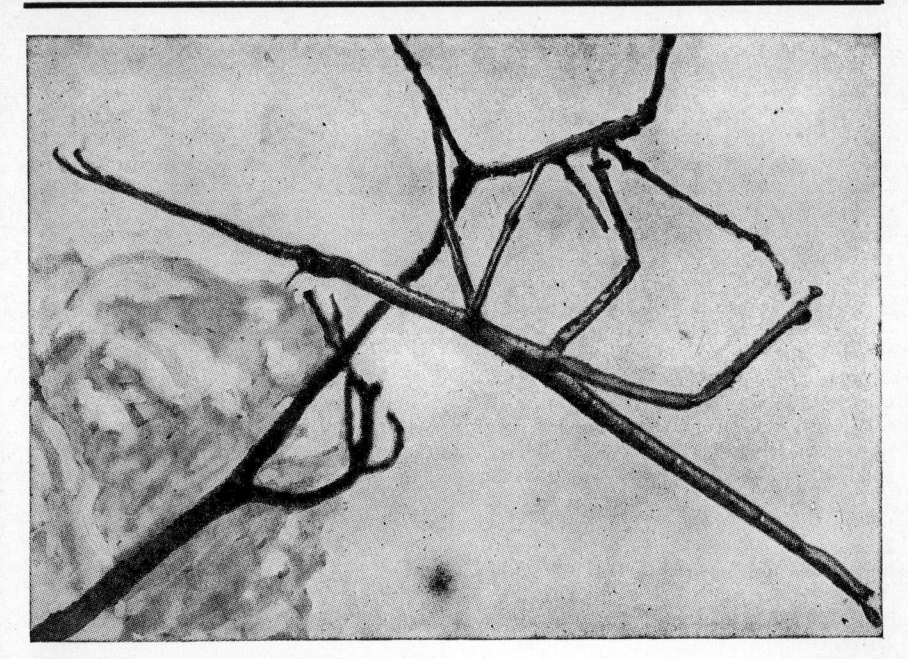

A tropical walking-stick insect, which looks like a twig

orous in diet, the walking sticks are very effectively concealed by their resemblance to the plants on which they rest and feed.

WALKLEY, ARTHUR BINGHAM (1855–1926), English dramatic critic, born in Bristol, and educated at Balliol and Corpus Christi colleges, Oxford University. He held important positions in the British postal service, but it was by his dramatic criticism that he became known over the English-speaking world to all interested in contemporary British dramatic and theatrical activities. He proved himself a sound and scholarly critic in his notices for the newspaper London *Times* and in contributions to various journals and reviews. Walkley's books include *Playhouse Impressions* (1892), *Frames of Mind* (1894), *Dramatic Criticism* (1903), and *Drama and Life* (1907).

WALKÜRE, DIE, music drama in three acts with music and text by the German composer Richard Wagner. It is the second in the series of dramatic compositions known collectively as *The Ring. Die Walküre* was first produced in Munich on June 24, 1870; its first American performance was given on January 30, 1835, in New York City. The scene is set in legendary times in northern Europe, and the plot continues the story of the *Rheingold* (q.v.), in which Wotan, king of the gods, founded a family of demigods to engender a hero great enough to retrieve the magical Ring made by the Nibelungen.

The scene of Act One is Hunding's forest hut, into which staggers the exhausted Siegmund. He is given shelter by Sieglinde, wife of Hunding, who many years ago forcibly carried the girl away from her home and twin brother. When Hunding returns, he recognizes in Siegmund his mortal enemy, and challenges him to combat the following morning. Hunding retires, after Sieglinde, irresistibly drawn to Siegmund, gives her husband a sleep-producing drink. She shows Siegmund a sword thrust into the trunk of a tree, and tells him the weapon was plunged there on her wedding day by a stranger who declared that whosoever could withdraw the sword would be her protector. Siegmund, recalling that his father promised him an invincible sword, draws the weapon from the tree. The two now realize they are brother and sister, children of Wotan, and together flee the hut.

Act Two takes place in a mountain pass. Wotan has destined that his two children shall meet and mate, but his wife Fricka, goddess of marriage, demands that he uphold Hunding and punish the pair for their unlawful union. Reluctantly, Wotan summons Brünnhilde, his daughter and favorite of the Valkyrie (Ger. *Walküre*) warrior maidens in whose care he has placed Siegmund, and bids her protect Hunding instead. Brünnhilde pleads in vain. When Siegmund and Hunding engage in battle, she disobeys and shields Siegmund, but Wotan, enraged, shatters Siegmund's sword with his spear. Hunding slays Siegmund, and then is struck dead by Wotan. Brünnhilde snatches the broken pieces of the sword, and with Sieglinde, flies from their father's wrath. Act Three finds Brünnhilde on the Rock of Valkyries. Her sisters fear to help her but promise to watch over Sieglinde. After telling Sieglinde to save the sword fragments for the son she will bear, Brünnhilde sends her away. Now Wotan appears and harshly reprimands Brünnhilde. He deprives her of her godhood and condemns her to a magic sleep. She will be awakened by the first passing stranger, who will then become her husband. Wotan is moved to pity by her pleas, however, and mitigates his punishment. Tenderly he places a kiss on his beloved daughter's eyes, and she sinks down on a rock. Wotan summons Loki, the god of fire, who surrounds the rock with flames which only a fearless hero can penetrate to reach the sleeping Brünnhilde. Sorrowfully, Wotan bids her farewell and departs.

WALL, a vertical structure forming a partition, enclosure, or dividing member, or a solid barrier for defense; especially and more generally such a structure built of masonry of stone, brick, or concrete. The term is also applied, irrespective of material, to the vertical enclosing structure of a wooden house, and to its internal partitions of studding, lath, and plaster, which form the walls of its rooms. In anatomy and biology the term is applied to the partitions and enclosing membranes of the organs of animals and human beings.

Walls for defense, with gates and towers at intervals, were in ancient days the chief reliance of cities for protection against invasion. Such walls were high and massive, sometimes forming a double or triple circuit with an ex-

Metropolitan Opera Assn.

Scene from Act Two of the Wagnerian opera "Die Walküre"

terior moat. Those of Troy, Thebes, and Babylon were the most famous in classical antiquity; those of Constantinople, of Avignon, Carcassonne, and Aigues Mortes in France, of Gothenburg in Germany, and of Lucerne in Switzerland are the finest of medieval examples now extant. The most colossal of all such walls is the Great Wall of China.

WALLABY. See KANGAROO.

WALLACE, county seat of Shoshone Co., Ida., situated on the Coeur d'Alene R., about 75 miles S.E. of Spokane, Wash. It is served by two railroads, and is the center of a mining and lumbering area. Lead, silver, and zinc are mined in extensive quantities in the surrounding region. Places of interest in the vicinity include the old Mission of the Sacred Heart, built in 1853 by three Jesuit missionaries. Wallace was settled in 1884 and incorporated as a city in 1892. Pop. (1940) 3839.

WALLACE, ALFRED RUSSEL (1823–1913), English naturalist and philosopher, born in Usk, Monmouth. He spent four years on the Amazon with Bates, and eight among the Malay Islands, making zoological collections. Unaware of Darwin's cognate researches and speculations, Wallace's reputation rest mainly on his discovery of natural selection. His native amiability and high-mindedness of character were shown by his rare self-abnegation of any claim for the discovery of natural selection, and by his uninterrupted friendship with Darwin. Darwin and he differed, however, on the subject of psychic phenomena, in which Wallace was deeply interested.

Wallace's most important works are, besides the 1858 essay, his epoch-making paper "On the Phenomenon of Variation and Geographical Distribution as Illustrated by the Papilionidæ of the Malayan Region", published in the *Transactions of the Linnean Society of London* (1865), *Contributions to the Theory of Natural Selection* (1870), *The Malay Archipelago* (2 vols., 1869), *The Geographical Distribution of Animals* (2 vols., 1876), *Tropical Nature* (1878), and *Darwinism* (1889). Other works are *Man's Place in the Universe* (1903), *My Life: A Record of Events and Opinions* (2 vols., 1905), *Is Mars Habitable?* (1907), and *The Revolt of Democracy* (1914).

WALLACE, CHARLES WILLIAM (1865–1932), American Shakespearean scholar. He was educated at the University of Nebraska, in connection with which he founded a preparatory school. Of the latter he was principal and director until 1900, and thereafter was a member of the English department of the university, becoming associate professor

Alfred Russel Wallace

in 1907. He studied at several German universities and carried on extensive researches in European archives. Important documents relating to theatrical conditions in Shakespeare's time, discovered by him especially in the Public Record Office in London, aroused great interest among scholars. These documents formed the basis of Wallace's books, including *The Children of the Chapel at Blackfriars, 1579–1603* (1908); *Three London Theaters of Shakespeare's Time* (1909); *Shakespeare and his London Associates as Revealed in Recently Discovered Documents* (1910); *The Evolution of the English Drama up to Shakespeare* (1912); and *The First London Theater, Materials for a History* (1913).

WALLACE, SIR DONALD MACKENZIE (1841–1919), British journalist and author, born in Scotland. He served the London *Times* as correspondent in various European capitals and later became private secretary to the viceroy of India, Frederick Blackwood, Lord Dufferin, and to his successor, Henry Petty-Fitzmaurice, Lord Lansdowne. From 1891 to 1899 Wallace had charge of the foreign department of the London *Times*.

WALLACE, EDGAR (1875–1932), British author and playwright. He started life as a newsboy, and was later a composer of popular songs, reporter, war correspondent, playwright, and prolific writer of mystery and detective stories.

WALLACE, HENRY AGARD (1888–   ), American editor and statesman, born in Adair County, Iowa, and educated at Iowa State College. He served on the editorial staff of *Wallace's Farmer,* 1910–29, and was editor of the merged *Wallace's Farmer* and *Iowa Homestead,* 1929–33. In 1933 he became secretary of agriculture in the cabinet of President Franklin Delano Roosevelt. He served as Vice-President of the United States from 1940 to 1944. In 1948 he ran unsuccessfully for President as the candidate of the Progressive Party (q.v.). He is the author of agricultural books and treatises on contemporary issues.

WALLACE, HENRY CANTWELL (1866–1924), American agriculturalist and cabinet member, born in Rock Island, Ill. He engaged in farming in Iowa from 1887 to 1891, taught for a while in the Iowa State College of Agriculture, and was associated editorially with *Wallace's Farmer* (1895–1924). He was secretary of agriculture from 1921 to 1924.

WALLACE, HUGH (1863–1930), American banker and diplomat, born in Lexington, Mo., and educated in public and private schools. In 1887 he moved to Tacoma, Wash., where he achieved prominence in banking and in real estate circles. For several years Wallace was active in the councils of the Democratic Party, but never was a candidate for office. He was a delegate to several Democratic National conventions and took conspicuous parts in the Presidential campaigns of 1912 and 1916. Although he was credited with being closer to President Wilson than any other Westerner, the exact nature of his work never was made known. In 1919 Wallace succeeded William Graves Sharp as United States ambassador in Paris, where he became extremely popular during his two years of office. The Grand Cross of the Legion of Honor, the highest decoration in the gift of the French government, was conferred on him. After President Wilson returned to the United States from Paris at the time the Treaty of Versailles was concluded, Wallace sat on the Supreme Allied Council as representative of the United States and was on terms of cordiality with Georges Clemenceau, premier of France, and other French leaders.

WALLACE, JOHN FINDLEY (1852–1921), American civil engineer, born in Fall River, Mass., and educated at the University of Wooster. In 1871–76 he was assistant engineer on the upper Mississippi River, and Rock Island Rapids. He was county surveyor and city engineer (1876–78), and from 1878 to 1904 held appointments as engineer, and subsequently as manager, on various railroads. In 1904 he became chief engineer of the Panama Canal, but resigned his position soon afterward. In 1906 he was elected president of the New York Electric Properties Company.

WALLACE, LEWIS, known as LEW WALLACE (1827–1905), American soldier and novelist, born in Brookville, Ind. His law studies were interrupted by the Mexican War, through which he served in a volunteer regiment as second lieutenant. He returned to the law, but on the outbreak of the Civil War he again volunteered, and after service in the West Virginia campaign was gazetted brigadier general (1861). For services at Fort Donelson, Shiloh, and Monocacy, he was promoted to the rank of major general. He served on several military commissions at the close of the war. He was thereafter governor of New Mexico Territory (1878–81), minister to Turkey (1881–85), and a distinguished lecturer and author. His *Ben Hur* (1880) won him a world-wide reputation. A play based on the book was very successful, as has also been a motion picture. Wallace also wrote *The Fair God* (1873) and *The Prince of India* (1893).

WALLACE, SIR RICHARD (1818–90), English art collector and philanthropist, born in London. He was probably the natural son of Maria, Marchioness of Hertford, although reputed to be her grandson. He was educated chiefly in Paris, where the greater part of his life was passed. He was known as an art connoisseur and was much beloved on account of his many benefactions during the Franco-Prussian War. In 1870 he inherited the property and the priceless art collection of the fourth Marquis of Hertford, and on the death of Sir Richard's wife in 1897 this collection was bequeathed to the British nation, and housed in Hertford House, London, as the Wallace collection.

WALLACE, ROBERT (1853–1939), Scottish agriculturist. He was professor of agriculture at the Royal Agricultural College, Cirencester, from 1882 to 1885, and professor of agriculture and rural economy at the University of Edinburgh, from 1885 to 1922, serving from 1900 as Garton lecturer on colonial and Indian agriculture. He traveled extensively, frequently in an official or advisory capacity, and studying the agriculture of various countries. The results of these studies are embodied in reports and in volumes of travels. Wallace came to be recognized as an expert in his field, and was active in promoting agricultural education in Scotland. His principal works are *Farm Live Stock of Great Britain* (1885), *Indian Agriculture* (1888), *The Agriculture and Rural Economy of Australia and New Zealand* (1891), *Farming Industries of Cape Colony* (1896), and *British Breeds of Live Stock* (1910–13).

WALLACE, SIR WILLIAM (1272?–1305), Scottish patriot, son of Sir Malcolm Wallace, of Elderslie in Renfrewshire. He first stands out clearly in 1297 as chief of a patriotic force against Edward I of England. He attacked the English garrison at Lanark, and slew William de Hazelrig; he attempted to surprise the English justiciar at Scone; and with a large company he lay in the Forest of Selkirk. Edward was at the time in Flanders, but his general in Scotland was Warenne, Earl of Surrey. He defeated Surrey at Stirling Bridge, after which the whole kingdom submitted to him. He was appointed "governor of Scotland in name of King John [Baliol]". In 1298 Edward in person invaded Scotland at the head of 88,000 men, and at Falkirk (July 22) totally routed Wallace. With this defeat Wallace's martial career terminated. He lived in France for a time, but returned and was captured near Glasgow by Sir John Menteith, Edward's governor of Dumbarton. He was brought to London, was tried for treason, and was executed.

WALLACE, WILLIAM (1844–97), British philosopher, born in Cupar-Fife, Scotland, and educated at the University of St. Andrews and at Balliol College, Oxford. He became a fellow of Merton College in 1867, and Whyte professor of moral philosophy at Oxford in 1882; he held both offices until his death. His works include *The Logic of Hegel, Epicureanism,* and *Lectures and Essays on Natural Theology and Ethics.*

WALLACE, WILLIAM (1860–1922), British composer, born in Greenock, Scotland. He studied ophthalmic surgery in Vienna and Glasgow, but later in 1889 entered the Royal Academy of Music in London, at which he spent two terms. From the very beginning his compositions attracted attention. His principal works include six symphonic poems, a choral symphony, an orchestral suite, several cantatas, chamber music, and two song cycles. He also wrote *The Musical Faculty, Its Origins and Processes.*

WALLACE, WILLIAM VINCENT (1814–65), Irish musician, born in Waterford. In 1845 he went to England and wrote his opera, *Maritana,* which was an immediate success. *Matilda of Hungary* followed it in 1847. After visiting America he composed *Lurline,* which was brought out in London in 1860, with even greater success than *Maritana.* In 1861 he composed *The Amber Witch;* in 1862, *Love's Triumph;* and in 1863, *The Desert Flower.*

WALLACEBURG, town of Kent County, Ontario, Canada, on the Sydenham River, 38 miles E.N.E. of Detroit. It is served by the Pere Marquette, Grand Trunk, and Canadian Pacific railways. The industrial establishments include planing and flour mills, and manufactures are glass, sugar, and canned goods. Pop. (1941) 4986.

WALLACHIA. See ROMANIA.

WALLACK, JAMES WILLIAM (about 1795–1864), English actor, born in London. His parents were actors and he also adopted the stage as a profession, making his first appearance at Drury Lane in 1807. In 1818 he visited New York, where he appeared with success as Macbeth in the play of the same name, and in other parts. He settled permanently in New York City about 1850, opened Wallack's Theater at Broadway and Broome Street in 1852, and the theater of the same name at Broadway and Thirteenth Street in 1861.

WALLACK, JOHN JOHNSTONE, known as LESTER WALLACK (1820–88), son of James William Wallack, born in New York City during a visit of his parents to America. In 1847 he made his debut in New York City as Sir Charles Coldstream in *Used Up* at the Broadway Theater. From 1852 to 1864 he played leading parts and also acted as stage manager at his father's theater. On his father's death (1864) he succeeded him as proprietor of Wallack's Theater, and retired from the stage in 1888. He married a sister of Sir John Millais, the eminent English painter. He published *Memories of Fifty Years* (1889).

WALLAROO. See KANGAROO.

WALLAS, GRAHAM (1858–1932), British economist, born in Sunderland. He was lecturer at the London School of Economics, and later a member of the Royal Commission on Civil Service. In 1914 he held the chair of political science at London University, and in that year was also Lowell Lecturer in Boston. In 1919 he was Dodge Lecturer at Yale. A member of the Fabian Society from 1886 to 1904, he published one of the *Fabian Essays* in 1889. His writings include also *Human Nature in Politics* (1909), *The Great Society* (1914), *Our Social Heritage* (1921), and *The Art of Thought* (1926).

WALLASEY, a manufacturing town in Cheshire, England, on the west bank of the Mersey estuary, 4 miles w. of Liverpool. It is

Albrecht Wallenstein (painting by A. Vandyck)

practically a suburb of Birkenhead and its chief feature is its immense dock formed from a former marsh called Wallasey Pool. Pop., about 94,000.

WALLAWALLA, a tribe of American Indians of Shahaptian stock formerly occupying the territory about the river of the same name and the adjacent banks of the Columbia, in Washington and Oregon, and since 1855 associated with the Cayuse and Umatilla upon the Umatilla Reservation, Oregon. They were visited by Lewis and Clark in 1804 and were Christianized by Jesuit missionaries about forty years later. They lived originally on fish, roots, and game, but are now fairly prosperous farmers and stock raisers. They now number about 400.

WALLA WALLA, county seat of Walla Walla Co., Wash., situated in the S.E. corner of the State 12 miles N. of the Oregon boundary and about 200 miles S.E. of Spokane. It is served by three railroads and maintains a municipal airport. The city is the chief trading, distributing, shipping, and manufacturing center for S.E. Washington and N.E. Oregon. The surrounding agricultural area, the vast and fertile Walla Walla Valley, is noted for the production of apples, prunes, plums, cherries, strawberries, melons, green peas, asparagus, carrots, lettuce, onions, spinach, tomatoes, potatoes, sugar beets, dry peas, wheat, alfalfa, barley, oats, livestock, wool, and poultry. A considerable portion of the region is irrigated. Industrial establishments in the city include flour and feed mills, fruit and vegetable canneries and packing houses, grain elevators, meat-packing plants, creameries, bottling works, a brewery, and factories making cans and farm machinery. About one fifth of the total U.S. output of canned green peas is produced in the city and vicinity. Wholesale and retail trading houses in Walla Walla number approximately 550.

Walla Walla is the site of Whitman College, established in 1859, of Walla Walla College (Adventist), founded in 1892, of a business college, of the Whitman Conservatory of Music, of a U.S. veterans hospital, and of the Washington State Penitentiary. Whitman National Monument (q.v.), w. of the city, commemorates the pioneer settlers of the area, notably the missionary Marcus Whitman, who, with his associates, was massacred by Indians on the site in 1847. Fort Walla Walla, a U.S. Army post, was established on the site of the present city in 1857 and a settlement developed around the fort in the following year. It was incorporated as a town in 1859 and chartered as a city in 1862. Pop. (1950) 24,071.

WALLENSTEIN, ALBRECHT EUSEBIUS WENZEL VON, DUKE OF FRIEDLAND AND MECKLENBURG, and PRINCE OF SAGAN (1583–1634), Austrian soldier, born near Königgrätz. He became general in chief of all the imperial armies (1625), and received from the emperor Ferdinand absolute authority in the field. Wallenstein at once marched for the Elbe and defeated Count von Mansfeld at Dessau, and held him and his ally, Bethlen Gabor of Transylvania, in check until Mansfeld's death and a truce with Bethlen freed Ferdinand from both these enemies. In the following year (1627) Wallenstein, co-operating with Tilly, won the Jutland peninsula and the Mecklenburg duchies from the Danes and the Protestant princes. For this, he received the duchy of Mecklenburg.

When Gustavus Adolphus invaded northern Germany, Ferdinand's allies, the old princes of the empire, insisted upon the dismissal of Wallenstein. Wallenstein quietly resigned (1630) his command and retired to Gitschin, the capital of his principality. But the inability of the Duke of Bavaria soon induced Ferdinand to restore Wallenstein to the supreme command.

This he did and, having driven the Saxons

out of Bohemia, Wallenstein immediately marched against the Swedes in Bavaria; he repulsed the attempt of Gustavus Adolphus to storm his entrenched camp near Nuremberg (September 3, 1632), but failed to get the better of the Swedish king at Lützen.

After invading Silesia, Wallenstein once more incurred the jealousy of Maximilian of Bavaria and the Catholic princes. He then tried to win over his officers to resist all attempts to effect his disgrace. In this he failed, and on February 24, 1634, he was assassinated by some Irish and Scottish officers. He was a man of transcendent ability, but of unscrupulous character.

WALLER, EDMUND (1606–87), English poet, born in Coleshill near Amersham, Buckinghamshire. He was one of the commissioners to Charles I at Oxford in 1643. He plunged into a plot on the king's behalf, was expelled from the House of Commons, and banished for life. He was permitted to return in 1652. Waller's poems have an easy, flowing, felicitous style. Pope eulogized his sweetness. His importance in English poetry is that he revived the heroic couplet in that form which it retained for over a hundred years.

WALLER, FRANK (1842–1923), American architect and artist, born in New York City. In 1870 he went to Rome, studying under John Chapman for a year. The year following he traveled in Egypt, making many studies and sketches. He was one of the incorporators of the Art Students League and was its first president. For many years he devoted himself to architecture in New York.

WALLER, LEWIS (1860–1915), English actor-manager, born in Bilbao, Spain. His first appearance on the professional stage was at Toole's Theatre, London, in 1883. During the next ten years he played a wide range of parts, both in the London theaters and in the provinces, and by hard work forged his way to the front rank of his profession. In 1895 he was associated with Sir Charles Wyndham in the production of *The Home Secretary,* and under Sir Herbert Beerbohm Tree's management played in *The Three Musketeers.* In the same year he assumed the management of the Shaftesbury Theatre. During the next decade he managed the Lyceum, the Comedy, the Lyric, the Imperial, and other theaters for short periods. His best-known role was Monsieur Beaucaire in Booth Tarkington's play of that name, which at the first production ran for over four hundred nights. Waller visited America for the first time in 1911, appearing at the Century Theatre in *The Garden of Allah* and later at Daly's, of which he had assumed the management, in a revival of *Monsieur Beaucaire.*

The common wallflower

WALLER, SIR WILLIAM (1597?–1668), parliamentary general, son of Sir Thomas Waller, lieutenant of Dover. He studied at Magdalen Hall, Oxford, and became a soldier of fortune. In 1640 he was elected to the Long Parliament as a member of the popular party. When the Great Rebellion began he entered the parliamentary army as colonel of a regiment of horse and gained numerous successes, but was defeated at Roundway Down in July, 1643. He was given another army and gained several successes, but in June, 1644, was defeated by King Charles I at Cropredy Bridge. In the early part of 1645 he led the expedition for the relief of Taunton. An ordinance which forbade members of Parliament to hold a command in the army put an end to his military career, and he then became one of the Presbyterian leaders in Parliament, gained the enmity of the army, and in 1647 fled to France. Returning to England, he supported the proposed treaty with the king, and in December, 1648, was imprisoned on a charge of having instigated the Scots to invade England. He was later active in negotiating for the return of Charles II. In February, 1660, he sat in the Long Parliament. He was a member of the last council of state, promoted the calling of a free Parliament, and sat in the Convention. *A Vindication of the Character and Conduct of Sir William Waller,* written by himself, was published posthumously in 1797.

WALLEYED PIKE. See PIKE PERCH.

WALLFLOWER (*Cheiranthus*), a genus of plants of the family Cruciferae. The common wallflower, *C. cheiri,* is found in rocky places and on old walls in the south of Europe, and also, but less abundantly, in the middle of Europe and in Britain. In its wild state its flowers are always yellow; in cultivation they exhibit a considerable diversity of colors, chiefly brown, purple, and variegated, and they attain a larger size.

WALLIN, JOHAN OLOF (1779–1839), Swedish poet and archbishop, born in Dalarna. He entered the ministry, and in 1837 was made archbishop of Uppsala. He obtained general recognition in 1815 through the didactic poem *Uppfostraren* ("The Educator"), which was awarded the highest prize by the Academy. On account of his great success in writing hymns he was called by Tegnér "David's Harp of the North". His *Psalmbook,* of which 128 hymns were his own, was authorized as the hymnbook of the country in 1819 and is still in use.

WALLING, WILLIAM ENGLISH (1877–1936), American Socialist writer, born in Louisville, Ky., and educated at the University of Chicago. He became a director of the National Association for the Advancement of the Colored People, and a member of the executive committee of the Intercollegiate Socialist Society. His later publications include *Sovietism* (1920), *American Labor and American Democracy* (1927), *The Mexican Question under Calles and Obregon* (1927), and *Our Next Step—A National Economic Policy* (with Matthew Woll, 1933).

WALLINGFORD, a borough and also a town of New Haven Co., Conn., situated on the Quinnipiac R., 12 miles N.N.E. of the city of New Haven. Transportation facilities include a railroad. In addition to the borough, the town includes several villages, notably Yalesville. The principal industries are the manufacture of silverware, silver-plated ware, nickelware, brass goods, hardware, edge tools, insulated wire, rubber goods, firearms, steel, and shirts. Wallingford is the site of the Choate School, a private preparatory school for boys, of the Gaylord Farm tuberculosis sanatorium, and of a Masonic home. The Samuel Parsons House, built in 1759, contains the collection of the Wallingford Historical Society. The site of the present town was settled about 1670 and named Wallingford after a town of the same name in Berkshire, England. It was incorporated in 1853. Population of town of Wallingford, including borough (1950) 16,914.

WALLINGTON, a borough of Bergen Co., N.J., situated 9 miles N. of Newark, and adjoining Passaic. The principal industries are the manufacture of lumber, paints, and curtains. Pop. (1940) 8981.

WALLIS, JOHN (1616–1703), English theologian and mathematician, born in Ashford. He systematized and extended the new geometry, extended the application of Kepler's law of continuity, first made popular the present meaning of fractional and negative exponents, and introduced the symbol ∞ for infinity. His attempt at interpolation was the beginning of a more general method employed by mathematicians of the 17th century, which later enabled Newton to generalize the binomial formula. He increased the power of algebra by the systematic use of formulas, gave the law for forming the successive convergents of a continued fraction, and suggested a modern graphic interpretation of imaginaries. Wallis was a student of polemics, language, mechanics, and theology, but his genius for mathematics eclipsed his other talents. His complete works were published at Oxford (1693–99).

WALLIS, SEVERN TEACKLE (1816–94), American lawyer, born in Baltimore, and educated at St. Mary's College. After studying law, he was admitted to the bar (1837). Early in life he devoted himself to literary pursuits, became an authority on Spanish literature and history, and in 1849 was sent by the United States government on a special mission to Spain to investigate the subject of Spanish land grants in Florida. Until the organization of the "Know-Nothing" Party he was a Whig, but afterward became a Democrat. He was elected to the Maryland House of Delegates in 1861, was chairman of the Committee on Federal Relations, and because of his sympathies with the Confederacy was arrested with other members of the legislature, and imprisoned for fourteen months. His works include *Glimpses of Spain* and *Spain: Her Institutions, Politics, and Public Men.*

WALLOONS, the name given to those among the Belgians whose mother tongue is French or a French dialect, in contrast to the Flemings, who speak Dutch or Dutch dialects. The Walloons in Belgium at the present time number some 3,150,000, as compared with about 4,100,000 Flemings. They are mostly confined to the south and southwest.

The Walloons are the remnants of the romanized Celts of northern Gaul, the so-called Belgæ of Julius Cæsar. After having offered a stubborn resistance to the Romans, they were finally conquered by them and like the other tribes of Gaul gradually abandoned their Celtic speech for Latin, which is therefore the source of Wallonian dialects. The north of Belgium, barren and unprotected, was soon raided by Teutonic tribes. Among these, the Toxanders settled in the heaths and marshes of the Campinian plain, with the consent of the Romans. Flanders, the land of the Menopii, was also devastated, and the whole north of Belgium was invaded by the Franks. The south remained for some time under the protection of the Roman legions in Tournay, but at the end of the 5th century the Franks took possession of the greater part of Gaul. This, however, was a mere conquest and did not result in any Teutonization of the country. The Teutonic settlements extended only as far south as the Carbonaria silva in the center of Belgium, for the Teutons, being agriculturists, were able to cultivate the more barren soil. In the wooded region of Hainault and the Ardennes, they simply appropriated large estates that were being cultivated by the Gallo-Romans. This explains why the language has remained Romance, while a great many place names are Teutonic.

In the Middle Ages the Wallonian provinces did not play so conspicuous a part as Flanders and Brabant. The communes of Liége and Dinant, however, were famous for their prosperity and their independence. The severe treatment inflicted upon Dinant by Charles of Burgundy has remained memorable. Liége was an episcopal principality notorious for the contests between bishops and citizens. In the 16th century, during the religious wars, the Walloons (the "Malcontents") sided principally with Spain and helped in the reconquest of the Flemish country. Only in Tournay, Valenciennes, and Artois were there Protestant communities, whose members later emigrated to the Dutch Republic. Some also went to America, among them Jean de Forest, from Avesnes, one of the founders of the city of New York.

Although the Flemings and Walloons have been politically united for centuries, their physical and moral characteristics are still easily distinguishable. The Walloons, like the French, are mostly of the brunette type, and are more nervous and vivacious than the Flemings. They are more industrious and thrifty than their neighbors, but less consistent in feeling. The lower classes are somewhat careless personally, in contrast with the proverbial Flemish and Dutch cleanliness, but they have more natural distinction than their Teutonic neighbors.

WALLPAPER, paper made to decorate walls. The printing of the common kinds is done with a roller-printing machine something like that used in calico printing, but the better class of wallpapers are block-printed by hand. The rollers or blocks are either entirely of wood, in which case the pattern is cut on their surface, or they are wood faced with a pattern formed of felt, and outlined with thin brass fixed edgewise into the wood. Flock-paper, sometimes called velvet-paper, is made by printing the pattern in strong size, and then dusting this over with ground wool dyed various colors, and called "flock". The superfluous flock which does not adhere to the size is shaken off. Such parts of a pattern as are to be finished in bronze or gold leaf are first printed in gold size.

One reason that block-printed papers are superior to roller prints is that the block surface is softer, being mostly of wood, and carries the ink better; also, in block printing each color dries before the next is applied, while in roller printing the colors follow one another immediately.

Wallpaper painted in China was used in Europe as early as the middle of the 16th century, though it did not become fashionable until a century later. The invention of the block as it is used in printing wallpaper is attributed to Jean Papillon, a French engraver, in 1688. In 1692 a patent was granted in England to William Bayley for the manufacture of paper hangings.

In the 19th century the wallpaper industry was transformed, and the production of huge quantities at a trifling price was made possible, by the introduction of continuous paper, the roller, and power. Paper in continuous rolls was first made in 1829 by Zuber in Alsace, who sold the English rights for $5000. Previously rolls had been made by pasting together sheets 18 in. wide. About 1850 Zuber brought from Manchester in England a six-color roller-printing machine based on the one used in

Metropolitan Museum of Art; H. Birge & Sons, N.Y.
AMERICAN WALLPAPERS. *Top: 18th century. Bottom: 20th century.*

Modern American wallpaper designs

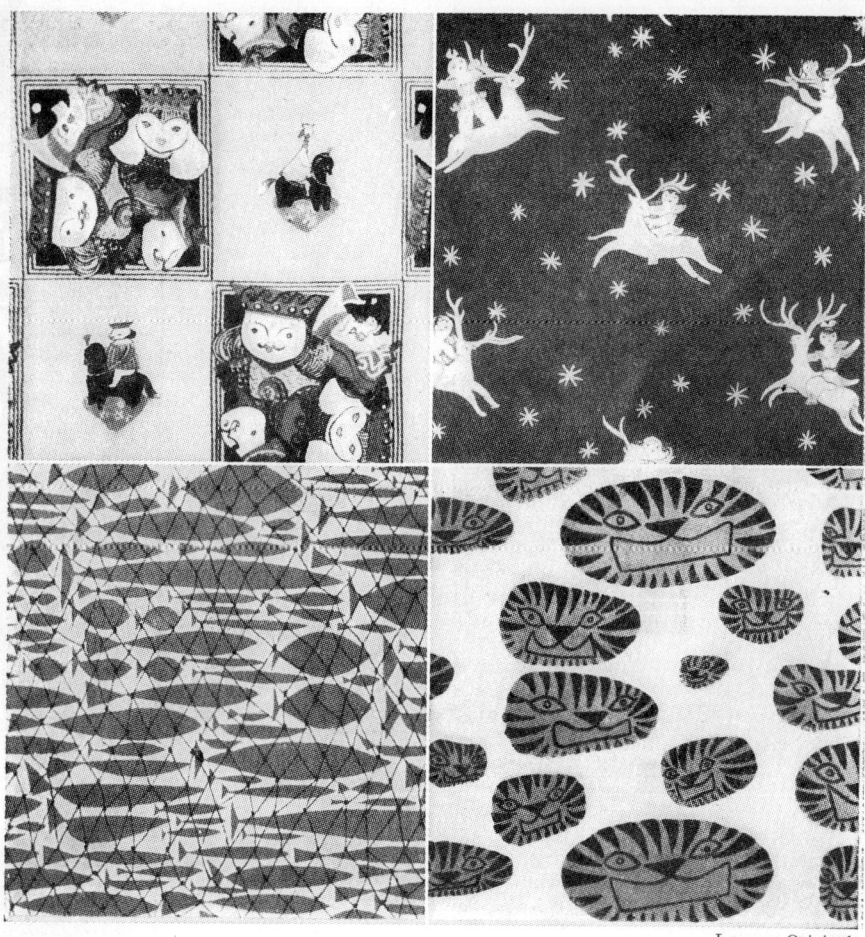

Laverne Originals

printing cottons. Henceforth the majority of papers were machine made.

WALLSEND, town of Northumberland, England, 4 miles N.E. of Newcastle, named from its being at the end of the Roman wall. Many Roman relics have been found there. It is a shipping center, and has lead-smelting, copper-smelting, and engineering works, and coal mines. Pop., about 45,000.

WALL STREET, a street in New York City extending from Broadway to the East River, following the line of the early city wall across Manhattan Island. The United States Sub-Treasury and numerous banking institutions are located on Wall Street, and the street is the center of financial operations in the United States. See NEW YORK CITY.

WALMER CASTLE, a round-towered castle, 2 miles s.w. of Deal, Kent, England, built by Henry VIII. Until 1905, it was the official residence of the lord warden of the Cinque Ports. It was the favorite residence of the Duke of Wellington, who died there; it contains relics of him, of Pitt, and of other lord wardens.

WALNUT, a genus, *Juglans,* of beautiful trees comprising seven or eight species of the Juglandaceae family. The common walnut, *J. regia,* is a native of Iran and the Himalayas, but has long been cultivated in all parts of the s. of Europe. It is a lofty tree of 60 to 90 ft., with large spreading branches. The leaves have two to four pairs of leaflets and a terminal one. The ripe fruit is one of the best of nuts, and is

Flowering branch of the common walnut tree

an important article of export from many parts of the s. of Europe. Walnuts yield by expression a bland fixed oil, which, under the names of *walnut oil* and *nut oil,* is much used by painters as a drying oil. The timber of the walnut is of great value, and is much used by cabinetmakers.

WALNUT CANYON NATIONAL MONUMENT, a national monument in central Arizona, established in 1915, and containing the remains of about 300 prehistoric Indian cliff dwellings. The monument, situated a few miles S.E of Flagstaff, covers an area of 1642 acres on both sides of Walnut Canyon, a limestone chasm. The cliff dwellings, built in the side of the canyon walls, are believed to have been inhabited between 900 and 1300 A.D. Each separate dwelling contains 6 to 8 rooms, apparently accommodating single family units. A solitary butte in the center of the canyon floor was probably used as a fort by the cliff dwellers, as remains of masonry fortifications have been found along its slopes.

WALPOLE, a town of Norfolk Co., Mass., situated on the Neponset R., 18 miles s.s.w. of Boston. Transportation facilities include a railroad. Walpole is a manufacturing center, producing twine, yarn, cotton batting, woolen textiles, paper, emery, flooring, roofing, boxes, chairs, and machinery. Pop. (1947) 8409.

WALPOLE, a town of Cheshire Co., N.H., situated on the Connecticut R., 4 miles s. of Bellows Falls, Vt. The town, which includes several villages, is served by a railroad. The surrounding area is agricultural, and Walpole is chiefly a residential community. It contains several fine old mansions, notably the Peck or General Allen House, built in 1792. The town was founded in 1749. Pop. (1940) 2400.

WALPOLE, HORACE, 4th EARL OF ORFORD (1717–97), English author and virtuoso, born in London, the third son of Sir Robert Walpole. He became a collector and connoisseur, dabbling lightly in verse and *jeux d'esprit*, trifling with history and art criticism, and corresponding voluminously with his friends. In 1791, by the death of his eldest brother's son, he became fourth Earl of Orford.

Walpole had gifts as a verse writer and was also skilled in the realm of fiction. In the *Castle of Otranto* (1764) he inaugurated a new era of supernatural romance. His tragedy *The Mysterious Mother* (1768) is extremely powerful.

Walpole's literary reputation now rests chiefly upon his letters, of which those to Mann, continued assiduously for forty years, form the staple. Croker, reiterating Byron's opinion that they are incomparable, says that they are "a perfect encyclopedia of information from the very best sources". The standard collection of Walpole's *Letters* (16 vols., 1903–05) was edited by Mrs. Toynbee.

WALPOLE, HUGH SEYMOUR (1884–1941), English novelist, son of the Right Reverend G.H.S. Walpole, Bishop of Edinburgh, born in New Zealand, and educated at King's School, Canterbury, and at Emmanuel College, Cambridge. He subsequently taught school for a time. He wrote his first novel, *The Wooden Horse,* in 1909, and after its publication turned to literature as a profession. He served with the Russian Red Cross during 1914–16, and became a commander of the Order of the British Empire (1918), and holder of the Georgian Medal. In addition to that mentioned, his long list of novels includes *Maradick at Forty* (1910), *Mr. Perrin and Mr. Trail* (1911), *The Prelude to Adventure* (1912), *Fortitude* (1913), *The Duchess of Wrexe* (1914), *The Golden Scarecrow*

(1915), *The Dark Forest* (1916), *The Green Mirror* (1918), *Jeremy* (1919), *The Captives* (1920), *The Thirteen Travellers* (1921), *The Young Enchanted* (1922), *Jeremy and Hamlet* (1923), *The Old Ladies* (1924), *Portrait of a Man with Red Hair* (1925), *Harmer John* (1926), *Judith Paris* (1931), *Fortress* (1932), *Vanessa* (1933), *The Inquisitor* (1935), *John Cornelius* (1937), *The Sea Tower* (1939), and *The Bright Pavilions* (1940).

WALPOLE, Sir Robert, 1st Earl of Orford (1676–1745), English statesman, born in Norfolk. In 1701 he was returned to Parliament for Castle Rising. In 1702 he was member for King's Lynn, and soon won the esteem of Godolphin, Marlborough, and other Whig leaders. In 1708 he was secretary of war, and in 1710 treasurer of the navy. Shortly after this he was found guilty by a Tory House of Commons of "breach of trust and notorious corruption", and on January 17, 1712, was sent to the Tower; but the charge was due to party animosity. He had always been a strong Hanoverian, and on the accession of George I he was restored to fortune. On the impeachment of Bolingbroke and others he became in 1715 chancellor of the exchequer and first lord of the treasury. In 1717 he resigned office. Sunderland gave Walpole (1720) the post of paymaster general, and after the collapse of the South Sea Scheme the public looked to Walpole to restore order in public affairs; in 1721 he became first lord of the treasury and chancellor of the exchequer, and from this time to his retirement in 1742 the life of Walpole may be said to be the history of England. He was the first to give to the cabinet the necessary unity. By systematic bribery he secured a Whig House of Commons, and in the House of Commons secured majorities. He resigned on February 2, 1742, when he was created Earl of Orford, with a pension of $20,000 a year.

Walpole had strong common sense, with clearness of political vision, and seems to have understood the true interests of his country beyond any of his contemporaries.

WALPOLE, Sir Spencer (1839–1907), English writer, known chiefly for his historical works. His *History of England from 1815*, which appeared in five volumes from 1878 to 1886, is in some respects the best work that appeared on England in the 19th century. In 1898 Walpole was knighted. Other works by him are *The Electorate and the Legislature, Foreign Relations, Life of Lord John Russell, The History of Twenty-Five Years,* and *Essays Political and Biographical.*

WALPURGA, Saint (710?–77), English saint, sister of St. Wilibald. She came with him from England to Germany, and was abbess of Heidenheim. Her feast day is May 1, hence she has been associated with some popular superstitions connected with this date. During "Walpurgis Night", the witches were supposed to ride on broomsticks to the ancient places of sacrifice, to revel with Satan. One of the best known of witch hills was the highest point of the Harz, the Brocken, the scene of the witches' Sabbath in Goethe's *Faust*.

WALRUS, a large marine mammal, *Odobenus rosmarus,* found in the Arctic regions of both hemispheres and related to the eared seals. The Pacific walruses differ in some minor respects from Atlantic walruses, and are usually classified as a distinct subspecies, *O. rosmarus divergens.* The walrus averages 11 to 14 feet in length, although larger animals have been reliably reported. A full-grown male ranges in weight from 1000 to 3000 pounds, and the female from 1500 to 2500 pounds. The anterior portion of the skull is greatly enlarged and the upper canine teeth are enormously elongated and laterally compressed to form tusks. Walrus tusks may measure from 15 to 30 inches in length. A young walrus possesses thirty teeth altogether, but in the adult this number is reduced to eighteen. All but the upper canine adult teeth have blunt crowns adapted to crushing and grinding the

Horace Walpole

The Atlantic walrus (Odobenus rosmarus)
— N.Y. Zoological Society

mollusks which comprise the major portion of their diet. The head of the walrus is rather small in relation to the size of the body; it is squared off, or truncated, in front and rounded behind. External ear apparatus is completely lacking. The broad muzzle, or cheek structure, is equipped with a number of very stout bristles which are translucent in appearance. The eyes are extremely small and set well back on the head. The lower jaw comes to a point between the tusks. The neck is short and thick. The body of the walrus is massive, diminishing in size from the shoulders to the hind quarters. The tail is rudimentary and the limbs are largely enclosed within the body skin. The exposed portions of the limbs are swimming appendages called flippers. Young walruses are covered with thick, short, reddish-brown fur. Fur of older walruses is scanty and may even disappear in large areas of the hide. The skin lies in wrinkled folds over the body, the folds being most numerous in the shoulder region. The Pacific walrus differs from the Atlantic variety by its longer, more slender tusks and shorter muzzle bristles.

Walruses were formerly indigenous to most waters of the Temperate Zone, but they were so persistently hunted and slaughtered for their ivory tusks, hides, and oil that their range is now restricted to the extreme northern latitudes.

Walruses are highly social animals, and are usually seen in the neighborhood of shores or masses of floating ice blocks congregated in herds. They are excellent, agile swimmers but are clumsy on solid surfaces on which they usually rest huddled closely together. They breed from April to June, remaining then on shore. Usually one calf is born each year. The gestation period is nine months and the young are suckled for three years. Walruses have loud voices, approximating a roar, and the noise made by a herd can be heard for several miles. The animal is gentle unless attacked; the whole herd comes to the defense of an attacked member. Polar bears and man are the chief enemies of the walrus.

WALSALL, a municipal, parliamentary, and county borough in Staffordshire, England, 8 miles N.N.W. of Birmingham. It stands on the edge of the Staffordshire coal field, and has manufactures of saddlers' ironmongery and all kinds of saddlery, carriages, iron and brass, and leather, while in the vicinity are coal pits, limestone quarries, and brickyards. Pop., about 107,000.

WALSENBURG, county seat of Huerfano Co., Colo., situated on the Cucharas R., about 175 miles s. of Denver. It is served by two railroads, and is the distributing center of an extensive farming and stock-raising area. Pop. (1948 est.) 7000.

WALSH, EDWARD ARTHUR (1882–   ), American professional baseball player, born in Plains, Pa. Walsh was a noted right-hand pitcher, especially remarkable for his mastery of the "spitball" pitching delivery. In this delivery the baseball, a portion of its cover well moistened by saliva, describes, after being thrown, curves that are extraordinarily sharp, and unpredictable and baffling to the batter; the spitball and other so-called "freak" deliveries are currently banned in baseball. After a career in minor leagues, Walsh was from 1906 to 1912 a member of the Chicago team ("White Sox") of the American League; subsequently he was briefly on the Boston team of the National League. Walsh was especially noted for the number of games in which he pitched during a season; he appeared in 66 games in 1908, a record number for more than forty years, and in 62 games in 1912. Altogether he pitched 432 games during his major-league career, winning 181 and losing 117 for a percentage of .607. He was appointed to the Baseball Hall of Fame (q.v.) in 1946.

WALSH, FRANCIS PATRICK (1864–1939), American lawyer and investigator, born in St. Louis, and educated at St. Patrick's Academy in that city. He was admitted to the Missouri bar in 1889, and was a member of the Kansas City Tenement Commission from 1906 to 1908. In the same city Walsh became attorney of the Board of Public Welfare in 1908 and president of the Board of Civil Service in 1911. In 1913, President Woodrow Wilson made him chairman of the Federal Commission on Industrial Relations, in which office he attracted attention by his investigation of industrial conditions in Colorado. In 1920 he was chairman and promoter of the Irish Bond Drive, and for a while the legal representative in the United States of Irish Republicans. In 1929 he was appointed a member of the New York Commission on revision of Public Utility Laws, and in 1931, chairman of the Power Authority of New York State.

WALSH, JAMES ANTHONY (1867–1936), American clergyman and educator, born in Cambridge, Mass., and educated at Boston College and Harvard University. After his ordination to the priesthood, he served for a time as assistant pastor at St. Patrick's Church, Boston, In 1903 he was appointed archdiocesan director of the Society for the Propagation of the Faith; in 1911 he was made president of the Catholic Foreign Mission Society of America and, also, in the same year, became Superior of the American Foreign Seminary at Maryknoll, Ossining, N.Y., a position which he held until his death. At Maryknoll Seminary students are prepared for the priesthood to serve in foreign mission fields, especially in the Orient.

WALSH, JAMES JOSEPH (1865–1942), American physician and author, born in Archbald, Pa., and educated at Fordham College and the University of Pennsylvania. After postgraduate work in Paris, Vienna, and Berlin he settled in New York, where in 1906 he became professor of physiological psychology at Cathedral College and professor of nervous diseases in, and dean of, the Fordham Medical School. He resigned his Fordham offices in 1912. In 1916 he received the Lætare Medal. He contributed to medical and other journals, and published various works of popular type, including *Catholic Churchmen in Science, Makers of Modern Medicine, The Popes and Science, Modern Progress and History,* and *American Jesuits.*

WALSH, ROBERT (1784–1859), American author, born in Baltimore. In 1811 he began the publication of *The American Review of History and Politics,* which was the first American quarterly, and in 1817–18 he edited the *American Register.* In 1819 he founded, and until 1836 was editor of, the Philadelphia *National Gazette.* From 1845 to 1851 he was United States consul in Paris, where he resided until his death. His works include *Letter on the Genius and Disposition of the French Government* (1810), *Correspondence Respecting Russia* (1813), *Essay on the Future State of Europe* (1813), and *An Appeal from the Judgments of Great Britain Respecting the United States* (1819).

WALSH, STEPHEN (1859–1929), English labor leader, born in Liverpool. He attended an industrial school at Kirkdale near there, and at the age of thirteen went to work in the Wigan coal field, where he soon gained a reputation among the miners as a leader. In 1906 he was elected to represent the Ince Division, Lancashire, and was re-elected periodically until his death. He had an important part in the labor legislation of Parliament and, from 1914 to 1920, served as chairman of the miner's section of the English Conciliation Board. He was parliamentary secretary to the Ministry of National Service in 1927, and to the Local Government Board, 1917–19. In 1921–22 he was vice-chairman of the Labor Party in the House of Commons, and in 1924, during the first Labor administration of England he was secretary of state for war.

Bruno Walter — Columbia Records, Inc.

WALSH, THOMAS JAMES (1859–1933), American legislator, born in Two Rivers, Wis., and educated at the University of Wisconsin. He took up the practice of law in Redfield, S.Dak. Moving to Helena, Mont., in 1890, he became interested in land and cattle companies in that State in addition to his law practice. Walsh was unsuccessful as Democratic candidate for representative in Congress in 1906 and for senator in 1910, but was elected to the latter office for the term 1913–19. He was re-elected senator from Montana in 1931 for the period ending March 4, 1937. As chairman of a subcommittee of the Senate Committee on Public Lands, Senator Walsh conducted a searching investigation of government oil-land leases in 1924. He also was active as a member of the foreign relations committee.

WALSH, WILLIAM J. (1841–1921), Irish Roman Catholic prelate, born in Dublin and educated at Maynooth College, where he became professor of dogmatic and moral theology in 1867. He was made vice-president in 1878, and in 1881 was unanimously chosen president. He was consecrated archbishop of Dublin in 1885. He played an important part in the Irish politics of his time. In addition to religious works, he wrote *Bimetallism and Monometallism.*

WALSINGHAM, a town in the county of Norfolk, England. It is noted for the ruins of an Augustinian priory, traditionally dated from 1016. To "Our Lady of Walsingham" came barefoot pilgrims from all over Europe, including Erasmus and Henry VIII. Pop., about 1100.

WALSINGHAM, SIR FRANCIS (about 1536–90), English statesman, born in Chiselhurst, Kent. In 1573 he was appointed one of the principal secretaries of state to Queen Elizabeth. He was regarded by the adherents of Mary, Queen of Scots, as the most insidious of her enemies. He intercepted her letters, and after deciphering them sent them to their destination. He soon held Mary in the toils. Walsingham was distinguished for acuteness of penetration and profound acquaintance with human nature. He had in his pay agents and spies in various countries; nevertheless, his personal integrity and patriotism were undoubted.

WALTER, BRUNO (1876–   ), German conductor, born in Berlin, and trained under Ehrlich, Bussler, and Radecke at Stern's Conservatory. After short periods as conductor in Cologne, Hamburg, Breslau, Pressburg, Riga, and Berlin, he rose rapidly to a position of pre-eminence through his brilliant work at the Hofoper in Vienna (1901–13). He was Hofkapellmeister and General-musikdirektor in Munich, 1914–22, conductor of the Leipzig Gewandhaus Orchestra, 1929–33, and Vienna State Opera, 1935–38. He made extensive tours as a guest conductor and in 1923 visited the United States, where his appearances with the New York, Boston, Minneapolis, and Detroit Symphony orchestras made a profound impression. He was the regular conductor of the German operas at Covent Garden after 1924. He has made guest appearances all over the U.S., conducting the National Broadcasting Orchestra, at the San Francisco World's Fair, and Metropolitan Opera House in New York where he assumed a conductorship in 1940.

WALTER, EUGENE (1874–1941), American playwright, born in Cleveland, Ohio. He began his career as a reporter on the Cleveland *Plain Dealer* and was later connected with several newspapers in different parts of the country. Subsequently he acted as advance agent and business manager for various traveling theatrical companies. He began writing for the stage in 1900, and his first successful play, *Paid in Full,* was produced in New York in 1908. His later plays include *The Easiest Way*

(1908), *Fine Feathers* (1911), *Just a Woman* (1916), *Little Shepherd of Kingdom Come* (1916), *The Assassin* (1917), *The Challenge* (1919), *The Toy Girl* (1921), and *Thieves in Clover* (1923). Walter also wrote numerous moving picture scenarios.

WALTER, HUBERT (about 1150–1205), English statesman and ecclesiastic. He accompanied Richard I on the Crusade. Returning to England (1193), Walter superintended the collection of money for Richard's ransom. At the same time he was chosen archbishop of Canterbury, and when King Richard returned he appointed Hubert justiciar of the realm, and left him virtual ruler of England. But the Cathedral Chapter objected to the employment of the archbishop in the royal service, and in 1198 Innocent III compelled him to resign by forbidding priests to hold secular offices

WALTER, JOHN (1739–1812), the founder of the London *Times*. He was born in London, the son of a coal merchant, to whose business he succeeded in 1755. He was very successful and established the coal exchange. In 1781, however, he retired from the coal business in order to take up the vocation of an underwriter. While at first successful, his speculations resulted in his failure in 1782. He succeeded in paying his creditors, who thereupon made him a gift of money. With this sum Walter purchased the patents of a new printing process and established the printing office in Blackfriars (1784), which is still the seat of *The Times*. On Jan. 1, 1785, appeared the first issue of *The Daily Universal Register,* which on Jan. 1, 1788, was changed to *The Times,* or *Daily Universal Register,* and on March 18 of that year became simply *The Times*. From the first it showed that attention to Parliamentary debates and that independence of attitude which have always been its distinguishing characteristics. Indeed, Walter was twice imprisoned and five times fined for libel, in consequence of the freedom of his comments.

WALTER, THOMAS USTICK (1804–87), American architect, born in Philadelphia, and trained under William Strickland. He began practice in 1830. He designed many important buildings in Philadelphia, including the Chester County Bank, Saint George's Hall, Girard College, and the Philadelphia Savings Bank. The breakwater at La Guaira, Venezuela, was also designed by him, and in 1848 he was commissioned by President Fillmore to superintend the enlargement of the Capitol in Washington. During the fourteen years he was engaged in this work he completed the Treasury Building and the Washington Post Office. In 1876 he was elected president of the American Institute of Architects.

WALTERS COLLECTION, one of the most important art collections in the United States, located in Baltimore, Md. It was begun by William Thompson Walters (1820–94), merchant and capitalist, who had been art commissioner from the United States to the Paris expositions of 1867 and 1878 and to the Vienna Exposition in 1873. He acquired an extraordinary collection of modern French paintings, including many celebrated pieces, the most extensive existing collection of bronzes and water colors by the French sculptor Barye, and a unique collection of Chinese porcelains, especially peach blooms. His collection was much increased by his son Henry Walters, who constructed the building which was opened to the public in 1909. To him the museum owes its collection of ancient art, particularly Greek and Roman sculptures, and Italian paintings.

WALTHAM, a city of Middlesex Co., Mass., situated on the Charles R., 9 miles w. of Boston. Transportation facilities include two railroads. The city is the retail trading center of an area with a radius of 15 miles and a population of about 300,000, and is also an important manufacturing center, with diversified industries. Waltham is especially famous for the manufacture of precision parts and products, notably the watches produced by the Waltham Watch Company, founded in 1849, the first successful watch factory in the U.S. and one of the largest in the world. Among other products of the more than 150 industrial establishments in the city are radar equipment, rivets, tower clocks, gauges, small machined parts, bearing jewels, salesbooks, screws, lathes, electrical transformers, and vitreous enameled products. Waltham is the site of Brandeis University, established in 1948. Other educational institutions in the city include the Waltham Training School for Nurses (1885), first institution of its kind in the U.S., Notre Dame Training School, Chapel Hill School for Girls, and the Massachusetts State College Field Station. Waltham was incorporated as a town in 1738 and as a city in 1884. It is said to be the site of the first cotton mill in the U.S. in which all the operations of manufacturing cotton cloth were performed under one roof, and of the first factory manufacturing chalk rayons. Pop. (1950) 47,198.

WALTHAM ABBEY, or WALTHAM HOLY CROSS, market town in the county of Essex, England, on the Lea, 12 miles N. of London.

Izaak Walton instructing a pupil in the methods of catching fish (from a painting)

The town takes its name from the Abbey of the Holy Cross, founded by King Harold, who is buried there. Of the magnificent Norman church only the nave remains, but this is held to be one of the finest specimens of this style in England. The reconstructed Temple Bar, which from 1670 to 1880 stood at the west end of Fleet Street, London, marks one of the entrances to Theobald's Park. The government gunpowder and flour mills, operated by the water power of the Lea, the government Enfield factory for rifles, at Enfield Lock, and large cordite factories at Quinton Hill just outside the town, are the chief industrial establishments. Pop., about 7000.

WALTHAMSTOW, an urban district in Essex, England, 6 miles N.E. of St. Paul's, London. Brewing is its chief industry. It contains a number of educational institutions, the most important of which is a large public school for boys, called the Forest School. Pop., about 130,000.

WALTHER VON DER VOGELWEIDE (about 1160–1230), German poet of the Middle Ages, born probably in Tirol. In 1180–98 he was in high favor in Vienna, at the court of the dukes of Austria, and later at Mainz and Magdeburg; in 1204 he outshone his rivals in the poetical contest at the Wartburg.

WALTON, a village of Delaware Co., N.Y., situated on the Delaware R., about 68 miles s. of Utica. Transportation facilities include a railroad. The village is surrounded by a farming and dairying region. The principal industrial establishments in Walton are condenseries, creameries, woodworking shops, iron foundries, and factories producing cheese and silk goods. Walton was incorporated as a village in 1851. Pop. (1940) 3697.

WALTON, BRIAN (1600–61), editor of the London Polyglot Bible, born in Seymour, Yorkshire, England. After 1641 he found refuge in London, where he devoted himself to his great work, which was published in six folio volumes (1654–57). Walton was consecrated bishop of Chester in December 1660, and died in London. Some portions of his Polyglot are printed in seven languages, all open at one view. No one book is given in nine languages, but nine are used in the course of the work. They are Hebrew, Chaldee, Samaritan, Syriac, Arabic, Persian, Ethiopic, Greek, and Latin.

WALTON, GEORGE (1740–1804), American lawyer, born in Frederick County, Va. He was admitted to the Georgia bar in 1774. He began practice in Augusta, Ga., took a prominent part in opposing the policy of the British government, and in 1776–81 was a member of the Continental Congress. In 1778 he served as a colonel of militia, was taken prisoner at the capture of Savannah, but was exchanged in 1779, and later in the same year was elected governor of Georgia. During 1783–93 he was chief justice of the State, was elected to the legislature several times, and was a member of the United States Senate in 1795–96. He was one of the signers of the Declaration of Independence.

WALTON, IZAAK (1593–1683), English essayist and poet, known as the "Father of Angling", born in Stafford, England. In 1624 he settled near Chancery Lane, London, as a linen draper. Later he removed into Chancery Lane itself. About 1644 he retired from business. Wood tells us that Izaak Walton spent most of his time "in the families of the eminent clergymen of England, of whom he was much beloved". He had been a friend of Donne, and Donne's sermons being about to be reprinted without a life history, Walton took up the task, and produced one of the most delightful biographies in miniature in English literature. In his later years Walton lived much of the time at Winchester.

The first edition of *The Compleat Angler, or the Contemplative Man's Recreation,* appeared in 1653; the fourth, grown from thirteen chapters to twenty-one, in 1676. Appearing in five editions in Walton's lifetime, it has since been published more than one hundred times, and the demand for "Waltoniana" has given a high value to the earlier copies. A supplement upon fly fishing, by his close friend, Charles Cotton, was added to the fifth edition and now forms the second part of the work. The discourse is interspersed with dialogue, quaint verses, songs, and idyllic glimpses of country life, and the whole breathes such cheerful contentment, and sweet freshness, as to give the book a charm altogether its own.

WALTON, WILLIAM TURNER (1902–   ), English composer, born in Oldham, and trained as a chorister at Christ Church Cathedral, Oxford University. In his youth he was associated with the English writers Osbert and Edith Sitwell; his first notable composition was a satiric suite, *Façade* (1923), composed to accompany recitations of poems by Edith Sitwell. In the same year he reached a wider, international audience with a string quartet, which was selected by a jury for performance at an international festival of contemporary music given in Salzburg, Austria. Walton's subsequent work forms a distinguished contribution to the body of modern music often called neo-Romantic. His style is generally marked by brilliant orchestration and musical wit; in more abstract works, however, his music exhibits a meditative strain, often with overtones of tragedy or pathos. Among his other works are the overture *Portsmouth Point* (1925), a *Viola Concerto* (1929), the oratorio *Belshazzar's Feast* (1931), a *Symphony* (1935), and a *Violin Concerto* (1939).

WALTZ, German dance which first became a fashionable dance in other countries in the early part of the 19th century, being introduced into England in 1813. The *Valse à Deux Temps* is a form of the waltz not so graceful as the older one, because not so correspondent to the rhythm of the music. Strauss, Gungl, and Godfrey are well-known waltz composers; and there are idealized concert-waltzes by Chopin, Liszt, and Brahms.

WALVIS BAY. See WALFISH BAY.

WAMPANOAG, an Algonquian tribe that formerly held the eastern shore of Narragansett Bay. They owned some thirty villages

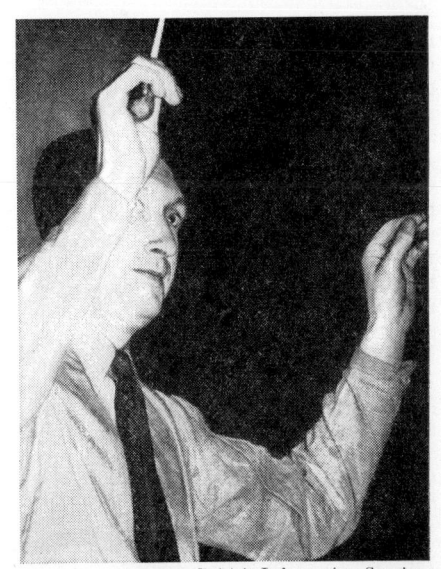

British Information Services
William Turner Walton

and numbered several thousands. By the pestilence of 1617 and King Philip's War they were nearly exterminated. The remnant of the tribe was either sold into slavery or amalgamated with the friendly Indians at Saconnet, R.I., who also became extinct during the next century.

WAMPUM, beads formed of the interior parts of shells strung on threads, formerly used among the American Indians as currency, and worn also in necklaces, bracelets, belts, and scabbards. The fathom was the name for a count, the number varying with the exchange.

Perhaps the most important use of wampum was in the symbolic record belts and strings which gave the stamp of authority to every intertribal transaction. No message from one tribe or council to another was considered official without the delivery at the same time of a string or belt of wampum, which was thenceforth preserved by the recipients as proof of the negotiation, the belt being handed over to the keeping of the custodian of the records. Such belts usually had the beads arranged in symbolic figures more or less suggestive of the transaction thus ratified. Wampum belts were used in the ratification of every important treaty negotiated with the Eastern tribes from the early colonial period down to the great intertribal treaty of Prairie du Chien in 1825. In 1843, at the intertribal council at Tahlequah, the Cherokee produced the belts which attested the peace made with the Iroquois before the Revolutionary War. The Iroquois themselves still preserve several of their ancient record belts; others of historic importance are preserved among the archives of New York State in Albany and elsewhere.

WANAMAKER, JOHN (1838–1922), American merchant and cabinet officer, born in Philadelphia. He entered mercantile life in Philadelphia in 1856 and gradually built up a large retail business. In 1896 he reopened the department store founded in New York by A.T. Stewart. He was president of the Young Men's Christian Association in Philadelphia from 1870 to 1883, was one of the founders of the Christian Commission at the time of the Civil War, and was the founder of Bethany Sunday School, of which he was for many years the superintendent. From 1889 to 1893 he was postmaster general in President Harrison's cabinet.

WANAMAKER, (LEWIS) RODMAN (1863–1928), American merchant, son of John Wanamaker, born in Philadelphia. He became associated in business with his father as vice-president of the John Wanamaker stores in New York and Philadelphia. Following the death of his father, in 1922, he became head of the business. Wanamaker was a leader in numerous civic and philanthropic movements. He presented to New York the perpetually burning light and altar of liberty, in Madison Square, as a memorial to the American dead in World War I. In his later years he devoted much interest to the advancement of aviation.

WANDERING JEW, in botany. See COMMELINACEAE.

WANDERING JEW, THE, the central figure of a medieval legend about a Jew who refused to allow Jesus Christ to rest at his door as he bore his cross toward Calvary. Thereafter, the Jew was condemned to wander over the face of the earth till the end of the world. The legend describes him as Ahasuerus, a cobbler, who hustled Jesus away, saying "Away with you, away!" Jesus replied, "Truly I go away, and that quickly, but tarry thou till I come."

A second legend (*Chronicle of St. Albans Abbey,* 1228) describes the Wandering Jew as Kartaphilos, the doorkeeper of the judgment hall and in the service of Pontius Pilate. He struck Jesus as he led Him forth, saying, "Go on faster, Jesus"; whereupon the Man of Sorrows replied, "I am going, but thou shalt tarry till I come again."

According to the same *Chronicle,* continued by Matthew Paris, Kartaphilos was baptized by Ananias, and received the name of Joseph. At the end of every hundred years he falls into a trance, and wakes up a young man about thirty.

In German legend the Wandering Jew is associated with John Buttadæus, seen in Antwerp in the 13th century, again in the 15th, and a third time in the 16th. His last appearance was in 1774 in Brussels. In a French version he is named Isaac Laquedem, or Lakedion. Another story describes him as Salatheil ben Sadi, who appeared and disappeared toward the close of the 16th century, in Venice, in so sudden a manner as to attract the notice of all Europe.

WANDEROO. See LANGUR.

WANDSWORTH, metropolitan borough of the city of London, England. It has oil mills, dye and paper works, as well as breweries and manufactures of calico. Pop. (1945) 289,780.

WANG AN-SHIH (fl. 1021–86), Chinese economic reformer. After becoming state councilor in 1069, Wang instituted measures

A full-grown wapiti stag

N.Y. Zoological Society

for nationalization of agrarian resources. A state monopoly in commerce was intended to dispose of the crops, lighten the burden of the farmer, and bring in a revenue to the government. A loan to farmers, which they would be forced to accept, was to bring the government interest at the rate of 2 percent, and taxation of land was to be in proportion to fertility. Wang's policies, unpopular generally, were reversed by his successor.

WAPAKONETA, county seat of Auglaize Co., Ohio, situated on the Auglaize R., about 56 miles N. of Dayton. It is served by two railroads. The city is surrounded by a fertile agricultural area in which are fields of oil and natural gas. Wapakoneta is an important churn-manufacturing center. Other leading industries in the city are the processing of dairy products and the manufacture of canned goods, beverages, machine knives, tool and shovel handles, farm and garden tools, trailers, soles and heels, furniture, and toys. Historical landmarks include a monument marking the site of old Fort Amanda, a stockade used during the War of 1812. The village was founded in 1833 on the site of a former Indian settlement. Pop. (1948 est.) 6000.

WAPENTAKE, in English law, an equivalent of the word "hundred", meaning a subdivision of a county. Originally it signified a gathering of the male citizens of a district to prepare for a military expedition or defense, the word itself being derived from two Saxon words meaning to take or touch weapons. By popular usage the term was later applied to a district from which a certain number of men capable of bearing arms were raised. The term was also applied to a Saxon court held at regular intervals by the chief men of a hundred. The wapentake is obsolete as a subdivision of a county, although the word is sometimes used as a matter of description in speaking of a district.

WAPITI, a ruminant mammal, *Cervus canadensis,* belonging to the Deer family. The animal, native to the northern part of the Western Hemisphere, has dark-brown fur on the head and neck, and creamy-gray fur on the back and flanks. A full-grown stag stands about 5½ feet high at the shoulder, and weighs about 700 pounds. The antlers are smooth and attain a great size, averaging over 4 feet each in length. The antlers are shed in March, begin to grow again in late spring, and are fully grown by fall. The wapiti formerly ranged throughout the temperate regions of the Western Hemisphere, but the advance of civilization, limiting its range and causing huge herds to be slaughtered for food and sport, effected a great reduction in numbers; the animal is now largely restricted to the western mountainous areas of western United States and Canada. The stags live apart from the main herd during most of the year, joining the herd only during the mating season. At this time the stags fight furiously over the right to the females, accompanying these fights with a braying call which has earned the animals the name of "jackass deer" in certain sections of the Rocky Mountains. In late spring wapitis leave the lowlands and migrate to the upper reaches of the mountain forests. The doe bears a single fawn soon after reaching the forest. Wapiti feed early in the morning and late in the afternoon, but never at night as do most deer. They eat almost any kind of plant.

WAPPÄUS, JOHANN EDUARD (1812–79), German geographer and statistician, born in Hamburg, and educated at the universities of Göttingen and Berlin. Wappäus was the first to impress upon his countrymen the possibilities of South America as a field for national enterprise. In 1845 he was made professor extraordinary, and in 1854 professor, at Göttingen. His works include *Untersuchungen über die Geographischen Entdeckungen der Portugiesen unter Heinrich dem Seefahrer* (1842), *Die Republiken von Südamerika* (1843), *Deutsche Auswanderung und Kolonisation* (2 parts, 1846–48), *Allgemeine Bevölkerungsstatistik* (2 vols., 1859–61), and *Einleitung in das Studium der Statistik* (published posthumously, 1881). The great work of Wappäus' life was the editing, 1847–71, of the seventh edition (10 vols.) of the monumental *Handbuch der Geographie und Statistik* by Stein and Hörschelmann. He himself contributed the introductory volume on universal geography (1849) and the three volumes devoted to the American continents (1855–67).

WAPPERS, BARON GUSTAVE (1803–74), Belgian historical and genre painter, born and trained in Antwerp. He went to The Hague, Amsterdam, and Paris, where he studied the old Flemish, Dutch, and Venetian masters. At Paris he fell for a time under the classical influence, and in 1823 painted a "Regulus" in that manner. Upon his return to Antwerp in 1830 he exhibited "Burgomaster van der Werff at the Siege of Leyden" (Utrecht Museum), a picture which in its color and fullness of life showed the influence of the old Flemish masters, and he was hailed as the deliverer of Belgian art from French bondage. In 1832 he became professor and in 1840 director of the Antwerp Academy, and from 1846 to 1853 was president of the National Museum. In 1859 he removed to Paris, where he died. His "Episode of the Belgian Revolution of 1830" (1834, Brussels Museum) confirmed him as the leader of the reaction against classicism, a position corresponding to that of the French painter Ferdinand Victor Eugène Delacroix in France. Wappers' fame has since declined. His pictures are chiefly to be found in the museums of Holland and Belgium.

WAPPINGERS FALLS, village in Dutchess County, N.Y., 7 miles s. of Poughkeepsie. Manufactured products include overalls, print cloths, dyes, sheets, and pillow cases. Pop. (1940) 3427.

WAR, in international law (q.v.), armed conflict between two or more governments or states. War between states or nations is termed international or public war; war between different parts or factions of the same nation is termed civil war. A rebellion (q.v.) is not war; to entitle the armed forces of the rebels to the rights and privileges of belligerents (see

BELLIGERENT), the government which they serve must be organized so as to be in a position to meet the duties resting on belligerents, that is, they must have the power to maintain law and order within the regions occupied by them and to carry on war on a large scale by land, sea, or air. War may begin formally with a declaration, or informally by an act of hostility. Under the provisions of the Hague Convention of 1907 (See HAGUE CONFERENCES) relative to the opening of hostilities, the contracting powers agreed that, before the actual commencement of war, there should be explicit warning "in the form either of a reasoned declaration of war or of an ultimatum with conditional declaration of war" (see DECLARATION OF WAR). Examples of formal declarations of war were the German ultimatum to Russia in 1914, and the proclamation of war by the United States against Germany in 1941. Nations may engage in hostilities without a formal declaration of war, as was the case with China and Japan in 1894 and again in 1931. International wars are generally terminated by treaty (q.v.), and civil wars by a peace proclamation. The usages, customs, and treaties of nations have formulated a code or system of laws of war (see BLOCKADE; NEUTRALITY; PRISONERS OF WAR; PRIZE; SEARCH, RIGHT OF).

In the United States only Congress is given the power under the Constitution (Art. 1. Sec. 8) "to declare war, grant letters of marque and reprisal, and make rules concerning captures on land and water". Congress also is authorized to "raise and support armies, but no appropriation of money to that use shall be for a longer term than two years". Under Art. 1, Sec. 10 of the Constitution, no State may "without the consent of Congress engage in war, unless actually invaded, or in such imminent danger as will not admit of delay". The President of the United States is the "Commander-in-Chief of the Army and Navy and of the militia of the several States when called into the actual service of the United States". The President may use the armed forces of the country without waiting for Congress to make a declaration of war, in the case of sudden invasion to repel foreign aggression.

WARBECK, PERKIN (1474–99), pretender to the English throne, born in Tournai. In 1491 he went to Cork and agreed at the instigation of opponents of Henry VII to set up a claim that he was Richard, Duke of York, second son of Edward IV. For a while he received some support, especially among foreign powers hostile to England and Henry VII. James IV of Scotland even gave him his own cousin, Catherine Gordon, as wife in 1495. In 1497 he made an expedition into England, but was captured. He confessed his imposture and, engaging in new conspiracies, he was condemned to death and executed at Tyburn.

WARBLER, popular name often applied to birds of the family Sylviidae. The grasshopper warbler is found in most parts of the center and south of Europe, at least during summer, being a bird of passage. It is of a greenish-brown color, the centers of the feathers dark brown, producing a spotted appearance; the lower parts pale brown. The sedge warbler, *A. schœnobaenus,* is generally found in thick patches of reeds or willows in marshes, or in other locations near water. The reed warbler, *A. streperus,* abounds in Holland and in many parts of Europe, and its range extends to the north of India. The chiffchaff, *P. collybita,* so named from its two-noted cry, is a familiar early migrant to Britain. The willow warbler, *P. trochilus,* frequents woods, shrubberies, thick hedgerows, and bushes, but builds its nest on the ground. Numerous species of warblers are found in North America, but these belong to a distinct family, Mniotiltidae, which appear to graduate into the tanagers. They are birds of brighter plumage than the Old World warblers, but resemble them in their habits, and are also migrants. See MYRTLE BIRD.

WARBURG, PAUL MORITZ (1868–1932), American banker and financier, born in Germany, and educated in Hamburg. He traveled extensively and in 1894 became a member of his father's Hamburg banking house, M.M. Warburg and Company. In 1902 he became a partner in Kuhn, Loeb, and Company, New York, and was the representative of his firm in the five-power group that conducted unsuccessful negotiations for a Chinese loan in 1911–12. Warburg was a leader in the agitation for a central banking system for the United States, and his appointment by President Woodrow Wilson to the Federal Reserve Board in 1914 aided in gaining the approval of the financial interests to the new currency scheme. He wrote *Essays on Banking Reform in the United States* (1914).

WARBURTON, PETER EGERTON (1813–89), English traveler in Australia, born near Norwich, and educated in Orléans and Paris. He traveled through the northwestern part of Australia on camel back and, on several occasions, nearly starved in the desert. He wrote *Major Warburton's Diary* (1866) and *Journey* across the Western Interior of Australia (1875).

WARBURTON, WILLIAM (1698–1779), English prelate and author, born in Newark. His *Divine Legation of Moses* formed the foundation of his fame. In a series of letters he defended the orthodoxy of Pope's *Essay on Man* and won the friendship of the poet. Warburton became dean of Bristol (1757) and bishop of Gloucester (1759). To literature he contributed an edition of Shakespeare, a work on *Julian the Apostate,* an edition of Pope, and *Lord Bolingbroke's Philosophy.*

WAR COLLEGE, THE NATIONAL, a military institution situated in Washington, D.C., under the supervision of the Joint Chiefs of Staff. Its purpose is the training of selected officers of the Army, Navy, and Air Force, and of the State and other executive departments, for joint-staff and command duties in the interest of national security. Almost half of the academic year is devoted to the study of international relations and world affairs, United States commitments and responsibilities abroad, and the formulation and implementation of foreign policy. The remainder is devoted to the study of overall strategy, the strategic areas of the world, scientific and technological advances, and logistics. Founded in 1900 as the Army War College, the institution was reorganized under its present name during the unification of the armed forces following World War II. The permanent staff consists of a commandant, three deputy commandants, an executive officer, and several instructors including representatives of the Army, Navy, Air Force, and State Department.

WARD. See GUARDIAN.

WARD, SIR ADOLPHUS WILLIAM (1837–1924), English dramatic historian, born in London. His *History of English Dramatic Literature to the Death of Queen Anne* is the standard work on this subject. In 1900 he was elected master of Peterhouse, Cambridge, and from 1911 to 1913 he served as president of the British Academy. He also wrote *Chaucer* (1880); *Dickens* (1882); *Life of Sir Henry Wotton* (1897); and *Collected Papers, Historical, Literary, and Miscellaneous* (1921–22, 5 vols.).

WARD, ARTEMUS. See BROWNE, CHARLES FARRAR.

WARD, EDGAR MELVILLE (1839–1915), American genre painter, born in Urbana, Ohio. In 1883 he became a member of the National Academy and afterward was made a professor there. His paintings include "The Coppersmith" (Metropolitan Museum of Art, New York City).

WARD, EDWARD MATTHEW (1816–79), English historical painter, born in London. He painted several historical pictures for the corridor of the House of Commons and in 1855 became a member of the Royal Academy. His son LESLIE WARD was illustrator on the staff of *Vanity Fair* (1873–1909), known also for his representations of contemporary celebrities in the *World.*

WARD, FREDERICK TOWNSEND (1831–62), American military adventurer, born in Salem, Mass. He served as a lieutenant in the French army during the Crimean War. During the Taiping rebellion he went to China (1860), offered his services to the authorities, and for a reward of $200,000 recaptured Sungkiang. He acquired a position of influence, and was made an admiral general in the service of the emperor. In 1862 while leading an assault on Tsekil, he was mortally wounded.

WARD, GENEVIÈVE, COUNTESS DE GUERBEL (1838–1922), American actress, born in New York. As Ginevra Guerrabella she commenced her operatic career as Lucrezia Borgia in Milan, Italy (1856). On the stage, she made her first appearance at Manchester, England, in 1873 as Lady Macbeth. Later she acted in England with Sir Henry Irving in *Becket, Richard III,* and other plays.

WARD, HENRY AUGUSTUS (1834–1906), American naturalist, born in Rochester, N.Y. He made numerous collections of mineralogy and geology for American and European universities and museums. His works include *Descriptions of Celebrated Fossil Animals in Museums of Europe* (1866).

WARD, MRS. HUMPHRY, nee MARY AUGUSTA ARNOLD (1851–1920), English novelist, born in Hobart, Tasmania, the daughter of Thomas Arnold (1823–1900), granddaughter of Thomas Arnold (1795–1842), and niece of Matthew Arnold (1822–88). In 1872 she married Thomas Humphry Ward. She contributed four biographical introductions to the first volume of her husband's *English Poets* (1880–81). Her first success was *Robert Elsmere* (1888), which caused a sensation at the time because of its attack on Evangelical Christianity. Her later works include *England's Effort* (1916), *Toward the Goal* (1917), *Missing* (1917), *A Writer's Recollections* (1918), *The War and Elizabeth* (1918), and *Fields of Victory* (1919).

WARD, JAMES (1769–1859), English painter and engraver, born in London. He exhibited his first picture in 1790, and afterward received the official title of painter and mezzotint engraver to the Prince of Wales. His early paintings were principally genre pictures, but he won distinction in animal subjects. A characteristic painting is his portrait of himself painted when he was seventy-nine years old (National Portrait Gallery). Among the best of Ward's plates are the "Centurion Cornelius", after Rembrandt; "Daniel in the Lion's Den", after Rubens; "Juvenile Retirement", after Hoppner; and "Mrs. Billington", after Reynolds. Ward was elected an Academician in 1811. A complete set of his engravings is in the British Museum.

WARD, JAMES (1843–1925), British philosopher and psychologist, born in Hull, and educated at the universities of Berlin and Göttingen, and at Trinity College, Cambridge University. He became a fellow at Trinity College in 1875, and in 1897 became professor of mental philosophy at Cambridge University. His *Psychological Principles,* published in 1918, contains a systematic exposition of mental life from the point of view of the Act school. In it he defined the mind as a "continuum of presentations". His works also include *Naturalism and Agnosticism* (1899), *Heredity and Memory* (1913), *A Study of Kant* (1922), and *Essays in Philosophy* (1927).

WARD, JOHN QUINCY ADAMS (1830–1910), American sculptor, born in Urbana, Ohio. He opened a studio in New York City in 1861. He was elected a member of the National Academy of Design in 1863, became its president in 1872, and in 1896 was elected president of the newly organized National Sculpture Society. His "Indian Hunter" (1864) was the first statue erected in Central Park, New York City. Later works include the Soldiers' and Sailors' Monument in Syracuse, equestrian statue of General Sheridan in Washington, and the bronze equestrian statue of General Hancock in Philadelphia.

WARD, SIR JOSEPH (GEORGE), 1st BARONET (1856–1930), New Zealand statesman. As leader of the Liberal Party he sponsored much of New Zealand's progressive legislation. He served his first premiership during 1906–12. In 1915 Sir Joseph entered the National Ministry, a coalition of the Liberal and Reform parties brought about by World War I, as finance minister and postmaster general. During 1917–18 he represented New Zealand in the Imperial War Cabinet in London, and in 1919 at the Paris Peace Conference. In 1928, as leader of the United Party, he again became premier, but resigned this office in May, 1930, two months before his death.

WARD, LESTER FRANK (1841–1913), American geologist, paleontologist, sociologist, and philosophical writer, born in Joliet, Ill., and educated at the Columbian University. After sixteen years service in the United States Treasury Department, in 1881 he transferred to the Geological Survey, serving as geologist until 1892, and then as paleontologist until 1906. In 1906 he became professor of sociology at Brown University. He was a pioneer in American sociology. His works include *Geographical Distribution of Fossil Plants* (1888), *Outlines of Sociology* (1898), and *Glimpses of the Cosmos: a Mental Autobiography* (1913–18).

WARD, MARVIN HARVEY (1913–   ), American amateur golf player, born in Olympia, Wash. He won the United States Golf Association Amateur Championship in 1939 and 1941; the Washington State Open and Amateur Championships in 1938; the Pacific Northwest Open in 1939, 1941, 1946, and 1947; and the Western Amateur in 1941 and 1947. Ward was a member of the American Walker Cup Team in 1938 and 1947.

WARD, NATHANIEL (1578–1652), American colonial clergyman, born in Haverhill, Suffolk, England. He emigrated to the Massachusetts Bay Colony in 1634. In 1641 he compiled for the colony of Massachusetts the "Body of Liberties", which was adopted by the General Court. He returned to England (1646), and, under the pen name of "Theodore de la Guard" he wrote *The Simple Cobbler of Agawam in America* (1647).

WARD, (THOMAS) HUMPHRY (1845–1926), English author and journalist, born in Hull. He edited *The English Poets* (4 vols., 1880), a notable anthology; *The Reign of Queen Victoria* (1887); and *Men of the Time* (12th ed.); and wrote alone *Humphry Sandwith, a Memoir* (1884), and jointly *The Oxford Spectator* (1868) and *Romney* (1904). For his wife, see WARD, MRS. HUMPHRY.

WARD, WILLIAM GEORGE (1812–82), English philosopher and Roman Catholic theologian, born in London, and educated at Winchester College and at Christ Church and at Lincoln College, Oxford University. His theological views were ill-defined until he made the personal acquaintance of the English theologian John Henry Newman, against whom he had previously been prejudiced. By the single argument that the Catholic church of the 3rd or 4th century could never have developed from anything resembling modern Protestantism, Newman made him an ardent Tractarian (see TRACTARIANISM) and a bitter assailant of Anglican Protestantism. He became a deacon in 1838, a priest in 1840, editor of the Tractarian organ, the *British Critic,* in 1839, and, after 1841, when he openly defended Newman's *Tract XC*, and was deprived of his lectureship at Balliol College, an open advocate of union with Rome. His position was definitely stated in 1844 in *The Ideal of a Christian Church Considered in Comparison with Existing Practice.* The book was censured by the Convocation of Oxford, and Ward was deprived of his degrees. This was in February, 1845, and in September of the same year he joined the Roman Catholic communion. He settled at St. Edmund's College, Ware, became professor of moral philosophy there in 1852, and held this chair until 1858. He was made PH.D. by the pope in 1854. In 1861 he returned to St. Edmund's. In the preceding year he had published *On Nature and Grace,* an able attack on agnosticism. He was editor of the *Dublin Review* from 1863 to 1878, and a leader of the Roman Catholic factions known as the Ultramontanists and Infallibilists. His breadth of vision and sympathy is indicated by his place as a founder of the Metaphysical Society (1869), and a fellow member in it of such men as the agnostic biologist Thomas Henry Huxley and the Unitarian theologian James Martineau; and by his friendship with Archbishop Archibald Campbell Tait, his antagonist even in university days, and with the philosopher and economist John Stuart Mill, though their views were so divergent.

WARD, WILLIAM HAYES (1835–1916), American clergyman, editor, and Orientalist, born in Abington, Mass. Joining the editorial staff of the New York *Independent* in 1868, he became superintending editor in 1870, and was editor in chief from 1896 to 1913. Ward gave special attention to Oriental studies, and was lecturer on Assyriology at Yale University in 1878-79, and president of the American Oriental Society, 1890–94 and 1909–10.

WARDE, FREDERICK (1851–1935), American actor, born in Wardington, England. He came to the United States in 1874 and was leading man at Booth's Theatre, New York, for three years, afterward starring in Shakespearian tragedies. From 1893 to 1903 he was in partnership with Louis James. After 1907 he lectured frequently on dramatic subjects.

WAR DEBTS, WORLD WAR I, financial obligations contracted by belligerent nations in World War I. Repayments to the United States of twenty-two billion dollars in principal and interest were distributed over a period of sixty-two years. The amount was approximately two-thirds of the sum originally charged against Germany by the Reparation Commission in 1921. In terms of value it was approximately three fifths of the total payments levied against Germany in the Young Plan. See BANK FOR INTERNATIONAL SETTLEMENTS; REPARATIONS.

War Debt Negotiations. After the Lausanne conference (see REPARATIONS), the nations gave little discussion to payments due the U.S. However, the U.S. has been outspoken against cancellation. Indebtedness of Germany to the United States on account of costs of army of occupation and awards under Settlement of War Claims Act of 1928, as amended, was $1,285,617,000 (including interest accrued under unpaid moratorium annuities) as of July, 1942; originally $1,103,506,925, which was reduced by payment of $33,587,810.

WAR, DEPARTMENT OF, a former executive department of the United States government, created by Act of Congress of Aug. 7, 1789, and incorporated in the National Military Establishment (q.v.) in 1947 under the title of Department of the Army. It had at its head a secretary appointed by the President, who ranked third among the cabinet members in the line of succession to the Presidency and received a salary of $12,000 a year.

The secretary of war had charge of all matters relating to military affairs, subject to the direction of the President, the distribution of stores, the signal service, the survey and improvement of harbors, and the administration of the insular possessions. The business of the War Department was distributed among a number of subdivisions of bureaus, each of which was under the supervision of a chief and under the general supervision of the chief of staff. These included the headquarters of the army, through which the orders of the President were issued by the chief of staff. Offices of the War Department worked in close co-operation with the army itself. In March, 1942, the army's Services of Supply assumed direction of those parts of the Department's office engaged in procurement and production.

WARDHOLDING, in the Scottish feudal system, military tenure of land by which a vassal held of a superior lord on condition of rendering military services when required by the latter. When such lands descended to an heir who had not attained his majority, and who therefore could not render satisfactory military services, the lord was allowed the guardianship of his person and possession of his lands during his minority. This right was sometimes waived in consideration of an annual tax. The lord of such vassal was also entitled to the payment of a sum of money upon the marriage of the latter. The vassal could not alienate his fee without the consent of the lord, and the estate was forfeited if he attempted to do so. This form of tenure was abolished in 1747 by statute.

WARDIAN CASE, a nearly airtight glass case in which plants are either grown for ornament or transported upon long sea voyages. It was invented about 1836 by the English botanist Nathaniel Bagshaw Ward (1791–1842). The cases were proved to be of great value by a successful shipment of 20,000 tea plants from Shanghai to the Himalaya Mountains, and their use made possible the transportation of cinchona and rubber-tree seedlings to Ceylon and India. The cases protect plants from frost, salt spray, and injurious gases, and conserve moisture, demanding little attention.

WARDLAW, LADY ELIZABETH (1677–1727), Scottish poet, born in Pitfirrane, Fifeshire. She married (1696) Sir Henry Wardlaw, of Pitcruivie. There was published in 1719 a ballad entitled "Hardyknute", which had been previously circulated by her as the copy of an ancient manuscript found in a vault at Dunfermline. The authorship of this work has never been satisfactorily settled, but as no one ever saw the original manuscript and certain of Lady Wardlaw's friends stated positively that it was of her own composition, it seems probable that such was the case. Even if a forgery, "Hardyknute" is a remarkably fine imitation of the genuine ballads. "Sir Patrick Spens" has also been ascribed to Lady Wardlaw's pen, but this attribution is untenable, though it is possible that she amended a copy of it as well as certain other ballads, such as "Gilderoy".

WARDLAW, RALPH (1779–1853), Scottish Congregational minister, born in Oalkeith, in Midlothian, and educated at the school of the Associate Secession Church. At the end of his course he became a Congregationalist. In 1800 he began to preach, and in 1803 settled in Glasgow as pastor of an independent church. In 1811 he was appointed professor of theology to the Congregational body in Scotland, and held the position, with his pastorate, till his death. Wardlaw was a voluminous author, often involved in theological controversy, and a prominent actor in the public religious and philanthropical movements of the day. The most important of his works are *Essays on Assurance of Faith, and on the Extent of the Atonement and Universal Pardon* (1830); *Discourses on the Sabbath* (1832); *Christian Ethics* (1833); *Discourses on the Nature and Extent of the Atonement of Christ* (1843); *Congregational Independency* (1847); and *Lectures on Systematic Theology* (posthumously published, 1856–57).

WARE, a town of Hampshire Co., Mass., situated on the Ware R., about 25 miles N.E. of Springfield. It is served by two railroads, and contains factories producing cotton, woolen, and knit goods, iron castings, gummed paper, and shoes. Ware was settled prior to 1700, and was incorporated as a town in 1775. Pop. (1940) 7557.

WARE, market town in Hertfordshire, England, 2½ miles N.E. of Hertford. Malting and brewing are the chief industries. Ware is celebrated in Cowper's poem of John Gilpin, and at Rye House, 4 m. distant (the scene of the Rye House Plot in 1683) is to be seen the bed of Ware mentioned in Shakespeare's *Twelfth Night*. Pop., about 6000.

WARE, EUGENE FITCH (1841–1911), American lawyer and poet, born in Hartford, Conn. He served in the Civil War, and was admitted to the bar in Fort Scott, Kans. He took an active part in Republican State politics, serving for five years as a member of the State senate. In 1902–05 he was United States commissioner of pensions. He became widely known as a contributor to magazines, particularly through the verse written under the pseudonym Ironquill. His publications include *The Indian Campaign of 1864* (1908); *From Court to Court* (1909), and *Ithuriel* (1909).

WARE, HARRIET (1877?–   ), American composer, born in Waupun, Wis. She wrote numerous songs and song cycles, and her tone poem *The Artisan* (words by the American poet Edwin Markham) was given by the New York Symphony Orchestra in 1929. Her three-part chorus, *Woman's Triumphal March*, was made the national song of the General Federation of Women's Clubs of America.

WARE, HENRY (1764–1845), American Unitarian clergyman, born in Sherburne, Mass. He was pastor of the First Church in Hingham, Mass., from 1787 to 1805, when he was called to the Hollis professorship of divinity at Harvard College. This event precipitated the separation of Unitarians and Congregationalists, and led to the founding of Andover Seminary. Ware carried on a controversy with Leonard Woods, whose *Letters to Unitarians* he answered in *Letters to Trinitarians and Calvinists* (1820). He also wrote *Foundation, Evidences, and Truths of Religion* (1842).

WARE, WILLIAM ROBERT (1832–1915), American architect, born in Cambridge, Mass. He was professor of architecture at the Massachusetts Institute of Technology (1865–81), and at Columbia University (1881–1903). He designed the American School of Classical Studies in Athens, Greece, and, with Henry van Brunt, the Memorial Hall at Harvard and the First Church in Boston. He wrote *Architectural Shades and Shadows* (1912).

WAREHAM, a town of Plymouth Co., Mass., situated on Buzzard's Bay, 50 miles S.E. of Boston. Transportation facilities include a railroad. The town, which includes the villages of Wareham, East Wareham, West Wareham, Onset, and South Wareham, is a summer resort, and the shipping point of an area producing cranberries, garden truck, oysters, scallops, and clams. Nails and horseshoes are manufactured in the town. Wareham was first settled in 1678, and was incorporated in 1739. In the 18th and 19th centuries the town was first a whaling and then a shipbuilding center. Pop. (1940) 6364.

WAREHOUSEMAN, in the law of bailments (see BAILMENT) in the United States, an individual or business establishment engaged in the business of storing the goods of others for compensation. A warehouseman is a bailee whose contract with the owner of goods usually commits him only to the exercise of ordinary care and diligence; if the goods in his care are damaged or lost, he is not responsible unless the owner proves that ordinary care has not been exercised. (A warehouseman may, however, enter into a contract calling for greater responsibility on his part, and may receive goods on any terms to which the owner and he agree.) Thus, the degree of care to be exercised by a warehouseman is generally less than that required of a common carrier or innkeeper, who are insurers of goods. In the case of a common carrier the highest degree of responsibility exists only while goods are in transit; for example, if baggage is left at a station or depot for a certain time after it has reached its destination, the responsibility of the railroad becomes that of a warehouseman and is no longer that of a common carrier. The method of enforcement of the lien of a warehouseman is usually fixed by statute. It consists in a public sale of goods after a certain period of time to meet delinquent storage charges. Any proceeds remaining over the warehouseman's charges and the expenses of sale belong to the owner of the goods. See also BONDED WAREHOUSES.

WAREHOUSE RECEIPT, in law in the United States, a form of negotiable paper (q.v.) evidencing the delivery of goods and chattels to a warehouseman for storage. Under the Uniform Warehouse Receipts Act, adopted by all forty-eight States, the warehouse receipt must list the location of the warehouse, the date of issue of the receipt, the rate of storage charges, a description of the warehoused goods, and a statement of any lien claimed by the warehouseman. A purchaser of a warehouse receipt takes only such property as the depositor had at the time the goods were warehoused; thus, if a thief deposits goods, the purchaser of the warehouse receipt has no claim to such goods as against the rightful owner. Warehouse receipts are often used as collateral or security for loans.

At common law a warehouse receipt was not negotiable, but could be assigned (see ASSIGNMENT) by the party depositing the goods in a warehouse; delivery of the receipt had the same effect as delivery of the goods themselves. Under modern statutes the warehouse receipt may be made non-negotiable by marking the word "non-negotiable" on the instrument or by stating on the instrument that the goods are deliverable only to a particular individual. See BONDED WAREHOUSES.

WAREHOUSING. See BONDED WAREHOUSES.

WARFIELD, DAVID (1866–   ), American actor, born in San Francisco, Calif. He first became prominent in 1901, when he was starred by David Belasco in *The Auctioneer,* in which he played fourteen hundred times. He was noted also for his performances in *The Music Master* (1904–07); *The Return of Peter Grimm* (1911); and *The Merchant of Venice* (1922), in which he played Shylock and in which he toured the country (1923–24).

WAR GAME. See KRIEGSPIEL.

WARGLA or **OUARGLA,** an oasis in the southern part of Algeria, 500 miles S. of the city of Algeria. Some 3 miles long and 2½ miles wide, it has a population of about 15,000, mostly Berbers and Negroes. Wargla, the most important town, has an export trade in dates and other tropical fruits, the trees being fed by over three hundred springs. It is also important as a junction point of several caravan routes. The population of the town is about 4000. Wargla was first occupied by native French troops in 1853. Previous to that time it was under the administration of the sultan of Morocco. The French administrative buildings, barracks, and hospital are south of the town.

WARHAM, WILLIAM (1450?–1532), English churchman and statesman, born in Church Oakley, Hampshire. He became archbishop of Canterbury (1503–32) and lord chancellor (1504–15). In the latter office he was succeeded by Cardinal Wolsey. A generous patron of learning, he was elected in 1506 chancellor of Oxford University.

WARMAN, CY (1855–1914), American journalist and author, born near Greenup, Ill. In 1888 he established the *Western Railway*, a semimonthly magazine, in Denver, and in 1892 the short-lived *Daily Chronicle* in Creede, Colo. Characterized as the "Poet of the Rockies", his verse and his railroad stories became widely popular.

WAR MANPOWER COMMISSION, a commission established by an Executive Order of April 18, 1942, within the Office for Emergency Management (q.v.), to assure the most effective mobilization and utilization of national manpower. The chairman planned the necessary policies after consultation with representatives of eight Federal departments. The functions of the Commission were extended to the armed forces by an Executive Order of Dec. 5, 1942, which transferred the Selective Service System to the W.M.C. On Sept. 18, 1945, the W.M.C. was merged into the Labor Department. At the same time the Office of Economic Stabilization was taken over by the Office of War Mobilization and Reconversion.

WARM-BLOODED ANIMALS. See COLD-BLOODED ANIMALS.

WARMOUTH, or GOGGLE EYE, a small, fresh-water bass, closely related to the rock bass of the eastern and central United States, which is more elongated than the sunfish, variable in color and markings, and noted for its large mouth and great voracity.

WARMSPRING, a collective designation for several remnant tribes of Shahaptian stock now residing with the Wasco upon the Warmspring Reservation in northern Oregon, upon which they were collected in 1855.

WARNER, ANNA BARTLETT, pseudonym AMY LOTHROP (1820–1915), American novel-

David Warfield

ist. She collaborated much with her sister, Susan Warner. The two sisters lived on Constitution Island in the Hudson near West Point, and conducted a Bible class for the cadets of the United States Military Academy. In 1908, with Mrs. Russell Sage, she gave Constitution Island to the government. Among her many books are *Dollars and Cents* (1852); *Stories of Vinegar Hill* (1872); *Cross Corner* (1887); *Patience* (1891); *West Point Colors* (1903); and a biography, *Susan Warner ("Elizabeth Wetherell")* (1909).

WARNER, ANNE (1869–1913), American author, born in St. Paul, Minn. Her writings include *A Woman's Will* (1904); a series of books dealing with the adventures of a maiden lady, Susan Clegg; *The Rejuvenation of Aunt Mary* (1905), which was also dramatized; *The Panther* (1908); *Your Child and Mine* (1909); *The Gay and Festive Claverhouse* (1914); and *The Taming of Amorette* (1915).

WARNER, CHARLES, real name CHARLES JOHN LICKFORD (1846–1909), English actor, born in London. He made his theatrical debut in *Richelieu* at Windsor Castle at the age of fifteen. He appeared at various times in *Romeo and Juliet, Our Boys,* and *It's Never Too Late to Mend*; but his claim to fame rests upon his portrayal of Coupeau in *Drink,* a melodrama which was originally produced in 1879, and

Charles Dudley Warner

continued in Warner's repertoire throughout the remainder of his life.

WARNER, CHARLES DUDLEY (1829–1900), American author, born in Plainfield, Mass. He practiced law in Chicago till 1860, and settled in Hartford, where he conducted the Hartford *Press* during General Hawley's absence in the Civil War, and on the paper's consolidation with the Hartford *Courant* became part owner and coeditor. In 1884 he became coeditor of *Harper's Magazine,* to which his papers on the South, on Mexico, and the Great West were contributed. In 1873 he wrote, with Mark Twain, *The Gilded Age;* he had then published *My Summer in a Garden* (1870), relating the experiences of an amateur gardener, and *Back-log Studies* (1872). Other works are *Being a Boy* (1877), *Washington Irving* (1881), *Captain John Smith* (1881), *In the Levant* (1893), *The Golden House* (1895), and *That Fortune* (1899).

WARNER, EDWARD PEARSON (1894–   ), American aeronautical engineer, born in Pittsburgh, Pa., and educated at Harvard University and the Massachusetts Institute of Technology. He was engaged in aeronautical work continuously after 1916, with the U.S. Army and with the National Advisory Committee for Aeronautics. In 1920 he became associate professor of aeronautics, and in 1924, professor, at the the Massachusetts Institute of Technology. He was assistant secretary of the navy for aeronautics from 1926 to 1929, when he became editor of *Aviation.* In 1939 he became vice-chairman of the Civil Aeronautics Board, resigning in 1945 to become president of the Interim Council of Provisional International Civil Aviation Organization. Among his works are *Airplane Design—Aërodynamics* (1927), *Aviation Handbook* (1931), and *Airplane Design Performance* (1936).

WARNER, EVERETT LONGLEY (1877–   ), American landscape painter and etcher, born in Vinton, Iowa. His works include "Broadway on a Rainy Evening" (Corcoran Art Gallery, Washington); "Quebec" (Pennsylvania Academy of Fine Arts, Philadelphia); "Along the River Front, New York"; and six etchings, in the Toledo Art Museum. He was elected an associate of the National Academy of Design in 1913, and was awarded medals in Philadelphia (1908), Buenos Aires (1910), and San Francisco (1915). During World War I he was the originator of a camouflage system adopted by the War Risk Bureau.

WARNER, GLENN SCOBEY, known as "POP" WARNER (1871–   ), American football coach, born in Springville, N.Y., and educated at Cornell University. Warner was one of the outstanding football coaches of his time; he was active as a coach for forty-five years. The universities, colleges, and schools at which Warner coached include the University of Georgia (1895–96); Cornell University (1897–98 and 1904–06); the Carlisle (Pa.) Indian Industrial School (1899–1903 and 1907–14), which he brought to a high place in football ranks; Stanford University (1924–32), and Temple University (1933–39). He was advisory coach at the San Jose (Calif.) State College from 1940 to 1945, when he retired.

WARNER, OLIN LEVI (1844–96), American sculptor, born in West Suffield, Conn. Among his most important works are busts of Alden Weir, the artist, and of Maud Morgan, the musician; statues of William Lloyd Garrison and General Charles Devens, in Boston; colossal heads of Michelangelo, Rembrandt, Raphael, Titian, and Velasquez for the Art Building at the Chicago Exposition (1893), and his nude figure "Diana" at the Metropolitan Museum of Art, New York City. In 1889 he was elected a member of the National Academy of Design.

WARNER, SETH (1743–84), American patriot, born in Roxbury, Conn. At the outbreak of the Revolutionary War he joined the patriot party, was second in command at the capture of Ticonderoga, and led the detachment of "Green Mountain Boys" which captured Crown Point (May, 1775). He participated in the unsuccessful expedition against Canada, was promoted colonel in the Continental Army (1776), commanded the rear guard of the army in the retreat from Ticonderoga (1777), and rendered good service in the operations which culminated in the surrender of Burgoyne.

WARNER, SUSAN, pseudonym ELIZABETH WETHERELL (1819–85), American authoress, born in New York City. She wrote *The Wide, Wide World* (1851), which proved to be one of the most successful of American stories. *Queechy* followed the year after, *The Hills of Shatemuc* in 1856, *The Old Helmet* in 1863, *Melbourne House* in 1864, *Daisy* in 1868, and *A Story of Small Beginnings* in 1872.

WARNER, WILLIAM (1558?–1609), English poet, born in London, and educated at Magdalen College, Oxford University. He settled in London as an attorney. Warner is chiefly known for *Albion's England* (1586), a long poem in fourteen-syllable lines treating of history and legend from Noah to William the Conqueror. Originally in four books, the poem was enlarged in subsequent editions to sixteen books, and in 1612 the history was brought down into the reign of James I. Warner also wrote a translation (1595) of *Menœchmi* by the ancient Roman playwright Titus Maccius Plautus and a collection of tales under the title *Pan His Syrinx* (1585).

WARNING COLORATION, conspicuous markings upon certain animals to protect them from the attacks of other animals. Most species so marked secrete a repugnant fluid which is either ejected from special glands or which, in the case of insects, gives them a bad taste, so that they are repulsive to monkeys, birds, lizards, or insects.

Inedible species of this type are often marked with bright colors, spots, or bands, and such colors are said to warn off intruders, which after their first experience recognize them as unfit to eat. A familiar example is the skunk, whose conspicuous black and white markings render it visible even in a rather dark night. Warning coloration is especially common in insects, especially gaily colored caterpillars and butterflies, like the milkweed butterfly. The brightly colored caterpillars, like the currant worm and a number of others, when fed to birds are rejected with disgust. Hence they enjoy immunity from attacks by birds.

WARNSDORF or **VARNSDORF,** a town in Czechoslovakia, 59 miles N. by E. of Prague. It is especially known for its large cotton manufactures. Woolen and linen goods, velvet, cement, and machinery are also produced. Pop., about 23,000.

WAR OF 1812, GENERAL SOCIETY OF THE, a hereditary patriotic society organized in Philadelphia, Pa., in 1891. It has for its object the preservation of the memories and victories of the War of 1812. It admits to membership any lineal descendant of one who served in the War of 1812, in the army, navy, revenue marine, or privateer service of the United States.

WAR OF 1812, THE, a conflict against Great Britain by the United States (1812–14) over an invasion of American rights. Bent on crushing Napoleon, Britain in 1803 forbade any direct trade in American ships between the West Indian islands possessed by any European power and the continent of Europe. Then followed between the two European powers a war of proclamation and counter-proclamation which practically ruined the American trade to Europe. In addition, the United States justly objected to the searching of her vessels by British cruisers off her coasts, to the impressing of her seamen into the British service, carried on despite papers of naturalization, and to the British intrigues inciting the Indian tribes to a frontier war. President Thomas Jefferson's policy in the face of these provocations was embodied in the Non-importation Act of 1806, which instituted a boycott of British-made goods. A wanton attack on the United States frigate *Chesapeake,* by the British ship *Leopard,* in June, 1807, should have precipitated matters, but Jefferson adhered to his policy, and when smuggling was resorted to in order to evade his legislation, he enacted his Force Act (1809) to compel obedience. On the accession of the Madison administration (1809), a firmer policy was inaugurated, and by the Macon Bill of that year the United States restored trade with both belligerents, offering at the same time that if either nation would suspend its Decrees or Orders, trade with the other would be suspended. Feeling against Britain, fanned by the eloquence of Clay and Calhoun, continued to rise, and despite tardy concessions by Britain, war was declared on June 18, 1812. Operations were at once commenced on the Canadian frontier. Three expeditions were simultaneously launched, their objective being Montreal. Hull, crossing at Detroit, was driven back and forced to surrender at Detroit. Van Rensselaer moved across the Niagara R., but was defeated at Queenstown, and Dearborn leading the third expedition halted on the frontier of New

The naval battle between the Constitution (right) and the Guerrière in the War of 1812

York State. The Ohio command was then given to William Henry Harrison, who successfully repelled a counter raid of the British by his masterful defense of forts Meigs and Stephenson, Ohio. Meantime an American fleet commanded by Oliver H. Perry had been organized on Lake Erie. With his flotilla he inflicted a crushing defeat on the British off Sandusky, capturing their entire fleet. Harrison was now able to invade Canada, and on the Thames R. defeated the British and Indian forces. Toronto (York) was burned on a succeeding raid, and an expedition downriver to Montreal was planned, but was not carried out. In 1814 the American forces under Jacob Brown and Winfield Scott won the battles of Chippewa and Lundy's Lane, but the British, being reinforced, drove them back to the American side.

Naval honors in the war rested with the United States. In 1812 sea fights between the *Constitution* and the *Guerrière*, the *United States* and the *Macedonian*, in 1813 between the *Constitution* and the *Java*, the *Hornet* and the *Peacock*, and the *Enterprize* and the *Boxer*, ended in victories for the United States Navy. The most notable British victory was that of the *Shannon* over the *Chesapeake*. Stung by this blow to her naval supremacy, Britain largely augmented her fleet, and a general blockade was instituted. Several landings were made, and a force from Bermuda under General Ross burned Washington, but was repulsed before Baltimore. In 1814 this force made a renewed attack from Jamaica as a base on New Orleans. The valor and military genius of Andrew Jackson repelled the British attack with a loss of 2036 men (January 8, 1815). Meantime a treaty of peace had been concluded at Ghent (December 14, 1814), and on the arrival of the news hostilities were suspended. The treaty left most of the points at issue unsettled. The war, despite the weaknesses it revealed, did much to consolidate the Union and to create a naval tradition invaluable to a young and rising nation.

WAR OF INDEPENDENCE. See REVOLUTION, THE AMERICAN.

WAR OF THE PACIFIC, also known as the CHILE-PERUVIAN WAR, the war which took place between 1879 and 1884 between Chile and the allied nations of Bolivia and Peru. The cause was a dispute between Chile and Bolivia regarding Chilean economic penetration of the Bolivian province of Atacama, rich in nitrate deposits. In 1878 Bolivia placed a heavy tax on nitrate exported from the country; the tax was protested by the Chilean Nitrate Company of Antofagasta (then the principal port of Atacama), and when the Chilean government sought to obtain remission of the tax by the Bolivian government, the latter cancelled its contract with the Chilean Nitrate Company. To protect the interests of its nationals, the Chilean government sent a force of 500 troops to occupy Antofagasta, whereupon Bolivia declared war (March, 1879) upon Chile. Chile requested Peru, which had made a treaty of alliance with Bolivia in 1873, to declare its neutrality, and when Peru refused, Chile declared war (April 5) upon both Bolivia and Peru.

Chilean troops at once occupied all the coastal towns of Bolivia, and the Chilean navy blockaded the ports of southern Peru. In October, 1879, Chile won control of the sea in an action off Angamos (on the coast of Atacama) in which Chilean warships sank the Peruvian ironclad *Huascar*; other elements of the Peruvian navy had been previously destroyed. In early November a Chilean expeditionary force captured Pisagua and Iquique, important coastal towns in the Peruvian province of Tarapacá. Combined Bolivian and Peruvian forces defeated the Chilean invading army in the battle of Tarapacá, but then instead of advancing, inexplicably chose to retreat. By the end of 1879 the Chileans had complete possession of Tarapacá.

In 1880 Chilean forces carried out an invasion by sea of the provinces of Tacna and Arica in southern Peru. The invaders defeated a Peruvian army at Cuesta de los Angeles and on May 26 won the decisive battle of Tacna; the victory gave Chile control of the two provinces. In November, 1880, Chilean troops landed on the Peruvian coast at Pisco and marched northward upon the Peruvian capital of Lima. They completely defeated the Peruvian army at Chorrillos and at Miraflores, outside Lima, and on January 17, 1881, occupied that city. Thereafter the Peruvians, led by General Andrés Cáceres (q.v.), kept up guerrilla warfare against the Chileans until finally subdued by a Chilean expedition, in 1883.

The war between Chile and Peru was ended by the Treaty of Ancón on October 20, 1883, by which Peru ceded to Chile the province of Tarapacá; in addition Chile was to hold the provinces of Tacna and Arica for ten years, and then a plebiscite was to be held to decide which nation was to retain permanent possession. The final disposition of the two provinces caused a dispute between Peru and Chile which was not finally resolved until 1929 (see TACNA-ARICA DISPUTE). Hostilities between Chile and Bolivia were ended by the Treaty of Valparaiso on April 4, 1884. This treated provided for an indefinite period of truce during which Chile was to keep possession of the Bolivian province of Atacama. The formal end of the war between Chile and Bolivia took place with the conclusion of a treaty on October 20, 1904. By terms of this agreement Chile gained permanent possession of Atacama in return for the construction of a railroad between Arica (in dispute between Chile and Peru at the time) and La Paz, the capital of Bolivia; the part of the railroad lying within Bolivia was to belong to that country fifteen years after completion of the entire railroad. See BOLIVIA: *History*; CHILE: *History*; PERU: *History*.

WARRANT, a writ issued by a judicial officer, directed to another officer, requiring the second officer to arrest a person.

WARRANTY, in the law of contracts in England and the United States, an undertaking, expressed or implied, given by one contracting party to another that a fact alleged with respect to the subject matter of the contract is as represented. A breach of warranty results from failure of the subject matter of the contract to conform to the facts as represented, and gives the injured party a cause of action for the breach. An "express warranty" is a warranty explicitly made by a seller; an "implied warranty" is a warranty which the law infers from the conduct of the parties or the nature of the transaction. An example of express warranty is that made in a warranty deed (q.v.) whereby the seller covenants that he has title to the property and that the property is free from encumbrances. Examples of implied warranties are the warranty of a retailer that the food sold by him to his customers is wholesome, the warranty of a manufacturer from whom a specific article has been ordered for a specified purpose that the article shall be fit for that purpose, and the warranty of any seller of personal property that he has title to the goods sold and that there are no liens on such goods. General praise of his goods by the vendor does not constitute a warranty.

When a breach of warranty occurs in a sale (q.v.) of goods the purchaser has a choice of two remedies: he may reject the goods, that is, rescind (see RESCISSION) the contract, and treat the transaction as if there had been no sale to him; or he may retain the goods. In the latter case he may, if he has paid for the goods, institute a legal action to recover on the seller's agreement to indemnify him; if the goods have not been paid for he may allege the breach of warranty as a partial setoff to the purchase price. If he rejects the goods he can bring an action for damages for breach of warranty, and for the payment he has made for the goods, if any. A purchaser is deemed to have waived his right to rescind if he accepts the goods with knowledge of their defective condition. Generally the purchaser alone has a right to be indemnified by the seller for the seller's breach of warranty; the seller may also be liable to the ultimate consumer for a breach of implied warranty, however, when a defective article is injurious to health or human life.

In the law of insurance (q.v.), a warranty is a statement which the insured makes with regard to some material fact, and on which the underwriter's liability is dependent. It is an essential condition of the contract, any breach of which renders the policy void.

WARREN, a town of Worcester Co., Mass., situated on the Allegheny R., 120 miles N.E of the city of Worcester. Transportation facilities include a railroad. Among the industrial establishments in the town are factories producing woolens, pumps, and valves. The town, which includes the villages of Warren and West Warren, was settled in 1664 and incorporated in 1742. It was called Western until 1834, when the name was changed to Warren, in honor of Gen. Joseph Warren, a hero of the battle of Bunker Hill. Pop. (1940) 3531.

WARREN, county seat of Trumbull Co., Ohio, situated on the Mahoning R., 14 miles N.W. of Youngstown. It is served by three railroads, and is an important manufacturing center in the Ohio-Pennsylvania steel-producing area Industrial establishments in the city include extensive blast furnaces, rolling mills, steel plants, and factories manufacturing electrical supplies, resistance welders, sinks, tubing, electrical transformers, electric motors, electric cable, fire extinguishers, and drinking fountains. Warren was settled in 1798, incorporated as a village in 1834, and chartered as a city in 1869. It became the county seat in 1800. Pop. (1950) 49,674.

WARREN, county seat of Warren Co., Pa., situated on the Allegheny R., 120 miles N.E. of Pittsburgh. It is served by two railroads. The borough is surrounded by a region rich in agriculture and in the production of natural gas and oil, and is an important manufacturing and oil-refining center. In addition to oil refining and the manufacture of oil-well equipment, the principal industries are the manufacture of steel tanks, steel-processing equipment, iron products, furnaces, steel cabinets, tools, axes, valves, flexible couplings, furniture, lumber, and barrels. Warren is the site of a State hospital for the insane, and is the headquarters of the Cornplanter State Forest and of the Allegheny National Forest. It was settled in 1795 and named for Gen. Joseph Warren, who served in the Continental army during the American Revolution. Warren was incorporated as a borough in 1832. Pop. (1940) 14,891.

WARREN, a town of Bristol Co., R.I., situated on the E. shore of Narragansett Bay at the mouth of the Warren R., 10 miles S.E. of Providence. Transportation facilities include a railroad. The principal industries in the town are the manufacture of automotive equipment, rubber goods, and cotton goods. The town, which was first settled about 1632, contains many fine old houses. It was incorporated in 1747, and from 1764 to 1770 was the site of the College of Rhode Island, now Brown University. Pop. (1940) 8158.

WARREN, FREDERICK MORRIS (1859–1931), American-French scholar, born in Durham, Maine. He was Street professor of modern languages at Yale University from 1900 to 1926. Warren was also president of the Modern Language Association of America in 1908 and became an editor of *Modern Philology*. His writings include *A History of the French Novel Previous to the Seventeenth Century* (1895).

WARREN, GEORGE FREDERICK (1874–1938), American agricultural expert and economist, born in Harvard, Nebr. Besides being professor of farm management at Cornell University after 1906, he is the author of *Elements of Agriculture* (1909) and *Farm Management* (1913), and joint author of *Dairy Farming* (1916) and the *Agricultural Situation* (1924). In 1933 he was a consultant of President Franklin Delano Roosevelt on the gold and currency policy and was named among the members of the Brain Trust.

WARREN, GOUVERNEUR KEMBLE (1830–82), American soldier, born in Cold Spring, N.Y. In the Civil War he commanded a brigade at the battles of Gaines Mill, Second Bull Run, and Antietam. During the final campaign against General Lee he commanded the 5th Army Corps.

WARREN, HOWARD CROSBY (1867–1934), American psychologist, born in Montclair, N.J. At Princeton University he was Stuart professor of psychology from 1904 to 1924, and chairman of the department from 1919 to 1931. He was the compiler of the *Psychological Index* (1894–1907 and 1910–14); associate editor of the *American Naturalist* in 1896–97; and associate editor and, later, coeditor (1904–10) of the *Psychological Review*. In

1910 he became senior editor of *Psychological Review Publications,* and was president of the Psychological Review Company from 1911 to 1925. He compiled a dictionary of psychological terms, and wrote *Human Psychology* (1910) and *Elements of Human Psychology* (1922).

WARREN, JOHN (1753–1815), American surgeon, brother of Joseph Warren, and father of John Collins Warren (1778–1856). He was born in Roxbury, Mass., and educated at Harvard University. He attended the wounded at the Battle of Bunker Hill, and afterward accompanied the American army to New York and New Jersey as hospital surgeon. From 1777 to the close of the war he superintended the military hospitals in Boston. In 1783 he was one of the founders and the first professor of anatomy and surgery in the newly established medical school at Harvard. He was the first president of the Massachusetts Medical Society (1804–15).

WARREN, JOHN COLLINS (1778–1856), American surgeon, son of John Warren, born in Boston, and educated at Harvard University. He succeeded his father as professor of surgery there. He was one of the founders and long an editor of the *Boston Medical and Surgical Journal* (1828). He was also one of the founders of the McLean Asylum for the Insane, and of the Massachusetts General Hospital, of which he was chief surgeon. In 1846 he performed the first public operation on a patient anesthetized by ether, in the Massachusetts General Hospital. He was a pioneer in the excision of bones and joints, and introduced an operation for fissure of the soft palate. Warren made a collection of specimens in anatomy, osteology, and paleontology, now known as the Warren Museum, to which he bequeathed his own skeleton. In 1849 he served as president of the American Medical Association. He was the author of numerous treatises on medical subjects.

WARREN, JOHN COLLINS (1842–1927), American surgeon, son of John Collins Warren (1778–1856), born in Boston. He graduated from Harvard Medical School (1866), where he taught after 1871 (as professor of surgery from 1893 till his retirement in 1907). From 1873 to 1881 he was editor of the *Boston Medical and Surgical Journal* and in 1896 served as president of the American Surgical Association. He wrote *Surgical Pathology and Therapeutics* (1895) and edited *International Textbook of Surgery* (1900).

WARREN, JOSEPH (1741–75), American patriot, born in Roxbury, Mass. In 1772 he was chairman of the first committee of correspondence of Boston, and in 1774 drafted the famous "Suffolk Resolves", which urged forcible opposition to Great Britain. He was a member of the first three provincial congresses of Massachusetts (1774–75), was president of the third, and was also a prominent member of the committee of public safety. He participated in the Lexington-Concord engagement, and took part in the Battle of Bunker's Hill, where he was killed.

WARREN, JOSIAH (1799–1874), American philosophical anarchist, born near Boston. He participated in the Welsh reformer Robert Owen's communistic experiment in New Harmony, Ind., in 1825–26. In the following year he opened in Cincinnati, Ohio, a time store, in which goods were sold at cost with seven percent added for rent, fuel, etc., and every customer was timed and charged so much an hour for the time of the salesman. In connection with this business Warren issued labor notes, which were used as money. Having demonstrated the feasibility of the experiment, he closed the store. Subsequently he established a community in Ohio, and later founded Modern Times, a community on Long Island. Warren is considered by many philosophical anarchists to be, with the French anarchist Pierre Joseph Proudhon (q.v.), the founder of their system of thought. He wrote *True Civilization* (1846) and *Equitable Commerce* (1852).

WARREN, LAVINIA (about 1841–88), American dwarf, born in Middleboro, Mass. She was less than 2 ft. tall, and her name was originally Mercy Lavinia Bumpus, but after becoming a member of P.T. Barnum's show her name was changed. In 1863, she married Charles S. Stratton, better known as Tom Thumb. Her husband died in 1883, and two years later she married an Italian dwarf named Count Primo Magri.

WARREN, LLOYD (ELIOT) (1868–1922), American architect, born in Paris, and educated at Columbia University and the École des Beaux-Arts. In 1899 he returned to the United States, where he was for a time with his brother Whitney Warren in the architectural firm, Warren and Wetmore. Later he became identified with the Society of Beaux Arts Architects, which from little more than a social architectural organization soon grew to be an educational system, with schools in many cities of the United States and Canada, and with its associated Institute of Design offering criticism to architectural students of more than twenty universities. During World

Harcourt, Brace
Robert Penn Warren

War I Warren was director of education and dean of the faculty in the Education Corps of the American Expeditionary Force, at Belleville, France. He was also a member of the *Fraternité des Artistes,* which came to the assistance of the families of French painters and architects. The French government awarded him the Legion of Honor.

WARREN, MERCY (1728–1814), American dramatist, poet, and historian, born in Barnstable, Mass. She was a sister of the American Revolutionary statesman James Otis. In 1754 she married James Warren, a merchant in Plymouth, who afterward became one of the Revolutionary leaders. Her dramas *The Adulator* (1773) and *The Group* (1775) are satires on the Massachusetts Loyalists. Her other works include *Poems, Dramatic and Miscellaneous* (1790) and *History of the American Revolution* (3 vols., 1805).

WARREN, SIR PETER (about 1703–52), British naval officer. He commanded (1745) an armament intended to attack Louisburg. His fleet, co-operating with Sir William Pepperell's forces, made serious breaches in the walls and the fortress surrendered. He married Susan, eldest daughter of Stephen De Lancey of New York, who brought him a valuable estate in the Mohawk Valley.

WARREN, ROBERT PENN (1905–   ), American writer and educator, born in Guthrie, Ky., and educated at Vanderbilt and Yale universities, the University of California, and Oxford University, England. While a student at Vanderbilt, Warren was associated with a group of Southern regional writers known as the Fugitive Group, and regional influences are discernible in most of his later literary work. He taught English from 1930 to 1931 at Southwestern College, from 1931 to 1934 at Vanderbilt University, and from 1934 to 1942 at Louisiana State University; after 1942 he was professor of English at the University of Minnesota. Warren's work in both poetry and fiction, usually concerned with themes drawn from Southern life, exhibits a powerful and imaginative style and keen psychological insight. He first came to the attention of a large audience with *All the King's Men* (1946; Pulitzer Prize, 1947), a realistic novel dealing with the career of a demagogue in an unnamed southern State, whose career closely parallels that of the American politician Huey Pierce Long. His other books include the novels *Night Rider* (1939), *At Heaven's Gate* (1943), and *World Enough and Time* (1950), and the collections of verse *Thirty-Six Poems* (1936), *Eleven Poems on the Same Theme* (1942), and *Selected Poems* (1944). Warren collaborated with the American critic Cleanth Brooks on the widely used college textbooks *Understanding Poetry* (1938) and *Understanding Fiction* (1943).

WARREN, SAMUEL (1781–1862), English clergyman. He entered the ministry of the Wesleyan Methodist Church in 1802, but in 1834 was suspended for opposing the formation of a theological institution at Manchester. His appeal to the lord high chancellor was denied in 1835, and in the same year he was expelled from the denomination. Many of his sympathizers, first known as Warrenites, united with the Leeds seceders of 1828 (Protestant Methodists; from 1835 Wesleyan Association Methodists). In 1857 they united with other seceders to form the United Methodist Free Church. Eventually Warren grew tired of continuous controversy and joined the Church of England, spending the last years of his life as the incumbent of All Souls' Church, Ancoats, Manchester. He was the author of *A Digest of the Laws and Regulations of the Wesleyan Methodists* (1827), *Sermons on Various Subjects* (1833), and *Remarks on the Wesleyan Theological Situation* (1834).

WARREN, SAMUEL (1807–77), British legal scholar and novelist, born in Denbighshire, Wales, and educated at the University of Edinburgh and at the Inner Temple, London. He was called to the bar in 1837, and in 1851 was appointed queen's counsel. He served as recorder of Hull (1854–74), as member of Parliament for Midhurst (1856–59), and then as master in lunacy. A Conservative in politics, it was in the interests of his party that he wrote *Ten Thousand a Year* (1839), a novel which made him famous. It first appeared in *Blackwood's Magazine,* and retained its popularity in numerous editions and translations throughout the 19th century. Warren also wrote several valuable legal treatises. A collection of all his writings was issued in five volumes (1854–55).

WARREN, SIR (THOMAS) HERBERT (1853–1930), English educator, scholar, and author, born in Bristol, and educated at Clifton College and at Balliol College, Oxford. From 1877 to 1885 he was fellow and tutor of Magdalen College, and president from 1885 to 1928. He served also as vice-chancellor of Oxford University (1906–10) and then was professor of poetry. He was knighted in 1914. His publications include *Plato's Republic* (four vols., 1888); *Education and Equality* (1895); *By Severn Sea and Other Poems* (1897); *Magdalen College, an Historical Sketch* (1907); *Essays of Poetry and the Poets* (1909); *Tennyson's Poems* (1910); *Oxford and Poetry* (1911); *Robert Bridges, Poet Laureate* (1913); *R. D. Blackmore's Lorna Doone* (1914); and *War and Poetry* (1915).

WARREN, WHITNEY (1864?–1943), American architect, born in New York. As a member of the firm of Warren and Wetmore he collaborated in the design of the monumental Grand Central Station in New York, completed in 1913; of the Belmont and Ritz-Carlton and other hotels, of the Automobile Club, and of the Chelsea Docks, all in New York; of important residences in New York and Toronto; of the Grand Trunk Station in Winnipeg, Canada; the John Paul Jones crypt at the Naval Academy, Annapolis; bronze gates in the Cathedral of St. John the Divine, New York; and many other important works. Following the bombardment of Reims Cathedral by the Germans during World War I, he made an examination of the damage done and prepared a report on restoration. He also prepared plans for and supervised the reconstruction (1928) of the University of Louvain in Belgium, destroyed by the Germans in 1914. Warren was awarded a silver medal at the Paris Exposition in 1900, was made a member of the Académie des Beaux-Arts of the French Institute in 1905, received an honorary degree from Harvard University in 1913, and was elected to the National Institute of Arts and Letters.

WARREN, WILLIAM (1812–88), American actor, born in Philadelphia. He made his debut in 1832 as Young Norval in Home's *Douglas*. After appearing with success in New York City and in London, he became a member of the stock company at the Boston Museum (1847), where he remained as chief comedian until 1883, when he retired.

WARRENSBURG, county seat of Johnson Co., Mo., situated on the Black R., 65 miles S.E. of Kansas City. Transportation facilities include a railroad. The city is surrounded by an agricultural area containing deposits of sandstone. The principal industries are meat packing and the manufacture of flour, stock feed, cotton goods, work clothing, shoes, and lawn mowers. Warrensburg is the site of the Central Missouri State Teachers College, established in 1871. Pop. (1948 est.) 7200.

WARRINGTON, a county borough and manufacturing town of Lancashire, England, on the right bank of the Mersey R., 18 miles E. of Liverpool. Manufactures include iron, wire, pins, files, cottons, glass, leather, chemicals, and soap. Pop., about 78,000.

WARSAW, county seat of Kosciusko Co., Ind., situated on the Tippecanoe R., 40 miles N.W. of Fort Wayne. The city is served by rail, is the trading center of an agricultural area, and is a noted vacation resort. The principal industries in Warsaw are the manufacture of breakfast foods, paper boxes, tools, surgical equipment, toys, furniture, and foundry products. In the vicinity of the city are more than 90 lakes, including Wawasee Lake, covering about 3600 acres, the largest lake in Indiana. Warsaw was incorporated as a town in 1854 and as a city in 1867. Pop. (1940) 6378.

WARSAW, county seat of Wyoming Co., N.Y., situated in the Wyoming Valley, 42 miles E. of Buffalo and 44 miles S.W. of Rochester. It is served by two railroads. The village is a manufacturing center, with factories producing livestock feed, paper boxes, cotton and knit goods, vegetable-ivory buttons, bottle caps, lanterns, highway torches, radio knobs, concrete burial vaults, and passenger and freight elevators. A library and a museum in the village contain collections of historical interest. Warsaw was settled in 1803 and incorporated as a village in 1843. Pop. (1940) 3554.

WARSAW (Pol. *Warszawa*), the capital of Poland on the left bank of the Vistula, 404

SCENES IN WARSAW, POLAND. *Top: Headquarters building of the Warsaw Friends of Science. Bottom: Clearing debris of buildings shattered by aerial bombs during World War II.*

m. by rail E. of Berlin. There is much corn and flax exported, and coal and manufactured goods imported. Warsaw has manufactures of electroplate, machinery, boots, leather goods, woolens, glass, and surgical instruments. Of over one hundred Catholic churches, the cathedral of St. John is the most notable. The university, suppressed in 1832, was reopened in 1864. Pop. (1949 est.) 606,778.

In World War I, Hindenburg, commanding the Austro-German forces, progressed steadily into Poland in the autumn of 1914, and claimed possession of all the country except Warsaw by the middle of October. The fight for Warsaw began on October 16 and continued till the evening of the 19th. The grand duke Nicholas, in command of the Russian forces, relied principally for defense upon his Siberian corps, with whom were Japanese guns and gunners, and at first the issue hung in the balance. On the next day the Russians crossed the river Vistula at Novo Alexandria, and opened the battle south of Pilitza, the heaviest fighting occurring around Glovaczov on the river Radonka. By October 22 the Germans were in retreat, making their last stand between Blonie and Paoechno.

A second attempt to take Warsaw was made in December, 1914, by the Germans, hoping by this means to divert Russian attention from Cracow. On November 15–16 the Russians had failed near Kutno to check Morgen's advance, and the following day Mackensen drove the Russians opposing him along the Bzura toward Lowicz. Heavy fighting followed around Mlava and Petrokov during the second week in December, and gradually the Russians gave way, finally making a stand on the Bzura-Rawka-Pilica line, 30 miles s.w. of Warsaw.

While the Germans were making almost uninterrupted progress in Galicia, in the summer of 1915, Mackensen prepared to strike the third German blow at Warsaw. The weakness of the Russian position in Poland was the precarious salient which depended upon the two long railroad lines connecting Warsaw with Petrograd, Moscow, and Kiev. On July 19 Gallwitz crossed the Narew, near Pultusk, while Bülow moved from the Dubissa toward the Aa and Sventa. Gallwitz and Scholtz, advancing from the Narew, made further defense of the salient impracticable and the Russian army left Prince Leopold of Bavaria free to enter Warsaw on the morning of August 4. In World War II, Warsaw, completely isolated, resisted furious enemy bombardment for almost two weeks, finally surrendering on Sept. 27, 1939.

WARSAW, UNIVERSITY OF, a university founded in 1816 and opened in 1818. After the Polish Revolution of 1830, it was suppressed. In 1857 a medical school was opened in Warsaw, and in 1861 a higher institution of learning was established, which was organized into a university in 1869. The library is particularly rich in Polish literature and history. It contains now over 570,000 volumes and nearly 1400 manuscripts. The ethnographical museum also contains valuable manuscripts. In 1820 the astronomical observatory was erected. During the German occupation the university was reconstituted with a Polish faculty.

WARSHIP, a vessel armed and equipped for purposes of war. All fully efficient fighting ships are designed and built as such, the characteristics of a warship and merchant vessel being so different that it is impossible to transform the latter into an efficient fighting craft. Warships are divided into aircraft carriers, battleships, battle cruisers, coast-defense ships, light cruisers, gun boats, destroyers, torpedo boats, and submarines. Merchant vessels, when armed for scouting or other service, are called auxiliary cruisers. Fleet auxiliaries, such as supply, repair, and hospital ships, are not regarded as warships; if they carry an armament it is light. See NAVY; VESSELS, NAVAL.

WARS, THE NAPOLEONIC, the series of wars that took place between France and a number of European nations from 1799, when France came under the domination of Napoleon Bonaparte, then the principal member of the Consulate during the French Revolution (qq.v.), until 1815, when he met his downfall as Emperor Napoleon I (q.v.). The Napoleonic Wars were a continuation of the wars of the French Revolution, in which the dynastic rulers of Europe combined in an effort to overthrow the Revolutionary government of France and restore the rule of the French monarchy. In the War of the First Coalition (1793–97), in which France fought against an alliance consisting of Austria, Prussia, Great Britain, Spain, Holland, and Sardinia, Napoleon was entrusted by the government of France, the Directory (q.v.), with conducting military operations against Austrian forces in northern Italy (1796–97). Subsequently he was made the leader of an expedition (1798–99) to conquer Egypt as a base for future attack against the British possession of India. Although they took place before the Consulate was established, these two campaigns (for details, see NAPOLEON I) are generally regarded as the opening phases of the

Napoleonic wars because they were the first in which Napoleon displayed on a large scale his genius as a commander; early battles of the War of the Second Coalition (see below) are also included in this category.

Napoleon's success against Austria in his northern Italian campaign of 1796–97 had put an end to the First Coalition. During his absence in Egypt, however, a new alliance known as the Second Coalition was formed on December 24, 1798; this alliance comprised Russia, Great Britain, Austria, the Kingdom of Naples, Portugal, and the Ottoman Empire. The principal fighting of the War of the Second Coalition, which broke out at the end of 1798, took place during the following year in northern Italy and in Switzerland. In the former area the Austrians and Russians, under the leadership chiefly of the noted Russian general Count Aleksandr Suvorov, were uniformly successful. They defeated the French in the battles of Magnano (April 5), Cassano (April 27), the Trebbia (June 17–19), and Novi (August 15); captured Milan; put an end to the Cisalpine Republic (q.v.), which had been formed under French auspices in 1797; occupied Turin; and in general deprived the French of the fruits of the victories they had won in Italy under Napoleon. In Switzerland matters went better for the French. After a defeat at Zurich (June 4–7) by the Austrian army under the Archduke Charles, French forces under General André Masséna defeated (September 26) a Russian army under General Alexander Mikhailov Korsakov. The victorious General Suvorov led his forces from northern Italy across the Alps to join those of Korsakov in Switzerland. He found Korsakov's forces already defeated and scattered; he himself was forced by the French to take refuge in the mountains of the canton of Grisons where, during the early fall, his army was practically destroyed by cold and starvation. On October 22, alleging lack of co-operation by the Austrians, the Russians withdrew from the Second Coalition.

After he returned to France from Egypt (October, 1799) and became one of the Consulate (November, 1799), Napoleon offered to make peace with the allies. The Coalition refused, and Napoleon planned a series of moves against Austria, and various German states in alliance with Austria for the spring of 1800. He himself crossed the Alps into northern Italy with a newly raised army of 40,000 men, and on June 14 defeated the Austrians in the battle of Marengo. In the meantime French forces under General Jean Victor Moreau had crossed the Rhine into southern Germany, taken Munich, signally defeated the Austrians under Archduke John in the battle of Hohenlinden in Bavaria (December 3) and, advancing into Austria, reached the city of Linz. These and other French successes caused Austria to capitulate. By the Treaty of Lunéville (February 9, 1801), Austria and its German allies ceded the left bank of the Rhine River to France, recognized the Batavian, Helvetian, Cisalpine, and Ligurian republics, and made other concessions. The Treaty of Lunéville also marked the breakup of the Second Coalition; the only Allied nation which continued fighting was Great Britain, whose troops had unsuccessfully engaged the French on Dutch soil in 1799, and made some territorial gains at the expense of France in Asia and elsewhere. On March 27, 1802, Great Britain itself made peace with France through the Peace of Amiens (see AMIENS, PEACE OF).

This peace, however, turned out to be a mere truce. In 1803 a dispute broke out between the two nations because of the refusal of France to surrender the island of Malta (taken June 12, 1798, by Napoleon's forces, while on their way to Egypt) to its original possessors, the Knights of Malta, as provided in the Treaty of Amiens; and war again broke out between Great Britain and France. An important consequence of this war was Napoleon's abandonment, due to the need to concentrate his resources in Europe, of his plan to establish a great French colonial empire in the region known as Louisiana in North America, west of the United States. Instead, he sold Louisiana to the United States (see LOUISIANA PURCHASE; UNITED STATES: *History*). In 1805 Great Britain was joined in its new war by Austria, Russia, and Sweden; and Spain allied itself to France; the ensuing war is known as the War of the Third Coalition.

Napoleon quickly moved against the new alliance. Since 1798 he had exerted pressure on Great Britain by keeping an army concentrated at Boulogne on the English Channel ostensibly preparing to invade England; and during the dissensions leading to the outbreak of war in 1803, Napoleon had greatly increased the French forces at Boulogne. After the formation of the Third Coalition against France, he moved his troops from Boulogne to meet the Austrians who, under the archduke Ferdinand and General Karl Mack von Leiberich, had invaded Bavaria. A number of German states, including Bavaria, Württemberg, and Baden, allied themselves with France. Napoleon defeated the Austrians at

Napoleon Bonaparte as commander in chief of the army of Italy (painting by A. J. Gros)

Ulm (q.v.), taking 20,000 prisoners, and then marched his troops along the Danube River and captured Vienna. Russian armies under General Mikhail Ilarionovich Kutuzov (1745–1813) and Czar Alexander I reinforced the Austrians, but Napoleon crushed the combined Austro-Russian forces in the Battle of Austerlitz (see AUSTERLITZ, BATTLE OF), sometimes known as the Battle of the Three Emperors. Austria again capitulated, signing the Treaty of Pressburg on December 26, 1805. Among the terms of this treaty were the concession by Austria to France of territory in northern Italy, and to Bavaria of territory in Austria itself; in addition, Austria recognized the duchies of Württemberg and Baden as kingdoms.

In Italy, where French forces under Masséna had defeated the Austrians under the Archduke Charles, Napoleon now made his elder brother, Joseph, King of Naples in 1806. Elsewhere in Europe, he made his third brother, Louis, King of Holland (the former Batavian Republic); and on July 12 established the Confederation of the Rhine (q.v.), which eventually consisted of all the states of Germany excepting Austria, Prussia, Brunswick, and Hesse. The formation of the Confederation put an end to the Holy Roman Empire (q.v.), and brought most of Germany under Napoleon's control. His Continental successes, however, were largely offset by the victory on October 21, 1805, of the British fleet under Admiral Horatio Nelson off Cape Trafalgar over the combined fleets of France and Spain; this victory gave Great Britain mastery of the sea throughout the remainder of the Napoleonic era. In 1806 economic warfare between Great Britain and France was initiated. Napoleon formulated his so-called

NAPOLEONIC WARS. *The Spanish capitulate to Napoleon at Madrid (painting by A. J. Gros).*

Continental System (q.v.), issuing decrees, in 1806 and later, forbidding British trade with all European nations; Great Britain retaliated by the Orders in Council, which in effect prohibited neutrals from trading between the ports of any nations obeying Napoleon's decrees. British mastery of the sea made it impossible for Napoleon to enforce the Continental System, and resulted eventually in the failure of his economic policy for Europe.

Before the effect of British sea power could be manifest, however, Napoleon increased his power over the Continent. In 1806 Prussia, aroused by Napoleon's growing strength in Germany, joined in a Fourth Coalition with Great Britain, Russia, and Sweden. Napoleon signally defeated the Prussians in the Battle of Jena on October 14, 1806 and captured Berlin. He then defeated the Russians in the Battle of Friedland (see FRIEDLAND, BATTLE OF) and forced the czar, Alexander I, to make peace. By the principal terms of the Peace of Tilsit (see TILSIT, TREATY OF) Russia gave up its Polish possessions and became an ally of France, and Prussia was reduced to the status of a third-rate power, deprived of almost half its territory and crippled by heavy indemnity payments and severe restrictions on the size of its standing army. Through military action against Sweden on the part of Russia and Denmark, the Swedish king, Gustavus IV, was forced to abdicate in favor of his uncle, Charles XIII, on the condition that the latter name as his heir General Jean Baptiste Jules Bernadotte, one of Napoleon's marshals. Bernadotte actually became king in 1818, as Charles XIV John, founding the present Swedish royal line.

In 1808 Napoleon was master of all of Europe excepting Russia and Great Britain, but from this time on his power began to decline. The chief reasons for this decline were the rise of a nationalistic spirit in the various defeated nations of Europe; and the persistent opposition of Great Britain, which, safe from invasion because of its superior navy, never ceased to organize and subsidize new coalitions against Napoleon.

In Spain Napoleon first encountered the nationalistic spirit that led to his downfall. In 1808, after dethroning Charles IV of Spain, Napoleon made his own brother Joseph king of that country. The Spaniards revolted and drove Joseph out of Madrid. A violent struggle (1808–13) known as the Peninsular War (q.v.) then took place between the French, intent on restoring Joseph, and the Spaniards, aided by British forces under Arthur

NAPOLEONIC WARS. *Napoleon's men wounded and dying in the retreat from Russia (painting).*

Wellesley (later Duke of Wellington). The Allies eventually defeated the French, inflicting losses in manpower that severely handicapped Napoleon when he was later forced to meet new enemies in the east and north of Europe. The first of these new enemies was Austria, which, inflamed by patriotic feeling, entered the Fifth Coalition, with Great Britain in 1809. Napoleon defeated the Austrians at Wagram (July, 1809), and inflicted upon them the Treaty of Vienna, by which Austria lost much territory. He also divorced his wife, Josephine, and married Marie Louise, daughter of the Austrian emperor, Francis I, in the vain hope of keeping Austria out of further coalitions against him.

The turning point of Napoleon's career came in 1812 when war again broke out between France and Russia because of Czar Alexander I's refusal to enforce the Continental System. Napoleon invaded Russia with an army of 400,000. He defeated the Russians at Borodino (see BORODINO, BATTLE OF), and then took Moscow (September 14, 1812). The Russians burned the city, making it impossible for Napoleon's troops to establish winter quarters there. The French retreated across Russia into Germany, suffering the loss of most of their men through cold, starvation, and Russian guerrilla attacks. Russia then joined the Sixth Coalition, which also included Prussia, Great Britain, and Sweden. In 1813, in a burst of patriotic fervor caused by the political and economic reforms that had taken place in the nation since its defeat at Jena, Prussia opened a War of Liberation against Napoleon. He defeated the Prussians at Lutzen and Bautzen, but was forced by the Battle of Leipzig (October, 1813) to retreat across the Rhine, thus freeing Germany. The following year the Russians, Austrians, and Prussians invaded France from the north; in March, 1814, they took Paris, whereupon Napoleon abdicated and was sent into exile on the island of Elba in the Mediterranean Sea.

The Allies then called the Congress of Vienna (see VIENNA, CONGRESS OF) to restore in Europe the monarchies Napoleon had overthrown. During their deliberations Napoleon escaped from Elba to France, quickly raised an army, and marched into Belgium to meet the forces of Great Britain, Prussia, Russia, and Austria. He defeated his enemies at Ligny, was defeated by them at Quatre Bras, and met final defeat (June 18, 1815) at Waterloo (see WATERLOO, BATTLE OF). Waterloo marked the end of the Napoleonic Wars. Napoleon returned to Paris, once more abdicated, and was sent into permanent exile on the island of St. Helena in the South Atlantic Ocean.

Napoleon himself was indifferent to the ideals of the French Revolution and fought the powers of Europe not to impose these ideals but for his own aggrandizement. For his own purposes, however, he abolished feudalism and serfdom in the states he conquered, and instituted political and, through the Code Napoleon (q.v.), social equality. In this way, although it was not his intention, he imbued Europe with the ideas of the French Revolution. The Napoleonic Wars were also largely responsible for the rise of nationalistic sentiment that took place in Europe during the 19th century, which, on the one hand, resulted in much social, economic, and political progress; and on the other, created the national jealousies and hatreds that in large part brought about World War I (q.v.).

WART (*Verrucae*), collections of lengthened papillae of the skin, closely adherent and ensheathed by a thick covering of hard dry cuticle. From friction and exposure to the air their surface presents a horny texture, and is rounded off into a small, button-like shape. *Subungual warts* originate beneath the nail, and as they increase they crop out either at the free extremity or the side of the nail, and are usually troublesome and often very painful. *Venereal warts* are caused by the direct irritation of the discharges of gonorrhea or syphilis.

WARTBURG, a castle near Eisenach in Saxe-Weimar, Germany, situated on a hill 565 feet above the town. It was begun about 1070 and till the year 1247 was the residence of the landgraves of Thuringia, attaining its greatest splendor under Hermann I (1190–1217), who was a noted patron of the arts. The restoration of the castle was begun in 1847 after designs by Ritzen, who succeeded in reproducing with great faithfulness the original plan of the structure.

The Sängersaal in the Hofburg is noted as the scene of the legendary Wartburg Krieg or Sängerkrieg of 1207, in which the most celebrated of German minstrels competed for supremacy. Walther von der Vogelweide, Wolfram von Eschenbach, and Heinrich von Ofterdingen participated in the musical tourney, and to the first of these fell the prize. This legend, dating from the early part of the 13th century, was blended in time with a West German tradition regarding the contest between the pious Wolfram and the magician Klingsor aided by the devil. The story in its modified form became the subject of an early poem which attained wide currency before the end of the 13th century. From this source Wagner, among others, drew part of the material he used in writing the libretto of *Tannhäuser*. See EISENACH.

WARTHE (Pol. *Warta*), a river of Germany and Poland, the largest tributary of the Oder. It rises in southwest Poland and flows in a general northwesterly direction, traverses Posen through the Warthe swamps, of which 140 square miles are protected by dikes, and joins the Oder at Küstrin. Of its total length of over 540 miles, 265 miles are navigable. As the principal river of Posen, the Warthe has considerable traffic and is connected by canal with the Vistula.

WART HOG, a large, bush-ranging, wild pig of Africa, of which there are two species, *Phacochoerus africanus,* of eastern Africa, called "halluf" in Ethiopia, and *Phacochoerus aethiopicus* of South Africa. Both have very long and broad heads with enormous tusks, and the face is made ugly by pairs of great wartlike protuberances on each side of the nose, with one pair just below the eyes.

WARTON, JOSEPH (1722–1800), English literary critic, born in Dunsfold, Surrey, and educated at Oriel College, Oxford University. He took orders in 1744, and was curate in Basingstoke (1744–45), and subsequently in Chelsea. In 1744 he wrote a book of verse with the title *Ode on Reading West's Pindar,* and in 1746 a collection of *Odes on Various Subjects,* in which he declared against the didactic school of poetry represented by the English poet Alexander Pope. In 1753 he published a four-volume edition of the ancient Roman poet Vergil in Latin and English, himself contributing translations of the *Eclogues and Georgics,* critical essays, annotations, and a *Life* of the poet. He did not achieve any important preferment in the Church of England, and in 1755 became second master of Winchester School. From 1766 to 1793 he was headmaster. While at Winchester he wrote the two volumes (1757–82) of his *Essay on the Genius and Writings of Pope,* his most important work. Warton became prebendary of London in 1782, and of Winchester in 1788.

WARTON, THOMAS (1728–90), English poet and critic, born in Basingstoke. In 1785 he was appointed Camden professor of history at Oxford, and poet laureate in succession to William Whitehead. His poems (sonnets, odes, and lyrics), collected in 1777, reached a fourth edition in 1789. Written in imitation of Spenser and Milton, they are interesting as links between the older English poetry and the

The South African wart hog (Phacochoerus aethiopicus)
N.Y. Zoological Society

poetic outburst beginning with Wordsworth and Coleridge. Warton gained his reputation as a critic with *Observations on the Faerie Queene,* a pioneer work in the revival of enthusiasm for magic and mystery. In 1774 appeared the first volume of his *History of English Poetry,* which still possesses great value. Judged historically, it marks an epoch in English literary history. Warton's last important undertaking was an edition of *Poems upon Several Occasions by John Milton* (1785).

WARWICK, a village of Orange Co., N.Y., situated on Wawayanda Creek, 5 miles N. of the New Jersey boundary. It is served by a railroad and contains railroad repair shops. The village is surrounded by an agricultural area containing several lakes. Warwick is the site of a State training school for boys. The village was settled in 1746 and has several old buildings, notably Baird Tavern, built in 1776. Warwick was incorporated as a village in 1867. Pop. (1940) 2534.

WARWICK, a city of Kent Co., R.I., situated on the Pawtuxet and Providence rivers, and on a branch of Narragansett Bay, 6 miles s. of Providence. Transportation facilities include a railroad and air-line service. Warwick is principally a residential community. Industries there are the manufacture of pipe fittings, stapling machines, brass castings and moldings, and textiles. In addition, the city is a shipping point for clams, oysters, and scallops. The first settlement was established in 1648 by Samuel Gorton (q.v.) and named by him after Robert, Earl of Warwick, who had assisted him in gaining a royal charter. It was the birthplace of Gen. Nathanael Greene, one of the heroes of the American Revolution. Warwick was chartered as a city in 1931. Pop. (1950) 43,027.

WARWICK, county town of Warwickshire, England, on the Avon, 21 miles S.E. of Birmingham. Warwick's chief glory is its stately castle, on a rocky elevation, overhanging the river. Besides relics of Guy of Warwick, the "Kingmaker", and Cromwell, it contains paintings by Vandyke, Rubens, Holbein, and other masters, the "Grimani table", and the Greek "Warwick vase", 7 ft. in diameter, from Hadrian's Villa in Tivoli. The industries include the making of art furniture, gelatine, and agricultural implements; there is a considerable trade in agricultural produce. Pop., about 13,000.

WARWICK, FRANCES EVELYN, COUNTESS OF (1861–1938), British humanitarian. After her marriage to the fifth Earl of Warwick she became generally known for her interest in public movements. She founded a complete organization, both at Warwick Castle and at Easton Lodge, for the welfare of the poor and nursing of the sick; the Lady Warwick College (housed in Studley Castle, Warwickshire) for training young women in horticulture, dairy, bee, and poultry keeping; a science and technical school on her Essex estate; and a home for crippled children at Warwick. Lady Warwick became an active Socialist, and lectured on socialism in the United States. She wrote *Warwick Castle and Its Earls* (2 vols., 1903), *William Morris, His Home and Haunts* (1912), *A Woman and the War* (1916), *Life's Ebb and Flow* (1929), *After-thoughts* (1931), *Branch Lines* (1932), and *The Prime Minister's Pyjamas* (1933).

WARWICK, LEOPOLD GUY FRANCIS MAYNARD GREVILLE, EARL OF (1882–1928), English soldier, born in Warwick Castle, Warwickshire. He was at Eton when the Boer War began, and not able to get parental consent to join the colors, he sold his gun and his fur coats for funds to get to South Africa. There he was attached to the staff of Sir John French.

During the Russo-Japanese War, 1904–05, Warwick became a correspondent for Reuter's, and later wrote a book on his experiences. In 1908 he was appointed aide-de-camp to Sir John French. In 1914 he commanded the Fourth and Twelfth Canadian Infantry brigades, with the rank of brigadier general. He was wounded in 1915, and received various British and foreign orders. He served also as liaison officer with the American army. In 1924 he succeeded his father as Earl of Warwick, being the sixth holder of the title, of the present peerage.

WARWICK, RICHARD BEAUCHAMP, EARL OF. See BEAUCHAMP, RICHARD DE.

WARWICK, RICHARD NEVILLE, EARL OF. See NEVILLE (family).

WARWICK, ROBERT RICH, 2nd EARL OF (1587–1658), English Puritan nobleman and naval commander, educated at Cambridge University. He was the eldest son of Lord Robert Rich, who was created Earl of Warwick in 1618. In the following year the son succeeded to the title. He studied law, was admitted to the bar in 1604, and became member of Parliament for Maldon in 1610. Joining the Puritan movement, he played an important part in the colonization of Rhode Island and Connecticut. In the Great Rebellion he was a supporter of the Parliamentarian cause. In 1642 he served as lieutenant of the fleet under Northumberland, whom he succeeded as admiral in 1643. During the protectorship of Cromwell he was chosen to bear the sword of state in the latter's presence.

WARWICKSHIRE, a midland county of England. The county is traversed by the river Avon. Five sixths of its area is under cultivation, including pastures; wheat is the chief crop, while dairying receives much attention. The north portion is industrial and its mechanical industries are very important, especially founding and the manufacture of machinery, automobiles, jewelry, and instruments. Official reports of the Executive Board placed the coal output at about 4,700,000 tons annually. The county town is Warwick, and the largest cities are Birmingham and Coventry. Area, 976 sq.m.; pop., about 1,652,000.

WAR ZONE. In warfare, especially in naval warfare, the ever-present problem is to reconcile the military necessity of the belligerents with the personal and commercial rights of neutrals. The belligerent state must be free to put effective pressure upon its antagonist, but the rights of a neutral state, being inherent in sovereignty, may not be abridged by belligerent action. These principles, if rigidly insisted on, would produce inevitable clash; hence experience has suggested compromise, and international law has accorded to the belligerent the right of visit and search with a view to prevent carriage of contraband or unneutral service, as well as the more extreme right of blockade.

The actual zone of battle, on sea as on land, has always been considered as interdicted to neutrals, and if damage is sustained through necessary acts of war no claims for indemnity arise. But it is unsafe to press the analogy further, for while on land the theater of operations is always under the jurisdiction either of the local sovereign or the military occupant, naval warfare is conducted in large part upon the high seas which lie outside the jurisdiction of any state and upon which all, neutrals and belligerents alike, have an equal right to be.

The restriction implied in the war zone, however, is primarily a result of new methods of warfare, such as the mine, the submarine, and the use of radiotelegraph. It was employed for the first time in the Russo-Japanese War both by way of the laying of mines on the high seas and the designation of strategical areas through which the passage of all vessels was regulated and in certain cases prohibited.

The policy of the belligerents in World War I went far beyond this limited idea of defense sea areas. Belligerents proceeded to pre-empt for hostile uses large areas of the high seas which were mined and became the scene of an unregulated submarine warfare.

For so-called combat areas or war zones, established by the U.S. neutrality legislation of 1939, see NEUTRALITY; see also TERRITORIAL WATERS.

WASATCH MOUNTAINS, a mountain range belonging to the Rocky Mountain system. It begins in southeast Idaho, and runs southward, east of the Great Salt Lake and through the center of Utah, gradually turning to the southwest, and ending at the southwest corner of the State. Its average height is about 10,000 feet, and several of its peaks are over 12,000 feet high. The range is a recent uplift, and of a composition similar to that of the minor Basin Ranges. It consists in the north of a ridge of Carboniferous rocks flanked by Tertiary and Cretaceous strata, and in the south of great masses of igneous rocks. Coal, iron, and silver constitute its chief mineral wealth.

WASCO, the easternmost tribe of Chinookan stock, formerly claiming the country on the south side of the Columbia River, about The Dalles, Oregon, and now gathered with other tribes upon the Warmspring Reservation in the same vicinity.

WASECA, county seat of Waseca Co., Minn., situated on Clear Lake, 76 miles S. of Minneapolis. It is served by two railroads, and is the center of a farming and stock-raising area. Industrial establishments in Waseca include grain elevators, a vegetable cannery, machine shops, and factories manufacturing sporting goods and radios. In the vicinity of the city is a State agricultural experiment station. Pop. (1940) 4270.

WASH, or WASH SALE, a term used in financial circles to describe a sale of stock or other securities at a stock exchange between parties solely for the purpose of attracting attention by reason of the apparent activity of the market, of creating a market price, or both. The term is also used of individual transactions in buying and selling "short" where both purchase and sale are consummated without the actual exchange of the securities, but merely as a book transaction. Although contrary to the regulations of most stock exchange associations, the practice is general.

WASH, a wide estuary on the east coast of England, between the counties of Lincoln and Norfolk, 22 m. in length and 15 m. in average breadth.

WASH BOTTLE, in chemistry, an apparatus for washing gases and precipitates. It consists usually of a tightly stoppered glass flask or bottle with two tubes passing into the vessel, one of them extending to the bottom of the liquid contained in the vessel. The gas passes into the liquid through the longer tube, bubbles up through the liquid, and makes its exit through the shorter tube, which is above the level of the liquid. When the apparatus is used for washing precipitates, as on a filter, a stream of liquid, usually water, is forced out at the longer tube by air pressure.

WASHBURN, county seat of Bayfield Co., Wis., situated on Chequamegon Bay, an arm of Lake Superior, 60 miles E. of Superior. It is served by a railroad and by lake steamers, and is a distribution point for coal. The city is also a commercial fishing center, and the center of a farming, dairying, lumbering, and quarrying area. Among the products of the surrounding region are poultry, fruits, and brownstone. The principal industry in the city is the manufacture of dynamite. Washburn was settled in 1883 and incorporated in 1904. Pop. (1940) 2363.

WASHBURN, ALBERT HENRY (1866–1930), American diplomat and lawyer, born in Middleborough, Mass. In 1919 he became professor of political science and international law at Dartmouth College. He represented the United States on the commission of jurists sitting at The Hague from December, 1922, to March, 1923, to consider amendment of the laws of war in accordance with a resolution of the Washington Disarmament Conference. The following year he was named president of the mixed commission appointed to adjust differences between Austria and Yugoslavia arising out of provisional trade agreements. He resigned as minister to Austria early in 1930 so as to accept the post of ambassador to Japan.

WASHBURN, CADWALLADER COLDEN (1818–82), American soldier and political leader, born in Livermore, Me. At the outbreak of the Civil War he became colonel of the 2nd Wisconsin cavalry, was promoted brigadier general and major general (1862), assisted in the capture of Vicksburg (1863), and subsequently commanded the District of West Tennessee. In 1872–74 he was governor of Wisconsin. He founded an orphan asylum in

Minneapolis, and the Washburn Observatory of the University of Wisconsin.

WASHBURN, CHARLES AMES (1822–89), American editor, born in Livermore, Me. He was editor and owner of the *Alta Californian* (San Francisco) in 1853–58, and of the San Francisco *Daily Times* (1858–60), and commissioner and later minister to Paraguay (1861–68). He was accused of conspiracy during the war between Brazil and Paraguay and was forced to return to the United States. He later invented a form of typewriter which he named the typograph. He wrote *Philip Thaxter* (1861), *A History of Paraguay* (1870), *Political Evolution* (1887), and *From Poverty to Competence* (1887).

WASHBURN, EDWARD WIGHT (1881–1934), American chemist, born in Beatrice, Nebr. From 1913 to 1916 he was professor of physical chemistry and from 1916 to 1922 professor of ceramic chemistry and head of the department of ceramic engineering at the University of Chicago. In 1926 he became chief chemist of the U.S. Bureau of Standards, in 1929 chairman of the International Commission on Physico-Chemical Standards, and member of the International Committee of Thermochemistry. He is the author of *Introduction to the Principles of Physical Chemistry* (1915).

WASHBURN, FREDERIC LEONARD (1860–1927), American entomologist, born in Brookline, Mass. After serving as instructor in zoology at the University of Michigan, he was appointed in 1889 professor of zoology at the Oregon Agricultural College, where he remained until 1895, when he went to the University of Oregon as professor of biology. During part of this period he was State biologist of Oregon. His appointment to the faculty of the University of Minnesota as professor of entomology followed in 1902 and from then until 1918 he was State entomologist of Minnesota. In 1918 he was made professor of economic vertebrate zoology at the University of Minnesota.

WASHBURN, MARGARET FLOY (1871–1939), American psychologist, born in New York City, and educated at Vassar College and Cornell University. She served as professor of psychology and ethics at Wells College from 1894 to 1900. At Cornell she was warden of Sage College and lecturer in psychology from 1900 to 1902, and at the University of Cincinatti was assistant professor psychology in 1902–03. Afterward she was associate professor, and professor at Vassar from 1908 to 1937. Her contributions to periodicals deal largely with problems of sensation and perception. She translated *Principles of Morality* (1901), which is Vol. III of Wundt's *Ethics*, and wrote *Animal Mind: Textbook of Comparative Psychology* (1908) and *Movement and Mental Imagery* (1916).

WASHBURN, STANLEY (1878–1950), American war correspondent and author, born in Minneapolis, Minn. He reported the major developments of the Russo-Japanese War and World War I and saw service in France with the 26th Division of the American Expeditionary Force. His works include *Victory in Defeat* (1916) and *The Russian Offensive* (1917); and a play *The Man in Hiding* (1914). In 1921 he was a secretary of the American delegation to the Disarmament Conference in Washington, D.C., and after 1926 he was a prominent coal mine operator in North Dakota.

WASHBURN, WILLIAM DREW (1831–1912), American capitalist, born in Livermore, Me. In 1857 he built the first commercial flour mill in Minneapolis and was made secretary of the Minneapolis Mill Company, which became one of the most important milling companies in the United States. Washburn played a major part in the development of the railroad interests in Minnesota, being one of the contractors in building a part of the Northern Pacific railroad, president of the construction company for the Minneapolis and Duluth and the Minneapolis and St. Louis railway companies, and organizer of the Minneapolis and Pacific Railroad Company. He was a member of the House of Representatives (1879–85), and United States senator (1889–95).

WASHBURNE, CARLETON WOLSEY (1889–), American educator, born in Chicago, Ill. He was head of the department of science at San Francisco State Teachers College (1914–19), and was appointed superintendent of schools in Winnetka, Ill., in 1919. He is known for his research in school administration and is the author of *Individual Speller* (1923), *My Sound Book* (1926), *Washburne Individual Arithmetics* (1927–29), *Better Schools* (1928), and *A Living Philosophy of Education* (1940); coauthor of *The Right Book for the Right Child* (1933); and editor of the Social Study Series (1928–31).

WASHBURNE, ELIHU BENJAMIN (1816–87), American diplomat and politician, born in Livermore, Me. He was a member of Congress, 1852–69, and was secretary of state under President Grant. He resigned this position to become United States minister to France, and during the dark days of the Paris

WASHBURN, MOUNT   12,967   WASHBURNE MUNICIPAL U.

General Electric Co.

WASHING MACHINES
Above: Dishes and silverware in the rack of a dishwashing machine, seen from above the tub. Right: Clothes-washing machine of the vertical-impeller type, with wringer.

Commune was the only foreign minister who remained at his post. He wrote *Recollections of a Minister to France, 1869–1877* (2 vols., 1887), and edited *The Edwards Papers* (1884).

WASHBURN, MOUNT, a mountain peak in Yellowstone National Park in Wyoming. The summit is 10,317 ft. above sea level.

WASHBURN MUNICIPAL UNIVERSITY, a coeducational, municipally controlled institution of higher education, situated in Topeka, Kans. It was founded in 1865 by the General Association of the Congregational Churches of Kansas, under the name of Lincoln College; the name was changed to Washburn College in 1868, and in 1941 the present name was adopted and municipal control instituted. The university comprises colleges of liberal arts, law, and music; courses are offered leading to the degrees of B.A., B.S., B.MUS., B.B.A., LL.D., and J.D. In a recent year over 2000 students were enrolled and the faculty numbered over 100.

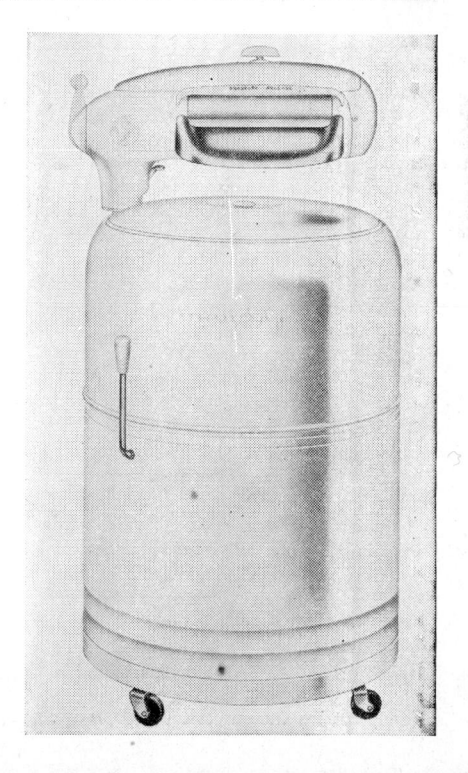

WASH DRILL, a boring apparatus consisting of pipe ending in a tubular bit. A jet of water under high pressure is forced through this nozzle, the drill sinking deeper as the earth is washed away; the surplus water and debris are sucked up by means of pumps. This method is of especial value in sand and soft loam.

WASHER, in mechanics, a small, flat, perforated disk, either of metal, rubber, fiber, or leather, used for placing beneath a nut or pivot head, or at an axle head or joint, to serve as a cushion or packing. A spring washer is a metal ring, cut through and with the ends thrown out of line, which thus acts as a spring. By exerting pressure against the nut, it insures tightness and lessens the possibility of the nut being loosened through vibration or other cause. In plumbing, a washer is an outlet pipe, as for a cistern, which is plugged when not in use. An unperforated washer is known as a blind washer.

WASHINGER, WILLIAM HENRY (1862–1918), American clergyman, bishop of the United Brethren Church, born in Greythorne, Pa. He was educated at Lebanon Valley College, and was pastor of a church in Harrisburg, Pa., 1890–94. In that year he was ordained in the ministry of the United Brethren Church and became pastor of a congregation in Chambersburg, Pa., where he remained until 1902. From 1902 to 1917 he was superintendent of the Pennsylvania Conference of the church, and then became bishop of the Pacific District, with his seat at Portland, Ore. He lectured on social, economic, educational, and religious topics, and wrote *City Evangelization* (1906). Washinger was a vice-president of the Federal Council of Churches of Christ in America.

WASHING MACHINE, any device for the cleaning of clothes or dishes by mechanical means. Modern machines for washing clothes in the home laundry are of two types. One consists of a vertical cylindrical tub in which the clothes are placed. In the center of the tub is a vertical impeller, equipped with vanes, which turns back and forth to agitate the clothes during the washing process and during rinsing. In some models of this type of washer the tub is filled by means of a hose from the domestic hot-water supply and is emptied by means of a built-in pump which expels the dirty water through another hose to a drain. The most modern machines of this type have permanent connections to the water supply and the drainage system and are operated by an automatic-sequence switch so that the machine performs the successive acts of filling, washing, emptying, filling, rinsing, and emptying without attention from the operator. The other type of home-laundry washing machine employs a perforated horizontal cylinder which is arranged to revolve in a tub of water. Vanes on the inside of the cylinder agitate or tumble the clothes as the cylinder revolves, producing the necessary washing action. Such machines are usually entirely automatic in action, performing the same sequence of operations as the agitator type of washer and, in addition, partially drying the clothes centrifugally by spinning the cylinder rapidly at the end of the sequence. Both types of home-laundry washing machine are impelled by gears powered by electric motors, and many modern washing machines are fitted with an automatic soap-feeding device which supplies soap during or immediately after filling. The large washing machines used by commercial laundries are described in the article LAUNDRY.

Dishwashing machines for home use consist of enclosed tubs equipped with wire racks in which dishes, glassware, and silverware are placed. Soap in powder form is placed in a special compartment, and the machine automatically sprays the dishes with jets of hot, soapy water, and then with a rinsing spray of hot water. In some types of dishwashers, the dishes are allowed to dry from their own heat, and in others provision is made to dry them by means of a heating unit. In all cases the sequence of operation of the machines is automatically controlled.

WASHINGS, CEREMONIAL, a religious observance common to the Christian, Jewish, Mohammedan and other creeds, involving partial or complete ablution for the purpose of actual or ritual cleanliness. There are three kinds of ablution recognized by Biblical and rabbinical law: (1) washing of the hands; (2) washing of the hands and feet; and (3) immersion of the entire body in water, as in the modern rite of baptism.

Washing of the hands and feet is prescribed by the Mosaic Law only for those desiring to perform priestly functions. The washing of the whole body is the form of ablution most frequently ordained in Scripture, and for the greatest number of causes, such as the eating of unclean flesh, or contact with a corpse or grave. In modern usage most of the old forms of purification are in abeyance, although the immersions for the sake of ritual purity at the festivals are still observed by the pious.

Following the custom of the priests, the pious Israelite bathed, or at least washed his hands, every morning before prayer. So fixed

Washington State Progress Commission

Washington State Capitol in the city of Olympia

did this custom become that the Christian Church adopted the Jewish custom of providing the worshipers with fountains or basins of water.

Among the Mohammedans ablution is also required before prayer, before touching the Koran, and after each ritual defilement.

WASHINGTON, a Pacific State and the most northwesterly State of the United States, bounded on the E. by Idaho, on the S. by Oregon, from which Washington is partially separated by the Columbia R., on the W. by the Pacific Ocean, on the N.W. by the Juan de Fuca Strait, Puget Sound, and Haro Strait, all of which separate Washington from Canada's Vancouver Island, and on the N. by the mainland portion of the Canadian province of British Columbia. Washington ranks as the 19th State in the Union in area, 23rd in the order of population (1950), and 42nd in the order of admission to the Union, having entered on Nov. 11, 1889. The State capital is Olympia (q.v.). In descending order of population (1950), the leading cities of the State are Seattle, Spokane, Tacoma, Yakima, Bellingham, Everett, Vancouver, Bremerton, and Walla Walla (qq.v.). From E. to W. the extreme length of the State is 360 m. and from N. to S. the extreme width is 240 m. The total area is 68,192 sq.m., including 1215 sq.m. of inland water surface. In 1940 the population was 1,736,191; the 1950 population, 2,378,963, represented an increase of more than 37 percent in ten years.

Washington is divided into two main regions, eastern and western Washington, by the Cascade Range (q.v.) which traverses the State in a S. to N. direction. Eastern Washington comprises about three fifths of the State's area, and western Washington encompasses the remainder. The Cascades vary in width from 50 m. at the southern margin of the State to over 100 m. at the international boundary. The peaks of the range reach an average elevation of 8000 ft. above sea level, and few of the passes through the mountains are below 6000 ft. Six glacier-covered, extinct volcanoes tower above the general level of the range. These include the highest point in the State, Mt. Rainier (14,408 ft.), which is also the third-highest peak in continental U.S., and Mt. Adams (12,307 ft.), Mt. Baker (10,730 ft.), Glacier Peak (10,436 ft.), Mt. St. Helens (9697 ft.), and Mt. Stuart (9470 ft.). The slopes of the Cascades, particularly on the west, are covered with forests of giant cedars, firs, and spruces. To the W. of the Cascades and lying between that range and another highland region called the Coast Range, is the Puget Sound Basin, a longitudinal depression which, at its highest points, is scarcely 500 ft. above sea level. The Basin, which extends from near the southern border of the State to British Columbia, is penetrated through more than half its length by the numerous branching arms of Puget Sound (q.v.), and forms one of the best systems of harbors in the world. The most densely populated sections of Washington, and four of the five largest cities in the State, are contained in the Basin. The Strait of Juan de Fuca, which separates Vancouver Island and Washington, connects the Pacific Ocean and Puget Sound. A narrow fiord, the Hood Canal, which somewhat resembles a fish hook in shape, projects about 60 miles inland from Puget Sound in a southwesterly direction, and then swings sharply to the N.E. The Sound contains numerous islands; the largest, Whidby Island, possesses a N. to S. extent of approximately 50 miles. Major indentations of the State along the Pacific Ocean include Grays Harbor and Willapa Bay, both situated on the southern portion of Washington's coast. Although the State possesses a general coast line of only 157 miles, the over-all length of the coast line measured around islands and bays, inlets, and estuaries reached by tidal water is 2846 miles. The lowest point in the State is at sea level along the Pacific Ocean, and the average elevation is 1700 ft. above sea level.

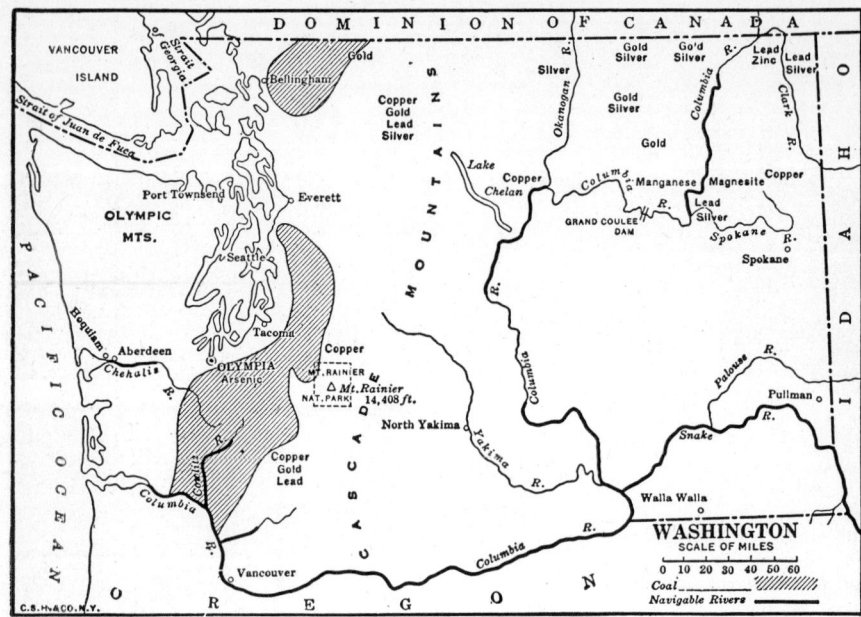

The Coast Range, situated w. of the Puget Sound Basin, traverses the State in a S.E. to N.W. direction, and increases in ruggedness and elevation toward the north. The southern portion of the range consists of broad irregular masses having a maximum elevation of about 3000 ft., while the northern portion of the highland rises into a well-defined group called the Olympic Mts. The Olympic Mts. are situated just w. of the Hood Canal, in the peninsula lying between Puget Sound and the Pacific Ocean; the highest peak, Mount Olympus, is 7954 ft. above sea level.

East of the Cascades the topography of Washington differs widely from that of the western portion of the State. It consists of three main physiographic provinces: the fertile Columbia Plain, which occupies most of southeastern Washington, and which is famed as the "Inland Empire" of the State; the Okanogan Highlands, a western extension of the Rockies which cover the northeastern portion of the State; and the Blue Mountain Range, a highland situated in the extreme southeastern portion of the State. The Columbia Plain consists of a vast basaltic plateau, an undulating treeless plain lying between 500 and 2000 ft. above sea level. The region is dissected by a number of river valleys and by depressions called coulees. The plains are bordered on the N. by the Columbia and Spokane rivers, which form the southern boundary of the Okanogan Highlands, a region of rolling

Wash. State Prog. Comm.

CITIES IN THE STATE OF WASHINGTON
Above: Skyline view of Seattle from Puget Sound. Right: Buildings in Tacoma. Mount Rainier is seen in the background.

hills which reach elevations exceeding 5000 ft. The Blue Mts. border the plains in the S.E. and possess elevations of more than 7000 ft. above sea level.

The only large independent river in Washington is the Columbia River (q.v.), which drains the entire eastern section of the State. Its principal tributaries are the Spokane, Pend Oreille, and Okanogan in the N.E., and the Snake River (q.v.) in the S.E. The Columbia's chief affluent from the E. slope of the Cascades is the Yakima. Western Washington is drained by a large number of comparatively small streams flowing into Puget Sound and the Pacific Ocean. The largest of those entering the sound are the Skagit in the N. and the Nisqually in the S. There are a number of lakes in eastern Washington; most of them are either expanded rivers such as the long and narrow Lake Chelan, the largest lake in the State, or remnants of old rivers. The largest concrete dam in the world, the Grand Coulee Dam (see DAMS), is situated in Washington on the Columbia R. The dam possesses a reservoir more than 150 miles long, and with Bonneville Dam and McNary Dam comprises the Columbia River Reclamation Project. Eventually, the system will irrigate 1,200,000 acres of land, in addition to providing a tremendous source of hydroelectric power.

Great contrast in climatic conditions exists between western and eastern Washington, the latter section having a less equable climate because the Cascade Range acts as a barrier against the moisture-carrying west winds and the tempering influence of the sea. Western Washington possesses a mild, moist climate and eastern Washington is subject to extremes of temperature in summer and winter, and a lesser amount of precipitation than the remainder of the State. The coastal region and the western section of the country receive from 21 to 120 inches of rain annually; the yearly amount of rainfall in eastern Washing-

Sheep grazing in Kittitas Valley, a leading wool-producing area in Washington State
(Washington State Progress Commission)

ton varies between 6 and 25 inches. Snowfall is light in the western region and heavy in the mountains and the east. The average annual temperature for the State as a whole is about 50°F.

Recreation facilities in Washington are excellent and include Mount Rainier National Park and Olympic National Park (qq.v.), noted for mountain climbing, winter sports, and hunting and fishing. Washington is the leading game-fishing State in the U.S. Fishermen are attracted by the salmon which spawn in the rivers of the State; trout and bass fishing are also notable. Wildlife includes panthers, black bears, wildcats, mountain goats, elk, deer, coyotes, and quail, pheasants, waterfowl, and other game birds.

The State is the site of eighteen Indian reservations, of which the largest are the Colville, Yakima, Spokane, and the Quinalt reservations; nine national forests, and a number of State parks and forests. National forest land in the State in a recent year exceeded 10,738,000 acres. Yearly, the State leads the nation in the production of lumber. Douglas fir, spruce, white and yellow pine, cedar, and larch are the principal trees. Recently the annual production of lumber in the State exceeded 3,257,000 million board feet, and the production of wood pulp, paper, and paperboard was more than 1,332,000 tons.

Of Washington's total area, approximately 33% is devoted to agriculture, which is the leading occupation of the people. The State leads the nation in the production of commercial apples, raising about 25% of the country's supply. In a recent year about 33,480,000 bushels of apples were produced. Other important fruits cultivated in Washington are cherries, pears, peaches, and plums. The State ranks fifth in the Nation as a wheat producer; Washington's Whitman, Lincoln, and Adams counties are the largest wheat-producing counties in the U.S. Other important agricultural products are corn, oats, barley, potatoes, hops, flower bulbs and seeds, and honey. Recently Washington possessed about 80,000 farms having more than 16,719,000 acres, which were valued at (land and buildings) more than $900,000,000. The raising of livestock is also important and in a recent year domestic animals in the State numbered 868,000 cattle (including 377,000 milch cows), 331,000 sheep, 158,000 swine, 75,000 horses, and 2000 mules.

Wash. State Prog. Comm.

IN WASHINGTON. *Above: Grand Coulee, largest concrete dam in the world. Right: Bridge on the San Juan Islands, in the northwestern part of the State of Washington.*

The cash income derived from crops and livestock in a recent year exceeded $512,200,000, and Federal subsidies added over $12,000,000.

The major manufacturing industries of the State are shipbuilding, airplane manufacture, food processing, and the manufacture of lumber and paper. Other industries include the manufacture of furniture, the refining of aluminum, and printing and publishing. Washington's industries, particularly shipbuilding and airplane manufacture, expanded greatly during the war years. At the peak of this production the output of the shipbuilding industry was valued at $1,750,000,000, and the aggregate of airplane manufacture was $2,373,000,000. Another industrial by-product of World War II in Washington was the establishment of the world's first full-scale plant for the manufacture of atomic bombs at the Hanford Engineering Works near Pasco. Other major industries are mining and fishing. Coal is the most important mineral found and its production represents half of the total value of mineral products in the State. In a recent year approximately 1,000,000 tons of coal were produced. Other minerals mined include gold, silver, marble, limestone, mercury, zinc, copper, clay, granite, antimony, sandstone, tungsten, platinum, diatomite, olivine, and magnesite. The total annual value of mineral products recently was more than $33,000,000. The State produces more than 200 varieties of sea food, the five species of salmon being the most important. Other important catches are oysters, halibut, crabs, clams, shrimp, cod, mackerel, and herring.

Transportation in Washington is provided by more than 5200 miles of main-track railway and more than 6100 miles of State-maintained, surfaced highways. In addition, more than 110 airports are in the State, of which 49 are municipal and 29 are equipped for night flying. Attendance at the elementary and secondary schools of Washington is free for all children between the ages of six and twenty-one, and compulsory throughout the full school year for all children between the ages of eight and sixteen. In a recent year there were more than 1460 elementary schools and junior and senior high schools, attended by more than 390,000 students and staffed by more than 12,750 teachers. Institutions of higher learning include the following State-supported schools: the University of Washington at Seattle, Washington State College at Pullman, and Western, Central, and Eastern State colleges of education at Bellingham, Ellensburg, and Cheney, respectively. Among the 23 other colleges and special schools in Washington are Whitman College at Walla Walla, Walla Walla College at College Place, Whitworth College and Gonzaga University at Spokane, and Seattle College and Seattle Pacific College at Seattle.

Washington is governed according to the terms of the constitution of 1889, as amended. Executive authority is vested in a governor, lieutenant governor, secretary of state, treasurer, attorney-general, auditor, superintendent of public instruction, commissioner of public lands, and insurance commissioner, all elected for four-year terms. Legislative authority is vested in a senate of 46 members, half of whom are elected every two years for four-year terms, and a house of representatives of 99 members, all elected for two-year terms. Judicial authority is vested in a supreme court, county superior courts, and courts of justices of the peace. Qualified voters are all U.S. citizens, twenty-one years of age or older, who have lived in the State a minimum of one year, the county three months, and the election district one month. Washington is divided into 39 counties and is represented in the Congress of the U.S. by 2 senators and 6 representatives.

History. According to some historians, the English navigator Sir Francis Drake, who explored the w. coast of North America in 1578–79, was the first European to sight the region comprising present-day Washington. Before the close of the 16th century the region was also seen by Juan de Fuca, a Greek sailing under the Spanish flag. He discovered (1592) the strait which now bears his name. Almost two centuries elapsed before the next significant discovery, the mouth of the river later called Columbia. This river, which was found in 1775 by the Spanish explorer Bruno Heceta, was named in 1792 by Robert Gray, a New England ship captain. Gray explored the river's estuary. Subsequent American claims to the region were partly based on Gray's visit. British navigators, including Captain John Cook, had meanwhile voyaged along the coast, and in 1792 George Vancouver circumnavigated what is now Vancouver Island.

The first exploration of the interior of the region, which had become known as the Oregon Country, was accomplished in 1805-06 by the Lewis and Clark Expedition (q.v.). Attracted by the potential fur trade in Oregon Country, the British also intensified their activities in the region. In 1810 the British explorer and fur trader David Thompson founded a settlement at the confluence of the Little Spokane and Spokane rivers. The American merchant John Jacob Astor sent a fur-trading expedition to Oregon Country in 1811. This expedition established a trading post, called Astoria (q.v.), near the mouth of the Columbia R. and a fort at the mouth of the Okanogan R. American occupation of the Oregon Country ended temporarily with the start of the War of 1812, leaving the ownership of the territory still in dispute. Negotiations in 1818 led to the establishment of the 49th parallel as the boundary between the U.S. and British possessions as far west as the Rocky Mts. However, as a settlement could not be reached regarding the boundary w. of the Rocky Mts. to the Pacific Ocean, and n. of the 42nd parallel, the two countries agreed to a ten-year period of joint occupancy of the Oregon Country. In 1819 Spain, which also had laid claim to the area, relinquished its claims to all Pacific coast territory n. of the 42nd parallel (the present northernmost extension of California's boundary); and in 1824 and 1825, by treaties with the U.S. and Great Britain, claim to the territory s. of the parallel 54° 40′ (the present southernmost extension of Alaska's boundary), was relinquished by Russia. In 1827 the Anglo-American convention of joint occupancy of the Oregon Country was extended for an indefinite period of time subject to termination by either party following a year's notice.

Although the British Hudson's Bay Company controlled the Northwest fur trade, organized American emigration to the Oregon Country began in the 1820's. The matter of the split jurisdiction of the region became a national problem and the so-called "Oregon question" came to occupy the attention of Congress. By the late 1830's many Americans were demanding that Great Britain relinquish all jurisdiction s. of 54° 40′ latitude; in 1844 the Democratic Party slogan, on which James K. Polk was elected President of the U.S., was "Fifty-four forty or fight". In 1846 Great Britain and the U.S. agreed, in the Oregon

Washington State Progress Commission

IN STATE OF WASHINGTON. *Top: Sugar factory in Yakima Valley, largest sugar-beet producing area in the State. Bottom: Harvesting wheat on a plain in eastern Washington.*

Treaty, to a compromise measure which set the northern limits of United States territory at the 49th parallel, except for the southern tip of Vancouver Island, which was to remain British. Two years later the U.S. established the Territory of Oregon; it included the present States of Washington and Oregon, and portions of Idaho, Wyoming, and Montana. On March 2, 1853, Washington was constituted as a separate Territory. It then included all of its present area in addition to portions of present-day Montana. In 1863 the Territory of Idaho (see IDAHO: *History*) was formed, and Washington assumed its present boundaries. Upon the organization of the Territory of Washington, the population was less than 4000. With the discovery of gold in eastern Washington a great influx of settlers followed, alarming the Indians of the region, who feared for their hunting grounds. The so-called Washington-Oregon Indian War occurred in 1855-56. Again in 1857 there were serious Indian troubles concurrent with the rush of population to the gold fields of British Columbia. The greatest population influx to Washington occurred after the discovery of gold at Salmon R. in 1860.

At the time of the boundary treaty between Great Britain and the U.S., the 49th parallel was accepted as the boundary from the Rockies to the channel between Vancouver Island and the mainland of the U.S. At that point the international boundary passed s.w. through the channel to the sea. In 1859 a dispute arose as to which channel was meant; the settlement of this dispute would decide the possession of the Haro Archipelago. George Edward Pickett (q.v.), then a captain in the U.S. Army, occupied San Juan Island of the archipelago with his men and prevented the landing of British troops. An actual military engagement was averted by the arrival of a British admiral, who refused to resort to force. The question was finally settled in favor of the U.S. by the decision of an arbitrator, the German emperor, on Oct. 21, 1872.

In 1885 and 1886 the people of the Territory entered into violent agitation against Chinese laborers who had been immigrating to the Pacific Coast in increasing numbers. Mobs burned Chinese homes, forcing them to leave their communities, and in some cases resorted to murder. In order to put an end to the outrages the Territorial governor called for the aid of Federal troops and subjected Seattle to martial law. Washington was admitted into the Union as a State in 1889, when Congress passed the Omnibus Statehood Bill admitting North and South Dakota, Montana, and Washington. The discovery of gold in the Klondike (q.v.) in 1897 hastened the commercial development of the State, as did the increasing trade with the Pacific island possessions of the U.S.

In the fifteen Presidential elections that have been held through 1948 since the admission of Washington to the Union as a State, Washington's voters have cast a majority or plurality of their ballots for the Democratic Party candidate seven times, the Republican Party candidate seven times, and once for Theodore Roosevelt, Progressive Party candidate in 1912. In the 1948 Presidential election Harry S. Truman, the Democratic incumbent, received 462,781 votes, Thomas E. Dewey, the Republican candidate, received 376,277 votes, and Henry A. Wallace, the Progressive Party candidate, received 29,745 votes.

WASHINGTON, the capital of the United States of America, situated on the E. bank and at the head of navigation of the Potomac R., about 30 miles s.w. of the center of Baltimore, Md., and about 226 miles s.w. of New York, N.Y. Washington is coextensive with the District of Columbia, the Federal District of the United States. The reader is directed to the article on the District of Columbia for important data on various aspects of the city, including site, transportation facilities, industries, public school system, institutions of higher learning, and government.

By virtue of its picturesque site, systematic plan, lovely parks, and magnificent public buildings and memorials, Washington ranks among the most beautiful cities in the world. The plan of the original city was drafted in 1791 by Pierre Charles L'Enfant (q.v.), a French engineer and veteran of the American Revolution. L'Enfant worked under the close supervision of President George Washington, who had selected the site of the Federal District. The outstanding feature of L'Enfant's design, the first ever prepared for a national capital, was the street layout, essentially a modification of the gridiron, or rectangular-block, pattern. The site of the Capitol of the United States (q.v.), occupying the approximate center of the original city, was selected as the focal point of the street system. North Capitol Street, extending due N. of the site, and South Capitol Street, extending due s., became the N. and s. axis of the city; East Capitol Street, extending due E. of the site, and the Mall, a broad park extending west-

The Capitol of the United States of America in Washington, District of Columbia

ward to the Potomac, became the E. and W. axis. Streets extending parallel to these axes completed the basic design, which was modified by the superimposition of a system of diagonal avenues. The diagonal avenues, now numbering twenty-one and named for various States of the Union, radiate from several central sites, particularly those of the Capitol and the Executive Mansion. Streets to the N. of the east-west axis were designated by consecutive letters of the alphabet, beginning with "A", and those to the S. were similarly named; streets to the E. of the north-south axis were designated by sequential numbers, beginning with "1", and those to the W. were similarly named. To facilitate identification, the quadrantal districts into which the city was divided by the two axes were designated Northeast, Southeast, Southwest, and Northwest.

Besides the regularity of layout, the principal features of the capital street system are the unusual breadth of the thoroughfares and the profusion of bordering shade trees. Pennsylvania Avenue, the main thoroughfare of the city, is 160 ft. wide. The section of the avenue extending from the Capitol to the Executive Mansion is the traditional site of the Presidential inaugural parades. With few exceptions, all of the avenues and streets in Washington range from 160 to 60 ft. in width. Sixteenth Street, which extends due N. from the Executive Mansion, is another important thoroughfare, and the other notable avenues include Constitution (originally known as B Street), Maryland, New York, Rhode Island, Connecticut, and Massachusetts avenues. The last-named avenue, four-and-one-half miles long, is lined with double rows of shade trees. In the aggregate, more than 600 m. of Washington streets are fringed with trees, including such varieties as red oak, oriental plane, maple, elm, and ginkgo. Four bridges span the Potomac at Washington, linking the city with Arlington (q.v.) and other Virginia communities.

The dismissal of L'Enfant in 1792, the subsequent loss of his designs, and various additional factors resulted in frequent violations of his plan for the development of the city, especially with respect to projected building sites, parks, and squares. Although the street layout was extended to the unoccupied portions of the Federal District, Washington developed in a generally haphazard fashion prior to 1871. In that year an extensive program for the improvement of the city was initiated. Pavements were constructed, a sewage system installed, shade trees set out, and a new water-supply system provided. Congressional action later led to beautification of the Mall, acquisition of new park areas, and adoption of zoning regulations. In 1926, responsibility for city planning was vested in a central governmental agency, the National Capital Park and Planning Commission. Among other things, this commission added considerably to the Washington park system, developed plans for the guidance of Federal building-construction projects, secured important changes in street layouts, and otherwise provided for the systematic improvement of Washington. One of the city's most distinctive characteristics, generally low structures, results from the timely adoption of zoning regulations.

As indicated above, Washington has been provided with a comprehensive park system in recent years. The system, covering more than 6000 acres and comprising numerous playgrounds and squares, the spacious grounds surrounding many of the public buildings, and several large recreation areas, contributes enormously to the beauty of the city. Among the units of the system, the most impressive is the Mall, with the Capitol and the Lincoln Memorial (q.v.) respectively dominating its E. and W. extremities. On the axis between these two structures and approximately due E. of the Executive Mansion stands the Washington Monument (q.v.), the highest masonry structure in the world. Other features of the Mall are the Reflecting Pools between Washington Monument and Lincoln Memorial, the approach to Arlington Memorial Bridge, the U.S. Botanic Garden, the neighboring museums, the Mall and Adams drives, and Union Square, containing the Ulysses S. Grant Memorial.

Rock Creek Park, in Washington N.W., is the largest unit of the city park system. This park consists of more than 1800 acres of woodland. Among its noteworthy features are about 30 m. of bridle paths and Fort De Russey, an important outpost of the capital defense system during the American Civil War. The newest and next-largest park in Washington is Anacostia Park, comprising about 1100 acres along both banks of the Anacostia R., a tributary of the Potomac. The park, situated in Washington S.E. and N.E., is the site of a golf course and Kenilworth Aquatic Gardens, with a bird sanctuary and interesting collections of water plants. In Washington S.W. is East Potomac Park, which is enclosed by Washington Channel, an arm of the Anacostia R., by the Potomac R., and by the Tidal Basin, an artificial lake. The N. shore of Tidal Basin adjoins the Mall. A scenic speedway along the perimeter of the Tidal Basin and East Potomac Park is connected with Rock Creek and Potomac Parkway, leading to the National Zoological Park (175 acres) and beyond to Rock Creek Park. The Thomas Jefferson Memorial, an impressive structure modeled after the ancient Pantheon in Rome, stands in East Potomac Park. Both this park and adjacent West Potomac Park contain a profusion of plants, shrubs, and trees, including about 3000 Japanese cherry trees, a gift (1912) from the people of Tokyo, Japan. The annual spectacle afforded by the cherry trees in bloom, usually beginning about the first week of April, attracts visitors from all parts of the nation. Other well-known units of the capital park system are Fort Stevens Park, Theodore Roosevelt Island, Glover-Archbold Park, Brentwood Park, Lincoln Park, Meridian Hill Park, and Montrose Park. Washington also contains a large number of smaller parks and squares, mainly comprising areas at the intersection of streets and avenues. Dupont Circle, Scott Circle, Logan Circle, Lafayette Park, Mount Vernon Square, and Stanton Park are typical of these areas, many of which are dominated by statues commemorating prominent American military heroes and statesmen. The chief private recreational facility in the city is Griffith Stadium (seating capacity about 32,000), the home grounds of the Washington baseball team ("Senators") of the American League.

Many of the numerous public buildings in Washington are architectural masterpieces, which together with the various parks and memorials give the city an atmosphere of dignified splendor. The stateliest and most conspicuous structure in the city is the Capitol of the United States, which is described in detail in a separate article. The Executive Mansion, popularly known as the White House (q.v.), is the oldest public edifice in Washington. Constructed (1792–99) from designs by the Irish-born architect James Hoban, the mansion is notable for its simple dignity. In 1814, during the War of 1812,

Aerial view of the White House and surrounding grounds in Washington, D.C.

invading British troops set fire to the Capitol, the Executive Mansion, and other buildings in the capital. The mansion was subsequently rebuilt. It was remodeled in 1902–03, and extensive repairs, necessitating its closing, were authorized in 1948 and begun in 1949. The other outstanding public buildings in the capital are grouped chiefly in the vicinity of the Capitol, the Mall, and Executive Mansion. Flanking the Capitol to the N.E. and S.E. are, respectively, the Senate Office Building and the House of Representatives Office Building, marble structures with imposing Corinthian colonnades. The Supreme Court Building, seat of the highest judicial tribunal of the U.S. government, occupies a site opposite and E. of the Capitol. Designed by the American architect Cass Gilbert and completed in 1935, the structure, with its huge portico containing eight Corinthian columns and a sculptured pediment, is one of the most beautiful and imposing in Washington. The main building of the Library of Congress, adjoining the Supreme Court Building on the S., is of gray granite, in Italian Renaissance style. The interior of the building is remarkably rich in decorations, mainly the work of noted American artists. Completed in 1897, the Library of Congress main building is adjoined by a modern annex in white marble.

The triangle formed by the intersection of Pennsylvania Avenue, Constitution Avenue, and Fifteenth Street is the site of the largest grouping of modern public buildings in the capital. At the base of the triangle and a short distance s.w. of the Executive Mansion is the Department of Commerce Office Building, completed in 1932. The foundation area (8 acres) of this structure, architecturally an adaptation of the Italian Renaissance style, is the largest in Washington. Harmoniously designed but somewhat smaller, the other structures in the so-called "Government Triangle" include the Post Office Department Building (1934), the Department of Justice Building (1934), the Department of Labor Building (1935), the National Archives Building (1935), and the Federal Trade Commission Building. The last-named building, occupying the triangle apex, is one of the most impressive in the entire group. Except for the Department of Agriculture Building, a white marble edifice situated a short distance s.w. of Washington Monument, and the nearby building of the Bureau of Engraving and Printing, all of the structures along the N. and S. sides of the Mall house museums and art galleries which are described in the following section of this article. The New National Museum Building, constructed of white marble in the neoclassic style; the original buildings of the Smithsonian Institution in the turreted Norman style; and the building of the National Gallery of Art, completed in 1941 and one of the most magnificent structures in the city, are especially interesting from an architectural standpoint.

Of the public structures in the immediate

vicinity of the Executive Mansion, the Treasury Department Building is the most imposing. The building is of granite construction, in Greek Ionic style, and its main section was completed in 1842. On the opposite (w.) side of the Executive Mansion is the building which formerly housed the State, War, and Navy Departments, a massive and uninspired edifice, completed in 1888, in French Renaissance style.

In addition to the structures cited, scores of other imposing public buildings, as well as numerous semipublic and privately owned buildings, are situated in Washington. Among these structures are the Federal Reserve Building (1937); the building housing the Corcoran Gallery of Art, the Washington Public Library, the National Academy of Sciences, and the Folger Shakespeare Library; the Department of Interior Building; the Pan American Building; Memorial Continental Hall, headquarters of the Daughters of the American Revolution; the Social Security Building; Union Railroad Station; and a large number of palatial hotels, private mansions, and foreign embassies. The Pentagon Building, housing the War Department and finished in 1942, is situated opposite the city, in Virginia. One of the largest office buildings in the world, it contains more than 3,600,000 sq.ft. of floor space. Other outstanding points of interest within the city are the U.S. Naval Observatory, the U.S. Soldiers Home, the U.S. Navy Yard, the Army Medical School, Walter Reed General Hospital, the Army War College, the Army Medical Center, the Bureau of Standards, Scottish Rite Temple, and institutions of higher learning, including Georgetown University, George Washington University, American University, Howard University, and the Catholic University of America (qq.v.). The city is the site of several famous ecclesiastical edifices, notably the Cathedral of St. Peter and St. Paul, seat of the Protestant Episcopal Diocese of Washington. Still under construction in a recent year, this edifice, when completed, will rank among the largest cathedrals in the world. Other noteworthy ecclesiastical edifices in the city are the National Shrine of the Immaculate Conception, the Franciscan Monastery, and St. John's Church (Episcopal). The last-named edifice is frequently identified as the "President's Church", because its parishioners have included many Presidents of the U.S. The Church of the Pilgrims (Presbyterian), the National Baptist Memorial Church, the Swedenborgian Church of the Holy City, and the Metropolitan Methodist Church are among other well-known places of worship in Washington.

Few other cities in the world are better equipped with educational and cultural facilities than Washington. Besides the prominent institutions of higher learning cited in the foregoing paragraph, many additional schools in the city provide advanced, specialized, and professional courses of study. Sectarian colleges include St. John's College (Roman Catholic), National Catholic School of Social Science, Trinity College (Roman Catholic), Washington Missionary School (Seventh Day Adventist), and National Methodist University. Other schools of higher learning in the city include the Washington College of Law, Washington Christian College, Columbus University, United States College of Veterinary Surgeons, Miner Teachers College, James Ormond Wilson Teachers College, and Army Medical College. There are several outstanding schools of art, including Critcher-Hill School of Art, Yard School of Fine Arts, Washington School of Art, National School of Fine and Applied Art, and the Corcoran School of Art. Gallaudet College, the first school of higher learning for deaf mutes in the U.S., is situated in Washington. The Carnegie Institution of Washington and the Brookings Institution (qq.v.) afford facilities for advanced research in various fields.

The libraries, museums, and art galleries of Washington contain unsurpassed collections, and with few exceptions are available to the general public without cost. The Library of Congress (q.v.), the largest library in the U.S. and one of the largest in the world, numbers about 9,000,000 books and pamphlets, nearly as many manuscripts, almost 2,000,000 maps and views, and considerable other valuable material among its collections. Supplementing the Library of Congress are the U.S. Army Medical Library which, with more than 1,100,000 books and pamphlets, is one of the largest of its kind in the world; the Washington Public Library, with more than 700,000 volumes; the Folger Shakespeare Library, with a variety of priceless collections, including many original and early editions of Shakespeare's works; the Dumbarton Oaks Research Library and Collection, with about 10,000 volumes relating to Byzantine culture; the Library of the Daughters of the American Revolution; and the libraries maintained by various departments of the Federal government, by several of the city's museums, and

Black Star; Ewing Galloway

WASHINGTON, D.C. *Above:* U.S. Supreme Court Building (left) and Library of Congress. *Right:* Jefferson Memorial at cherry-blossom time. *Below:* Pennsylvania Avenue, looking toward Capitol.

by schools of higher education in the city.

The collections of the Smithsonian Institution (q.v.) and its various branches embrace practically the entire realm of human culture. Of special importance among the Smithsonian branches are the National Collection of Fine Arts (q.v.); the United States National Museum, which has comprehensive exhibits relating to the archeology, natural history, ethnology, paleontology, and history of America; and the National Gallery of Art, with numerous paintings by the masters, including Rembrandt, Rubens, Goya, El Greco, Raphael, Titian, Van Eyck, and Gainsborough. The collections of the National Gallery also include priceless sculptures, tapestries, porcelains, and other rare works of art. Additional famous art exhibits in Washington are those of the Corcoran Gallery of Art (q.v.), the Phillips Memorial Gallery, the Folger Shakespeare Library, and the Dumbarton Oaks Collection.

Various nationally prominent learned societies maintain headquarters in Washington. Among these societies are the National Geographic Society, National Academy of Sciences, American Association for the Advancement of Science, American Historical Association, Washington Academy of Sciences, Philosophical Society of Washington, American Institute of Architects, Entomological Society of America, and the American Civic Association.

History. Pertinent information concerning the acquisition and evolution of the site of Washington will be found in the article dealing with the District of Columbia (also see CAPITALS OF THE UNITED STATES). The projected city was officially named in September, 1791. Within the next two years construction work began on the Executive Mansion and the Capitol. President John Adams became the first resident of the Executive Mansion in 1799. In November, 1800, one wing of the Capitol having been completed, the Congress of the U.S. held its first session in Washington. Growth of the city had proceeded, however, very slowly during the final years of the 18th century, and contemporary humorists occasionally referred to it as the City of Magnificent Distances, the City of Streets without Houses, the Wilderness City, and the Capital of Miserable Huts. Much of the expansion achieved in the first decade of the next century was wiped out by the British attack on the city in 1814, during the War of 1812. Made possible by the American defeat (August 24) at Bladensburg (q.v.), the attack caused the total or partial destruction of all except two of the public buildings in Washington. Following the close of hostilities the buildings were rapidly repaired or replaced. Because of its strategic location, the city figured significantly in the American Civil War. A major supply depot and hospital center for the Union armies, it was repeatedly threatened by Confederate forces. Troops under General Jubal Anderson Early were halted, in July, 1865, only a few miles from the city limits. Pierre L'Enfant's *Plan of the City of Washington* was rediscovered in 1887. Insofar as accomplished violations permitted, subsequent planning for the improvement of the city was based on the original designs. Pop. (1950) 797,670.

WASHINGTON, county seat of Wilkes Co., Ga., situated 61 miles N.W. of Augusta. Transportation facilities include a railroad. The city is the center of a farming, dairying, and lumbering area. Among the industrial establishments in Washington are a milk condensery, a clothing factory, lumber mills, machine shops, and factories producing furniture and fertilizers. The town was founded on Jan. 23, 1780, and is said to be the first incorporated town in the U.S. named in honor of George Washington. Pop. (1949 est.) 4500.

WASHINGTON, county seat of Daviess Co., Ind., situated near the White R., 100 miles s.w. of Indianapolis. It is served by two railroads, and contains extensive railroad repair shops. The city is the trading center of a rich farming, stock-raising, and mineral-producing area. In addition to farm products, the surrounding area yields coal, oil, and natural gas. Among the industrial establishments in the city are flour mills, fruit and vegetable canneries, and factories producing lumber, wood veneers, furniture, refrigeration units, clothes hangers, clothing, rubber goods, and tile. Washington was founded in 1816 and chartered as a city in 1870. Pop. (1949 est.) 13,000.

WASHINGTON, county seat of Washington Co., Iowa, situated 66 miles s.w. of Davenport. It has important horse-breeding and stock-raising interests and manufactures flour, buttons, and hog-oilers. Pop. (1940) 5227.

WASHINGTON, a city in Franklin Co., Mo., situated 54 miles w. of St. Louis, on the Missouri River. It contains manufactories of pipes, boxes, shoes, and zithers. Pop. (1940) 6756.

WASHINGTON, a borough of Warren Co., N.J., situated 65 miles w. of New York City. It is served by a railroad, and is a manufacturing center, surrounded by an agricultural area. The principal industries in the borough are the manufacture of hosiery, lingerie, printed linens, brass products, porcelain products, metal tile, and wooden articles. Pop. (1948 est.) 5200.

WASHINGTON, county seat of Beaufort Co., N.C., situated 127 miles E. by S. of Raleigh, on the Pamlico River. It carries on a considerable trade in cotton, corn, rice, farm produce, lumber, and naval stores. Oyster fishing and shipbuilding are important industries; there are also steam gins, lumber and planing mills, cooperages, and manufactories of fertilizers, buggies, and shirts. The city is the site of the Washington Collegiate Institute. Pop. (1940) 8569.

WASHINGTON, county seat of Washington Co., Pa., situated on Chartiers Creek, 32 miles s.w. of Pittsburgh. It is served by two railroads, and lies in a fertile agricultural area also noted for the production of bituminous coal, oil, and natural gas. The principal industries in the city are the production of a wide variety of glassware, including glass food containers and table glassware, steel for high-speed tools, molybdenum, ferroalloys, annealing boxes, tungsten, tin and terne plate, chemicals, and corrugated boxes. Washington is the site of Washington and Jefferson College, established in 1780, on the campus of which is a memorial library founded by a gift from Benjamin Franklin. Another notable educational institution in the city is Washington Seminary for girls, established in 1836. Places of historic interest in the city include the house, built in 1788, which served as headquarters for David Bradford, leader of the Whisky Insurrection (q.v.) in 1794. The town of Washington was founded in 1781 by David Hoge, who had bought land in the region in 1771; two lots in the town were presented by him to George and Martha Washington. In 1876 the first crematory in the U.S. was established there by Francis Julius Le Moyne (1798–1879), an abolitionist noted for his efforts on behalf of runaway slaves from the South. The town was incorporated as a borough in 1810 and chartered as a city in 1924. Pop. (1950) 25,898.

WASHINGTON, BOOKER TALIAFERRO (about 1858–1915), American Negro educator, born on a plantation near Hale's Ford, Franklin Co., Va., the son of a mulatto slave woman. His first education was obtained at a night school. In 1872 he traveled five hundred miles to the Hampton (Virginia) Normal and Agricultural Institute, at which, dur-

Tuskegee Institute
Monument to Booker T. Washington

ing three years, he paid for his board and education by acting as janitor. He was graduated in 1875, and taught for some time in Malden, W.Va., then studied at Wayland Seminary, Washington, D.C. Appointed instructor in Hampton Institute, he trained seventy-five Indians under the American soldier and educator General Samuel Chapman Armstrong, and developed a night school. In 1881 he was appointed organizer and principal of a Negro school in Tuskegee, Ala. In advancing the interests of this institution, Washington became a well-known public speaker, and was recognized as the foremost exponent of the education and advancement of the Negro. In 1892 he founded the Tuskegee Conference, and in 1900 organized the National Negro Business League. His works include *The Future of the American Negro* (1899), *Up from Slavery* (1901), *Character Building* (1902), *Working with the Hands* (1904), *Tuskegee and Its People* (1905), *Life of Frederick Douglas* (1907), *the Story of the Negro*

(1909), and *My Larger Education* (1911).

WASHINGTON, GEORGE (1732–99), American Revolutionary soldier and statesman, first President of the United States, called the father of his country. He was born in Bridges Creek, Westmoreland County, Virginia, the eldest son of a Virginia planter, Augustine Washington (d. 1743), and his second wife, Mary Ball (1708–89). Washington was educated partly at a neighborhood school, and partly by his older half brother, Lawrence. His principal studies, geometry and trigonometry, prepared him to perform the work of a surveyor, an important occupation in view of the wild state of the country and the increasing demand for accurate surveys. In 1748 Washington was certified as a public surveyor by the colonial government. He passed the summer months of the next three years practicing his profession, particularly on the immense tracts of land in the Shenandoah Valley owned by his chief employer, Thomas Fairfax, 6th Baron Fairfax (see FAIRFAX). Surveyors were scarce, and the remuneration for their services was consequently high; Washington managed to save a considerable sum of money, with which he purchased extensive tracts of land long before he attained his majority. His prudence, together with the other admirable qualities of character which he displayed, soon gained hm the esteem and confidence of the leading men in the Colony of Virginia.

In 1751 the frontiers of Virginia were threatened by frequent French and Indian attacks (see FRENCH AND INDIAN WAR), necessitating the institution of measures for public safety. The colony was accordingly divided into military districts, to each of which an adjutant general was appointed. One of these appointments was granted to Washington, who forthwith entered upon the study of military tactics and strategy. These studies were interrupted toward the close of the year when Washington accompanied his half brother Lawrence, who was dying of tuberculosis, to Barbados in the West Indies. Upon the death of Lawrence in July, 1752, Washington inherited the family estate of Mount Vernon, on the Potomac River, Virginia. Returning to the colonies, he was commissioned by the lieutenant governor of Virginia, Robert Dinwiddie (q.v.), to warn the French, who had advanced with a military expedition to the headwaters of the Ohio River, against trespassing on territory claimed by Virginia. The British warning was rejected, and Washington returned to Williamsburg.

In the spring of 1754 he was appointed lieutenant colonel of the regiment which formed the military establishment of Virginia, and, with half the regiment (150 men), was sent forward to set up an outpost on the site of the modern city of Pittsburgh. There Washington found the French firmly established in strategic Fort Duquesne, and accordingly took up his own position in Fort Necessity, at Great Meadows. He withstood the initial French attack, but was finally forced to capitulate after a ten-hour enemy siege. Some time later, an order was issued from the British military headquarters to the effect that any British field officer holding a royal commission was thenceforth to have a higher rank than any colonial officer. As this reorganization entailed a demotion for Washington, he at once resigned and retired to Mount Vernon. In 1755, however, he accepted a post as aide on the staff of General Edward Braddock (q.v.), serving under him in the British campaign to take Fort Duquesne. Washington's personal bravery under fire was conspicuously demonstrated in the disastrous battle of the Monongahela River, in the course of which the British troops were ambushed by French and Indian forces, and General Braddock was mortally wounded. Braddock's defeat was due largely to his disregard of the military tactics proposed by Washington, who was more experienced in the art of Indian warfare than was his British-trained commanding officer.

Following the death of Braddock, Washington was made commander in chief of the Virginia forces and vested with the responsibility for the defense of the Colony's frontier against French and Indian incursions. He thereupon reorganized his troops, retaining command of them until November, 1758, when Fort Duquesne was surrendered by the French and occupied by the British. On January 6, 1759, Washington married Martha Dandridge Custis (1732–1802), a wealthy young widow with two children. Having been elected to the Virginia House of Burgesses shortly before his marriage, he began to take an increasingly prominent part in public affairs, regularly attending every meeting of the colonial assembly.

When the American Revolution began, Washington took the position that only in the last extremity should arms be taken up by the colonists for the redress of their grievances against Great Britain. His respect for law and order made him look with apprehension on any violent rupture; nevertheless,

George Washington (painting by Gilbert Stuart)
New-York Historical Society

he drew up in 1769 a Nonimportation (q.v.) Act providing for the imposition by the colonies of an embargo on various British goods; the act was ratified by the House of Burgesses. At the provincial convention held on August 1, 1774 at Williamsburg, Washington was among the foremost in asserting the right of the colonies to self-government. He was one of the six Virginia delegates appointed to the first Continental Congress (q.v.), which met in September, 1774, and on June 15, 1775, he was chosen by the second Continental Congress commander in chief of the Continental Army. For this important post Washington's previous education and experience had singularly qualified him. Not only was he skilled in military affairs, but his thorough knowledge of the geographical character of the country and his familiarity with the organization and fighting methods of the British royal army made him the most formidable adversary whom the British could have faced.

Washington left Philadelphia on June 21, 1775, joined the Continental Army at Cambridge, Massachusetts, and assumed command on July 3rd. The army, numbering about 16,000 men, was low in virtually everything that could make it an effective fighting force

General Cornwallis surrendering to George Washington on October 19, 1781

—arms, ammunition, accouterments, and, above all, morale. Washington at once instituted an effective organization of his army, forming it into six brigades of six regiments each; keeping together, as far as practicable, the troops from each colony; and placing these troops under a commander from their own colony. In addition to his pressing military duties, Washington maintained a voluminous correspondence with the heads of the various colonies, and afterward with the governors of the several States, at length becoming the sole channel of communication between the Continental Army and the numerous organs of governmental authority. In his conduct of the Revolutionary War, Washington exhibited the same qualities of leadership, fortitude, and sound judgment which had characterized his previous undertakings, both military and civil. He drove the British from Boston, Massachusetts (March 17, 1776); defeated the mercenary Hessian troops at Trenton, New Jersey (December 25, 1776); expelled the British from Princeton (January 3, 1777); succeeded in holding together the hard-pressed Continental Army at Valley Forge, Pennsylvania, during the bitterly cold winter of 1777-78; and finally forced the surrender of the British general Lord Charles Cornwallis (q.v.) on October 19, 1781. See REVOLUTION, THE AMERICAN; UNITED STATES:

History. On November 25, 1783, the British evacuated New York; nine days later Washington delivered his memorable Farewell Address to the army; and on December 23, at Annapolis, he resigned his commission to the United States Congress and retired to private life.

Four years later, however, he was once more called to public duty, becoming president of the Philadelphia convention of 1787, which framed the Constitution of the United States. Washington was unanimously chosen the first President of the United States, and on April 30, 1789, took the oath of office in New York City, where Congress was then sitting. The new President thoroughly informed himself concerning all affairs of state, and personally directed the organization of the different departments of the government in accordance with the provisions of the Constitution. He appointed as heads of departments such able and distinguished men as Thomas Jefferson, Alexander Hamilton, Henry Knox, and Edmund Jennings Randolph (qq.v.). Meanwhile, before the work of Congress began, Washington made a tour through the eastern States of the Union for the purpose of familiarizing himself with the sentiments and opinions of the men who were presently to lay the foundations of the industrial and commercial greatness of the

George Washington and his troops entering New York City in 1783

United States. In his first message to Congress, he presented a series of judicious suggestions for laws and regulations, which were at once made the basis of national legislation. He scrupulously refrained from allying himself with either of the two political parties, Federalist (see FEDERALIST PARTY) and Republican (see DEMOCRATIC PARTY), which were then forming under Hamilton and Jefferson; on the contrary, he strove to reconcile the differences between the two leaders, which he feared would bring about wider differences among the people in the future.

The success of Washington's first administration, and the universal sense of security experienced under his leadership, gave rise to a general desire that he accept the presidency for a second term. Hamilton and Jefferson, divided by strong personal and political differences, were nevertheless in complete agreement on the subject of a second term for Washington, and each addressed a letter to the President urging his accession to the popular will. Washington complied, was unanimously re-elected, and on March 4, 1793, took the oath of office for the second time. At the outset of Washington's second administration, the new American republic became involved in European affairs. Great Britain and France were at war, and a considerable portion of the population in the United States was in favor of rendering aid to the French out of gratitude for the assistance granted by France to the American colonies during the Revolutionary War. Washington, however, was strongly opposed to foreign entanglements; he recognized the new French Republic (see FRANCE: *History*; FRENCH REVOLUTION), and received its representative, but steadfastly adhered to his resolution to avoid interference in European issues. He therefore issued a proclamation of neutrality on April 22, 1793.

Two major factions then arose in the United States, one advocating adherence to the cause of France, and the other supporting Washington and the principle of neutrality. Dissensions and resignations occurred in the President's cabinet. Among the people, radical Jacobin (see JACOBINS) clubs were formed, as vociferous in the expression of their animosities as were their prototypes in France. In the midst of this excitement, Washington sent the jurist and statesman John Jay (q.v.) as envoy extraordinary to England. Jay negotiated with the British a commercial treaty (see JAY'S TREATY) which was signed by Washington on August 18, 1795. By his wisdom and determination, Washington successfully prevented his country, just emerging from the trials and vicissitudes of the Revolutionary War, from engaging in entangling

Met. Mus. of Art; N.Y. Hist. Soc.; Bklyn. Mus.

Above: "The Washington Family," painting by Edward Savage. Left: "Martha Washington," by Rembrandt Peale. Below: "Lady Washington's Reception," by Daniel Huntington.

alliances which would certainly have precipitated renewed warfare and perhaps have rendered impossible the growth of the republic.

Among the significant events of Washington's second administration were the admission of Vermont, Kentucky, and Tennessee into the Union; the assumption by the Federal government of the war debts of the several States; the chartering of the Bank of the United States; the establishment of the national mint; the Whisky Insurrection (q.v.) of 1794 in western Pennsylvania; and the decisive victory achieved by General Anthony Wayne (q.v.) over the hostile Indians of the northwest at Fallen Timbers, near the present-day city of Toledo, Ohio, on August 20, 1794. On September 19, 1796, Washington, declining to serve again, issued his farewell address to the country he had been so largely instrumental in forming almost out of chaos. He delivered his last Presidential message to Congress, turned over his office to his successor, John Adams (q.v.), and retired to his estate at Mount Vernon. In 1798 the prospect of war with France led to Washington's appointment as commander in chief of the United States Army. On December 12, 1799, he contracted a severe cold; respiratory complications supervened, and he died on December 14th.

The public mourning for Washington was almost as widespread in Europe as it was in the United States. Homage was paid to him by the armies of Napoleon Bonaparte, afterward Napoleon I of France, and by the Channel fleet of Great Britain. On all sides it was acknowledged that the world had lost a statesman of the highest rank. The general estimate of Washington is admirably epitomized in the tribute of the American soldier and statesman Henry Lee, that he was "first in war, first in peace, and first in the hearts of his countrymen". Although he was, like almost all the proprietied Americans of his time, a slaveholder, he was a humane and considerate master. He possessed at his death 124 slaves; in his will, he directed that they be emancipated at the death of his wife. As early as 1786 he expressed himself in favor of abolition by legislative authority. All of Washington's biographers have attested to his courage, his indestructible spirit in adversity, his sound judgment, and his absolute integrity of motive.

WASHINGTON, WILLIAM (1752-1810), American soldier, a kinsman of George Washington, born in Stafford County, Va. He was educated for the ministry, but on the outbreak of the Revolutionary War entered the Continental Army as a captain under Colonel Hugh Mercer. He was wounded in the battles of Long Island and Trenton, fought at Princeton, and later became a major in a corps of cavalry. In 1779 he joined General Benjamin Lincoln's army in the South and became a lieutenant colonel in March, 1780. At the battle of Cowpens he made a charge upon Sir Banastre Tarleton's troops that decided the day, and in the pursuit he had a personal encounter with the British leader. He assisted in covering the rear of General Nathanael Greene's army in the famous retreat before Cornwallis, and fought with great distinction at Guilford Court House and Hobkirk's Hill. At Eutaw Springs he was taken prisoner, and was not released until the close of the war. He later settled in Charleston, and became a member of the South Carolina legislature. When war with France became imminent in 1798, he was, upon the recommendation of General Washington, made a brigadier general.

WASHINGTON AND LEE UNIVERSITY, a nonsectarian, privately controlled institution of higher education for men, situated in Lexington, Va. It was founded in 1749 as a secondary school under the name of Augusta Academy; its name was changed to Liberty Hall Academy in 1776, and in 1782 the institution was chartered as a college. In 1798 George Washington endowed it with a gift of $50,000, and the name was changed, with his authorization, to Washington Academy. The name was changed again, in 1813, to Washington College, and in 1871, after the death of General Robert E. Lee, who had been president of the institution from 1865 to 1870, the present name was adopted. The divisions of the university are the School of Arts and Science, offering curricula in humanities, languages, and mathematics and science; the School of Commerce; and the School of Law. The university awards the degrees of B.A., B.S., and LL.B.; in some courses of study accelerated programs are available by which students may earn degrees in three instead of the customary four years. In a recent year over 1300 students were enrolled and the faculty numbered about 80.

WASHINGTON CONFERENCE, a meeting of representatives of the United States, Great Britain, France, Japan, China, Italy, Belgium, the Netherlands, and Portugal, called by the United States and convening in Washington, D.C., from November 12, 1921, to February, 1922. As a result of the discussions the following five treaties were adopted.

(1) A treaty between the United States, the British Empire, France, Italy, and Japan with respect to the limitation of naval armament. This so-called Five-power Naval Treaty established a 5–5–3 ratio for the capital ships of the United States, Great Britain, and Japan, and maintained the *status quo* in respect to American, British, and Japanese fortifications in the Pacific.

(2) A treaty between the same powers in relation to the use of submarines and poisonous gases in warfare.

(3) A treaty between the United States, the British Empire, France, and Japan relating to their insular possessions and dominions in the Pacific Ocean. This is known as the Four-power Treaty and was bound up with the naval pact. It also maintained the *status quo* in respect to insular possessions in the Pacific.

(4) A treaty between the United States, Belgium, the British Empire, China, France, Italy, Japan, the Netherlands, and Portugal relating to policies in matters concerning China. It guaranteed Chinese independence and maintained the "open door" policy.

(5) A treaty between the same nine powers relating to the Chinese customs tariff.

In addition, twelve resolutions were adopted relating to such matters as proposals for the amendment of the laws of war; extraterritoriality in China; reduction of Chinese military forces; the Chinese Eastern Railway; and radio stations and foreign postal agencies in China.

The validity of some of these treaties, especially those relating to China, virtually lost its value with the Japanese aggression against China (see CHINA: *Sino-Japanese Relations*). Japan also opposed the ratio for capital ships by giving notice (1934) that she would terminate the agreement at the earliest possible date, December, 1936.

See FAR EASTERN QUESTION; NAVAL TREATIES.

WASHINGTON COURT HOUSE, city and county seat of Fayette Co., Ohio, on Sugar Creek, situated 40 miles s.w. of Columbus. The city contains a poultry-packing house, and factories making stoves, furniture, soap, and fertilizers. Pop. (1940) 9402.

WASHINGTON, FORT. See FORT WASHINGTON.

WASHINGTON MONUMENT, a monument to George Washington, consisting of an obelisk in the city of Washington, D.C., begun in 1848 and finished in 1884. It has a height of 555 ft., an area at the foundation of 16,000 sq.ft., and a weight of 36,912 tons. The apex has an aluminum point. There are 262 marble pieces, an elevator, and an iron stairway of 898 steps. The monument cost $1,187,710. The Washington National Monument Society originated the project.

WASHINGTON, MOUNT, the highest peak of the White Mountains in New Hampshire, and, with the exception of a number of peaks in North Carolina and Tennessee, the highest point in the United States east of the Rocky Mountains. It rises from the Presidential Range near the center of the White Mountain group, east of the Crawford Notch, and has an altitude of 6290 ft. above sea level. It is composed chiefly of granite; its west slope is steep, and on the north and east it is broken by deep gorges. The lower slopes are covered with forest, but the summit is bare and rocky.

WASHINGTON, TREATY OF, a treaty concluded in Washington in 1871, designed to bring about a settlement of differences between the United States and Great Britain. By its provisions the *Alabama* and *San Juan* claims were referred to arbitration; the free navigation of the St. Lawrence was granted to the United States in return for the free use of Lake Michigan and certain Alaskan rivers; and the fisheries dispute with Canada was referred to a commission.

WASHINGTON UNIVERSITY, a coeducational, nonsectarian, privately controlled institution of higher education, situated in St. Louis, Mo. It was founded in 1853 as the Eliot Seminary and Evening School for Boys; women were first admitted and the present name was adopted in 1857. The university includes the University College, schools of architecture, botany, business and public administration, dentistry, engineering, fine arts, law, liberal arts, medicine, and nursing, and a graduate school; it awards the degrees of B.A., B.S. in various engineering curricula, business administration and nursing, and the degrees of B.F.A., D.D.S., M.D., LL.B., M.A., and PH.D. The University College includes the Adult Study Center, established in 1939, which offers courses and lectures to students who do not wish to earn academic credit. Among the institutions affiliated with the university are the Barnes Hospital, the St. Louis Maternity Hospital, and the St. Louis Children's Hospital. In a recent year about 14,000 men and women were enrolled, of whom about 7200 were matriculated for full-time study; the faculty numbered about 1150.

WASHINGTON, UNIVERSITY OF, a coeducational, State-controlled institution of higher education, situated in Seattle, Wash.,

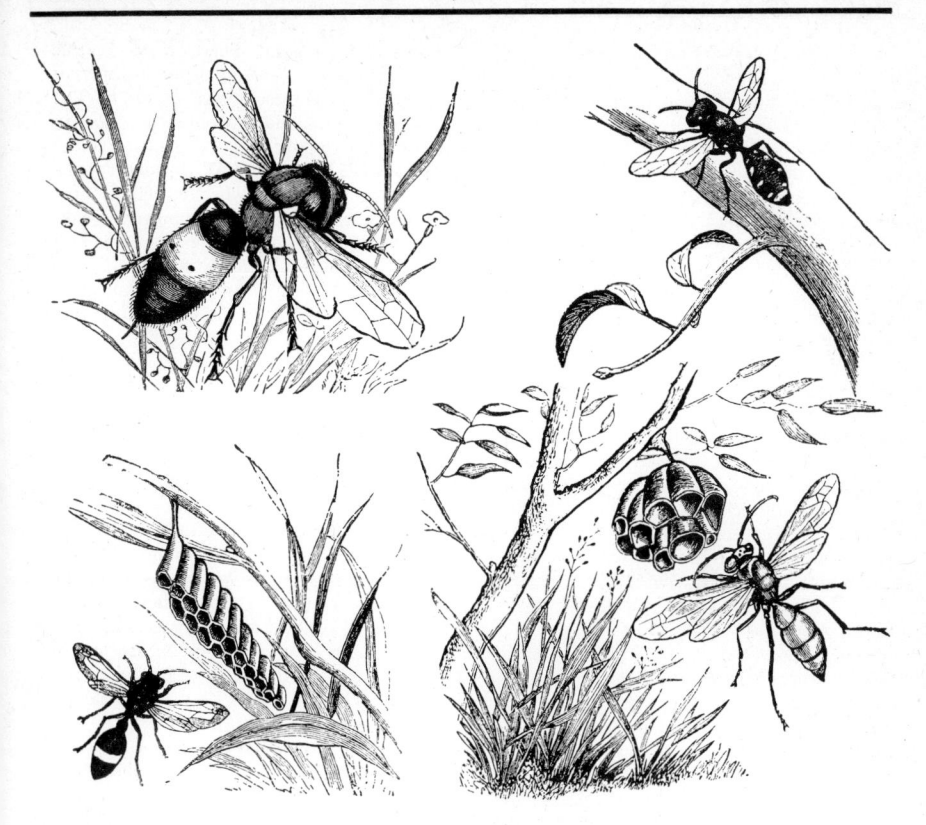

WASPS. *Top, left:* Vespa cincta. *Top, right:* Crabro subterraneus. *Bottom, left:* Icaria ferruginea. *Bottom, right:* Polistes tasmaniensis

and opened for instruction in 1861. Its divisions are the College of Arts and Sciences, which includes semiprofessional schools of architecture, art, fisheries, home economics, journalism, librarianship, music, nursing education, and physical education; the College of Education; the College of Economics and Business; the College of Engineering; the College of Forestry; the College of Mines; the College of Medicine and Dentistry; the College of Pharmacy; the School of Librarianship; the School of Law; the Graduate School; and the University Extension Service. The university awards the degrees of B.A., B.S., B.S. in various engineering curricula, D.D.S., M.D., LL.B., J.D., and PH.D. An accelerated program is available by which students may earn baccalaureate degrees in three instead of the customary four years. In a recent year over 18,000 men and women were enrolled and the faculty numbered about 1000.

WASHITA RIVER. See OUACHITA.

WASHO, a small American Indian tribe, settled west of Reno and Carson City, Nev. Distinct in language from surrounding tribes, they are thought to be the remnant of a once-flourishing tribe decimated by war. They are now almost extinct.

WASH, THE, a drowned plain on the E. coast of England, between the counties of Lincoln and Norfolk. It is about 22 miles in length, 15 miles in average breadth, and receives the rivers Witham, Welland, Ouse, and Nene. The shores are low and marshy, and the Wash is largely occupied by sandbanks, which are dry at low water. Two wide areas, called Lynn and Boston deeps, afford anchorage for vessels.

WASP, a hymenopterous insect belonging to the family Vespidae, or a closely related family. The true wasps of the family Vespidae are characterized by the way in which the anterior wings are longitudinally folded, each being doubled on itself down the middle, and by the nature of the antennae, which are usually "kneed" at the end of the first joint, and have thirteen joints and a clubbed end in the males, and twelve joints and hardly any apical thickening in the females.

The social wasps, species of *Vespa* and *Polistes,* build papery nests. Begun by the queen wasp, which alone survives the winter, and completed by those of her offspring which develop into workers, these nests are composed of masticated vegetable matter, generally woody fibers worked into a paste with the viscid secretion of the salivary glands. A variable number of combs, each one cell deep, are connected by a scaffolding of the same material, and often surrounded by external walls; there is one door in aerial nests, and usually two in those built underground. The cells, which are used as cradles for the developing eggs and grubs, are hexagonal. The food consists of the juices of plants and fruits, and the nectar of flowers; but they are sometimes carnivorous.

The solitary wasps, also of the family Vespidae, have no workers. They usually build single cells of clay or sand. They are distinguishable structurally from the social forms. The mandibles are generally long and narrow, not broad, and the tarsal claws are toothed. They are generally smaller than the social wasps, and darker in color. The nest is often in a hole, and is generally provisioned with insects or insect larvae for the use of the offspring.

Besides the Vespidae, there are the burrowing sand wasps, or Crabronidae; the related Pompilidae, with similar habits; and others.

WASSERMANN, AUGUST VON (1866–1925), German therapeutist and pathologist, born in Bamberg. After teaching at the University of Berlin (1902–13), he became, in 1913, director of an institute for the experiment of therapeutics, and was able to carry on the work previously started by him. In 1906 he discovered the reaction test for syphilis, for which he is best known, and which is called the Wassermann reaction. He also developed a precipitin reaction which distinguishes between the blood of men and animals by differentiating albumin bodies contained therein.

WASSERMANN, JAKOB (1873–1934), German novelist, born in Fürth, near Nuremberg, Bavaria. At the age of twenty-five he moved to Austria, where he passed the remainder of his life, first in Vienna, and subsequently in Alt-Aussee, Styria. During his later life he traveled extensively in Europe, Africa, and the United States. Wassermann's literary career was inaugurated in 1896, when he began to contribute short stories and verse to *Simplicissimus,* an illustrated satirical weekly magazine founded at Munich in the same year. In 1897 appeared *Die Juden von Zirndorf* ("The Jews of Zirndorf"), the first of his long, analytical problem novels. The principal themes of these works are the conflict between the older and younger generations, the problem of evil in human relations, man's inhumanity to man, and the difficulties of the generation growing up in Germany after World War I. The other notable novels of Wassermann are *Caspar Hauser* (1909), *Das Gänsemännchen* ("The Goose Man", 1915), *Christian Wahnschaffe* ("The World's Illusion", 1918), *Ulrike Woytich* (1923), *Der Aufruhr um den Junker Ernst* ("The Triumph of Youth", 1926), and *Der Fall Maurizius* ("The Maurizius Case", 1928).

WASTE, in the law of real property in England and the United States, a term designating injury or damage to property committed by a tenant for life, for years, or from year to year (see TENANT) which results in a permanent reduction of the value of the property. The injury is to the future estate of the remainderman or reversioner. Waste is called "voluntary waste" when the injury to the property is the result of a willful act on the part of the tenant, such as the cutting down of fruit trees or the ploughing up of a flower garden. It is designated "permissive waste" when the tenant is negligent in failing to take measures to prevent the injury or to maintain the property in a reasonable manner, as in neglecting to make reasonable repairs to a building to prevent ruin and decay. It is usual in leases of housing accommodation in the United States for the landlord to provide that "throughout said term, the tenant shall take good care of the demised premises, its appurtenances, fixtures and equipment; shall not drill into, disfigure or deface any part of the building or suffer same to be done. At the end of the term the tenant shall quit and surrender the demised premises in as good order and condition as they were at the beginning of the term, reasonable wear and damage by the elements excepted."

A tenant who commits waste is said to be "impeachable for waste", that is, he is liable for damages in an action at law by the reversioner or remainderman. In certain cases a proceeding in equity for an injunction may be instituted. Thus, equity will enjoin threatened acts of waste by a tenant, as, for example, when a tenant attempts to alter the property by making material changes in its structure; in such cases, if the waste is committed, an action in law for damages may be brought. A mortgagee may also institute an equity proceeding to restrain a mortgagor from committing any acts which may affect the mortgagee's security. Equity will likewise enjoin any alterations in property which may be considered as an improvement of the property, unless such changes are authorized either expressly or by implication in the terms of the instrument by which the tenant acquired his interest. In other cases, however, in which a tenant acquires an interest in property "without impeachment of waste", he is not liable at law for any acts of injury or destruction to the premises, because he is authorized to do anything which might at law be considered waste. Equity in this latter class of cases will, however, enjoin threatened acts of destruction to the property which are so extreme as to be unconscionable.

WASTE LAND, an uncultivated and unprofitable tract in a populous and cultivated country. The lands generally included embrace swamps, moors, rocky or sandy tracts, and chalk downs. The reclaiming of waste land, by irrigation and fertilizing, or drainage, is sometimes successfully undertaken; but in most cases it is more profitable to improve lands already cultivated.

WATAUGA ASSOCIATION, the name of the first independent civil government established by white settlers on the continent of North America. The association was founded in 1772, in the eastern part of the present State of Tennessee, by the American pioneer John Sevier and a group of colonists most of whom had migrated from the Colony of Virginia. The territory governed by the association had been ceded to the Virginia colonists in 1768 by the Six Nations, the principal federation of North American Indians at that time; it comprised a considerable area lying between the Ohio and Tennessee rivers. The first settlement established by Sevier and his associates was founded in 1769 on the banks of the Watauga River. The settlers drew up a constitution known as the "Articles of the Watauga Association", the first such document ever drafted by freemen born in North America; this document has not survived. Later, the association constituted itself the State of Franklin, with a view to petitioning Congress for admission into the United States; see FRANKLIN, STATE OF.

WATCH, a small, portable, spring-driven, mechanical device for measuring and indicating time. Watches were developed from the early clocks about the end of the 15th century, and the mechanisms of the two types of timepieces have undergone similar development since then; see CLOCK; CHRONOMETER; see also TIME, STANDARD. The first watches were made by Philip Hele, a locksmith of Nuremberg, Germany, and were called *Nuremberg eggs,* from the shape of the case. Too large to be carried in the pocket, the Nuremberg eggs were carried suspended from the girdle or hanging about the neck, or were carried in saddle bags. They had circular dials, with a single pointer to indicate the hour; later, as the skill of watchmakers increased, other dials and pointers were often added, to show the day of the week, the date, the month, the phase of the moon, and the sign of the zodiac. During the 16th century, smaller watch mechanisms were produced in Europe, and these movements were enclosed in such articles as canes, crosses, pendants, or bracelets, or in richly jeweled cases of elaborate shape and ornamentation. Watches were worn on the wrist, in rings, and in lapel studs or buttons. The watch dials and hands, as well as the cases, were enameled and jeweled. Modern watches are occasionally mounted in such elaborate and ornamental cases, but the great majority are made in wafer-shaped cases for carrying in the pocket or as a pendant, or in curved or rectangular cases for wearing on the wrist.

The first important improvement in the watch mechanism was made about the middle of the 16th century, when the fusee (q.v.) was generally adopted to equalize the force applied to the works by the mainspring when fully wound and when partially unwound. In 1658 the English scientist Robert Hooke introduced the use of a hairspring to regulate the motion of the balance wheel. The mechanism and the hand for indicating minutes was added in 1687; the use of jeweled bearings was introduced in 1700, and the stemwinding, keyless watch was invented about the same year. Several kinds of escapement (q.v.) were invented in the latter half of the 18th century; most of them are in use today, in essentially the same form. The last step in the evolution of the modern watch was the introduction in 1849 of automatic machinery for the manufacture of the parts by the Boston watchmaker Aaron Dennison. This improvement achieved a high degree of accuracy, and permitted large-scale production at moderate cost. In a recent year the number of fine watches produced in the United States was about 3,000,000; the production of moderate-priced

EARLY WATCHES. *Top, left to right: Nuremberg egg; German, 16th century; calendar, 1690. Middle: English fusee, 1725; rococo alarm in openwork case; 40-hour, Nuremberg. Bottom: Baroque, carved iron case; 17th-century astronomical; 17th-century striker.*

watches totaled about 10,000,000. Of the moderate-priced watches, practically all were manufactured entirely in the United States. The fine watches, however, were in large part assembled in the United States from movements imported from Switzerland, which country produces most of the fine watch movements used by watchmakers throughout the world.

WATCH, a term used to designate the part of a ship's company that is employed in active duty at one time. The deck force is divided into starboard and port watches; the fireroom and engine-room forces are usually divided into three watches. The starboard and port watches may also be subdivided into first and second parts called quarter watches. In cases of emergency, or when the ship is getting under way, coming to anchor, or performing some other evolution requiring all available men, both watches (all hands) are called. In port, all hands are engaged during working hours of the day, but only a small anchor watch is on deck at night except in unusual circumstances. The term "watch" is also used to designate the two- or four-hour period of time during which a watch of men is on deck. The watches are named as follows: midwatch, midnight to 4 A.M.; morning watch, 4 to 8 A.M.; forenoon watch, 8 A.M. to noon; afternoon watch, noon to 4 P.M.; first dog watch, 4 to 6 P.M.; second dog watch, 6 to 8 P.M.; and first watch, 8 P.M. to midnight. The dog watches are designed to shift the order of the watch so that the same men will not have the same watch every night.

WATCH NIGHT. See NEW YEAR'S DAY.

WATCH OFFICER, an officer having charge of a ship during a particular time, or watch. The number of such officers depends upon the character of the vessel. In many large steamers two officers are usually on watch at a time. On large naval vessels the younger ensigns act as junior officers of the watch under the regular watch officers, who are lieutenants or ensigns of more experience. The senior officer on duty is called the officer of the deck or officer of the watch.

WATER, a substance composed of hydrogen oxide, H_2O, and surpassing all other known substances in importance and abundance. It was regarded by the ancients as a cold, moist "element" which typified all the substances recognized as liquids. In 1781 the English chemist Henry Cavendish obtained water by detonating mixtures of common air and hydrogen. His results, however, were not clearly interpreted until several years later, when the French chemist Antoine Lavoisier showed water to be a compound consisting of two volumes of hydrogen united with one volume of oxygen; or sixteen parts by weight of oxygen united with two parts by weight of hydrogen, to form eighteen parts by weight of water.

Natural waters are usually classified according to their origin, and include rain water, surface water, well water, spring water, and sea water. Rain water, also occurring as snow and hail (qq.v.), forms by the condensation of water vapor in the air, and is the purest of all natural water. In its passage from the clouds to the earth, however, it takes up foreign substances from the atmosphere, and always contains varying amounts of nitrogen, carbon dioxide, ammonia, sulfuric and sulfurous acids, and calcium and magnesium salts, as well as traces of organic matter and insoluble suspended material.

Surface water, which includes the water from rivers, lakes, and streams, is usually less pure than rain water. Its composition is determined largely by the nature of the soil and rocks over which it passes, and by the surface vegetation. The minerals contained in solution usually consist of carbonates, chlorides, iron, manganese, and alkaline-earth sulfates, and the organic material is mostly of vegetable origin. In limestone areas, surface waters are usually rich in dissolved calcium compounds. Well water, which is derived from wells or bore holes made in the surface of the earth, includes the water from both shallow and deep wells. Shallow wells serve mostly as a source of domestic water, and contain chiefly nitrates, nitrites, and ammonia of organic origin. Water from wells more than 100 feet in depth, especially artesian wells, contains only minerals in solution, and is the purest form of well water. Spring water, or mineral water (q.v.), usually contains concentrated amounts of carbonates, sulfides, sulfates, chlorides, and silicates, and frequently possesses marked medicinal properties. Sea water is the water which forms oceans. It constantly receives impure water from rivers and streams, and at the same time loses pure water by evaporation. The impurities that remain give this water its saline character; see OCEAN AND OCEANOGRAPHY.

Water is well known in the liquid, solid, and gaseous states. Under normal atmospheric pressure (760 mm. of mercury), and between 0°C. (32°F.) and 100°C. (212°F.), it exists as a tasteless, odorless liquid, generally colorless, but bluish or greenish when sufficiently deep. Pure liquid water has a specific gravity of 1.00 at 4°C. (39°F.), and is practically incompressible, 1,000,000 volumes decreasing by only 50 volumes when the atmospheric pressure is doubled. Its specific heat of 1.00 at 15°C. (59°F.), is greater than that of any other substance except hydrogen (q.v.). Pure water may be produced by exploding a mixture of two volumes of hydrogen and one volume of oxygen, by passing hydrogen over the hot oxide of almost any metal, or by distillation.

Excess amounts of dissolved calcium and magnesium carbonates, which are retained in solution by the action of carbon dioxide, impart a temporary "hardness" to water. Boiling the water expels the carbon dioxide, and the carbonates are deposited as "fur" or "boiler crust". The chlorides and sulfates of mag-

U.S.D.A., Bur. of Ent. & Plant Quar.
Water beetle (Hydrophilus triangularis)

nesium and calcium cannot be deposited, and therefore cause a permanent hardness. Temporary hardness can be corrected by adding to the water calcium hydroxide, which combines with the excess carbon dioxide and causes the carbonates to precipitate; see HARDNESS, in water.

When cooled below 0°C. (32°F.), water passes from the liquid to the solid state known as ice, and undergoes an expansion equal to one eleventh of the original volume. In a vacuum, water can be cooled far below its freezing point; it is then in an unstable state, and is rapidly frozen upon contact with the air or on any disturbance, the temperature simultaneously rising to the normal freezing point. Ice is transparent and highly coherent, and has a specific gravitiy at 0°C. of .917. It may exist in several forms, according to the manner in which the water is cooled; see ICE. The heat necessary to transform one gram of ice at 0°C. into liquid at 0°C. is 79.06 calories, and is known as the heat of fusion of ice. After contracting on changing from ice to liquid, water expands with rising temperautres until it reaches a temperature of 4°C. (39.2°F.), after which it contracts gradually, reaching a specific gravity of 0.9749 at 100°C.

Liquid water passes into water vapor, or gaseous water, at the boiling point (q.v.), 100°C. (212°F.), the heat necessary for this change (heat of vaporization) being 595.9 calories per gram of water. Water vapor is colorless and transparent, and has a density of 0.000596. It can exist as a vapor only below a maximum, or critical, pressure of 217 atmospheres. Higher pressure causes liquefaction, unless the temperature is above the critical temperature, 374°C. (705.2°F.); see CRITICAL POINT.

Water covers approximately 75 percent of the earth's surface, and composes, as vapor, a considerable portion of the earth's atmosphere. It is the most important substance involved in the life cycles of plants and animals, and is a constituent of all living cells. In chemistry, water is involved, as a solvent, catalyzer, electrolyte, or reagent, in practically every chemical reaction (see CHEMISTRY; SOLUTION). Water employed for domestic purposes must first be treated to remove excessive amounts of chlorine, ammonia, nitrates, organic matter, and poisonous metals such as lead and copper; see WATER PURIFICATION.

Heavy Water. Ordinary water, described above, is composed of oxygen combined with hydrogen which has an atomic weight of 1; heavy water contains a hydrogen isotope which has an atomic weight of 2, and has the formula D_2O. Heavy water is present in all naturally occurring waters to the extent of about 15 parts per 100,000. It differs from ordinary water in physical properties, having a density of 1.1 times that of ordinary water, a boiling point of 101.42°C., and a melting point of 3.802°C. See DEUTERIUM.

WATER BATH, an implement used in chemcal laboratories for evaporating solutions or heating substances under such conditions that the temperature can never surpass that of boiling water.

WATER BEETLE, common name for any of numerous aquatic beetles (q.v.) of the families Dytiscidae, Gyrinidae, and Hydrophilidae, belonging to the order Coleoptera. The family Dytiscidae, which contains the true, or diving, water beetles, contains approximately 2000 species native to land areas throughout the world. Its principal genus, *Dytiscus,* is commonly found in temperate and subtropical regions of America. The adult is usually brilliant greenish black with reddish-brown, black, or yellow stripes. The long, flattened hind legs are covered with hair and serve as modified paddles for swimming. The hardened elytra, which are usually grooved in the female and smooth in the male, form a cavity above the body proper. Periodically, the beetles rise to the surface of the water to draw a fresh supply of air into the elytra cavity. The males of most species have the three basal segments of the front tarsi modified to form cuplike suckers that enable them to cling to the females during copulation. During the breeding season, the female prepares several slits in underwater plant stems, and deposits a minute egg in each slit. The larvae which emerge from the eggs are equipped with hollow, sucking mandibles, and continuously attack and suck juices from small, aquatic insects. Because of their rapacity, water beetles are commonly known as water tigers. After approximately ten days of feeding, the larvae dig a round hole in the moist earth at the water's edge, in which they pupate. The adults hibernate in the underwater earth during a large part of the year, but are usually active in spring; they feed on insects and aquatic vegetation. The principal species include *D. fasciventris,* having reddish-brown abdominal segments, and reaching a length of 1 inch; and *D. hybridus,* having the abdomen uniformly black, and reaching a length of 1½ inches.

The family Gyrinidae, consisting of the whirligig beetles, contains approximately 350 species native to temperate and tropical regions throughout the world. Whirligig beetles spend most of their life on the surface of the water, but can dive to considerable depths; like the diving beetles, they are equipped with an air cavity under the elytra. They usually assemble on the surface in large numbers, and dart about in rapid, spiral movements. When disturbed, they rub the tip of the abdomen against the elytra, thereby producing a squeaking sound. The front legs of the adult are very long and modified for grasping; the hind legs are flattened, and propel the insect through the water. During the breeding season, the female lays numerous elongated, oval eggs, end to end, on the leaves of underwater plants. The larvae have sharp mandibles and resemble a centipede (q.v.) in external appearance; like the larvae of the diving beetle, they are extremely predaceous. During August the larvae live on land and spin a grayish, pointed cocoon, in which they pupate. The adults emerge several weeks later, and feed mainly on vegetation. They hibernate during the cold months of the year, but come to the surface periodically for their characteristic whirling "dances". The principal genus, *Dineutes,* contains approximately 30 widely distributed species. The adults are lustrous black above, and are yellow, black, or brown below. The body, like that of the diving beetle, is elliptical and convex. Typical species include *D. vittatus,* which averages ½ inch in length and is colored yellow below; *D. emarginatus,* smaller than *D. vittatus* and colored black below; and *D. americanus,* tinged with brown below and attaining a length of ½ inch.

The family Hydrophilidae consists of the water scavenger beetles, and contains about 1200 species native to North America and Europe. The adults usually feed on vegetable matter, but sometimes prey upon small aquatic animals. They are usually dark colored and shiny, and elliptical in shape. They do not swim as rapidly as the diving or whirligig beetles; most species are aquatic or amphibian, but a few are terrestrial. The principal breathing tubes open through a notch between the head and thorax. During the breeding season, the female constructs several silken cocoons from gland secretions, and lays from 20 to 100 eggs in each cocoon. The cocoons become attached to the female or to aquatic plants, or float on the surface of the water; the eggs hatch in several days. The larvae subsist mainly on other insects, but are not as voracious as the larvae discussed above. They pupate on moist earth near the shore, and emerge as adults within two weeks. Typical water scavenger beetles belong to the genus *Hydrophilus*. *H. triangularis,* the typical species, has triangular abdominal segments and is spotted yellow at the sides; it reaches a length of 1½ inches. The name "water beetle" is sometimes applied to *Platypsyllus castoris,* which lives as a skin parasite on the beaver.

WATER BOATMAN. See BOAT BUG.

WATER BUCK, or KOB, a large African antelope of aquatic habit in the genus *Cobus* or *Kobus,* several species of which are known by such common names as singsing. The water buck proper, *Cobus ellipsiprymnus,* is more than 4 feet tall, and remarkable for its long, shaggy, reddish coat. It is numerous throughout southern and eastern Africa, roving in small bands near marshes or rivers, to which it runs for refuge when alarmed. See WATER DEER.

WATER BUG, the popular name of any aquatic insect (Hydrocorisa) in the order Rhynchota, or Hemiptera. The term *bug* is specially applicable to insects of the Heteroptera, of which Hemiptera is a suborder. One of the most distinctive characteristics of the water bugs is the shortness of their antennae.

WATERBURY, city and one of the county seats of New Haven Co., Conn., situated on the Naugatuck River, 32 miles s.w. of Hartford. Waterbury is the leading center of the United States for the manufacture of brassware (including castings and finishings), and is noted for the manufacture of watches and clocks. There are also copper, oroide, silver, and aluminum works, foundries and machine shops, woolen mills and manufactories of presses, stamp and steel dies, machinery of many kinds, pressure gauges, brass and steel oilers, rivets, chains, hardware and nails, boilers, cloth, lamps and reflectors, cutlery, bicycle and automobile trimmings, buckles, cartridges, insulated wire, and silk thread. Pop. (1950) 104,242.

WATERBURY, a town of Washington Co., Vt., situated on the Winooski R., 11 m. by rail N.W. of Montpelier. It is surrounded by a farming, dairying, quarrying, and lumbering area. The principal industries in the town are the processing of dairy products and the manufacture of maple syrup and other maple products, lumber, clothespins, granite monuments, foundry products, and gasoline engines. Waterbury is the site of a State hospital for the insane, and maintains facilities for both summer and winter sports, including golf and skiing. Pop. (1940) 3074.

WATER CALTROP, or WATER CHESTNUT, common name applied to perennial, aquatic herbs of the genus *Trapa,* belonging to the Evening-primrose family. The genus contains three species native to warm areas of the Eastern Hemisphere, and is cultivated in many countries as an aquarium plant. The underwater leaf stalks are inflated near the apex, and each bears a loose rosette of floating leaves and numerous long, slender, submerged leaves. The small, white, solitary flowers, which are arranged on short peduncles among the floating leaves, have a four-parted calyx, four petals, four stamens, and a solitary pistil. The fruit is a leathery, single-seeded, indehiscent capsule; its two or four spinelike projections closely resemble the caltrop of warfare, for which the genus is commonly named. *T. natans,* also known as Jesuits' nut, is native to Europe and the Orient, and bears floating leaves 4 inches in length. The fruit has four spines and, like the common chestnut, is often roasted and eaten in some parts of Europe. *T. bispinosa,* commonly known as the singhara nut, is native to India and Ceylon, and bears floating leaves 6 inches in length. The fruit is usually two-horned and very sweet, and is often used as food.

WATER CHESTNUT. See WATER CALTROP.

WATER CLOCK. See CLEPSYDRA.

WATER-COLOR PAINTING, or AQUARELLE, the process of painting by means of colors mixed with water and some adhesive, as gum or size, instead of oil, now used for such painting upon paper which shows through as a ground. It differs from gouache painting, in which the color is applied in successive layers, as in oil. The processes of painting in vogue before the introduction of oil colors were, for the most part, varieties of water color, e.g., fresco painting (q.v.), in which water colors are applied to the wet lime of the plaster, and tempera (q.v.).

In early Christian miniatures and book illustrations water color was the medium usually employed. During the Byzantine and Romanesque periods the gouache technique was preferred, but the Gothic age saw a revival of the aquarelle.

From the later 15th to the 17th century water colors were used in coloring prints from wood and line engravings. They were used in colored sketches by many of the masters, and this was the origin of modern water color. It was the custom of Dürer and certain of the German, Dutch, and Flemish artists to outline drawings with a reed pen and fill in those outlines with an auxiliary flat wash. Gradually the hard lines were replaced by touches with the brush, and the result was a monochrome in browns, and grays, bistre, or India ink. These again came to be tinted, and so suggested the full use of colors. The stained drawing gradually gave way to tinted drawing which predominated till 1790. Paul Sandby (1725–1809), often called "the father of water-color art", improved upon the tinted drawings by working in body color. Whateley, Westall, and Gilpin used water colors as well as oil. Rowlandson, Cristall, Hills, Wright, Mortimer, Gresse, Hearne, and John Robert Cozens (1752–99?) developed fine atmospheric effects. J.M.W. Turner (1775–1851) soon surpassed all his predecessors and contemporaries, and in his hands water-color painting became a new art.

Other important names are those of Varley, Samuel Prout, Peter de Wint, Cotman, David Cox, Copley Fielding, Cattermole, and Birket Foster. Millais, Rossetti, Holman Hunt, Ford Maddox Brown, and other members of the Pre-Raphaelite Brotherhood achieved success in water color, as did also Sir Hubert Herkomer, Walter Crane, Frederick Taylor, H.B. Brabazon, Frederick Walker, and Arthur Melville.

The impetus toward water color in France first came in the early twenties from the Englishman Bonington and from Géricault. It was soon practiced by all important artists, among them Delacroix, Isabey, and Decamps. Among French aquarellists of a later date were Leloir, Meissonier, Regnault, Detaille, Vibert, and Jaquemart; in the 20th century, Henri Matisse, Maurice de Vlaminck, Othon Friesz, and Moishe Kiesling.

Fan painting upon silk and satin is done with water colors, which have also been applied with success to paintings upon canvas and other materials as well.

In Germany water colors were used by Schwind in the portrayal of his fables, but the first important German aquarellist was Hildebrandt, a pupil of Isabey. Other important representatives are Menzel in Berlin,

Karl Werner, and B. Fiedler (Triest). Both in Holland (Israels) and Belgium are flourishing schools, and in Spain and Italy the example of Fortuny gave rise to a particularly brilliant development. Among Scandinavians of the 20th century is Edvard Munch; among Germans, Lovis Corinth and Emil Nolde; and among Swiss, Paul Klee.

Several exhibitions of water-color paintings are held yearly in the United States, particularly in New York City and Philadelphia, but no distinctive American school has as yet been developed. Among the artists prominent in figure painting are Winslow Homer, J.S. Sargent, William M. Chase, C.Y. Turner, Robert Blum, Irving R. Wiles, Frank Benson, and Cecilia Beaux; in landscape may be mentioned Alexander Wyant, J. Francis Murphy, Samuel Coleman, R. Swain Gifford, Henry Farrer, Childe Hassam, C.C. Cooper, Gifford Beal, Adolf Dehn, Ernest Fiene, John Marin, and Lyonel Feininger; in marine painting, William T. Richards, Charles Woodbury, and Charles A. Platt; in genre, Walter Gay, and the Russian-American Marc Chagall. Among others, belonging to a younger group are Hilda Belcher, Helen Turner, Harold Camp, C.K. Chatterton, H.B. Demuth, Arthur Davies, John Sloan, Samuel Halpert, and John Martin.

The earliest organized society for the promotion of the art was the British Society of Painters in Water Colors, founded in 1804, and known since 1882 as the Royal Society. The American Water-Color Society holds yearly exhibits in New York City, and the New York and Philadelphia Water-Color clubs hold annual exhibitions. The Victoria and Albert Museum possesses what is probably the finest collection of water colors.

WATER COLORS, pigments mixed with water, with the addition of some adhesive material such as gum or size. When prepared for artists' use, the pigments are formed in dry cakes with gum, or mixed with water and glycerin to a pasty consistency; pigments used for sign painting or coloring walls are mixed with glue or size. The latter are sometimes called distemper colors, their application being only of a temporary character.

WATERCOURSE, in the law of real property in England and the United States, a stream of water, having a permanent and substantial source of supply, and usually flowing in a well-defined bed or channel into some other body of water. The source of supply of the water may be springs or natural percolation, but must be sufficient to supply water during the greater part of the year; a stream does not lose its character as a watercourse if it becomes dry in times of drought. A watercourse is said to be a natural watercourse when the stream is formed by the natural flow of water; it is termed an "artificial" watercourse when the flow of the stream is created by man, as in the case of a canal. For a discussion of the rights of owners of land along watercourses, see RIPARIAN RIGHTS; WATER RIGHTS.

WATER CRESS, common name applied to an aquatic perennial herb, *Radicula nasturtium-aquaticum,* belonging to the Mustard family. The herb, which is native to Europe, is cultivated in springs and wet grounds in temperate climates, for use as food in salads and garnishes. The yellow or white flowers have four sepals, four petals, six stamens, and a solitary pistil. The fruit is a slender or globular, indehiscent pod. Water cress is grown from either seed or cuttings. After the flower buds bloom, the leaves become extremely pungent, and can no longer be used as food; see CRESS.

WATER CURE. See HYDROTHERAPY.

WATER DEER, common name for *Hydropotes inermis,* a small Chinese deer of aquatic habits. The deer do not bear antlers, but the male has tusklike canine teeth in the upper jaw. The name is also applied to the water chevrotain (see CHEVROTAIN), and to the water buck, *Kobus ellipsiprymnus,* a South African antelope, commonly found near lakes and watercourses, and possessing exceptional powers of swimming.

WATER DROPWORT, common name for a plant, *Oenanthe crocata,* of the Carrot family. It has compound or decompound leaves, which have a disagreeable odor. It is common in wet places throughout Europe. The roots have some resemblance to small parsnips, but are very poisonous. The fine-leaved water dropwort, *O. phellandrium,* called water fennel by the Germans, is also common in similar situations in Europe. It is characterized by a jointed rootstalk, with tufted whorled rootlets and a strong zigzag stem dilated at the base.

WATEREE RIVER, a river rising in the Blue Ridge Mts., N.C. Its upper course is known as the Catawba. It flows generally s. into South Carolina, where it unites with the Congaree R. to form the Santee R. Length, 300 m.

WATERFALL, a sudden descent of a stream of water over a declivity or over the edge of a cliff or precipice. Geologically, waterfall precipices may be formed either by faulting

FAMOUS WATERFALLS
Above: Niagara Falls, in the United States (left) and Canada (right). Left: Two of a series of bridges spanning the Trummelbach Falls in Switzerland.

or thrusting of portions of the earth's crust or by variation in erosion of hard and soft rocks in the path of a stream. Waterfalls are among the most remarkable of natural spectacles and many thousands of large falls are found in all parts of the world. From the point of view of height alone, the largest fall in the world is the Angel Waterfall, in Venezuela, which has two descents, one 3300 and the other 5000 feet in height. Other noteworthy falls of the world include the Victoria (354 ft.) and Tugela (2810 ft.) waterfalls in Africa, the Gersoppa (830 ft.) and Cauvery falls (299 ft.) in India, Wollomombie Falls (1100 ft.) in Australia, Sutherland Falls (1904 ft.) in New Zealand, Gavarnie Falls (1385 ft.) in France, Vettis Falls (850 ft.) in Norway, Trummelbach Falls (950 ft.) in Switzerland, Takkakaw Falls (1200 ft.) in Canada, Niagara Falls (168 ft.) between Canada and the United States, and the Ribbon (1612 ft.), Yosemite (1430 ft.), and Multnomah (850 ft.) falls in the United States. In terms of the average amount of water flowing over the crest, Guayra Falls on the borders of Brazil and Paraguay is the largest in the world. This waterfall is 130 ft. high and has an average flow of 470,000 cu.ft. of water per second. The volume of flow of the Khon waterfall in the Mekong R. in Indo-China is approximately 410,000 cu.ft. per second. The flow of water over Niagara Falls is 212,000 cu.ft. per second.

WATER FLEA, common name applied to fresh-water crustaceans belonging to the division Entomostraca, and so named for their rapid, darting movements; see CRUSTACEA. Water fleas are found in ponds and ditches throughout the United States and Europe, and average $\frac{1}{8}$ in. in length; the males are usually smaller than the females. The common water flea or cyclops, *Cyclops viridis,* belongs to the class Copepoda. It has a greenish-white, pear-shaped body and bears a single crimson, sparkling, median eye. The female is equipped with two sacs which hang from the external opening of the oviduct, and which bear the eggs fertilized by the male. Cyclops eat both animal and vegetable matter, and reproduce many times during the year. *Daphnia pulex,* belonging to the class Branchiopoda, is globular in shape and reddish in color. It is marked by a sharp caudal spine and a ventral beak, and bears a pair of large, sessile, compound eyes and a single, simple, median eye. *Cypris pubera,* belonging to the class Ostracoda, has a dainty, elastic shell and a pair of simple eyes. The female usually lays its eggs on underwater rocks or plants.

WATERFORD, a town in New London Co., Conn., situated on Long Island Sound, 46 miles E. of New Haven. It contains granite and paper-cutting industries. Pop. (1940) 100.

WATERFORD, a village of Saratoga Co., N.Y., situated on the Hudson River, about 10 miles N. of Albany, at the junction of the Erie and Champlain divisions of the New York State barge canal. There are manufactories of knit goods, gloves, fire hydrants, valves, stocks and dies, brush-making machinery, cooperage products, and lathes. Pop. (1940) 2903.

WATERFORD, a maritime county in the province of Munster, Eire, E. of Cork. The surface is in general mountainous, the principal ranges being Knockmeledown (2609 ft. above sea level) and Cummeragh (2478 ft. above sea level). The Suir and the Blackwater are the chief rivers. Lead, iron, and copper are mined, the latter having been worked at Knockmahon for many years. Marble of several colors is quarried, and potter's clay of good quality is found. The fisheries are important. Area, including county borough, 708 sq.m.; pop. (1943) 75,968.

WATERFORD, county borough and port of Eire, situated on the Suir River, 97 miles s.s.w. of Dublin. It is one of Eire's chief ports. The chief trade is with England, to which butter, pork, bacon, corn, flour, eggs, and livestock are exported. There are shipyards, distilleries, breweries, foundries, and flour mills. Pop. (1943) 27,825.

WATER HEN or **MOOR HEN.** See GALLINULE.

WATERHOUSE, ALFRED (1830–1905), English architect, born in Liverpool. His important works are the Court of Assize in Manchester; the new buildings of Balliol College, Oxford University, and of Caius and Pembroke colleges, Cambridge University; Manchester City Hall; Owens College, Manchester; the South Kensington Natural History Museum, London; Eaton Hall, Cheshire; and Iwerne Minster, Dorsetshire. Waterhouse was one of the most noted of the architects who adapted the Victorian Gothic styles to modern secular purposes.

WATERHOUSE, JOHN WILLIAM (1849–1917), English figure painter, born in Rome, Italy. At first he painted in the manner of the classic school of the English painters Frederick Leighton and Sir Lawrence Alma-Tadema, but his later works suggest Pre-Raphaelite influence (see PRE-RAPHAELITES). They include "The Oracle" (1884); "St. Eulalia", "The Magic Circle" (1886), and "The Lady of Shalott" (1888), all in the Tate Gallery, London; "Hylas and the Nymphs" (1897, Manchester Art Gallery); "Echo and Narcissus" (1903, Liverpool Art Gallery); "The Soul of the Rose" (1908); and "Thisbe" (1909). Waterhouse became a Royal Academician in 1895.

WATER HYACINTH, common name applied to a perennial, tropical, aquatic herb, *Eichhornia crassipes,* belonging to the Pickerel-weed family. The herb is native to Brazil, and is cultivated in many areas as a tank or pond plant. The yellow-spotted, light-blue flowers, which are arranged in a loose spike about 12 inches above the leaves, have a six-parted calyx, a six-lobed corolla, three stamens, and a solitary pistil. The fruit is a many-seeded capsule. Water hyacinths bear large stems which are equipped with air bladders to support the heavy mass of tufted, centrally constricted leaves. It grows so abundantly in the rivers of many warm countries as to obstruct the passage of ships. In Florida it is known as the "million-dollar weed" because of the great sums of money expended in attempts to control it. The plant is sometimes used as a source of fiber for paper and cardboard, and it is also dried and used as industrial fuel.

WATERING-POT SHELL, See ASPERGILLUM.

WATER LEAF, common name applied to hardy, perennial herbs of the family Hydrophyllaceae, and especially to its principal genus, *Hydrophyllum.* The genus contains approximately six species native to North America, and is cultivated in some areas as an ornamental plant. The small white, lilac, blue, or purple flowers, which are arranged in cymes,

The sweet-scented water lily

have five sepals, five petals, five stamens, and a solitary pistil. The fruit is a spherical, one-to-four-seeded capsule. The leaves are lobbed and palm shaped, often reaching a breadth of 12 inches. *H. appendiculatum,* native to Vermont, bears violet or purple flowers and reaches a height of 2 feet. *H. capitatum,* which is native to Colorado, bears purple or white flowers and grows to a height of 9 inches. *H. virginianum,* found in w. and s. Quebec, Canada, bears white or violet-purple flowers and reaches a height of 2½ feet. *H. canadense,* which bears greenish-white or purple flowers, is native to E. United States and grows as tall as *H. virginianum.*

WATER LILY, common name applied to aquatic, perennial herbs of the family Nymphaeaceae, and to its principal genus *Nymphaea.* The genus, which contains approximately 40 distinct species and numerous varieties, is native to the Northern and Southern hemispheres and is cultivated throughout the world. The solitary, showy flowers are white, yellow, blue, or red, and have four sepals, numerous petals, numerous stamens, and a solitary pistil. The fruit is naked and ovoid, and usually ripens above the surface of the water. Water lilies float on the surface of the water or rise a few inches above the surface; the leaves are round or oval, and are 2 to 24 inches in diameter. Water lilies are classified as hardy or as tropical, and the tropical species are further classified as day-blooming and night-blooming. Hardy water lilies are cultivated as perennials; the flowers are pure white and deep vermilion to bronze and copper. Tropical water lilies are cultivated as annuals, and are showier than hardy species. The fragrant flowers are colored mainly in shades of blue, purple, and pink, and lack the yellow tints of the hardy species.

The sweet-scented water lily, *N. odorata,* is a common, day-blooming, tropical species; it is native to E. United States and bears white flowers. Its most important varieties include, var. *rosea,* the Cape Cod water lily, which is native to Massachusetts and bears pink flowers, and the rice-field water lily, var. *gigantea,* native to E. United States, Mexico, Cuba, and British Guiana, and bearing white flowers. Other day-blooming tropicals include *N. flavovirens,* a white-flowered species native to Mexico; *N. gigantea,* found in Australia and bearing light-blue flowers; *N. zanzibariensis,* native to Zanzibar and bearing dark-blue flowers; *N. alba,* native to Europe and North Africa and bearing white flowers; and *N. mexicana,* a canary-yellow species native to Florida and Mexico. The common night-blooming tropical *N. lotus,* commonly called white lotus, bears pure white flowers and is native to Egypt and Hungary. Other night-bloomers, all bearing pink or reddish flowers include *N. rubra,* found throughout India; *N. amazonum,* native to tropical America; and *N. rudgeana,* native to tropical America.

Practically all hardy water lilies are hybrid varieties of species described above, and are classified by common name according to general coloration. Common yellow hardy varieties are usually shaded with red, and include the Paul Hariot, Sioux, Northern Indiana, and Phoenix. Common pink or red varieties include William Doogue, Mark Hanna, Leviathan, W.B. Shaw, Arethusa, James Gurney, James Brydon, William Falconer, and Mrs. Richmond. The Aurora and Comanche are apricot-yellow to copper-red; the Goliath is pure white. Among the tropical day-bloomers are such common horticultural varieties as the white-flowered Mrs. George H. Pring, the blue-flowered Mrs. Edwards Whittaker, the pink-flowered General Pershing and Mrs. C. W. Ward, and the purple-flowered Panama Pacific and August Koch. Among the tropical night-blooming hybrids are the pink- or red-flowered varieties Frank Trelease and Bissett.

Numerous insect pests frequently attack the water lily, causing considerable damage to the leaves. The aphid pests of the family Aphididae are usually controlled by introducing their natural enemies, such as the lady bug or lady bird of the family Coccinellidae. Lepidopterous leaf miners are destroyed by spraying the plants with a kerosene emulsion; the leaf cutter, *Hydrocampa obliteralis*, is usually controlled with arsenate and lead sprays. The damage caused by fungus diseases, such as leaf spot, is reduced by the use of Bordeaux mixture sprays.

WATERLOO, city and county seat of Monroe County, Ill., situated 23 miles s. of St. Louis. The leading manufactures are flour, condensed milk, and cigars. Noteworthy features are the courthouse and city library. Pop. (1940) 2361.

WATERLOO, city and county seat of Blackhawk County, Iowa, situated 53 miles N.W. of Cedar Rapids, on the Red Cedar River. Waterloo carries on a large jobbing and wholesale trade and has considerable industrial importance. There are beef- and pork-packing and corn-canning establishments, brickyards, large cream-separator works, and manufactures of concrete work, gasoline engines, farming implements, well drills, refrigerators, cigars, flour, creamery supplies, and foundry and machine-shop products. The Illinois Central Railroad maintains extensive repair and construction shops in the city. Pop. (1950) 64,354.

WATERLOO, a village and one of the county seats of Seneca County, N.Y. It has manufactures of woolen goods, wagons, and flour. Pop. (1940) 4010.

WATERLOO, BATTLE OF, the decisive military engagement of the Napoleonic Wars and the culminating battle in the brief campaign which finally annihilated the power of Napoleon (see NAPOLEON I; FRANCE: *History*; ENGLAND: *History*; EUROPE: *History*). The participants of the battle, which was fought on June 18, 1815, 2 miles from the Belgian village of Waterloo and 12 miles s. of Brussels, were the French, under the command of Napoleon; and the Allies, consisting of English, Dutch, Belgian, Hanover, Brunswick, and Nassau forces under the command of the British Duke of Wellington (see WELLINGTON, 1ST DUKE OF, ARTHUR WELLESLEY) and the forces of Prussia, Saxony, and several other German states under the command of Gebhard Leberecht von Blücher (q.v.).

The events leading up to the battle were as follows. In Feb., 1815, Napoleon escaped from the island of Elba, on which he had been in exile since spring, 1814, and with a small force made his way to Paris, entering the French capital on March 20. He immediately prepared to resume the war which had ended with his abdication and exile in 1814. At this time the Congress of Vienna (see VIENNA, CONGRESS OF) was still in progress. The Allies suspended negotiations and prepared to resume the struggle. The armies of Wellington and Blücher were distributed in the Belgian Netherlands, Wellington having his headquarters at Brussels, and Blücher at Namur. The Austrians gathered an army on the eastern frontier of France, which was to be joined by a Russian army, the united force to be commanded by Prince Karl Philipp von Schwarzenberg (q.v.). Napoleon's plan of action was based upon the tactics of rapid and aggressive action responsible for his early successes. He planned to destroy the Anglo-Dutch army, on the north, before the Austrian and Russian forces could be made effective. His plan for defeating the Allied army in Belgium was to dispose of Wellington and Blücher separately. Accordingly, in June he moved his army, which consisted of a force of about 124,000 men, to the Franco-Belgian frontier. Wellington's Anglo-Dutch forces were distributed in numerous, widely distant cantonments southwest of Brussels and Blücher's forces were dispersed near Wellington's eastern flank and southeast of Brussels. Prussian outposts guarded the combined front, which extended E. to W. for about 90 miles and possessed a mean depth of about 30 miles. The Allied forces outnumbered the French and consisted of about 93,000 men under Wellington and about 116,000 men under Blücher.

On June 14 Napoleon succeeded in concentrating his forces on the frontier s. of the Sambre R., in position to strike and split the Allies at the towns of Charleroi and Quatre Bras. The Allies had received no advance warning of the proximity of the French army's position. As a result, they had been unable to consolidate their armies and had not moved a soldier to meet Napoleon.

On June 15 Napoleon's forces, the left wing commanded by Michel Ney and the right wing commanded by Marquis Emmanuel de Grouchy (qq.v.), crossed the Sambre R., catching the Allies unprepared. The French moved forward to Charleroi, and engaged their enemy. Ney's force, the left wing, was sent on to Frasnes, just s. of Quatre Bras, and Grouchy's force, the right wing, advanced to the Prussian positions at Gilly, E. of Charleroi. Wellington, learning of the advance on Quatre Bras, located about 12 miles N. of Charleroi, began to concentrate his forces near the former town. In the early evening the right wing of Napoleon's army captured Gilly and moved northward to a position s. of the town of Fleurus. At the end of the day Napoleon's forces possessed the strategical advantage. He had succeeded in placing his army between Wellington's and Blücher's, and his main force was in a position to swing left to encounter the Anglo-Dutch army, or right to close with the Prussians.

On the morning of June 16 Napoleon dispatched a letter to Ney which outlined the strategy of his campaign: "I have adopted as the general principle for this campaign to divide my army into two wings and a reserve. ... I shall bring [the reserve] into action on either wing just as circumstances dictate." Napoleon thus determined to throw his reserve into action to strengthen one wing in order to bring about a decisive victory over one of the two armies, while using his other wing, unsupported, exclusively to neutralize the other army by containing it. Based upon this general plan, Napoleon's strategy was to push an advance guard N.E. to the town of Gembloux to forestall Blücher, move his reserve up to Fleurus, and move his left wing under Ney into Quatre Bras. When this maneuver was accomplished, the reserve was to swing N.W. and join Ney at Quatre Bras, and then both the left and center wings were to advance on Brussels, thus completing the split of the two allied armies. Ney failed to take advantage of the comparative helplessness of Quatre Bras on the morning of the 16th and he did not move against the town until Napoleon ordered him for the second time to secure it while Napoleon attacked Blücher. Because at this time Napoleon did not know which would be the decisive flank, his orders were flexible: the wing first to succeed in its mission was to turn inward to reinforce the other. On the afternoon of June 16, Napoleon engaged Blücher in a battle at Ligny, a town just N. of Fleurus, and Ney engaged Wellington at Quatre Bras.

Quatre Bras. At 2 P.M. Ney attacked and made some headway, but at 3 P.M. the Dutch-Belgian troops, who were under the command of the Prince of Orange, were reinforced by Wellington, who had been conferring with Blücher near Ligny. The French attacked Wellington at 4:15 but the Duke's group was reinforced at 5:00. Ney then realized that he would need reinforcements. The French marshal ordered the 1st corps, which had moved S.E. to help at Ligny, back to Quatre Bras. At 5:30 Ney received an order from Napoleon which directed him to seize Quatre Bras and then turn S.E. to help against Blücher, who was pinned at Ligny. A few minutes later Ney received another order from Napoleon directing him to allow the 1st corps to assist at Ligny no matter the outcome of the battle at Quatre Bras. Ney, however, refused to rescind his command to the 1st corps. At about 7 P.M. the Anglo-Dutch troops were reinforced again, and possessing the numerical advantage for the first time in the day, they succeeded in driving Ney back to Frasnes. In the meantime, the 1st corps, which numbered about 20,000 men, had received the order to return to Quatre Bras just as they reached the Ligny battlefield. The corps turned about and arrived at Ney's position after the conclusion of the battle. They saw no action at either Quatre Bras or Ligny that day. It was a drastic error, for if the 1st corps had been used exclusively at Ligny, it would have insured the Prussian destruction, and if the corps had been used exclusively at Quatre Bras, Wellington's forces would have been crushed.

Ligny. Napoleon, as he became aware of the dispostion of the Prussian forces exposed on open slopes, decided to make the battle against Blücher the action at which the decisive result would be aimed. At about 3 P.M., after hearing the guns from Quatre Bras, Napoleon launched his attack. He planned to smash the center of the Prussian line and at the same time use the 1st corps to attack the Prussian flank. The battle for the town of Ligny was furious, and although the French held the advantage throughout the day, a series of misunderstandings and mistakes, including the advancement of the 1st corps at the wrong time and in the wrong direction, and then its subsequent withdrawal, forced Napoleon to fight without the aid of a force at his flank. As a result, although Napoleon defeated Blücher by the end of the day, he was unable to destroy the Prussian forces, which retreated northward. Blücher's forces during the retreat were still able to maintain contact with Wellington's forces.

The position of the armies on the next day, June 17th, remained to Napoleon's advantage. Wellington was still confronted by Ney's force and his left flank was unprotected as a result of Blücher's retreat. Wellington's position at Quatre Bras was therefore impossible to maintain. The Duke received intelligence that Blücher was retiring to Wavre in the N. and he therefore decided to retire to the village of Mt. S. Jean, w. of Wavre and s. of Waterloo. In this way Wellington would be assured of support from Blücher. On the morning of the 17th Napoleon ordered Ney to take up a position at Quatre Bras; if a rear guard were at the town, they were to be driven off by Ney, and if Wellington were there, he was to be contained until Napoleon could reach Quatre Bras to engage and crush the Anglo-Dutch forces. Wellington was at Quatre Bras but Ney again erred and did not move against him. At 10 A.M. Wellington began his retreat unhindered, thus ending the opportunity for a decisive French victory. At 11 A.M. Napoleon decided to send a force under the command of Marquis Emmanuel de Grouchy to Gembloux, where a Prussian force had been encountered. After a slovenly, unhurried march, Grouchy reached the town, but the Prussian force, a small unit of cavalry, was allowed to slip away. Grouchy, who by this time knew that the Prussians had marched to Wavre and not Namur, should then have marched to the front. Instead, he halted at Gembloux and settled there for the night. Napoleon joined Ney at Quatre Bras with the remainder of the army and set out in pursuit of Wellington. The French forces did not catch up to Wellington until nightfall. Both armies encamped for the night north of Genappe, a village a few miles s. of Mt. S. Jean and Waterloo. During the night Wellington made his plans for the impending battle. The Duke needlessly dispatched 17,000 men to the town of Hal, about 8 miles w. of Waterloo, in the event that Napoleon should attempt to outflank him. Wellington then arranged the mass of his army, 67,600 men and 156 guns, south of Mt. S. Jean under the cover of a low ridge. The Duke also contacted Blücher, who assured Wellington that he would support him by bringing up his Prussian force from the east to close with Napoleon's exposed right flank when the French emperor began his attack.

Waterloo. It rained during the night, but at about 8 A.M. on the morning of the Battle of Waterloo, June 18, the rain ceased. Napoleon deployed his force of 74,000 men and 246 guns in three lines about 1300 yards from the Anglo-Dutch position. The French army formed a formidable array as Napoleon reviewed it amid enthusiastic acclaim. At 10 A.M. Napoleon ordered Grouchy to march for Wavre with his 33,000 men. The emperor planned to use Grouchy's force to intercept Blücher's inner flank to keep the Prussian from the main battle, but this plan was not clearly outlined in the written instructions to Grouchy. The battle opened at 11:30 A.M. with a diversionary attack on Wellington's right flank. A little more than an hour and a half later Napoleon signaled the beginning of the main battle by sending Ney into Wellington's center with the 1st corps. Napoleon then saw the Prussian advance corps in the distance on his right flank. The emperor hurriedly sent a second message to Grouchy informing him that the battle was now joined and that Grouchy was to hurry to the scene of the action to contain the Prussians. Grouchy received the command too late to carry it out and Napoleon was forced to dispatch a portion of his main line of troops to neutralize the Prussian corps. Ney's initial attack at the center of the line was successful, but in pursuing the routed Anglo-Dutch, the 1st corps met a severe fire from infantry and cavalry, and was repulsed. The Prussian corps, although they disrupted the symmetry of Napoleon's attack by drawing off a portion of the French army, still had not joined the action. At 4 P.M. Ney led a second attack against the line. It comprised a cavalry charge of eighty squadrons against the Anglo-Dutch positions, which consisted of "squares" of infantry. The attack began with a fierce cannonade against Wellington's forces and was followed by the advance of the French horsemen, who fought a dramatic battle, but were beaten back. It is probable, military tacticians believe, that Ney's charge would have been successful had his cavalry received the support of French infantry.

At about 4:30 the Prussian advance guard entered the battle and engaged the force that Napoleon had sent out to protect his right flank. The French on the flank were forced back beyond the village of Plancenoit, endangering Napoleon's right flank and rear. The emperor further weakened his main forces by

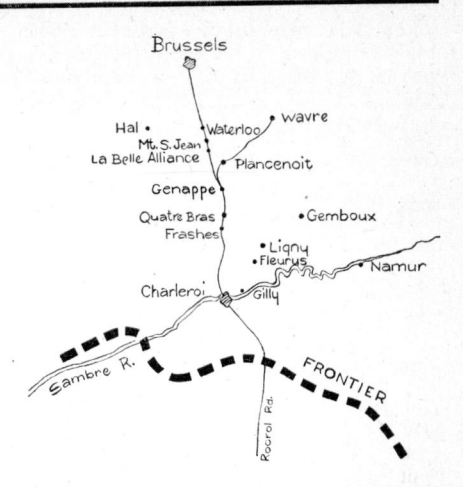

Scene of operations of Battle of Waterloo

dispatching aid to this threatened right flank, and with these reserves the French troops recaptured Plancenoit and drove the Prussians back. With his right flank again secure Napoleon ordered Ney to advance for the third time and to capture the Anglo-Dutch position in the center of Wellington's line at all costs. Marshal Ney succeeded, giving Napoleon his first important advantage of the day. But the French advantage in occupying a commanding position in the center of the line was short-lived, because the village of Plancenoit had meanwhile been recaptured by the Prussians, who had been bolstered by reserves. Before Napoleon could press his newly won advantage in the center of the weakened Anglo-Dutch line, he was forced again to buttress his right flank, which he secured by recapturing Plancenoit for a second time, but the delay had allowed Wellington to strengthen his position by moving a portion of his troops from his left flank to a position behind his torn center. Prussian troops took the place of Wellington's newly shifted reserve. The shift of troops was extremely important. Napoleon now fiercely attacked Wellington all along the line, but the key French attack in the center failed as a result of the combined actions of the new British reserves and their Dutch-Belgian allies. At approximately 8 P.M., when the French were recoiling in the center of the line, the Prussian forces, which had taken up positions on the extreme left of Wellington's line, drove through the right corner of the French line, throwing most of Napoleon's troops into a rout. Napoleon's retreat along the road to Charleroi was kept free by the action of two French battalions which managed to hold Plancenoit to the last possible moment. During the night that followed, the Prussians maintained the pursuit of the scattered French forces, forced them from seven successive bivouacs, and finally drove them back across the Sambre R. The fighting during the day had been so fierce that approximately 45,000 men had been killed or wounded within an area of three square miles. The losses during the battle on June 18 were more than 40,000 casualties for the French, about 15,000 from Wellington's groups, and about 7000 Prussians.

On June 18, Grouchy, although he heard the sound of the fighting at Waterloo, marched instead for Wavre, and there encountered a force of about 16,000 Prussians. The two armies fought throughout the day and the Prussians, despite their inferior numbers, managed to maintain a superior position until near the end of the day. Fighting for the night stopped at 11 P.M. When the action resumed again in the morning, the French compelled the Prussians to retreat. Grouchy, then hearing of the disaster at Waterloo, succeeded in carrying out a successful retreat, slipping by Blücher's army and returning to Paris with the remainder of his force intact.

In reviewing the causes for Napoleon's failure at Waterloo it may be seen that the French emperor did not show his usual care and thoroughness in his orders, nor his usual broad judgment in execution. In addition, Ney and Grouchy both failed in judgment at critical times. The timely arrival of the Prussians was the final factor in Napoleon's defeat. Napoleon later laid the principal blame for the disaster on Grouchy, who might possibly have contained the Prussians had he advanced to Waterloo.

WATERLOO BRIDGE, a stone bridge over the Thames River in London, built by private enterprise (1811–17) from designs by the Scottish civil engineer John Rennie and sold to the London Metropolitan Board of Works in 1878. It rests upon nine arches and has a length of 1380 feet and a breadth of 42 feet.

WATERLOO WITH SEAFORTH, a town on the southwest coast of Lancashire, England, situated at the mouth of the Mersey River, 5 miles N.N.W. of Liverpool. It is a favorite seaside suburb for Liverpool merchants. Pop., about 31,000.

WATERLOW, SIR ERNEST ALBERT (1854–1919), English landscape painter, born in London. In 1890 he was elected a Royal Academician and in 1897 he became the president of the Royal Society of Painters in Water Color. Characteristic works are "Galway Gossips" (1887), "Friends or Foes" (1890), "Golden Autumn" (1896), "A Summer Shower" (Walker Art Gallery, Liverpool), "Suffolk Marshes" (1902), "Sketch in Essex" (1905), and "The Banks of the Loing".

WATERMELON, an annual vine, *Citrullus vulgaris,* of the family Cucurbitaceae, native to tropical Africa, and extensively cultivated in warm climates, particularly in southern U.S.S.R. and in the United States. In the latter country, more than 200,000 acres, especially in Texas, Georgia, and Missouri, are annually devoted to the cultivation of the watermelon. The refreshing red, greenish, or yellow pulp of its ripe fruit contains about 93 percent water and 2 percent sugar. A number of varieties, especially red-fleshed ones, are in cultivation. The white-fleshed, rather solid form used in preserving is generally known as a

Swimmers playing a game of water polo. One of the two goals is seen at right.

citron or preserving melon. The watermelon is sensitive to frost and is easily stunted by cold. It thrives in a rich, warm, sandy loam which is well supplied with humus.

WATER METER, any type of mechanical device used to measure the volume of flow of water through a pipe or channel. Water meters are of three general types: those which measure flow by means of pistons in cylinders which fill with water; those which measure flow by means of the turning of vanes, buckets, or propeller screws which are actuated by the flow; and those which measure flow by the difference in pressure in a constricted portion of the water channel; see VENTURI TUBE.

WATER NET, common name applied to fresh-water, green algae of the genus *Hyrodictyon,* belonging to the family Chlorophyceae (q.v.). The genus, which is colonial in habit, derives its common name from the elongated, saclike net formed by the end-to-end attachment of the numerous cylindrical cells of the colony.

WATER OATS. See WILD RICE.
WATER PARTING. See WATERSHED.
WATER POLO, a game played by two teams of seven swimmers each. The object of the game is to pass an inflated ball about 27 inches in circumference between goal posts set 10 feet apart and under a cross bar 3 feet above the surface of the water. The players of each side are divided into three forwards, two backs, one halfback, and one goalkeeper. One hand only may be used in handling the ball, and it is a foul to interfere with an opponent not in possession of the ball. Other fouls are also recognized; the usual penalty for the commission of a foul is a free pass by the opposing side.

WATER POWER, term applied to the power which is, or can be, derived from the fall of water in the gradient of a stream from a higher to a lower level. Water power is a natural resource, available wherever a sufficient volume of water flow exists; its development, however, requires construction of expensive works, such as canals, dams, and aqueducts (qq.v.); the installation of turbines (see TURBINE) or water wheels; and, as is generally the case today, the erection and equipment of hydroelectric powerhouses. Because of the large amount of capital required, the development of water power is often uneconomical for regions in which coal is cheap, even though the fuel cost for a steam-powered generating plant is higher than the cost of running a hydroelectric plant.

The availability of water power was an important factor in the development of early American industrial cities. Coal was scarce and wood fuel unsatisfactory; substantial development of an industrial area could therefore be achieved only in localities with ample supplies of water power. The first development of water power was undertaken to supply power to sawmills and grist mills along the rivers of New England, but the first important installations were made at Pawtucket, Rhode Island, in 1790, at Paterson, New Jersey, in 1791, and at Fall River, Massachusetts, in 1813. At such installations the rivers were damned, and, from the pools above the dams, canals were run along the banks in order to use as many water wheels as the water supply would permit. Where the drop was more than 16 feet, which was then the working limit, the discharge from the first set of wheels was collected in a second canal, and used to operate a lower set. As many as five levels were used, the tail water of one group of water wheels becoming the head water of the next lower group. Such water-power developments were used to supply power to mill machinery through shafting or belting.

In modern plants the water-driven turbine is connected directly with an electric generator (see DYNAMOELECTRIC MACHINERY), even when the power is used locally. In such installations, especially in those having a substantial head of water available, water is brought through strong pipes from storage or impounding pools above the dam to the lowest level above tail water, and then is run in solid streams through turbine wheels equipped with vanes or impulse buckets, which are designed for maximum efficiency at the particular head available. Installations are classified as low-head if the difference in level of the head and tail water is 100 feet or less, and as high-head if the difference is greater than 500 feet. The highest head employed is more than 5400 feet, in the hydroelectric installation at Lac Fully, Switzerland. Before World War II the capacity of developed water power installations throughout the world totaled 55 million horsepower, with a potential, undeveloped capacity of 417 million horsepower; North America and Europe had approximately equal capacities of slightly more than 24 million horsepower each. Since that time the United States has forged ahead, mainly because of the building of such navigation, irrigation, and hydroelectric projects as the Hoover, Norris, Bonneville, and Grand Coulee Dams (see DAMS) and the developments of such various governmental agencies as the Tennessee Valley Authority (see below). Present developed water power in the United States amounts to 22 million horsepower, with a potential undeveloped capacity of 1210 million horsepower.

The development of the hydroelectric resources of the United States was given a strong impetus by the establishment in 1920 of the Federal Power Commission (q.v.) to study, develop, and regulate the water-power resources of the country. Another important governmental agency is the Tennessee Valley Authority, created by Congress in 1933, for the purpose of providing the unified development of the Tennessee River and all its tributaries. This watershed comprises an area of 41,000 square miles, and supports a population of about 3,200,000 persons; it includes portions of seven States: Virginia, North Carolina, Tennessee, Georgia, Alabama, Mississippi, and Kentucky. The primary function of the T.V.A. includes the construction and maintenance of twenty-one dams on the main river and its tributaries for the purpose of flood control, hydroelectric development, and making the river navigable for 630 miles, from its mouth near Paducah, Kentucky, to Knoxville, Tennessee. The system provides for the storage of about 12 million acre-feet of flood waters, for the generation of 3.35 million horsepower of electrical energy, and for navigation of the river, which in 1948 carried 410 million ton-miles of freight. Other functions of the T.V.A. include the distribution of surplus electric power; the development of improvements in the manufacture and distribution of synthetic fertilizers; and, in time of national emergency, the manufacture of electrochemical products for war supplies.

Governmental agencies with similar functions include the Bonneville Power Administration, operating in the Columbia River Valley, and the Southwestern Power Authority, operating in the States of Arkansas and Louisiana, and in parts of Kansas, Missouri, Texas, and Oklahoma.

Water-purification unit operated by U.S. Army in the Solomon Islands during World War II

WATERPROOFING, the coating of articles made of textile fabrics, paper, and other substances, so as to render them impervious to water. Besides a solution of rubber for waterproofing, various preparations are used, such as a mixture of beeswax and yellow rosin in boiled oil. Fabrics may also be rendered waterproof by thoroughly impregnating them with a solution of soap and then dipping them into a solution of alum.

WATER PURIFICATION, the removal of contaminating bodies or substances from water which is to be used for human consumption or for industrial purposes. The types of impurities encountered in water include: solid inorganic matter such as silt particles; living organisms such as bacteria and algae; inorganic substances in solution; and organic substances in solution.

For the removal of organic and inorganic matter suspended in water, two methods are usually employed, sedimentation and filtration. In purification by sedimentation, the water to be treated is allowed to stand in a settling basin, or to flow very slowly through some form of settling channel. By the action of gravity the solid particles in the still or slow-moving water fall to the bottom of the settling vessel and can be removed. Sedimentation was formerly extensively practiced, but most modern water-supply systems use the more rapid method of filtration, for purifying the water.

The filters used in water purification are beds of fine sand through which water is allowed to flow either by gravity, by positive pressure, or by suction. The older type of sand filter, the so-called "slow" sand filter, consisted of a bed of very large area, through which water percolated by gravity. The efficiency of the filter in straining particles from the water was increased by the natural formation of a jellylike layer of bacterial material on the surface of the filter. This layer had extremely fine pores and served to strain out the most minute solid particles. Slow sand filters are not effective in the clearing of water having a high degree of turbidity, as they become clogged, and must be cleaned by flushing with clean water in the reverse direction to the normal flow through the filter. Because of the large area of the filter beds, this flushing is mechanically difficult and expensive.

In most installations, slow sand filters have been supplanted by rapid sand filters having a smaller area, and operating under either positive or negative pressure. These filters are used in conjunction with chemical pretreatment of the water with coagulating or flocculating agents, such as alum, which combine with the mineral salts dissolved in the water to form a gelatinous "floc" or precipitate. This

Water scorpion (Nepa cinerea)

floc enters the upper portion of the sand filter to form an additional filter medium. Rapid sand filters are cleaned quickly and economically by flushing them with clean water in a direction opposite to the normal flow of water through the filter. The flow of water through a rapid sand filter is approximately 125,000,000 gallons of water per day per acre of filter surface. The rate of filtration in a slow sand filter is from 12 to 40 times slower.

Chemical Treatment. Besides the treatment with alum for flocculation mentioned above, water usually undergoes other forms of chemical treatment in the course of purification. Such treatments include various forms of water softening for the removal of calcium salts (see HARDNESS), and the addition of disinfecting agent, usually calcium chloride or sodium hypochlorite, to kill any bacteria which may have survived the filtration process. Normally, modern rapid sand filters remove from 80 to 98 percent of all the solid material, including bacteria, in the raw water. The addition of chemicals, as, for example, $2\frac{1}{2}$ to 5 lb. of chlorine to each 1,000,000 gal. of water, is then sufficient to free the water of bacteria.

WATER RAT, common name for any vole of the genus *Arvicola,* especially *A. amphibius.* This animal is about $8\frac{1}{2}$ inches in length, reddish-brown in general color, and is numerous throughout Europe. It is closely related to the voles and meadow mice of the United States, and has similar habits, except that it is more aquatic and diurnal than members of the genus *Microtus,* to which other voles belong.

WATER-RECOVERY APPARATUS, apparatus carried on an airship for condensing and recovering the water contained in the exhaust gases of internal combustion engines in order to avoid the necessity of releasing gas as the fuel is consumed.

WATER RICE. See WILD RICE.

WATER RIGHTS, in the law of real property in England and the United States, a general term used to designate the legal control or use of water. The owner of land does not have exclusive ownership of water in a stream on, or flowing through, his land; he is, however, entitled to a reasonable use of such water for such purposes as watering animals, irrigation, power in running mills, and drainage. He must not interfere with the rights of owners of adjoining land, as by diverting, polluting, damming, or lessening the steady flow of the stream (see RIPARIAN RIGHTS). The lower proprietor, i.e., the party owning the land lower down bordering on the stream, has an easement (q.v.) in the stream flowing from the land of an upper proprietor. Also, the owner of land may himself create an easement granting others the right to take water from his land or the right to fish or cut ice. A riparian owner who owns land on a nonnavigable stream cannot be deprived of his rights by the state without fair compensation

Water percolating through the soil or water collected in wells, cisterns or artificial ponds is regarded as part of the land and belongs to the owner of the land. An owner of land may use waters percolating through the soil or surface waters other than streams in any way he pleases; he may dig a well and consume all the water, even though it renders a well on the land of an adjoining owner dry. He has no easement of drainage on the land of the adjoining owner; nor has he any cause of action against an adjoining owner who takes measures to prevent the flow of percolating or surface waters on his land.

The public is entitled to the use of waters, whether private or not, which are capable of navigation or transportation. The public has the right of anchoring and fishing from boats in navigable water. It has no right of landing on the shore. On land between the high- and low-water mark of tidal waters, the public may pass and repass, dry nets thereon, fish, or take shellfish.

WATER SCAVENGER BEETLE. See WATER BEETLE.

WATER SCORPION, any of the water bugs of the family Nepidae. These insects have swollen forelegs fitted for grasping, thus distantly resembling the chelicerae of a true scorpion. The anal end of the body is furnished with two thin, long, grooved, terminal bristles or sheaths, which when pressed together form a tube, through which the insect obtains its supply of air from above the surface of the water. The water scorpions are carnivorous, feeding upon fishes' eggs, small fish, and water insects.

WATERSHED, WATER PARTING, or DIVIDE, a boundary, such as a mountain ridge, which separates the waters flowing into two different river systems. The location of a divide is dependent upon the contours of the land, and sections of a divide sometimes shift position with the change in contour caused by unequal erosion rates of two adjoining streams. In the United States, the streams which flow into the Pacific and those which flow into the Gulf of Mexico through the Mississippi River system are separated by a line known as the Continental Divide, or Great Divide (q.v.). The term "watershed" is also commonly applied to the entire area, delimited by divides, comprising the drainage basin of a river system.

WATER SHIELD. See BRASENIA.

WATERSNAKE, a harmless colubrine serpent of the genus *Natrix* or *Tropidonotus*, closely related to the garter snakes. The common watersnake of the United States is *T. fasciatus*, with several varieties of the species, of which all are southern except for the variety *sipedon*, the numerous and well-known watersnake of the northern and eastern States, which occurs as far west as the dry plains. The average adult length of a watersnake is 3 feet. Its color is a variable brown, with large, dark-brown markings on the back and sides, and with the belly yellowish or reddish, spotted with reddish-brown, rounded spots. These colors, together with its habits and somewhat broad head, lead to its often being mistaken for the venomous moccasin snake, of which some naturalists consider it a mimic. This snake is semiaquatic in its habits, being usually found on the borders of the water. It is an expert swimmer and diver, and skillful at catching fishes, on which it mainly subsists. When cornered it is pugnacious, but its bite is insignificant. Its young, 16 to 33 in number, are born alive, when about 8 inches long.

The watersnake of Europe is *N. natrix*, much like the American snake in form, colors, and habits, and commonly known in England as grass snake. The main difference between it and the American watersnake is that the former is more active on land, and lays eggs, which are buried in loose loam, or in manure or dust heaps. Several other species of the genus occur in the Malayan Archipelago and two in Africa; some of them are large and of savage appearance, but all are harmless.

WATERS OF MEROM, the scene of the great battle, described in the Old Testament, between the Hebrews under Joshua and the allied kings of Canaan. The waters of Merom have been identified with the more northern of the two lakes through which the Jordan River flows in its course to the Dead Sea. The lake is now called Huleh, or, more fully, Baheiret el Huleh.

WATER SOLDIER, common name for a plant, *Stratiotes aloides*, in the family Hydrocharideae. It is a singular plant with numerous leaves, which are strap shaped and spring from the root, from which also springs the two-edged flower stem, bearing a spathe with delicate white flowers.

WATER SPANIEL, a curly-haired spaniel of aquatic habits. The English water spaniel is usually black and white with medium-sized

Red-bellied watersnake, the common watersnake of the United States

The Irish water spaniel

ears; the Irish water spaniel is liver colored, with very long ears. The former is seldom seen. See SPANIEL.

WATER SPIDER, in America any spider, especially those of the genus *Lycosa,* living near the water and at times running over the surface or diving beneath it. True water spiders belong to the species *Argyroneta aquatica,* found in European and Asiatic waters. They construct submarine, silken nests, resembling a diving bell, which the spiders fill with air, carrying one tiny bubble at a time.

WATERSPOUT, a small, rapidly whirling column of air, extending from a cloud down to an ocean or lake. Its central axis becomes visible as a column of water or cloudy vapor. The formation of a waterspout is due to a strong upward draft beneath the base of a cumulous cloud. The air that supplies this draft acquires a rapid rotary motion as it ascends. The resulting centrifugal tendency of air in rotation leads to a very low pressure in the central axis of the eddy. The rising air flowing into this region expands as it passes into places of low pressure, and is therefore cooled dynamically and becomes visible by the cloudy condensation of a part of its moisture.

WATER STRIDER, a slender, long-legged water bug of the family Hydrobatidae. They live upon the surface of quiet waters and dart about with great rapidity. A common species upon ponds and in the United States is *Hygrotrechus remigis,* a moderately stout, dark-brown insect about ½ in. long. It hibernates in mud, beneath leaves upon the banks, or at the bottom of the water under stones. While truly aquatic, water striders are structurally more nearly related to the land bugs than to the other water bugs.

WATER SUPPLY AND WATER WORKS, respectively, the provision of a supply of water for irrigation, industrial, and domestic needs, and the engineering installation necessary to provide such a supply. Primitive man had no need of engineering works to supply his water; hunters and nomads camped near such natural sources of fresh water as springs, rivers, and lakes, and populations were so sparse that pollution of the water supply was not a serious problem. After community life developed, however, and agricultural villages became urban centers, the problem of supplying water for all the inhabitants of a city became important, and, in many cases, a supply of irrigation (q.v.) water became necessary for the farms surrounding the city and producing the food for its peoples. Irrigation works were constructed in prehistoric times, and before 2000 B.C. the rulers of Egypt and of Babylonia constructed systems of dams and canals (qq.v.) to impound the flood waters of the Nile and Euphrates rivers, controlling floods and providing irrigation water throughout the dry season. Such irrigation canals also served to supply water for domestic purposes. The first people to consider the sanitation of their water supply were the ancient Romans, who constructed a vast system of aqueducts (see AQUEDUCT) to bring the clean waters of the Apennine Mountains into the city, and built settling basins and filters (see WATER PURIFICATION) along these mains to insure the clarity of the water. The construction of such extensive water-supply systems declined when the Roman Empire disintegrated, and for several centuries local springs and wells (see WELL-SINKING) formed the principal source of domestic and industrial water, even in cities of substantial size.

The invention of the force pump (see PUMPS AND PUMPING MACHINERY) in England in the middle of the 16th century greatly extended the possibilities of development of water-supply systems. At London in 1562 the first pumping water works was completed; it pumped river water to a reservoir 120 feet above the level of the Thames, and from the reservoir the water was distributed by gravity, through lead pipes, to buildings in the vicinity. The first municipal pumping station in the United States was erected about 1760 to supply water to the town of Bethlehem, Pennsylvania. It consisted of a 5-inch wooden pump which raised the water 70 feet through pipes made of bored hemlock logs. By 1800 sixteen American cities had water-supply systems, and since that time almost every city and town in the country has been provided with municipal water works, most of them publicly owned and operated. In addition to the municipal systems, many State and Federal developments provide water for irrigation, industrial, or domestic uses as a by-product of navigation control, hydroelectric-power generation, and flood control; see FLOODS, CONTROL OF; WATER POWER; DAMS; IRRIGATION.

The ultimate source of all natural potable water on the earth is rain, which is rarely used as a direct source except on islands in salt

Water spider (Argyroneta aquatica)

water, such as Bermuda, where the rain is collected and led into cisterns to serve as the only available water supply. When rain falls, it runs off into streams, in the case of heavy rains, or soaks into the ground, percolating through porous strata until it reaches an impervious stratum, upon which it collects, forming the ground water which is the source of wells and of the springs which feed streams, rivers, and lakes. In its course underground water dissolves soluble mineral matter, and often the waters of rivers and lakes are polluted by the influx of sewage or industrial wastes. Examination of potential sources of water supplies, therefore, in addition to measurement of the amount of water available, includes determination of the feasibility of economically rendering the water suitable for use. Undesirable tastes and odors can often be removed by aeration; bacteria can be destroyed by the addition of a few parts per million of chlorine, and the taste of chlorine can then be removed with sodium sulfite; excessive hardness (q.v.), which renders the water unsuitable for many industrial purposes, is reduced by the addition of slaked lime or by the zeolite (q.v.) process; and suspended organic matter, which supports bacterial life,

WATER-SUPPLY SYSTEMS

Above: Water in an underground cistern in the city of Istanbul, Turkey. Left: Ancient Roman aqueduct in Segovia, Spain.

and suspended mineral matter, as well, are removed by the addition of a flocculating and precipitating agent, such as alum, before settling or filtration; see WATER PURIFICATION.

In modern water-supply systems an entire watershed is made into a reservation to control pollution. The waters are impounded by a system of dams, and flow by gravity, or are pumped, to the local distribution system; see CATSKILL AQUEDUCT; DELAWARE AQUEDUCT. Local distribution systems may be laid out in the form of a "tree" of mains progressively decreasing in diameter, but, where possible, they are in the form of a gridiron or of a closed loop, to guard against the necessity of shutting off the entire supply when any one main is damaged. Frequently local standpipes or reservoirs are maintained to avoid subjecting the entire system to excessive pressure and to consequent leakage and wastage.

The use of water from municipal systems depends greatly on the nature of the community, the amount of industry, and the standards of living. In rural English towns with no industrialization, it varies from 20 to 40 gallons per capita daily; in industrial Brit-

WATER SUPPLY. *Top, left: Fresh-water vendor on the island of Curaçao, in the Caribbean Sea. Top, right: Nomads take water from a brook in Tozeur Oasis, North Africa. Bottom: In Bermuda each house has a tank to store rain, the only source of fresh water.*

Laying a water pipe in the Catskill Aqueduct system to supply New York City — Ewing Galloway

ish cities it is 50 to 75 gallons, and in the United States it varies from 100 to 254 gallons per capita daily consumption.

WATER TIGER. See WATER BEETLE.

WATERTOWN, a town of Litchfield Co., Conn., situated about 25 miles s.w. of Hartford. It is served by a railroad, and is a manufacturing center. The principal industries in the town are the manufacture of silk and rayon goods, plastics, pins and tacks, hardware, and wire products. Watertown was settled about 1701 as a part of Waterbury. It was separated from Waterbury in 1738 and incorporated as Watertown in 1780. Pop. (1940) 8787.

WATERTOWN, a town including several villages, in Middlesex Co., Mass., 7 miles w. of Boston. It has a large public library and a United States arsenal. A prominent residential suburb of Boston, it is also largely interested in manufacturing. The leading products are automobiles, rubber goods, shirts, soap, woolen goods, stoves, and furnaces. Watertown was settled and incorporated in 1630. Pop. (1950) 37,339.

WATERTOWN, county seat of Jefferson Co., N.Y., on the Black R., 70 miles N. of Syracuse. It is served by a railroad, and maintains a municipal airport. Watertown, which derives its name from the use of the water power furnished by the 112-foot drop of the falls in the river at this point, is the largest city of N. New York, an important manufacturing center, and the commercial center of an area abounding in dairy farms and vacation resorts. In the vicinity are extensive deposits of iron and limestone. The principal industrial products of the city are railroad air brakes and paper-mill machinery. Other products are paper, paper boxes, textiles, women's clothing, knit goods, mattresses, thermometers, optical goods, sanitary plumbing fixtures, electrical machinery, ammunition, foundry and machine-shop products, metalwork, flour, and breakfast foods. In addition, the city is the headquarters of two large insurance companies. Notable public buildings in Watertown include the Flower Memorial Library, built in 1904 as a memorial to Roswell P. Flower, a Watertown resident who was governor of New York from 1892 to 1895; the Jefferson County Historical Museum, and a Naval Militia armory. Watertown is a gateway to vacation resorts in the Thousand Islands and the Adirondack Mountains. Nearby is Pine Camp, a large U.S. Army training post.

Watertown was founded in 1800 and incorporated as a city in 1869. The development of the paper industry there dates from 1809, and the first portable steam engine in the U.S. was manufactured there in 1847. F.W. Woolworth, operator of the first successful five-cent store, originated the idea of specializing in items priced at five and ten cents while employed as a salesclerk in a store in Watertown in 1878. Pop. (1950) **34,280.**

WATERTOWN, county seat of Codington Co., S.Dak., situated on the Big Sioux R., 210 miles w. of Minneapolis, Minn. It is served by nine railroads and maintains a municipal airport. The city is a lake-resort center, and the principal trading center and shipping point of the N.E. quarter of the State, a rich farming and stock-raising area. Among the industrial establishments in Watertown are a large meat-packing plant, a large flour mill, a horse abattoir, rendering plants, creameries, bottling works, food-processing plants, machine shops, and factories producing sash and doors and other lumber products, cement, concrete, and mausoleums. Nearby are several extensive chick hatcheries, and deposits of sand and gravel. The chief trading commodities are agricultural machinery and tools, and seeds and feeds. Watertown was founded in 1881 and incorporated in 1885. Pop. (1948) 12,861.

WATERTOWN, city of Dodge and Jefferson counties, Wis., situated on both sides of Rock River, 44 miles N.W. of Milwaukee. The city contains manufactures of flour, chairs, and blinds, and is the site of Northwestern College and Sacred Heart College. Pop. (1940) 11,301.

WATER VALLEY, one of two county seats of Yalobusha Co., Miss., situated about 120 miles N.N.E. of Jackson. Transportation facilities include a railroad. The city is surrounded by a farming, dairying, and lumbering area, in which cotton and watermelons are important crops. Among the industrial establishments in Water Valley are sawmills, lumber mills, a foundry, a silage mill, cotton mills, plants processing dairy products, and factories producing wooden articles, iron products, garments, and work clothing. Water Valley was settled in 1855, incorporated as a town in 1858, and chartered as a city in 1890. Pop. (1940) 3340.

WATERVILLE, a city of Kennebec Co., Me., situated on the w. bank of the Kennebec R., opposite Winslow (q.v.), and 18 miles N. of Augusta. It is served by a railroad, contains railroad repair shops, and maintains a municipal airport. Waterville is a manufacturing center, the trading center of an area with a population of about 82,000, and the gateway to the Belgrade Lakes region. The city is surrounded by a fertile agricultural area. The Ticonic Falls in the river at Waterville furnish abundant water power. The principal industries are the manufacture of paper, paper pulp, cotton goods, worsteds, men's shirts, fiber products, flour, small boats, canoes, foundry and machine-shop products, and traction engines. Waterville is the site of Colby College, established in 1818, of Coburn Classical Institute, a coeducational preparatory school, and of the Central Maine Sanatorium. The site of the present city was settled about 1760. The town of Waterville was incorporated in 1802 and in 1883 it was incorporated as a city. Pop. (1950) 18,232.

WATER VIOLET, or FEATHERFOIL, common name applied to perennial, aquatic herbs of the genus *Hottonia,* belonging to the Primrose family. The genus contains two species native to Europe and America, respectively, and is cultivated as an aquarium plant. The white or purplish flowers, which are borne in racemes, have a five-parted calyx, a five-lobed corolla, five stamens, and a solitary pistil. The fruit is a globular, many-seeded capsule. *H. palustris,* the European species, is found throughout Europe and bears attractive, pale-purple flowers. The American species, *H. inflata,* also known as water feather and water yarrow, is native to E. United States and bears white flowers. Both the European and American species either float freely or take root in the muddy bottoms of shallow, stagnant pools.

WATERVLIET, a city of Albany Co., N.Y., situated at the head of navigation on the Hudson R., opposite Troy, with which it is connected by bridge, and about 5 miles N. of the city of Albany. It is served by a railroad and contains railroad repair shops. The city is a manufacturing center, with industrial establishments producing ladders, brushes, gauges, sandpaper, paper and wooden boxes, asbestos products, stoves, boats, machine-shop products, metal articles, leather products, spun silk, and men's clothing. Watervliet is the site of the oldest arsenal in the U.S., established in 1807 and still an important source of heavy ordnance material for the U.S. Army. Watervliet was incorporated as the village of West Troy in 1836 and in 1896 was chartered under its present name. The first Shaker (q.v.) settlement in the U.S. was established near Watervliet in 1776. Pop. (1950) 15,036.

WATER YAM. See LATTICE PLANT.

WATFORD, a town of Hertfordshire, England, situated on the Colne River, 15 miles N.W. of London. It contains an ancient Perpendicular church, and breweries, malt works, and corn mills. Pop., about 66,000.

WATKINS GLEN, county seat of Schuyler Co., N.Y., situated at the s. end of Seneca Lake, about 20 miles N. of Elmira. It is served by two railroads. The village is a salt-producing center, and a resort noted for its scenic beauty and medicinal springs. The village is also a shipping point for the surrounding grape-growing area. The numerous brine wells and saltworks in the village and vicinity produce approximately 170,000 tons of salt annually. Adjoining the village is the famous Watkins Glen State Park, covering 540 acres and containing Watkins Glen, a narrow canyon, 2 miles in length and rising as high as 300 ft., through which a stream falls in a series of cascades, rapids, and pools for a drop of 1200 ft. The renowned mineral springs at Watkins Glen are similar in type to those of Bad Nauheim in Germany, but exceed those springs approximately five times in mineral content. The site of the present village was settled in 1788 and the settlement was known as Salubria until 1842, when it was incorporated as Jefferson. It was named Watkins Glen in 1852 in honor of Dr. Samuel Watkins, an early resident. Pop. (1940) 2913.

WATLINGS ISLAND. See SAN SALVADOR.

WATLING STREET, one of the great Roman highways of Britain, commencing at Dover, passing through Canterbury and Rochester to London, and thence to Chester and York, and northward in two branches to Carlisle and the Roman Wall in the neighborhood of Newcastle. Traces of the ancient road are still to be found in many parts of its course, and in some it is still an important highway; a street in London retains its name.

WATROUS, HARRY WILSON (1857–95), American figure and genre painter, born in San Francisco, Calif. He was a member of the National Academy after 1895, and its secretary in 1898. His work includes "Passing the Summer" (Metropolitan Museum of Art, New York City), "A Study in Black" (St. Louis Museum), "The Drop Sinister" (1914), "Who Cares" (1915), and "The Line of Love" (1915).

WATSEKA, county seat of Iroquois Co., Ill., situated on the Iroquois River, 80 miles s. of Chicago. The principal manufactures are flour, carriages, iron products, canned goods, and knitted goods. Pop. (1940), 3744.

WATSON, HENRY BRERETON MARRIOTT (1863–1921), English novelist, born in Caulfield, Australia. He is known through his contributions to *The National Observer* and as assistant editor of *Black and White* and of the *Pall Mall Gazette*. His writings, mostly stories of adventure, include *Marahuna* (1888), *Lady Faintheart* (1890), *Diogenes of London* (1893), *Galloping Dick* (1895), *The Adventurers* (1898), *The Princess Xenia* (1899), *The Rebel* (1900), *The House Divided* (1901), *Hurricane Island* (1905), *Twisted Eglantine* (1905), *At a Venture* (1911), *The Big Fish* (1912), and *Chapman's Wares* (1915).

WATSON, JAMES CRAIG (1838–80), American astronomer, born in Ontario, Canada, of American parents, and educated at the University of Michigan. He became professor of astronomy at the University of Michigan in 1859, professor of physics and mathematics in 1860, and director of the observatory in 1863. Watson discovered many planetoids, and had charge of the American expedition to observe the transit of Venus at Peking, China, 1874. His principal work is *Theoretical Astronomy* (1868), a classic treatise on the theory of the motions of comets and planets. Watson left a large sum of money to the National Academy of Sciences (the Watson Fund), the interest of which is used to further astronomical research.

WATSON, JOHN (1847–1939), Canadian philosopher, born in Glasgow. At the age of twenty-five he was appointed professor of logic, metaphysics, and ethics at Queen's University, Kingston, Canada. Aside from numerous papers in philosophical journals, his publications include *Kant and His English Critics* (1881), *Schelling's Transcendental Idealism* (1882), *The Philosophy of Kant as Contained in Extracts from His Own Writings* (1888), *Comte, Mill, and Spencer* (1895), *An Outline of Philosophy* (1898), *The Philosophical Basis of Religion* (1907), *The Philosophy of Kant Explained* (1908), *The Interpretation of Religious Experience* (1912), and *The State in Peace and War* (1919).

WATSON, JOHN, better known by his pen name IAN MACLAREN (1850–1907), British clergyman and author, born of Scottish parentage in Manningtree, Essex, England. He was ordained minister of Logiealmond Free Church in 1875, and from 1880 to 1905 was minister of Sefton Park Presbyterian Church, Liverpool. Watson was Lyman Beecher lecturer at Yale University in 1896, and published his lectures under the title *The Cure of Souls* (1896). Among his best-known stories of Scottish life are *Beside the Bonnie Brier Bush* (1894; dramatized 1905), *The Days of Auld Lang Syne* (1895), *Kate Carnegie* (1896), *The Life of the Master* (1901), and *Graham of Claverhouse* (1907).

WATSON, JOHN BROADUS (1878–), American psychologist, born in Greenville, S.C., and educated at Furman University and the University of Chicago. He served as instructor in psychology at the University of Chicago until 1908, when he was appointed professor of experimental and comparative psychology and director of the psychological laboratory at Johns Hopkins University. There he served until 1920, when he announced his retirement from academic life. He lectured at the New School for Social Research, however, for several semesters following 1921. In 1924 he became a vice-president of the J. Walter Thompson advertising agency, and later, of the William Esty and Company agency. Watson was a vigorous exponent of the psychological school of thought known as behaviorism (q.v.; see also PSYCHOLOGY: *Types of Behavior*). He was editor of the *Psychological Review* from 1908 to 1915, joint editor of the *Journal of Animal Behavior,* and editor of the *Journal of Experimental Psychology* from 1915 to 1927. His works include *Animal Education* (1903), *Behavior—An Introduction to Comparative Psychology* (1914), *Behaviorism* (1925), *Psychological Care of Infant and Child* (1928), and *Ways of Behaviorism* (1928).

WATSON, JOHN CRITTENDEN (1842–1923), American naval officer, born in Frankfort, Ky. He became a master in the navy in 1861, and served throughout the Civil War. In the Spanish-American War he commanded the blockading squadron on the North Cuban coast and subsequently was made commander in chief of the Eastern Squadron, which was to threaten the Spanish coast and thus force the return of the Spanish fleet, bound for Manila. News of the movement having reached Spain, the Spanish fleet was recalled before Watson could execute his orders, and Watson resumed charge of the blockade of the northern coast of Cuba. He was commandant of the Mare Island Navy Yard (1898–99) and afterward commander in chief of the naval forces on the Asiatic Station (1899–1900). In 1902 he was president of the Naval Examining and Retiring Boards.

WATSON, SERENO (1826–92), American botanist, born in East Windsor Hill, Conn., and educated at Yale University and the University of New York. He was botanist of the United States Geological Survey, making collections in the Great Basin region, under Clarence King, the first head of the U.S. Geographical Survey; Watson's findings were published as a volume of King's *Report* in 1870. Upon his return from this survey, Watson became an assistant in the Gray Herbarium at Harvard University, and at the death of Dr. Asa Gray in 1888, he was made curator. He also wrote *Botany of California* (1876), with Gray and W.H. Brewer; *Bibliographical Index to North American Botany* (1878); numerous papers, collected and published as *Contributions to American Botany* (1873–91); and, with J.M. Coulter, he revised and extended Gray's *Manual of Botany* (1890).

WATSON, THOMAS (about 1557–92), English poet, born probably in London. He wrote mainly in Latin but is best known for his English works *Hecatompathia* (1582) and *Teares of Fancy* (1593).

WATSON, THOMAS E(DWARD) (1856–1922), American politician and author, born in Columbia Co., Ga. In 1896 he secured the nomination on the People's Party ticket with the American political leader William Jennings Bryan. In 1904 he was nominated for President by the People's Party. Several magazines owned by Watson opposed conscription for service abroad, and were barred from the mails in 1917. He was elected to the United States Senate for the term 1921–27. His writings include *Napoleon* (1902; 1913), *Life and Times of Thomas Jefferson* (1903), and *Life and Times of Andrew Jackson* (1907).

WATSON, THOMAS LEONARD (1871–1924), American geologist, born in Chatham, Va. He was professor of economic geology at the University of Virginia and afterward became head of the school of geology there. With H. Ries he was associated in the authorship of *Engineering Geology* (1914) and *Elements of Engineering Geology* (1921).

WATSON, SIR WILLIAM (1858–1935), English poet, born in Burley-in-Wharfedale, Yorkshire. His *Epigrams of Art, Life, and Nature* (1884) was his first book to attract attention. In 1885 he attacked the British policy in Egypt in sonnets entitled *Ver Tenebrosum.* Following the death of Alfred Austin in 1913, the honor of the laureateship was conferred on Robert Bridges, Watson having been passed over because, as rumor alleged, of his authorship of *The Woman with a Serpent's Tongue,* said to have been aimed at the wife of the prime minister. His sonnets in the *Purple East* contain some of his best work. He was knighted in 1917. Among his later books are *Lyric Love* (1892), *The Eloping Angels* (1893), *Excursions in Criticism* (1893), *Odes and Other Poems* (1894), *The Father of the Forest* (1895), *Sable and Purple* (1910), *Heralds of the Dawn* (1912), *The Muse in Exile* (1913), *Retrogression* (1916), *Ireland Unfreed* (1922), *Poems Brief and New* (1925), and *Selected Poems with Notes by the Author* (1928).

WATSONVILLE, a city of Santa Cruz Co., Calif., situated on the Pajaro R., 47 miles s.

Fisher Scientific Co.

Above: It is believed that the young James Watt first became interested in steam pressure by observing the action of a boiling teakettle. Left: James Watt (from drawing).

of San Jose. It is served by a railroad, maintains a municipal airport, and is the shipping point of a fertile agricultural region noted for vegetables, fruits and berries, and livestock. More than 20,000 carloads of lettuce are shipped annually from Watsonville, and the city is an important center of the frozen-food industry. Among the industrial establishments in the city are food processing and freezing plants, canneries, packing plants, creameries, dehydrating plants, saltworks, lumber and planing mills, and factories producing ice, cider, vinegar, tobacco products, fertilizers, magnesia products, neon signs, concrete pipe, building materials, harmonicas, toys, dental equipment, and wooden boxes. Watsonville was first settled in 1851. It was organized as a village in 1868 and incorporated as a city in 1903. Pop. (1947) 11,458.

WATT. See ELECTRICAL UNITS.

WATT, JAMES (1736–1819), Scottish inventor and mechanical engineer, born in Greenock. At the age of eighteen he went to London to serve an apprenticeship as a mathematical-instrument maker; his apprenticeship was interrupted by illness, and never completed. Nevertheless he succeeded in obtaining an appointment to the University of Glasgow in 1757 as mathematical-instrument maker. He early became interested in making improvements in the steam-driven engine, invented by the English engineer Thomas Newcomen and applied to the removal of water from mines. After performing various experiments to determine the properties of steam,

Detail from a signboard painted by Antoine Watteau depicting an art dealer's shop

Watt devised a separate condenser which prevented loss of steam in the cylinder, and in 1769 took out his first patent, which covered this device and other improvements on Newcomen's engine, such as steam-jacketing and a closed cylinder. At this time he was the partner of John Roebuck, who had financed his researches, in the manufacture of steam engines; in 1775 Roebuck's interest was taken over by Matthew Boulton, owner of the Soho Engineering Works at Birmingham. The partnership was on the verge of bankruptcy for almost twenty years, before it became a financial success. Watt retired from the firm in 1800.

In 1775 Watt obtained a twenty-five year extension of the original steam engine patent, and between 1781 and 1785, he took out patents for several other inventions, including a planetary gear system, a double engine, a centrifugal governor, a recording steam indicator, and a smokeless furnace. Watt opposed the use of high-pressure steam and the compound expansion engine, which have since become features of the modern steam engine (see STEAM AND STEAM ENGINEERING), as well as the proposal to use the steam engine as a source of power for a rail-borne vehicle.

Watt introduced the term horsepower, (q.v.), and the electrical unit of power, the *watt,* was named in his honor. Watt also acquired a reputation as a civil engineer, making several surveys of canal routes and inventing, in 1767, an attachment which adapted telescopes for use in measurement of distance. Among other inventions credited to Watt are devices for copying sculptures and manuscripts.

WATTEAU, ANTOINE (1684–1721), French genre painter, born in Valenciennes. In 1702 he went to Paris, where he earned a livelihood by hack work for a picture dealer. He later got employment with the decorator of the Luxembourg, and in 1711 became a student at the Academy. In 1717 he was made a member of the Academy, and became famous as the creator of a new type of art. He died of consumption in Nogent, near Paris. In virtue of their charm and graceful design, the pictures of this master of the rococo age are still much favored. He is represented in nearly all the large public galleries of Europe, including the Hermitage, Leningrad; the Dresden Gallery, the Prado, Madrid; Chantilly Museum, Paris; the National galleries of Scotland and Ireland; the Dulwich Gallery, London; Buckingham Palace, London; and the Wallace collection, London.

WATTERSON, HENRY (1840–1921), American journalist and orator, born in Washington, D.C. He entered journalism in Washington as reporter and editorial writer for the *States.* Watterson served in the Confederate Army in 1861–62 as private soldier and aide-de-camp successively to generals Nathaniel Bedford Forrest and Leonidas Polk. In 1862–63 he edited the Chattanooga *Rebel.* In 1864 he was again in military service as chief of scouts to Gen. Joseph Eggleston Johnston. He edited the *Republican Banner* of Nashville, 1865–68, and then became editor in chief of the Louisville *Journal.* The latter newspaper was merged with the *Democrat* in 1868 to make the *Courier-Journal,* of which Watterson became the editor. Under his direction this newspaper came to occupy a foremost place in American journalism. In 1912 he became involved in the disagreement between the American statesman Woodrow Wilson and the journalist George Brinton McClellan Harvey. Watterson opposed Wilson's nomination and only casually supported the Democratic ticket, but in 1915 the President and he were partially reconciled. He was sometimes spoken of as "Marse Henry" Watterson. His writings include *Oddities in Southern Life and Character* (1882), *History of the Spanish-American War* (1899), and *The Compromises of Life: Lectures and Addresses* (1903; 1906).

WATTLE, a method of marking range cattle for identification; it was at one time used in addition to the brand (see BRANDING) as a substitute for, or in addition to, the earmark. The wattle was made by slitting the dewlap in such a manner that when the animal was viewed in profile, characteristic knobs, loops, or pendants would show. Wattles were occasionally made on the jaw or shoulder.

WATTLEBIRD, common name applied to an oscine bird, the Australian honey eater (q.v.), *Coleia (Anthochaera) carunculata,* belonging to the family Meliphagidae. The bird is colored grayish brown above and below, each feather on the upper parts being striped and bordered with white. It reaches a length of 12 inches; the long, wide, tapering tail, which constitutes one third of the total length, is brown, tipped with white. The wattlebird derives its name from the reddish 6-inch long wattle that hangs on each side of the throat. Several other birds are commonly, but erroneously, called wattlebirds. The wattle crow, or *kokako,* of New Zealand belongs to the genus *Callaeas* and is closely related to the jays (q.v.). It is slate gray and brown above and below, and has a black face; a fleshy wattle hangs from each side of the lower mandible. *Callaeas cinerea,* native to the South Island of New Zealand, bears orange wattles; *Callaeas wilsoni,* of the North Island, bears blue wattles.

WATTS, ALARIC ALEXANDER (1794–1864), English journalist and poet, born in London. He was editor of the *Leeds Intelligencer* (1822–25) and the *Manchester Courier* (1825–26), took part in establishing (1827) the London *Standard,* a Conservative newspaper, and founded the *United Service Gazette* (1833). In the meantime he had begun the *Literary Souvenir* (1824), which became one of the most successful of the annuals. It was suspended in 1838. During the next ten years he was engaged in starting several provincial newspapers in the Conservative interest. Though these undertakings led to bankruptcy (1850), he had organized the subsequently popular plan of supplying sheets of general news printed in London to supplement the local news of country newspapers. In 1856 he projected and edited *Men of the Time,* a useful biographical dictionary of contemporary men. The dictionary was continued, under varying titles, until 1901, when it was incorporated with *Who's Who.* As a poet, Watts enjoyed a wide reputation for *Poetical Sketches* (1823; privately printed, 1822) and *Lyrics of the Heart* (1850).

WATTS, GEORGE FREDERICK (1817–1904) English painter and sculptor, born in London. He attracted notice by his cartoon of *Caractacus* sent to Westminster Hall in 1843, and again by pictures of *Echo* and *King Alfred* in 1847. Watts was essentially a painter of literary subject matter, notable for his individuality, dignity, extreme correctness in drawing, splendid color, and exquisite purity of atmosphere. Among his more important paintings are "Paolo and Francesca" (1848), "Fata Morgana" (1848), "Life's Illusions" (1849), "Love and Death" (1877), "Watchman, what of the Night?" (1880), "Hope" (1886), and "Love Triumphant" (1898). "Love and Life", exhibited at the Columbian Exposition in Chicago (1893), was afterward presented to the United States, and is now in the White House. The exhibition of his works at the Grosvenor Gallery (1882) included one of his admirable sculptures. Among his notable works of sculpture were also a fresco of St. George in the houses of Parliament, and another in Lincoln's Inn. He presented and bequeathed a large number of his pictures to the National Portrait Gallery, and to the galleries of Edinburgh, Dublin, Nottingham, Manchester, and Norwich.

WATTS, ISAAC (1674–1748), English clergyman and hymn writer, born in Southampton. He became minister of the Independent Church in Mark Lane, London (1702). He was counted among the best preachers of his time. His theological works were numerous. His treatise on *Logic* was for a time a textbook at Oxford University. Watts' best-known work is his *Divine and Moral Songs for Children* (1715). His *Horæ Lyricæ* (1705), *Hymns and Spiritual Songs* (1707–09), and *Psalms of David Imitated* (1719) contain some of the most popular hymns in the English language.

WATTS, SIR PHILIP (1850–1926), British naval constructor, educated at the College of Naval Architecture. Watts designed and built many notable ships. As director of naval construction in the Admiralty (1901–11), he revolutionized naval tactics and battleship design by bringing out the battleship *Dreadnought* (q.v.) and the first battle cruisers.

WATTS, ROBERT (1820–95), Irish Presbyterian minister and theologian, born in Moneylane, County Down. He came to the United States in early manhood, and graduated from Washington College, Lexington, Va., in 1849, and from Princeton Theological Seminary in 1852. He founded in Philadelphia in 1852 a Presbyterian mission which was organized under his pastorate as the Westminster Church in 1856. In 1863 he accepted a call to the Lower Gloucester Street Church, Dublin. He became professor of systematic theology in the Assembly's College, Belfast, in 1866. Watts was a strong conservative in theology, and was especially opposed to the influence of German exegesis. He was the author of *Calvin and Calvinism* (1866), *Utilitarianism* (1868), *What Is Presbyterianism?* (1870), *Arminian Departures from Reformation Principles* (1871), *Dr. Briggs's Theology Traced to Its Organic Principle* (1891), and *Driver's Introduction Examined* (1892).

WATTS, THOMAS HILL (1819–92), American lawyer and politician, born in Butler Co., Ala. During the Civil War he served for a time as colonel in the Confederate Army and as attorney general in the cabinet of the president of the Confederacy, Jefferson Davis (1862–63). He was governor of Alabama (1863–65).

WATTS-DUNTON, THEODORE (1832–1914), English critic and poet, born in St. Ives, Huntingdonshire. In 1897 he added his mother's name Dunton to his father's. He studied law,

Farrar, Straus & Company
Alec Waugh

and was called to the bar in 1863, but soon turned to literature and became one of the most influential literary and art critics of the day, contributing important critical articles to works of reference and to the more important magazines and reviews. The English poets Dante Gabriel Rossetti and Algernon Charles Swinburne were his intimate friends. He edited the English writer George Borrow's *Lavengro* and *Romany Rye,* and his writings include *The Coming of Love* (poems, 1897), and *Alwyn,* a gypsy romance, in which he depicted Rossetti as D'Arcy (1898).

WAUGH, the name of a distinguished British literary family, the most notable members of which are the following.

1. ARTHUR WAUGH (1866–1943), biographer, editor, and literary critic, born in Midsomer Norton, Somersetshire, and educated at New College, Oxford University. In 1896 he edited the *Lives of the Poets* by the 18th-century critic and lexicographer Samuel Johnson (q.v.). He also wrote biographies of the Victorian poets Robert Browning and Alfred, Lord Tennyson. Representative specimens of his literary criticism are contained in *Reticence in Literature* (1915) and *One Man's Road* (1931). Waugh served as director (1902–30) and chairman (1926–36) of the publishing firm of Chapman and Hall, Ltd., of London.

2. ALEC, in full, ALEXANDER RABAN WAUGH (1898–   ), son of Arthur Waugh, author, editorial consultant, and traveler, born in London, and educated during World War I at the Royal Military College, Sandhurst. He had a military career, serving in World Wars I and II with the British Expeditionary Force in France (1917–18; 1940), and in World War II with the Middle East Force (1941) and with the Persia and Iraq Command, known as the Paiforce (1942–45). Waugh is the author of novels and short stories. His most notable works are *The Loom of Youth* (1917), *Kept* (1925), *Nor Many Waters* (1928), *Most Women* (1931), *Wheels within Wheels* (1933), *The Balliols* (1934), *Eight Short Stories* (1937), *Going Their Own Ways* (1938), *No Truce with Time* (1941), and *Unclouded Summer* (1948).

3. EVELYN ARTHUR ST. JOHN WAUGH (1903–   ), brother of Alec Waugh, writer, born in London, and educated at Hertford College, Oxford University. In 1930 he became a convert to Roman Catholicism. During World War II, Waugh received a commission in the Royal Marines (1939), served with the eighth Commando (q.v.) unit in the Middle East, and was subsequently transferred to the Royal House Guards, being discharged in 1945 with the rank of captain. Waugh is the author of novels distinguished for their brilliant satire on the manners and morals of decadent British aristocracy. His works include *Decline and Fall* (1928), *Vile Bodies* (1930), *Remote People* (1932), *Black Mischief* (1932), *Handful of Dust* (1934), *Put Out More Flags* (1942), *Brideshead Revisited* (1945), *The Loved One* (1948), *Scott King's Modern Europe* (1948), and *Helena* (1950).

WAUGH, FREDERICK JUDD (1861–1940), American marine painter and illustrator, born in Bordentown, N.J. He is represented in most American and in some English public collections, among his paintings being "The Great Deep" and "The Roaring Forties" (Metropolitan Museum of Art, New York City). The National Academy of Design awarded him the Palmer Memorial marine prize (1929).

WAUKEGAN, city and county seat of Lake County, Ill., on Lake Michigan, 35 miles N. of Chicago. It is a popular summer resort and residential suburb of Chicago. It has a fine harbor and mineral springs. Pop. (1940) 34,241.

WAUKESHA, county seat of Waukesha Co., Wis., situated on the Fox R., 16 miles w. of Milwaukee. It is served by rail and maintains a municipal airport. The city is the center and shipping point of a rich farming, dairying, stock-raising, and quarrying area, and is a noted health resort, renowned for its mineral springs. Pure-bred cattle, raw and certified milk, and a famous mineral water known as "White Rock" are shipped in vast quantities from the city. Among the industries in the city are the bottling of mineral water, brewing, and the manufacture of milk products, ice cream, gelatin desserts, bottle-washing machinery, carbonated beverages, lumber, sash and doors, residential and industrial shades, leather products, church furniture, cement tile, concrete products, iron, aluminum, and steel castings, agricultural machinery, tools, foundry patterns, hydraulic jacks, automobile parts, metal stampings, trucks, steel fences, stainless-steel tanks, steel sash, janitor supplies, and veterinary medicines. Waukesha is the site of Carroll College (Presbyterian), founded in 1846 and the oldest college in the State, of the Wisconsin Industrial School for Boys, and of a U.S. veterans hospital. In the city and vicinity are numerous sanatoriums and health resorts, and the city maintains a municipal park system with abundant recreational facilities. Waukesha was founded in 1834 as Prairieville. It was incorporated as the village of Waukesha in 1852 and chartered as a city in 1896. Pop. (1950) 21,186.

WAUKON, county seat of Allamakee County, Iowa, 90 miles N.W. of Dubuque. It is in a rich farming district, and is a shipping point for livestock and grain. Pop. (1940) 2972.

WAUPACA, county seat of Waupaca Co., Wis., situated about 45 miles N.W. of Oshkosh. It is served by two railroads, and is surrounded by a farming and stock-raising area, in which potatoes are an important crop. Waupaca is especially noted as a summer resort; in the vicinity are numerous lakes and streams providing excellent recreational facilities, and nearby are medicinal springs. Pop. (1948 est.) 4000.

WAUPUN, a city of Dodge and Fond du Lac counties, Wis., situated about 65 miles N.W. of Milwaukee, in a dairying and farming area. Among the industrial establishments in the city are a milk condensery, vegetable canneries, and factories producing shoes, rivets, vulcanizers, metal tanks, ladders, and windmills. Waupun is the site of the Wisconsin State Prison and of the State Central Hospital for the Insane. The city was founded in 1838 and incorporated in 1857. Pop. (1940) 6798.

WAURIKA, county seat of Jefferson County, Okla., 100 miles s. by w. of Oklahoma City. Pop. (1940) 2458.

WAUSAU, county seat of Marathon County, Wis., on the Wisconsin River, 85 miles N.W. of Green Bay. It is a popular summer and winter resort. The Big Bull Falls furnishes power for its varied industries. Pop. (1950) 30,386.

WAUSEON, county seat of Fulton Co., Ohio, situated 33 miles w. of Toledo. It is served by three railroads. The canning of various food products is a principal industry in the village. Wauseon was settled in 1835 and incorporated as a village in 1854. Pop. (1948) 3154.

WAUWATOSA, a city of Milwaukee Co., Wis., adjoining the city of Milwaukee on the w. Wauwatosa is a residential suburb of Milwaukee, with some industries, notably the manufacture of chemicals, metal products, concrete products, metal castings, and lumber products. The city was settled in 1834 and incorporated in 1897. Pop. (1950) 33,300.

WAVE, a displacement of some part of a medium due to the propagation of a disturbance through the medium. Many waves come in groups called *trains,* in which one wave follows another, so that the movement of the displaced elements of the medium is a periodic vibration. Any vibrating object can set up a train of waves, and the transmission of vibration is always by means of waves; see VIBRATION. Waves are caused by the application of energy, and are the most important means of transmission of energy between objects which are not contiguous. Much of the development of modern science has followed from the elaboration of the theory of waves and wave motion.

If one end of a long rope is tied to a wall and the other end is vigorously shaken once, a single wave proceeds along the rope to the wall; under some circumstances, the wave may be reflected back from the wall along the rope. In this example of a simple type of wave, it is obvious that the transmission of the wave does not involve the transmission of any matter. Only energy is transmitted along the rope. As the wave passes, each part of the rope moves up and down once, and then remains where it was before the wave passed. This type of wave is called a *transverse wave,* because the motion of each part of the rope is in a direction perpendicular to the direction of wave propagation.

Another type of wave, called a *longitudinal wave,* consists of motions of the particles in the direction of the wave propagation or exactly opposite to that direction. If, instead of a rope, a coiled spring is used, and stretched abruptly, a longitudinal wave proceeds down the spring. As it passes each point on the spring, that part is alternately stretched and relaxed, gradually returning to normal. As before, the movement of the wave is accompanied by a transfer of energy, but no material accompanies the progress of the disturbance. The waves described above are called *simple* because they are single, not part of a wave train.

Simple waves illustrate two of the important characteristics of all waves: *velocity* and *amplitude.* The velocity is the speed of propagation of the disturbance; the amplitude is the extent of the disturbance. A fundamental property of waves is the dependence of velocity on the nature of the medium alone, so that velocity is the same for waves of greatly different amplitudes and frequencies. For example, the velocity of the wave along the rope described above depends only on the weight of the rope and the tension on the rope. The velocity can be doubled by quadrupling the tension; it can be halved by quadrupling the weight per foot of the rope; but it cannot be changed in any way by the vigor or nature of the disturbance which originates it. In the case of the spring the velocity is somewhat more complex, and depends among other things on the elastic properties of the spring; nonetheless, it does not depend on amplitude or frequency.

When the disturbance which originates a wave is a periodic motion, such as a vibration, waves progress continuously through the medium, one wave beginning as the previous wave ends. In the first example above, shaking the rope continuously up and down, produces a continuous train of waves along the rope. Each point along the rope (ignoring for the moment the result of reflected waves) moves periodically up and down; as the *crest* of each wave passes a particular point on the rope, it is at its highest position; as the wave passes on and the *trough* reaches this point, the rope is at its lowest position.

For illustration, assume that the rope has such tension and weight that the waves move along it at ten feet per second; assume also that the rope is shaken up and down once each second. Then the crests of the wave would occur once in each ten feet along the rope, and a crest would pass any point once every second. In technical terms, the *wave length* would then be ten feet, and the *frequency* one cycle

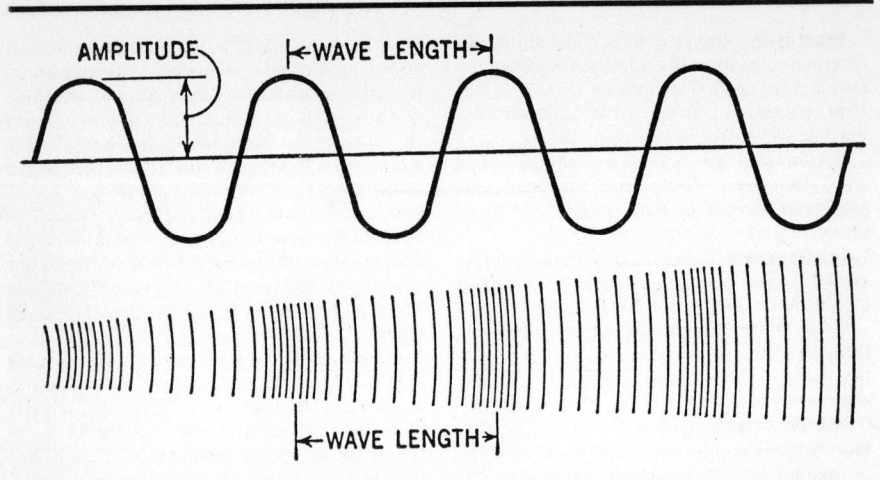

Diagram showing principles of wave amplitude and wave length. Bottom: A sound wave.

per second. If the shaking were done twice as fast, once up and down every half second, the velocity of the waves would still be ten feet per second, but the wave length would be reduced to five feet, and the frequency would become two cycles per second. These examples illustrate the fundamental rule of wave trains: the velocity of propagation is equal to the wave length times the frequency.

Interference. When two waves meet at a point, they may meet crest to crest, or trough to trough, and so reinforce one another; on the other hand, they may be crest to trough, or trough to crest, and so counteract one another. This latter phenomenon is called interference (q.v.; see also BEAT; DIFFRACTION). In the example above of continuous shaking of the rope, reflection was ignored. If reflection from the wall is perfectly efficient, then two waves of equal amplitude and frequency move through the rope with the same velocity, but in opposite directions, and interference results. At certain points in the rope, one wave is always half a wave length ahead of the other, so that the crest of one wave arrives at the same time as the trough of the other. Because velocity of the waves is the same in each direction, such points do not move at all, and are called *nodes*. At points midway between the nodes, both crests arrive at once, and a half cycle later both troughs arrive at once. Such points move rapidly back and forth with an amplitude twice as great as that of the unreflected wave. At intermediate points, the amplitude is intermediate between this double amplitude and the zero amplitude of the node. Thus the rope is divided into sections one wave length long by the nodes, which do not progress along the rope, while the rope between nodes vibrates back and forth. The resultant wave is called a *standing wave* or *stationary wave*.

Standing waves are present in vibrating strings such as the strings of musical instruments. A violin string, for instance, when bowed or plucked, vibrates as a whole, with nodes only at the ends, and also vibrates in halves, with a node at the center, and in thirds with two equally spaced nodes, and in various other fractions, all simultaneously. The vibration as a whole produces the fundamental note, and the other vibrations produce the various harmonics (q.v.). The motion of any particular point element of the string is extremely complex, as it consists of the sum of all the different motions in response to all the different modes of vibration. Each mode of vibration may be thought of as a simple vibration, or as a standing wave caused by waves moving along the string and being repeatedly reflected at each end. Nodes in vibrating plates produce Chladni (q.v.) figures.

The most modern theory of the atom is explained by analogy to a set of standing waves, the amplitude of each wave at any point being a measure of the probability that a particle will be found at that point. Much of modern theoretical physics is based on similar standing waves. See QUANTUM MECHANICS.

Sound is a longitudinal wave of alternate condensations and rarefactions, transmitted through solid, liquid, or gaseous matter. The amplitude determines the **intensity** of sound (q.v.), and the frequency determines pitch.

Light is a transverse wave. The amplitude determines the intensity and the frequency determines the color. The medium through which light waves are transmitted is not easily defined, however; see WAVES, ELECTROMAGNETIC.

Earthquakes are waves, both longitudinal and transverse, transmitted through the ground as a result of some violent motion in the earth's crust. At the extremely large amplitudes characteristic of earthquakes the velocity is slightly increased, an exception to the rule of constant velocity. See EARTHQUAKE.

Ocean Waves. Sound waves travel efficiently through water with a speed of almost a mile per second. The various types of familiar waves on the surface of water are essentially transverse waves which move along the surface at considerably lower speeds than a mile per second, and have little or no effect on the interior of the water, so long as the depth exceeds the amplitude of the waves.

If a rock is dropped into a pool, a group of circular waves spreads out from the point of impact. A cork floating in the pool bobs up and down as the waves pass, but does not move with the waves. These waves are less complex than ocean waves and swells, which are created by the wind. If wind blows upon the surface of water, it almost immediately creates tiny waves with a wave length of about one inch, moving in the direction toward which the wind is blowing, at a velocity considerably less than that of the wind. If the wind continues to blow over these waves they increase in size and speed. Some hundreds of miles of open water are necessary for maximum size and speed to be reached with even a moderate wind. When such an equilibrium has been reached, the waves move at only two to three knots (nautical miles per hour) less than the wind; their height in feet is about equal to their speed in knots, and their wave length is very great; waves traveling at 60 knots, for example, have a wave length of about 2000 feet. Inasmuch as doubling their velocity doubles the height of the waves, but quadruples their length, the rapidly moving waves of storms are less steep than the slower waves of milder weather; however, high wave crests may hide the horizon from a person on the deck of a ship, and without the horizon as a reference the observer is likely to overestimate the height of the waves while underestimating their length, and thus to believe that they are far steeper than is actually the case.

If the wind blows over the open ocean long enough to build up such waves as described above, and then dies down, the waves continue on for hundreds of miles, virtually without abatement. Such waves without wind constitute a *swell,* and often persist through a region where a wind is causing waves in quite a different direction; the wind-borne waves and the swell may be superimposed on one another without mutual effect, just as a violin string can vibrate in fundamental and overtones simultaneously, or the air can carry to the ear at one time all of the different simultaneous sounds of an orchestra.

When waves or swell reach shallow water, the nature of the wave movement changes. When the depth of the bottom becomes less

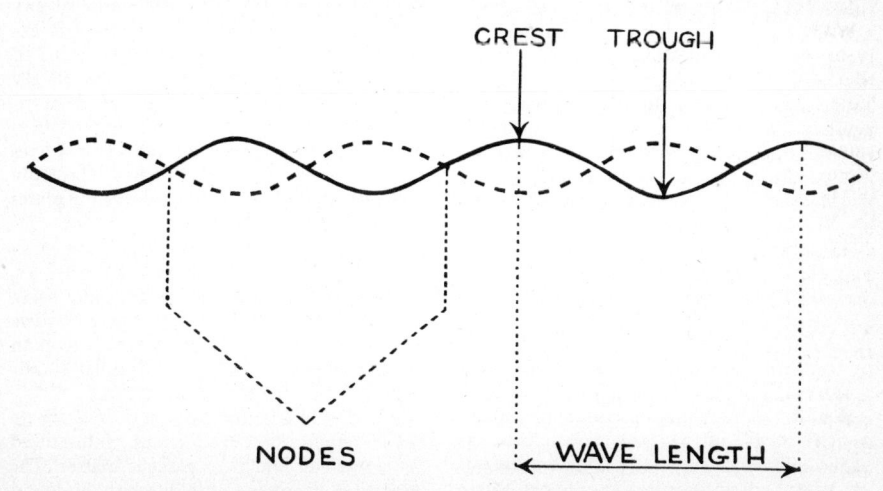

Diagram illustrating the principle of continuous wave motion

Sir Archibald Percival Wavell

than the wave length, the speed and wave length begin to decrease; when the depth becomes less than the amplitude, the troughs of the waves are slowed down more than the crests, so that the wave front gradually becomes steeper, and the crest eventually curves over and falls, forming a breaker. By this time the character of the wave has so changed that the water is transported with the wave front, and the wave rushing into shore is composed of moving water, much like a miniature bore (q.v.).

WAVELL, SIR ARCHIBALD PERCIVAL (1883–1950), British soldier, born in Colchester, and educated at Royal Military College, Sandhurst, and Staff College. He served in the South African War, Indian frontier campaigns, World War I, and was promoted through the ranks, becoming major general in 1933. Most familiar with the conditions in the Middle East, he was chief of this command in 1940–41, when the Italian armies in Libya were subjected to heavy defeats (Dec., 1940–Feb., 1941). He was later transferred to India, appointed supreme commander, Unified Southwest Pacific Area Command, in 1942. He was made viceroy of India and was raised to the peerage in 1943.

WAVELLITE, a rare, translucent mineral, composed of hydrous aluminum phosphate, $Al_2(OH)_3(PO_4)_2 \cdot 5H_2O$, and crystallizing in the orthorhombic system. It has a hardness of $3\frac{1}{2}$ to 4, a specific gravity of 2.33, and shines with a vitreous luster. The color ranges from white, yellow, or green, to brown. Wavellite is found in radiating globular aggregates, principally in the minerals limonite and phosphorite. It occurs in the United States in several areas of Pennsylvania and Arkansas, and is also found in Devonshire, England.

WAVERLY, county seat of Bremer Co., Iowa, situated on the Cedar R., about 70 miles N.W. of Cedar Rapids. It is served by four railroads, and is the center of an agricultural area in which livestock, poultry, and general farm crops are the principal products. Industrial establishments in the city include creameries, condenseries, corn canneries, printing and publishing plants, and factories manufacturing cheese, chemicals, and furniture. Waverly is the site of Wartburg College (Lutheran), established in 1868, on the campus of which is the Waverly Museum, containing collections of artifacts of New Guinea and an extensive ornithological exhibit. Pop. (1940) 4156.

WAVERLY, a village of Tioga Co., N.Y., situated on the Chemung R., 18 miles S.E. of Elmira, and adjoining the Pennsylvania boroughs of South Waverly, Sayre, and Athens, which are separated from Waverly only by the State line. Waverly is served by three railroads, and is a shipping point for an agricultural area producing vegetables, fruits, poultry, and dairy products. The village was incorporated in 1863. Pop. (1940) 5450.

WAVES. See WOMEN ACCEPTED FOR VOLUNTEER EMERGENCY SERVICE.

WAVES, ELECTROMAGNETIC, collective term for the waves (radio waves) which are propagated outward from a source of electramagnetic disturbance (such as a spark), and for a large number of related forms of radiation, including light, which show more or less similar properties. The concept of electromagnetic waves originated almost entirely with one man, the Scottish physicist James Clerk Maxwell. In a series of papers which he wrote in the 1860's and 1870's, Maxwell advanced the idea of the electromagnetic wave, discovered its major properties (with the aid of extremely complex mathematics), proposed that light consisted of such waves, and made a number of specific predictions. The German physicist Heinrich Hertz verified a number of these predictions about 1887, when he generated electromagnetic waves by means of an electric spark, and showed that they possessed many of the properties of light, such as reflection, refraction, and polarization.

A number of properties of light indicate its

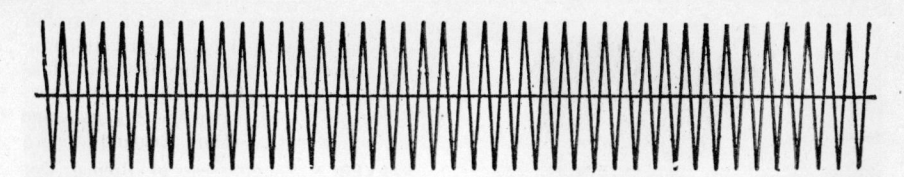

Diagram showing the form of electromagnetic waves

connection with electricity and magnetism. For example, in the Kerr effect (discovered in 1875 by the Scottish physicist John Kerr), the effect of a liquid on a beam of polarized light is changed by applying an electric field to the liquid. In the Faraday effect (discovered in 1845 by the English scientist Michael Faraday), the effect of a piece of glass on a beam of polarized light is changed by applying a magnetic field to the glass. These and similar phenomena strongly suggest that light is electromagnetic in nature. The strongest evidence for this, however, is a quantitative prediction made by Maxwell and confirmed in numerous experiments by later physicists, that the speed of light in a vacuum is exactly equal to the ratio of an electromagnetic unit of electric current to an electrostatic unit of electric current; see ELECTRICAL UNITS. There is no apparent reason why this ratio should have any relation to the speed of light; that the two numbers are precisely equal is strong proof of the validity of Maxwell's theory of the electromagnetic nature of light, and has been hailed as one of the great unifications in physical science.

Physicists had known since the early 19th century that light consists of a transverse wave (see WAVE), but they originally assumed that the wave is mechanical, involving the yielding of some extremely diffuse and highly elastic medium which they called ether (q.v.). According to Maxwell's electromagnetic theory, the movement is not of a material object, but of an electric and a magnetic field. The concepts of such fields had been introduced by Michael Faraday some years before; see FIELD. Scientists knew that the collapse of an electric field creates a magnetic field, while the collapse of a magnetic field creates an electric field. An electromagnetic wave, according to Maxwell, consists of a transverse electric wave in one plane, and a transverse magnetic wave in a perpendicular plane; the line of intersection of these planes is the direction of motion of the wave. As the magnetic wave decreases the electric wave grows, and vice versa, so that they support one another in their transfer of energy across empty space. Maxwell still postulated an "ether" in which his waves move, but according to his concept, ether is much more tenuous than the mechanical ether which had been postulated earlier, and the theory suffered little change when all concept of ether was dropped with the advent of the theory of relativity (q.v.).

Electromagnetic waves include radio, infrared or radiant heat, visible light, ultraviolet, and X rays. These waves differ from each other only in their frequencies. The entire group occupies a range some fifty times the range of visible light; see FREQUENCY. In the regions commonly called radio waves, of long wave length and comparatively low frequency, the Maxwell theory is still valid: no experimental exceptions have yet been found to indicate that the nature of such radiation is other than electromagnetic, undulatory, and continuous. In the remaining regions of the electromagnetic spectrum, however, particularly those in which the wave length is short and the frequency high, there is increasing evidence that the energy is radiated in discrete units called *quanta,* and not as waves; see QUANTUM MECHANICS.

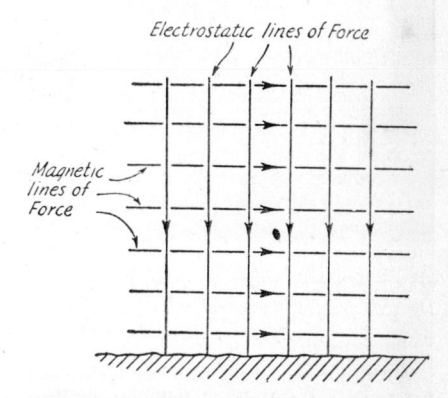

Direction of electromagnetic waves is determined by directions of intersecting electrostatic and magnetic lines of force. Here a wave is moving out of page, toward reader.

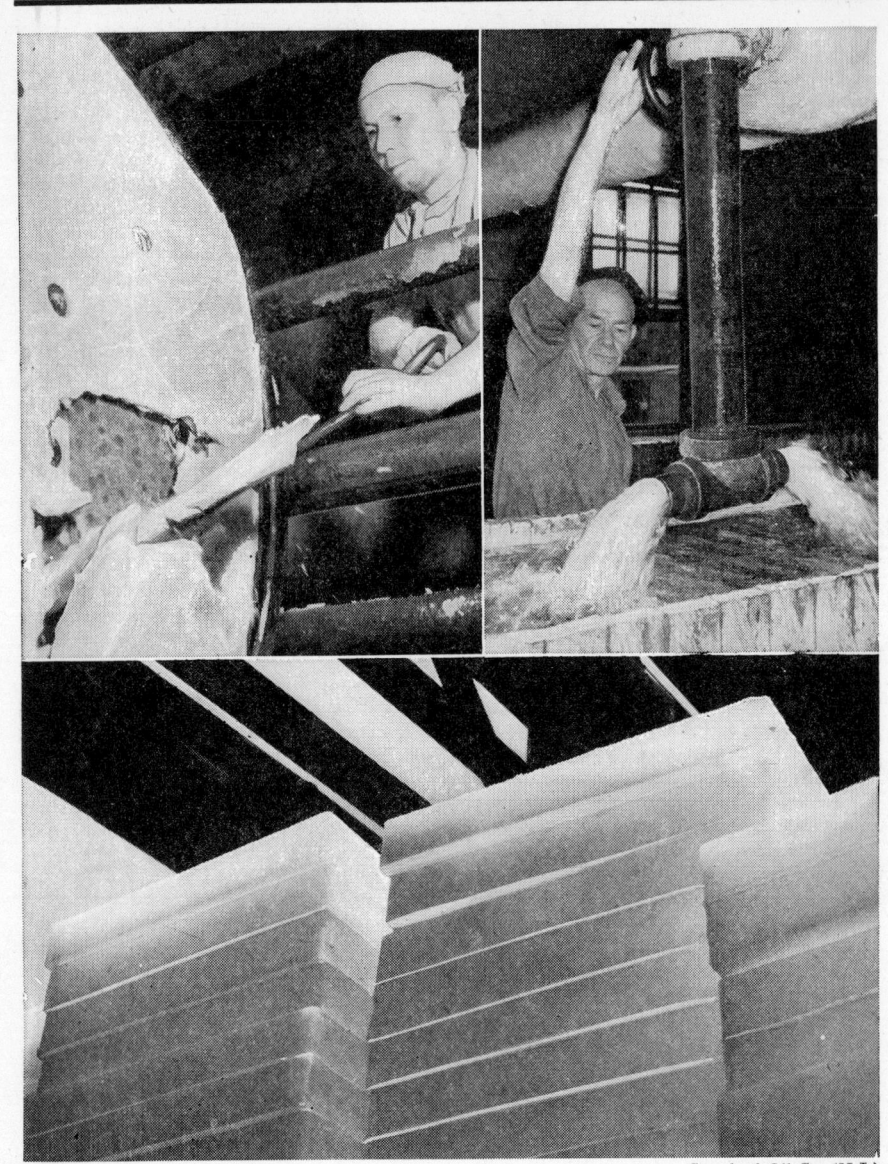

MANUFACTURING PARAFFIN WAX. *Top, left: Removing wax from press which is used to separate the wax fraction in petroleum distillation. Top, right: Remelted wax being run off into a mold. Bottom: Refined-paraffin cakes ready for packing and shipment.*

Standard Oil Co. (N.J.)

WAVRE, town of the province of Brabant, Belgium, on the Dyle, 15 miles s.e. of Brussels. It has breweries, tanneries, paper mills, and cotton manufactures. In Wavre on June 18, 1815, after their defeat at Ligny, the Prussians under Johann von Thielmann repulsed a superior force of the French under Emmanuel de Grouchy, and thereby prevented the latter from bringing timely assistance to Napoleon at Waterloo. Pop., about 8500.

WAX, name applied to various animal and vegetable substances, and to several mineral hydrocarbons, all of which resemble beeswax in physical qualities and appearance, in chemical composition, or in both. The physical qualities of waxes include a typical dull luster and somewhat soapy or greasy texture, and the property of softening gradually upon moderate heating from a semibrittle state to a flaccid, malleable consistency, and ultimately to a liquid state. Chemically, waxes are related to the fats and fixed oils (see FATS AND FIXED OILS); all three classes of substances are esters of fatty acids. Fats and fixed oils, however, are formed from fatty acids and glycerin; waxes are primarily composed of one or more esters formed from a mono- or di-hydric alcohol (q.v.), and a fatty acid, both of high molecular weight. Waxes resist saponification (hydrolysis into component acid and alcohol) by treatment with alkali, whereas fats yield readily to such treatment.

Typical animal waxes are: beeswax (q.v.), secreted by bees in constructing their honeycomb; sperm oil, a liquid wax from the sperm whale; spermaceti (q.v.), a solid constituent refined from sperm oil; lanolin, the principal constituent of the natural wool fat of sheep; and Chinese wax, the secretion of wax insects (see WAX INSECT). Vegetable waxes occur on the exposed surfaces of many plants, particularly on leaves, acting as a protection against excessive loss or gain of water by the plant. Some plants are a sufficiently abundant source of wax to have commercial importance; among their products are myrtle wax (see BAYBERRY), used by early Americans in candle making; Carnauba wax, exported from Brazil (see WAX-PALM; CARNAUBA PALM); and Japan wax, extracted from an oriental species of sumac, and used as a substitute or adulterant for beeswax. The last-named substance is chemically not a true wax but a fat, and possesses a characteristic rancid odor which makes it unsuitable for many purposes. Paraffin waxes have the physical but not the chemical characteristics of wax. They are saturated hydrocarbons (q.v.) of high molecular weight, and are found in the high-melting-point residue obtained from fractional distillation of petroleum, and in the native form as the mineral ozocerite. So-called sealing wax is actually a mixture of resins.

Waxes are used in the manufacture of candles, which, although no longer in general use as a practical source of illumination, are still employed in large quantities for decoration and in religious ceremonies. Waxes are also used in polishes, in lubricants, in chewing gum, in painting as vehicles, for pigments, in surgery for casts and molds, in etching (q.v.) processes, in laundries as detergents, in pharmacy as ointments, and in modeling (see WAXWORKS).

WAXAHACHIE, county seat of Ellis Co., Tex., situated about 45 miles S.E. of Fort Worth. It is served by four railroads, and is the center and shipping point of an area noted for the production of cotton, corn, oats, clover seed, wheat, onions, livestock, dairy products, honey, clay, limestone, and lumber. Among the industrial establishments in Waxahachie are cotton gins, a cotton compress, a cottonseed-oil mill, a flour mill, lumber yards, a textile mill, plant nurseries, a honey-processing plant, and factories producing cosmetics, garments, and furniture. The city is the site of the Southwestern Bible Institute. Waxahachie was settled in 1847 and incorporated in 1860. Pop. (1948 est.) 12,500.

WAXBERRY. See BAYBERRY.

WAX CLUSTER. See GAULTHERIA.

WAX INSECT, common name for any of several homopterous scale insects (q.v.) belonging chiefly to the family Coccidae. The insects are so named because of their waxlike secretions. They are native to temperate and tropical regions throughout the world, and subsist on the juice which they suck from various plants. The oval, scale-covered body is usually dull colored, and reaches a length of one eighth of an inch. The female and young are wingless; the males have a single pair of wings, the hind wings being represented by two clublike *halters*, or sense organs. Reproduction takes place several times during the year.

The Chinese wax insect, *Coccus sinensis,* known to the Chinese as *lah-shoo,* deposits its wax secretions on the branches of sumac and other trees. Toward the end of August, the wax is scraped from the branches of the trees, melted with boiling water, and strained through tightly woven cloth; it is ready for use after cooling, and is usually employed in the manufacture of candles. The East Indian wax insect, *Apis dorsata,* produces a wax which burns with a dim, smoky light and emits a resinous odor. Although unsuitable for candlemaking, the wax is sweet when fresh, and is eaten by native children as candy. Certain of the lantern flies (q.v.) of the superfamily Fulgoroidea (q.v.), also secrete large quantities of a white, flocculent wax which is used in China and tropical America in the manufacture of candles. The term "wax insect" is sometimes extended to include various plant lice, or aphids (q.v.), of the genera *Pemphigus, Chermes,* and *Schizoneura.* See WAX.

WAX MYRTLE. See BAYBERRY.

WAX PALM, common name applied to perennial palms of the genera *Ceroxylon* and *Copernicia,* which contain approximately five and eight species, respectively. They are native to tropical America, and yield a resinous wax used in the manufacture of candles, wax polishes, and other products. *Ceroxylon andicolum,* native to the Columbian and Ecuadorian Andes, reaches a height of 200 feet. Its inconspicuous white flowers have three sepals, three petals, nine to fifteen stamens, and a solitary pistil. The fruit is round, bony, and nutlike, and is enclosed in a soft integument. The tree is cultivated in many warm areas, and has a wax coating on the outside of the trunk. *Copernicia cerifera,* also known as the Carnauba palm (q.v.) is native to South America, and reaches a height of 35 feet.

WAX PLANT, any one of various plants so called from the waxlike appearances of the flowers or leaves or both, including any species of *Hoya,* any one of several begonias, one of the honeyworts, *Cerinthe major,* and the Indian pipe.

WAXWING, common name for birds of the genus *Bombycilla,* formerly *Ampelis,* type genus of the family Bombycillidae (q.v.). The secondary feathers of the wings, and sometimes other feathers of the wings and tail, are tipped with horny appendages resembling drops of sealing wax. In the United States the commonest species are *B. cedrorum,* the cedar bird or cedar waxwing, and *B. garrula,* the Bohemian waxwing. The cedar waxwing is about 7.2 inches in length. The head and neck are brown, the back olive, shading into yellow on the abdomen. They feed on insects, which they catch on the wing, and on small fruits. In summer they are found in Canada and in the United States as far south as the Carolinas; in winter they range as far as the West Indies and Costa Rica. The Bohemian waxwing is slightly larger, and has reddish-brown patches on the forehead and cheeks. It ranges from northern Canada to central United States.

WAXWORK or **BITTERSWEET,** common name applied to climbing, perennial shrubs of the genus *Celastrus,* belonging to the Staff-tree family. The genus contains approximately thirty species native to Asia, Australia, and America, some of which are cultivated as ornamental plants. The inconspicuous white flowers, which are arranged in panicles or racemes, have a five-parted calyx, a five-lobed corolla, five stamens, and a solitary pistil. The fruit is an orange-colored loculicidal capsule. The climbing bittersweet, or false bittersweet, *C. scandens,* is native to Canada and central U.S., and climbs to a height of 20 feet. Other members of the genus include *C. orbiculatus,* native to Japan and China, and slightly smaller than *C. scandens; C. paniculatus;* and *C. hypoleucus.* The last two are both native to China, and grow to a height of 15 feet.

WAXWORK, the use of wax, generally beeswax, with or without the addition of other material, for the execution of statues, busts, and medallions, as well as for modeling a great variety of objects from which metal castings are to be made. Wax is used extensively by sculptors to embody an initial conception later to be worked out in clay or other material. From very early times in imitative art, wax-working was practiced in various parts of the world. The Egyptians made wax figures of their deities and at one period of Greek art wax dolls were quite common. Pliny records that Lysistratus, about 300 B.C., made colored portraits in wax from plaster molds; while in Rome, patrician families commonly placed wax masks of ancestors as well as of living members of the family in the vestibules of their houses. During the Middle Ages, especially in Italy, wax was widely used for making portraits, figures of the saints, and ecclesiastical objects, and Spanish art boasts many such beautiful specimens. In the 15th century Andrea del Verrocchio and Orsino were the first to make human figures of wax on a wooden framework or skeleton, and having glass eyes and natural hair. About the close of the 18th century, wax portraits acquired wide vogue. Later, life-size figures of notable persons were made for purposes of popular exhibition, as in Madame Tussaud's in London, and the Eden Musée in New York City.

WAXY DEGENERATION, or AMYLOID DEGENERATION, a morbid process in which the healthy tissue of various organs is replaced by a nitrogenous substance, resembling in some respects amyloid compounds. Organs affected by this degeneration have a certain resemblance in consistency and physical character to wax. They are abnormally translucent, increased in volume, solidity, and weight. Amyloid degeneration is common to many tissues and organs, but the parts most frequently affected are the spleen, liver, and kidneys. Waxy degeneration is rarely met with as a primary condition. It is caused by chronic suppuration, syphilis, tuberculosis, cancer, and possibly gout.

WAY. See RIGHT OF WAY.

Penna. Dept. of Commerce Photo
Left: Anthony Wayne. Right: Blockhouse in Erie, Pennsylvania, where Anthony Wayne died.

WAYCROSS, county seat of Ware Co., Ga., situated 95 miles s.w. of Savannah. It is an important railroad and highway center, a leading bright-leaf tobacco market, and the commercial center of an area in which tobacco, corn, sugar cane, cotton, pecans, livestock, lumber, and naval stores are the chief products. Industrial establishments in the city include railroad shops, meat-packing plants, chick hatcheries, refrigerating plants, lumber mills, plants processing gum turpentine and other naval stores, and factories producing apiaries, carbonated beverages, wood veneers, caskets, and shoes. In the vicinity of the city is Okefenokee Swamp (q.v.), a vast marshy area covering about 660 sq.m., one of the largest swamps in the U.S. and noted as a wildlife refuge. Waycross was settled in 1870, incorporated as a town in 1874, and chartered as a city in 1909. Pop. (1950) 18,842.

WAYLAND, town of Middlesex County, Mass., on the Sudbury River, 18 miles w. of Boston. The chief industry is the manufacture of shoes. Pop. (1940) 921.

WAYLAND, FRANCIS (1796–1865), American educator, born in New York City, and educated at Union College and Andover Theological Seminary. In 1827 he was elected president of Brown University, which appointment he held until 1855. The rapid development of that institution during his administration marked him as a leader in educational reform. The later years of his life were largely devoted to the cause of prison reform. His writings include *Elements of Moral Science* (1835) and *The Present Collegiate System in the United States* (1842).

WAYLAND THE SMITH (Norse, *Völund*), a hero of English and Teutonic legends. In the folklore of Great Britain he was a mythical wizard and blacksmith appearing in many forms. Sir Walter Scott's *Kenilworth* immortalized the cromlech in Berkshire which bears the name of Wayland Smith's Cave and where, the legend runs, if a traveler leaves his horse with a fee, he will find him shod on his return. The Teutonic Völund, corresponding to the Roman Vulcan, was a wonderful smith and king of the elves. His adventures are told in *Elder Edda.* Wayland also appears as Galant in the French *chansons de geste.*

WAYNE, county seat of Wayne Co., Nebr., situated 90 miles N.W. of Omaha. Transportation facilities include a railroad and an airport. The city is the center and shipping point of an agricultural area yielding wheat, corn, sugar beets, hay, vegetables, potatoes, cattle, and hogs. Among the industrial establishments in the city is a poultry-processing plant. The city was founded in 1881, and is the site of the largest of the Nebraska State Teachers colleges, established in 1921. Pop. (1940) 2719.

WAYNE, ANTHONY (1745–96), American soldier, born in Easttown, Pa. Raising a regiment of volunteers, he was appointed colonel of it in 1776, and sent to Canada, where he covered the retreat of the provincial forces at Three Rivers. He commanded at Ticonderoga until 1777, when he was made brigadier general, and joined George Washington in New Jersey. He fought at Brandywine; led the attack at Germantown; captured supplies for the distressed army at Valley Forge; distinguished himself at Monmouth; was defeated at Paoli; and finally achieved a brilliant victory in the storming of Stony Point in 1779. His courage and skill greatly aided the Marquis de Lafayette in Virginia in 1781, and he took part in the siege of Yorktown. "Mad Anthony", as he was called, sat in Congress for Georgia in 1791-92, and was then appointed general in chief of the army. He commanded a successful expedition against the Indians of the Northwest, and in 1795 signed the Treaty of Greenville with twelve tribes, by which the United States acquired a large tract of territory.

WAYNE, JAMES MOORE (1790-1867), American jurist, born in Savannah, Ga., and educated at Princeton College. He then studied law, was admitted to the bar, and practiced in Savannah. From 1829 to 1835 he was a member of Congress. He was appointed associate justice of the United States Supreme Court in 1835. Wayne was an able orator and logician, and an authority on admiralty jurisprudence.

WAYNESBORO, county seat of Burke Co., Ga., situated about 30 miles s. of Augusta. It is served by two railroads, and is the center and shipping point of a rich agricultural region. Cotton, asparagus, pecans, and fruits are the principal crops produced in the area. Industrial establishments in the city include cotton gins, cottonseed-oil mills, fruit and vegetable canneries, lumber mills, and factories manufacturing wooden spools, wood veneers, fertilizers, clothing, furniture, and metal products. Waynesboro was founded in 1783 and incorporated in 1888. Pop. (1940) 3793.

WAYNESBORO, borough of Franklin County, Pa., about 14 miles S.E. of Chambersburg. It has manufactures of engines, agricultural and other machinery, and tools. Pop. (1940) 10,231.

WAYNESBURG, county seat of Greene County, Pa., 45 miles s. by w. of Pittsburgh. It is the seat of Waynesburg College and is a center for the shipment of livestock and wool. Pop. (1940) 4891.

WAYNESVILLE, county seat of Haywood Co., N.C., situated about 25 m. by rail s.w. of Asheville, in a scenic mountain region at an altitude of 3000 ft. above sea level. The principal industries in the town are the manufacture of shoes, furniture, leather products, rubber goods, and tapestries. Pop. (1949 est.) 4500.

WAYNE UNIVERSITY, a coeducational, municipally controlled institution of higher education, situated in Detroit, Mich. It was established in 1929, as a federation of those units of the Detroit public-school system devoted to higher education, under the name of the Colleges of the City of Detroit; the present name was adopted in 1933. The divisions of the university comprise schools of education, engineering, general studies, law, liberal arts, medicine, pharmacy, public affairs, and social work, and a graduate school; the degrees awarded include the B.A., B.A. in education, B.S., B.S. in education, B.S. in nursing, LL.B., M.D., M.A., M.S., ED.D., and PH.D. In a recent year over 24,000 students were enrolled and the faculty numbered almost 950.

WAYNFLETE or **WAINFLEET, WILLIAM OF** (1395?-1486), English bishop and statesman, born in Wainfleet. He was ordained priest in 1426, became a fellow of Eton College in 1440, and second provost in 1443. He succeeded Cardinal Beaufort as bishop of Winchester in 1447 and a year later obtained letters patent for the foundation of a hall at Oxford to promote the study of theology and philosophy, which ten years later he merged into his foundation of Magdalen College. He was lord chancellor from 1456 to 1460. After 1470 he was occupied with the completion of Eton and Magdalen colleges. In 1484 he founded a free school in Wainfleet.

WAYS AND MEANS, COMMITTEE OF, the most important committee of the U.S. House of Representatives, twenty-five in number, charged with the raising of revenue and the payment of national debt. It is appointed by the speaker of the House, and the chairmanship usually goes to a leader of the majority party. The minority party is usually given from one fourth to one third of the places on the committee.

WAYZGOOSE or **WAY-GOOSE,** in England, a yearly dinner given at Bartholomew's Tide, especially by printers, at which the wayzgoose or stubble goose was the principal dish. Formerly the dinner was given by the apprentices to their fellow-workmen. The custom is mentioned by Joseph Moxon in *Mechanical Exercises* (1683), but the serving of wayzgoose at various festivals had been popular since its introduction by Edward IV (1461-83) at Michaelmas time. It was the chief dish at Queen Elizabeth's feast celebrating the defeat of the Spanish Armada.

WAZAN, holy city of Morocco, situated about 53 miles N. of Fez, containing a number of mosques and a palace. The shereef, to whose residence Wazan owes its importance, is regarded as the spiritual ruler of Morocco, and as such is superior even to the sultan. The town is outside the jurisdiction of the sultan and is regarded as an asylum by fugitives from justice, whence it is known as Dar D'manah ("House of Safety"). The inhabitants of Wazan, estimated at 10,000, are mostly descendants of the shereefs and are engaged in the manufacture of the white woolen cloth from which *jirbahs* or hooded Moorish cloaks are made.

WAZIRISTAN, a mountainous region in northwest India bordering upon Afghanistan and included in the territory between the Gomul and Tochi rivers. It consists of two political agencies, Northern and Southern Waziristan. Iron mining and the breeding of horses and donkeys are the principal industries.

WEA (abbreviated from *Wawiatenong,* an American Indian term meaning a settlement near an eddy in a stream), a subtribe of the Miami branch of the Algonquian linguistic stock. At the beginning of the 19th century they were resident upon the Upper Wabash River, with their principal village, known to the French as Quiatenon, just below the mouth of Wea Creek, near the present site of Lafayette, Ind. In 1820 the Wea sold their reserved lands in Indiana and removed with the Piankishaw to Illinois and Missouri. They afterward removed to Kansas. In 1854 the two tribes, reduced to a mere remnant, united with the remnants of the Peoria and Kaskaskia tribes, all that were left of the ancient Illinois (q.v.).

WEAKFISH, or SQUETEAGUE, common name for any of several marine acanthopterygian food fishes of *Cynoscion* and related genera, belonging to the family Otolithidae. The weakfish receives its name from its weak, easily lacerated mouth. It is pale brown tinged with green above, and silvery along the sides and under parts. Numerous brown blotches, some of which form undulating lines, run downward or forward along the sides of the body. The fish average 5 pounds in weight and 2 feet in length, but sometimes attain a weight of 30 pounds. It spawns in May and June; the eggs, after being laid, are buoyed up by tiny oil drops and hatch in approximately 48 hours. From its shape and habit of biting at a hook, the weakfish is often called sea trout, and is sold in many markets under this name. The common weakfish, *C. regalis,* also known as gray trout, is found abundantly off the E. coast of the United States, from Cape Cod to Florida, and is an important food fish. A similar species, *C. arenarius,* is native to the Gulf of Mexico, and is commonly known as the sand squeteague, sand trout, and white trout. *C. nothus,* commonly known as the bastard weakfish, bastard trout, and silver squeteague, and *Eriscion nebulosus,* known as spotted squeteague and spotted sea trout, are found off the shores of the South Atlantic and Gulf States.

WEALDEN FORMATION, an important series of fresh-water strata belonging to the lowest division of the Lower Cretaceous series as developed in England. It was originally studied in the parts of Kent, Surrey, and Sussex called the Weald, hence its name. The layer is composed of the Weald clay above, and the Hasting sands below.

WEALTH, in economics, a store or accumulation of those material objects that have exchangeable value, such as real or personal property, especially when in the possession of a particular man or of a community or mass of men. As a rule, objects which fall under the category of wealth are useful, limited in supply, and transferable. See PROPERTY; ECONOMICS; CAPITAL.

WEANING, the stage in the feeding of infants during which other food is substituted for milk from the breast. Nine months is generally accepted by modern medical authorities as a sufficient time for nursing by the breast. Weaning is done gradually, when possible, in order to avoid indigestion and possible undesirable psychological reactions in the infant, and the discomfort of painful breasts in the mother. Weaning is easiest for infants who have previously been given occasional bottle feedings; it can be accomplished by the gradual substitution of bottle feeding for breast feeding over a period of two weeks, until the bottle is used exclusively. Although it was once held that weaning should not be done in hot weather, because of increased possibility of contamination of milk, modern methods of food preservation have removed this objection. Acute diseases such as pneumonia, tuberculosis, Bright's disease, typhoid fever, or inflammatory conditions of the breast, or the occurrence of pregnancy, may necessitate the abrupt termination of breast feeding, but weaning is not necessitated by minor illnesses or the resumption of menstruation. If the disease is of a temporary nature, the breasts may be emptied at regular intervals with a pump, and the child may be fed from a bottle until resumption of breast feeding when the mother recovers.

The eastern or New York weasel, common in the eastern United States

When the mother has no milk, the child is weaned as soon as the mother's breasts have been emptied of colostrum. When the mother's milk is scanty, supplementary bottle feeding is usually instituted. Milk banks of frozen breast milk are available in some of the larger cities. Weaning is indicated if, after two or three weeks, a mother is still not yielding more than 10 ounces of milk a day. When weaning is sudden, artificial food must be introduced with care; that is, a five-month-old child must not be put at once on a diet for that age, but gradually accustomed to it after beginning with food which is proper for a child one month old. See INFANTS, FEEDING OF.

Certain modern social scientists, such as the American anthropoligist Margaret Mead, have attempted to correlate the age at which weaning characteristically takes place in a society, and certain typical personality traits of the members of the society. In primitive cultures in which the weaning period is late, optimistic, carefree personalities develop, despite scantiness of food and other difficulties of survival; in other primitive societies, in which weaning takes place at a very early age, the typical cultural personality traits are often caution and hoarding, regardless of living conditions.

WEARE, MESHECH (1713–86), American political leader, born in Hampton, N.H. He was a commissioner to the colonial congress in Albany in 1754, chairman of the Committee of Public Safety in 1775, and president of the State from 1776 to 1784. During the Revolution he was active in raising troops to oppose the British.

WEARING OF THE GREEN, THE, an Irish ballad by an unknown writer. It first appeared in 1797, during the activities of the revolutionary group known as the United Irishmen. Later, at the time of the Fenian troubles, a revised version was introduced by Dion Boucicault (q.v.) in his play *Arrah na Pogue,* the hero being Napper Tandy (see TANDY, JAMES NAPPER).

WEASEL, common name for carnivorous mammals of the genus *Mustela,* closely related to the marten, sable, polecat, mink, and stoat. In the common European weasel, *M. vulgaris,* the body of the male is about 8 in. in length, the tail 2½ in. ; the eastern or New York weasel, *M. noveboracensis,* common in E. U.S., is 16 in. long, the female 13 in. A smaller species, more widely distributed through the northern United States and Canada, is the short-tailed, or Bonaparte's, weasel, *M. cicognani,* which supplies most of the ermine procured in British America in winter, although the Arctic least weasel, *M. rixosus,* supplies some. The color of a weasel's upper parts is generally reddish brown, of the under parts, white. In northern regions and in very cold winters the weasel occasionally becomes pure white, just as the stoat becomes the white ermine. It has a disagreeable smell, hunts by night, and is characterized by agility and pertinacious blood-thirstiness, preying on rats, mice, birds, and young rabbits. It is often troublesome in poultry yards. It may be tamed when taken young.

WEATHER. See CLIMATE; METEOROLOGY. For information on various weather pheno-

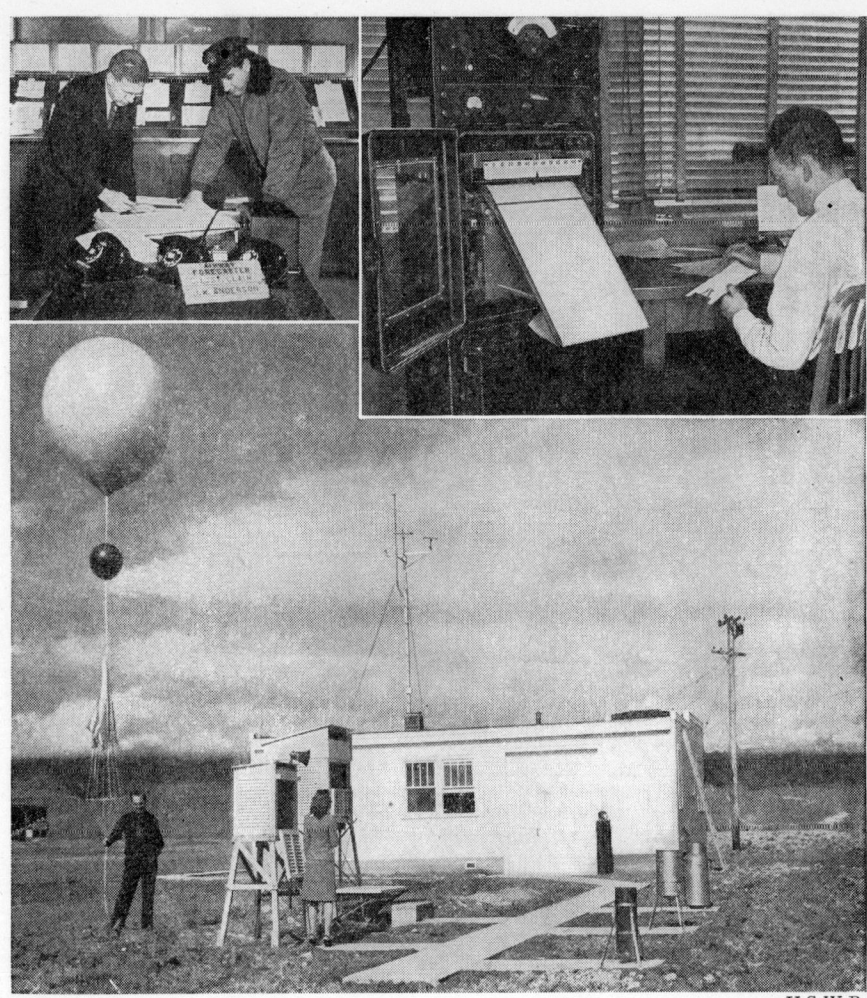

U.S. WEATHER BUREAU. *Top, left: An Air Corps pilot checking weather data with forecaster before taking off on a flight. Top, right: Observer receiving signals from radiosonde sent aloft on balloon. Bottom: Radiosonde balloon being released at a weather station.*

mena, see CLOUD; CYCLONE; DEW; FOG; HAIL; RAIN; SLEET; SNOW; TORNADO; WIND.

WEATHER BUREAU, UNITED STATES, in the Department of Commerce, a meteorological agency organized in 1870 as a unit of the Signal Corps and transferred to the Department of Agriculture in 1891 as a civilian bureau "for the purpose of forecasting weather conditions throughout the United States, for taking meteorological observations, and for the diffusion of meteorological information and the display of storm and flood signals".

The bureau was transferred by Presidential Reorganization Order in 1940 from the Department of Agriculture to the Department of Commerce.

The functions of the Weather Bureau are to provide weather forecasts, current meteorological reports, warnings of storms and other meteorological phenomena, and statistical compilations relating to the climate of the United States and its possessions to all activities requiring these services. For day-to-day forecasting and storm-warning work, opera-

WEATHER BUREAU   13,038   WEATHER BUREAU

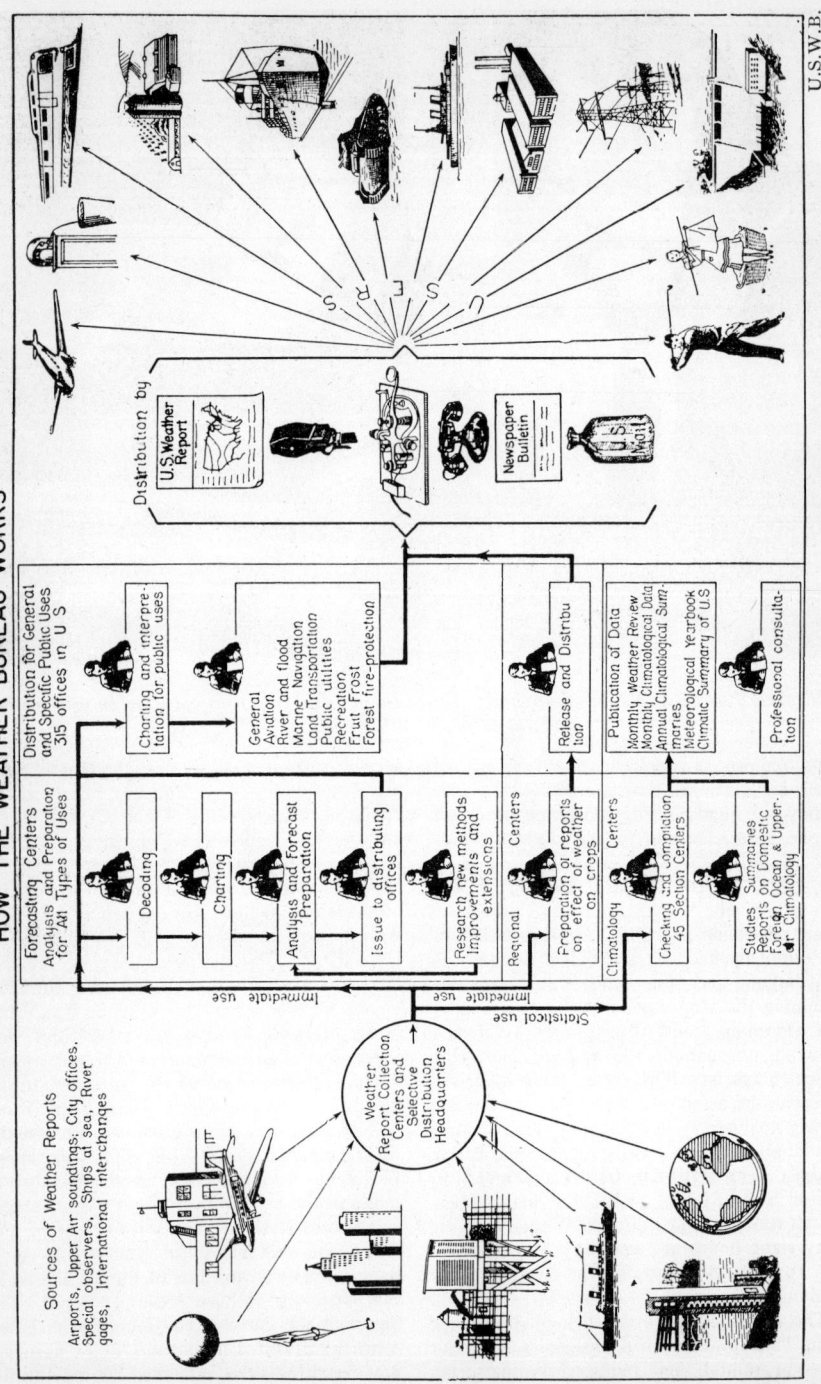

A chart showing how weather data is collected, organized, and distributed to the public

A Weather Bureau unit supervisor checks data with a plotter (left) for accuracy in preparation of a daily weather map.

tions require a comprehensive network of observing stations, which number approximately five hundred, for reporting at intervals of one, three, six, and twelve hours the current conditions of weather at the surface of the earth. These stations are distributed throughout the United States, Alaska, the island possessions, and the Caribbean Sea, and are supplemented by a smaller number of pilot-balloon and radio-sonde stations for determining the atmospheric pressure, temperature, humidity, and direction and velocity of winds throughout the active atmosphere above the surface. The surface and upper-air observations, assembled by a teletype network of approximately 56,000 miles, are charted and analyzed four times a day at thirteen forecast centers distributed throughout the United States, where predictions of impending weather for the subsequent thirty-six to forty-eight hours are issued. From observation to completed forecast the time required is about three hours.

The statistical records include the foregoing "synoptic" reports plus daily observations of rainfall and temperature made by approximately five thousand co-operative observing stations (about one hundred in each State and territory) established to record the climatic characteristics of the United States and its possessions. The observers at these stations, who for the most part serve without pay, render monthly tabulations of their daily observations, which are subsequently summarized and published in the *Climatological Data of the United States.*

The numerous uses of the Weather Bureau's service include service for aviation and other transportation, agriculture, marketing, and other forms of commerce. The Hurricane Warning Service aids greatly in safeguarding human life and property. The Fruit Frost Service warns of freezing temperatures in the citrus orchard regions of the South and West. The River and Flood Service predicts river stages in the navigable rivers and flood stages on all larger streams to aid inland shipping and to prevent destruction of livestock in low-lying farm areas and loss of human life when evacuation is necessary during floods. The Fire-weather Service, co-operating with the National Forest Service and State agencies, keeps such agencies informed during the fire hazard season of impending weather condi-

Rufous-necked weaver bird of India — N.Y. Zoological Society

tions likely to start or to encourage forest fires.

The Weather Bureau's climatic records are used by architects in the design of homes, schools, and factories; they play an important part in the location of manufacturing plants; they are of basic importance in studies of health and disease; they suggest the areas for various forms of crop experiment; and they provide invaluable guidance to physicians and patients in the selection of homes for invalids.

The national cost of the Weather Bureau is approximately $10,000,000 a year.

WEATHERFORD, county seat of Parker Co., Tex., situated 30 miles w. of Fort Worth. It is served by three railroads, and is the trading center and shipping point of a fertile agricultural area. Watermelons, peanuts, peaches, pecans, apples, plums, grapes, corn, oats, wheat, grain sorghums, Hereford cattle, hogs, horses, and dairy products are among the diversified agricultural products of the surrounding region, which also contains deposits of clay, sand, and gravel. Industrial establishments in the city include grain elevators, flour mills, a cottonseed-oil mill, a peanut-oil mill, bottling works, and factories producing clothing and oil-field equipment. The city is the site of Weatherford College, a junior college established in 1869, affiliated with Southwestern University at Georgetown. The site of the present city was first settled in 1850. It was incorporated as a town in 1856 and chartered as a city in 1858. Pop. (1948 est.) 8500.

WEATHERFORD, WILLIAM (about 1780–1826), a mixed-blood chief of the Creek Indians, born in the Creek settlement, Ala. He led the Creek Indians against the United States forces in the attack on Fort Mims, the battles of the Holy Ground, and of the Horseshoe Bend (1812–14), but surrendered in 1814 to General Andrew Jackson.

WEATHERLEY, FREDERIC EDWARD (1848–1928), English song writer and barrister. Beginning with *Muriel and Other Poems* (1870), he wrote many popular songs, especially for children. His most famous song was "Roses of Picardy". His best-known works include *Lays for Little Ones* (1898).

WEAVER, JAMES BAIRD (1833–1912), American political leader, born in Dayton, Ohio. During the Civil War he rose to the brevet rank of brigadier general of volunteers in the Union army. He was elected to Congress in 1878, and in 1880 was a candidate for the Presidency, receiving a popular vote of 308,578. In 1884 and 1886 he was elected to Congress by a fusion of Democrat and Greenback votes, but was defeated in 1888. In 1892 he was the candidate of the People's Party for the Presidency.

WEAVER, JOHN VAN ALSTYN (1893–1938), American author, born in Charlotte, N.C. In 1916–17 he was a member of the editorial staff of the *Chicago Daily News,* and again in 1919–20. He was literary editor of the *Brooklyn Daily Eagle* (1920–24), and after 1928 writer for the Paramount-Famous-Lasky Corp., film producers. A well-known contributor to many magazines, Weaver wrote *In American* (verse, 1921), *Margie Wins the Game* (novel, 1922), *More in American* (verse, 1925), *Love 'em and Leave 'em* (play, with George Abbott, 1926), *To Youth* (verse, 1927), *Her Knight Comes Riding* (novel, 1928), and *Joy-Girl* (1932).

WEAVER BIRD, the popular name for a group of birds, forming the family Ploceidae, similar to the finches. The name refers to the structure of the nests of these birds, which are woven of various vegetable substances. About 275 species of Ploceidae are known, of which over 200 are found in Africa, and the remainder in tropical Asia, the Philippines and other East Indian islands, and Australia. They are small birds, with a strong conical bill, sometimes coral red. One of the best-known species is the yellow weaver, *Ploceus philippinus,* the baya of India. Many weaver birds construct nests much on the same plan—pouches elongated into tubes, entered from below; some are kidney-shaped, with entrance at the side. They often suspend their nests from the extremities of branches, and prefer branches which hang over water. The social weaver birds, *Philetaerus socius,* of South Africa construct in communities an umbrella-shaped roof in a tree, beneath which may be 300

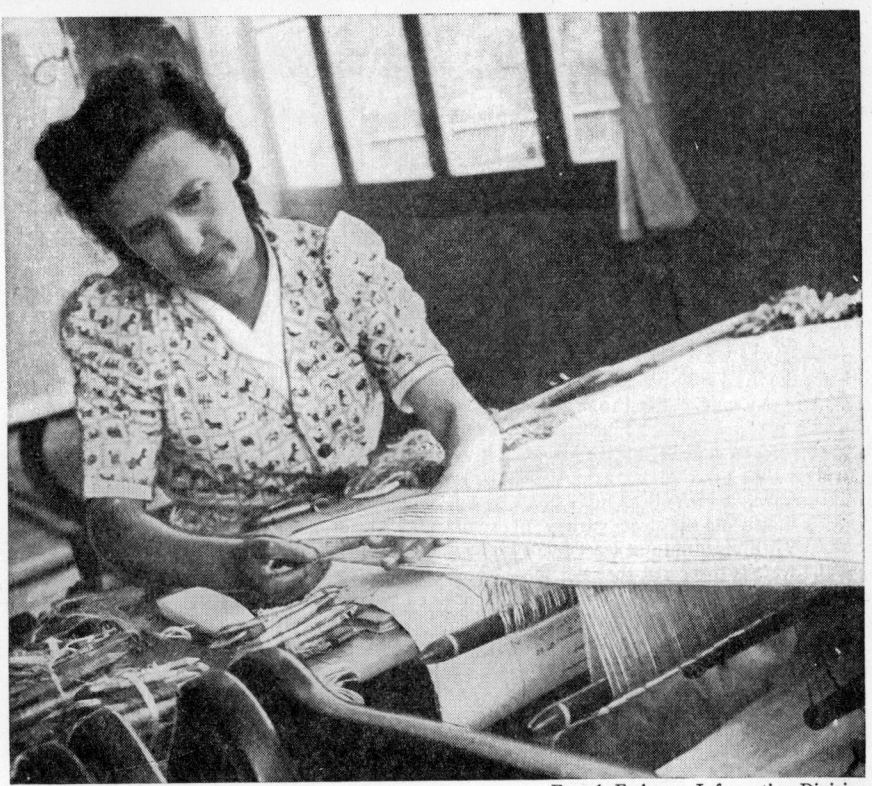

Weaving tapestry in France. Since each weft line is composed of numerous short lengths of thread, the weaver puts her hand in the shed at point where weft is to be stopped.

bird homes. The waxbills, nutmeg birds, African oxpeckers, and other species belong to this large family.

WEAVER'S-SHUTTLE SHELL, a smooth, usually white gastropod, related to the cowrie (q.v.) shells. Its aperture is drawn out into a long canal at each end. The foot is narrow and adapted for clasping the round stems of the alcyonarian coral *Gorgonia,* on which the mollusk feeds. The best-known species is *Ovulum volva.* The genus contains many species inhabiting all warm seas, and the group is sometimes called China shells.

WEAVING, the art of making cloth on a loom which in its simplest form is merely a frame to hold the warp threads parallel and regular, and enables *sheds* to be formed through which the wefts can move freely in a straight line without the necessity of passing over and under, as in plaiting. The three fundamental steps in weaving after the loom has been warped are: (1) pulling the lisses or healds to form the new shed; (2) passing the weft (usually called *filling* in machine weaving) through the shed; and (3) pressing home the weft.

The three fundamental weaves are plain, twill, and satin. All others are merely variations and complications of these. In plain weave the warp is divided into only two systems, the odd threads being attached to one set of lisses, the even threads to another. The passes of the weft to the left are through a shed that has the odd warps next to the weaver; the passes of the weft back to the right are through a shed that has the even warps next to the weaver. In twill weave the warp is divided into at least three systems, and there is not complete alternation of warp and weft as there is in plain weave. In a two-one twill the first weft passes over warp one, under warps two and three, over warp four, under warps five and six, etc.; the second weft over warps two, five, eight, etc., and under the

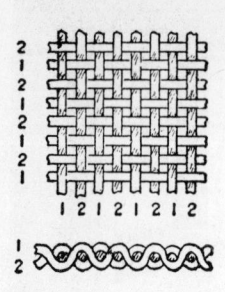

Plain weave 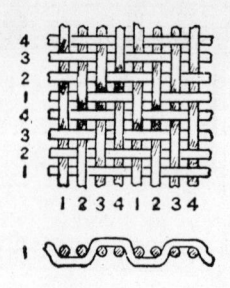   *Twill weave* 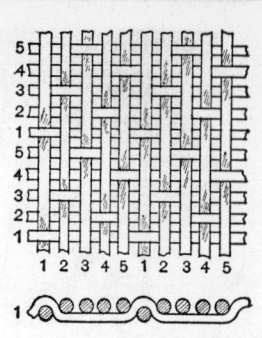   *Satin weave*

others; the third weft passes over warps three, six, nine, etc., and under the others. This of course leaves only half as much weft as warp on the surface, and forms the diagonal ribs or ridges that are characteristic of twills. In satin weave, which demands small silky threads taken up a great variety of twill the warp is divided into at least five systems, and the weft is so passed that not more than one fourth as much weft as warp remains on the surface; also the points where the weft comes to the surface are placed irregularly to avoid twill or diagonal effects. The result is that the wefts are practically negligible, and the surface appears to consist entirely of short lengths of parallel warps, thus giving the glossy effect characteristic of satin.

The plain weave is the simplest form of weaving, requiring but two different movements of the warp threads. The twill weave is a weave in which the filling threads pass over or under two or more adjacent warp threads, and which is primarily a silk weave each of the picks being alike except that each is stepped one thread to the right or the left of the one preceding it. The twill weave is distinguished by having a distinct wale or diagonal pattern, and by changing the number of threads at a time, at least once in a repeat, weaves may be produced. Twill weaves are designated as right twills and left twills, as the diagonal, when traced from the bottom of a piece of cloth held lengthwise, leads to the right or left respectively. In the satin weave the stitching of the warp threads to the filling is so distributed that no two intersections are adjacent. In order to make a smooth surface the warp threads stitch down to but one filling thread in a repeat of the weave. The weave as shown produces a fabric with warp satin face and filling satin back.

Rep and Taffeta Weaves. The simplest forms of plain weave have warp and weft threads of equal size and equal number to the inch, and showing equally on the surface, as in hard-spun etamines or rough-spun burlaps. Increasing the size and hardness of the warps, and decreasing the size while increasing the number and softness of the wefts, and pressing the wefts home hard, buries the warps entirely and produces a ribbed surface consisting entirely of wefts, the ribs marking the position of the hidden warps. This is the so-called rep weave, except that usually on the shuttle loom the warps are fine and the wefts are coarse, and the result is a warp rep instead of a weft rep. When the weft rep on a bobbin loom is figured by blocking in the colors with short passes, instead of sending the weft the full width of the warp as on the shuttle loom, the result is true tapestry. If on a shuttle loom we have coarse wefts with fine warps, but the warps are so few that instead of covering the wefts they serve merely as binders, the result is taffeta. If the warps are numerous, but the wefts are inserted in a satin weave, then the result will be warp satin on one side and a taffeta finish on the other.

Damasks and Brocades. Damask is a weave with warp satin ground and weft satin, twill, or taffeta figures, or vice versa. Brocade, derived from the Spanish for brocaded, and ultimately from the broche, i.e., the pointed bobbin of the high-warp loom, originally meant the combination of bobbin and shuttle effects; in other words, figures inserted with bobbins during the process of weaving a shuttle fabric. Ancient shuttle silks containing gold are usually called brocades, because the gold thread was inserted from bobbins, even in what would otherwise be damasks. Nowadays the brocaded effects, even on many hand looms, are usually inserted with extra shuttles. Brocaded figures are weft effects, apt to be small and detached and in relief and in color, as contrasted with most damask figures that

Early drawing showing a hand loom of 1778, used for weaving taffeta

are large and flat and usually in the same color as the ground, but with contrasting tone produced by the contrast of weaves.

Velvet. Velvets are also primarily a silk weave, corresponding in wool to the hand-knotted Oriental rugs. Brussels and Wilton carpets, and their printed imitations called tapestry carpets and velvet carpets, are merely the velvet weave applied to floor coverings of wool; see CARPETS AND RUGS. Corduroys and velveteens are fabrics with pile surface, formed by bringing weft threads in loops to the surface and then cutting the loops. The pile of modern velvets is produced not by extra wefts, but by extra warps that loop over wires which are withdrawn after the passage of the binding weft. The introduction of crossing threads that differ in color or count from the rest, as well as variations in the number of threads that cross and in the weft threads that are crossed, and the combination of gauze with twill, satin, brocade, or velvet weaves, produces some of the most delightful and unconventional stuffs that are known. See LOOM.

WEBB, ALEXANDER STEWART (1835–1911), American soldier and educator, born in New York City, and educated at the United States Military Academy. During the Civil War he served in the defense of Fort Pickens, at the first battle of Bull Run, and in the Peninsular and Maryland campaigns, and was made a brigadier general of volunteers in June, 1863. At Gettysburg his brigade played a conspicuous part in repelling Pickett's famous charge. He commanded a division in the Rapidan campaign, and a brigade in the campaign of the Wilderness; was severely wounded at Spottsylvania; and, after his return to active service, acted as chief of staff to General Meade. In 1864 he was brevetted major general of volunteers, and in 1865 was brevetted major general. From 1869 until 1903 he was president of the College of the City of New York. He wrote *The Peninsula: McClellan's Campaign of 1862* (1882).

WEBB, SIR ASTON (1849–1930), British architect, born in London. He gained renown as the most prominent British architect of his time. He designed, among other buildings, the Admiralty Arch at the east end of the Mall, London, and the London offices of the Grand Trunk Railway of Canada and of the Metropolitan Life Assurance Company. He also restored churches in different parts of England, including the beautiful St. Bartholomew's the Great in Smithfield, London. The most famous examples of his work are the new façade of Buckingham Palace and the buildings of the Victoria and Albert Museum in South Kensington.

WEBB, BEATRICE POTTER (1858–1943), English economist. After receiving a private education, she engaged in the investigation of social and industrial conditions. She married Sidney Webb (see WEBB, SIDNEY) in 1892. In 1905–09 she served on the Royal Commission on Poor Law and Unemployment, of whose minority report she was joint author, and after 1909 was honorary secretary of the National Committee for the Prevention of Destitution. She became one of the leading members of the Fabian Society. She was a member of several important committees during and after World War I, including the reconstruction committee in 1917–18, the war cabinet committee on women in industry in 1918–19, and the lord chancellor's advisory committee for women justices in 1919–20. From 1919 to 1927 she was a justice of the peace in London. She wrote *The Cooperative Movement in Great Britain* (1891), *Men's and Women's Wages: Should They Be Equal?* (1919), *My Apprenticeship* (1926), and *Methods of Social Study* (1932).

WEBB, CHARLES HENRY (1834–1905), American author, born in Rouses Point, N.Y. He ran away to sea in his youth, and later founded a periodical, *The Californian,* which he edited until 1866. He subsequently contributed to the New York *Tribune* humorous articles over the signature John Paul. Webb's works include *Parodies, Prose, and Verse* (1876); *Vagrom Verse* (1889); and *With Lead and Line along Varying Shores* (1901).

WEBB, JAMES WATSON (1802–84), American journalist, born in Claverack, N.Y. In 1827 he became editor of the New York *Morning Courier,* and having united with this the *Enquirer,* he edited the *Morning Courier and New York Enquirer* until 1861. In 1843 he was appointed engineer in chief of the State of New York, with rank of major general, and in 1861 minister and envoy extraordinary to Brazil. In 1865 he negotiated the secret treaty with the French emperor for the removal of French troops from Mexico. Webb wrote *Altowan, or Incidents of Life and Adventure in the Rocky Mountains* (1846); *Slavery and Its Tendencies* (1856); and *National Currency,* a pamphlet (1875).

WEBB, JOHN RICHMOND (about 1667–1724), English general, born in Wiltshire. He distinguished himself under Marlborough at the battle of Blenheim and at Oudenarde, where he commanded the left. He became brigadier general in 1704 and major general in 1706. In 1708 he won a victory at Wynendaele, Belgium, over a French force three times as large as his own. In 1709 he became lieutenant general and was wounded at Malplaquet. From 1712 to 1715 he was general and commander of the land forces in Great Britain, but the Whigs turned him out, and in 1722 by charging him with membership in a Jacobite society forced his retirement from public life. His character is portrayed in *Henry Esmond* by Thackeray, who, through his paternal grandmother, was descended from Richmond Webb, the general's second cousin.

WEBB, MATTHEW (1848–83), English sailor, born in Dawley, Shropshire. He served in the mercantile marine until 1875, when he became a professional swimmer, making his first attempt, August 12, to swim the English Channel, which ended in failure, but succeeding on the second attempt, August 24. To maintain a waning popularity, he undertook to swim the rapids and whirlpool of Niagara, and perished in the attempt.

WEBB, SAMUEL BLATCHLEY (1753–1807), American soldier, born in Wethersfield, Conn. He served with great gallantry and was wounded at Bunker Hill, and in 1775 became aide-de-camp to General Putnam, with the rank of major. In 1776 he was chosen by George Washington as his private secretary and aid, with the rank of lieutenant colonel, and as such wrote the order for promulgating the Declaration of Independence in New York City. He participated in the battles of Long Island, White Plains, Trenton, and Brandywine, being wounded at White Plains and Trenton, and on Dec. 10, 1777, during an expedition to Long Island, was taken prisoner. He was exchanged in December, 1780, and was transferred to the Third Connecticut Regiment in January, 1781; in September, 1783, he was brevetted brigadier general. He was one of the sixteen officers who on June 19, 1783, founded the Society of the Cincinatti.

WEBB, SIDNEY JAMES, 1st BARON PASSFIELD (1859–1948), English economist and socialist, born in London. He was a founder of the London School of Economics and Political Science and became honorary professor of public administration at the University of London. One of the first members of the Fabian Society, he contributed to *Fabian Essays* and wrote *Socialism in England* (1890). As editor of the *New Statesman* and through his speeches and writings Webb exerted a powerful influence on the development of English public opinion on political, economic, and especially social questions. He served on many governmental committees, including the Coal Industry Commission (1919), entered Parliament as a Labor member (1922), and was president of the Board of Trade in the MacDonald government (1924). In June, 1929, he was appointed secretary of state for dominion affairs and the colonies in the second Labor cabinet, and shortly afterward was created

Sidney James Webb
British Information Services

Baron Passfield. His works include *The Prevention of Destitution* (1911), *Towards Social Democracy?* (1916), and *The Story of the Durham Miners (1662-1921)* (1921). He edited *How to Pay for the War* (1916) and *Fabian Essays* (1920 edition). In collaboration with his wife, Beatrice Webb, he wrote, among other works, *A Constitution for the Social Commonwealth of Great Britain* (1920), *The Consumers Co-operative Movement* (1921), *The Decay of Capitalist Civilization* (1923), *English Poor Law History* (3 vols., 1927-29), and *The Truth about Soviet Russia* (1942).

WEBB, THOMAS (1724-96), British soldier and Methodist preacher, born in England. He served with distinction as an officer in the Royal American Army, and was severely wounded at the storming of Louisburg, Nova Scotia, in 1758. In 1765 he came under the influence of John Wesley, and thereafter took up the life of an itinerant preacher. With the exception of brief visits to England and Ireland, to solicit aid for struggling Methodist churches, he preached in the American colonies till the outbreak of the Revolution.

WEBB, THOMAS EBENEZER (1821-1903), British philosophical scholar, born in Pontscatho, Cornwall. He became professor of moral philosophy at the University of Dublin in 1857, regius professor of laws in 1867, and public orator in 1879. He withdrew from academic life in 1887, and until his death was county court judge for Donegal. Webb wrote *The Intellectualism of Locke* (1857), *The Veil of Isis* (1885), *The Irish Land Question* (1886), and *The Mystery of William Shakespeare: A Summary of Evidence* (1902).

WEBB CITY, a city of Jasper Co., Mo., situated 5 miles N.E. of Joplin, and adjoining Carterville. It is served by two railroads. Webb City and Carterville form practically a single industrial community, and are the center of a rich lead and zinc mining area. Agriculture is another important industry in the surrounding region. Among the industrial establishments in the city and vicinity are foundries, stockyards, and factories manufacturing fertilizers, chemicals, blasting powder, heavy industrial and mining machinery, garments, and caskets. The industrial development of the city dates from the discovery of lead in 1873 on the farm of John C. Webb, for whom the city was named. Pop. (1948 est.) 8000.

WEBBE, WILLIAM (d. 1591?), English author. He was educated at St. John's College, Cambridge, where he made the acquaintance of Gabriel Harvey and Edmund Spenser. About 1583 he became a private tutor in the household of Edward Sulyard of Flemyngs in Essex. Webbe's chief work, *A Discourse of English Poetrie* (1586), is of interest for the light it throws upon the poets of the author's day, and upon contemporary literature and canons of criticism. To it are appended the first two eclogues of Vergil in hexameter verse. Webbe belonged to the school which advocated the abolishment of the use of rhyme and classical meters in English verse.

WEBBER, CHARLES WILKINS (1819-56), American journalist and explorer, born in Russellville, Ky. As one of the Texan Rangers, he experienced much of the wild frontier life. Afterward he studied medicine and then theology, but abandoned both professions and became a journalist. He organized an expedition to the Colorado and Gila rivers in 1849. In 1855 he went to Central America. He was killed in Nicaragua, while a member of the filibustering party commanded by William Walker (q.v.). He wrote *Old Hicks, the Guide, or Adventures in the Comanche Country in Search of a Gold Mine* (1848); *The Gold Mines of the Gila* (1849); *Tales of the Southern Border* (1852); and *Shot in the Eye* and *Adventures with the Texan Rifle Rangers* (1853).

WEBBER, HERBERT JOHN (1865–1946), American plant physiologist, born in Lawton, Mich., and educated at the University of Washington. He was employed by the United States Department of Agriculture to investigate orange diseases in Florida from 1893 to 1897 and from 1889 to 1907 had charge of the department's plant-breeding investigations. He served as professor of experimental plant biology at Cornell in 1907–08, and as acting director in 1909–10. He was then appointed professor of plant breeding at the New York State College of Agriculture. In 1912 he went to the University of California to be director of the Citrus Experiment Station, dean of the Graduate School of Tropical Agriculture, and professor of plant breeding. He was professor of subtropical horticulture there from 1929 to 1936, when he became professor emeritus.

WEBER, ALBRECHT (1825–1901), German Orientalist, born in Breslau, and educated at the universities of Breslau, Bonn, and Berlin. He was Privatdocent at the University of Berlin from 1848 to 1856. In 1856 he became assistant professor and in 1867 professor of Indian languages and literature, holding this position until his death. His most important works are his edition of the *White Yajur Veda* (1849–59); *Indische Studien* (18 vols., 1850–98); *Indische Litteraturgeschichte* (1852); *Indische Skizzen* (1857); *Verzeichnis der Berliner Sanskrithandschriften* (2 vols., 1853–92); a translation of Kalidasa's drama *Mālavikā und Agnimitra* (1856); an edition of Hala's *Saptaśataka* (1881); *Indische Streifen* (3 vols., 1868–79); contributions, especially from Vedic literature, to the *Sanskrit-Wörterbuch* of Otto von Böhtlingk and Rudolf von Roth; and numerous briefer articles in Oriental periodicals.

WEBER, ERNST HEINRICH (1795–1878), German physiologist and anatomist, born in Wittenberg. He was appointed professor of comparative anatomy at Leipzig in 1818, professor of human anatomy in 1821, and, in addition, professor of physiology in 1840. Weber is well known for his discoveries in anatomy, notably that of the existence of a rudimentary uterus in male mammals, but his greater fame rests upon his pioneer work in the exploration of the sense organs. His work upon the ear and upon the cutaneous senses of pressure, temperature, and what was then called the space sense, gave the deciding impulse to the introduction of the experimental movement into psychology. The important generalization which bears his name (see WEBER'S LAW) was the first valid generalization in psychophysics.

WEBER, JOSEPH M. (1867–1942), American comedian, born in New York City. He began his stage career in 1877 in company with Lewis M. Fields (Lew Fields), with whom he formed the theatrical firm of Weber and Fields in 1885. Besides several other enterprises this firm managed the Broadway Music Hall from 1895 to 1904. Thereafter Weber was proprietor and manager of Weber's Theater, New York City. He was one of the best-known comedians of his day, especially clever in burlesques.

WEBER, KARL JULIUS (1767–1832), German writer, born in Langenburg, Württemberg, and educated at the universities of Erlangen and Göttingen. In 1792 he became private secretary to the Count of Erbach-Schönberg, whom he left in 1799 to accept the post of government councilor at König in Odenwald. He held various administrative offices until his retirement, in 1804. From 1820 to 1824 he was a member of the popular chamber of the Württemberg Estates. Weber is best known for his writings, in which he displays a fresh, original spirit, fine powers of observation, and a talent for witty satire. He was largely influenced by the humanistic teachings of French literature and philosophy, but his reading and his sympathies were cosmopolitan. The most celebrated of his works is *Demokritos, oder Hinterlassene Papiere eines lachenden Philosophen* (1832–40). He also wrote *Möncherei* (1818–20); *Das Ritterwesen* (1822–24); and *Deutschland, oder Briefe eines in Deutschland Reisenden Deutschen* (1826–28). His collected works (30 vols.) were published between 1834 and 1845.

WEBER, KARL MARIA FRIEDRICH ERNST VON (1786–1826), German composer and pianist, born in Eutin, near Lübeck. In Vienna in 1803 Weber was warmly welcomed as a pupil by Abbé Vogler, who obtained for him the conductorship of the opera in Breslau. This post Weber held for two years. He afterward left Breslau at the invitation of Duke Eugene of Württemberg for Schloss Carlsruhe. His host subsequently had him appointed secretary to his brother, Duke Ludwig, in Stuttgart. From 1813 to 1816 he was director of the opera in Prague, and in 1817 he undertook the direction of the German opera in Dresden, an appointment which he held until his death. He died in London, where he had gone to direct the production of *Oberon,* the opera commissioned by Charles Kemble.

Weber's *Freischütz* struck a national note, and through it he became the founder of the Romantic school of German opera. His influence on Wagner was very marked. The finale of the first act and the march in the second act of *Tannhäuser*, and the first finale in *Lohengrin*, besides minor passages in both these works, show unmistakably the influence of Weber in structure. Wagner's admiration for Weber was unbounded. Weber's *Leyer und Schwert* are among the most spirited German patriotic songs, and several of his piano works, notably the *Invitation à la Valse*, the E flat major *Polonaise*, and the *Concertstück* for piano and orchestra, are brilliantly effective compositions.

WEBER, MAX (1881–   ), American artist, born in Bialystok, Russia. Brought by his parents to the United States in 1891, he graduated from Pratt Institute, Brooklyn, in 1900. He taught at the Art Students League, New York in 1920–21, and from 1925 to 1927. He is represented in many American galleries and museums. In 1928 he was awarded the Potter Palmer gold medal and $1000, in 1941, the Temple gold medal of Pennsylvania Academy of Fine Arts, and the Clark bronze medal and $1000 by the Corcoran Art Gallery, Washington, D.C. Weber was one of the leading exponents of modernism in art.

WEBER, WILHELM EDUARD (1804–91), German physicist, born in Wittenberg, and educated at the University of Halle. In 1825, in association with his brother Ernst Heinrich Weber he published *Die Wellenlehre*. He became assistant professor of physics at Halle in 1827, and professor at Göttingen in 1831. He was one of the seven professors of Göttingen who were removed in 1837 for having protested against the violation of the constitution. He held the chair of physics at Leipzig from 1843 until 1849, when he was restored to his former position at Göttingen. While living in that city he became acquainted with the German scientist Karl Friedrich Gauss, and in 1833 they jointly devised an electromagnetic telegraph. They also founded the Magnetic Union and made many observations on terrestrial magnetism. Weber's most important achievement was the introduction of the absolute system of electrical units, modeled on the work of Gauss, who first devised such a system of units for magnetic quantities. Weber determined the value of the practical units in absolute measure and, at the International Electrical Congress held in Paris in 1881, his system was adopted and the volt, ampere, coulomb, and farad were defined. Weber's works were published by the Göttingen Academy of Science in 1892, and his more important papers on absolute measurement of current and resistance were republished in Leipzig in 1904 as *Fünf Abhandlungen über . . . Strom und Widerstandsmessung*.

Karl Maria von Weber

WEBERN, ANTON VON (1883–1945), Austrian composer, born in Vienna, and educated at the University of Vienna. He studied with the composer Arnold Schönberg (q.v.), adopting Schönberg's twelve-tone system (q.v.) in his own works. Webern conducted theater orchestras in provincial German cities, subsequently securing a post as teacher of composition at Schönberg's musical academy in Vienna. His principal works are *Passacaglia* for orchestra; *Six Pieces* for orchestra; *Four Songs* with orchestra; *Geistliche Lieder* ("Sacred Songs") for soprano, clarinet, flute, harp, trumpet, and double bass; and *Five Movements* and *Six Bagatelles* for string quartet.

WEBER'S LAW, in psychology, the formula expressing the relation of sensation to intensity of stimulus. In 1834 Ernst Heinrich Weber proposed the theorem that the ratio of the increment of stimulus necessary to give a noticeably different sensation to the original stimulus is constant, or, as he expressed it, $\frac{V-U}{U} = C$, where V is the comparison stimulus, U the standard stimulus, and C a constant. The principle can be more explicitly stated in other forms, for example, (a) if sensations increase in intensity by equal amounts,

Daniel Webster

their stimuli increase by relatively equal amounts; (b) the difference which is relatively the same for stimulus is absolutely the same for sensation; and (c) the intensity of the stimulus increases in geometrical ratio as the intensity of the apperceived sensation increases in arithmetical ratio. The validity of this theorem was confirmed by the German physicist Gustav Fechner by the use of various psychophysical methods. He also extended its range to other sense departments than those investigated by Weber, and gave it the name "Weber's Law". Since Fechner's time the investigation of the applicability of the law has been carried on by many experimenters, and its significance is attested by its prominence in the literature of psychophysics.

WEBSTER, a town of Worcester Co., Mass., situated on the French R., about 15 miles s.w. of the city of Worcester. It is served by two railroads. The surrounding region is agricultural; the principal industries in the town are the manufacture of machine-shop products, shoes, and cotton and woolen goods. Within the limits of the town is Lake Chaubunagungamaug, covering an area of 2 sq.m. Webster was founded in 1812 by Samuel Slater, an industrialist who established cotton and woolen mills there. It was incorporated in 1832. Pop. (1945) 13,534.

WEBSTER, (ALICE) JEAN (1876–1916), American author, born in Fredonia, N.Y. For some years she lived in Italy, and in 1906–07 she made a trip around the world. Jean Webster was a niece of Mark Twain. Besides short stories contributed to magazines, she wrote *Just Patty* (1911), *Daddy Long-Legs* (1912), and *Dear Enemy* (1915). *Daddy Long-Legs,* by which she became best known, was dramatized by her and produced in New York in 1914, and in 1931 it was made into a motion picture.

WEBSTER, ARTHUR GORDON (1863–1923), American physicist, born in Brookline, Mass., and educated at Harvard College and the universities of Paris, Stockholm, and Berlin. In 1895 he was awarded the Thomson prize (Paris) of 5000 francs for experimental research on the period of electrical oscillations. He became professor of physics in 1900 at Clark University, where he had taught since 1890. In 1903–04 he was president of the American Physical Society, and in 1915 was appointed to the Naval Consulting Board. He came to be recognized as a leading authority on sound in the United States, inventing several instruments in this field. Among his works are *Dynamics of Particles of Rigid, Elastic, and Fluid Bodies* (1903) and *Harrison Lectures on Sound, University of Pennsylvania* (1911).

WEBSTER, DANIEL (1782–1852), American statesman and orator, born in Salisbury (now Franklin), N.H. His father was a member of the State legislature and a county judge. Daniel graduated from Dartmouth College in 1801, studied law at Salisbury and Boston, was admitted to the bar in 1805, and quickly attracted notice in Portsmouth. Political discussion also enlisted his energies, and with the New England Federalists he opposed the second war with Britain. Sent to Congress in 1813, he served two terms, maintaining an honorable position in an unpopular party. In 1816 Webster removed to Boston, and for nearly seven years devoted himself to the practice of law. He soon rose to the position of one of the foremost advocates of the country and appeared before the United States Supreme Court in several famous constitutional cases. In 1820 he aided greatly in the revision of the constitution of Massachusetts. In the same year he delivered three addresses which established his fame as one of the greatest of orators. In the meantime, in 1822, Webster had been elected to Congress from the Boston district. As chairman of the Judiciary Committee he was instrumental in securing a codification of the criminal jurisprudence of the United States. He made notable speeches in opposition to the protective tariff measure of 1824. In 1827 he was elected to the United States Senate. He now abandoned his opposition to protective tariffs and became a supporter of the measure of 1828 known as the "tariff of abominations".

In 1830 his fame as an orator reached its culmination in his reply to the speech of Robert Y. Hayne, senator from South Carolina, on the nature of the Union and the right of nullification. In this epoch-making oration Webster successfully combated the theory of nullification and ably vindicated the nationalist view of the Union. His argument was later supplemented and reinforced in debate with Calhoun on the Force Bill (see NULLIFICATION). In the controversy over the renewal of the charter of the United States Bank, Webster advocated renewal and opposed President Jackson's financial policy in general (see BANKS AND BANKING). Many of the principles of sound finance, developed by his speeches at this time, have been incorporated in the Federal Reserve System. Upon the organization of the Whig Party, Webster became one of its leaders, and in 1836 received the electoral vote of Massachusetts for President. In 1840 the Whigs offered Webster the Vice-Presidency but he refused. Upon the election of Harrison, however, Webster was appointed secretary of state, a position which he retained under Tyler. In this capacity he managed with tact the cases growing out of the McLeod and *Creole* affairs and brought to a successful conclusion the negotiations with Lord Ashburton chiefly for the settlement of the northeast boundary dispute with Great Britain (see NORTHEAST BOUNDARY DISPUTE).

In 1844 he was again suggested for the Presidency, but his following was small, and in the succeeding year he re-entered the Senate as the successor of Rufus Choate, in which capacity he opposed the annexation of Texas and the war with Mexico. Webster at first declined to support Taylor's candidacy for the Presidency in 1848, but later ably defended the Whig administration. His last years in the Senate were devoted to efforts to preserve the Union and maintain peace between the North and the South by means of compromise. His last great speech was that delivered in the Senate, March 7, 1850, on the Compromise Measures of 1850. The speech aroused indignation in the North, where it was said that he was truckling to the South in order to gain support in his candidacy for President. Upon the succession of Fillmore to the Presidency in 1850, Webster became secretary of state. During this second tenure of the office he carried on a memorable correspondence with Chevalier Hülsemann, the Austrian minister, boldly championing the right of the United States to recognize the new Hungarian Republic and its head, Kossuth.

Again in 1852 he was disappointed in not receiving the Whig nomination for the Presidency, refused to support the candidacy of General Scott, and took no part in the campaign. He returned to his home in Marshfield, Mass., in September, and there died on October 24. Hardly in the history of the country has there been a more general expression of sorrow. The mourning can only be compared with that which followed the deaths of Washington and Lincoln.

WEBSTER, HENRY KITCHELL (1875–1932), American novelist, born in Evanston, Ill. His works include *The Innocents* (1924), *The Corbin Necklace* (1926), *The Beginners* (1927), *The Clock Strikes Two* (1928), and *The Sealed Trunk* (1929).

WEBSTER, JOHN (1580?–1625?), English dramatist. Virtually nothing is known about his life. He is thought to have begun writing plays as early as 1601, collaborating with such Elizabethan dramatists as Henry Chettle, Thomas Dekker, Michael Drayton, John Heywood, and John Marston. In conjunction with Drayton, Webster wrote *Cæsar's Fate* (produced in 1602). His revised version of Marston's *Malcontent* appeared in 1604. With Dekker he wrote two comedies, *Westward Hoe* and *Northward Hoe,* both first produced in the winter of 1604–05 and printed in 1607. He may also have collaborated with Heywood in writing *Appius and Virginia* (produced about 1609). Webster's individual genius was first revealed in its full stature in the tragedy *The White Devil, or Vittoria Corombona,* which was printed in 1612, having been produced some two years before. The other work upon which his reputation is principally based is *The Duchess of Malfi,* staged around 1614 but not printed until 1623. Webster's tragicomedy *The Devil's Law Case,* inferior in construction to both *The White Devil* and *The Duchess of Malfi,* was produced around 1619 or 1620. The 19th-century English poet and literary critic Algernon Charles Swinburne assigned Webster a place beside Shakespeare among the English dramatists.

WEBSTER, MARGARET (1905–   ), American actress and director, born in New York City, and educated in England. She made her debut

Noah Webster (from a painting)

on the professional stage in 1924, and in the following year she appeared at the Haymarket, London, as the Gentlewoman in *Hamlet.* During the next ten years her engagements included leading roles in numerous Shakespearean plays, including *Macbeth,* and in plays by George Bernard Shaw and Henrik Ibsen. Her first American appearance, as Mrs. Anna Steele in *Parnell,* took place in New York City in 1938. She had meanwhile (1935) produced a number of plays in London, and from 1937 to 1939 she directed several Shakespearean presentations in New York. In 1943 she produced *Othello* in New York, with Paul Robeson in the leading role. This production, in which she played the part of Emilia, had a record run of 295 successive performances. Her works include *Shakespeare without Tears* (1942).

WEBSTER, NOAH (1758–1843), American educator and lexicographer, born in West Hartford, Connecticut, and educated at Yale College. From 1779 to 1781 he taught school in Hartford, and studied law. Deciding against legal practice, he opened a classical school at Goshen, New York, in 1782. The following year he returned to Hartford, and there in 1783 the first part of his *Grammatical Institute of the English Language,* a spelling book subsequently known by the popular names *Webster's Spelling Book* or *Blue-Backed Speller,* was published. In 1889 it was estimated that more than 62,000,000 copies of this volume had been printed and sold since its publication. In 1787, following the adjournment of the Constitutional Convention (see CONSTITUTION OF THE UNITED STATES: *The Constitutional Convention*), Webster issued a pamphlet entitled *Examination of the Leading Principles of the Federal Constitution.* In December of the same year he established in New York City *The American Magazine,* but discontinued it after a year and went back to Hartford in 1789.

Returning to New York four years later, he founded a daily newspaper, *The Minerva* (afterward *The Commercial Advertiser*), and a semiweekly edition of *The Herald* (afterward *The Spectator*), both in support of the Federalist Party (q.v.). In 1795, under the signature of Curtius, he wrote a series of cogent articles for the periodical, *The Minerva,* defending the commercial treaty negotiated the previous year by the American statesman John Jay (see JAY'S TREATY). Three years later, Webster moved to New Haven, where he wrote *A Brief History of Epidemic and Pestilential Diseases* (2 vols., 1799), long the standard authoritative work on the subject; *Historical Notices of the Origin and State of Banking Institutions and Insurance Offices* (1802); *Rights of Neutral Nations in Time of War* (1802); *A Compendious Dictionary of the English Language* (1806); and *A Philosophical and Practical Grammar of the English Language* (1807). From 1812 to 1822 Webster resided at Amherst, Massachusetts; during this period he represented Hampshire County in the Massachusetts legislature (1815, 1819), served as trustee (1816–21) and president (1820–21) of Amherst Academy, and helped to found Amherst College (1819–21).

After devoting over twenty years to the study of the English language, during which he visited both England and France (1824–25), Webster returned to the United States in 1825 to complete his *American Dictionary of the English Language,* the first edition of which was published in two volumes in 1828. This work contained 12,000 more words and about 40,000 more definitions than had previously appeared in any English dictionary, but Webster's importance as a lexicographer does not rest merely upon the scope of his work. He was the first to emphasize American rather than British usage, and the first to organize meanings in the chronological order of their first appearance in the language. His precise definitions and accurate etymologies are now generally considered models of dictionary style. Finally, by the inclusion of thousands of contemporary technical and scientific terms, Webster laid the groundwork for the modern comprehensive, rather than purely literary, type of dictionary; see DICTIONARY. A second edition of Webster's dictionary was issued in 1840. His other works include *Dissertations on the English Language* (1789), *Manual of Useful Studies* (1832), *History of the United States* (1832), and *A Collection of Papers on Political, Literary, and Moral Subjects* (1843).

WEBSTER, RICHARD EVERARD, VISCOUNT ALVERSTONE (1842–1915), English jurist. He was created lord chief justice of England in 1900. He was called to the bar in 1868, became queen's council in 1878, and attorney general in 1885. As a jurist he was expert in commercial, railroad, and patent cases. He represented Great Britain in the Bering Sea arbitration (1893), before the Venezuela Boundary Commission (1898), and in the Alaska Boundary problem (1903). In the Parnell libel suit against the London *Times* he was leading counsel for the owners (1890).

WEBSTER-ASHBURTON TREATY. See NORTHEAST BOUNDARY DISPUTE.

WEBSTER CITY, county seat of Hamilton Co., Iowa, situated on the Boone R., 72 miles N.W. of Des Moines. It is served by three railroads and maintains a municipal airport. The city is the trading center of an agricultural area. The principal industries in Webster City are the packing of meat, poultry, and eggs, the processing of dairy products, and the manufacture of flour, food products, stock feeds and medicines, troughs and sieves, tilling spades, cultivator shovels and sweeps, washing machines, concrete products, scoreboards and timers, metal castings, tools and dies, machine tools, ornamental iron products, thresher screens, and automobile trailers. Three magazines of national circulation, the *National Chiropractic Journal,* the *Aberdeen Angus Journal,* and *Healthways,* are printed in Webster City. Educational institutions in the city include Webster City Junior College. Webster City was settled in 1859. Pop. (1948 est.) 8000.

WEBSTER GROVES, a city of St. Louis Co., Mo., adjoining the city of St. Louis, of which it is a residential suburb. It is the site of Webster College (Roman Catholic), established in 1916, an affiliate of St. Louis University, of the German Evangelical Missouri College, a theological seminary established in 1850, and of the Eden Theological Seminary. Webster Groves was incorporated in 1896. Pop. (1950) 23,289.

WEBWORM, common name applied to the caterpillar larvae of various widely distributed lepidopterous moths (see LEPIDOPTERA), for their habit of spinning large communal webs. The fall webworm, *Hyphantria cunea,* belongs to the family Arctiidae and reaches a length of ¾ inch. Fall webworms spin a common web enclosing several leaves or whole branches of trees; after devouring the leaves or parts of the branches, they move to another tree. They are usually dark green in color and are covered with rough, long hairs. The garden webworm, *Loxostege similalis,* belonging to the family Pyralididae, feeds on garden vegetables by drawing the leaves into its web. It is yellow, spotted with black, and averages one inch in length. The family Pyralididae also includes the grass webworm, *Crambus vulvigagellus*; these worms spin a web around the stalks and roots of various grasses. They are dark brown above and lighter below, and feed only at night. During the day, they retire to a tube of cut grass and silk below the surface of the ground. Methods of protecting crops against webworms include the burning of webs and the spraying of foliage with arsenic solutions.

WECKHERLIN, GEORG RUDOLPH (1584–1653), German poet, born in Stuttgart, and educated at the University of Tübingen. After serving as secretary to Duke John Frederick, he removed to England, where he served (1624–41) as an undersecretary of state. At the outbreak of the Great Rebellion, he chose the side of Parliament and from 1644 to 1649 held the position of secretary for foreign tongues. Upon his retirement he was succeeded by John Milton. In 1652 he was appointed assistant to the latter, but continued in office only a few months. Weckherlin's German poems are for the most part influenced by the works of the French Pléiade, especially those of Pierre de Ronsard. He ranks as foremost of the poets before Optiz who tried to introduce Renaissance forms and feelings into German verse. His lyrics are poetic in tone, though some may be considered hard and unwieldy in form. His chief English poems are *Triumphal Shows Set Forth Lately at Stuttgart* (1616) and *Panegyricke to Lord Hay, Viscount of Doncaster* (1619). His collected poems were edited by H. Fischer (Stuttgart, 1893–95).

WEDDIGEN, OTTO (1882–1914), German naval officer, born in Herford. At the outset of World War I he was commander of the submarine *U-9,* which, on September 22, 1914, torpedoed the British cruisers *Aboukir, Hogue,* and *Cressy,* in the North Sea. This exploit was followed on October 4 by the sinking of the British cruiser *Hawke,* and Weddigen became a popular hero in Germany. His victories provided the first striking example of the effective value of the submarine. In command of the *U-29,* Weddigen perished a few weeks later, when his boat was caught in a fishing seine in the Straits of Dover.

WEDDING ANNIVERSARIES. The names given to the several anniversaries of a marriage are said to be of quite ancient origin, and arose from the gift which was regarded as the most suitable offering from the husband to the wife. The names commonly given to such anniversaries are for the first, paper; second, straw; third, candy; fourth, leather; fifth, wooden; seventh, floral; tenth, tin; twelfth, linen; fifteenth, crystal; twentieth, china; twenty-fifth, silver; thirtieth, pearl; thirty-fifth, coral; fortieth, emerald; forty-fifth, ruby; fiftieth, golden; and seventy-fifth, diamond. The diamond wedding is often celebrated at the sixtieth anniversary. Those most frequently celebrated are the paper, wooden, tin, crystal, silver, and golden.

WEDEKIND, FRANK (1864–1918), German playwright, born in Hanover, West Prussia, and educated at the universities of Munich and Zurich. After leading a Bohemian existence in Paris and London, he returned to Munich, where he obtained a position on the staff of the celebrated satirical magazine *Simplicissimus.* His plays *Der Erdgeist* ("The Earth Spirit", 1895), *Der Kammersänger* ("The Singer", 1899), and *Der Liebestrank* ("The Love Potion", 1900) were produced at Leipzig with notable success. In consequence of unflattering allusions to the German emperor, William II, which Wedekind introduced into his writings, the dramatist was sentenced to a term of imprisonment, but evaded the punishment by fleeing from Munich to Paris. He soon returned, however, to serve out his sentence. Thereafter he went to Berlin, where he acted for a time in his own plays. Wedekind was deeply influenced by the works of the playwrights Henrik Ibsen and August Strindberg. Although he often equals these dramatists in emotional power, he is inferior to them in both technique and style. The plays of Wedekind, in which the theme of sexual depravity frequently figures, are pervaded by a strong cynicism and pessimism. His other dramatic works include *Frühlings Erwachen* ("The Awakening of Spring", 1891), *So Ist das Leben* ("Such is Life", 1902), *Hidalla* (1904), *Totentanz* ("The Dance of Death", 1906), *Der Stein der Weisen* ("The Philosopher's Stone", 1909), *Simson* (1914), and *Herakles* (1917).

WEDEMEYER, ALBERT COADY (1897–   ), American military officer, born in Omaha, Nebr., and educated at the United States Military Academy, West Point, N.Y. He entered the United States Army in 1918 as second lieutenant and rose through the ranks to brigadier general in 1942, major general in 1943, and lieutenant general in 1945. In 1944, during World War II, he was appointed commander of the United States forces in the China Theater and chief of staff to the commander in chief of the Chinese forces, Generalissimo Chiang Kai-shek. In 1947 General Wedemeyer made a survey of conditions in China and Korea for President Harry S. Truman. Though the text of his report was not released to the public by the Department of State for reasons of national security, statements issued by Wedemeyer indicated that he had criticized both the Kuomintang (q.v.) and the communist forces in China, and had concluded that communism could not be eliminated in China by military force alone.

WEDGE, a simple machine based on the principle of the inclined plane (q.v.). The wedge consists of an object of triangular cross-section, usually having two faces, which are inclined planes, forming an isosceles triangle with a narrow base. Force is applied to the wedge in a direction perpendicular to the base, and the mechanical advantage given by the wedge is proportional to the ratio of the length of the wedge to the width of its base. No simple formula for the mechanical advantage given by an actual wedge is possible, because of the effects of friction. Wedges are frequently used for lifting heavy objects, and the wedge principle is employed in such cutting tools as the axe and the chisel, in which a comparatively small force is used to exert a large force for the cutting or splitting of wood or other material.

WEDGWOOD, HENSLEIGH (1803–91), English philologist, grandson of Josiah Wedgwood, born in Gunville, Dorset. He was one of the original members of the English Philological Society, and a scholar of wide learning. He wrote *On the Development of the Understanding* (1848), *A Dictionary of English Etymology* (1857), and *Contested Etymologies* (1882).

WEDGWOOD, JOSIAH (1730–95), the most celebrated of English potterists, born in Burslem, Staffordshire. His earliest efforts were

Metropolitan Museum of Art
WEDGWOOD WARE, 18TH CENTURY
Above, left: Vase bearing Josiah Wedgwood's characteristic classical cameos and figures. Above, right: Black basalt-ware tea set. At right: Queen's-ware dinner plate.

directed to the refining of the material, and in 1763 he took out a patent for a beautiful cream-colored porcelain, which became popularly known as queen's ware, Queen Charlotte having much admired it, and extended her patronage to the manufacturer. Black ware had been made in England from time immemorial, but Wedgwood's improvement, known as basalt, was so great as to amount to a creation. Wedgwood was assisted by John Flaxman, who modeled the most characteristic designs. The ware cosisted of tinted bodies of blue, sage green, and various colors, on which small cameo reliefs in white or tinted paste were applied while they were soft, and were then fired. The figures are classical and the microscopic delicacy of the detail is astonishing. Toward the end of the 18th century many imitations of the Wedgwood wares were made by different English manufacturers and they were copied at Sèvres, but with French designs. The famous Barberini or Portland vase, produced from the original antique, is probably the most famous example of Wedgwood jasper. In 1769 Wedgwood had removed his works some little way from Burslem, and to the new site he gave the fanciful name Etruria.

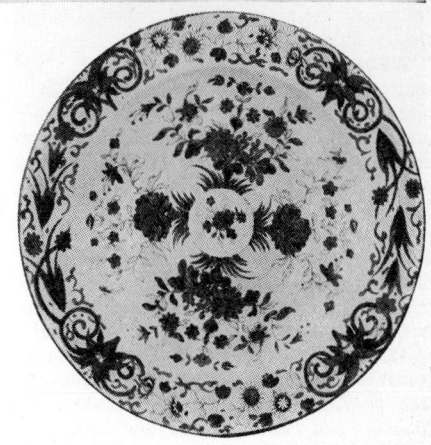

WEDGWOOD, THOMAS (1771–1805), English physicist and philanthropist, son of Josiah Wedgwood. It is said that Wedgwood was the first photographer, as he was the first to discover that a silhouette of any object might be obtained when its shadow was thrown on a surface moistened with nitrate of silver. He did not, however, discover any way of fixing the images, and so was obliged to keep them in the dark. He aided several men, among whom was Samuel Taylor Coleridge, the poet.

WEDGWOOD WARE. See WEDGWOOD, JOSIAH.

WEDMORE, SIR FREDERICK (1844–1921), English art critic and writer, born in Clifton.

Standard Oil Co. (N.J.)
Hoeing weeds in a field of tobacco

In 1885 he visited the United States to deliver art lectures at Harvard and Johns Hopkins universities. Among his many books on art are *Studies in English Art* (two series, 1876, 1880), *Masters of Genre Painting* (1877), *Turner and Ruskin* (1900), *Some of the Moderns* (1909), *Etchings* (1911), and *Painters and Painting* (1913).

WEDNESBURY, a municipal borough in Staffordshire, England, near the source of the Tame, 7½ miles N.W. of Birmingham. Its chief industry is the manufacture of heavy iron and steel goods. The city is named after the Saxon god Woden. The site of an ancient temple dedicated to pagan worship is occupied by a fine Perpendicular church. Pop, about 32,000.

WEDNESDAY, the fourth day of the week, the *Dies Mercurii* of the Romans, the *Mittwoch* of the modern Germans. The Anglo-Saxon form was *Wōodnes dæg*; the Dutch, *Woensdag*; and the Swedish and Danish, *Onsdag*.

WEED, THURLOW (1797–1882), American journalist and political leader, born in Cairo, N.Y. In 1815 he went to New York City, and after a brief career in printing establishments there he founded succesively the *Agriculturist* in Norwich and the *Onondaga County Republican* in Manlius, N.Y. He became editor of the Rochester daily *Telegraph* in 1822, and, in 1825, owner. In 1826 he established the *Anti-Masonic Enquirer*. He was for several years a member of the State legislature. In 1830 Weed removed to Albany and established the Albany *Evening Journal,* an anti-Jackson organ, which he edited for thirty-three years. From 1840 to 1860 he played a leading part in national and New York State politics. After the Civil War he served on the editorial staff of the *New York Times,* and from 1867 to 1878 was editor of the *Commercial Advertiser*. In 1866 he published *Letters from Europe and the West Indies*. His *Autobiography* was published in 1884.

WEEDEN, WILLIAM BABCOCK (1834–1912), American economist and historian, born in Bristol, R.I. In 1851 he entered upon the business of woolen manufacture in Providence, R.I. He served in the Civil War, resigning as captain. Weeden's works include *Morality of Prohibitory Liquor Laws* (1875); *Social Law of Labor* (1882); *Economic and Social History of New England* (1890); *War Government, Federal and State* (1906); and *Early Rhode Island, a Social History of the People* (1910).

WEEDS, undesirable plants growing wild, usually in cultivated ground. No systematic classification of weeds is possible; a plant may be considered desirable under one set of circumstances, and be a rank pest under another; for example, the white clover is often intentionally cultivated in a lawn, but in a strawberry patch it becomes a nuisance. Weeds harm the cultivated crop by competing with it for moisture, minerals, and sunlight, thereby reducing the size of the crop, and accelerating exhaustion of the soil. They also provide shelter and incubation for diseases and insect pests, which damage the crop, and increase the labor required in cultivation. In ornamental cultivation, they also injure the appearance of the plot, and reduce the value of the property. On fallow land weeds may form a cover crop, preventing erosion and furnishing a green manure for plowing under, but this advantage is offset by the harm done in allowing undesirable plants to gain a foothold and to form a focus for seeding the plot and adjacent lands.

Methods for the control of weeds depend for their effectiveness on the life history of the particular species. Annual weeds, such as goosefoot, shepherds' purse, and chickweed, are most easily controlled by prevention of seeding, cutting off the tops of the plants before the seed forms; by cultivation, such as hoeing, raking, or forking, early in the season, to destroy the young plants; or by pulling up the weeds by hand. Biennial weeds, such as burdock and wild carrot, can be controlled by the same methods as the annual species, but perennial weeds, especially those which propagate by roots and rootstocks as well as by seed, must have the root destroyed, for effective control. Repeated tillage is effective in eradicating perennial weeds, especially when it is combined with the planting of a competitive crop, such as clover alfalfa, soybeans, or cowpeas, which smothers the weed plants. Other methods of weed control include mowing, burning, smothering the growth with a mulch of hay, straw, or paper, and the use of chemical herbicides.

Herbicides include soil sterilizing agents and contact herbicides. Temporary sterilizing agents, such as chlorpicrin and carbon bisulfide, are volatile, and, after killing all root tissue with which they come in contact, evaporate, leaving the soil ready for cultivation after several weeks. Permanent sterilizing agents, such as borax and the borates, are used only where cropping is not intended, as in establishing permanent firebreaks. Contact herbicides are spread or sprayed on the top growths; certain petroleum oils, sulfuric acid, sodium chlorate and other salts kill all plant tissue with which they come in contact; other contact agents have a selective action. Cereals, onions, and peas, for example, are resistant to the action of sodium dinitroorthocresylate, which kills most broad-leafed annual weeds; plants of the carrot family withstand the action of stove oil, which kills most weeds and grasses. See TWO-FOUR-D.

WEEHAWKEN, a township of Hudson Co., N.J., situated on the Hudson R., adjoining Hoboken and opposite midtown New York City. Transportation facilities include several railroads, and the extensive water front is lined with wharves accommodating the largest ocean-going vessels. Weehawken is an important coal depot, and a manufacturing center, with numerous varied industrial establishments. The township lies along the s. end of the Palisades. At a point in Weehawken just below the summit of the Palisades, is the ledge which was the site of the famous duel between Alexander Hamilton and Aaron Burr, on July 11, 1804, in which Hamilton was fatally wounded. Weehawken was incorporated in 1859. Pop. (1940) 14,363.

WEEK, the period of seven days now in universal use as a division of time. It is of Hebrew or Chaldean origin. Originally regarded as a memorial of the creation of the world, it is obviously the most convenient division of the lunar month. From the designations of the planets have been formed the modern names for the days of the week, Sunday (Sol), Monday (Moon), Tuesday (Tui, the Saxon Mars), Wednesday (Woden, or Mercury), Thursday (Thor, or Jupiter), Friday (Frygga, or Venus), and Saturday (Saturn). See CALENDAR.

WEEKS, EDWIN LORD (1849–1903), American painter, born in Boston, and educated in Paris, where he studied under Jean Gérôme and Léon Bonnat. He traveled extensively in Egypt and Asia, and the Oriental motif predominates in most of his paintings. He received the grand diploma of honor at Berlin in 1891, and a special medal and prize at the Empire of India Exhibition in London (1896), and was made Chevalier of the Legion of Honor of France in 1896, and officer of the Order of St. Michael of Bavaria in 1898. His work, which shows accuracy of observation and detail, is well represented in the Corcoran Gallery, Washington, the Academy of Fine Arts, Philadelphia, and the Metropolitan Museum of Art, New York City, and the Brooklyn Institute Museum.

WEEKS, JOHN WINGATE (1860–1926), American banker and public official, born in Lancaster, N.H. In 1888 he became a member of the banking house of Hornblower & Weeks of Boston, Mass. A Republican, he served as mayor of Newton (1903–04) and as representative in Congress (1905–13). He also served in the United States Senate (1912–19). President Warren Gamaliel Harding appointed Weeks secretary of war in 1921. He remained in President Calvin Coolidge's cabinet until October, 1925, when he resigned.

WEEKS, FEAST OF. See PENTECOST.

WEELKES, THOMAS (1575?–1623), English organist and composer of madrigals (see MADRIGAL), educated at New College, Oxford University. He became a member of the Chapel Royal, and from 1602 to 1623 was organist at Chichester Cathedral. The collection of madrigals of Weelkes upon which his reputation is chiefly based were first published in 1597; his *Ayres or Phantasticke Spirites,* another collection of madrigals, appeared in 1608. See also SERVICE.

WEEMS, MASON LOCKE (about 1760–1825), American preacher and writer, born in Dumfries, Va. He is chiefly remembered for his *Life of Washington* (1800). The fifth edition (1806) contained such anecdotes as that of the hatchet and the cherry tree, now generally discredited. His other works include a *Life of General Francis Marion* (1805), *God's Revenge against Gambling* (1816), and *The Bad Wife's Looking-glass, or God's Revenge against Cruelty to Husbands* (1823).

WEENIX, JAN (1640–1719), Dutch animal and still-life painter, born in Amsterdam. From 1702 to 1712 he was court painter to the elector in Düsseldorf, for whom he decorated the Castle of Bensberg with paintings, most of which are now in the Munich Gallery and in Schleissheim. Nearly all the chief galleries of Europe and America possess his pictures, which are characterized by delicate brush work and good color.

WEEPING TREE, a term applied to a tree the branches of which droop toward the ground. Notable examples are afforded by the weeping willow, elm, and birch. Most of these trees cannot be propagated by means of seeds, but are increased by means of grafting, the graft being applied to a young tree of the upright growing form.

WEEVER, or STINGFISH (*Trachinus*), a genus of fishes, mainly European, of which two species, the greater, *T. draco,* 12 or 13 in. long, and the smaller, *T. vipera,* are both British, and are excellent food fish. They have sharp dorsal and opercular spines, with which they can inflict serious wounds.

WEEVER, JOHN (1576–1632), English poet and antiquary, born in Lancashire, and educated at Queens' College, Cambridge. In 1599 he wrote *Epigrammes in the Oldest Cut and Newest Fashion,* chiefly valued because its references to William Shakespeare, Michael Drayton, Ben Johnson, Thomas Middleton, and others throw light on contemporary opinion of those poets. In 1601 Weever wrote *The Mirror of Martyrs,* which relates to Sir John Oldcastle. His antiquarian researches were of value despite occasional inaccuracies.

WEEVIL, common name for any of numerous coleopterous beetles (q.v.) of the division Rhynchophora, belonging mainly to the families Curculionidae and Scolytidae. The adult weevil is usually dull in color and is herbivorous; it is characterized by a prolongation of the anterior part of the head into a *rostrum*; the apex of the rostrum contains the biting mouthparts, and two clubbed antennae are attached in depressions at each side. The oval body, which is covered with a rough, hard integument, bears four-jointed tarsi. A single median suture traverses the lower part of the head. Weevils exhibit complete metamorphosis; the larvae are white, semicircular, fleshy grubs with vestigial legs, strong jaws, and rudimentary eyes; they feed entirely on plant life, causing much damage to crops. The adults usually hibernate during most of the winter.

The family Curculionidae consists of the true weevils, and contains approximately 20,000 species native to temperate and subtropical regions of North America and Eurasia. Most weevils of this family are grouped under the subfamily Curculioninae, of which *Curculio* is the characteristic genus. *Curculio,* which contains the nut and acorn weevils, is characterized by a bulky body and a long, slender beak. In the female, the beak is usually longer than the entire body; it is used for drilling holes in nuts or acorns, and for placing the eggs in the kernels. Squirrels often open acorns in search of the larvae. When the nuts fall to the ground during the autumn, the larvae burrow underground and pupate the following July. The adults average .3 inch from the front margin of the head to the tip of the abdomen. *C. auriger,* the lesser chestnut weevil, is black, with brownish scales, and has bands of pale yellow spots crossing the elytra. The hickory nut weevil, or pecan weevil, *C. caryae,* has an overall brownish-yellow color. The hazel nut weevil, *C. ottusus,* is dark brown, and is covered with sparse, yellow hairs. Other curculionid weevils include the curculios, or fruit weevils, which are a quarter of an inch in length, and spend most of the adult and larval stage within various fruits. The most important of these weevils is the plum curculio, *Conotrachelus nenuphar,* which feeds on plums, peaches, cherries, and other stone fruits. It is found throughout the United States, and is usually dark brown, varied with black. Numerous eggs, deposited by the female under the skin of the fruit, hatch within several days into small, white grubs, which eat their way through the flesh of the fruit. The larvae attain full growth in eighteen days; they then bore their way out of the fruit and enter the soil to pupate. The grape curculio, *Craponius inequalis,* is dark brown, with scattered patches of white. The adult feeds on grape leaves; the female deposits numerous eggs within the fruit. After feeding on the seeds, the larvae drop to the ground and pupate underground. *Tachypterellus quadrigibbus,* the apple curculio, is usually colored dark red

U.S.D.A., Bur. of Entomology & Plant Quarantine

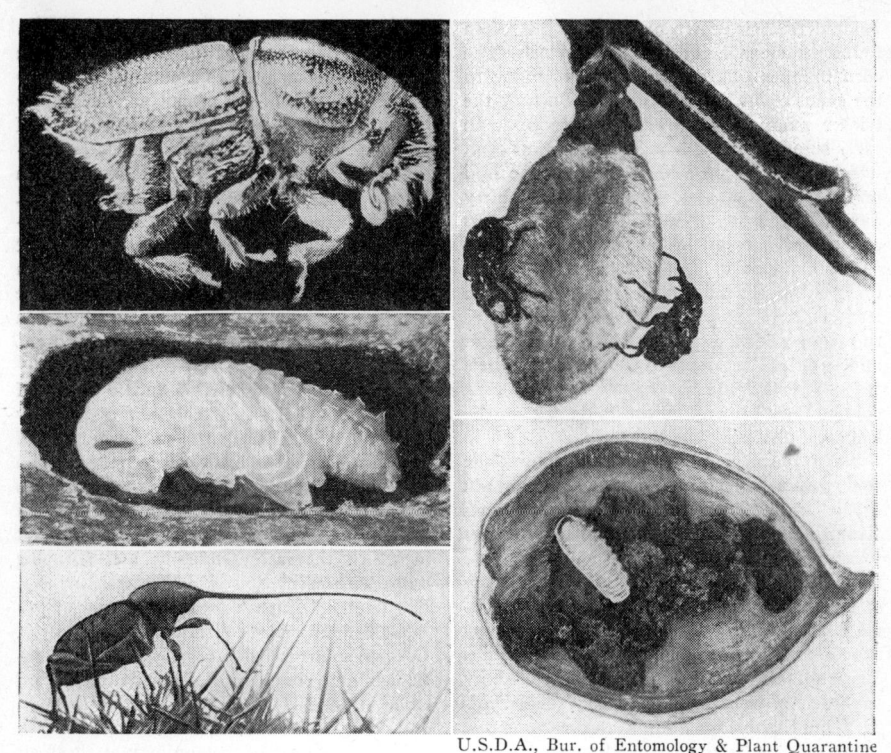

WEEVILS. *Left, from top to bottom:* Elm-tree fruit beetle (*Scolytus multistriatus*); pupa of elm-tree fruit beetle; chestnut weevil (*Curculio proboscideus*). *Right top:* Plum curculio (*Conotrachelus nenuphar*) on peach. *Right, bottom:* Plum-curculio larva.

and bears two large tubercles on the back of each elytron. The adults feed on the shoots or fruit of apple trees; the female deposits its eggs within the flesh of the fruit. The larvae eat their way through the fruit, and pupate there after three weeks. The grape weevil, *Ampeloglypter sesostris,* is pale reddish-brown and attains a length of .12 inch; it lays its eggs in grape canes, producing galls approximately twice the diameter of the cane. *A. ater,* a black species, deposits its eggs in a girdle around the cane, causing the vine to break off. The strawberry weevil, *Anthonomus signatus,* is black or dark brown in color and averages .13 inch in length. The females, after depositing their eggs in strawberry buds, cut the stems so that the buds fall to the ground. Strawberry plants are also dwarfed or killed by the larvae of another weevil, the strawberry crown borer, *Tyloderma fragrariae,* which digs out the interior of the crown. The cotton-boll weevil, *Anthonomus grandis,* commonly known as boll weevil, has an over-all grayish color and averages .13 inch in length. It is native to s. Mexico and Central America, and is widespread in the U.S., causing considerable damage to the cotton crop. The adults infest the cotton plant; the female lays its eggs in the squares and bolls, upon which the larvae feed; see COTTON.

The subfamily Calendrinae contains the grain weevils and billbugs, the larvae of which either bore into the stems of plants or feed on grain. The granary weevil, *Calendra,* or *Sitophilus, granaria,* has been widely distributed through the shipment of grain in commerce, and destroys large quantities of cereals each year. It is colored chestnut-brown or black, is wingless, and averages .13 inch in length. The females produce numerous eggs six times during the year, and deposits them inside the kernels, where the larvae feed and grow. *C. oryzae,* commonly known as the rice weevil, is native to India and infests rice and other grains throughout the world. It is colored reddish brown or black, and is often found in crackers or packaged cereals. The corn billbugs or elephant bugs, belonging to the genus *Sphenophorus,* hibernate during the winter among dead leaves and rubbish. In early summer, the female lays numerous eggs, which hatch within a month; the larvae feed on the roots of grasses, and pupate after thirty days. The cabbage weevil, *Rhynchophorus cruentatus,* lives in the cabbage palmetto and is abundant in s. United States. It is shiny black or partly red, and averages .75 inch in length. *R. ferrugineus,* commonly known as the palm weevil, is native to the West Indies and tropical America; see GRUGRU. The alfalfa weevil, *Phytonomus posticus,* is usually colored dark brown and causes damage to the leaves of alfalfa.

The subfamily Otiorhynchinae contains the root weevils, the larvae of which subsist on the roots of numerous plants. *Brachyrhinus,* the principal genus, is characterized by the presence of two short spurs on each hind tibia, and reaches a length of .3 inch. The strawberry root weevil, *B. sulcatus,* is brownish black; in the adult stage it eats young shoots, and destroys many ornamental shrubs. The subfamily Attelabinae is constituted by the single genus *Attelabus,* the larvae of which feed on thimblelike rolls of leaves prepared by the female adult. The seed weevils, whose larvae live in and destroy the seeds of many trees, belong to the genus *Apion* of the subfamily Apioninae. They are pear shaped and usually dark brown in color, and are commonly found in wild indigo trees of the genus *Baptisia.*

The family Scolytidae contains the bark, or engraver, beetles, which create numerous tunnels by burrowing between the bark and wood of trees. The principal genus, *Scolytus,* has a shiny, black thorax, dark-red elytra, and light-brown legs; it averages .12 inch in length. During the breeding season, the female tunnels into the bark or sapwood of various trees, digs several small pockets along the sides of the tunnel, and deposits a single egg in each pocket. Each larva tunnels at right angles to the main burrow, pupating at the end of its burrow. Adults emerging from the pupae bore "straight out", producing numerous small "wormholes" in the bark. Typical species are the fruit-tree bark beetle, *S. rugulosus*; elm-tree fruit beetle, *S. multistriatus*; and hickory-tree beetle, *S. spinosus.*

Various other insects, not included in the division Rhynchophora, are commonly known as weevils. The pea weevil, *Mylabris pisorum,* belongs to the family Mylabridae; it is mainly black, covered with reddish-brown and white hairs, and has a notch on the middle of each side of the pronotum. The female lays numerous eggs once a year on the pod of young peas, the larvae boring inside and pupating within the seed. *M. obtectus,* the bean weevil, is black above, reddish brown below, and lacks the notch on the side of the pronotum. The female lays its eggs throughout the year on or within the bean pod, in which the larvae pupate. The flour beetles, of the family Tenebrionidae, are commonly found in meal, grain, and other vegetables; see MEAL WORM.

Weevils cause millions of dollars worth of damage to American and Eurasian crops every year. They are difficult to control because of their small size and because of the hidden positions of the larvae and pupae. Common methods of control consist of burning infested fruits, nuts, or stems; plowing up the ground in which the insects pupate; and spraying crops with carbon bisulphide insecticides. See ENTOMOLOGY, ECONOMIC.

WEGENER, ALFRED LOTHAR (1880–1930), German meteorologist, geophysicist, and arctic explorer, born in Berlin. He conducted explorations in Greenland from 1906 to 1908, and from 1912 to 1917. In 1924 he was appointed professor of meteorology at the University of Graz. He conducted two additional expeditions into Greenland in 1929 and in 1930, losing his life during the latter exploration. Wegener is particularly noted for a hypothesis which states that the continents now in existence were originally a single area of land, and have attained their present positions by a process of drifting. He is also noted for research in atmospheric thermodynamics.

WEIERSTRASS, KARL (1815–97), German mathematician, born in Ostenfelde, Westphalia, and educated at the universities of Bonn and Münster. In 1842 he became a teacher at the Gymnasium in Münster, and in 1848 was appointed to a similar position in Braunsberg. In 1856 he became instructor at the Industrial Institute in Berlin, and in 1864 was appointed professor of mathematics at the university of that city. His works relate chiefly to Abelian integrals and differential equations, and he is generally regarded as being the founder of the modern treatment of the general theory of functions. His *Abhandlungen aus der Funktionenlehre* was published in Berlin in 1886. His other works, including *Zur Theorie der Abel'schen Integrale* (1849), *Formeln u. s. w.*

Fairbanks, Morse & Co. Signal Corps Photo

WEIGHING MACHINES. *Right, top to bottom: Even-balance scale; household scale; meat beam scale. Above: Vegetable spring scale.*

der Elliptischen Funktionen (1885), and his numerous memoirs, appear in his *Mathematische Werke,* published under the patronage of the Prussian Academy of Sciences (Berlin, 1894–1903). He also edited the works of Jacobi (1881–91) and Steiner (1881–82).

WEIGALL, ARTHUR EDWARD PEARSE BROME (1880–1934), English Egyptologist and antiquarian. He served many years on the staff of the Egypt Exploration Fund. In 1914 he retired as inspector general of antiquities of Egypt. Weigall was present at the opening of Tutankhamen's tomb. Among his works are *Nero* (1930), *Life of Marc Antony* (1931), and *Laura Was My Camel* (1933).

WEIGEL, VALENTIN (1533–88), German mystic, born in Grossenhain, and educated at the universities of Leipzig and Wittenberg. From 1567 to his death he preached at Zschopau, near Chemnitz. He emphasized the necessity of internal unction and illumination. His main thesis was that knowledge does not come from without, but from the eye of the cognitive subject. In cosmology his position approximates that of Paracelsus. Of his writings only an unimportant funeral sermon appeared before his death. His works were published from 1604 to 1618 in various places, and Weigelianism became widely spread. His opponents represented him as a dangerous revolutionary, who aimed at the overthrow of all political and social order. Weigel's most prominent writings include *Libellus de Vita Beata* (1609), *Ein Schön Gebetbüchlein* (1612), *Philosophia Theologica* (1614), *Principal und Haupttractat von der Gelassenheit* (1618), and *Soli Deo Gloria* (1618).

WEIGELIA, genus of deciduous shrubs in the Honeysuckle family, formerly called *Diervilla.* The flowers are crimson, pink, or yellowish white in color, one of which, *W. florida,* was introduced into cultivation from China. Two American species are known as bush honeysuckle. The northern species, *W. lonicera,* is common in the middle and northern States. It grows from 1 to 4 feet high, bears oblong-ovate petioled leaves, and pale-yellow axillary flowers. The southern species, *W. sessilifolia,* grows along the southern Alleghenies, and has sessile leaves. The shrubs are extensively cultivated and many hybrid forms have been developed.

WEIGHING MACHINE, any apparatus for ascertaining weight, especially an apparatus for weighing very heavy bodies. Early weighing machines were all based on the old Roman steelyard principle, where the article to be weighed had to be suspended and balanced. Modern weighing machines date from 1830 with the invention of the platform scale by Thaddeus Fairbanks, which determined weights by a system of levers.

Some scales work automatically, taking material from a large hopper, weighing out a certain amount and discharging it, and then repeating the operation. Such contrivances are used for bagging such products as sugar and coffee, and for weighing grain or coal in or out of bin or elevator. Scales are built which have a capacity for weighing very heavy loads; examples of these are railway car and locomotive scales, cattle scales with a capacity of weighing from 20 to 200 head of cattle, and grain scales of 500 bushels capacity and more. Besides scales operating on the principle of the balance, there are weighing machines which operate by compressing a coiled spring or by twisting a bar of metal. The spring scale is a very common device, and in the form of a dynamometer for registering the pull of locomotives is made with very large capacities. For the most part, however, spring scales are of small capacity. They are not as reliable as balance scales.

Weighing machines have been adapted to many purposes, and are commonly called scales. They derive their names either from some constructional feature or from the use to which they are specially fitted, as *combination* scales, having several beams or several sets of graduations upon one beam; *lever* scales, a special adaptation of the steelyard; *registering* scales, having a device, usually operated by pushing a button, which records the weight of an article on a card or paper; *suspension* scales, suspended from a traveling crane and used to weigh the load carried by the crane; *creamery* scales, a platform scale having several beams, for weighing at the same time the lots of milk brought by several persons; *grocers'* scales, having a large receptacle on the platform; *railroad* scales, a large platform scale bearing a railroad track, and arranged for weighing rolling stock, or the load on a car; *canal-boat* scales, an arrangement of a canal lock for weighing canal boats, also called weigh-lock scales; and *grain* scales or *sample* scales, lever scales of great accuracy for weighing minute quantities.

WEIGHTS AND MEASURES. To measure a a given unknown quantity of any kind is to find how many times that quantity contains another known quantity of the same kind. The latter quantity is called the "unit" in which the result is expressed. A concrete representation of a unit is called a standard. Of the earliest standards of length the principal were the palm, or hand, breadth, the foot, and the cubit (the length from elbow to tip of middle finger). The obvious objection to such standards as these is their liability to vary, yet it was only within modern times that definite standards of measurement were adopted. In the United States and Great Britain the unit of linear measurement is the yard; the standard yard, which was established in 1854, is the distance between two lines crossing two gold studs set in a certain bar of platinum kept in London, the measurement being made when the temperature is 62° F. and the barometric pressure is 30 in. The fundamental units in common use in the United States today are the yard as the unit of length; the pound avoirdupois and the pound troy as units of weight; and the gallon as unit of capacity. The legal standards fixing these units are carefully preserved at the National Bureau of Standards, and certified copies are supplied. From the simple units named, other units are derived, connected with these by simple arithmetical relation. These relations constitute the tables of measurement. The separate States have enacted statutes dealing with the use of false weights and measures, and for securing uniformity in different trades and industries.

THE CHIEF WEIGHTS AND MEASURES OF THE WORLD [1]

Abbreviations

a.	= are.	i.bu.	= imperial bushel.	m.²	= square meter.
bu.	= bushel.	i.gal.	= imperial gallon.	mi.	= mile or miles.
cwt.	= hundredweight.	in.	= inch.	oz.	= ounce (avoirdupois).
ft.	= foot or feet.	kg.	= kilogram.	pk.	= peck.
g.	= gram.	kl.	= kiloliter.	qt.	= quart.
gal.	= gallon.	km.	= kilometer.	rd.	= rod.
gr.	= grain.	l.	= liter.	sq.	= square.
ha.	= hectare.	m.	= meter.	yd.	= yard.
lb.	= pound (avoirdupois).				

[1] Due to the advent of World War II, foreign weights and measures are corrected only up to 1939.

WEIGHTS AND MEASURES

Country	Weight or Measure	English or American Equivalent	Metric Equivalent
Afghanistan †	charak	4 lbs.	1.82 kg.
	gaz	40 in.	1.016 m.
	kharwar	1,280 lbs.	581.82 kg.
	khurd	.25 lb.	.114 kg.
	maund	80 lbs.	36.27 kg.
	pao	1 lb.	.454 kg.
	seer	16 lbs.	7.273 kg.
Algeria [1]			
Argentine Republic *			
Australia		Weights and measures of Great Britain.	
Austria * [2]	centner (100 pfund)	123.46 lbs.	56.06 kg.
	eimer	12.49 gals.	56.59 l.
	fuss	12.446 in.	0.316 m.
	jach	1.43 acres	5,754.64 sq.m.
	meile	4.714 mi.	7.586 km.
	metzen	1.7 i.bu.	61.49 l.
	pfund	1.235 lbs.	280 g.
Belgian Congo	Metric System		
Belgium *	aune [3]		= meter
	litron [3]		= liter
	livre [3]		= kilogram
Bolivia * [4]	mare (mining produce)	507 lbs.	229.97 kg.
Brazil * [5]	alqueire	1 i.bu.	40 l.
	arroba	32.379 lbs.	14,687.4 g.
	libra	1.012 lbs.	459,033 g.
	oitava } outava	55.34 grs.	3.65 g.
	quintal	129.54 lbs.	58.749 kg.
Canada [7]		Weights and measures of Great Britain.	
Central America	arroba	26.075 lbs.	11.827 kg.
	cantara	4.263 gals.	16.137 l.
	cuartilla	1.065 gals.	4.031 l.
	"	also 0.393 gal.	1.487 l.
	fanega	1.574 bu.	55.48 l.
	libra	1.043 lbs.	0.473 kg.
	vara	32.874 in.	0.835 m.
Chile †	fanega	2.575 bu.	90.743 l.
	libra	1.043 lbs.	473 g.
	quartillo	10.656 in.	0.27 m.
	vara	33.367 in.	0.847 m.
China † [8]	chang	125.99 in.	3.2 m.
	ch'ih	1 ft.	0.32 m.
	chin (catty)	1.333 lbs.	604.78 g.
	li	0.333 mi.	576 m.
	liang (tael)	1.32 oz.	37.301 g.
	mow	0.167 acres	0.067 ha.
	picul	133.333 lbs.	60.478 kg.
	tou	10.946 qts.	10.355 l.
	ts'un	1 in.	0.025 m.
Colombia [4]	Metric System		
Cuba	Metric System		
Denmark	Metric System		
Egypt [9]	ardeb	43.555 gal.	164.855 l.
		5.444 bu.	191.837 l.
	diraa baladi (for textiles)	22.835 in.	.571 m.
	diraa mimâri (for building)	29.528 in.	0.738 m.
	feddân	1.038 acres	4,200.833 m.
	heml	550.274 lbs.	249.549 kg.
	kadah	3.63 pints	1.999 l.
	keila	3.63 gal.	13.74 l.
	oke	2.75 lbs.	1.247 kg.
	pic (square)	6.055 sq.ft.	0.563 sq.m.
	qantar	99.049 lbs.	44.927 kg.
	qasabar	3.882 yds.	3.55 m.
	rob	1.815 gal	6.87 l.
	rotl	0.991 lbs.	0.45 kg.

WEIGHTS AND MEASURES

Country	Weight or Measure	English or American Equivalent	Metric Equivalent
Ethiopia †	dawala	176 lbs.	80 kg.
	farasula	37.5 lbs.	17 kg.
	gasha	80 acres	198 ha.
	goundo	3.3 qt.	3 l.
	kantar	100 lbs.	45.45 kg.
	khalad	71 yds.	65 m.
	kounna	8.8 lbs.	4 kg.
	kund	19.75 in.	.502 m.
	ladan	88 lbs.	.40 kg.
	natr	1.875 lbs.	0.85 kg.
	ookia	1 oz.	28.067 g.
	waggia		
	(for ivory)	$480 weight	....
	(for rubber)	$649 weight	....
	wanche	3.3 qt.	3 l.
France	Metric System		
Germany	Metric System		
Great Britain [10]	chaldron	36 bu.	1.308 kl.
	stone	14 lbs.	6.35 kg.
Greece *	kantar	124.608 lbs.	56.511 kg.
	oke	2.832 lbs.	1.285 kg.
	pik	27 in.	0.686 m.
	pound (Great Venetian)	1.053 lbs.	0.478 kg.
	stremma	0.247 acres	0.01 ha.
Guatemala †	arroba	25.35 lbs.	11.498 kg.
	cantara	4.263 gals.	16.137 l.
	fanega	1.5 i.bu.	54.525 l.
	libra	1.014 lbs.	459.94 g.
	quintal	101.40 lbs.	45.994 kg.
	tonelada	18.1 cwt.	919.514 kg.
Haiti *	Metric System		
Hawaii		Weights and measures of United States	
Honduras † [11]	arroba	25 lbs.	11.34 kg.
	quintal	100 lbs.	45.359 kg.
	tonelada	2,000 lbs.	907.184 kg.
	vara	32 in.	0.813 m.
Hong Kong [12]	catty	1.333 lbs.	604.78 g.
	chek	14.625 in.	0.371 m.
	cheung	12.187 ft.	3.714 m.
	picul (100 catties)	133.333 lbs.	60.478 kg.
	tael	1.333 oz.	37.789 g.
Hungary *	Metric System		
India [6]	maund	82.26 lbs.	37.39 kg.
	seer	2.507 lbs.	0.935 kg.
	tola	180 gr. troy	11.664 g.
Iran *	abbasi (5 sîr)	5,680 grs.	368,064 g.
	batman (same as MAN)		
	gez	40.95 in.	1.04 m.
	kervankeh (same as ABBASI)		
	man [14]	6.49 lbs. to 116.80 "	2.933 kg. 52.98 kg.
	miskal	71 grs.	4.6 g.
	sîr (16 miskals)	1,136 grs.	73.613 g.
	wakkeh (same as ABBASI)		
	zar (same as GEZ)		
Italy *	Metric System		
Japan	chô (60 ken)	352 ft.	107,289 m.
	chô (square)	2.45 acres	9,915.15 m.
	ken	5.965 ft.	1.818 m.
	kin	1.323 lbs.	0.6 kg.
	koku (liquid)	39.68 gals.	156.202 l.
	koku (dry)	4.96 bu.	174.781 l.
	kwan	8.267 lbs.	3.76 kg.
	picul	132.27 lbs.	59.997 kg.
	ri (36 chô)	2.44 mi.	3.91 km.
	ri (square)	5.955 sq.mi.	15.54 sq.km.
	shaku	11.93 in.	0.303 m.
	sün	1.193 in.	0.03 m.
	to (liquid)	3.97 gals.	15.016 l.
	to (dry)	1.985 pks.	17.487 l.
	tsubo	3.954 sq.yds.	3.306 sq.m.

WEIGHTS AND MEASURES

Country	Weight or Measure	English or American Equivalent	Metric Equivalent
Liberia		Weights, etc., of Gr. Brit. or U.S.	
Mexico *	arroba	25.357 lbs.	11.501 kg.
	barril	20 gals.	75.7 l.
	fanega	1.55 bu.	56.342 l.
	libra	1.014 lbs.	0.46 kg.
	vara	32.9 in.	0.835 m.
Netherlands *			
Nicaragua *			
Norway *			
Panama [13]			
Paraguay *			
Peru *	arroba		
	(weight)	25.36 lbs.	11.503 kg.
	(liquid)	6.70 i.gals.	30.438 l.
	libra	1.014 lbs.	459.94 g.
	ounce	1.014 oz.	28.746 g.
	quintal	101.44 lbs.	45.994 kg.
	vara (length)	33.367 in.	0.847 m.
	" (square)	7.731 sq.ft.	0.718 sq.m.
Philippine Islands * [15]	anega (dry)	2.724 qts.	2.999 l.
	apatan (dry)	0.085 qt.	0.094 l.
	" (liqu.d)	0.085 qt.	.081 l.
	arroba		
	(liquid)	16.907 qts.	16 l.
	(weight)	25.35 lbs.	11.502 kg.
	balita	110.773 sq.rds.	27.9 a.
	bitic	16.538 sq.rds.	4.183 a.
	catty (16 taels)	1.38 lbs.	632.64 g.
	cavan	2.128 bu.	75 l.
	fanega	1.574 bu.	55.5 l.
	ganta	2.724 qts.	2.999 l.
	league (lagua, legua, loague)	3.462 mi.	5.573 km.
	line	0.83 in.	0.002 m.
	onza	1.002 oz.	29 g.
	palma	7.874 in.	0.2 m.
	pico } picul}	139.46 lbs.	63.262 kg.
	quintal	101.403 lbs.	46.009 kg.
	real	0.431 acre	1,746.875 sq.in.
	tael	603.798 grs.	39 g.
	vara	32.913 in.	0.836 m.
	vara (sq.)	7.305 sq.ft.	0.6987 sq.m.
Portugal *	almude		
	(Lisbon)	3.7 i.gals.	16.809 l.
	(Oporto)	5.6 i.gals.	25.44 l.
	alqueire		
	(Lisbon)	0.36 bu.	12.686 l.
	moio	77.64 lbs.	35.185 kg.
Puerto Rico *			
Romania *			
Siam (Thailand) *	ban	264.178 gals.	1,000 l.
	carat	0.006 troy oz.	0.2 g.
	catty	1.323 lbs.	600 g.
	keup	0.273 yds.	0.25 m.
	kwien	528.356 gals.	2,000 l.
	ngan	478,394 sq.yds.	400 sq.m.
	picul	132.277 lbs.	60 kg.
	rai	1,913.573 sq.yds.	1,600 sq.m.
	sat	5.284 gals.	20 l.
	sawk	0.547 yds	0.5 m.
	sen	43.744 yds.	40 m.
	tanan	0.264 gals.	1 l.
	wah	2.187 yds.	2 m.
	wah (sq.)	4.784 sq.yds.	4 sq.m.
Spain *	arroba		
	(wine)	3.5 i.gals.	15.89 l.
	(oil)	2.75 i.gals.	12.49 l.
	fanega	1.5 i.bu.	54.525 l.
	libra	1.014 lbs.	441.688 g.
	quintal	220.4 lbs.	99.972 kg.
	vara (sq.)	1 yd.	0.914 m.
Sweden *			
Switzerland *	arpent	0.889 acre	0.36 sq.in.
	centner	110.231 lbs.	50 kg.
	pfund	1.102 lbs.	0.5 kg.
	quintal	220.462 lbs.	100 kg.

Country	Weight or Measure	English or American Equivalent	Metric Equivalent
Turkey *	almud	1.151 i.gal.	5.228 l.
	arshin ⎫ archine ⎭	29.528 in.	0.750 m.
	cantar	125 lbs.	56.698 kg.
	endaze ⎫ endaseh (cloth) ⎭	25.70 in.	0.652 m.
	kile	0.36 i.qt.	0.408 l.
	kileh	0.912 i.bu.	32.138 l.
	kintal (same as CANTAR)		
	oke	2.832 lbs.	1.284 kg.
Union of Soviet Socialist Republics	arshin	28 in.	0.711 m.
	chetvert	5.771 i.bu.	203.37 l.
	dessiatine	2.699 acres	1.922 ha.
	pood	36 lbs.	16.329 kg.
	pound	0.9 lb.	408 g.
	sazhen	7 ft.	2.133 m.
	vedro	2.705 i.gals.	12.278 l.
	verst (length)	0.662 mi.	1.06 km.
	(square)	0.439 sq.mi.	113.704 ha.
United States [10]		See Weights and Measures in Common Use.	
Uruguay *	arroba	25.35 lbs.	11.498 kg.
	fanega	30 gals.	113.55 l.
	quintal	101.4 lbs.	45.994 kg.
Venezuela *			

NOTES ON PRECEDING ENTRIES.

* Metric system legal and obligatory, though some old weights and measures may still be in use.
† Metric system legal, but not obligatory, or not in general use among the people.
[1] The weights and measures of France are used.
[2] The metric system is legal and obligatory throughout the Republic of Austria.
[3] Name only occasionally used.
[4] Spanish measures still in use.
[5] Former Portuguese system still largely used.
[6] A great variety of weights and measures, more than can be here enumerated, are found in different provinces. Grains and liquids are largely measured by weight. The Standards of Weight Act, 1939, fixed the legal measures as here recorded. The standard ounce, pound, hundredweight, and ton were also established as legal weights.
[7] The weights and measures of Canada are the same as those of Great Britain, but in some parts of Lower Canada various old French terms are still used.
[8] The standard metric unit came into use in the Customs' Service, 1934, in accordance with the new standards promulgated by the government in 1929. The government also set up a temporary system, based on the metric system ("constituting the so-called 1-2-3 system of Chinese weights and measures based on international metric standard"—*Statesman's Yearbook*, 1942), to accustom the people to use of the metric system and designed for market use only. Some of the old units of weight, capacity, and length are here recorded.
[9] In 1939 the government established the meter, kilogram, and liter as the legal weights and measures of Egypt. In practice, however, the existing system, here recorded, continues in use; their metric equivalents, however, have to be given as well.
[10] The weights and measures of Great Britain are practically the same as those of the United States, which are derived from them. The common United States standard (Winchester) gallon contains 231 cubic inches; the British imperial gallon 277.274 cubic inches. The United States (Winchester) bushel contains 2,150.4 cubic inches; the British imperial bushel 2,218.2 cubic inches. Certain British units little used in the United States are noted in the table given above. For all others see the tables of Weights and Measures in Common Use.
[11] The metric system has been legal since 1897; English pounds and yards, however, and the old Spanish system are still in general use.
[12] The weights and measures of Great Britain are in general use in the crown colony of Hong Kong.
[13] In general use are the English and American weights and measures as well as those of the metric system.
[14] The *mans* are many and various, from the *man-ı-tabriz* (6.49 lbs.) to the *man-i-hâsheni* (116.80 lbs.).
[15] The metric system was in operation at the time the United States took possession, and its continued use was authorized by act of the Philippine Commission, Sept. 17, 1901. The weights and measures given in the table above are from the official tables of the *United States Census of the Philippine Islands*, 1903, Vol. IV, Pp. 448 et seq. Great variations in the quantities represented by these names are found in different islands and provinces.

WEIGHTS AND MEASURES IN COMMON USE

Long or Linear Measure

12 inches (in.)	= 1 foot (ft.).
3 feet	= 1 yard (yd.).
5½ yds. or 16½ ft.	= 1 rod (rd.) or pole (p.).
40 rods	= 1 furlong (fur.).
8 fur ongs	= 1 mile (mi.).
320 rods or 5280 ft.	= 1 mile.
3 miles	= 1 league.

Square Measure

144 square inches	= 1 square foot (sq.ft.).
9 square feet	= 1 square yard (sq.yd.).
30¼ sq.yds. or 272¼ sq.ft.	= 1 square rod (sq.rd.).
160 square rods	= 1 acre (A.).
640 acres	= 1 square mile (sq.mi.).

Cubic Measure

1728 cubic inches (cu.in.)	= 1 cubic foot (cu.ft.).
27 cubic feet	= 1 cubic yard (cu.yd.).
24¾ cubic feet	= 1 perch (P.).

Wood Measure

16 cubic feet	= 1 cord foot.
8 cord feet or 128 cubic feet	= 1 cord (cd.).

Note. A cord of wood, as generally piled, is 8 ft. long, 4 ft. wide, and 4 ft high.

Liquid Measure

4 gills (gi.)	= 1 pint (pt.).
2 pints	= 1 quart (qt.).
4 quarts	= 1 gallon (gal.).

Note. 31.5 gallons are considered a barrel (bbl.), and 63 gallons a hogshead (hhd.); but barrels and hogsheads are made of various sizes.

Apothecaries' Fluid Measure

60 minims (♏)	= 1 fluid dram (f ʒ).
8 fluid drams	= 1 fluid ounce (f ℥).
16 fluid ounces	= 1 pint (O.).
2 pints	= 1 quart (qt.)
8 pints	= 1 gallon (C.)

Dry Measure

2 pints (pt.).	= 1 quart (qt.).
8 quarts	= 1 peck (pk.).
4 pecks	= 1 bushel (bu.).

Note. In the United States, a bushel contains 2150.42 cu.in.; in Great Britain 2219.36 cu.in.

Troy Weight

24 grains (gr.)	= 1 pennyweight (pwt. or dwt.).
20 pennyweights	= 1 ounce (oz.) troy.
12 ounces troy	= 1 pound (lb.) troy.

Note. 1 lb. troy = 5760 grains. In weighing diamonds 1 carat = 3.168 troy grains, and is divided into quarters, which are called carat grains, or into hundredths, which are called points.

Apothecaries' Weight

20 grains (gr.)	= 1 scruple (℈).
3 scruples	= 1 dram (ʒ).
8 drams ap.	= 1 ounce (℥).
12 ounces ap.	= 1 pound (lb).

Note. The pound, ounce, and grain have the same weight as those of troy weight.

Avoirdupois Weight

27¹¹⁄₃₂ grains	= 1 dram (dr.).
16 drams	= 1 ounce (oz.)
16 ounces	= 1 pound (lb.).
25 pounds	= 1 quarter.
4 quarters or 100 pounds (U.S.)	= 1 hundredweight (cwt.).
112 pounds (Great Britain) 20 long hundredweight or	= 1 long or gross hundredweight. = 1 ton (T.).
2000 pounds (U.S.) "net" or "short" 2240 pounds (Great Britain)	= 1 long ton.

Note. 1 lb. avoirdupois = 7000 grains or 0.4535924277 kilograms. The long ton is also used in the United States.

TIME MEASURE

60 seconds (sec.)	=	1 minute (min.).
60 minutes	=	1 hour (hr.).
24 hours	=	1 day (da.).
7 days	=	1 week (wk.).
365 days } 12 months }	=	1 common year (yr.).
366 days	=	1 leap year.
100 years	=	1 century.

MARINERS' MEASURE

6 feet	=	1 fathom.
100 fathoms	=	1 cable length (or cable).
7 1/2 cable lgths.	=	1 mile.
5280 feet	=	1 statute mile.
6076.097 feet	=	1 nautical mile.

MEASURE OF ANGLES OR ARCS

60 seconds (″)	=	1 minute (′).
60 minutes	=	1 degree (°).
90 degrees	=	1 right angle or quadrant (**L**).
360 degrees	=	1 circle.

THE METRIC SYSTEM

MEASURES OF LENGTH

myriameter	10,000	m.	6.214	miles
kilometer	1000	m.	0.62137	mile (3280 feet, 10 inches)
hectometer	100	m.	328	feet 0.6 inches
decameter	10	m.	393.7	inches
meter	1	m.	39.37	inches
decimeter	0.1	m.	3.937	inches
centimeter	0.01	m.	0.3937	inch
millimeter	0.001	m.	0.03937	inch

Factors for Conversion. 1 inch = 0.0254 meter; 1 foot = 0.3048 meter; 1 mile = 1609.3472 meters.
Abbreviations. cm. = centimeter, dm. = decimeter, km. = kilometer, m. = meter, mm. = millimeter.

MEASURES OF SURFACE

hectare	10,000 m.²	2.471	acres
are	100 m.²	119.596	square yards
centare	1 m.²	1550	square inches

Factors for Conversion. 1 square inch = 0.06452 square meter; 1 square yard = 0.836 square meter; 1 acre = 4047 square meters.
Abbreviations. a. = are, ha. = hectare, m.² = square meter.

MEASURES OF CAPACITY

Name	Liter	Cubic Measure	Dry Measure
kiloliter (stere)	1000	1 m.³	1.308 cu.yds.
hectoliter	100	0.1 m.³	2.8 bush., 11.35 pecks
decaliter	10	10 dm.³	9.08 qts.
liter	1	1 dm.³	0.908 qt.
deciliter	0.1	0.01 dm.³	6.1022 cu.in.
centiliter	0.01	10 cm.³	0.6102 cu.in.
milliliter	0.001	1 cm.³	0.061 cu.in.

Name	Liter	Cubic Measure	Liquid Measure
kiloliter (stere)	1000	1 m.³	264.17 gals.
hectoliter	100	0.1 m.³	26.418 gals.
decaliter	10	10 dm.³	2.642 gals.
liter	1	1 dm.³	1.057 qts. liquid
deciliter	0.1	0.1 dm.³	0.845 gill.
centiliter	0.01	10 cm.³	0.338 fl.oz.
milliliter	0.001	1 cm.³	0.271 fl.dr.

Factors for Conversion. 1 cubic inch = 0.0164 liter; 1 bushel = (U.S.) 35.235 or (British) 36.37 liters; 1 quart (dry measure) = 1.1011 liters; 1 peck = (U.S.) 8.81 or (British) 9.09 liters; 1 cubic yard = 765 liters; 1 fluid dram = 0.00389 liter; 1 fluid ounce = 0.0296 liter; 1 gill = 0.1183 liter; 1 quart (liquid measure) = 0.9463 liter; 1 gallon standard (231 cubic inches) = 3.785 liters; 1 gallon imperial (277.42 cubic inches) = 4.546 liters.

Abbreviations. cl. = centiliter, cm.³ or cc. = cubic centimeter, dal. = decaliter, dl. = deciliter, dm.³ = cubic decimeter, hl. = hectoliter, l. = liter, m.³ = cubic meter, ml. = milliliter, mm.³ = cubic millimeter.

WEIGHTS AND MEASURES

WEIGHTS

Name	Gram	Water at Maximum Density	Avoirdupois Weight
millier (tonneau)	1,000,000	1 m.³	2204.6 lbs.
quintal	100,000	1 hl.	220.46 lbs.
myriagram	10,000	10 l.	22.046 lbs.
kilogram	1,000	1 l.	2.204 lbs.
hectogram	100	1 dl.	3.527 ozs.
decagram	10	10 cm.³	0.353 oz.
gram	1	1 cm.³	15.432 grs.
decigram	0.1	0.1 cm.³	1.543 grs.
centigram	0.01	10 mm.³	0.154 gr.
milligram	0.001	1 mm.³	0.015 gr.

Factors for Conversion. 1 grain = 0.0648 gram; 1 avoirdupois ounce = 28.3495 grams; 1 troy ounce = 31.103 grams; 1 pound = 453.59 grams.

Abbreviations. cg. = centigram, dg. = decigram, g. = gram, kg. = kilogram, mg. = milligram, q. = quintal, t. = tonneau (millier).

TABLES OF INTERRELATION OF UNITS OF MEASUREMENT [1]

UNITS OF LENGTH

Units	Inches	Links	Feet	Yards	Rods
1 inch =	1	0.126 263	0.083 333 3	0.027 777 8	0.005 050 51
1 link =	7.92	1	0.66	0.22	0.04
1 foot =	12	1.515 152	1	0.333 333	0.060 606 1
1 yard =	36	4.545 45	3	1	0.181 818
1 rod =	198	25	16.5	5.5	1
1 chain =	792	100	66	22	4
1 mile =	63,360	8,000	5,280	1,760	320
1 centimeter =	0.3937	0.049 70 60	0.032 808 33	0.010 936 111	0.001 988 384
1 meter =	39.37	4.970 9609	3.280 833	1.093 611 1	0.198 838 4

Units	Chains	Miles	Centimeters	Meters
1 inch =	0.001 262 63	0.000 015 782 8	2.540 005	0.025 400 05
1 link =	0.01	0.000 125	20.166 84	0.201 168 4
1 foot =	0.015 151 5	0.000 189 393 9	30.480 06	0.304 800 6
1 yard =	0.045 454 5	0.000 568 182	91.440 18	0.914 401 8
1 rod =	0.25	0.003 125	502.9210	5.029 210
1 chain =	1	0.0125	2,011.684	20.116 84
1 mile =	80	1	160,934.72	1,609.3472
1 centimeter =	0.000 497 096 0	0.000 006 213 699	1	0.01
1 meter =	0.049 709 60	0.000 621 369 9	100	1

[1] National Bureau of Standards.

UNITS OF AREA

Units	Square Inches	Square Links	Square Feet	Square Yards	Square Rods	Square Chains
1 square inch =	1.	0.015 942 3	0.006 944 44	0.000 771 605	0.000 025 507 6	0.000 001 594 23
1 square link =	62.7264	1	0.4356	0.0484	0.0016	0.0001
1 square foot =	144	2.295 684	1	0.111 111 1	0.003 673 09	0.000 229 568
1 square yard =	1,296	20.6612	9	1	0.033 057 85	0.002 066 12
1 square rod =	39,204	625	272.25	30.25	1	0.0625
1 square chain =	627,264	10,000	4,356	484	16	1
1 acre =	6,272,640	100,000	43,560	4,840	160	10
1 square mile =	4,014,489,600	64,000,000	27,878,400	3,097,600	102,400	6,400
1 square centimeter =	0.154 999 7	0.002 471 04	0.001 076 387	0.000 119 598 5	0.000 003 953 67	0.000 000 247 104
1 square meter =	1,549.9969	24.7104	10.763 87	1.195 985	0.039 536 7	0.002 471 04
1 hectare =	15,499,969	247 104	107,638.7	11,959.85	395.367	24.7104

Units	Acres	Square Miles	Square Centimeters	Square Meters	Hectares
1 square inch =	0.000 000 159 423	0.000 000 000 249 1	6.451 626	0.000 645 162 6	0.000 000 064 516
1 square link =	0.000 01	0.000 000 015 625	404.6873	0.040 468 73	0.000 004 046 87
1 square foot =	0.000 022 956 8	0.000 000 035 870 1	929.0341	0.092 903 41	0.000 009 290 34
1 square yard =	0.000 206 612	0.000 000 322 831	8,361.307	0.836 130 7	0.000 083 613 1
1 square rod =	0.006 25	0.000 009 765 625	252,929.5	25.292 95	0.002 529 295
1 square chain =	0.1	0.000 156 25	4,046,873	404.6873	0.040 468 7
1 acre =	1	0.001 562 5	40,468,726	4,046.873	0.404 687
1 square mile =	640	1	25,899,984,703	2,589,998	258.9998
1 square centimeter =	0.000 000 024 710 4	0.000 000 000 038 610 06	1	0.0001	0.000 000 01
1 square meter =	0.000 247 104	0.000 000 386 100 6	10,000	1	0.0001
1 hectare =	2.471 04	0.003 861 006	100,000,000	10,000	1

Units of Volume

Units	Cubic Inches	Cubic Feet	Cubic Yards	Cubic Centimeters	Cubic Decimeters	Cubic Meters
1 cubic inch =	1	0.000 578 704	0.000 021 433 47	16.387 162	0.016 387 16	0.000 016 387 16
1 cubic foot =	1,728	1	0.037 037 0	29,317.016	28.317 016	0.028 317 016
1 cubic yard =	46,656	27	1	764,559.4	764.5594	0.764 559 4
1 cubic centimeter =	0.061 023 38	0.000 035 314 45	0.000 001 307 94	1	0.001	0.000 001
1 cubic decimeter =	61.023 38	0.035 314 45	0.001 307 943	1,000	1	0.001
1 cubic meter =	61,023.38	35.314 45	1.307 942 8	1,000,000	1,000	1

Units of Capacity Dry Measure

Units	Dry Pints	Dry Quarts	Pecks	Bushels	Liters	Dekaliters	Cubic Inches
1 dry pint =	1	0.5	0.0625	0.015 625	0.550 599	0.055 060	33.600 312 5
1 dry quart =	2	1	0.125	0.031 25	1.101 198	0.110 120	67.200 625
1 peck =	16	8	1	0.25	8.809 58	0.880 958	537.605
1 bushel =	64	32	4	1	35.2383	3.523 83	2,150.42
1 liter =	1.816 20	0.908 102	0.113 513	0.028 378	1	0.1	61.0250
1 dekaliter =	18.1620	9.081 02	1.135 13	0.283 78	10	1	610.250
1 cubic inch =	0.029 761 6	0.014 880 8	0.001 860 10	0.000 465 025	0.016 386 7	0.001 638 67	1

Units of Mass Greater than Avoirdupois Ounces

Units	Avoirdupois Ounces	Avoirdupois Pounds	Short Hundred-weights	Short Tons	Long Tons	Kilograms	Metric Tons
1 avoirdupois ounce =	1	0.0625	0.000 625	0.000 031 25	0.000 027 901 79	0.028 349 53	0.000 028 349 53
1 avoirdupois pound =	16	1	0.01	0.0005	0.000 446 428 6	0.453 592 427 7	0.000 453 592 43
1 short hundredweight =	1,600	100	1	0.05	0.044 642 86	45.359 243	0.045 359 243
1 short ton =	32,000	2,000	20	1	0.892 857 1	907.184 86	0.907 184 86
1 long ton =	35,840	2,240	22.4	1.12	1	1,016.047 04	1.016 047 04
1 kilogram =	35.273 957	2.204 622 34	0.022 046 223	0.001 102 3112	0.000 984 206 4	1	0.001
1 metric ton =	35,273.957	2,204.622 34	22.046 223	1.102 311 2	0.984 206 40	1,000	1

Units of Capacity Liquid Measure

Units	Minims	Fluid Drams	Fluid Ounces	Gills	Liquid Pints
1 minim =	1	0.016 666 7	0.002 083 33	0.000 520 833	0.000 130 208
1 fluid dram =	60	1	0.125	0.031 25	0.007 812 5
1 fluid ounce =	480	8	1	0.25	0.0625
1 gill =	1,920	32	4	1	0.25
1 liquid pint =	7,680	128	16	4	1
1 liquid quart =	15,360	256	32	8	2
1 gallon =	61,440	1,024	128	32	8
1 milliliter =	16.2311	0.270 518	0.033 814 7	0.008 453 68	0.002 113 42
1 liter =	16,231.1	270.518	33.8147	8.453 68	2.113 42
1 cubic inch =	265.974	4.432 90	0.554 113	0.138 528	0.034 632 0

Units	Liquid Quarts	Gallons	Milliliters	Liters	Cubic Inches
1 min m =	0.000 065 104	0.000 016 276	0.061 610 2	0.000 061 610 2	0.003 759 77
1 fluid dram =	0.003 906 25	0.000 976 562	3.696 61	0.003 696 61	0.225 586
1 fluid ounce =	0.031 25	0.007 812 5	29.5729	0.029 572 9	1 804 69
1 gill =	0.125	0.031 25	118.292	0.118 292	7.218 75
1 liquid pint =	0.5	0.125	473.167	0.473 167	28.875
1 liquid quart =	1	0.25	946.333	0.946 333	57.75
1 gallon =	4	1	3,785.332	3,785 332	231
1 milliliter =	0.001 056 71	0.000 264 178	1	0.001	0.061 025 0
1 liter =	1.056 71	0.264 178	1,000	1	61.0250
1 cubic inch =	0.017 316 0	0.004 329 00	16.3867	0.016 386 7	1

WEIGL, JOSEPH (1766-1846), Austrian composer, born in Eisenstadt, Hungary. He studied with Johann Albrechtsberger and Antonio Salieri, and when but sixteen years of age wrote an opera, *Die Unnütze Vorsicht*. His first opera produced, however, was *Il Pazzo per Forza*, which appeared in 1788 and won critical acclaim. Encouraged by this success, he brought out, between that year and 1825, thirty more operas, both Italian and German, and a number of ballets. He also wrote two oratorios and many German and Italian cantatas. Upon the death of Salieri, in 1825, he received the position of second court conductor and devoted his entire time to masses, offertories, and graduals. His opera *Die Schweizer Familie,* produced in Vienna in 1809, became exceedingly popular.

WEIHAIWEI, port on the north coast of the promontory of Shantung, China, about 40 miles E. of Chifu, and about the same distance west of Yung-ching-hien. It was fortified by the Chinese (1883-85), was made a naval station, and an arsenal was established. In 1895 the Japanese captured it from the landward side. It was evacuated in 1898, and shortly thereafter leased by Great Britain to be held by her so long as Russia should hold Port Arthur, on the opposite coast. In 1905, when Japan took over the lease of Port Arthur, the British lease was amended to run as long as the Japanese occupied Port Arthur. With the concession went a strip of land 10 miles wide, lying east of 121° 40′ E., and covering an area of about 285 square miles. Following a treaty signed on April 18, 1930, the district of Weihaiwei was formally restored to China on October 1, 1930. Pop., about 154,000.

WEIL'S DISEASE, an acute, infectious, febrile disease chiefly attacking rats but often occurring in humans and in other vertebrates, including mice, cats, dogs, swine, and horses. The disease, which is caused by a spirillum *Leptospira icterohemorrhagiae*, is so called because it was first described by the German physician Adolf Weil (1848-1916) in 1886. The causative organisms are eliminated in the urine of infected rats and are transmitted to man by direct contact, or by drinking water contaminated with such urine. The organisms are capable of entering the body through small abrasions in the skin or mucous membranes. Weil's disease is often epidemic among humans in Japan, northern Africa, and along the shores of the Mediterranean Sea; it occurs sporadically in most temperate countries of the world. Persons, such as dock workers and workers in flooded rice paddys, who labor in wet, exposed places, are most often attacked by the disease because of increased possibility of contact with rat urine. During wartime Weil's disease is often so prevalent as to reach epidemic proportions in regions where only sporadic cases occurred before; conditions for its spread are enhanced in moist trenches or foxholes. In various epidemic outbreaks in Europe during wartime the mortality rate of persons attacked by the disease ranged from four to thirty-two percent; in epidemics in the Orient the mortality rate has reached almost fifty percent.

The incubation period of Weil's disease ranges from six to twelve days. The onset of the disease is sudden, marked by fever of 102° to 104°F. (38.5° to 40°C.), chills, headache, vomiting, aches, and pains. These symptoms persist for six to seven days and constitute the *initial stage* of the disease. Toward the close of the initial stage the temperature usually returns to normal. The *second stage* of the disease, which lasts for about five days, is marked by the appearance of large numbers of the causative organisms in the urine of the infected person. Small hemorrhages, caused by toxins produced by the spirilla, often develop in the skin, mucous membranes, and internal organs. Jaundice (q.v.) of mild to severe degree may occur, indicative of damage to the liver. In about forty percent of affected persons jaundice does not develop; such cases usually recover completely. In severely jaundiced patients, the liver becomes enlarged, and the kidneys are often damaged; in such cases death usually occurs during the second stage of the disease. In surviving victims the temperature rises slightly at the end of the second stage; during the *third* or *convalescent stage* of Weil's disease, the temperature falls once again, and the jaundice slowly disappears. In surviving victims, anemia and emaciation are often seen as aftereffects of the disease. One attack of the disease confers immunity for more than five years.

In many of its manifestations Weil's disease resembles yellow fever and malaria (qq.v.). It is distinguished from such diseases by several diagnostic laboratory examinations, including serological tests (see IMMUNITY), and injection of young guinea pigs or mice with blood or urine of victims. The serum of convalescent victims has been used in the treatment of Weil's disease with moderate success; sulfa drugs and penicillin combined with immune serum are successfully employed in many cases of this condition.

Weimaraner dog

Among other names given to Weil's disease are *icterohemorrhagic fever, leptospiral jaundice, infectious jaundice, epidemic jaundice, hemorrhagic jaundice,* and *leptospirosis icterohemorrhagica.*

WEIMAR, city in Thuringia, Germany, situated 50 miles w.s.w. of Leipzig. With it are connected several names prominent in the German art world. It has a natural history museum, with ethnological and antiquarian collections, the Liszt museum, and a geographical institute. Weimar has manufactures of iron, wood, straw, cloth, leather, and stoves, and is an important center of the book trade. Weimar dates from the 9th century. It passed to the Ernestine line of Saxony about 1500. Owing to the patronage of Duke Charles Augustus it is famous for literary associations pertaining to the classic epoch of German literature. Johann Wolfgang von Goethe resided here during more than fifty years of his life; Johann Friedrich von Schiller, Christoph Martin Wieland, Johann Gottfried von Herder, and Franz von Liszt also lived here. Pop., about 46,000.

WEIMARANER, a breed of hunting dog which originated in Weimar, Germany, at the beginning of the 19th century, and is believed to have been derived chiefly from a variety of bloodhound. The dog was bred by members of a club known as the Weimaraner Club, which strictly limited its membership and imposed breeding standards so rigid that the number of Weimaraner dogs in Germany has never exceeded fifteen hundred. The breed was imported into the United States in 1929 by an American who had become a member of the club; the dog is currently beginning to win popularity in this country. The dog runs with great speed, having been known to exceed thirty-eight miles an hour; thus, with the whippet, it is the fastest of domesticated animals. Originally the Weimaraner was used for hunting large game, such as wolves, deer, and wild boars, and later for hunting birds. The dog is often kept as a watch dog or a pet. The animal has an aristocratic-looking head; slightly folded ears which are placed fairly high; intelligent eyes that are blue-gray or amber in color; straight, muscular forelegs and powerful hindlegs; and a tail that is cropped when the puppy is about three days old and which grows to a maximum length of about six inches. It has a short coat which may be one of various shades of gray. The male is from 24 to 26 inches high at the withers and weighs between 65 and 85 pounds; the female is from 22 to 25 inches high and weighs between 55 and 75 pounds.

WEINGARTNER, FELIX (1868–1942), Austrian musical conductor, born in Zara, Dalmatia. In 1884 he produced his opera *Sakuntala* in Weimar. He was conductor of the theaters in Königsberg, Danzig, and Hamburg, and for two years in Mannheim. In 1891 he was appointed Kapellmeister at the Berlin Court Opera, and also of the Royal Symphony concerts. From 1898 to 1904 he was conductor of the Kaim orchestra, Munich, and from 1908 to 1910 director of the Vienna Opera and conductor of the symphony concerts. From 1912 to 1914 he was first conductor at the Stadttheater in Hamburg, and thereafter was general musical director in Darmstadt and director of the conservatory. He visited the United States in 1905 as guest conductor of the New York Philharmonic Society. During the seasons 1912 to 1914 he conducted the Wagner performances of the Boston Opera Company. From 1919 to 1924, he was chief conductor and general director of the Volksoper in Vienna. In the fall of 1924 he became general director of the Deutsches Opernhaus in Charlottenburg (Berlin). In 1927 he settled in Basel as director of the Conservatory and conductor of the Allgemeine Musikgesellschaft. His later works include two operas, *Meister Andrea* and *Terokayn*; an overture, *Aus Schwerer Zeit*; a second violin concerto; and two symphonies, No. 4 (in F) and No. 5 (in C minor).

WEINHOLD, KARL (1823–1901), German philologist and student of Germanic culture, born in Reichenbach, Silesia, and educated at the universities of Breslau and Berlin. He became Privatdocent at Halle in 1847, removed to Breslau in 1849, and became professor of German language and literature at Cracow in the following year, at Gratz in 1851, at Kiel in 1861, at Breslau in 1876, and at Berlin in 1889. His services to Germanic grammar and anthropology are valuable. The more important of his works include *Die Deutschen Frauen in Mittelalter* (1851); *Altnordisches Leben* (1856); *Die Riesen des Germanischen Mythus* (1859); *Die Heidnische Totenbestattung in Deutschland* (1859); *Alemannische Grammatik* (1863); *Bayrische Grammatik* (1867); editions of the Old High German *Isidorfragment* (1847), and of the *Pilatusfragment* (1877) of Lampricht's *St. Francisken Leben und Tochter Syon* (1880); *Mittelhochdeutsche Grammatik* (1877); *Mittelhochdeutsches Lesebuch* (1850); *Verbreitung und Herkunft der Deutschen in Schlesien* (1887); *Ueber den Mythus vom Wanenkrieg* (1890); *Zur Geschichte des Heidnischen Ritus* (1896); *Mystische Neunzahl* (1897); and *Die Verehrung der Quellen in Deutschland* (1898). He was editor of *Germanistsche Abhandlungen* from 1882 to 1891, and in the latter year founded and edited the *Zeitschrift des Vereins für Volkskunde*.

WEIR, a raised barrier which impedes the flow of water in a stream or other channel. In the United States the term is limited to barriers used for the measurement of liquid flow, but in England and elsewhere it is applied to any form of dam over which water flows continuously. Weirs used to measure water flow may have sharp or flat crests, may be rectangular or V-shaped in opening, and may be partially or totally submerged. The overflow channels of dams are often employed as weirs for measuring water flow. The amount of flow can usually be calculated by simple formulas involving the dimensions of the weir and the depth of water above the edge of the weir.

WEIR, JOHN FERGUSON (1841–1926), American painter and sculptor, son of Robert Walter Weir, born in West Point, N.Y. In 1861 he opened a studio in New York and in 1866 became a member of the National Academy. From 1869 until 1913 he served as director of the School of Fine Arts at Yale University. Among his best-known paintings are "The Gun Foundry" (1867), "Forging the Shaft" (1868, Metropolitan Museum of Art, New York City), "Tapping the Furnace", and various portraits, including those of Admiral Farragut, President Dwight of Yale, and Wells Williams. Examples of his sculpture may be found at Yale University and in New Haven. He wrote *Human Destiny in the Light of Revelation* (1903).

WEIR, J(ULIAN) ALDEN (1852–1919), American portrait, genre, and landscape painter and etcher, born in West Point, N.Y. He received his first instruction from his father, Robert Walter Weir (q.v.), and then studied at the National Academy of Design, New York, and at the Beaux-Arts, Paris, under Jean Gérôme. After his return to America he was one of the founders of the Society of American Artists (1877), and at one time its president. He was elected a member of the National Academy in 1886, and its president in 1915. He was chosen a member of the American Academy of Arts and Letters and received numerous important prizes, including gold medals at St. Louis (1904), National Academy of Design, New York (1906), and the Corcoran Art Gallery, Washington (1914). Weir's work, which is impressionistic, is characterized by a skillful and original handling of delicate color, and a harmonious arrangement of masses. He combines much refinement of feeling with an able and sure technique. Examples of his paintings are to be found in most public collections in America, including the Metropolitan Museum of Art, New York City, the Art Institute, Chicago, the Albright

Musical Courier
Felix Weingartner

Detail from "The Green Bodice," painting by J. Alden Weir
Metropolitan Museum of Art

Art Gallery, Buffalo, the National and Corcoran galleries, Washington, and the Pennsylvania Academy of Fine Arts, Philadelphia. In the Luxembourg Museum, Paris, is his "Portrait of a Young Girl".

WEIR, ROBERT WALTER (1803–89), American historical and genre painter, born in New Rochelle, N.Y. In 1834 he was appointed professor of drawing at the West Point Military Academy, which position he held until 1876. Among his many pictures are "The Embarkment of the Pilgrims" (in the Capitol in Washington, 1845); "The Landing of Hendrik Hudson" (1842); "Columbus before the Council of Salamanca"; and a large allegorical painting, "Peace and War", which is in the Chapel at West Point.

WEISBACH, JULIUS (1806–71), German mathematician and mining engineer, born near Annaberg, and educated at the universities of Freiburg, Göttingen, and Vienna. He became professor at the school of mines in Freiberg in 1833. He is principally known for his work in hydraulics and mechanics, his introduction and development of the surveying of mines, and the extension of axonometry. He wrote *Handbuch der Bergmaschinenmechanik* (1836), *Experimentalhydraulik* (1855), *Lehrbuch der Ingenieur- und Maschinenmechanik* (1845–60), *Der Ingenieur* (1848), *Die Neue Markscheidekunst* (1851–59), and *Anleitung zum Axonometrischen Zeichnen* (1857).

WEISER, county seat of Washington Co., Idaho, situated at the confluence of the Weiser and Snake rivers, on the Oregon boundary and 72 miles N.W. of Boise. It is served by a railroad, and is the trading center and shipping point of a fertile agricultural area. The principal products of the surrounding area are sugar beets, onions, celery, wheat, fruits, and livestock. Farm implements are an important commodity in Weiser's trade, and among the industrial establishments in the city are a flour mill, a dairy-products plant, bottling works, an iron foundry, and a brick plant. In the vicinity of the city are copper, silver, and gold mines. Pop. (1948 est.) 5935.

WEISHAUPT, ADAM (1748–1830), German mystic and religious leader, born in Ingolstadt, and educated at the University of Ingolstadt. After 1772 he was professor of canon law in the university. In 1776 he turned against the Jesuits, whose pupil he had been, and on May 1 of that year founded the Order of the Illuminati, or, as it was at first called, *Gesellschaft der Perfectabilisten,* the members of which were entirely subservient to their superiors, though theoretically vowed to the propagation of liberty. Weishaupt attracted great numbers of young men by his teaching, and made Ingolstadt a cosmopolitan centre until 1785, when his lecture hall was burned by his enemies. He then removed to Gotha, where he died. Among his writings are *Apologie der Illuminaten* (1786), *Geschichte der Verfolgung der Illuminaten* (1786), and *Das Verbesserte System der Illuminaten* (1787).

WEISMANN, AUGUST (1834–1914), German zoologist, born in Frankfort on the Main. He was professor of zoology at the University of Freiburg from 1871 to 1912. Weismann's zoological investigations, especially those dealing with the embryology of insects and crustaceans, were of the greatest importance. *The Origin of Species* of Charles Darwin came to his attention in 1861 and he at once accepted the evolution theory and was one of the first scientific men in Germany publicly to defend it. Weismann aided in establishing the present theory that heredity has a physical basis. Subsequently he proposed a theory of germinal selection. Weismann was a leader of the Neo-Darwinian or Weismannian school of evolutionists. His theories have been criticized as superscientific speculations and assumptions, especially that related to the architecture or mechanical arrangement of his hypothetical elements or determinants of the germ plasm. His works include *Die Entwicklung der Dipteren* (1864), *Studien zur Deszendentheorie* (2 vols., 1875–76), and *Das Keimplasma, eine Theorie der Vererbung* (1892).

WEISS, ANDRÉ (1858–1928), French statesman, born in Mülhausen, Alsace-Lorraine. He lectured on law at the University of Dijon from 1881 to 1891, and was professor of civil law at the University of Paris from 1896 to 1908, becoming in the latter year, professor of international law. In 1909 and 1911 he represented France at The Hague court, and in 1919 was a member of The Hague Court of Permanent Arbitration, and French vice-president of the Court of International Justice in The Hague. He wrote a number of authoritative books on international and civil law.

WEISS, JOHN (1818–79), American author and clergyman, born in Boston. He preached at Watertown and New Bedford, Mass., till failing health compelled him to devote several years to travel. In 1859 he returned to Watertown, where he remained till 1870 in charge of the Unitarian church. He was a zealous abolitionist, a transcendentalist in philosophy, an advocate of woman's rights, and a champion of rationalism in religion. His works include a *Life and Correspondence of Theodore Parker* (1864), *American Religion* (1871), and a translation of Schiller's *Philosophical and Æsthetic Letters and Essays.*

WEISSE, CHRISTIAN HERMANN (1801–66), German philosopher, born in Leipzig, and educated at the University of Leipzig. After taking his degree in 1823 he taught at the university until 1837, when he retired to his estate near the city; but he was recalled to academic activity in 1846 by an appointment as professor. Weisse was with Johann Fichte one of the founders of the system of speculative theism which opposed the pantheistic idealism of Georg Hegel. His most important writings include *System der Aesthetik als Wissenschaft von der Idee der Schönheit* (2 vols., 1830), *Die Idee der Gottheit* (1833), *Grundzuge der Metaphysik* (1835), *Kritik und Erläuterung des Goetheschen Faust* (1837), *Die Christologie Luthers* (1852), *Philosophische Dogmatik oder Philosophie des Christenthums* (3 vols., 1855–62), and *Psychologie und Unsterblichkeitslehre* (1869).

WEISSE, FANEUIL DUNKIN (1842–1915), American surgeon, born in Watertown, Mass., and educated at the University Medical College, New York. At that institution between 1865 and 1888 he was successively clinical professor of dermatology, professor of surgical pathology, and professor of practieal and surgical anatomy. He was also professor of surgical pathology of the New York College of Veterinary Surgeons. After helping to found the New York College of Dentistry in 1865, he served as professor of anatomy, surgical pathology, and oral surgery until his death. His works include *Practical Human Anatomy* (1886).

WEISSENFELS, a city of the State of Saxony-Anhalt, Eastern Germany, situated about 23 miles s.w. of Leipzig. Its principal manufactures include machinery, boots, sugar, nails, and paper. Coal is mined in the vicinity. Pop. about 40,000.

H. S. Moskovitz drawing, Harper & Bros.
Chaim Weizmann

WEITENKAMPF, FRANK (1866–   ), American library official and authority on engraving, born in New York. He was placed in charge of the department of art and prints of the New York Public Library, which became widely known through the interesting print exhibitions he arranged. Weitenkampf gained recognition as one of the foremost authorities on engraving in the United States. Among his works are *American Graphic Art* (2nd ed., 1924), *How to Appreciate Prints* (4th ed., 1929), and many contributions to periodicals. He was a member of the editorial staff of the *Standard Dictionary* and contributed to several encyclopedias, among them the *New International*.

WEITLING, WILHELM (1808–71), German socialist, born in Magdeburg. He was a tailor by trade, but traveled through his native country preaching communism and other radical doctrines. After taking part in the revolutionary movement of 1848 he settled in America, which he had previously visited, and formed a socialist society, in New York City, called the Arbeiterbund. He was identified with a socialistic colony in Wisconsin, but lived and worked in New York. The ideal society of Weitling was to be fashioned on the old ethnic lines, a federation of the families of the world, with leaders chosen by acclamation. The leaders should divide the products of labor, giving to every one a fixed share. He wrote *Die Menschheit Wie Sie Ist und Sein Soll* (1838), *Garantien der Harmonie und Freiheit* (1842), and *Das Evangelium Eines Armen Sünders.*

WEITZENKORN, LOUIS (1893–1943), American editor, born in Wilkes-Barre, Pa. He started his newspaper career as a reporter for the New York *Tribune* in 1914. In 1915 he was with the *New York Times*; in 1916–17 he conducted a column of verse, "The Guillotine", for the New York *Call*; from 1924 to 1929 was Sunday feature editor for the New York *World*; and for a time managing editor of the New York *Graphic.* He is the author of the plays *First Mortgage* (1929), *Five Star Final* (1930), made into a motion picture, 1931, and *The Burglar Strike* (1937).

WEIZMANN, CHAIM (1874–   ), statesman, chemist, and scholar, the first president of Israel, born in Motol, Grodno Province (now part of Byelorussian S.S.R.), Russia, and educated at the universities of Berlin, in Germany, and Fribourg, in Switzerland. He joined the Zionist movement between 1901 and 1904, while serving as a lecturer on organic chemistry at the University of Geneva. In 1906 he went to England, where he became a lecturer on organic chemistry and, later, a reader in biochemistry at the University of Manchester. He was naturalized as a British subject in 1910. Weizmann was subsequently a delegate to numerous congresses of the World Zionist Organization, and quickly won recognition as one of the ablest spokesmen for the Zionist cause. He also acquired renown as a brilliant chemist, and in 1916 was appointed director of the British Admiralty Laboratories. In that capacity he performed a notable service for the British government during World War I by discovering and developing a method for synthesizing acetone, a substance essential to the manufacture of a smokeless powder called cordite. In 1917, Prime Minister David Lloyd George offered him any honor he might choose as a reward for this service; in reply, Weizmann declared that a national home for the Jewish people was his sole desire. In November, 1917, the British government issued the celebrated Balfour Declaration (q.v.), in which it formally announced its favorable attitude toward the establishment in Palestine of a national home for the Jewish people. For an account of subsequent developments in Palestine leading to the establishment of the Jewish state of Israel, see ISRAEL: *History.*

In 1921 Weizmann was elected president of the World Zionist Organization. He served in that post for eight years, acting as a force for compromise between the Zionist extremists, who demanded the immediate fulfillment of the Balfour Declaration, and those British and Arab authorities who resisted all attempts at the realization of the Declaration. From 1929 to 1931, and from 1935 to 1946, he was president of the Jewish Agency for Palestine, the quasi-governmental organization exercising limited authority over the Jewish population of Palestine under the supervision of the British mandatory authorities. In 1942, during World War II, Weizmann offered his services to the U.S. government as a consultant on the manufacture of synthetic rubber; his services were accepted and he made a substantial contribution to the development of the synthetic-rubber industry, a key factor in U.S. war production. Late in 1946 he retired, because of certain differences with other Zionist leaders, from active participation in the leadership of the Zionist movement. On May 16, 1948, one day after the termination of the British mandate in Palestine and the proclamation of the formation of the Jewish state, Weizmann was elected president of the new provisional government of Israel. In February, 1949, upon the formal establishment of the Israel government, he was voted its first president.

WEKA, native Maori name for the peculiar New Zealand rails of the genus *Ocydromus,* which, although provided with wings, are unable to fly because of the wide angle between the scapula and coracoid bones of the pectoral girdle. They are generally brown, and are found along the seashore, feeding on shellfish carried ashore with kelp.

WEKERLE, SÁNDOR (1848–1921), Hungarian political leader, born in Moor. He became ministerial councilor in 1884 and two years later was made undersecretary of state in the Ministry of Finance, and was elected to the lower house of the Diet. In 1889 he became minister of finance. In November, 1892, he succeeded Szapáry as president of the Ministerial Council, resigning in 1894. From 1897 to 1906 he was president of the Hungarian Court of Administration. After more than a year of crisis precipitated by the refusal of the Independence Party to take office, Wekerle was premier and minister of finance in a compromise cabinet from 1906 to 1910.

WELCH, ASHBEL (1809–82), American civil engineer, born in Nelson, N.Y. In 1835 he was appointed chief engineer of the Delaware and Raritan Canal, which position he held for nearly forty years. In 1865 he devised, for the New York and Philadelphia Railroad, a method of safety signaling, which was afterward developed into the block system now in use by nearly all railroads. He became president of the United Railroads and Canals of New Jersey in 1867, and after this system was acquired by the Pennsylvania Railroad in 1871, he acted as consulting engineer for various enterprises.

WELCH, WILLIAM HENRY (1850–1934), American pathologist, born in Norfolk, Conn. From 1879 to 1884 he was professor of pathological anatomy at Bellevue Hospital Medical College, New York. He then became professor in Johns Hopkins University and pathologist to the Johns Hopkins Hospital, being also dean of the medical school from 1893 to 1898. He became eminent as an authority in bacteriology and pathology. In 1901 he was elected president of the board of directors of the Rockefeller Institute for Medical Research in New York, and in 1906 trustee of the Carnegie Institution of Washington. He was president of the Congress of American Physicians (1897), the Association of American Physicians (1901), the American Association for the Advancement of Science (1906–07), the American Medical Association (1910–11), and the National Academy of Sciences (for the term 1913–19). In 1921 he became editor of the American Journal of Hygiene and in 1926 professor of medical history at Johns Hopkins. Among his works are *General Pathology of Fever* (1888), *Biology of Bacteria* (1894), *Infection and Immunity* (1894), and *Bacteriology of Surgical Infection* (1895).

WELCKER, FRIEDRICH GOTTLIEB (1784–1868), German classical archeologist and philologist, born in Grünberg, Hesse-Darmstadt, and educated at the University of Giessen. In 1806 he went to Rome, where he remained two years as tutor in the family of Wilhelm von Humboldt, who became his warm friend. On his return from Italy, he was appointed to a professorship of ancient literature at Giessen. In 1814 he served in the War of Liberation. For political reasons he left Giessen, went the following year to Copenhagen to edit the posthumous works of the Danish archeologist Jörgen Zoëga, and accepted a chair at Göttingen in 1816. In 1819 he was called to Bonn, where he remained until his death, though he resigned his chair in 1859. Welcker's studies covered a wide range, but his chief influence was exerted in the fields of Greek literature, art, and mythology. He belonged to that school of German philologists who took as their aim the complete reconstruction of the ancient life, in distinction from the school of Gottfried Hermann, who was disposed to limit the field to the language and text of the Greek and Roman writers. Welcker was thoroughly imbued with the harmony of the whole Greek conception, whether expressed in art, literature, or religion, and it was to the presentation of this as a complete whole that he devoted his efforts. Among his editions of Greek texts are the collection of the fragments of Hipponax (1817), Theognis (1826), Philostratus (1825), and the *Theogony of Hesiod* (1845). His other works include *Der Epische Cyklus* (1835, 1849; reprinted 1865, 1882); *Die Æschyleische Trilogie Prometheus, und Nachtrag* (1824, 1826); *Die Griechischen Tragödien mit Rücksicht auf den Epischen Cyklus Geordnet* (1839–41); and *Griechische Götterlehere* (1857–62).

WELD, Woold, Dyer's Rocket, Dyer's Weed, or Yellow Weed, common name for an herbaceous weed, *Reseda luteola,* of the same genus as mignonette (q.v.). Weld is native to Europe, and naturalized in N.E. United States. Growing to a height of one to two feet, it has alternate lanceolate leaves, and greenish four-petaled flowers in racemes. Weld was formerly much cultivated in Europe as the source of a yellow dye, which has largely been supplanted by synthetic dyestuffs.

WELD, Isaac (1774–1856), Irish topographical writer, born in Dublin, and educated in England. In 1795–97 he traveled through the United States and Canada, visiting not only the long-settled eastern seaboard, but also the unbroken wildernesses of the West. After his return to Europe he wrote *Travels through the States of North America and the Provinces of Upper and Lower Canada during the Years 1795, 1796, and 1797* (1799). Several editions were issued, and translations were made into French, German, and Dutch. Among his other publications were a paper by which he sought to divert Irish emigration from the United States to Canada (1801); *Illustrations of the Scenery of Killarney and the Surrounding Country* (1807); and a *Statistical Survey of the County of Roscommon* (1838).

WELD, Theodore Dwight (1803–95), American reformer and abolitionist, born in Hampton, Conn. In 1833 he entered the Lane Theological Seminary in Cincinnati, where, during the famous antislavery debate, he took the lead among the students by his eloquence. On the suppression of the antislavery society by the trustees of the seminary, he was one of the students who withdrew, and during the next three years he devoted himself to lecturing on slavery and its evils. He edited the publications of the American Anti-slavery Society, and in 1854 opened a school in Perth Amboy, N.J., where he received boys and girls of both races. In 1864 he removed his school to Hyde Park, Mass., where he passed the remainder of his life. His works include *The Bible against Slavery* (1837); *American Slavery as It Is: or, the Testimony of a Thousand Witnesses* (1839), composed of extracts from Southern papers; and *Slavery and the Internal Slave Trade in the United States* (1841).

WELD, WELDE, or **WELLS,** Thomas (about 1590–1662), Puritan divine, born in England. His Puritan sympathies drew him to America, and settling to a charge in Roxbury, Mass., he distinguished himself by his denunciation of Anne Hutchinson and the Antinomians, and by compiling the *Bay Psalm Book,* the first book printed in the United States. He was sent to England in 1641 as agent for the colony, but was dismissed in 1646; and preferring to remain in England, was appointed to a charge in Gateshead on Tyne, whence he was ejected in 1662. Among his works are *Antinomians and Familists Condemned* (1644) and *The Perfect Pharisee under Monkish Holiness* (1654).

WELDING, any process of joining together pieces of metal by fusing the pieces under the influence of temperature, pressure, or both. Welded joints that are correctly made have as much strength as the original metal. With the development of suitable equipment and techniques for welding, this method of joining metals has supplanted bolting and riveting in many types of metal structures. An important advantage of welding is that by its use the overlapping joints needed to secure fastenings may be eliminated. Welding also makes practicable the direct fabrication of complex machinery parts which could formerly be made only in the form of heavy castings; see Founding. A typical example of this application of welding is the construction of lightweight welded blocks for internal combustion engines. By the use of suitable techniques almost any metal or alloy can be welded, including even such inflammable materials as magnesium and its alloys. Welding has been applied to all types of metal from massive castings and large structural shapes to the thinnest of metal sheets.

The two main types of welding process are those in which a joint is made by the direct fusion of two pieces and those in which additional metal is added to the joint. Welding techniques can also be classified according to

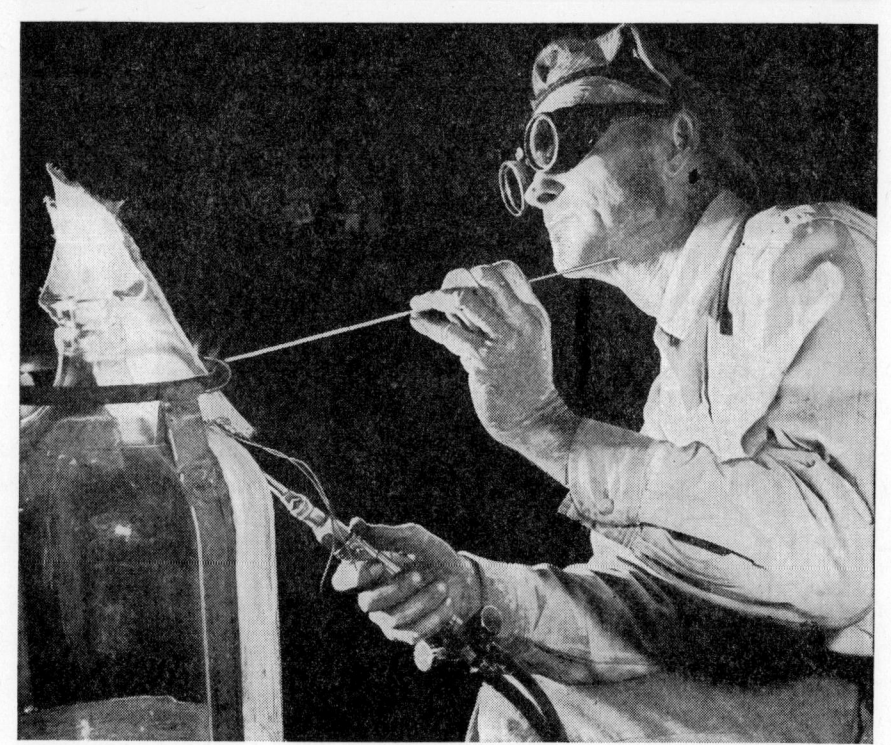

Tinsmith welding metal carrier on laboratory bottle with an oxyacetylene torch

the heat and pressure sources which are used. The types of welding commonly employed include forge welding, electric-arc welding, gas welding, resistance welding, and thermit welding. In addition, a number of special welding techniques are sometimes employed. These special methods include atomic-hydrogen arc welding, heliarc welding, and a process of cold-pressure welding, introduced in 1949, in which metals are joined and interfused by pressure alone, without heating.

Forge Welding. This is the simplest and oldest form of welding, and has been practiced by blacksmiths and other artisans for centuries. It consists of heating the parts to be joined to a red heat and forcing them together by means of repeated, heavy, hammer blows. Forge welding is usually only adaptable to comparatively heavy metal sections, and is little used in modern manufacturing.

Electric-Arc Welding. The joints in electric-arc welding are heated to the fusing point by means of an electric arc formed between the material being welded and a metallic electrode which melts and deposits fused metal in the heated joints. The equipment consists of some form of generator which supplies direct or alternating current at a low voltage and high amperage. One side of the output of the generator is connected to the work and the other to the welding electrode. When the electrode is touched or brought close to the work an arc is formed which utilizes almost the entire output of the generator in the form of heat. In some cases of arc welding, and also in gas welding, fluxes (see FLUX) are utilized to clean from the surfaces to be joined oxides which might impair the solidity of the weld. Electric-arc welding is well adapted to automatic welding processes in which long seams or joints are welded by machine. In such machines, for example, those used in the manufacture of welded pipe, the work passes along under the arc, and a ribbon of joint metal is fed continuously to the arc.

Gas Welding. In this type of welding, heat is supplied by a flame formed by mixing oxygen and acetylene gas in a torch and burning the mixture. This flame is applied to the joint, and a welding rod of the same metal as the

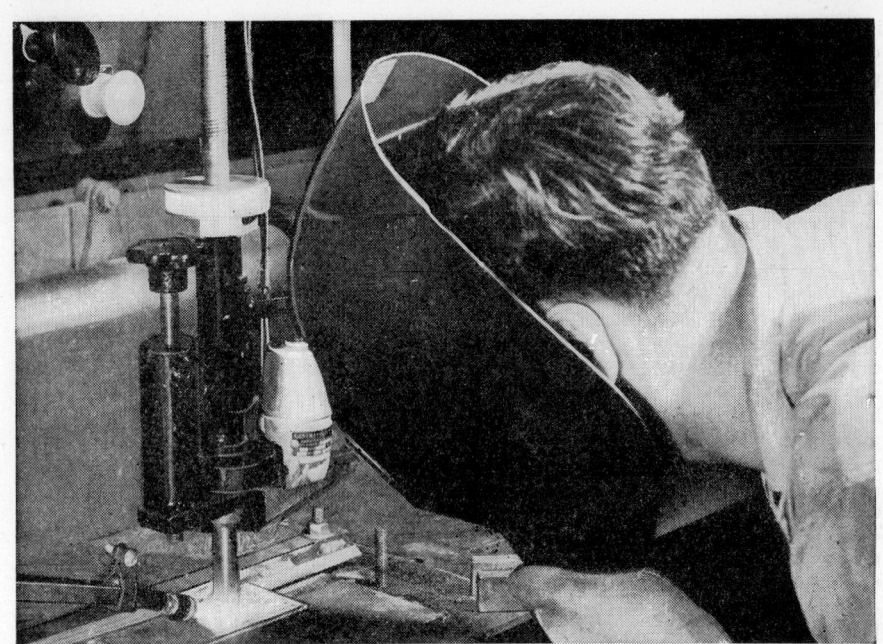

Arc-welding a metal part with automatic equipment, electronically controlled

work is usually also held in the flame and melted into the joint. Gas welding has the advantage of using apparatus that is readily portable, and independent of a source of electrical supply or other elaborate equipment. The welding apparatus consists of cylinders containing oxygen and acetylene under high pressure, reducing valves to lower the gas pressure, and a torch for mixing and burning the gases.

Resistance Welding. The characteristic of resistance welding is that heat is obtained by the effect of an electric current passing through the metal itself. The currents used are very high and are applied only momentarily. In a typical resistance-welding operation electrodes are clamped on either side of the joint and a pressure of 50,000 lb. per sq. in. is applied. A current of 60,000 amperes is passed through the electrodes and the joint for a small fraction of a second. The combination of high pressure and large current fuses the halves of the joint together. Resistance welding is extensively employed in many fields of manufacturing, and is particularly adaptable to repetitive welds made by automatic or semiautomatic machines.

Thermit Welding. In this form of welding, which is adaptable only to the welding of iron and steel, heat is generated by the chemical reaction which results when a mixture of aluminum and iron oxide (called thermit) is ignited. The temperature of this reaction is about 2500°C. (4532°F.) and molten iron is produced which serves as filler metal for the weld. Thermit welding is chiefly employed for welding breaks or seams in heavy iron and steel sections. The powdered thermit is held in place about the joint to be welded by some form of refractory mold.

Atomic-Hydrogen Welding. This process, a combination of gas and arc welding, uses as a source of heat a jet of hydrogen gas passing through an electric arc. The hydrogen gas, which is normally in the form of molecules containing two atoms of hydrogen, is dissociated into single atoms by the arc, and recombines at the surface of the work into the molecular form, releasing large quantities of heat during recombination. An advantage of this form of welding is that the joint is covered by a layer of hydrogen during the welding operation, thus preventing oxidation of the metal.

Heliarc Welding. This form of welding is a refinement of atomic-hydrogen technique, in which inert helium gas is used instead of hydrogen. It is used chiefly for the welding of inflammable metals such as magnesium, because the inert gas blankets the joint and prevents the burning of the metal, which otherwise takes place when the heat of the welding arc is applied.

WELDON, WALTER (1832–85), English chemist, born in Loughborough, Leicestershire. He was for a time engaged in his father's manufacturing business, and in 1860 he founded a monthly entitled *Weldon's Register of Facts and Occurrences Relating to Literature, the Sciences, and the Arts,* which continued for four years. He then began a scientific career which was the more remarkable because he had no practical knowledge of chemistry when he took out the first patents for his manganese regeneration process. By this process, which was patented in 1867 and applied commercially in 1869, the cost of bleaching powder was reduced £6 a ton, and the cost of producing such materials as paper and calico became much lower in consequence of the cheaper process. Weldon was president of the Society of Chemical Industry in 1883–84.

WELFARE ISLAND, formerly BLACKWELLS ISLAND, an island situated in the East River between the borough of Manhattan, to which it belongs politically, and the borough of Queens on Long Island (see NEW YORK CITY). Welfare Island possesses a maximum length of a mile and three quarters and a maximum breadth of 750 ft. The island is used by the City of New York to house municipal welfare institutions, including a number of hospitals and a home for the aged. These institutions are the New York City Hospital, the Goldwater Memorial Hospital for Chronic Diseases, the New York City Home for Dependents, the Cancer Institute, and the Metropolitan Hospital. Other buildings on the island include the Central Nurses Residence, the Blackwell House for internes, and the Elevator Storehouse, a ten-story building which connects the Queensboro Bridge to Welfare Island. The bridge, connecting East 59th St. in Manhattan to Queens Boulevard in Queens, provides the only vehicular entrance to Welfare Island; the top floor of the Elevator Storehouse is flush with the roadway of the bridge. Elevators possessing a capacity of more than seventeen and a half tons lower ambulances and other vehicles from the bridge to the surface of the island. The building also contains Reception Hospital, an emergency ward. Pedestrian traffic reaches the island by means of a ferry which crosses the river from the north end of the island to East 78th St. in Manhattan.

In 1637 the island, then called Minnahannock by the Indians, was purchased by Wouter Van Twiller, the governor of New Netherland. Van Twiller established a piggery on the island, which soon came to be called Varcken (Hog). For a period after the seizure of New Netherland by the English, the island was known as Perkins Island. It subsequently became the property of one Robert Blackwell, by whose name the island was thereafter known for more than two centuries. New York City purchased Blackwells Island in 1828 and made it the site of several public institutions, including a penitentiary and a workhouse. The island eventually became notorious because of the corruption prevailing in its penal institutions, and in 1921 the municipal authorities, as part of a generally futile effort to remedy the situation, changed its name to Welfare Island. In 1934 a raid on the island led by Austin H. MacCormick, New York City commissioner of correction, disclosed the abuses in the penal system. Following this development, the prisoners were transferred to a new penitentiary, the ancient prison buildings were razed, and the island was given over entirely to welfare institutions.

WELFARE WORK. See SOCIAL WORK.

WELHAVEN, JOHAN SEBASTIAN CAMMERMEYER (1807–73), Norwegian poet, born in Bergen, and educated at the University of Christiania. In 1825, while yet a student, he opposed the attempts of Henrik Wergeland to form a national literature. In 1832 he attacked the latter's poetry in *Henrik Wergelands Digtekunst og Polemik,* which made Welhaven the champion of the conservative classes. He followed this up by the publication of a cycle of satirical sonnets, *Norges Dæmring* (1834). In 1840 he became lecturer and in 1846 professor of philosophy at the University of Christiania. Welhaven's poetry holds a permanent place in Norwegian literature. He published volumes of poems, as well as two literary studies, *Holberg* (1854) and *Ewald og de Norske Digtere* (1863).

WELL. See ARTESIAN WELLS; SPRING; WATER SUPPLY AND WATER WORKS; WELL-SINKING.

WELLAND CANAL, an important Canadian ship canal, 27 miles long, between Lake Erie and Lake Ontario, begun in 1824 and completed in 1833. In 1913 a new and enlarged canal was started which, in the main, follows the old line from Port Colbourne on Lake Erie to Allanburg, whence there is a new route to Lake Ontario. The new canal (opened, 1932) is 200 feet wide at the bottom and has a depth of 25 feet, later increased to 30 feet.

WELLES, (GEORGE) ORSON (1915–), American actor, producer, director, and writer, born in Kenosha, Wisconsin, and educated at the Todd School, Woodstock, Illinois. He appeared with the Gate Theater, Dublin, Eire, from 1931 to 1932, and in 1933 toured the United States as a member of the company of the American actress Katherine Cornell. In 1937 Welles founded his own theatrical company, the Mercury Theater, in New York City; the organization presented Shakespeare's *Julius Caesar* in its first year, and a number of plays, the most notable of which was George Bernard Shaw's *Heartbreak House,* in 1938. After 1938 the Mercury Theater appeared only sporadically. Among its later productions, all of which Welles produced, directed, and acted in, were *Five Kings* (1939) and *Native Son* (1941). After 1938 Welles also wrote, directed, and acted in radio plays. He contributed to a number of motion pictures as a writer, director, producer, and actor, frequently serving in two or more of these capacities in a single production; these motion pictures include *Citizen Kane, The Magnificent Ambersons, Journey into Fear, Lady from Shanghai, Jane Eyre, Macbeth,* and *The Prince of Foxes.*

WELLES, SUMNER (1892–   ), American statesman, born in New York City. After 1915 he held various public offices and diplomatic positions for the U.S. government. He was assistant secretary of state from 1933 to 1937 and undersecretary of state from 1937 until he resigned in 1943. He wrote *Naboth's Vineyard* (1928), *Time for Decision* (1944), and *We Need not Fall* (1948).

WELLESLEY, town of Norfolk County, Mass., 14 miles s.w. of Boston. It is the seat of a college for women. Pop. (1950) 20,847.

WELLESLEY, RICHARD COLLEY, 1st MARQUIS WELLESLEY (1760–1842), British colonial administrator in India, born in Dangan Castle, Ireland. He was governor-general of India from 1797 to 1805, and succeeded in making treaties with independent rulers and establishing several dependent principalities. In 1809 he became secretary of state for foreign affairs and in 1821 lord lieutenant of Ireland.

WELLESLEY COLLEGE, a nondenominational, privately controlled institution of higher education for women, situated in Wellesley, Mass., about 14 miles from Boston. It was founded in 1870, and opened for instruction in 1875. All undergraduate work at the college is concentrated in the liberal arts, and the B.A. is the only baccalaureate degree awarded; in graduate studies, however, a greater degree of specialization is permitted, and courses of study are offered leading to the degrees of M.A., M.S. in education, and M.S. in hygiene and physical education. In a recent year over 1700 women were enrolled and the faculty numbered over 200.

WELLESLEY PROVINCE. See PENANG.

WELLINGBOROUGH, town in Northamptonshire, England, located on a declivity near the confluence of the Ise with the Non, 10 miles N.E. of Northampton. It has important industries of boot making, iron smelting, and brewing. Pop., about 21,000.

WELLINGTON, county seat of Sumner County, Kansas, on State Creek, 30 miles s. by w. of Wichita. Pop. (1940) 7246.

WELLINGTON, a village of Lorain Co., Ohio, situated 36 m. by rail s.w. of Cleveland. It is served by two railroads, and is a railroad junction point. The principal industries in Wellington are the manufacture of iron castings, screw-machine products, warehouse trucks, automobile parts, glass cloth, and brickyard supplies. The village was settled in 1818 and incorporated in 1855. Pop. (1948 est.) 3340.

WELLINGTON, capital of New Zealand, on Port Nicholson, an inlet of Cook Strait, on the southern coast of North I., 150 miles from Nelson. It was the first settlement of the New Zealand Company. The harbor is a fine expanse of water, and has an excellent wharf, affording accommodation to ships of any tonnage. Among the industries are tanning; brewing; candle, soap, and boot making; meat preserving; flour milling; sawmilling; and shipbuilding. Pop. (1948 est.) 186,100.

WELLINGTON, ARTHUR MELLEN (1847–95), American civil engineer, born in Waltham, Mass., and educated at the Boston Latin School, and as an articled student with John B. Henck, an engineer and author of *Henck's Field Book.* After about a year as assistant engineer in the construction of Prospect Park, in Brooklyn, N.Y., he began a career of railway engineering in 1868, in charge of a locating party on the Blue Ridge Railroad, in South Carolina. After various other railway engineering engagements he became chief assistant in the engineering department of the New York, Pennsylvania, and Ohio Railway from 1878 to 1881, and afterward held positions with the Mexican Central and the Mexican National railways. He became an editor of the *Railway Gazette* in 1884, and one of the editors and owners of the *Engineering News* in 1887. With the latter journal he continued until his death, serving also as consulting engineer for many enterprises, including the abolition of grade crossings in Buffalo, the improvement of railway terminals and erection of the Board of Trade building in Toronto, and the planning for the Boston subway. He wrote *Computation of Railway Earthwork from Diagrams* (2 vols., 1874), *The Economic Theory of Railway Location* (1877 and 1887), *Car Builders' Dictionary* (1884), and *Field Work of Railway Location and Laying Out of Works* (1889).

WELLINGTON, ARTHUR WELLESLEY, 1st DUKE OF (1769–1852), English soldier and statesman, son of Garret, 1st Earl of Mornington, of Dangan Castle, County Meath, Ireland, and Anne Hill, daughter of Lord Dungannon.

Wellesley joined the army in 1787, and saw service in Holland. In 1796 he was sent to Calcutta, but his military genius was not conspicuous until 1803, when he distinguished himself in the Mahratta war.

In 1807 he was appointed Irish secretary, but after a few months was sent to Copenhagen, where he commanded the troops which drove the Danes out of Zealand. He then returned to the Irish Office, but in July embarked with some 10,000 men for the relief of the British forces in Portugal. His army landed at Mondego Bay in August, 1808, and on the 17th he defeated the French under General Andoche Junot at Roliça. On the 21st he inflicted a second defeat upon them at Vimiera. In the Peninsular War (1809–14) he inflicted defeat on Napoleon's best marshals, and as a result was made a field marshal, Marquis of Douro. For these services to the nation Parliament voted its thanks and a gift of £400,000. A dukedom was conferred upon him by the crown in 1814.

When Napoleon returned from Elba and took the field with his army once again, the defense of Belgium was allotted to Wellington, and a Prussian army commanded by Blücher. On June 18, 1815, Wellington inflicted a decisive defeat on Napoleon at Waterloo, which crushed Napoleon's power forever.

Wellington was created Prince of Waterloo in the Netherlands, and the estate of Strathfieldsaye, in Hampshire, was purchased from Lord Rivers and presented to Wellington by the nation.

On the death of George Canning in August, 1827, and the fall of Lord Goderich's cabinet in January following, the duke became prime minister at the earnest desire of King George IV. Becoming, with Robert Peel, convinced that Catholic emancipation was necessary, he

1st Duke of Wellington (by Francesco Goya)

brought in a bill to grant it in 1829. Failing to recognize the earnestness of the demand for parliamentary reform in 1830, he declared against it, and thus brought about the fall of his government, becoming so unpopular that he was hooted by the mob on the anniversary of Waterloo.

Called upon by King William IV in 1834 to form a cabinet, he recommended Sir Robert Peel as prime minister, reserving for himself the post of foreign secretary. Peel was in Italy, but the duke was sworn in as first lord and secretary of state for the Home Department, so as to enable him to act in all the other offices until Peel's return in three weeks' time. This brief dictatorship greatly raised his reputation as a statesman. In 1842 he was appointed commander in chief of the army for life. Upon his death he was buried with great pomp in St. Paul's Cathedral, London.

WELLMAN, WALTER (1858–1934), American journalist and explorer, born in Mentor, Ohio. In 1879 he founded the Cincinnati *Evening Post,* and from 1884 to 1911 was Washington correspondent of the Chicago *Herald* and *Record-Herald.* In 1892 he located the spot of Columbus' landing on Watling Island. He led an expedition to the Arctic regions in 1894 and reached latitude 81° N.E. of Spitzbergen, and in 1898–99 was leader of an expedition to Franz Josef Land which reached latitude 82°. After having a dirigible balloon constructed in Paris he took it to Dane's I., Spitzbergen, in the spring of 1906, and in 1909

H. G. Wells

made an unsuccessful attempt with it to reach the North Pole. He wrote *The Aerial Age* (1911), *The German Republic* (1916), and *The Force Supreme* (1918).

WELLS, BENJAMIN WILLIS (1856–1923), American scholar and editor, born in Walpole, N.H., and educated at Harvard University. He was an instructor in Friends' School, Providence, R.I. (1882–87), was professor of modern languages in the University of the South (1891–99), and after 1899 was on the editorial staff of the New York *Churchman.* Wells edited a large number of French and German text books, and was joint editor, with W.P. Trent, of *Colonial Prose and Poetry, 1607–1775* (1902). His other works include *Modern German Literature* (1895), *Modern French Literature* (1897), and *A Century of French Fiction* (1898).

WELLS, CAROLYN (1869–1942), American writer, born in Rahway, N.J. After 1895 she devoted herself to literary work. Her numerous writings include the "Patty" books, *At the Sign of the Sphinx* (1896), *Idle Idyls* (1900), *Folly in Fairyland* (1901), *A Matrimonial Bureau* (1905), *Whimsey Anthology* (1906), *Pleasant Day Diversions* (1909), *The White Alley* (1915), *Vicky Van* (1918), *The Come Back* (1921), *Book of Limericks* (1925), and the detective stories *Triple Murder* (1929), *The Master Murderer* (1933), and *Who Killed Caldwell?* (1942).

WELLS, CHARLES JEREMIAH (1799?–1879), English poet, born probably in London. He was a friend of John Keats, who dedicated a sonnet to him. Wells published anonymously a volume called *Stories after Nature* (prose) in 1822. In 1824 he wrote *Joseph and His Brethren, a Scriptural Drama,* which bore the pseudonym H.L. Howard on the title page. Neither work met with success, and Wells abandoned literature. Subsequently *Joseph* was lavishly praised by critics of the Swinburnian school. In 1876 a revision of it was published, with a critical introduction by Algernon Charles Swinburne. It is distinguished by brilliant character study and richness of diction.

WELLS, DAVID AMES (1828–98), American economist, born in Springfield, Mass. From 1866 to 1870 he was special commissioner of revenue, and in 1871 became commissioner of New York State commission on local taxation. He edited numerous scientific textbooks, and wrote *The Creed of the Free Trader* (1875), *Robinson Crusoe's Money* (1878), *Our Merchant Marine* (1882), *The Primer of Tariff Reform* (1884), *Principles of Taxation* (1886), *Recent Economic Changes* (1889), and *The Practise of Taxation* (1900).

WELLS, F(REDERIC) LYMAN (1884–   ), American psychiatrist, born in Boston, and educated at Columbia University. He was an assistant in psychology at Columbia in 1905–06, and lectured at Barnard College in 1906–07. He then became assistant pathological psychologist of McLean Hospital in Waverley, Mass. He became chief of the Psychological Laboratory at the Boston Psychopathic Hospital and instructor at the Harvard Medical School in 1921. He wrote *Mental Adjustments* (1917), *Pleasure and Behavior* (1924), and *Mental Tests in Clinical Practise* (1927).

WELLS, GRANT CARVETH (1887–   ), American author, lecturer, and radiologist, born in Surrey, England. He was one of the engineers on the original survey of the Grand Trunk Pacific Railway, Canada, and was later sent by the British government to the Malay Peninsula, where he lived in the jungle for six years, making notes of flora, fauna, and ethnological studies. He came to America in 1918. Wells also traveled in Lapland, Africa, Russia (Caucasus Mountains and Mt. Ararat), Mexico, and Panama. He wrote *Six Years in the Malay Jungle* (1925), *A Jungleman and His Animals* (1925), *In Coldest Africa* (1929), *Exploring the World* (1934), and *North of Singapore* (1940).

WELLS, HERBERT GEORGE (1866–1946), English novelist and lecturer, born in Bromley, Kent. He started his career as a science teacher, and became a journalist in 1890. His writing is highly imaginative and is concerned with scientific speculation and with forecasts of social or socialistic reform. In his novel *Mr. Britling Sees It Through* (1916), he created the famous character *Mr. Britling,* through whom he voiced the opinions and reactions of an Englishman at home during World War I. In his novel *The World Set Free* (1914) he predicted the atomic bomb. Among his other writings are *The Invisible Man* (1897); *Tales of Space and Time* (1899); *New Worlds for Old* (1908); *Marriage* (1912); *An Englishman Looks at the World* (1914); *Joan and Peter* (1918); *The Outline of History* (1920); *A Short History of the World* (1922); *The Science of Life* (with Julian Huxley and A.P. Wells, 1929); *The Shape of Things to Come* (1933); *Experiment in Autobiography* (1934); *The New America, The New World* (1935); *The Holy Terror* (1939); *Babes in the Darling Wood* (1940); and *Guide to the New World* (1941).

WELLS, HORACE (1815–48), American dentist, born in Hartford, Vt., and educated in Boston. In 1840 he began experimenting with nitrous oxide gas as an anesthetic, and is generally believed to have been the first to use this means of producing anesthesia in dental operations. He wrote *A History of the Application of Nitrous-oxide Gas, Ether, and Other Vapors in Surgical Operations* (1847).

WELLS, HORACE LEMUEL (1855–1924), American chemist, born in New Britain, Conn., and educated at Yale College. After serving as chemist to the Connecticut Agricultural Experiment Station and the Colorado Coal and Iron Co., in 1884 he returned to Yale, at which in 1894 he became professor of analytical chemistry and metallurgy. In 1903 he was elected to the National Academy of Sciences. Among his scientific researches the more important are concerned with the double halogen salts, and the double and triple salts, especially of the alkali elements. He translated Fresenius' *Qualitative Analysis,* and wrote *Studies from the Chemical Laboratory of the Sheffield Scientific School* (1901), *Chemical Calculations* (1903), and *Text Book of Chemical Arithmetic* (1905).

WELLS, SIR THOMAS SPENCER (1818–97), English surgeon, born in St. Albans, Hertfordshire, and educated at Trinity College, Dublin, and at St. Thomas's Hospital, London. In 1841 he was admitted to the Royal College of Surgeons. After serving in the Naval Hospital in Malta during the Crimean War, he studied under François Magendie in Paris, and in 1853 established himself as an ophthalmic surgeon in London. He was chosen surgeon at the Samaritan Free Hospital for Women and Children in 1854, and there he began the work in abdominal surgery which made his name famous. In 1858 he first performed the operation of ovariotomy. In 1882 he became president of the College of Surgeons and in the following year was created a baronet. Among his works are *Practical Observations on Gout and Its Complications* (1854), *Cancer Cures and Cancer Curers* (1860), *Diseases of the Ovaries: Their Diagnosis and Treatment* (1865–72), *On Ovarian and Uterine Tumors: Their Diagnosis and Treatment* (1882), and *Diagnosis and Surgical Treatment of Abdominal Tumours* (1885).

WELLS. WILLIAM CHARLES (1757–1817), American scientist, born in Charleston, S.C., and educated at the University of Edinburgh. In 1782 he accompanied the Loyalist troops to St. Augustine, Fla., where he was editor of the first weekly newspaper in the province. In 1784 he went to London, and in 1800 became chief physician of St. Thomas's Hospital. His scientific reputation is based upon his *Essay on Dew* (1814). In a paper read by him in 1813 before the Royal Society he recognized, according to the statement of Charles Darwin, the principle of natural selection. He also wrote *Single Vision with Two Eyes* (1792), *On the Color of the Blood* (1797), and *On Vision* (1811).

WELLSBORO, county seat of Tioga County, Pa., situated 40 miles N. by W. of Williamsport. It is the site of the Green Free Library, Woodland Park, and the Wellsboro Conservatorium of Music. Wellsboro is the shipping point and trading center for a large area, and has fruit evaporators, flour and woolen mills, and a milk-condensing plant. Pop. (1940) 3665.

WELLSBURG, county seat of Brooke Co., W.Va., situated on the Ohio R., 16 miles N.E. of Wheeling. It is served by two railroads, and lies in an area noted for the production of coal, wheat, apples, and sheep. The principal industries in the city are the manufacture of paper and paper products, foundry products, stamped-steel products, glassware, cement, and flour. Wellsburg, one of the oldest towns in West Virginia, was founded in 1791, and was first known as Charles Town. Pop. (1948 est.) 6900.

WELL-SINKING, the operation by which deep holes of comparatively small diameter

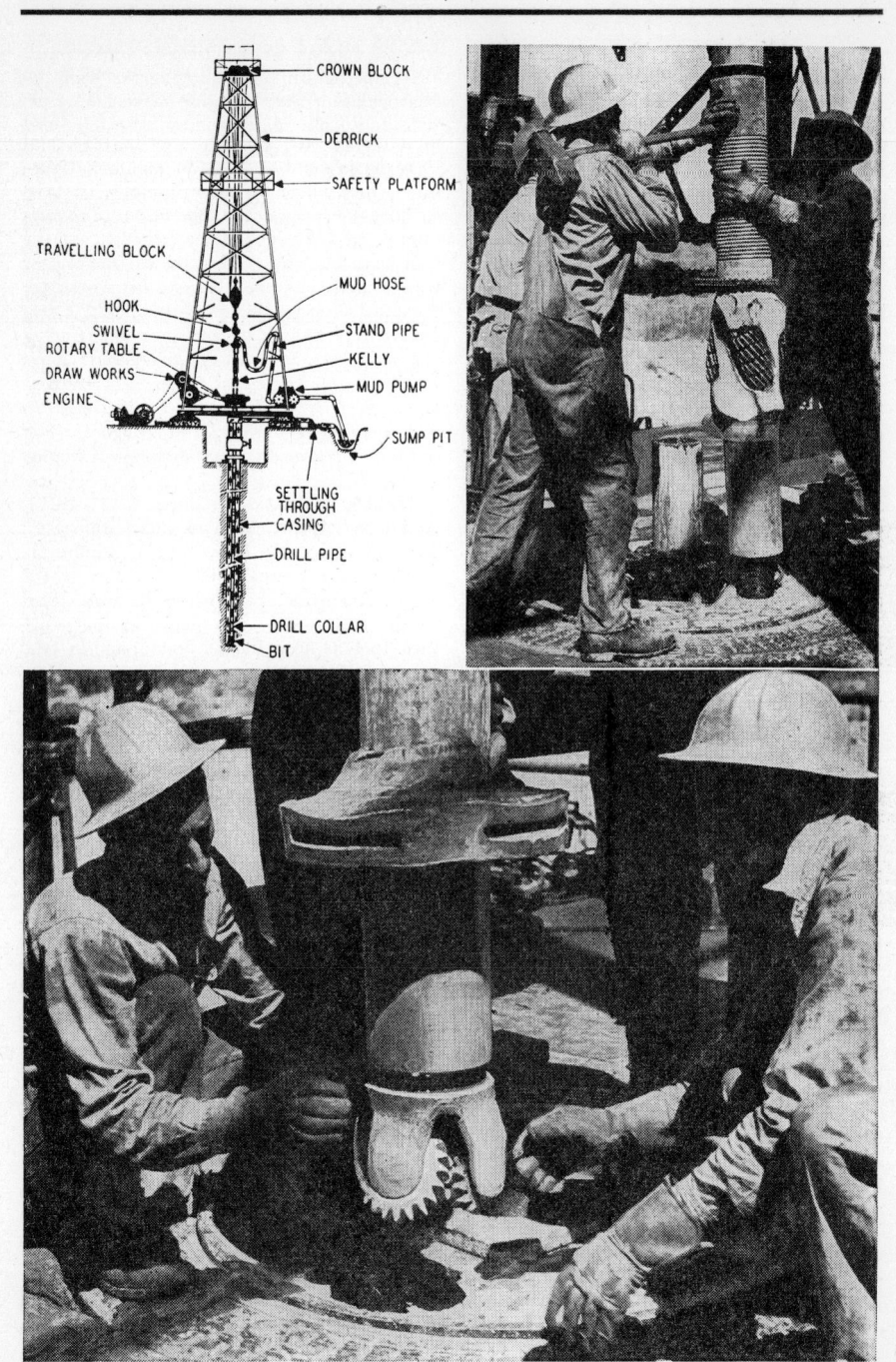

WELL-SINKING: PETROLEUM. *Top, left: Drawing showing parts of rotary-drilling rig. Top, right: Attaching reamer to drill pipe. Bottom: Screwing rock bit onto the drill pipe.*

are sunk into the earth for the development of subterranean resources, such as water, gas, petroleum, or salt. The process also includes the lining of the hole with curbing of stone or brick, or with iron or steel tubing, to prevent cave-ins of the earth or rock penetrated, or to shut out all liquids except those from the strata the well is designd to tap. The term "well-sinking" is also loosely applied to the sinking of any similar hole, such as those sunk in the prospecting for solid minerals, or in the determination of the character and depth of soil and rock strata for supporting foundations and other engineering structures.

Wells range in diameter from 1 inch to 100 feet, and in depth from 5 to 15,000 feet. The method of sinking a well depends on the character and depth of the material to be penetrated, rather than upon the objective for which the well is sunk. When sunk in ordinary loose soil, wells are dug by excavating with pick and shovel, or comparable mechanical means. The walls of the excavation are shored with timbers or planks to prevent cave-in, and are later lined with stone or brick.

When the bore of a well must pass through a stratum of rock, driving, boring, or drilling must be employed. Driven wells are sunk by a machine essentially similar to a pile driver (see PILES, in engineering); the drive head, consisting of a hardened steel point, is attached to the bottom of the tubular casing, which is driven into the ground. Entry ports in the bottom of the casing provide access for the fluid sought, when the appropriate stratum is reached; see ARTESIAN WELL.

Deep wells, such as those used for tapping resources of petroleum or natural gas, are sunk by boring or drilling. These terms boring and drilling are applied indiscriminately to two processes: one employing a circular drill, such as a diamond drill, which forms a circular or annular cut, and which is driven by rotation of the well casing, to which it is attached; the other using a fishtail or similar bit, weighing as much as several tons, which cuts and pulverizes the rock by dropping of its own weight. The circular drill can be used to drill inclined well holes; the bit, suspended from a flexible cable, can be used only for sinking vertical wells, and the well casing is placed in a separate operation. In both types the equipment used at the surface of the ground is essentially similar: it consists of an engine for supplying power; a tapering derrick 50 to 250 feet in height; a mechanism for imparting the rotary motion and downward thrust to the rotating drill, or reciprocating vertical motion to the fishtail; and an auxiliary mechanism for removing the drills for sharpening or dressing, and for removing debris and loose material from the bore. See PETROLEUM; WATER.

WELLSTON, a city of Jackson Co., Ohio, situated about 30 miles S.E. of Chillicothe. It is served by two railroads. The surrounding area is noted for the mining of iron, coal, clay, and limestone. The city is a manufacturing center, with factories producing coal-mining machinery, sheet metal, machine-shop products, metal containers, furniture, wooden articles, and clothing. Wellston was first settled in 1871, and was incorporated in 1876. Pop. (1940) 5537.

WELLSVILLE, a village of Allegany Co., N.Y., situated on the Genesee R., 26 miles S.W. of Hornell. It is served by two railroads, and lies in a farming, dairying, and oil-producing area. The principal industries in Wellsville are oil refining and the manufacture of machine-shop products, steam turbines, optical goods, lumber, caskets, upholstery, and gloves. The village was settled in 1795 and named for Gardiner Wells, an early settler. It was incorporated in 1871. Pop. (1940) 5942.

WELLSVILLE, city of Columbiana County, Ohio, situated on the Ohio R., about 48 miles W.N.W. of Pittsburgh. It has iron and tin plate works, car shops, and plants engaged in the manufacture of boilers, tanks, sewer pipes, and pottery. Railroad repair shops and machine shops are among other industrial establishments in the city. Rich deposits of clay and coal are found in the neighborhood, and natural gas and oil also occur. Pop. (1940) 7672.

WELSBACH, CARL AUER VON (1858–1929), Austrian chemist and inventor, born in Vienna, and educated at the University of Heidelberg. He discovered the rare earth (q.v.) elements neodymium and praseodymium, and in 1885 invented the incandescent mantle for gas lamps, since called by his name. In 1890 he became president of the Auergesellschaft, a company formed to manufacture gas burners and mantles under his patents. In 1897 he invented the osmium-filament lamp, and six years later invented the pyrophoric alloy of iron and cerium, which made possible the development of pocket lighters. He was a member of many technical societies, and of the scientific academies of Vienna, Berlin, and Stockholm.

WELSER, the name of a famous burgher family of Augsburg, Germany. **1.** BARTHOLOMÄUS WELSER (1488–1561), a merchant. He loaned the emperor Charles V a great sum of money, for which in 1528 he received as security the province of Venezuela. In consequence of their rapacious acts the Welsers were deprived of their rule before the emperor's reign was over. **2.** PHILIPPINE WELSER (1527–80), daughter of Franz Welser and niece of Bartholomäus, renowned for her learning and beauty. She secretly married the archduke Ferdinand, second son of the emperor Ferdinand I. Her children were debarred from inheriting their father's rank, but one of them became a cardinal and the other distinguished himself as a soldier and was created Margrave of Burgau. **3.** MARKUS WELSER (1558–1614), a scholar. Among his works are a Latin history of Bavaria.

WELSH LANGUAGE AND LITERATURE. The literature of Wales is more ancient and far more extensive than that of either Cornwall or Brittany, and is to be compared rather with that of Ireland. Irish is richer than Welsh as regards the quantity and interest of its ancient monuments, but modern Welsh has held its place as a literary language as successfully as Irish. In the history of Welsh, as in that of all the Celtic languages, three periods are regularly recognized: Old Welsh, extending from the time of the earliest monuments through the 10th century; Middle Welsh, from the 11th to the 16th century; and Modern Welsh, from the 16th century to the present time.

Old Welsh. The monuments of the earliest period are of the same sort in Wales as in Ireland, though much more scanty. The very oldest material is found in funeral inscriptions, some of which probably date back to the 5th century. A considerable number of Old Welsh glosses have been preserved in manuscripts ranging from the 8th to the 10th century, but no literary texts have come down from this period. The heroic age of Welsh history falls in the 6th century, and several great bards are supposed to have lived at that time. The most famous are the so-called *cynferdd*: Aneurin, Llywarch Hen, Merlin, and Taliesin. Many poems attributed to them exist in manuscripts of the 12th and succeeding centuries; only a few poems have come down to us, however, which were actually written by the *cynferdd*.

Middle Welsh. The earliest texts of assured date appear in the *Liber Landavensis* ("Book of Llandaff"), a manuscript of the 12th century. To the early Middle Welsh period belongs also the collection of ancient laws ascribed to Howel Dda and probably compiled in their substance in his time. The oldest manuscript of the laws belongs also to the 12th century. The Middle Welsh literature, properly speaking, falls into two main divisions—bardic poetry and prose romance.

During the ages of struggle between Saxons and Welshmen, the bards were an important class in society, and a considerable quantity of their poetry has been preserved. Their most flourishing period extends from the time of Gruffudd ab Cynan's return from Ireland in 1080 to the death of Llewelyn ab Gruffudd in 1282. Among the foremost of these Middle Welsh poets were Meilyr, Gwalchmai his son, Owain Kyveiliog and Howel ab Owain Gwynedd (both royal princes), Einion and Meilyr (sons of Gwalchmai), Dafydd Benvras, Llywarch ap Llewelyn, Cynddelw, Elidir Sais, and Phylip Brydydd.

After the reign of Llewelyn ab Iorwerth in the first half of the 13th century, a decline began in the work of the poets. But the elegy on Llewelyn ab Gruffudd by Gruffudd ab yr Ynad Goch ranks with the best productions of the earlier bards. The 14th century is called the Golden Age of Welsh poetry, the main characteristic of which is the adoption of the severe principles of versification known as the *cynghanedd*. Among the bards who lived in the 15th century were Rhys Goch Eryri, Iolo Goch, Llywelyn Goch, Gruffudd Llwyd, Sion Cent, Dafydd ap Edmwnd, Lewis Glyn Cothi, and Gutyn Owain.

The prose literature of the Middle Welsh period consists chiefly of chronicles and romantic tales. The first do not differ in character from the annals of the surrounding nations. The prose romances, on the other hand, form perhaps the most interesting, and are the most widely known, of all Welsh writings.

Modern Welsh. Welsh literature since the 16th century has relatively less interest than in the earlier periods of its history. With the decline of the bardic institution, poetry ceased to be cultivated as of old, and the prose of the modern period has been too largely confined to theological subjects to be of permanent interest. A few authors, however, deserve special mention. Huw Morus stands out among the poets in the 17th century and Goronwy Owen in the 18th. The publication of Evans' *De Bardis Dissertatio* in 1764 was an event of importance in the early history of the Romantic movement in England and one of the first signs among Welshmen of a revival of interest in their own national antiquities. At the beginning of the 19th century the *eisteddfod* was resumed once more as an important national institution, and a new enthusiasm was stimulated among both poets and prose writers.

One of the first monuments of modern Welsh prose was William Morgan's translation of the Bible, published in 1588. This version, revised in 1620 by Bishop Parry, is still in use. In the 17th century the most important prose writers were Morgan Llwyd and Charles Edwards. At the beginning of the 18th century stands Elis Wynn, whose *Gweledigœtheu y Bardd Cwsc* ("Visions of the Sleeping Bard") is generally recognized as the masterpiece of Welsh prose since the *Mabinogion*. A little later lived Theophilus Evans, whose *Drych y Prif Oesoedd* still ranks as a favorite Welsh classic. In the 19th century the principal prose writers have been Davin Owen (Brutus), Thomas Price (Carnhuanawc), Gweirdd ap Rhys, Gwallter Mechain, and Lewis Edwards. Throughout the century a thriving periodical literature was maintained, and in 1899 at least twenty-nine newspapers and thirty-nine magazines (secular and religious) were printed in Welsh. The Welsh, like all their Celtic neighbors, have been possessed of a rich and interesting folklore, but their tales are not as well preserved as those of the Gaelic peoples. Active efforts have been made in recent years to save what is left of these popular traditions, and an extensive collection of material has been published by Rhys under the title *Celtic Folk-Lore* (1901). See BARD; BRETON LITERATURE; IRISH LITERATURE; MANX LITERATURE; SCOTTISH GAELIC LITERATURE.

WELSH SPRINGER SPANIEL, a breed of spaniel (q.v.) known in Wales and western England for several centuries and popular today particularly in Scotland, England, the United States, Australia, India, and Siam. The Welsh springer spaniel, which weighs between thirty-three and forty pounds, is smaller than the English springer spaniel (q.v.) which it otherwise resembles in a number of ways. It is larger, however, than the cocker spaniel, and because of its longer legs it can cover ground more quickly than the cocker. The Welsh springer spaniel has a skull that is of moderate length and slightly domed; small ears that taper towards the tip; eyes of medium size that are hazel or dark in color; long and muscular shoulders and neck; and a strong, compact, muscular body. It has a silky coat, red and white or orange and white in color, which is straight or flat and thick. The animal is active, and is noted for its endurance and ability to stand extremes of heat and cold. It is most useful as a gun dog, is a good water

Welsh terrier

dog, and makes an excellent watch dog and pet.

WELSH TERRIER, a type of terrier which supposedly originated in Wales approximately two centuries ago, but was not recognized as a separate breed until 1884; up to that time the dog was known either by its present name or as the old English terrier. The Welsh terrier was imported into the United States in 1888 and its popularity since that time has steadily increased. The dog is used for hunting the otter, fox, and badger, and also makes an excellent watch dog and a pet. The Welsh terrier has a flat skull; a powerful jaw; v-shaped ears; small, dark-hazel eyes; a moderately long and thick neck; and straight, muscular legs. It has a wiry, hard, abundant coat, which is black and tan in color; it is 15 inches high at the shoulder and weighs about 20 pounds.

WELTE, MICHAEL (1807–80), German inventor and builder of mechanical musical instruments, born in Unterkirnach, Black Forest. After serving a five-year apprenticeship with Joseph Blessing, a maker of musical clocks, Welte established a musical-instrument factory in 1832 in Voehrenbach. In 1849 he exhibited at Karlsruhe his first "Orchestrion" (q.v.). In 1872 the factory was moved to larger quarters in Freiburg. Michael's oldest son, EMIL, came to the United States in 1865 to establish a branch. In 1884 he applied the newly invented perforated paper roll. Michael's grandson, EDWIN, applied his uncle's (Emil) invention to the pianoforte, and in 1904 exhibited the Welte-Mignon player piano which reproduced performances of great pianists. The application of the same principle to the organ resulted, in 1912, in the invention of the Philharmonic Organ.

WELWITSCH, FRIEDRICH (1806–72), Austrian botanist, born in Klagenfurt, Carinthia, and educated at the University of Vienna. In 1839 he was sent on a journey of botanical exploration to the Cape Verde Islands and Azores by the Reiseverein of Württemberg. Having been detained in Lisbon, he took up his residence in Portugal, and became director of the botanical gardens of Lisbon and Coimbra. He collected 56,000 botanical specimens in Portugal for the Reiseverein. From 1853 to 1861 he traveled in Africa, particularly Angola and Benguela, where he amassed an important botanical and zoological collection. The genus *Welwitschia* (q.v.), a unique African genus of gymnosperms, was named in his honor. After 1863 he lived in London. He wrote *Synopse Explicativa das Amostras de Madeiras e Drogas Medicinaes de Collegidas na Provincia de Angola* (1862).

WELWITSCHIA, a genus of plants, also called *Tumboa*, in the family Gnetaceae (q.v.), and containing a single species, *W. mirabilis*. The genus was named for the Austrian botanist Friedrich Welwitsch (q.v.), who discovered the plant in 1860 and described it in 1863. The plant has a heavy root, and a stem which rarely reaches one foot in height, but which has a circumference of 6 to 12 feet. Each plant bears a single pair of opposite, woody leaves, which are never replaced, but continue to grow through the life of the plant, forming ribbons lying on the ground, wearing off at the extremities, and becoming frayed and split with age. The inflorescences are axillary male and female cones; the female cones are larger than the male, and contain ovules which are scarlet when mature. Welwitschia is native to the deserts of s.w. Africa; the plant is rarely cultivated elsewhere, but dried specimens are displayed in museums throughout the world.

WEMYSS, EARL OF, a Scotch title of the Charteris family. The title was created in 1633 and the first bearer of it was Sir John Wemyss. After the death of the fifth earl the title was discontinued owing to the family's part in the 1745 rebellion. In 1821 the title was restored, being conferred on the member of the family who was then Baron Wemyss, as sixth earl of Wemyss. The family also bears the title Earl of March and the heir carries the courtesy title Lord Elcho. The present holder is the 12th Earl, FRANCIS DAVIS CHARTERIS (born 1912), who was appointed assistant district commissioner of Basutoland in 1937, and owns large estates in England and Scotland.

WEMYSS, WESTER, 1st BARON OF WEMYSS (1864–1933), British naval officer, born in Fife, Scotland. He entered the navy in 1877 and rose through the various grades to the rank of vice admiral in 1916 and admiral in 1918. He was commander of the Royal Naval Barracks (1911–12). In April, 1915, he commanded the squadron which landed the troops at Gallipoli. From 1916 to 1917 he was commander in chief of the East Indies and Egypt. He was a member of the War Cabinet of 1918, and first sea lord from 1917 to 1918. In November, 1918, he was chosen with Marshal Foch to receive the German armistice delegation. In recognition of his distinguished war record he received a knighthood in 1916 and a barony in 1919. In 1929 he retired from the Admiralty.

WENATCHEE, county seat of Chelan Co., Wash., situated on the Columbia R., at the mouth of the Wenatchee R., 167 miles E. of Seattle and 174 miles w. of Spokane. Transportation facilities include a railroad and an airport. Wenatchee is the shipping point and distributing center of five fertile valleys comprising one of the greatest apple-growing districts in the world. In addition, the surrounding agricultural area, much of which is irrigated, yields peaches, pears, cherries, prunes, apricots, and wheat. The Wenatchee area is also a dairying and mining region, especially noted for its copper mines. The city borders on the Columbia Basin Project, which, when completed, will provide irrigation for 1,200,000 acres of land. Near Wenatchee are two picturesque lakes, Chelan and Wenatchee, and the city is a gateway to a scenic area of the Cascade Mountains. In the vicinity of the city are beautiful alpine gardens, and Wenatchee is the site of an annual blossom festival. The city was chartered in 1892. Pop. (1948 est.) 13,000.

WEN CHOW or **YUNGKIA**, a city and port of Chekiang Province, China, situated on the Wu R., about 159 miles s. of Hangchow. Among the chief exports are tea, timber, and paper umbrellas. Pop., about 632,000.

WENDELL, BARRET (1855–1921), American college professor and author, born in Boston, Mass. He lectured at Harvard University and at Cambridge University, the Sorbonne, University of Berlin, and other European colleges. He wrote *The Duchess Emilia* (1885), *English Composition* (1891), *A Literary History of America* (1900), *The Mystery of Education* (1909), and numerous essays.

WENDS, the name given by the Germans to a branch of the Slavs which, as early as the 6th

The leaders of the Wends are forced by the Saxons to choose Christianity or death.

century, occupied N. and E. Germany from the Elbe along the coast of the Baltic to the Vistula, and as far S. as Bohemia. In a narrower sense the name of Wends is given to those remnants of the Slavic population of Lusatia who still speak the Wendish tongue. Of these Lusatian Wends there are about 200,000. They appealed to the Paris Peace Conference in 1919 for self-determination.

WENER, VÄNERN, or **WENER, LAKE,** the largest lake in the Scandinavian peninsula and one of the largest in Europe, situated in S.W. Sweden. It is nearly 100 m. in length, 50 m. in greatest breadth, and 300 ft. in greatest depth, and lies 150 ft. above sea level. Its area is about 2150 sq.m.

WENLOCK, a municipal borough of Shropshire, England, situated on the Severn R., about 14 miles S.E. of Shrewsbury. It has interesting remains of a Cluniac abbey, originally founded as a nunnery about 680. Coal, iron, and limestone are mined in the neighborhood. Pop., about 14,000.

WENNERBERG, GUNNAR (1817–1901), Swedish poet, composer, and statesman, born in Lidköping. He won fame with a collection of poems, *Gluntarne,* describing the life of students at Uppsala. He also composed melodies for these poems. The same success met his trios, his patriotic hymns, including *Hör Os,* *Svea, O, Gud som Styrer Folkens Oden, Stå Stark Du Ljusets Riddarvakt,* and the oratory *Jesu Födelse.* He was minister of education (1870–75 and 1888–91), governor (1875), and senator. His *Samlade Skrifter* were published in four volumes (1881–85).

WENTLETRAP, a small prosobranch gastropod of the family Scalariidae, also called staircase shell and ladder shell. The shell is spiral with many whorls, the whorls deeply divided, and crossed by remarkably elevated ribs. The aperture is round and rather small. The animal is furnished with a proboscis, and has the eyes placed on an external convexity, the foot short and oval. About 200 species are known, some found in northern seas, as *Scala (Scalaria) communis* on the coasts of Europe, and *S. graenlandica* on those of North America. The best known is probably the precious wentletrap, *S. pretiosa,* from the coasts of China and Australia, at one time highly valued by collectors.

WENTWORTH. See STRAFFORD, ROCKINGHAM.

WENTWORTH, BENNING (1696–1770), colonial governor of New Hampshire, born in Portsmouth N.H., and educated at Harvard College. In 1734 he was appointed a king's councilor, and (1741–67) was governor of New Hampshire. In 1749 he was authorized to grant patents of land in what is now Vermont. This territory was also claimed by the colonial governor of New York, and a bitter controversy arose over the "New Hampshire Grants". After his resignation (1767) he presented to Dartmouth College land now comprising its campus. The town of Bennington, Vt., was named in his honor.

WENTWORTH, GEORGE ALBERT (1835–1906), American mathematician, born in Wakefield, N.H. In 1858 he became instructor of ancient languages at Exeter Academy, and in 1859 he was appointed to the chair of mathematics at the same institution, a position which he retained until 1891. He wrote *Elements of Geometry* (1878), *Elements of Algebra* 1881, *Plane and Spherical Trigonometry* (1882), *Surveying and Navigation* (1882), *Five Place Tables of Logarithms* (1882), *Elements of Analytic Geometry* (1886), *School Algebra* (1887), *College Algebra* (1888), *Higher Algebra* (1891), and a large number of other textbooks.

WENTWORTH, SIR JOHN (1737–1820), colonial administrator and a nephew of Benning Wentworth, born in Portsmouth, N.H. In 1765 he went to England as agent for the province, and in the following year was appointed governor of New Hampshire. He did much to further the settlement of the country, and assisted in founding Dartmouth College (1770), to which he gave its charter and 44,000 acres of land. In 1775, for attempting to get men to assist General Gage in fortifying Boston, he was forced to take refuge in Fort William and Mary, and subsequently on a British man-of-war. He received a new commission as surveyor general of all the king's woods in British North America in 1783. He was created a baronet in 1795 and became lieutenant governor of Nova Scotia in 1792. He held this office until 1808, when he retired on a pension.

WENTWORTH, WILLIAM CHARLES (1793–1872), Australian statesman, born on Norfolk Island, New South Wales. He was called to the bar in Sydney in 1823. He founded *The Australian* and was a leader in the agitation for self-government. In 1852 he founded the University of Sydney. He died in England and his remains were brought back to Sydney and buried with public honors. The Commonwealth of Australia owes its autonomy to him.

WERDAU, a town of Saxony, Germany, situated on the Pleisse R., about 40 miles s. of Leipzig. It has important industries, including plants engaged in the manufacture of woolen fabrics, chemicals, machinery, shoes, paper, playing cards, motors, wagons, and upholstery goods. Pop., about 21,000.

WEREGILD or WERGELD, in Germanic and Anglo-Saxon law, the compensation by which homicide and other heinous crimes against the person were expiated. There was an established progressive rate of weregild for homicide, varying, at different times and among different Teutonic tribes, from the weregild of the churl or peasant to that of the king. In Anglo-Saxon times the value of the king was 7200 shillings. The value of an ealdorman was 2400 shillings, and that of a churl was 200 shillings.

WEREWOLF (from AS. *wer*, "man"; *wulf*, "wolf"), according to a widespread superstition, a man who is transformed, or who transforms himself, into a wolf in nature and appearance. This act or insane delusion, which is known as lycanthropy, is mentioned by classical writers; one of the earliest stories of the transformation of a man into a wolf appears in the Greek myth of Lycaon (q.v.), and an interesting tale of a werewolf is related by the Roman author Gaius Petronius Arbiter in his *Satyricon* (see PETRONIUS). Stories of werewolves are also found in the sagas of the northern races. Tales of persons who were changed into wolves by way of punishment were especially prevalent during the Middle Ages. Like witches (see WITCHCRAFT), werewolves were regarded as servants of the Devil, and it was believed that they took part in the Devil's Sabbath. Although the animal whose shape is taken is usually a wolf, mention is also made in the folklore of many European nations of the transformation of a human being into a dog, bull, bear, or other animal.

WERFEL, FRANZ (1890–1945), Austrian novelist, dramatist, and poet, born and privately educated in Prague. In 1912 he secured an editorial position in the publishing house of Kurt Wolff at Leipzig, Germany. The following year he helped to found *Der Jüngste Tag* ("The Youngest Day"), a publication devoted to the advancement of expressionist (see EXPRESSIONISM) literature. After serving in the German army during World War I, Werfel moved to Vienna, where he resided until the Nazi occupation of Austria in 1938. He subsequently lived in Paris and, after the fall of France in 1940, in the United States.

Werfel's basic philosophy, first expounded in his early collections of lyrical verse *Der Weltfreund* ("The World Friend", 1911), *Wir Sind* ("We Are", 1913), *Einander* ("Another", 1915), and *Gerichtstag* ("Judgment Day", 1919), is that of a universal brotherhood based on the individual and collective realization of God in human relationships. The dramatic works of Werfel, ranking among the best in the literature of the modern German theater, include *Spiegelmensch* ("Mirror Man", 1920), *Bocksgesang* ("Goat Song", 1922), *Juarez und Maximilian* ("Juarez and Maximilian", 1926), *Paulus Unter den Juden* ("Paul Among the Jews", 1926), and *Das Reich Gottes in Böhmen* ("The Kingdom of God in Bohemia", 1930). It was through his novels, however, that Werfel first achieved an international reputation. Notable among these works are *Nicht der Mörder, der Ermordete ist Schuldig* ("Not the Murderer, the Murdered is Guilty", 1920), *Verdi* (1924), *Der Tod des Kleinbürgers* ("The Man Who Conquered Death", 1926), *Der Abituriententag* ("The Class Reunion", 1928), *Die Geschwister von Neapel* ("The Pascarella Family", 1931), *Die Vierzig Tage des Musa Dagh* ("The Forty Days of Musa Dagh", 1933), and *Lied der Bernadette* ("The Song of Bernadette", 1941).

WERFF, ADRIAEN VAN DER (1659–1722), Dutch historical and genre painter, born in Kralingen. He was a pupil of Cornelis Picolet and of Eglon van der Neer. He resided in Rotterdam, where in 1696 he became known to Elector Palatine John William. The elector appointed him court painter. His minute, correctly drawn, and elegantly composed Biblical, mythological, and genre paintings are characterized by porcelainlike finish, pallid color, and conventionally academic style. Many of his compositions are among the collections of the principal European galleries.

WERGELAND, HENRIK ARNOLD (1808–45), Norwegian poet and dramatist, born in Kristiansund, and educated at the University of Christiania (now Oslo). His early work, romantic in tone and expressing a militant political liberalism, earned for him a wide popular following. The most representative specimen of this work is *Skabelsen, Mennesket, og Messias* ("Creation, Man, and Messiah", 1830), a long and rambling philosophico-dramatic poem, deficient alike in thought and style. Under the mordant critical attacks of his compatriot, the conservative poet and literary critic Johan Sebastian Welhaven (q.v.), Wergeland gradually improved and refined his poetic style. As his stylistic mastery grew, however, his popular following declined, and by 1840, when he had become a truly great lyric poet, he had completely lost his place in the esteem of his countrymen as the foremost literary exponent of political liberalism. Writing under the pseudonym of Siful Sifadda,

Franz Werfel

Wergeland satirized the conservative and doctrinaire views of Welhaven in the farces *Papegöien* (1833) and *Den Konstitutionelle* (1839). In 1836 Wergeland secured a post in the Norwegian state library; he was made custodian of the royal archives four years later. The most notable of Wergeland's dramatic works is *Campbellerne* (1837). His reputation, however, rests principally on his lyrical narrative poems *Jan van Huysums Blomsterstykke* (1840), *Svalen* (1841), *Jöden* (1842), *Jödinden* (1844), and *Den Engelske Lods* (1844), which are generally considered the best works of their kind in the Norwegian language.

WERGELD. See WEREGILD.

WERNER, ABRAHAM GOTTLOB (1750–1817), German geologist and mineralogist, born in Wehrau, Prussia. His first original work, *Ueber die Äussern Kennzeichen der Fossilien* (1764), won him a position as instructor at the Mining Academy of Freiberg. He arranged geological formations into groups and made a systematic classification of minerals.

WERNER, ALFRED (1866–1919), Swiss chemist, born in Mühlhausen, Alsace. He worked under Berthelot at the Collège de France, and by 1895 had become professor at the University of Zurich. In 1902 he was placed in charge of the lectures on inorganic chemistry at the last-named institution. His views on valence and co-ordination in complex compounds led to important advances in chemical theories. He was awarded the Nobel Prize in chemistry for 1913.

WERNER, ANTON ALEXANDER VON (1843–1915), German historical and portrait painter and illustrator, born in Frankfort on the Oder, and educated in Berlin, Karlsruhe, and Paris. His earliest, and perhaps his best, work was in illustration, particularly for *Der Trompeter von Säckingen* and other poems of Victor Scheffel. The first of his historical and genre paintings appeared in 1865. During the Franco-German War he accompanied the Third Army Corps and became practically the official German painter of the war. In 1875 he was appointed director of the Berlin Academy. His art is soberly realistic and typically Prussian, and his draftsmanship is excellent. Among his numerous patriotic paintings are "The Negotiations for Surrender at Sedan", "Meeting of Bismarck and Napoleon III at Donchery", "In Quarters before Paris, 1871", "The Proclamation at Versailles of William I as Emperor", "Close of the Congress of Berlin", "Opening of the Reichstag by Emperor William II, 1889", and "Unveiling of the Wagner Monument, Berlin". His portraits include several of Emperor William II.

WERNER, KARL (1808–94), German watercolor painter, born in Weimar. After studying in Leipzig, he spent almost twenty years in Italy. On a visit to England in 1851 he was made a member of the Society of Painters in Water Colors. Extensive travels in Italy, Spain, and the Orient furnished subjects, mostly architectural, for his drawings, some of which have been published, as "The Holy Places" (1866) and "Nilbilder". He is considered one of the best German aquarellists of the 19th century, and his work is distinguished for careful execution, brilliancy of color, and poetic conception. Among his easel pictures are "Partenkirchen" (1833) and "Cathedral of Cefalù" (1838), in the National Gallery, Berlin; and "Interior of House at Granada" (1856) and "View of Spalato", in the Leipzig Museum.

WERNER, REINHOLD VON (1825–1909), German admiral and writer, born in Weferlingen, Prussia. After a number of years' experience in the merchant marine, in the course of which he made numerous voyages to the East Indies, he became, in 1849, an officer in the newly organized German navy. In 1852 he entered the Prussian service, became lieutenant captain in 1856, took part in the East Asia expedition of 1859–62, and as commander of a corvette during the war with Denmark in 1864 fought at Jasmund. During the Seven Weeks' War Werner seized the Hanoverian ports on the North Sea. He became rear admiral in 1875, but was retired three years later. In 1898 he was nominated to be vice-admiral, and in 1901 was ennobled. He wrote *Die Preussische Expedition nach China, Japan, und Siam* (1863); *Die Schule des Seewesens* (1866); *Das Buch von der Deutschen Flotte* (1868); *Seebilder* (1876); *Erinnerungen und Bilder aus dem Seeleben* (1881; 7th ed., 1898); *Berühmte Seeleute* (2 vols., 1882–84); *Drei Monate an der Sklavenküste* (1885); *Dirk Mallinga* (1888); and *Bilder aus der Deutschen Seekriegsgeschichte von Germanicus bis Kaiser Wilhelm II* (1898).

WERNER, ZACHARIAS (1768–1823), German romantic dramatist, born in Königsberg (now Kaliningrad). He studied law at Königsberg, entered (1793) the Prussian civil service, and after sojourns in Warsaw and Berlin went to Rome, where he joined the Roman Catholic Church. He had earlier made the acquaintance of Goethe. He became a priest in 1814 and thereafter resided mainly in Vienna, where he became noted for the sensational eloquence of his preaching. Werner owes his place in literature to four dramas, *Die Söhne des Thals* (1803), *Das Kreuz und der Ostee* (1806), *Martin Luther* (1807), and especially *Der 24 Februar* (1809). His *Works* (13 vols., 1841) contain four other dramas and many poems, hymns, and sermons. The dramas are luridly romantic.

WERNHER, SIR JULIUS (CHARLES) (1850–1912), British South African capitalist, born in Germany. He was active in an Anglo-German firm in London in 1870, returned to Germany and served in the Franco-Prussian War, and later settled in Kimberly, where he developed a diamond-mining company. With Alfred Beit and Cecil Rhodes he subsequently formed the De Beers Corporation. In 1905 he was created a baronet.

WERNIGERODE, town in Saxony, Germany, situated about 43 miles s.w. of Magdeburg. It has a famous library, with a collection of hymns and other Biblical material. Its manufactures include chocolate, machinery, cigars, and dyestuffs. Pop., about 19,000.

WERRA, a river of Germany, rising in the southeastern part of the Thuringian Forest. It flows in a generally northwesterly direction, passing Meiningen and at Münden uniting with the Fulda to form the Weser. It is 170 m. long and is navigable N. of Wanfried.

WERRENRATH, REINALD (1883–   ), American concert baritone, born in Brooklyn,

N.Y. He studied with C. Dufft, A. Mees, and Percy Rector Stephens, and made his debut at the Worcester Festival of 1907. He then made several transcontinental tours and everywhere met with enormous success. In 1918–19 he was a member of the Metropolitan Opera Company. He was especially fine in oratorio. He wrote some male choruses and edited a collection of modern Scandinavian songs. In 1931 he conducted a series of broadcasts of the National Oratorio Society for the National Broadcasting Company.

WERTH or **WERDT**, JOHANN VON (1600?–52) German soldier, born in Büttgen, near Jülich. He entered the imperial army, and then the Bavarian army, and fought in the Thirty Years' War. A cavalry leader of ability, he rose to high rank. By a spirited charge at Nördlingen in 1634, he turned the day against the Swedes and was made baron and lieutenant marshal. In 1635 he took Speyer; and in 1636 he invaded France, threatened Paris, and finally retreated with immense booty. Two years afterward he was defeated by Bernhard of Saxe-Weimar at Rheinfelden, and was taken prisoner, but in 1642 was exchanged for the Swedish general Horn. In 1643 he helped the Imperialists to win the great victory of Tuttlingen. He shared in the defeat at Jankau in 1645. In the same year his cavalry decided the battle of Mergentheim against Turenne and he conducted the retreat of the Imperialists after the death of General Mercy at Allersheim. When the elector of Bavaria made peace with France and Sweden in 1647, Werth attempted to transfer a part of the Bavarian army into the service of the emperor, but his plan was discovered, and he escaped with only a few followers. When the elector again declared war, he was restored to command, but the Peace of Westphalia soon afterward brought an end to the long struggle.

WESCOTT, GLENWAY (1901–   ), American author, born in Kewaskum, Wis., and educated at the University of Chicago. Most of his life was spent in France and other European countries; as a writer, however, he is best known for novels and short stories dealing with his native region. Wescott's most important work, the novel *The Grandmothers* (1927), is a study of a pioneer family of the Midwest told from the point of view of a young expatriate. Another work on the same theme is his well-known collection of short stories, collectively entitled *Good-Bye, Wisconsin* (1928). Wescott also wrote *Apartment in Athens* (1945), a powerful and widely read novel dealing with the fate of a Greek family

Harper & Bros.
Glenway Wescott

during World War II. Among his other books are the collection of poems *Natives of Rock* (1925), and the novels *The Apple of the Eye* (1924), *The Babe's Bed* (1930), and *The Pilgrim Hawk* (1940).

WESEL, a city of the State of North Rhine-Westphalia, Western Germany, situated at the confluence of the Lippe and the Rhine rivers, about 35 miles N.W. of Düsseldorf. Its industries include flour milling, sugar refining, weaving, and soap making. Pottery and machinery are also manufactured. Pop., about 25,000.

WESER, a river of Germany, formed by the confluence of the Werra and the Fulda rivers. It flows generally northwestward from Münden, in the S.E. section of the West German State of North Rhine-Westphalia, to the North Sea, a distance of about 280 m. The Weser is navigable throughout its course.

WESLEY, CHARLES HARRIS (1891–   ), American Negro educator, author, and historian, born in Louisville, Ky., and educated at Fisk University, Nashville, Tenn., at Yale University, and at Harvard University. He taught history and modern languages at Howard University (1914–20), was professor of history and chairman of the history department

John Wesley preaching Methodism to the American Indians (from a painting)

(1920–42), and then became president of Wilberforce University, Wilberforce, Ohio. During World War I, he served with the Y.M.C.A. He was pastor and presiding elder of the Ebenezer and Campbell African Methodist Episcopal Church, Washington, D.C. (1918–38). He conducted extensive research into Negro labor from slave-trade days to modern times, and was active in social and educational reform circles. Among his works are *Negro Labor in the United States, 1850–1925* (1927); *Richard Allen, Apostle of Freedom* (1935); *The Collapse of the Confederacy* (1938); and *The Negro in the Americas* (1940).

WESLEY, JOHN (1703–91), English theologian, evangelist, and founder of Methodism, born in Epworth Rectory, Lincolnshire. He was ordained deacon in Christ Church Cathedral in 1725, and admitted to priest's orders in 1728. In 1735 Wesley undertook a mission to Georgia. He returned to England in 1738. Then came the ever memorable May 24, 1738, when Methodism as history knows it was born.

He made the great innovation first in Bristol, where he preached to 3000 persons. For half a century, he preached Methodism in a tireless itinerary of travel. Until his seventieth year all his journeys were done on horseback, 60 or 70 miles day after day. Perhaps his best single treatises were his *Notes on the Old and New Testaments* (1764) and his *Doctrine of Original Sin* (1757).

Wesley further prepared numerous collections of psalms, hymns, and sacred songs, with several works on music and collections of tunes. In addition, he published his own *Sermons* and *Journals,* and started in 1778 a monthly magazine which still exists.

For the organization, doctrine, and present condition of the societies founded by him, see METHODISTS.

WESLEYAN METHODIST CHURCHES, the designation of a number of Protestant (see PROTESTANTISM) denominations which developed from the Methodist Association founded at Oxford University, England, in 1729, by John Wesley (q.v.) and his brother Charles (1707–88). The followers of John Wesley first achieved ecclesiastical organization in Great Britain in 1739 under the name of the *Wesleyan Methodists.* The installation of an organ in the Brunswick Wesleyan Methodist Chapel of Leeds, in Yorkshire, England, in 1828, in contravention of a portion of Wesleyan Methodist doctrine pertaining to the use of music at devotional services, and against the wishes of the leaders of the congregation, resulted in the withdrawal of more than a thousand communicants, who thereupon organized themselves as the *Wesleyan Protestant Methodists.*

The next schism among the Wesleyan Methodists occurred in 1835 when a large number of the congregation withdrew to signify their support of Dr. Samuel Warren (1781-1832), a Wesleyan preacher ousted by the autocratic Wesleyan Methodist minister Jabez Bunting (q.v.) because of his opposition to Bunting's plan to found a Wesleyan theological institute. The dissident Wesleyans founded the *Wesleyan Methodist Association.* In 1857 the Wesleyan Protestant Methodists united with the Wesleyan Methodist Association to form the *United Methodist Free Churches;* for the later history of this body, see METHODISTS.

In the United States, the *Wesleyan Methodist Church* was organized at Utica, New York, in 1843, by Northern antislavery Methodists in protest against the acquiescent attitude toward slavery adopted by Methodist ministers and congregations in the Southern States. The Wesleyan Methodist Church, nonepiscopal (see BISHOP) in its ecclesiastical polity, is also opposed to secret societies, intemperance, and ostentatious dress. In a recent year it maintained about 650 churches and had about 22,000 communicants; see also METHODISTS, AMERICAN.

WESLEYAN UNIVERSITY, a nondenominational, privately controlled institution of higher education for men, situated in Middletown, Conn. It was established in 1831 under the auspices of the Methodist Episcopal Church; at no time since its founding, however, has the university been under sectarian control. The curriculum is restricted to the liberal arts, though a semiprofessional course in accounting is available to students majoring in economics; the only degrees awarded are those of B.A. and M.A. All students are required to pursue a general course in liberal arts during their first two years of undergraduate study. In a recent year about 900 men were enrolled and the faculty numbered about 100.

WESSEL, JOHAN HERMAN (1742-85), Norwegian poet, born in Jonsrud, Akershus Stift, and educated in Christiania and Copenhagen. With others he founded (1772) *Norske Selskab* and in the same year wrote the classic *Kierlighed Uden Strömper* ("Love Without Stockings"), an exceptional parody of formal and linguistic elegance. His stories, including *Gaffelen, Herremanden, Smeden og Bageren,* and *Hundemordet,* and his witty verses are also notable.

WESSEL or **WESSEL GANSFORT,** JOHANNES (1420?-89), mystic, religious reformer, and friend of Thomas a Kempis, born in Groningen and educated in Cologne, Louvain, and Paris. He visited Rome and taught philosophy at Heidelberg and at Paris. His later years were spent in monastic retirement in Holland. Wessel's friends, among whom was the bishop of Utrecht, called him *lux mundi* (Lat., "light of the world"), with reference to his evangelical views, but his critics called him master of contradictions, in allusion to his attitude to the Roman Catholic Church and to his mind, which held scholastic, mystic, and classical culture together with scientific knowledge in one consciousness. His friends saved his manuscripts and sent them to Martin Luther, who published a collection of them (1512), leaving out an essay on the Eucharist, because it advocated Huldreich Zwingli's views.

WESSEX, an Anglo-Saxon kingdom, situated in southern Britain and extending from Watling Street (q.v.), to the English Channel. The kingdom was founded early in the 6th century by a group of Saxons under a chieftain called Cerdic. They quickly overran what are now Hampshire and Wight, and during the succeeding century occupied most of the s. of Britain. Under Egbert they rose to the lordship of most of the other kingdoms on the island, and began the history of England.

WEST, ANDREW FLEMING (1853-1943), American classical scholar and educator, born in Allegheny, Pa., and educated at the College of New Jersey (now Princeton University). In 1883 he became Giger Professor of Latin, and in 1901 dean of the Graduate School, in Princeton University, and held both positions until his retirement in 1928. He was one of the founders of the American School of Classical Studies in Rome, and served for many years as the chairman of the school's managing committee. West was in charge of planning the residential Graduate College of Princeton University, which was opened in 1913. His works include *Alcuin and the Rise of the Christian Schools* (1892), *A Latin Grammar for Schools* (1902), *American Liberal Education* (1907), *The War and Education* (1919), and *American General Education* (1932).

WEST, BENJAMIN (1738-1820), American painter, born in Springfield, Pa. Self-taught, at the age of sixteen he practiced portrait paint-

Detail from "Death on the Pale Horse," painting by Benjamin West

ing in the villages near Philadelphia and painted his first historical picture, "The Death of Socrates". In 1760 he went to Italy to study. While in Italy, he painted his "Cimon and Iphigenia" and "Angelica and Medora", and was elected a member of the academies of Florence, Bologna, and Parma. In 1763 he visited England, where he spent the rest of his life. His "Agrippina Landing with the Ashes of Germanicus" attracted the attention of George III, who was West's steady friend and patron for forty years. Among his other works are "Penn's Treaty with the Indians", "Christ Healing the Sick", "Death on the Pale Horse", and "Battle of La Hogue".

WEST, MAE (1892–), American actress, born in Brooklyn, N.Y. Her career began on the vaudeville stage in 1911. She subsequently played leading roles in numerous productions, including *The Drag* (1927), *Sex* and *Pleasure Man* (1928), and *Diamond Lil* (1930). After 1932 she appeared in various motion pictures. Her hard-boiled roles, with pronounced emphasis on sex, won her international renown. During World War II a life preserver used by American airmen was popularly known by her name. She appeared on Broadway, New York City, during 1948 and 1949 in a successful revival of *Diamond Lil*.

WEST AFRICA, PORTUGUESE. See ANGOLA.

WEST ALLIS, a city of Milwaukee Co., Wis., adjoining the city of Milwaukee on the w. It is served by two railroads, and is a manufacturing center, with large industrial establishments producing engines, turbines, tractors, trucks, steam pumps, automobiles, steel castings, wheelbarrows, and tools. Pop. (1950) 42,945.

WEST BEND, county seat of Washington Co., Wis., situated on the Milwaukee R., 34 miles N.N.W. of Milwaukee and about 30 miles S.S.E. of Fond du Lac. It is served by a railroad, and is the center of an agricultural region yielding livestock, dairy products, and general farm crops. The chief industries in the city are the processing of dairy products and the manufacture of aluminum ware, leather goods, woolen goods, cheese boxes, farm machinery, industrial trucks, and automotive parts. The site of the present city was first settled about 1845. Pop. (1949 est.) 6500.

WESTBORO, a town of Worcester Co., Mass., situated 12 miles E. of the city of Worcester. It is served by a railroad, and is a manufacturing center. Industrial establishments in the town include tanneries, machine shops, and factories producing leather goods, narrow cotton fabrics, and abrasives. Westboro is noted as the birthplace of Eli Whitney, inventor of the cotton gin. The town was settled about 1659 and incorporated in 1717. Pop. (1945) 6665.

WEST BROMWICH, a parliamentary, municipal, and county borough of Staffordshire, England, situated 6 miles N.W. of Birmingham. The manufactures include puddling and sheet-iron rolling, sheet-glass making, coal-mining, and brick and tile making. Pop., about 82,000.

WESTBROOK, city of Cumberland County, Me., situated about 5 miles N.W. of Portland. Among the manufactures of the city are paper, silks, and cotton goods. Pop. (1940) 11,087.

WEST CHESTER, county seat of Chester County, Pa., situated about 27 miles W. of Philadelphia. The principal manfactures include cream separators, wheels, and planing-mill, foundry, and machine-shop products. Pop. (1950) 15,109.

WEST CHICAGO, city of Dupage County, Ill., situated 30 miles w. of Chicago. It has foundries, furniture plants, and other industrial establishments. Pop. (1940) 3355.

WEST CONSHOHOCKEN, a borough of Montgomery County, Pa., situated about 13 miles N.W. of Philadelphia, on the Schuylkill R. The manufacture of woolens and carpets is the chief industry. Pop. (1940) 2464.

WESTCOTT, BROOKE FOSS (1825–1901), English scholar and divine, born in Birmingham. In 1869 he became canon of Peterborough. He held this office until 1883. After 1870 he was also regius professor of divinity at Cambridge. In 1883 Gladstone appointed him a canon of Westminster, and in 1890 he was appointed bishop of Durham. Westcott was joint editor of Westcott and Hort's Greek New Testament. Among his more important writings are *The History of the Canon* (1855), *Introduction to the Study of the Gospels* (1860), *The New Testament in the Original Greek* (With Dr. Hort, 1881), *Social Aspects of Christianity* (1887), *The Epistle to the Hebrews* (Greek text with notes and essays, 1889), and *The Incarnation and Common Life* (1889).

WESTCOTT, EDWARD NOYES (1846–98), American author, born in Syracuse, N.Y. He is the author of *David Harum: A Story of American Life* (1895–96; published 1898). The work was immensely popular.

WESTERGAARD, NIELS LUDVIG (1815–78), Danish Orientalist and philologist, born and educated in Copenhagen. In 1838 he went to Bonn, where he studied Sanskrit, and then visited Paris, London, and Oxford, finally returning to Denmark. In 1841 he made a journey to India and in 1843–44 to Persia (now Iran) and Russia. From 1845 to 1878 he was professor of Indian philology at the University of Copenhagen. Noteworthy among his publications are *Radices Linguæ Sanskritæ* (1841), *Sanskrit Læsebog* (1846), and *Bundehesh, Liber Pehlvicus* (1851). His most important work was his edition of the *Zenda-vesta, or the Religious Books of the Zoroastrians* (1852–54).

WESTERLY, a town of Washington Co., R.I., situated on the Pawcatuck R., which there forms the Connecticut boundary, and about 70 miles E. of New Haven, Conn. Transportation facilities include a railroad and a 100-ft. bridge over the river. The town is a summer resort and a manufacturing center. In the town and vicinity are extensive granite quarries; other industrial establishments in Westerly are commercial fisheries, textile mills, and factories producing color-printing presses, elastic webbing, wire-stitching machines, airplane propellers, and cotton dyers and converters. The town, which comprises several villages, including Bradford and Watch Hill, provides 6 miles of bathing beaches. Westerly was once an important shipbuilding center. Oliver Hazard Perry, American naval hero of the War of 1812, built gunboats there prior to that war. The first settlement on the site of the present town was established in 1661, and the town was incorporated in 1669. Pop. (1949 est.) 12,400.

WESTERN AUSTRALIA, a State of Australia, occupying the western third of the continent. The Indian Ocean is to the N. and W., the Southern Ocean to the S., and South Australia, with its Northern Territory, to the E. It extends from 13° to 35° S. lat. and 113° to 129° E. long., being 1500 m. long by 1000 m. broad. Area, 975,920 sq.m.; pop. (1949 est.) 532,667. The central portions are stony or sandy, and the N. and S. coastal areas are poor in soil, but there is good land at the W. and in the N.E. Although this region is less hilly than eastern Australia, it is not so well watered. Perth (q.v.) is the capital. For climate and fauna, see AUSTRALIA.

Western Australia is one of the most sparsely settled regions in the world. Most of it is wholly uninhabited, the population being confined mainly to portions of the coast region and to the gold-mining settlements in the interior.

Education is compulsory, secular, and free. Higher education is aided by the state. The Church of England claims nearly half the population. Other important denominations are the Roman Catholic, Methodists, and Presbyterians.

Agriculture, stock raising, manufacturing, mining, lumbering, and fishing are the leading industries. The principal crops are wheat, oats, barley, hay, potatoes, tobacco, orchard fruits, including apples, and vines. State forests and timber reserves cover an area of about 5,000,-

Australian Official Photos

WESTERN AUSTRALIA. *Above: View of Perth, the capital of Western Australia. Left: Cattle herders near Wyndham. Below: Street in Kalgoorlie, important gold center.*

000 acres. Livestock includes horses, cattle, sheep, pigs, goats, camels, mules, and donkeys.

About 4250 miles of State-owned railway are maintained; there are about 250 miles of privately owned lines and 450 miles of Commonwealth lines.

Executive power is vested in a governor, acting through a responsible ministry, and legislative power in a parliament of two houses, namely the Legislative Council, consisting of thirty members elected for six years on a property qualification basis, and the Legislative Assembly, consisting of fifty members elected for three years by universal suffrage.

The coast of Western Australia was probably visited by Spanish and Portuguese navigators in the 16th century. In the following century the Dutch mariner Abel Tasman surveyed the north coast. The west coast was only surveyed during later explorations. The earliest settlement was founded by British colonists in 1825. The British took formal official possession of the land in 1827. The colonization of Western Australia on a planned basis was begun in 1829 by a British organization, which received large land grants. Several thousand convicts from Sydney were numbered among the early settlers. It was not until 1870, however, that extensive efforts were made by the British to facilitate the development of the colony. On Jan. 1, 1901, Western Australia became a State of the Australian Commonwealth.

WESTERN EMPIRE. See ROME.
WESTERN GHATS. See GHATS.
WESTERN ISLANDS. See HEBRIDES.
WESTERN PORT, a town in Alleghany County, Md., situated on the North Branch of the Potomac R., 28 miles s.w. of Cumberland. Its industries are coal mining and paper making. Pop. (1940) 3565.

WESTERN RESERVE, in United States history, that part of the public lands in Ohio claimed by Connecticut under its charter of 1662, and reserved to it by compromise under the Articles of Confederation. The region began at the Pennsylvania boundary, extended 120 m. westward, and comprised 3,667,000 acres. In 1800 Connecticut surrendered its jurisdiction to Ohio. Proceeds from sales of this land were allocated to the State school fund. Other parcels of land in New York belonged to the Connecticut reservation and were disposed of in the same way.

WESTERN RESERVE UNIVERSITY, a partly coeducational, nondenominational, privately controlled institution of higher education, situated in Cleveland, Ohio. It was founded as a men's college in 1826 at Hudson, Ohio, 20 miles s.e. of Cleveland, under the name of Western Reserve College; in 1844 the college was merged with the Cleveland Medical College (organized 1843), and in 1882 it was moved to Cleveland and named Adelbert College; the present name was adopted in 1884. At the present time Western Reserve University comprises thirteen distinct schools and colleges, affiliated with the university according to the by-laws of the university corporation and governed by a single group of officers. The schools include Adelbert College (an undergraduate school for men), Flora Stone Mather College (the corresponding undergraduate school for women), Cleveland College (a coeducational undergraduate school in Downtown Cleveland, 5 miles from the main campus, offering both full-time and part-time instruction), schools of architecture, applied social sciences, dentistry, education, law, library science, medicine, nursing, and pharmacy, and a graduate school. All constituent schools offer undergraduate degrees in their respective fields of instruction, and most offer master's and doctor's degrees as well. An accelerated program permits students to earn undergraduate degrees in some fields in three instead of the customary four years. In a recent year nearly 13,000 men and women were enrolled at the university and the faculty numbered over 1000.

WESTERN SAMOA, TERRITORY OF, formerly a German colony, occupied by the British in 1914, and mandated to New Zealand in 1920. It includes the islands of Savaii and Upoli. See SAMOA.

WESTERN SPRINGS, a town in Cook County, Illinois, situated about 15 miles s.w. of Chicago, of which it is a residential suburb. Pop. (1940) 4856.

WESTFIELD, a city of Hampden Co., Mass., situated on the Westfield R., 9 miles w. of Springfield. It is served by two railroads, is a railroad junction point, and maintains a municipal airport. The city is a manufacturing and distributing center of an area including about twenty other towns and comprising sections devoted to the cultivation of tobacco and garden truck. Westfield's industrial development dates from the manufacture there of whips and lashes early in the 18th century; during the 19th century, when Westfield was known as The Whip City, it contained more than forty establishments producing whips and lashes. The present leading industries are the manufacture of boilers, radiators, bicycles, textile machinery, grinding wheels and abrasives, name plates, electric motors, precision tools, plumbing supplies, hardware, fishing tackle, celluloid products, games and toys, concrete blocks, brick, lumber, wooden and paper boxes, paper, envelopes, greeting cards, thread, brushes and mops, needles, cigars, and dresses. In addition, Westfield contains marble and trap-rock quarries, printing plants, and a flower and shrub nursery.

The city is the site of Westfield State Teachers College, established in 1839, and of the Westfield State Sanitarium, for the treatment of tuberculosis and cancer. The Westfield Athenaeum contains museums of art and history. A trading post, called by the Indian name Woronoco, was established on the site of the present city about 1640. The settlement which developed was a part of Springfield until 1669, when it was set apart and incorporated as the town of Westfield. It was chartered as a city in 1921. Pop. (1950) 20,961.

WESTFIELD, town of Union County, N.J., situated 5 miles w. by s. of Elizabeth. It is largely a residential suburb of New York. Pop. (1950) 21,335.

WESTFIELD, a village of Chautauqua Co., N.Y., situated on Chautauqua Creek, near Lake Erie, and 30 miles E. of Erie, Pa. It is served by two railroads. The village is in the heart of the renowned Chautauqua grape-growing region, and is the site of the home office and largest factory of the Welch Grape Juice Company. In addition, the village contains fruit-processing plants and commercial fisheries. Westfield was incorporated as a village in 1833. Pop. (1940) 3434.

WEST FLANDERS. See FLANDERS, WEST.

WESTFORD, town of Middlesex County, Mass., about 7 miles s.w. of Lowell. The manufacture of worsteds is carried on. Pop. (1940) 350.

WEST FRANKFORT, a city in Franklin County, Illinois, 45 miles S.S.E. of Centralia. Brick making and coal mining are important industries. Pop. (1940) 12,383.

WEST HAM, a county and parliamentary borough of Essex County, England, forming an eastern suburb of London, from which it is separated by the Lea R., a tributary of the Thames. The borough contains the industrial center of Stratford (q.v.), site of extensive railway works. Other important industries in the borough include the manufacture of chemicals and artificial paving stone, shipbuilding, distilling, and silk printing. Among the recreation areas in the borough is 80-acre West Ham Park. West Ham was incorporated as a borough in 1886 and became a county borough in 1889. Pop., about 175,000.

WEST HARTFORD, a town of Hartford Co., Conn., adjoining the city of Hartford on the w. It is served by a railroad, and is a shipping point for a truck-farming, dairying, and tobacco-growing area. West Hartford is a manufacturing and residential suburb of Hartford. The principal industries in the town are the manufacture of tools and dies, sheet-metal products, burial vaults, steel balls, and rubber nipples. It is noted as the birthplace of Noah Webster, the American lexicographer. West Hartford was separated from Hartford and incorporated as a separate town in 1854. Pop. (1950) 44,401.

WEST HARTLEPOOL, a county borough of Durham, England, forming, with the municipal borough of Hartlepool (q.v.), which is sometimes called East Hartlepool, a parliamentary borough. The Hartlepools together form a single port on Hartlepool Bay just N. of the mouth of the Tees R. and 247 m. by rail N. of London. For information concerning the port and industries, see HARTLEPOOL. Pop., about 70,000.

WEST HAVEN, a town of New Haven Co., Conn., adjoining the city of New Haven, of which it is a residential and manufacturing suburb. The principal industries in the town are the manufacture of buckles, wire goods, elastic fabrics, pipe organs, glazed paper, motorboats, jewelry, tools, rubber tires, and beer. The site of the present town was first settled in 1648. It was established as a separate community from New Haven in 1715, and in 1822 it was officially separated from New Haven and made a part of North Milford, with which it formed the town of Orange. It was incorporated as an independent town in 1921. Pop. (1950) 31,876.

WEST HAZLETON, borough of Luzerne County, Pa., 31 miles s. of Wilkes-Barre. Pop. (1940) 7523.

WEST HOMESTEAD, a borough in Allegheny County, Pa., 8 miles S.E. of Pittsburgh, on the Monongahela River. There are steel mills, axle works, and brickworks, and manufactures of machinery and car wheels. Pop. (1940) 3526.

WEST INDIA COMPANY, FRENCH, an organization established in 1625 for the purpose of trading with and colonizing in the West Indies. In 1628 the company founded a settlement on the island of St. Christopher. The company was dissolved in 1674, some time after it had secured Grenada.

WEST INDIAN BOXWOOD or **ZAPATERO,** a yellow wood of great density and hardness chiefly used for turning, from *Casearia praecox,* a small tree, about a foot in diameter, belonging to the family Flacourtiaceae. The tree is found in northern South America, and in Cuba and other West Indian islands.

WEST INDIES, in physical geography, an archipelago in the Atlantic Ocean, extending from the vicinity of the Florida and Yucatán peninsulas of North America to the vicinity of the Venezuelan coast of South America and enclosing the Gulf of Mexico (see MEXICO, GULF OF) and the Caribbean Sea (q.v.). The northernmost extremity of the archipelago, which roughly resembles a crescent in shape, lies approximately at 27° N. latitude. Its s. extremity lies at about 10° N. latitude. The approximate easternmost and westernmost limits of the West Indies are delineated by 59° 40′ W. longitude and 85° W. longitude respectively. By geographic division, the West Indies islands comprise three main chains, namely the Bahamas, the Greater Antilles, and the Lesser Antilles (qq.v.). The Lesser Antilles, occasionally designated the Caribbees, include two subgroups, the Windward Islands and the Leeward Islands (qq.v.).

In political geography, the West Indies comprises three independent nations, including one that is coextensive with the largest island of the archipelago, and several colonial dependencies. Cuba (q.v.), consisting of the island of the same name and a number of off-lying islands, is the largest West Indian nation. The other two independent nations are Haiti and the Dominican Republic (qq.v.), which occupy Hispaniola (q.v.), the second-largest island of the archipelago. Both Hispaniola and Cuba form part of the Greater Antilles. Ownership of practically all of the remaining islands of the West Indies is distributed among the United States, France, the Netherlands, and the United Kingdom.

Puerto Rico (q.v.), fourth-largest island of the archipelago and another of the Greater Antilles, is a Territory of the United States. Part of the Virgin Islands, a group belonging geographically to the Leeward Islands, makes up the remainder of the West Indian possessions of the United States (see VIRGIN ISLANDS OF THE UNITED STATES). The French West Indies (q.v.), wholly confined to the Leeward group, includes Martinique, Guadelupe, Desirade, and Marie-Galante (qq.v.). Dutch possessions in the archipelago consist of Curaçao (q.v.) and five other islands of the Lesser Antilles (see WEST INDIES, NETHERLANDS).

With the exception of certain Lesser Antilles islands belonging to Venezuela, the remainder of the West Indian archipelago is owned by the United Kingdom (see BRITISH WEST INDIES). British possessions in the archipelago include Jamaica (q.v.), third-largest island of the West Indies and one of the Greater Antilles; the Bahamas; Trinidad, Dominica, Barbados (qq.v.), and various other islands of the Windward group; and several of the Virgin Islands (see VIRGIN ISLANDS, BRITISH). The total area of the West Indies is approximately 93,000 sq.m., and the total population is about 14,000,000.

Excluding the Bahamas, which are low coral formations, the West Indies are generally mountainous. The noncoral islands are mainly composed of the projecting remnants of a submerged chain of mountains, an extension of the Central American Cordillera. Many of the Lesser Antilles consist of volcanic cones, a number of which are still active. Elevations up to 10,000 ft. are common in the Great Antilles. In the Lesser Antilles elevations rarely exceed 5000 ft.

The islands possess a tropical climate, but temperate conditions prevail in the elevated regions and conditions at the lower levels are modified by oceanic influences. Throughout most of the archipelago, the average annual temperatures range between 77° F. and 82° F. Two sharply defined seasons are distinguishable in the West Indies, the dry season extending from December through May, and the wet season extending from April through November. Northeast winds prevail during the wet season. The prevailing winds during the dry season are southeast. Violent hurricanes, which frequently cause extensive damage to life and property, are an occasional phenomenon from early July through October, the hottest and wettest period in the islands. Precipitation averages about 60 inches annually.

The indigenous flora of the archipelago is closely related to that of tropical South America. Dense forests occur on many of the islands, and the vegetation includes various species of valuable timber and fruit trees. By virtue of the diversified climatic conditions, numerous imported species of plant life, particularly grains, vegetables, and other varieties that are indigenous to the temperate zone, flourish in the West Indies. The fauna of the archipelago is characterized by an abundance of tropical birds. Among representative birds are the parrot, trogon, and many species of

Office of Info. for Puerto Rico; Cuban Tourist Commission

WEST INDIES. *Top:* At a session of the senate of Puerto Rico, in the city of San Juan. *Bottom:* View of the city of Santiago de Cuba, on the island of Cuba.

Alcoa SS.; Pan Amer. Air.

WEST INDIES. *Above: Boat laden with produce in Grenada harbor, Windward Islands. Right: Street in Port-of-Spain, Trinidad, British West Indies. Below: Loading bananas, Port Antonio, Jamaica.*

Official Netherlands Photos

ON CURAÇAO ISLAND, NETHERLAND WEST INDIES
Above: Phosphate mines at Tafelberg. Left: Native at his house in San Pedro. Below: In Willemstad, the capital.

waterfowl. Large mammals are not found among the indigenous fauna. Of the smaller species of mammals, the armadillo, raccoon, opossum, and agouti are typical examples. Snakes, especially adders and boas, abound in the West Indies, and the reptilian fauna also includes various species of lizards. (For additional data on the physical features, climate, flora and fauna, natural resources, industries, history, and other features of the archipelago, see articles dealing with the various islands and island groups.)

WEST INDIES, NETHERLANDS or NETHERLANDS ANTILLES, designations applied to the West Indian possessions of the Netherlands. The possessions, which are situated in the Lesser Antilles, consist of the Netherlands Windward Islands and the Netherlands Leeward Islands and comprise part of the Netherlands Overseas Territories in America. Surinam (q.v.), on the N.E. coast of South America, is sometimes classified as part of the Netherlands West Indies. Curaçao (q.v.), the largest of the islands, Aruba, and Bonaire (qq.v.) form the Windward group. The Leeward group, which is situated about 550 miles N.E. of the Windward group, consists of Saba, St. Eustache, and the s. portion of St. Martin (qq.v.). The N. portion of St. Martin is a possession of France. Willemstad (q.v.), Curaçao, is the capital of the Netherlands West Indies. The principal industry is the refining of crude oil which is imported from Venezuela (q.v.). Other products are straw hats, phosphate of lime, and salt. Livestock raising is an important agrarian industry.

By the provisions of amendments (1948) to the constitution of the Netherlands, the Netherlands West Indies is a part of the Netherlands Kingdom within the Union of the Netherlands (see NETHERLANDS, THE). The Territory has limited autonomy. Legislative authority is vested in the *Staten,* a unicameral body consisting of twenty-one elected members. All male and female inhabitants of Dutch nationality, who are more than twenty-three years old, have the right to vote. Executive authority in the Territory is vested in a governor, an appointee of the Netherlands Crown. He is assisted by an executive board, which consists of a maximum of six members appointed by the governor with the concurrence of the *Staten.* The governor is also assisted by an advisory council, a body normally consisting of five royal appointees. (For further information on the Territory, see articles dealing with the separate islands.) Area, 403 sq.m.; pop. (1948) 148,530.

Westinghouse Electric Corp.
George Westinghouse

WESTINGHOUSE, GEORGE (1846–1914), American engineer and inventor, born in Central Bridge, N.Y., and educated at Union College. During the Civil War he served in the 12th New York Regiment until 1864, and then for two years as assistant engineer in the United States Navy. In 1868 he patented the air brake (see BRAKES), which was first used on passenger trains in the same year, and has since been adopted almost universally for railway and rapid-transit cars, and adapted for motor trucks and buses. He founded the Westinghouse Air Brake Co. at Pittsburgh in 1869. Westinghouse also became interested in railway-signal devices, and in 1882 was one of the organizers of the Union Switch and Signal Company. He then became interested in the field of electricity; he acquired patents on alternating current machinery, and pioneered in the introduction in the U.S. of the high-voltage, single-phase, alternating-current system of electrical transmission. In 1886 he organized the Westinghouse Electric Co. for the manufacture of alternating current devices. Under his direction the company manufactured the generators for the power plants at Niagara Falls and for the rapid-transit systems of New York City and London, England. Westinghouse also established large factories in Europe and was president of thirty corporations which were later amalgamated as the Westinghouse Electric and Manufacturing Company. During his lifetime he was granted more than 400 patents. In 1910 he was president of the American Society of Mechanical Engineers.

WESTINGHOUSE, HENRY HERMAN (1853–1933), American engineer and inventor, brother of George Westinghouse, born in Central Bridge, N.Y., and educated at Cornell University. After graduation from the university, he joined the Westinghouse Air Brake Company established by his brother, and was thereafter continuously connected with that firm. He is known for his invention of the Westinghouse single-acting steam engine. He also founded the engineering firm of Westinghouse, Church, Kerr & Co.

WEST LAFAYETTE, suburb of Lafayette, Tippecanoe County, Ind. It is the site of Purdue University. Pop. (1940) 6270.

WESTLAKE, JOHN (1828–1913), English legal scholar, born in Lostwithiel, Cornwall. In 1885 he was elected to Parliament as Liberal member for the Romford Division of Essex. From 1888 to 1908 he was professor of international law at Cambridge University. He was a member for Great Britain of the International Court of Arbitration at The Hague from 1900 to 1906. His works include *A Treatise on Private International Law* (1858), *Chapters on the Principles of International Law* (1894), and *International Law* (2 vols., 2nd ed., 1910–13).

WEST LOTHIAN, formerly LINLITHGOW, a southeastern county of Scotland, bounded on the N. by the Firth of Forth. The county seat is Linlithgow (q.v.). The surface of the county, which is hilly in the s., slopes downward from the interior to the Firth. Cairnnaple, 1016 ft. above sea level, is the highest point in West Lothian. The principal rivers are the Almond and the Avon, and the county is crossed in a S.E. to N.W. direction by the Union Canal, which connects Edinburgh, in Midlothian County, to the Firth and Clyde Canal, which crosses Scotland, connecting the North Sea to the Atlantic Ocean by way of the North Channel and Irish Sea. Agriculture is the chief industry and approximately two thirds of the area of the county is under cultivation. The chief crops are oats, barley, and wheat. Dairy farming is also important. Minerals found in West Lothian include coal, silver, shale, oil, clay, limestone, freestone, and whinstone. Manufactures include steel, iron, paper, and alcoholic beverages. Area of the county, 120 sq.m.; pop. (1949 est.) 87,100.

WESTMACOTT, SIR RICHARD (1775–1856), English sculptor, born in London. The works by which he is chiefly known are public monumental statues, including those of Addison, Pitt, Fox, and Percival in Westminster; the monuments to Abercromby, Collingwood, Captain Cook, and General Pakenham in St. Paul's; a colossal bronze statue of Achilles in Hyde Park; and groups representing the "Progress of Civilization", done for the British Museum (1847).

WESTMEATH, an inland county of Leinster Province, Eire, situated between Meath and Roscommon. The county seat is Mullingar. Area, 681 sq.m.; pop. (1946) 54,880.

WESTMINSTER, county seat of Carroll Co., Md., situated 28 miles N.W. of Baltimore. It is served by a railroad and is the commercial center of a rich agricultural area. The principal products of the surrounding region are vegetables, fruits, livestock, poultry, and poultry products. Industrial establishments in the city and vicinity include meat-packing plants, vegetable-packing plants, flour mills, fruit and vegetable canneries, plant nurseries, distilleries, and factories producing road signs, felt bases for linoleum products, poultry equipment, packing equipment, granite and marble memorials, clothing, shoes, and fertilizer. Westminster was settled in 1764, and is the site of Western Maryland College (Methodist), established in 1868, and of the Westminster Theological Seminary, established 1882, also a Methodist institution. Pop. (1940) 4692.

WESTMINSTER, a metropolitan borough of London, England, situated on the northern bank of the Thames R. and w. of the City of London. It is the site of the Houses of Parliament, the government offices, Westminster Abbey, St. James's Palace, Buckingham Palace, Belgrave Square, the eastern end of Hyde Park, Green Park, Trafalgar Square, the Mall, Pall Mall, Piccadilly, Whitehall, and Charing Cross and Victoria Railway stations. Pop. (1945) 83,260.

WESTMINSTER ABBEY, officially, the Collegiate Church of St. Peter, situated in the borough of Westminster, London. It is a national sanctuary and burial place. Originally Westminster Abbey was the abbey church of a monastery founded in the reign of King Offar of Mercia, and reorganized by Dunstan in 971. The first church is said to have been built by King Sebert of Essex (616) on

British Information Services

Above: Interior of Westminster Abbey, London, looking toward the High Altar. Right: Chapel of Henry VII in Westminster Abbey.

Thorney Isle, in the Thames. The foundation did not, however, achieve importance until the reign of Edward the Confessor, who had a palace at Westminster and who, during 1049–65, built a church on the present site, dedicated to St. Peter, whence the present official name. In the later 13th century Henry III undertook the reconstruction of the church. The choir and transepts were built between 1245 and 1258, and, with the eastern half of the nave, consecrated in 1269. The work was continued by his successors, but haltingly, with long interruptions, and the nave was not wholly completed till the end of the 15th century. The chapel of Henry VII was added between 1502 and 1520 under Henry VIII. The two west towers were constructed by Sir Christopher Wren and Nicholas Hawkesmoor (1722–40), and the north transept was restored in 1890. The abbey was heavily endowed and under the special protection of the kings of England, whose palace was at Westminster. It was disendowed during the Protestant Reformation as a cathedral (1540–50), but restored by Queen Mary, and received its present organization, under a dean and twelve prebendaries, from Queen Elizabeth.

Westminster Abbey is one of the largest and best examples of the early English architectural style. More than any other it shows the French influence, in its polygonal apse and chapels, the loftiness of the nave, and heavy flying buttresses. Its proportions are grandiose. The total exterior length, including Henry VII's chapel, is 423 feet, 6 inches; the breadth is 71 feet, 9 inches, for nave and aisles, and 203 feet, 2 inches across the transepts. The nave is the loftiest in England (101 feet, 8 inches); the towers measure 225 feet, 4 inches. The chapel of Henry VII, begun by him as a Lady chapel, but completed as his mausoleum chapel by his successor, is a very remarkable structure in the Perpendicular style, having a ceiling vaulted with fan tracery.

Of all English churches none is so intimately connected with national life and history. English kings since William the Conqueror have been crowned at the Abbey, and it was the repository of the ancient regalia until their destruction under the Commonwealth. The coronation chair, containing the ancient Stone of Scone, brought by Edward I from Scotland, still stands in the chapel of Edward the Confessor. In Westminster Abbey lie buried thirteen kings, including Edward the Confessor and others from Henry III to George II, and five sovereign queens, besides the consorts and descendants of kings. The practice of interring courtiers, statesmen, and soldiers in the abbey began under Richard II, and continues to the present time. The two Pitts, Fox, Palmerston, Warren Hastings, Gladstone, and other British statesmen too numerous to mention have been accorded this honor. In the Poets' Corner (South Transept) repose some of England's greatest poets, notably Chaucer, Spenser, Dryden, Gray, Browning, and Tennyson, and nearby rest the men of letters. There are places for theologians, actors, musicians, artists, and scientists. The House of Commons met for three hundred years in the Chapter House of the Abbey, and for the next three hundred years in St. Stephen's chapel, built by King Stephen. The Jerusalem Chamber, to the s.w. of the abbey and so called because of its former decorations, is celebrated as the death chamber of Henry IV. Westminster School, founded by Queen Elizabeth in 1560 from revenues of the abbey, occupies the ancient dormitory of the abbey as a classroom and its refectory as a dining room. The latter contains some ancient tapestry and stained glass.

WESTMINSTER ASSEMBLY or **ASSEMBLY OF DIVINES,** in British history, a convocation appointed by the Long Parliament in the reign of Charles I, for settling the doctrine and government of the Church of England. It consisted of 121 clergymen and 30 laymen, 10 of whom were lords and 20 commoners, together with 4 clerical and 2 lay commissioners from the Church of Scotland. The principal fruits of its deliberations were the *Directory of Public Worship,* the *Confession of Faith,* the *Shorter Catechism,* and the *Larger Catechism.* These several formularies, which contain a clear and rigid embodiment of Calvinistic theology and Presbyterian church government, constitute to this day the authorized Presbyterian standards. The Assembly remained in session until 1649.

WESTMINSTER HALL, a part of Westminster Palace, the Houses of the British Parliament. The Hall, begun by William Rufus in 1097, was destroyed by fire in 1291, later rebuilt and enlarged, and in 1397 reconstructed by Richard II and covered with a superb, open-timber, hammerbeam roof of oak. It escaped the fire which destroyed the palace in 1834. The ceiling, covering a hall 290 feet long, 68 feet broad, and 92 feet high, is one of the most remarkable pieces of timber architecture in existence, both as to beauty and constructive skill. No other hall in England is as rich in historical associations. Here the king, surrounded by his chaplains, heard legal cases and administered justice. A year after its completion its builder, Richard II, was deposed in it, as was Edward II before him; Charles I received in it the death sentence, and a few years later Oliver Cromwell was installed there. Among the great men condemned in the Hall were Sir William Wallace, Sir John Oldcastle, Sir Thomas More, and the Earl of Strafford. The seven bishops who opposed James II were acquitted there, as was Warren Hastings.

WESTMINSTER PALACE. See PARLIAMENT, HOUSES OF.

WESTMINSTER SCHOOL, one of the oldest of English public schools, situated in London. It was established by Henry VIII, refounded in 1560 by Queen Elizabeth, and reorganized in 1868 as one of the nine great public schools. The school is particularly famous for the Westminster Play, an annual presentation of a Latin comedy, produced by the scholars.

WESTMINSTER STANDARDS, collective name for the formularies drawn up by the Westminster Assembly, comprising (1) the *Confession of Faith;* (2) the *Larger* and *Smaller Catechisms;* (3) the *Directory of*

Public Worship; and (4) the *Directory for Church Polity and Discipline*. The name is often used for the first three formularies.

WESTMINSTER, STATUTE OF, an enactment of the British Parliament, in December, 1931, recognizing the full equality of the British dominions with the United Kingdom and establishing the British Commonwealth of Nations (q.v.), an association of independent states. The statute, incorporating principles adopted by the Imperial Conference of the statesmen of Great Britain and the self-governing dominions in 1926, stated that the United Kingdom and the "Dominions are autonomous communities within the British Empire, equal in status, in no way subordinate one to another in any aspect of their domestic or external affairs, though united by a common allegiance to the Crown, and freely associated as members of the British Commonwealth of Nations". By the provisions of the statute, the dominions are empowered to reject any law of the British Parliament if their own parliaments so decide, and to enact legislation concerning all domestic matters, including merchant shipping. Canada, Australia, New Zealand, South Africa, Newfoundland, and the Irish Free State were named as dominions in the statute. In 1937 the Irish Free State was reconstituted as Eire, an independent state associated with but outside of the British Commonwealth. Pakistan and the Union of India, chiefly comprising former British India, became dominions of the Commonwealth in 1947. Ceylon was admitted to the Commonwealth in 1948. In 1949 Newfoundland joined the Dominion of Canada.

WESTMORLAND, a northern county of England, bounded by Cumberland, Durham, Yorkshire, and Lancashire. The surface is mountainous, the highest summit being Helvellyn (3118 ft.), on the Cumberland boundary. The western portion of the county belongs to the Lake District. The moorlands are numerous and extensive. Coal, lead, copper, slate, and graphite are the chief mineral products. Area, 689 sq.m.; pop., about 64,000.

WEST NEWTON, borough of Westmoreland County, Pa., situated on the Youghiogheny River, 33 miles S.E. of Pittsburgh. Radiators and boilers are the chief manufactured products. Pop. (1940) 2765.

WEST NEW YORK, a town of Hudson Co., N.J., situated on the Hudson R., opposite New York City and adjoining Weehawken on the N. Waterfront facilities include docks and grain elevators. The town is an important manufacturing center, and one of the chief centers of the embroidery industry in the U.S. Other industries in West New York are the manufacture of textiles, rubber goods, and smoking pipes and accessories. The town was incorporated in 1898. Pop. (1950) 37,754.

WESTON, county seat of Lewis County, W.Va., 65 miles E.S.E. of Parkersburg, on the West Fork of the Monongahela River. Its chief manufactures are carbon, glass, and lumber. Pop. (1940) 8268.

WESTON, AGNES (1840–1918), English philanthropist, born in London. She was the founder of Royal Sailors' rests in Portsmouth and Davenport. She also had tracts sent in her name to every ship touching at a port in the United Kingdom. Her writings include a biographical work entitled *My Life Among the Bluejackets* (1910).

WESTON, EDWARD (1850–1936), American electrician, born in London, England. He came to the United States in 1870. In 1875 he founded in Newark, N.J., the first factory in America for the construction of electromagnetic machines. His business was consolidated with another company in 1881, and in 1888 he formed the Weston Electric Instrument Co. He was founder of the American Institute of Electrical Engineers.

WESTON, EDWARD PAYSON (1839–1929), American pedestrian, born in Providence, R.I. In 1861 he made his first long trip, walking from Boston to Washington, a distance of 443 miles, in 208 hours. He walked from Portland, Me., to Chicago (1326 miles) in 26 days in 1867, and 40 years later bettered his record by 29 hours. In 1909, at the age of seventy, he crossed the continent on foot (3895 miles) in 104 days and 7 hours, and returned in 1910, walking 3500 miles in 76 days and 23 hours.

WESTON SUPER MARE, a watering place in Somerset, England, situated on the Bristol Channel, 20 miles S.W. of Bristol. Pop., about 28,500.

WEST ORANGE, town of Essex County, N.J., situated 5 miles N.W. of Newark. It contains Llewellyn Park, a beautiful residential district on the S.E. slope of Orange Mt., and after 1887 was the home of Thomas A. Edison. Pop. (1950) 28,624.

WESTOVER, RUSSELL CHANNING (1886–), American cartoonist, born in Los Angeles, Calif. He was cartoonist for the San Francisco *Bulletin* (1904–08), Oakland *Herald* (1908–10), San Francisco *Chronicle* (1910–12), and for a short time with the San Francisco *Post* and the New York *Herald*. He was a contributor to *Life* and *Judge* (1918–21). Thereafter he was a cartoonist for King Features Syndicate. He originated the popular comic strip "Tillie the Toiler".

WESTPHAL, JOACHIM (1510–74), German theologian, born in Hamburg. He studied theology at Wittenberg under the guidance of Martin Luther, and later at the universities of Heidelberg, Strasbourg, and Basel. In 1541 he was appointed preacher in his native city. He became well known through his polemical activity on the Lutheran side in the controversy between the Swiss and German reformers concerning the Lord's Supper. Among the pamphlets written by Westphal on this controversy are *Recta Fides de Cœna Domini* (1553), *Collectanea Sententiarum Aurelii Augustini de Cœna Domini* (1555), and *Confutatio Aliquot Enormium Mendiorum I. Calvini* (1558).

WESTPHAL, KARL FRIEDRICH OTTO (1833–90), German alienist, born in Berlin, and educated at the universities of Berlin, Heidelberg, and Zurich. He settled in his native city, where he held several hospital positions and where he was professor of psychiatrics at the university from 1874 until his death. In 1868 he became editor of the *Archiv für Psychiatrie und Nervenkrankheiten*. In 1875 he pointed out the importance of the knee jerk in diagnosis and he described several forms of insanity.

WESTPHALIA, formerly a Prussian province, lying between Hanover and Hesse-Nassau, the Rhine Province, and Holland, and after World War II a part of the West German State of North Rhine-Westphalia. About 1180 Westphalia came under the archbishops of Cologne, as dukes of Westphalia. In 1807 Westphalia, with parts of Hesse, Hanover, Brunswick, and Saxony, was made into a kingdom for Jerome Bonaparte by Napoleon I, and incorporated in the Confederation of the Rhine. In 1813, following Napoleon's military reverses, the kingdom was dissolved, and the Congress of Vienna assigned Westphalia to Prussia. See PRUSSIA. The peace of Westphalia, concluded at Münster and Osnabrück, October 24, 1648, brought the Thirty Years' War to an end. The chief industries are coal mining and the manufacture of iron and steel. Linen and cotton goods are also produced. Area of former province, 7804 sq.m.; pop., about 5,000,000.

WESTPHALIA, PEACE OF, the treaty which closed the Thirty Years' War (q.v.) in 1648 and readjusted the religio-political affairs of Europe. It is so called from the fact that the envoys met in the cities of Münster and Osnabrück, in the Circle of Westphalia. It is sometimes spoken of as the Treaty of Münster. The minor German states had long sought relief from the devastations of war, and in 1641, at a convention held at Hamburg, preliminaries regarding the conduct of negotiations for peace were agreed upon. A peace congress, which had been called to meet in March, 1642, opened in 1644. The representatives of France, the Holy Roman Empire, Spain, and the German Catholics met at Münster, and those of Sweden, the Holy Roman Empire, and the German Protestants at Osnabrück. Portugal, the United Provinces, Savoy, Tuscany, Lorraine, Mantua, and Switzerland were also represented. The negotiations were long drawn out, but Torstenson's decisive campaign in 1644–45 and the successes of Turenne and Wrangel in southern Germany, together with the capture of part of Prague by Königsmark in July, 1648, forced the emperor Ferdinand III to give up his dilatory tactics. After the signing of treaties at Osnabrück and Münster the Osnabrück diplomats went to Münster in October, 1648, and the general Peace of Westphalia was signed there on the 24th. By its terms, the sovereignty and independence of the different states of the Holy Roman Empire were fully recognized, and liberty was given them to contract any alliances with each other, or with foreign powers, if these were not against the emperor or the empire. All religious persecution in Germany was interdicted. The Treaty of Passau of 1552 and the religious Peace of Augsburg of 1555 were confirmed. With respect to the secularization of ecclesiastical benefices, everything was to remain in Austria as it was in 1624, and in the Palatinate, Baden, and Württemberg as it was in 1618. The power of putting under the ban of the empire was to be exercised only with the consent of the Diet. The Reformed or Calvinist Protestants were put on a footing of equality as to privileges with the Lutherans. In every state the religion of the ruling prince might be made incumbent on his subjects, but the right of emigration for dissenters was guaranteed. The Lower Palatinate was restored to the eldest son of Frederick V, Elector Palatine, and an eighth electorate was created in his favor, but the Upper Palatinate was confirmed to Bavaria, on condition that, should the two states become united, one electorate was to be abolished. France was confirmed in the possession of the bishoprics of Metz, Toul, and Verdun, and obtained possession of the Austrian territories in Alsace, with suzerainty over the ten imperial cities of that

Cadets going to classes at the United States Military Academy, West Point, New York

region; Breisach, on the E. bank of the Rhine, remained in French hands. Sweden obtained Hither Pomerania, with Stettin, the island of Rügen, Wismar, and the secularized sees of Bremen and Verden, with minor territories. These remained fiefs of the Holy Roman Empire, and Sweden was given three deliberative voices in the Diet. Brandenburg obtained, as compensation for its cessions in Pomerania, the secularized bishoprics of Halberstadt, Minden, and Cammin, together with the succession to the see of Magdeburg. Mecklenburg was enlarged by the secularized sees of Schwerin and Ratzeburg. Hesse-Cassell obtained the rich abbacy of Hirschfeld. The elector of Saxony was allowed to retain Lusatia. The see of Osnabrück was to be alternately in the hands of a Catholic bishop and a prince of the house of Brunswick-Lüneburg. The independence of the United Provinces was recognized by Spain, and they, together with Switzerland, were declared independent of the Holy Roman Empire. France and Sweden became guarantors for the execution of the provisions of the treaty. The Peace of Westphalia, by weakening the central authority of the Holy Roman Empire, destroyed its unity, and afforded France, as one of the guarantors, a pretext for continual interference with its internal affairs. France now became the chief power of the continent, taking the place formerly occupied by Spain. The Peace of Westphalia marked the close of the period of religious wars. Thereafter, European armed struggles were mainly for political ends.

WEST PITTSTON, a borough of Luzerne Co., Pa., situated on the Susquehanna R., opposite Pittston (q.v.) and about 9 miles S.W. of Scranton. It is served by two railroads. The borough is a residential and manufacturing community, with coal mines, machine shops, knitting mills, silk mills, and factories producing glass, chains and cables, automobile accessories, and cigars. West Pittston received its present name in 1859, having been known formerly as Jenkins Fort. Pop. (1949 est.) 8180.

WEST PLAINS, county seat of Howell Co., Mo., situated 115 miles S.E. of Springfield. It is served by a railroad and is the center and shipping point of an area noted for livestock, dairy products, poultry, fruits and berries, and timber. The city is an important market for livestock and wool. Industrial establishments in West Plains include creameries, lumber mills, planing mills, and factories producing wooden handles, flooring, shoes, baseball bats, cheese, and ice cream. Pop. (1949 est.) 7500.

WEST POINT, county seat of Clay Co., Miss., situated about 35 miles N. of Macon. It is served by three railroads, and is the center of an agricultural area noted for cotton and cattle. West Point is an important manufacturing center, containing a large cheese plant, meat-packing plants, food-processing and packing plants, cotton gins, cottonseed-oil mills, textile mills, lumber mills, plants processing dairy products, and factories producing cotton yarns, garments, lumber products, and fabricated steel. Pop. (1949 est.) 7500.

WEST POINT, a military post of the United States, situated on the w. bank of the Hudson River, in Orange County, N.Y., and about 50 m. by rail from New York City. It is the site of the U.S. Military Academy (see MILITARY ACADEMY, UNITED STATES).

WESTPORT, town of Fairfield County, Conn., on the Saugatuck R., 10 miles w. of Bridgeport. The city is largely a residential center. Many artists and writers make it their home. Pop. (1940) 8258.

WESTPORT, a town of Bristol Co., Mass., situated on the Atlantic Ocean, about 5 miles S.E. of Fall River. It is a manufacturing center, and a popular summer resort, with a fine bathing beach. The principal industries in the town are the manufacture of textiles, wooden articles, metal bottle caps, and metal tanks. The first textile mill in Westport was established in 1812. Pop. (1940) 4134.

WEST RIDING. See YORKSHIRE.

WEST RUTLAND, a town in Rutland County, Vt., situated about 4 miles w. of Rutland. Marble quarrying is the leading industry. Pop. (1940) 2500.

WEST ST. PAUL, city of Dakota County, Minn., situated on the Mississippi R., about 5 miles s. of St. Paul. It is a residential suburb of St. Paul. Pop. (1940) 5733.

WEST SPITZBERGEN, the largest and most important of the islands of the Spitzbergen Archipelago, Norway. The island contains immense deposits of coal of high quality, the reserves being estimated at over 10,000 million tons. The largest settlement is Longyear City, at Ice Fiord. Area, 14,600 sq.m.; pop., about 2000.

WEST SPRINGFIELD, town of Hampden County, Mass., situated on the Connecticut R., opposite Springfield. It is an industrial center, with plants engaged in the manufacture of paper, oil burners, and electrical equipment. Pop. (1950) 20,398.

WEST TERRE HAUTE, town of Vigo County, Ind., situated about 1 mile w. of Terre Haute. Coal, clay, sand, and gravel are produced. Pop. (1940) 3729.

WESTVILLE, village of Vermilion County, Ill., 7 miles s. of Danville. Coal is mined in the vicinity. Pop. (1940) 3446.

WESTVILLE, a town in Pictou County, Nova Scotia, Canada, situated about 5 miles w. of New Glasgow. Its industries include coal mining, lumbering, woodworking, and brickmaking. Pop., about 4000.

WEST VIRGINIA, one of the South Atlantic States of the United States, bounded on the N. by Ohio, Pennsylvania, and Maryland, on the s. by Virginia and Kentucky, on the E. by Virginia and Maryland, and on the w. by Kentucky and Ohio. West Virginia ranks as the 40th State in the Union in area, 29th in the order of population (1950), and 35th in the order of admission to the Union, having entered on June 20, 1863. The state capital is Charleston. In descending order of population (1950) the leading cities of the State are Huntington, Charleston, Wheeling, Clarksburg, Parkersburgh, and Fairmont (qq.v). The general shape of West Virginia is that of an oval, about 210 m. long from N.E. to s.w., and about 125 m. wide. Two narrow tongues of land, known as panhandles, extend northward between Pennsylvania and Ohio and eastward between Maryland and Virginia, respectively. The area of the State is 24,181 sq.m., including 91 sq.m. of inland water surface. The population in 1950 was 2,005,552.

The surface of West Virginia is generally rugged; the eastern section, particularly, is mountainous. The main range of the Alleghany Mts. crosses the N.E. section, and farther s. forms the State boundary with Virginia. The greater part of the mountain region, occupying more than one third of the State, belongs to the Allegheny Plateau; the mountains in the extreme southern section of the State may be considered as a northern extension of the Cumberland Plateau. The mountains of the N.E. are chiefly in the form of parallel ridges with a s.w. and a N.E. trend; the southern mountains are irregularly dissected by river valleys, presenting broad domes with spurs running in all directions, with

West Virginia State Capitol in the city of Charleston
W. Virginia Industrial & Publicity Comm.

few definite ridges. The elevation of the valleys is about 2000 ft. above sea level, and the elevation of the ridges is from 3000 to over 4000 ft. The highest point in the State is Spruce Knob in Pendleton Co., which is 4860 ft. above sea level. The lowest point, in Jefferson Co., is 240 ft. above sea level; the average State elevation is 1500 ft. West of the mountains is a belt of broad, flat hills from 1000 to 2000 ft. in elevation, followed by a more gently rolling country which slopes towards the banks of the Ohio R., along which the altitude ranges between 500 to 650 ft. With the exception of the northeastern section, the entire State is drained by the Ohio R. and its tributaries. The largest of the tributaries are the Big Sandy, the Guyandot, the Kanawha, Little Kanawha, and the Monongahela headstreams. The extreme northeastern section of the State is drained by the Potomac and its tributaries. All of the rivers furnish abundant water power and many of them are navigable or have been made navigable. The State receives such excellent drainage that almost no marshland can be found there. The climate is healthful, and free from violent extremes of heat and cold. The mean temperature for the winter months ranges from 26°F. in the N.E. mountains to 34°F. in the S.W. part of the State. Summer temperatures range from 67°F. in the N.E. to 74°F. in the S.W. Annual precipitation is from 35 and 40 inches in the S.E. to more than 50 inches in the mountain regions. Hunting and fishing facilities in the State are abundant. The famous spa, White Sulphur Springs (q.v.) is located in the State.

About 70% of the total area in the State is covered with forests, consisting chiefly of hardwoods. The most important trees are beech, birch, white and chestnut oaks, the yellow poplar, walnut, ash, basswood, and maple. Softwood trees include white and yellow pine, spruce, and hemlock. National forest land in the State, which includes the George Washington and Monongahela national forests, covers more than 1,800,000 acres. In addition, there are seven State forests, twenty-two State parks, and a number of State roadside parks.

The State is the second-largest producer of hardwood in the U.S. (Arkansas leads), and possesses some of the largest hardwood lumber mills in the world. In a recent year more than 476,000,000 board ft. of lumber were produced in West Virginia. West Virginia is the leading coal-mining State in the U.S. It possesses such great deposits of bituminous coal that alone it could supply the country for a period of 250 years. A recent estimate of the coal reserves in West Virginia was 63,687,664,000 tons. The coal region covers 17,280 sq.m., or more than two thirds of the total area of the State. In a recent year approximately 152,000,000 short tons of coal were produced. The State is also an important source of natural gas, petroleum, and quarry products. Recently the annual output of oil from more than 17,000 wells exceeded 2,615,000 barrels. Approximately 56,545,000 gallons of natural gasoline and 203,000,000,000 cu.ft. of natural gas were also produced. Other minerals found in West Virginia include clay, lime, silica, sand, and salt. The quarry products are building stone, limestone, and sandstone. Recently, the total annual value of the mineral output of the State was over $632,650,000.

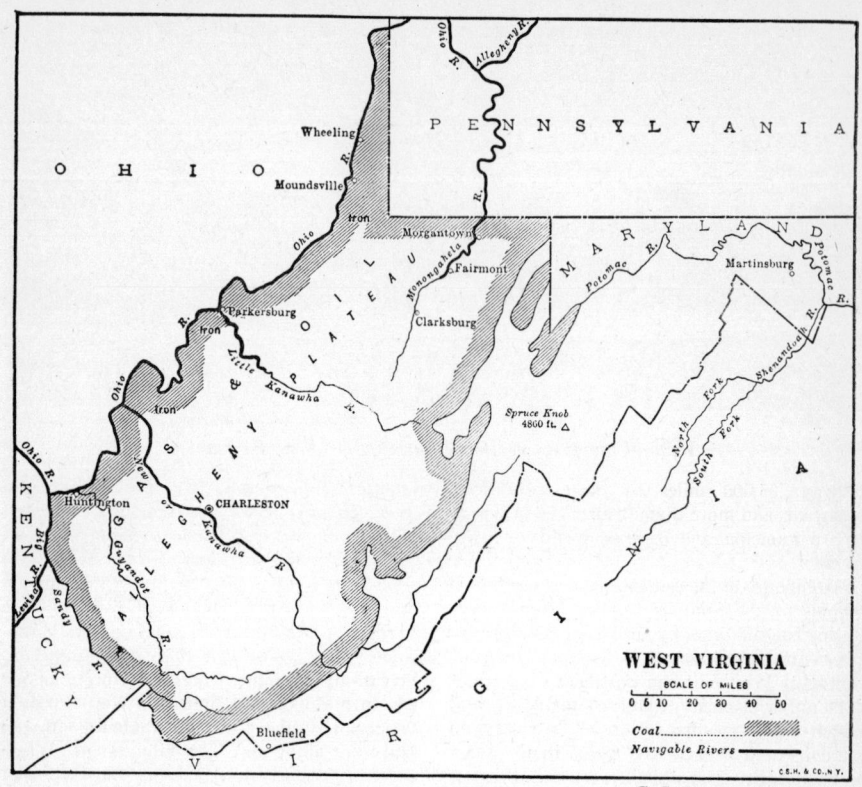

More than 30% of the total population of West Virginia is rural. The principal agricultural products are wheat, corn, oats, hay, potatoes, and tobacco. Other products include apples, peaches, plums, and grapes. The raising of livestock is also important in the State's economy. In a recent year livestock numbered 566,000 cattle (including 232,000 milch cows), 321,000 sheep, 279,000 swine, 97,000 horses, and 6000 mules. The recent annual wool clip from 289,000 sheep was about 1,532,000 pounds. Farms in the State number more than 97,000, possess a total area of more than 8,719,000 acres (1,505,000 acres devoted to crops), and are valued at (land and buildings) more than $341,000,000. The recent annual cash income from livestock and crops was approximately $111,000,000; Federal subsidies added over $4,300,000 to the total farm income.

Manufacturing industries in West Virginia have grown rapidly in the past fifty years. The State possesses some of the largest glass factories in the world and ranks first in the country as a glass producer. Its chemical plants are also important; one of the largest and most diversified chemical centers in the world is located at West Virginia's Kanawha Valley. Other important articles manufactured are steel and rolling-mill products, pottery, bricks, textiles, bread and bakery products, leather, and tobacco products. Oil refining and printing and publishing are also carried on. In a recent year the total value of industrial products and services was approximately $440,000,000.

Transportation in West Virginia is provided by more than 4000 miles of steam and electric

View of buildings in Charleston, capital of West Virginia

railway, 33,000 miles of State-maintained highways, and more than 30 airports, of which 10 are municipal and 7 are equipped for night flying.

Attendance in the elementary and secondary schools of the State is free and compulsory during the full school year for all children between the ages of seven and sixteen. In a recent year West Virginia possessed more than 4500 public elementary and secondary schools, which were attended by more than 423,000 students and staffed by more than 15,000 teachers. Institutions of higher learning in the State number nineteen and include nine universities and colleges, five teachers colleges, three Negro colleges, and two junior colleges. State-supported institutions include West Virginia University at Morgantown, West Virginia State College (for Negroes) at Institute, the Potomac State School at Keyser, West Virginia Institute of Technology at Montgomery, and Marshall College at Huntington. Private institutions of higher learning include Bethany College at Bethany, West Virginia Wesleyan College at Buckhannon, Morris Harvey College at Charleston, Salem College at Salem, and Greenbriar College (for women) at Lewisburg.

The city of Wheeling, West Virginia, looking south, down the Ohio River

West Virginia is governed according to the constitution of 1872, as amended. Executive authority is vested in a governor, who is ineligible to succeed himself, a secretary of state, auditor, treasurer, attorney-general, superintendent of schools, and commissioner of agriculture, all elected for four-year terms. Legislative authority is vested in a senate of 32 members, half of whom are elected every two years for four-year terms, and a house of delegates of 94 members, all elected for two-year terms. Judicial authority is vested in a supreme court of appeals consisting of 5 justices elected for twelve-year terms, and circuit courts, inferior courts, county courts, and justices of the peace. Electors are all U.S. citizens over twenty-one years of age, who have lived in the State a minimum period of one year and the county at least two months. West Virginia is divided into 55 counties and is represented in the Congress of the U.S. by 2 senators and 6 representatives.

History. Prior to 1863 the region which is now West Virginia was a part of the State of Virginia, and earlier had also been included in the Royal Province of Virginia. The first Euro-

Left: Coal-loading installation at Williamson, West Virginia. Below: Tipple in which coal from three mines is washed and graded, near Logan, West Virginia.

W. Virginia Indus. & Public. Comm.

Shaping and finishing hand-blown glassware in a factory at Milton, West Virginia
W. Virginia Industrial & Publicity Comm.

pean to explore the territory of West Virginia was probably John Lederer, a German surgeon in the employ of the colonial governor Sir William Berkeley (q.v.); Lederer traveled in the region in 1669. In the same year Robert Cavalier, Sieur de La Salle (q.v.), journeyed down the Ohio R. and landed at several places in the region. After 1732 the western portion of Virginia began to be settled by Scotch and Irish pioneers who soon came into conflict with the French, who also claimed the country (see FRENCH AND INDIAN WAR). The Six Nations (see IROQUOIS), a confederation of Indian tribes in New York, also claimed the western portion of Virginia by right of conquest (see TENNESSEE: *History*), but ceded their claims to the whites in 1754. However, the tribes which resided in the region refused to acknowledge the cession. In 1774, at Point Pleasant (see POINT PLEASANT, BATTLE OF), an extremely bloody battle was fought between Virginia settlers and militia and a confederacy of Shawnee, Delaware, Wyandot, Cayuga, and other Indian tribes led by Cornstalk (q.v.), a famous Shawnee Indian chief. The Virginians won the battle and elicited a treaty from the Indians which forced them to give up much of the disputed land (see DUNMORE'S WAR).

Following the American Revolution an en-tirely different society grew up in the western woods of Virginia as compared with that in the east. The backwoodsmen had few luxuries, few Negro slaves, and little contact with European culture. Jealousies ensued between the eastern and western sections (see VIRGINIA: *History*), and the western settlers complained bitterly that they had all the burdens of government without the corresponding benefits. The representation in the eastern counties was based partially upon the number of Negroes. The western counties of Virginia did not have the same representation because of the scarcity of slaves in the region. As early as 1776, during the Revolution, the settlers w. of the Allegheny Mts. had attempted, unsuccessfully, to create a new State called "Westsylvania". The Virginia counties w. of the Alleghenies protested strongly when, in 1829, a State convention drew up a constitution which favored, in regard to representation, the slave-holding counties of Virginia, and also kept property qualifications for suffrage. As a result, the trans-Allegheny counties voted, with one exception, to reject the document, which, however, was carried by the east's surplus of votes. The split between the eastern and western portions of Virginia grew more acute as the Civil War approached; a number of the western Vir-

W. Virginia Indus. & Public. Comm.
Above: A scene in the Allegheny Mountains of West Virginia. Left: Main entrance to the Greenbrier, resort hotel in White Sulphur Springs, West Virginia.

ginia counties bordered on the free States of Ohio and Pennsylvania, and many of the counties were Northern in sentiment. When Virginia passed the ordinance of secession in 1861 there was much dissatisfaction in the western part of the State. Of the 47 delegates from the trans-Allegheny counties, only 11 voted for secession. Numerous small meetings were held in western Virginia and on May 13, 1861, delegates from 25 counties met at Wheeling and called a convention to meet June 11th. Representatives from 40 counties attended, voted to void the acts of Virginia's secession convention, declared their independence from Virginia, and established a provisional government. On July 2 a legislature met and elected representatives to the United States Senate; the representatives were admittd by that body. The people also voted, 18,489 to 781, for the formation of a new State. Between November, 1861, and February, 1862, a constitution was framed and on May 13, the legislature of the so-called "Restored Government of Virginia" petitioned Congress for admission. On Dec. 31, 1862, President Lincoln approved the act of admission to the Union, to take effect upon the insertion into the State's constitution of a clause that would provide for the gradual emancipation of slaves. The provision was added to the constitution and on June 20, 1863, West Virginia was formally admitted to the Union.

During the Civil War an unusually large part of the population was in arms. More than 32,000 men from the new State served in the Federal army; about 8000 men served in the Confederate army. On Feb. 3, 1865, prior to the adoption of the 13th amendment, slavery was entirely abolished by West Virginia. The return of the Confederate soldiers, who came primarily from the southern and eastern counties of West Virginia, threatened the Republican Party control of the State, and caused a great deal of tension, which resulted, in 1866, in adding an amendment to the constitution disfranchising all who had given aid and comfort to the Confederacy after June, 1861. However, the amendment was abrogated in 1871, and in 1872 an entirely new constitution went into force as a result of a return to power of the Democratic Party.

The industrial growth of West Virginia dates from the closing decades of the 19th century, although petroleum was first obtained in large amounts as early as 1860. Coal mining also progressed following the close of the Civil War. In 1907 a suit was brought by the State of Virginia against the State of West Virginia in the United States Supreme Court to compel the latter State to assume its proportionate share of Virginia's State debt prior to the separation in 1861. In 1915 the Supreme Court handed down a decision which favored Virginia. West Virginia was required to pay $20,571,929 plus interest to Virginia, minus $2,966,000, which the court held was West Virginia's share of the assets arising from the original principal debt.

In the twenty Presidential elections held from 1872 through 1948, the voters of West Virginia have cast a majority or plurality of their ballots for the Democratic candidate ten times and for the Republican candidate ten times; however, the Democrats have won every election since 1932. In the 1948 Presidential election Harry S. Truman, the Democratic incumbent, received 429,188 votes, and Thomas E. Dewey, the Republican candidate, received 316,251 votes.

WEST VIRGINIA UNIVERSITY, a coeducational, State-controlled, land-grant institution of higher education, situated in Morgantown, W.Va. It was founded in 1867 as the Agricultural College of West Virginia; the present name was adopted the following year. The constituent schools of the university are the College of Arts and Sciences (established 1867), the College of Law (1878), the College of Engineering (1887), the College of Agriculture (1897), the School of Music (1897), and the School of Medicine (1902); the divisions of instruction include agriculture, arts and sciences, education, engineering and mechanic arts, forestry, home economics, journalism, law, medical sciences, mines, music, pharmacy, physical education and athletics, and graduate studies. The university awards the degrees of B.A., B.S. in business administration, journalism, and various engineering curricula, LL.B., M.A., and PH.D. An accelerated program permits students to earn undergraduate degrees in some fields in about two and a half rather than the customary four years. In a recent year over 7000 men and women were enrolled and the faculty numbered over 400.

WEST WARWICK, a town of Kent County, Rhode Island, 10 miles w.s.w. of Providence. The chief industry is the manufacture of cotton. Pop. (1950) 19,042.

WESTWOOD, JOHN OBADIAH (1805–93), English entomologist and antiquary, born in Sheffield. He was a founder of the Entomological Society of London, and became its honorary life president.

WETASKIWIN, a town in Alberta, Canada, situated about 39 miles s. of Edmonton. It is the trading center of a productive farming district. Pop., about 2100.

WETHERSFIELD, town of Hartford County, Conn., situated on the w. bank of the Connecticut River, about 3 miles s. of Hartford. The town is the site of the Connecticut State Prison. Farming implements are the chief manufactured product of the town. Pop. (1940) 9644.

WETMORE, ALEXANDER (1886–   ), American biologist, born in North Freedom, Wis. After service in various museums he became, in 1925, assistant secretary of the Smithsonian Institution, in charge of the United States National Museum. His works include *Observations on Birds of Argentina, Paraguay, Uruguay and Chile* (1926); *The Migration of Birds* (1927); *Birds of Porto Rico and the Virgin Islands* (1928); *Book of Birds* (1937); and *Check List of Fossil Birds of North America* (1940).

WETMORE, ELIZABETH BISLAND (1861–1929), American author, born on the Fairfax Plantation, La. In 1891 she married Charles W. Wetmore in New York. She was editor of the *Cosmopolitan*, and contributed to the *Atlantic Monthly* and the *North American Review*. Books written or edited by her, under her maiden name, include *Life and Letters of Lafcadio Hearn* (2 vols., 1906), *Japanese Letters of Lafcadio Hearn* (1910), and *The Case of John Smith* (1916).

WETTEREN, town in the province of East Flanders, Belgium, 8 miles E. by s. of Ghent, on the Scheldt River. It is of considerable industrial importance, having extensive bleaching establishments and plants engaged in the manufacture of cotton goods, lace, and gunpowder. Pop., about 18,000.

The Wetterhorn towering over the village of Grindelwald in Switzerland — Swiss Federal Railways

WETTERHORN, a peak of the Bernese Alps, s.w. Switzerland. It belongs to the Finsteraarhorn group, and is situated 8 miles s.E. of the Lake of Brienz. It has three summits, the highest of which has an altitude of 12,149 ft.

WETTER, or **VETTER, LAKE,** the second-largest lake in Sweden, situated in the s. portion of the country. It is 70 m. long, 13 m. in average breadth, has an area of 753 sq.m., is 370 ft. in greatest depth, and is 270 ft. above the level of the Baltic. An intricate chain of small lakes, continued westward by the Göta Canal, connects it with Lake Wener, and thus with the Kattegat.

WETTING AGENTS, chemical compounds having the property of reducing the surface tension of liquids exposed to a gas, such as air, or of reducing interfacial tension so as to permit the mixing of otherwise immiscible liquids, such as water and oil. Wetting agents are also applied to the surface of a solid, on which they are adsorbed, forming a microscopic film, and thereby permit the wetting of the surface by a liquid which otherwise would not cling to the surface as a smooth film. Wetting agents are most commonly used with water, and the most important of these agents are the sodium salts of fatty acids, collectively called soaps (q.v.). Other detergents have also come into common use, but the principle of action is the same in all cases.

According to the theory of action of wetting agents, the agent consists of a molecule containing two groups, one *hydrophyllic,* or water seeking, the other *hydrophobic,* or water avoiding. At the surface of the water, the molecules of the wetting agent are arranged so that the hydrophyllic group is directed toward the water, and the hydrophobic group is directed outward, and is adsorbed by the surface of the substance to be wet. The molecules of the wetting agent thus form a bond between two immiscible substances, such as water and oil, and allow the formation of an emulsion (q.v.; see also COLLOIDAL DISPERSION). In the soap sodium stearate,

$C_{17}H_{35}COONa$, the oil-soluble stearate chain $C_{17}H_{35}-$ is the hydrophobic group, and the water-soluble sodium-acid combination, -COONa, is the hydrophyllic group.

The presence in hard water of calcium, magnesium, and iron salts creates a disadvantage to the use of soaps, because these metals precipitate the soap as an insoluble curd, thereby wasting much of the soap. To obviate this difficulty, a new type of wetting agent was developed, and marketed under such trademark names as "Drene" and "Dreft". These compounds were produced by reducing fatty acids to the corresponding alcohols, forming the organic sulfate, and then the sodium salt of the organic sulfate. Such agents have the advantage of forming soluble compounds with the hard-water metals, and also may be used in acid solutions, which precipitate soaps as insoluble fatty acids. The sodium salts of many complex organic hydrogen sulfates are used as wetting agents, but the majority have limited applicability.

Wetting agents are widely used in the dyeing, bleaching, and flame-proofing of textiles; in the manufacture of metal and glass cleaners, and of insecticide sprays, and in the flotation (q.v.) process of ore refining. Wetting agents are also used in such products as wallpaper removers and in certain types of fire extinguishers; see FIRE EXTINGUISHER.

WETZLAR, a city of the West German State of Hesse, situated on the Lahn R., about 33 miles N.W. of Frankfort on the Main. Its cathedral dates from the 11th century. Wetzlar was formerly an imperial free city, and from 1691 to 1806 was the seat of the Imperial Court of Justice. On June 15, 1796, the archduke Charles defeated the French under Jourdan at Wetzlar. The town, which had been held by Prince Dalberg, was transferred to Prussia by the Congress of Vienna in 1815. Following World War II, it was incorporated into the new State of Hesse. Pop., about 17,000.

WEXFORD, maritime county of the province of Leinster, Eire, bordering on Wicklow, Carlow, Kilkenny, and Waterford. The coast line is irregular, and dangerous for shipping. The principal river is the Slaney, which enters the sea through Wexford Harbor. The Barrow R. forms part of the boundary. Farming and fishing are the principal industries, and the trade is chiefly in the export of agricultural produce, especially barley. Area, 908 sq.m.; pop. (1946) 91,704.

WEXFORD, county seat of Wexford County, Eire, situated at the mouth of the Slaney R., about 93 miles s. of Dublin. Fishing, shipbuilding, and the manufacture of rope and whisky are leading industries. Pop., about 12,000.

WEYDEN, ROGIER VAN DER (1399?–1464), Flemish painter, founder of the school of Brabant. About 1425 he established a studio in Brussels, and the office of painter to the city was subsequently created for him. To his most mature period belongs the altar of the "Epiphany" in Munich. Among his other paintings are the portraits "Man with an Arrow", in the Brussels Museum, and "Francesco d'Este", in the Metropolitan Museum of Art, New York City.

WEYERHAEUSER, FREDERICK (1834–1914), American capitalist, born in Neidersaulheim, Germany. He came to the United States in 1852 and settled in Pennsylvania, but moved to Illinois in 1856, and to St. Paul, Minn., in 1891. He subsequently established the Weyerhaeuser Timber Company and the so-called Weyerhaeuser Syndicate, which controlled millions of acres of timber lands, becoming known as the "Lumber King."

WEYER'S CAVE, a large, stalactite cavern, situated near Staunton, Va. The cave, which opens into a western spur of the Blue Ridge

Metropolitan Museum of Art
"Francesco d'Este," by Rogier van der Weyden

Mountains, contains several chambers, the largest of which is known as Washington's Hall.

WEYGAND, MAXIME (1867–   ), French soldier, born in Brussels, Belgium, and educated at St. Cyr. He was promoted through various grades to the rank of general in 1916. He was an assistant to Marshal Ferdinand Foch (q.v.), 1914–23, and credited with bringing about the Russian reverses before Warsaw, in 1920. He was high commissioner of Syria (1923–24), commander in chief of the French army (1930–35), and generalissimo of the British and French armies during the German blitzkrieg in the west (May–June 1940), during World War II. Sent as military commander to North Africa by Marshal Pétain in 1940, he was recalled the next year. He was imprisoned by the Germans in 1942 and freed in May, 1945.

WEYLER Y NICOLAU, VALERIANO, MARQUIS OF TENERIFE (1839–1930), Spanish general, born in Palma, Majorca. After quelling a revolution in Catalonia (1893) and ruling Barcelona, he replaced Marshal Campos in Cuba. His severe repressive measures against the Cuban revolutionists raised a storm of criticism in the United States, and he was recalled (1897). He was later minister of war in Spain. In 1926 he was implicated in the San Juan revolt and fined by Primo da Rivera.

WEYMAN, STANLEY JOHN (1855–1928), English novelist, born in Ludlow. His *A Gentleman of France,* which appeared in 1893, won critical acclaim. It was translated into several languages. Weyman's other works include *Ovington's Bank* (1922), *The Traveller in the Fur Cloak* (1925), and *Queen's Folly* (1925).

WEYMOUTH, a town, comprising several villages, of Norfolk Co., Mass., situated on Boston Harbor, about 12 m. by rail S.E. of Boston. Weymouth, with its constituent villages, is the second-largest town in the State. Within its limits are four islands. Weymouth is a manufacturing center, containing factories producing paper boxes and tubes, shoes, shoe counters, chemicals, fertilizers, electrical appliances, nails, and scouring pads. Cultural facilities include the Fogg Library, founded in 1898, and the Tufts Library, founded in 1879. The site of the present town was first permanently settled in 1623. It was incorporated in 1635. Pop. (1950) 32,695.

WEYMOUTH AND MELCOMBE REGIS, municipal borough and watering place of Dorsetshire, England, situated about 52 miles S.W. of Southampton, at the mouth of the Little Wey. A bridge, reconstructed in 1881, connects Weymouth with Melcombe Regis. There are very fine beaches and an esplanade more than 1 m. long. Pop., about 22,000.

WEYPRECHT, KARL (1838–81), German polar explorer, born near Michelstadt, Hesse. In 1871 he accompanied the Austrian explorer Julius von Payer to Novaya Zemlya. He also commanded (1872–73) the Austro-Hungarian expedition which discovered Franz Josef Land.

WEYR, RUDOLF VON (1847–1914), Austrian sculptor, born in Vienna. He became known through his marble reliefs for the hexedra of the Grillparzer Monument, Vienna (1878). He also executed the plastic works for the New Museum, the University, and the Burg Theater, the latter containing his masterpiece, a frieze of the "Triumphal Procession of Bacchus and Ariadne". Among his other sculptures in Vienna are several public monuments and portrait statues.

WHALE, common term for any of the marine, pisciform mammals of the order Cetacea (q.v.), but usually excluding the porpoise and the dolphin (qq.v.). The order is divided into three suborders. The order Zeuglodontia, also called Basilosauridae, consists of extinct fossil genera which are characterized by the possession of several types of teeth similar to the assortment of incisors, canines, and molars found in many extant mammals. Such fossils are to be found mostly in Eocene strata, and form a connecting link between the ancestral quadruped form and the extant fishlike animal. The order Mysticeti, also called Mystacoceti and Balaenoidea, comprises the whalebone whales of the family Balaenidae, including the sulfur-bottom, baleen, or right whale (q.v.), and the family Rachianectidae, the gray whale (q.v.). The order Odontoceti, toothed whales, includes the families Phatanistidae, river porpoises; Delphinidae, porpoises and dolphins; Ziphiidae, bottlenose whales (see BOTTLEHEAD); and Physeteridae, sperm whales. The sperm whale, or cachalot, *Physeter catadon* or *macrocephalus,* is found in the warm parts of all oceans. The bull attains a length of 50 to 70 feet; the cow is considerably smaller. Almost half the total length of the sperm whale consists of the head, which contains a large cavity, called the *case,* filled with spermaceti (q.v.) and oil. The blubber also produces a fine quality of whale oil. Ambergris (q.v.) is a pathological product of the intestines of the sperm whale.

The pygmy sperm whale of southern seas, comprising species of the genus *Kogia*, resembles the sperm whale except in size, being 9 to 15 feet in length. See WHALE FISHERY.

WHALEBACK, name applied to a type of freight steamer developed on the Great Lakes. The sides of a whaleback are curved in to meet a narrow flat deck several feet above the water line. Circular hatchways rise above this deck and support small deck houses and, in some instances, a flying fore-and-aft bridge. The waleback is well suited to the lake trade, but the poor accommodations for the crew on long voyages have prevented its general adoption in ocean traffic. The first whaleback to cross the Atlantic was the *Charles W. Wetmore,* of 3000 tons, which made the voyage to Liverpool in 1891. The shape of the whaleback makes it particularly steady at sea, and it is possible that vessels of this type may have increased use in carrying ore and similar heavy cargoes. A modification of the type, called the turret deck, has been developed in England. The sides are curved inward as in the whaleback, but at about one fourth the beam from the side they are curved up again to form a narrow superstructure, which extends from stem to stern.

WHALEBOAT, a narrow boat, sharp at both ends and with considerable sheer, that is, the ends rise considerably above the middle part. It received its name from its extensive use in whale fishery. Such boats are carried by many vessels in all trades and by men-of-war. They are suitable for nearly all uses at sea, and are generally fitted as lifeboats. The shape of the stern adapts them to use as surf boats or in rough seas, in which case they are steered with a heavy oar working in a crutch on the sternpost.

WHALE FISHERY, the pursuit and capture of whales from boats or ships, carried on as a commercial enterprise. The principal products include oil, whalebone, ambergris, spermaceti, glue, and fertilizer. The skin of small species is sometimes used for leather, and the flesh of the whale is sometimes used for food, as, for example, in Norway during the food shortages of World War II. Whale oil is used as a lubricant, in the tempering of steel, and in the machining of screws. It was the principal illuminating oil of the civilized world before it was supplanted, during the latter half of the 19th century, by petroleum products, such as kerosene. Numerous substances have been discovered or synthesized for replacing whalebone, and this condition has resulted in the elimination of the importance of natural whalebone as an article of commerce; see RIGHT WHALE.

In the early days of whale fishery, whales were captured from open boats by means of hand-thrown harpoons (see HARPOON); the floating carcass was then towed alongside the mother ship of the small-boat fleet and *flensed.* After flensing, that is, stripping the blubber from the carcass, the blubber was stored in barrels for rendering ashore, the whalebone and the jaw were removed and stored, and the rest of the carcass was abandoned. In modern practice the harpoon, sometimes weighing 100 pounds, is fired from a gun on the bow of the whaler, and usually contains in its head an explosive charge fuzed to explode and kill the whale a few seconds after impact. The carcass is then towed to a factory on a large ship or, sometimes, on shore. The carcass is then flensed and the blubber rendered, and the meat and bones are cut up and cooked by steam under pressure to recover the oil. The residue of meat and bone is then dried for sale as fertilizer.

History. The earliest evidences of whale fishery indicate that the Norwegians engaged in the pursuit in the 9th century. From 1300 to 1500 whaling in the Bay of Biscay was the principal occupation of the Basque provinces and Gascony. As the Biscayan fisheries died out, the coasts of Spitzbergen became the center of a successful whaling industry, carried on principally by the Dutch, who supplied most of the oil used in Europe during the latter half of the 17th century. In the 18th century Great Britain became the leading country in whale fishery, subsidizing the industry and paying bounties to whaling vessels, mainly for the purpose of training seamen for the Royal Navy. The Pacific Ocean was opened to whaling in 1787, and the famous Kodiak ground, off the coast of Alaska, was discovered in 1835. About this time the leadership of the industry passed to the United States, where it remained until the decline of the industry in the latter part of the century. In 1931 twenty-six maritime countries signed a Convention for the Regulation of Whaling, which had for its purpose the conservation of the rapidly disappearing herds.

The whaling fleet of the United States reached a peak of 167,000 gross tons in 1860; after that year it declined steadily until, in the years following World War II, only six vessels, totaling 1000 gross tons, were engaged in the whaling industry under United States registry. The catch of whale products fell from more than 10,000,000 pounds in

Norweg. Offic. Photos; Can. Nat. Rys.

WHALE FISHERY. *Above: Harpoon gun on the bow of a Norwegian whaling vessel. Left: Attaching the point on harpoon used for spearing whales, at Churchill, Manitoba. Below: Captured whale on a Norwegian shore.*

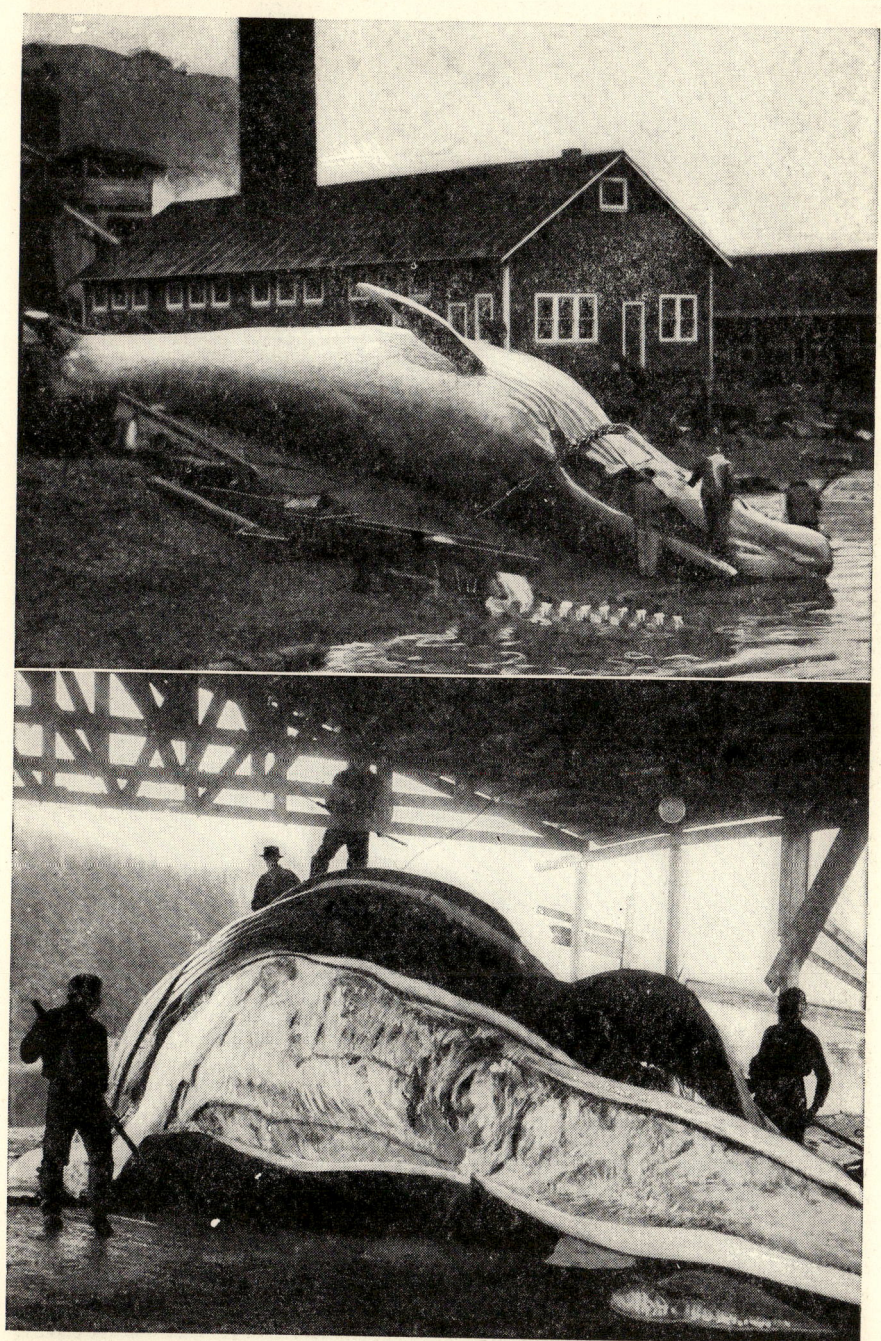

WHALE FISHERY. *Top: 75-foot finback whale being pulled up a ramp at a plant in Alaska. Bottom: Inside the plant the whale is cut apart to obtain the blubber, meat, and bones.*

Alaska Life Pub. Co.; Fishing Gazette

A whale shark, the largest of fishes, attaining a length of seventy feet — Bureau of Fisheries

1937, to less than 100,000 pounds in each postwar year.

WHALEN, GROVER ALOYSIUS (1886–   ), American merchant and public official, born in New York City. He was secretary to Mayor John F. Hylan of New York in 1917, commissioner of plant and structures, New York City (1919–24); general manager of the John Wanamaker department store, New York (1924–28); and New York City Police Commissioner (1928–30); after which he returned to John Wanamaker. Whalen was known as chairman of the city reception committee for distinguished guests, and as president of the New York World's Fair, 1939–40. In 1934 he resigned from Wanamaker's to serve as chairman of the board of Schenley Products Co. He became chairman of the Civilian Defense Volunteer Office of New York City in 1943.

WHALE SHARK, common name applied to a huge shark, *Rhineodon typus,* recognized as the largest fish in existence. Its body is dull colored, and covered with pale, circular blotches. It averages 18 to 25 feet in length, but sometimes reaches a length of 70 feet, attaining a weight of 150,000 pounds. Whale sharks are found in all warm seas, and swim very slowly at or just below the surface. Because of their extremely small throat, they feed on fish no larger than sardines. Most of their food consists of plankton strained out of the sea water by the numerous fine gill rakers located at the back and sides of the mouth cavity and throat. Whale sharks are protected by a strong, tough skin approximately 4 inches thick.

WHALLEY, EDWARD (d. 1678?), English regicide, born in Nottinghamshire. He fought with distinction under his cousin, Oliver Cromwell, in the Great Rebellion, and acted as custodian of Charles I. He was one of those who signed the king's death warrant, and was wounded in the battle of Dunbar. Afterward he assisted General John Lambert in defeating the Royalists at Hamilton, and also participated in the battle of Worcester. On Aug. 13, 1652, he presented to Parliament the petition of the army. When the Restoration came, he fled, in company with his son-in-law, Major General William Goffe (q.v.), to Boston, in the colony of Massachusetts. In 1661 they removed to New Haven and in 1664 to Hadley. Several attempts were made by the home government to secure their arrest, but all were unsuccessful.

WHARF. See DOCK; HARBOR.

WHARF, in the law of real property in the United States, a structure on the bank or margin of navigable waters (see RIVERS, NAVIGABLE) to which vessels can be moored and from which they may be loaded and unloaded. A riparian owner (see RIPARIAN RIGHTS) or one who owns land abutting on navigable waters which have been declared to be public waters has the right to erect a wharf; for the protection of the public's right of navigation, however, this right is subject to regulation by the State in which the land under water is situated. In some States a riparian owner may erect a wharf on the land between the high-water and low-water marks; in other States he may use land only to the high-water mark. Under its power of eminent domain (q.v.), a State may take shore property from a riparian owner for the construction of wharves for public use; the riparian owner is compensated both for the loss of his land and for the loss of his water rights (q.v.) resulting from cutting off the remainder of his land from the shore. A State may grant permission to a city to establish wharves on its water front, as was done by the State of New York to the City of New York. In such cases a city is authorized by the State legislature to condemn lands for the erection of any public wharves whose revenue is to be paid into the city treasury.

WHARFAGE. See WHARF.

WHARTON, borough of Morris County, N.J., situated about 10 miles N.N.W. of Morristown. Silk and paper are important manufactures. Pop. (1940) 3854.

WHARTON, ANNE HOLLINGSWORTH (1845–1928), American author, born in Cumberland County, Pa. She was the first historian of the National Society of Colonial Dames of America and a judge of the American Colonial exhibit at the World's Columbian Exposition, Chicago (1893). Her works include *A Rose of Old Quebec* (1913), *English Ancestral Homes of Noted Americans* (1915), and *In Old Pennsylvania Towns* (1920).

WHARTON, EDITH NEWBOLD JONES (1862–1937), American novelist, born in New York City, and privately educated. In 1885 she married Edward Wharton, a banker of Boston, Massachusetts. Edith Wharton's earliest writings, published shortly after her marriage, consisted of poems and short stories which appeared in *Scribner's Magazine*. Her first book, *The Greater Inclination*, a collection of short stories notable for their intellectual penetration and mature artistry, appeared in 1899, and was followed by two more volumes of short stories, *Crucial Instances* (1901) and *The Descent of Man and Other Stories* (1904). Mrs. Wharton's early novels include *The Valley of Decision* (1902), *The House of Mirth* (1905), *Madame de Treymes* (1907), and *The Fruit of the Tree* (1907). An extended sojourn abroad, both in Italy and France, resulted in the travel books *Italian Villas and Their Gardens* (1904), *Italian Backgrounds* (1905), and *A Motor Flight through France* (1908). Soon after completing these books, she settled in Europe; except for short visits to America and England, she lived and worked for the remainder of her life on the French Riviera. Among her major novels are *Ethan Frome* (1911), *The Age of Innocence* (1920), *Twilight Sleep* (1927), *The Children* (1928), *Hudson River Bracketed* (1929), *Certain People* (1930), *A Backward Glance* (1934), and *The Freebooters* (unfinished, 1937). Mrs. Wharton set forth the principles of her literary method in *The Writing of Fiction* (1925). Her work, the salient characteristics of which include a fine sense for character, a subtle irony, and an impeccable technique, has earned for her an enduring place in American literature.

WHARTON, FRANCIS (1820–89), American jurist and clergyman, born in Philadelphia. From 1856 to 1863 he was professor of English history and literature at Kenyon College, Ohio. In 1871 he was called to the Episcopal Theological Seminary, Cambridge, Mass. From 1885 to 1889 he was counsel to the United States Department of State and examiner of international claims.

WHARTON, THOMAS, 1st MARQUIS OF (1648–1715), English statesman and son of Baron Wharton, the Puritan statesman, born in Woburn, Bedfordshire. His interest in politics was not marked until 1679, when he supported the Exclusion Bill, legislation designed to exclude the Duke of York (later James II) from the throne. He was suspected of complicity with the pretender Monmouth and was certainly most active in arranging for the reception of William, Prince of Orange, in 1688. The preceding year he had composed the satirical ballad *Lilli Burlero, Bullen-a-la,* by means of which, as he used to boast, he had sung a king out of three kingdoms. On William's accession he was rewarded with numerous lucrative offices. In 1702, at the accession of Anne, he was removed from office, but by clever intriguing and the liberal use of money within the next few years he became one of the leaders of the Whig Party. After June, 1706, he was a member of the Whig Junto. In 1708 he was made lord lieutenant of Ireland, and held the post two years. For part of this time Joseph Addison was his secretary. Wharton was the shrewdest party manager of his day and a sincere if not disinterested Whig.

WHARTON, THOMAS (1735–78), American politician, born in Chester County, Pa. He was a prominent opponent of the Stamp Act, and in 1774 became a member of the Committee of Correspondence. He was elected president of the Council of Safety in 1776, and from 1777 until his death was president of Pennsylvania.

WHAT CHEER, a town of Keokuk Co., Iowa, situated on Coal Creek, 60 miles s.w. of Iowa City. It is served by two railroads, and is surrounded by a fertile agricultural area in which are valuable deposits of clay. The principal industries in the town are the manufacture of drain tile, sewer pipe, building blocks, wall coping, brick, terra cotta, and clay novelties. The town was formerly a coal-

Denver C. of C.; Standard Oil (N.J.)

Above: Wheat stacked at harvest time in a field in Colorado. Left: Stalks of wheat growing in the State of Texas.

mining center, but the coal deposits of the region were exhausted by the end of the 19th century. Pop. (1940) 1339.

WHATELY, RICHARD (1787–1863), English clergyman, born in London. In 1825 he was appointed principal of St. Alban's Hall, and professor of political economy in 1829, but had given only a few lectures when in 1831 he was made archbishop of Dublin. The success of the national system of education in Ireland was in large measure due to him.

WHEAT, common name for cereal grasses of the genus *Triticum*, cultivated for food since prehistoric times by the peoples of the temperate zones, and now the most important grain crop (see CEREALS) of those regions. Grains of wheat have been found among the relics of the Lake Dwellers of Switzerland, and in Egyptian and Mesopotamian tombs dating from the period before 5000 B.C. The cultivation of wheat was introduced into Mexico by the Spaniards in 1520; the grain was first planted in New England in 1602, and in Virginia in 1611.

Wheat is a tall, annual plant, growing to a height of about 4 feet; the leaves resemble the flat blades of other members of the Grass family (see GRASSES); the inflorescence (q.v.) is composed of a spike with many flowered spikelets arranged alternately; and the grain is a caryopsis (q.v.; see also FRUIT). Wheat (winter wheat) is usually sown in the autumn in regions where the winters are mild; in colder regions it is sown in the spring. Cultivation of wheat does not extend as far into the colder regions as does the culture of barley, oats, or rye.

The various species of wheat are classified according to the number of chromosomes (see CHROMOSOME; HEREDITY) in the vegetative cell. The genus *Triticum* is divided into three series: the haploid, or "einkorn", containing 14 chromosomes; the diploid, or "emmer", containing 28 chromosomes; and the triploid, or "spelt", series, containing 42 chromosomes. The einkorn series contains the species *T. monococcum*, or einkorn, and *T. spontaneum*, wild einkorn. Comprising the emmer series are *T. dicoccum*, or emmer (q.v.) wheat; *T.*

dicoccoides, or wild emmer wheat; *T. durum,* or durum wheat; *T. abyssinicum,* or Abyssinian wheat; *T. persicum,* Persian wheat; *T. polonicum,* Polish wheat; *T. turgidum,* poulard wheat; and *T. timopheevi,* timopheevi wheat. Five species constitute the spelt series: *T. spelta,* or spelt wheat; *T. vulgare* or *aestivum,* common wheat; *T. compactum,* club wheat; *T. sphaerococcum,* shot wheat; and *T. macha,* macha wheat. Many of these species are grown in the United States for experimental purposes, but only varieties of common, club, and durum wheats are of commercial importance. A limited amount of emmer, Polish, poulard, and spelt, however, is grown for cattle feed.

Varieties of common wheat include bearded and beardless, and also include those classified as winter and spring, and, according to the color of the grain, as white and red wheat. Most white wheats are of spring habit only. Closely related to the common wheats are the club wheats, which have especially square, compact spikes; and spelt, in which the glumes tightly enclose the grains. In poulard, the glumes are exceptionally tumid, and are always awned, or bearded; Polish wheat has empty papery glumes, and emmer has tight glumes, like those of spelt. Durum wheat (Lat. *durum,* "hard") is so called because of the hardness of the grain; it is grown chiefly in dry regions, and is used in the manufacture of semolina and macaroni.

Standards and Grading. The United States Grain Standards Act of 1916 authorized the Secretary of Agriculture to investigate the handling and grading of grain, establish official standards, and license grain inspectors. Under this law, all wheat in interstate and foreign commerce is graded by licensed inspectors according to the official wheat standards of the United States, as revised in 1927. These standards, based on color and texture of kernels, as indicating quality, comprise the following classes and subclasses: Class 1, hard red spring wheat, with subclasses (a) dark northern spring, (b) northern spring, and (c) red spring; Class 2, durum wheat, and subclasses (a) amber durum, (b) durum, and (c) red durum; Class 3, hard red winter wheat, including subclasses (a) dark hard winter, (b) hard winter, and (c) yellow hard winter; Class 4, soft red winter wheat, including subclasses (a) red winter, and (b) Western red; and Class 5, white wheat, with subclasses (a) hard white, (b) soft white, and (c) Western white. Each subclass is divided into five grades, determined by test weight per bushel,

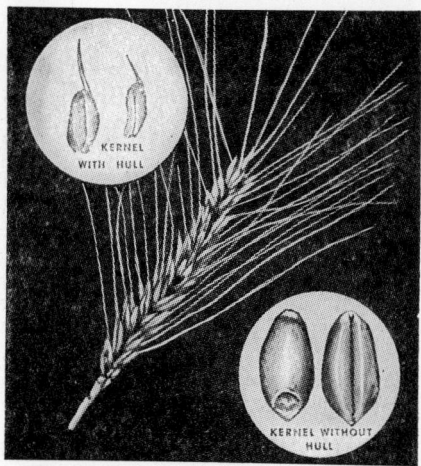

General Mills
Head of hard red winter wheat, and kernels

moisture content, percentage of damaged kernels, purity, cleanness, and condition. Wheat failing to meet the specifications for any of these grades is designated "sample grade". In addition grades are included for mixed wheat, mixed durum, treated wheat, and for wheats contaminated with garlic, infected with smut, or infested with weevils.

Since 1920 the quantity of protein in wheat has become an increasingly important price factor, and by 1928 a high protein content in the bread wheats quite generally commanded a premium. At present, testing wheat for protein content by either State or commercial laboratories is an accepted practice at the principal terminal markets of the Central West, which receive the winter and spring hard wheats.

The principal diseases of wheat are connected with the presence of parasitic fungi. The chief of these diseases are rust, bunt, and smut (qq.v.; see also FUNGI: *Structure and Reproduction*). Wheat is also liable to injury from several insect pests, especially the Hessian fly and sawfly (qq.v.).

Cultivation and Harvesting. In the United States wheat may be planted by hand on small acreages, but on large farms it is usually planted by sowing machines of the drill or broadcast types; see IMPLEMENTS, AGRICULTURAL. Little cultivation is necessary beyond preparation of the land by plowing and harrowing, and, sometimes, dusting to control pests. Wheat crops are generally rotated with corn, hay, and pasture in the East, and with oats and barley, or bare fallowing, in the drier western regions. Wheat is harvested by means of the combined harvester and thresher, or *combine,* which was used in the Pacific Coast States for fifty years before its general introduction into the Great Plains region about 1917. Since that time its use has spread to all important grain-producing sections of the United States and Canada. Combines are operated with tractors, and vary in size and type to meet local requirements. A combine, cutting a 16-foot swath, harvests and threshes the wheat on 30 acres in an 8-hour day. Crews with groups of combines begin harvesting in Texas in May, and, moving northward with the season, finish in North Dakota, Idaho, and Washington in August.

Uses. The principal use of wheat is the manufacture of flour (q.v.) for bread and pastries. In general, hard varieties are used for bread flour, and soft varieties for pastry flour. Wheat is used to a limited extent in the making of beer, whisky, and industrial alcohol. Low grades of wheat, and by-products of the flour-milling, brewing, and distilling industries are used as feed for livestock. In Europe especially, wheat grains are roasted and used as a substitute for coffee, and wheat starch is employed as a sizing for textile fabrics.

Statistics. In the years before World War II, the wheat crop of the world averaged about 160 million long tons. The leading countries were the U.S.S.R., with about 24 million tons; the United States, with 20 million; and Canada, with 14 million tons. The acreage devoted to the raising of wheat in the United States is about 50,000,000 in all. Production was high during World War I, and reached 945,403,000 bushels in 1919. It dropped to 513,213,000 bushels in 1934, but rose again to more than one billion bushels each year from 1944 to 1948, inclusive. It reached an all-time high of 1,364,919,000 bushels in 1947. The value of the wheat crop dropped from a high of $2,074,079,000 in 1919 to less than half a billion dollars in the 1930's, and then rose to a new high of $3,150,000,000 in 1947. In a recent year production amounted to about 1,290,000,000 bushels, with a value of $2,641,-000,000.

WHEATEAR, small European migratory song bird, *Saxicola aenanthe,* of the Thrush family, which is occasionally found on the north coasts of Asia and America. Its colors are gray, black, and white, the under parts buff. Its wings and legs are long.

WHEATON, county seat of Dupage County, Ill., 28 miles w. of Chicago. Wheaton College is located in the city. Pop. (1940) 7389.

WHEATON, HENRY (1785–1848), American jurist, born in Providence, R.I. From 1812 to 1815 he edited the *National Advocate* in New York, and from 1816 to 1827 was reporter for the United States Supreme Court. From 1827 to 1835 he was chargé d'affaires in Copenhagen, and from 1835 to 1846 minister in Berlin. Wheaton wrote *Elements of International Law* (1836).

WHEATON COLLEGE, a nondenominational, privately controlled institution of higher education for women, situated in Norton, Mass. It was founded in 1835 as the Norton Female Seminary; the name was changed to Wheaton Female Seminary in 1839, and in 1912, when the institution was authorized by the State legislature to confer degrees, the present name was adopted. The curriculum of the college is restricted to the liberal arts; the only degrees awarded are those of B.A. and M.A. In a recent year about 500 women were enrolled and the facutly numbered almost 70.

WHEATSTONE, SIR CHARLES (1802–75), English physicist and inventor, born in Gloucester, England. His first researches were in connection with sound. In 1834 he was appointed professor of experimental philosophy at King's College, London. Three years later he took out patents for an electric telegraph. He explained the principle of the stereoscope in 1838, and in 1843 he brought out instruments and processes for determining the constants of a voltaic series. The polar clock, another of his inventions, was an application of Brewster's discovery that the plane of polarization of the light of the sky always made an angle of 90° with the sun. In 1840 he showed that by means of electromagnetic regulating devices a number of clocks far apart could be kept going synchronously from a central clock. Wheatstone's bridge (q.v.), which was invented by Hunter Christy, was first brought into general use through his efforts in 1843, and has proved a fundamental method in the measurement of electrical resistance. Wheatstone was one of the first to recognize the importance of Ohm's law and to apply it in electrical measurements. He also had a share in the development of the dynamo, devising a method for making the magneto-machines then in use self-exciting by employing a shunt circuit passing around the field magnets.

WHEATSTONE BRIDGE. See ELECTRIC METERS.

WHEEL AND AXLE, a simple form of machine consisting of two wheels, one large and

$R = $ radius of large wheel

$r = $ radius of small wheel or axle

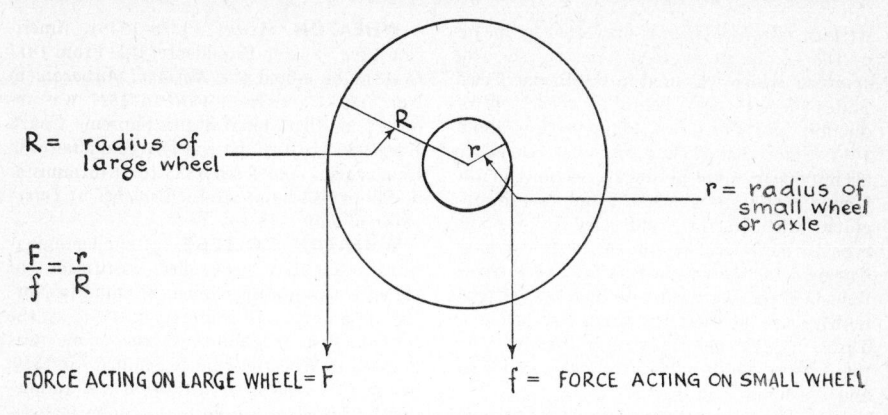

$$\frac{F}{f} = \frac{r}{R}$$

FORCE ACTING ON LARGE WHEEL = F $f = $ FORCE ACTING ON SMALL WHEEL

Diagram showing the principle of the wheel and axle

one small, mounted concentrically on the same axle. In most types of this machine the small wheel is the axle itself. From the point of view of mechanical analysis the wheel and axle is equivalent to a lever (q.v.) in which the fulcrum is the center of rotation of the machine. The force applied to one wheel necessary to balance a force applied to the other wheel is inversely proportional to the radii of the two wheels, as shown in the accompanying drawing. Wheels and axles are employed by themselves in weight-lifting machines such as winches and capstans, and are also extensively used as parts of more complicated mechanisms.

WHEEL ANIMALCULE. See ROTIFERA.

WHEEL, BREAKING ON THE, a method of inflicting the punishment of death. It originated among the ancient Greeks and Romans and was used in western Europe until the 19th century for assassins, incendiaries, highwaymen, and pillagers of churches.

WHEEL BUG. See KISSING BUG.

WHEELER, ANDREW CARPENTER (1835–1903), American author, born in New York City. He became a reporter on *The New York Times*. After the Civil War Wheeler served on the staffs of the New York *Leader* and the *World*. To the latter paper he contributed under the name Nym Crinkle. He also used the pseudonym J.P. Mobray.

WHEELER, BENJAMIN IDE (1854–1927), American educator and university president, born in Randolph, Mass. After acting as instructor in Latin and Greek at Brown University, and in German at Harvard University (1879–86), he was professor (1886–99) at Cornell University. From 1899 until 1919 he was president of the University of California.

WHEELER, BURTON KENDALL (1882–   ), American lawyer and politician, born in Hudson, Mass. He attracted attention by his success in winning damage suits in Butte, Mont., for the miners against the big copper companies. The liberal political element in Butte sent him to the State legislature in 1911, and he was Federal district attorney in Montana from 1913 to 1919. He was elected to the U.S. Senate in 1922 and served until 1947. While in charge of the investigation of former attorney general Harry Micajah Daugherty (q.v.; see also FALL, ALBERT), Wheeler was accused of accepting a fee illegally, but was exonerated. Prior to the attack on Pearl Harbor (q.v.), Wheeler was a leading isolationist.

WHEELER, EVERETT PEPPERRELL (1840–1925), American lawyer and author, born in New York City. He served as a member of the Board of Education of New York City (1877–79), as chairman of the New York City Civil Service Commission (1883–89 and 1895–97) and of the committee on law reform of the American Bar Association (1908–11), and as president of the Reform Club (1889–90). He was also president of the New York Civil Service Reform Association. His writings include *The Knowledge of Faith* (1904) and *Daniel Webster, Expounder of the Constitution* (1905).

WHEELER, HOWARD DURYEE (1880–   ), American editor, born in Montclair, N.J. After holding various reportorial posts, he was editor of the San Francisco *Daily News* (1906–08) and of the *Newspaper Enterprise Association* (1909–14). He was managing editor, *Harper's Weekly* (1914–15); editor in chief, *Everybody's Magazine* (1915–19); general manager, *Science Service* (1921–22); general manager, *McClure Newspaper Syndicate* (1923–26); editor *Condé Nast Syndicate* (1927–29); and chief editorial writer, *Daily Mirror,* New York City (1929–35). Among his works is *Interludes* (1934).

WHEELER, JOSEPH (1836–1906), American soldier, born in Augusta, Ga., and educated at the U.S. Military Academy. When the Civil War broke out he resigned his commission to enter the Confederate Army, and soon afterward was promoted colonel of the 19th Alabama Infantry. He commanded a brigade at Shiloh, was commander of the cavalry of the Army of the Mississippi, and of the Army of Tennessee, and was commissioned major general in 1863. He commanded the cavalry of the Confederate Army throughout the campaigns of Chickamauga, Chattanooga, and Atlanta, and greatly hindered General Sherman's army during the march to the sea. He commanded the cavalry of General Johnston's army in North Carolina, and was included in its surrender. After the war he was a representative in Congress (1885–1900). At the outbreak of the Spanish-American War (1898) he was appointed major general of volunteers, and assigned to the command of the cavalry division of Shafter's army in Cuba. He commanded in the actions of Guasimas and San Juan, served afterward in the Philippines, was commissioned brigadier general in the regular army in 1900, and retired in the same year.

WHEELER, SCHUYLER SKAATS (1860–1923), American engineer, born in New York City. In 1883 he was a member of Thomas Alva Edison's engineering staff. He organized the firm of Crocker and Wheeler in 1888, and in the following year became president of the Crocker-Wheeler Company in Ampere, N.J., manufacturers of electrical equipment. Wheeler had an important part in the development of the electric motor and in the direct application of electricity to driving tools, inventing an electric elevator, an electric fire engine, and other devices. For his invention of an electric fan he received the John Scott medal of the Franklin Institute in 1904.

WHEELER, WAYNE BIDWELL (1869–1927), American lawyer and temperance worker, born in Brookfield, Ohio. In 1915 he became general counsel of the Anti-Saloon League of America. He figured prominently in the struggle which culminated in the enactment and ratification (1919) of the 18th amendment to the U.S. Constitution.

WHEELER, WILLIAM ALMON (1819–87), American legislator, born in Malone, N.Y. He was a member of the State legislature (1849–50), a member of the U.S. House of Representatives (1861–63 and 1869–77), and was the author of the "Wheeler Compromise" (1875) which adjusted the differences between the contending political factions in Louisiana. From 1876 to 1881 he was Vice-President of the United States.

WHEELER, WILLIAM MORTON (1865–1937), American zoologist, born in Milwaukee, Wis. After two years as assistant professor of zoology at the University of Chicago, he became professor at the University of Texas (1899), was curator of invertebrate zoology in the American Museum of Natural History, New York City, from 1903 to 1908, and thereafter professor of economic entomology at Harvard. He remained connected with the Natural History Museum as honorary curator of social insects. He was on the editorial staffs of the *Biological Bulletin, Journal of Morphology, Journal of Animal Behavior,* and *Psyche.* His works include *Ants, Their Structure, Development, and Behavior* (1910) and *Social Life Among the Insects* (1923).

WHEELING, county seat of Ohio Co., W. Va., situated on the E. bank of the Ohio R., 66 miles s.w. of Pittsburgh, Pa. The city area includes Wheeling Island, in the Ohio R. Transportation facilities include three railroads, river steamers and barges, a municipal airport, and several bridges connecting Wheeling with cities and towns in Ohio, on the opposite bank of the river. Wheeling is the principal manufacturing center and the third-largest city in population in the State, and the center of a region rich in coal and natural gas. The leading industry in the city is the manufacture of steel; the city is also an important center for the manufacture of iron, tin plate, aluminum, zinc, china, porcelain, pottery, glassware, tile, plastics, tobacco products, nails, matches, furniture, paper and paper products, textiles, mattresses, patent medicines, and sausage. The municipal park system includes Oglebay Park, largest municipal park in the State, covering 754 acres on the outskirts of the city. Features of the park include a golf course, swimming pool, formal gardens, a conservatory and greenhouses, bridle paths, a museum of natural history, and the Mansion Museum, dating in part from 1801 and containing collections of art and historical material.

Wheeling was settled in 1769 by Col. Ebenezer Zane and his two brothers, colonists from Virginia. During the American Revolution the settlement was frequently attacked by hostile Indians and marauding parties of British and Indians, but was successfully defended. The settlement was incorporated as the town of Wheeling in 1806 and chartered as a city in 1836. Upon the secession of Virginia from the Union in 1861 Wheeling became the headquarters of those opposed to secession and was made capital of the "Restored Government of Virginia", which became the State of West Virginia in 1863. It was the capital of the new State until 1869 and again from 1875 to 1885. Pop. (1950) 58,447.

WHEELOCK, ELEAZAR (1711–79), American clergyman and educator, born in Windham, Conn. He was pastor of the Second Congregational Church in Lebanon, Conn., and there established a school for the education of Indian and white youths. In 1770 he removed to Hanover, N.H., where he established (1770) Dartmouth College. During the remaining nine years of his life Wheeler was president of the new college.

WHEELOCK, JOHN (1754–1817), American educator, and son of Eleazar Wheelock, born in Lebanon, Conn. In 1777 he entered the Continental Army, but resigned in 1779 to succeed his father as president of Dartmouth College. In 1815, owing to differences with the trustees in regard to religious matters, he was removed from his office, but was reinstated by the State legislature a few months before his death.

WHEELOCK, JOHN HALL (1886–   ), American author, born in Far Rockaway, Long Island (now part of New York City). In 1911 he became a member of the editorial force of Charles Scribner's Sons. Among his writings are *The Human Fantasy* (1911), *The Beloved Adventure* (1912), *Love and Liberation* (1913), *Dust and Light* (1919), *The Black Panther* (1922), and *The Bright Doom* (1927).

WHEELWRIGHT, EDMUND MARCH (1854–1912), American architect, born in Roxbury, Mass. From 1891 to 1895 he was city architect of Boston, and designed many important school buildings and Harvard Bridge (over the Charles River). Wheelwright also designed Jordan Hall, Boston, the Boston Opera House, the Cleveland Museum of Art, additions to the Massachusetts General Hospital, and Cambridge Bridge, Boston. In 1904 he was sent to Europe with R. Clipston Sturgis by the trustees of the Boston Museum of Fine Arts to study museum buildings, and they later served jointly, with Despradelle, as advisory architects to Guy Lowell, who designed the new Museum of Fine Arts. Boston.

WHEELWRIGHT, JOHN (1592–1679), English clergyman, born in Lincolnshire, England. In 1636 he came to America, where he became pastor of a Puritan church in Mount Wollaston (now Braintree), Mass. He adopted the antinomian views of his sister-in-law, Anne Hutchinson, and was banished from the colony in 1637. He then settled in New Hampshire, where he founded the town of Exeter. In 1643 he removed to Wells, Me. In 1644 the sentence of banishment was revoked and he returned to Massachusetts, where he was pastor of the church in Hampton (1646–54). In 1662 he became pastor of a church in Salisbury, N.H.

WHEELWRIGHT, WILLIAM (1798–1873), American capitalist, born in Newburyport, Mass. From 1824 to 1829 he was United States consul in Guayaquil, Ecuador. In 1829 he removed to Valparaiso, where he established a line of passenger steamers. He founded the Pacific Steam Navigation Company in 1840. He constructed a number of railroads in Chile and Argentina.

WHELK, a popular name for a number of marine Gastropods, of the family Buccinidae, and especially applied to the Buccinum common on the coast of northern seas. It occurs from low water to a depth of about 600 fathoms, and burrows in the sand for bivalves, such as Mya, on which it feeds. Its shell is sometimes 3 inches in length, is grayish or brownish white in color, and has a few ridged whorls, a wide aperture, and a short notch or canal for the respiratory siphon. The notch at the mouth of the shell, in which the siphon lies, is characteristic of most carnivorous Gastropods. It is used in Europe for food.

WHETSTONE, GEORGE (1544?–87?), English author, born in Lincolnshire. He served in the Low Countries in 1572 and was present at the battle of Zutphen (1586). He also accompanied Sir Humphrey Gilbert on the disastrous voyage to Newfoundland (1578–79). Whetstone is mainly of interest because his *Promos and Cassandra*, a play in rhymed verse (1578), and the prose tale with the same title, in his *Heptameron of Ciuill Discourses* (1582), furnished the plot for Shakespeare's *Measure for Measure.*

WHETSTONES. See HONES; ABRASIVE.

WHEWELL, WILLIAM (1794–1866), English philosopher and scholar, born in Lancaster. Between 1828 and 1832 he was professor of mineralogy at Cambridge University. He was later professor of moral theology at Cambridge. In 1841 he succeeded Wordsworth as master of Trinity. He became vice-chancellor of the university in 1855. His works include *History of the Inductive Sciences* (3 vols., 1837), *The Philosophy of the Inductive Sciences* (2 vols., 1840), and *The Elements of Morality Including Polity* (1855).

WHEY, a by-product obtained in the manufacture of cheese. When milk is curdled with rennet or any similar substance, the curd separates from the liquid portion of the milk, and the liquid portion is termed "whey". Its principal use is as a feed for pigs, calves, and sometimes for cows. It is less valuable for this purpose than skim milk or buttermilk, for the casein, which contributes largely to the value of both of these, is lacking in whey. It contains about 93 percent water (only 7 percent solids), 5 percent milk sugar, 0.9 percent casein and albumin, 0.3 to 0.5 percent fat, and about 0.5 percent ash. In large factories whey is used for making milk sugar. Whey cheese, made in some of the countries of northern Europe, is practically evaporated whey, with some cream added. Butter has been made from whey by running it through a separator, but in good cheese-making practice whey contains little butter fat. It is also used medicinally, especially in Europe, and is sometimes used as a source of water-soluble vitamins.

WHICKHAM, a town in Durham, England, 3 miles s.w. of Newcastle. It has iron foundries, chemical works, lumber yards and saw mills. Pop., about 21,000.

WHIDAH BIRD, or **WIDOW BIRD,** common name for birds of the subfamily Viduinae in the Weaver Bird (q.v.) family. The best known species is *Steganura paradisea,* the paradise whidah bird, or paradise weaver; it is the size of a canary, and it has black plumage, with orange-buff collar and breast. During the mating and breeding season, the males have long drooping tail feathers, almost a foot in length.

WHIFFEN, BLANCHE, better known as MRS. THOMAS WHIFFEN (1845–1936), American actress, born in London. Her maiden name was Galton. She made her stage debut at the Royalty Theatre, London, in 1865; came to America in 1868, and toured the United States under John Templeton's management. In 1879 she played Buttercup in the first American production of Gilbert and Sullivan's *Pinafore.* She joined Daniel Frohman's company at the Lyceum in 1887, and later Charles Frohman's company at the Empire. Blanche Whiffen in later years appeared in many plays, including *Zira* (1905), *The Great Divide* (1905–07), *Cousin Kate* (1912), *Rosemary* (1915), *The Goose Hangs High* (1924), *Trelawney of the Wells* (1925), and *Just Fancy* (1927).

WHIG and **TORY** (Whig, probably abbreviated from *whiggamore,* a nickname for the Presbyterian peasantry of the western lowlands of Scotland; Tory, from Ir. *toridhe, tornighe,* "pursuer", "plunderer"), the names which for about two centuries were popularly applied to the two great political parties in Great Britain. Both were at first names of reproach. Whig was meant to imply that those who were thus designated were no better than the Presbyterian rebels of Scotland, while the name Tory was intended to imply some connection with Irish brigands, who were supposed to desire a Catholic king. The names came into use about 1680. In general, the Tories were adherents of the ancient Constitution of England and the supporters of regal and ecclesiastical authority, while the Whigs as a rule favored reform in the direction of a more democratic government. In 1832, when the Reform Bill was passed through the efforts of a wing of the Whig Party, the two old parties really disappeared, the Tories being ultimately succeeded by the Conservatives and the Whigs by the Liberals.

WHIG PARTY, in United States history, a name originally applied to those who, in the colonial and Revolutionary periods, were opposed to British rule. At a later period it was the name adopted (1834) by the survivors of the old National Republican Party, after its overwhelming defeat by Andrew Jackson in 1832. In 1839 the Whig Party nominated William Henry Harrison for President and John Tyler for Vice-President. After a remarkable campaign, the Whigs triumphed, but their rejoicing was soon cut short by the death of President Harrison and the accession of Vice-President Tyler, who was not of their political faith and who shortly embittered the Whigs by his vetoes of the bank bill. In 1844 the Whig Party nominated its leader Henry Clay and for the first time adopted a platform of principles, which included "a well-regulated national currency; a tariff for revenue to defray the necessary expenses of the government, and discriminating with special reference to the protection of the domestic labor of the country; the distribution of the proceeds from the sales of the public lands; a single term for the presidency; a reform of executive usurpations".

The Whigs of both North and South supported the war with Mexico after it was once declared (1846), but the controversy over the question of admitting or excluding slavery from the territory acquired thereby (see WILMOT PROVISO) clearly revealed that Northern and Southern Whigs could not much longer stand together. The antislavery or "Conscience" wing of the Whig Party in Massachusetts soon arose in opposition to the so-called "Cotton Whigs". In the Presidential election of 1848 the Whigs, with General Zachary Taylor as their candidate, were for the second and last time successful. It was chiefly through the efforts of Henry Clay that the passage of the Compromise Measures of 1850 was effected. The election of 1852 resulted in the overwhelming defeat of the Whig candidate, General Winfield Scott. The Kansas-Nebraska Bill of 1854 led to the disruption of the Whig Party and to the formation of a new party in the North (see REPUBLICAN PARTY), which was finally joined by most of the Northern Whigs, many of whom were at first affiliated with the Know-Nothing movement. In the South most of the Whigs for a time acted with the Know-Nothing Party, but they were soon absorbed by the Southern Democratic Party.

WHIP, a term used in English politics to designate the party representative whose duty it is to notify members of Parliament belonging to his party of the near approach of a division and to compel their attendance while the vote is being taken. The whip of the party in power is appointed a junior lord of the Treasury, with some minor patronage, in order to increase his influence.

In the United States the party whip first came into being in 1900. His position, while in many respects similar to that of the English whip, differs in certain essentials. He is usually an influential member and is chosen by the congressional caucus of each party. The position is considered one of the highest after that of leader. One important duty is to sound the sentiments of the party and to determine how many votes can be depended upon in important legislation; also to attempt to influence other members to remain loyal to party issues. He also arranges for "pairings" of absent members. In Congress, the party caucus, of which the whip is a member, usually gives a "call" for the entire party to be present when matters of outstanding importance are to be voted upon.

WHIPPET, a breed of hound or sporting dog which hunts by sight, not by scent. The breed originated in England in the first half of the 19th century from a cross between the English greyhound and various breeds of terriers, the product of which was later crossed with the

The whippet

Italian greyhound; the whippet was first recognized as a show breed in 1891. The dog was formerly used as a rat killer and for rabbit coursing, but currently is valued as a pet and for racing. With the possible exception of the Weimaraner (q.v.), the whippet is the speediest of domesticated animals, being able to run as fast as thirty-five miles per hour. The sport of whippet racing originated in Lancashire and Yorkshire in the 19th century and was introduced into the United States by English mill workers employed in Lowell and Lawrence, Massachusetts; the sport is carried on throughout the United States today, particularly in Maryland and Florida. The dogs generally race on a circular track in pursuit of an artificial rabbit propelled along an electric rail.

Although delicate and almost fragile in appearance, the whippet is a strong and vigorous animal. The dog has a long, lean head, fairly wide between the ears; small, finely textured ears, thrown back and folded; intelligent eyes, dark hazel in color; a long, muscular neck; a deep and wide chest; long, tapering legs; powerful hindquarters; and a long, tapering tail. It has a smooth, firm coat, which may be of any of a number of colors. The whippet weighs about 20 pounds; the male is between 19 and 22 inches in height and the female between 18 and 21 inches.

WHIPPING. See FLOGGING.

WHIPPLE, ABRAHAM (1733–1819), American naval officer, born in Providence, R.I. Early in life he entered the navy, and soon won distinction as a commander against the French. In 1772 he commanded the party of volunteers which captured and burned the British revenue schooner *Gaspée,* in Narragansett Bay. During the Revolutionary War his

The whippoorwill

schooner *Providence* reputedly took more British prizes than any other American vessel. In July, 1779, with the *Providence* and two other vessels, he fell in with a British merchant fleet of nearly 150 sail, heavily convoyed, and succeeded in capturing 10 vessels. Eight of these vessels reached Boston, where they were sold for about $1,000,000. At the defense of Charleston, S.C., in 1780, he commanded the naval forces, was captured, and remained a prisoner until the end of the war.

WHIPPLE, ALLEN OLDFATHER (1881–   ), American surgeon, born in Urmia, Iran, and educated at Princeton University and the College of Physicians and Surgeons of Columbia University. He was professor of surgery at the College of Physicians and Surgeons and director of surgical service at the Presbyterian Hospital in New York City. He retired in 1946 to join the medical faculty of the University of Beirut, in Lebanon. Whipple was a fellow of the American College of Surgeons and an honorary fellow of the Royal College of Surgeons, London.

WHIPPLE, EDWIN PERCY (1819–86), American critic, born in Gloucester, Mass. He was long a distinguished lecturer on literary and biographical topics. His first book was *Essays and Reviews* (2 vols., 1848–49), which was followed by *Literature and Life* (1849), *Literature of the Age of Elizabeth* (1876), *Recollections of Eminent Men* (1887), and *American Literature and Other Papers* (1887).

WHIPPLE, GEORGE HOYT (1878–   ), American pathologist, born in Ashland, N.H. Until 1908 he was engaged in pathological research, and was pathologist at Johns Hopkins University and Hospital from 1909 to 1914. He then went to the University of California as director of medical research (1914–21) and dean of the medical school (1920–21). After 1921 he was dean and professor of pathology at the University of Rochester School of Medicine and Dentistry. In 1927 he became a trustee of the Rockefeller Foundation. He was elected a member of the National Academy of Science in 1929 and awarded the Nobel Prize for medicine in 1934.

WHIPPLE, GUY MONTROSE (1876–1941), American psychologist, born in Danvers, Mass. He began teaching in 1902 at Cornell and went to the University of Illinois in 1914. The Carnegie Institute of Technology employed him from 1917 to 1919 as acting director of its bureau of salesmanship and as professor of applied psychology. He was professor of experimental education at the University of Michigan from 1919 to 1925. During World War I, he was a member of the committee on mental examination of army recruits. His writings include *Questions in School Hygiene* (1909), *Manual of Mental and Physical Tests* (2nd ed., 1914), *How to Study Effectively* (1916), *Classes for Gifted Children* (1919), *Problems in Educational Psychology* (1922), and *Problems in Mental Testing* (with Helen D. Whipple, 1925).

WHIPPLE, HENRY BENJAMIN (1822–1901), American Protestant Episcopal bishop, born in Adams, N.Y. In 1847 he began to study theology privately, was ordained priest in 1850, and became rector in Rome, N.Y. In 1859 he was elected and consecrated bishop of Minnesota. He was a warm friend of the Indians, among whom he established successful missions. He also founded a group of schools in Faribault, Minn. He wrote *Lights and Shadows of a Long Episcopate* (New York, 1899).

WHIPPLE, SQUIRE (1804–88), American civil engineer, born in Hardwick, Mass., and educated at Union College. In 1840 he designed a successful scale for weighing canal boats and patented an iron bridge truss. This truss, a trapezoidal type, usually called the Whipple truss, made him known as the father of iron bridges. In 1872 he patented a lift drawbridge, and in the following year built one over the Erie Canal at Utica.

WHIPPLE, WILLIAM (1730–85), a signer of the Declaration of Independence, born in Kittery, Me. After being a sailor for a number of years, he settled as a merchant (1759) in Portsmouth, N.H. In 1775 he was elected a member of the Provincial Council of Safety. He was a member of the Continental Congress (1776–79). From 1777 to 1782 he was a brigadier general of militia, and held commands at the Battle of Saratoga and in the expedition to Rhode Island. He was a justice of the Superior Court of New Hampshire from 1782 to 1785.

WHIPPOORWILL (*Antrostomus vociferus*), a species of nightjar, a native of North America, common in the eastern parts of the United States. It is named for its cry which is loud and clear, and heard usually only at night. It is about 10 inches long. In the more southern parts of the United States a larger species, known from its cry as the chuck-will's-widow, is common.

WHIP SNAKE, common name given in North America to various species of swift, brownish blacksnake, especially *Zamenis flagelliformis,* the coach-whip snake, 4 to 5 ft. long, which is slender and harmless. The long, slender, whiplash-like green tree serpents of the family Dryophidae of India and the Malay countries are poisonous, and one species, *Dryophis nasutus,* of India is said by the natives to dart at the eyes of men passing it.

WHIPWORM, common name applied to nemotode worms of the genus *Trichuris,* of which one species, *T. trichiura,* is a common parasite of man in the United States. The worm, which is almost world-wide in distribution, attains a length of about 2 inches. Its anterior end is thin and threadlike; its posterior end is thick and, in the male, is usually coiled when the worm is at rest. The eggs of the whipworm are ingested by man with contaminated food or water, and hatch in the intestinal tract. The adult worms usually attach themselves to the mucous membrane of the large intestine, especially in the region of the caecum. Most frequently the worms produce no symptoms; occasionally, however, infestation with whipworms results in intestinal upsets, anemia, or even symptoms of nervous disturbance. Whipworms also occasionally cause inflammation of the vermiform appendix. The adults are particularly difficult to dislodge by present methods. The eggs of the whipworm are eliminated in the feces of an infested person. The brown, oval eggs, when viewed under the microscope, may be recognized by a characteristic buttonlike protuberance at each end. Other species of similar form and habit infest other animals as, for example, *T. ovis* attacks sheep, and *T. vulpis* infests dogs.

WHIRLIGIG BEETLE. See WATER BEETLE.

WHIRLIGIG MULLET, common name for a mullet, *Mugil brazilensis,* of the coastal waters of the southeastern United States. It is often found swimming round and round in great schools at the surface like whirligig beetles (see WATER BEETLE) ; it is usually mistaken for a young spearling or bluefish.

WHIRLPOOL, any body of water moving in a circular or vortical motion, usually having the center of the body depressed because of the centrifugal action of the moving water. Whirlpools may be caused by irregularities in the channel of a stream, as in the case of the whirlpool in the Niagara R., or by the meeting of opposing currents, as in the maelstrom (q.v.) in the Arctic Ocean off the coast of Norway. Whirlpools may also be caused, by the rotation of the earth, around a current flowing downward into an underwater outlet.

WHIRLPOOL RAPIDS, a remarkable series of rapids in the Niagara River, 3 m. below Niagara Falls. The central portion of the current is forced by the narrowness of the channel (300 feet) to a height of 20 to 30 feet above the edges. In spite of the dangerous character of the rapids, they have occasionally been navigated by persons in barrels.

WHIRLWIND, a term specifically applied to rotating windstorms that continue only a few seconds, seldom longer than a minute. The most violent storms of this type occur on hot, dry plains, as in India, Texas, and the eastern slope of the Rocky Mountains, and especially in the Sahara Desert. In the smaller whirlwinds rotation may be either clockwise or counterclockwise, but in the larger whirls the direction, like that of the tornado, is always the same as that of the storms attending areas of low pressure (see CYCLONE; TORNADO).

WHISKY (Gaelic, *uisgebeatha,* "water of life") an alcoholic liquor obtained by distilling the fermented mash of any of several cereal grains, and aging the distillate in wooden casks. The classification of the various types of whisky is based on the kind of grain used in the mash. *Rye whisky* is produced from a mash containing more than fifty percent of rye grain. *Bourbon whisky* (q.v.), is produced from a mash of fifty to eighty percent corn; and *corn whisky* from a mash of more than eighty percent corn. *Malt whisky* is made from malted barley; this type is not extensively produced in the United States, but a small percentage of barley malt is usually added to the mash of other types of whisky, because the malt ferments split the starch of the grain into sugar and make it available for fermentation. Rye whisky is made chiefly in the north and east of the United States, especially in Pennsylvania, Maryland, and Illinois. Bourbon and corn whisky are produced in central and southern States, notably Kentucky. Malt whisky is produced in Scotland and Ireland; the characteristic flavor of Scotch and Irish whiskies is produced during a stage in the preparation of the malt, in which it is toasted over an open peat fire. The term "whisky" is sometimes applied incorrectly to liquors obtained from starchy materials other than

MAKING SCOTCH WHISKEY. *Above, left: Barley is first allowed to germinate. Above right: Taking a sample from a fermentation vat. Below, left: Tester tapping a still.*

grains, such as potatoes; see BEVERAGES; DISTILLED LIQUORS.

The characteristic flavor of each kind of whisky is imparted by the grain, and modified by the particular strains of yeast used in fermentation (q.v.), the amount of higher alcohols and other organic constituents removed in rectification (see DISTILLATION), and the nature of the cask and the length of time the liquor is aged. Generally whiskies are aged in oaken barrels which are charred on the inside. The char assists in the chemical action by which the harsh constituents of raw spirit are gradually transformed into aldehydes and esters, giving the beverage a less fiery, mellower taste. The charred wood also contributes to the color of the liquor, which is water-white in the raw spirit, and amber to reddish brown in the properly aged product. In the United States *bonded whisky* is whisky from a single batch, aged at least four years in a government warehouse, and bottled for sale after the alcoholic content is adjusted to fifty percent. *Blended whisky* ranges from quality products which are mixtures of several whiskies, each qualified for the bonded label, to *spirit whisky*, which is a mixture of ninety-five percent neutral spirits (i.e., diluted grain alcohol) and five percent whisky.

The average per capita consumption of distilled liquors in the United States was 2.40 proof gallons before the time of the Civil War; between the Civil War and World War I, the average annual consumption was 1.40 gallons, and since the repeal of Prohibition (q.v.) it has been 1.08 gallons. In a recent year new whisky produced in the United States amounted to 168 million gallons; about 60 million gallons were used, and a stock for aging remained, amounting to 465 million gallons.

WHISKY INSURRECTION, the name given to an outbreak which occurred in western Pennsylvania in the summer of 1794. It arose from discontent with the excise regulations, and culminated in open riot and the destruction of private property. Because of the lack of transportation facilities, the Scotch-Irish farmers of western Pennsylvania could send their grain to the market only in the form of whisky. The State protested against the Federal excise law of 1791, and conventions were held. At one of these, held in Pittsburgh and attended by delegates from the four western counties, violent resolutions were passed. Meanwhile tax collectors had been tarred and feathered, and the Federal government, to appease the discontent, modified the law in March, 1792. Meetings of protest, however, continued, riots took place, and President Washington was compelled to issue a proclamation (September 5) calling upon all to obey the law. Although the situation was quieter during 1793, the trouble in the following year became so dangerous, after an excise officer had been shot, that the Federal government appointed a commission to meet two hundred delegates from western Pennsylvania at Parkinson's Ferry. No satisfactory result was attained, however, and Washington ordered 15,000 militiamen, under Governor Henry Lee of Virginia, to proceed to the disturbed districts and quell the disturbance. The leaders fled the country. Several hundred prisoners were taken, all of whom were soon afterward pardoned. The real significance of the disturbances, which never acquired the character of an insurrection, was that it was the first instance in which the strength of the new Federal government to maintain domestic tranquillity and enforce laws was put to the test. The promptness with which the resistance was put down won respect for the government and established precedents with regard to its power and duty on similar occasions in the future.

WHISKY RING, THE, in United States history, a secret association of distillers and Federal officials formed, during the administration of President Grant, for the purpose of defrauding the government of the tax imposed on distilled spirits. In 1875, through the active efforts of Benjamin H. Bristow, the secretary of the treasury, the frauds were discovered. On May 10, sixteen distilleries in St. Louis, Milwaukee, and Chicago were seized, and indictments were promptly found against some 240 distillers and revenue officials, the chief clerk in the Treasury Department, and O.E. Babcock, the private secretary and confidential adviser of the President. The trials began in Jefferson City, Mo., in October, 1875, and resulted in the conviction of a treasury agent and a supervisor. Babcock was acquitted in 1876. Most of the other offenders either pleaded guilty or were convicted. The leading defendants who were convicted were pardoned after a short interval. The revelations brought discredit on Grant's administration.

WHISPERING GALLERY, the name given to galleries on the interior of certain domed buildings which from their construction possess a peculiar echo, transmitting sounds with great intensity to distant points. The most noted of such whispering galleries is in the cupola of St. Paul's, London, where a low whisper uttered near one wall may be distinctly heard at the opposite wall 108 feet away.

WHIST, a four-handed game played by four persons, two in partnership against the other two. The origin of the game, like that of most card games, is obscure. Edward Hoyle, the first writer of any celebrity on whist, published his *Short Treatise* in 1742. The evolution of whist into a highly philosophical game took place in the decade following 1860, and was due to the labors of Henry Jones, better known as "Cavendish", James Clay, and William Pole. The first edition of *Cavendish on Whist* appeared in 1862, and two years later Clay produced his *Treatise on Short Whist*.

In America the game is seven points, each trick above six counting one, honors not counting. It is played with the full pack of cards, which are dealt, singly, to four players, beginning at the left, and continuing until all are dealt. The last card is turned up, and becomes the trump. Ace is the highest, and trumps take plain card suits. In straight whist, rubbers are played, the best two games out of three constituting a rubber.

Long whist, a game of ten points in which honors are scored, is now seldom played. Short whist, a game of five points, where honors are scored, is popular in England. Dummy whist is a game played by three persons, the fourth hand, called the dummy, being exposed on the table. Double dummy is played by two persons, each player having a dummy or exposed hand for his partner. In this game there is no misdeal and the laws are the same as for dummy whist. In duplicate whist the deal is played but once by each player, but in order to bring the play of teams, pairs, or individuals into comparison, each hand is played over again. See BRIDGE.

"Harmony in Yellow and Gold," by Whistler
Metropolitan Museum of Art

WHISTLER, JAMES ABBOTT MCNEILL (1834–1903), American painter and etcher, born in Lowell, Mass. He was the son of Major George Washington Whistler, consulting engineer of the St. Petersburg and Moscow Railroad (1800–49). In 1859 he began to exhibit in the London Royal Academy, showing "Two Etchings from Nature", which were followed in 1860 by five dry-point portraits and etchings of Thames subjects and a painting of a mother and child, "At the Piano". Three years later his "Little White Girl" was rejected by the jury of the Paris Salon, but attracted attention in the Salon des Refusés. He exhibited frequently in the Salon, the Academy, the Grosvenor Gallery, and the Society of British Artists, and in 1874 and 1892 he held exhibitions of his paintings in London.

The finest of his oil pictures are "The Artist's Mother", shown in the Royal Academy of 1872, awarded a gold medal in the Salon of 1884, and purchased for the Luxembourg Museum in 1891; the "Portrait of Thomas Carlyle", shown in the artist's exhibition of 1874, and purchased by the Glasgow Corporation in 1891; and the "Portrait of Miss Alexander". As a purely decorative artist he made his reputation by the "Peacock Room", painted in 1877 in Leyland's house at Prince's Gate, London, and by the "Music Room" in Sarasate's residence in Paris. As a dry-point etcher Whistler's eminence was even more widely recognized than as a worker in color.

The eccentricities of Whistler and his quarrels with English artists and critics during his long residence in London from 1859 were, for a long time, better known than his paintings. His central idea was that painting should appeal only to the eye, and that it was not a medium for the expression of ideas or emotions, the subject being absolutely irrelevant. Emphasizing the analogy with music, he called his paintings arrangements, symphonies, nocturnes, and the like, pitching them in one or two related color tones. Especially well known is his quarrel with John Ruskin, who in his *Fors Clavigera* (1877) had given vent to his feelings over one of Whistler's "Nocturnes" in the following language: "I have seen and heard much of cockney impudence before now; but never expected to hear a coxcomb ask 200 guineas for flinging a pot of paint in the public's face." The artist promptly sued for damages, and in the celebrated trial which followed he was awarded one farthing, which coin he triumphantly wore as a watch charm ever afterward. He was no less known for his wit, which usually carried a personal sting, and he left behind a wealth of anecdote.

Whistler retaliated against Ruskin in an amazingly clever and abusive pamphlet, *Whistler vs. Ruskin: Art and Art Critics,* which, along with a notable lecture, *Ten O'Clock,* and occasional letters on art and personal subjects, was published as *The Gentle Art of Making Enemies* (1890). *The Baronet and the Butterfly* (1899) was another philippic.

Few artists had as broad a range of subjects as Whistler. He discovered beauty in all about him, in the squalid quarters of London and in the commonplace of the drawing room as well as in the magic canals of Venice. Although he was a fine draftsman, color was to him the chief factor in painting, and not even Velázquez was a greater master of color values. The most comprehensive collection of Whistler's work was made by Charles L. Freer of Detroit, Mich., who presented it in 1906 to the

National Gallery, Washington, D.C. It contains about fifty paintings, water colors, and etchings.

WHISTON, WILLIAM (1667-1752), clergyman of the Church of England and mathematician, born in Norton, Leicestershire, and educated at Cambridge University. In 1690 he took his degree, and obtained a fellowship in 1691. In 1693 he became chaplain to John Moore, Bishop of Norwich, and in 1698 was presented to the living of Lowestoft, in Suffolk. His *New Theory of the Earth,* a work which earned him a considerable reputation, appeared in 1696. In 1701 he was appointed deputy to Sir Isaac Newton, and in 1703 succeeded him in the Lucasian professorship at Cambridge. In addition to his academic duties he engaged in clerical work, attaining considerable success as a preacher. The development of his theological opinions led him into Arian heresy, and his avowal of his views in his preaching and his writings led, in 1710, to expulsion from his professorship and the university. In 1711 appeared the most noted of his original writings, *An Historical Preface to Primitive Christianity Revived.* His subsequent prosecution in the Church of England courts was dropped after five years of litigation. Whiston remained formally a member of the Church of England until 1747, when he joined the Baptists. He continued to disseminate his religious opinions, and his publications were numerous. He also busied himself with scientific investigations, and he was one of the first persons to perform experiments while lecturing in London. In 1715 he instituted a society in London for promoting primitive Christianity. His translation (1737) of Josephus is the best known of his many works.

WHITAKER, JOSEPH (1820-95), English publisher. From 1856 to 1859 he edited the *Gentleman's Magazine.* He founded the monthly journal *The Bookseller* in 1858, and ten years later put ou the first annual *Whitaker's Almanac. A Reference Catalogue of Current Literature* (1874) was periodically revised and enlarged. With one of his sons, Joseph Vernon Whitaker, he founded the *Stationery Trades Journal* in 1880.

WHITAKER, MILTON (1870-   ), American chemist, born in Frazeysburg, Ohio, and educated at the University of Colorado. In 1903 he became chemist and general superintendent of the Welsbach Company, but resigned in 1911 to accept the professorship of chemical engineering at Columbia University. He served until 1917, when he was made vice-president of the United States Industrial Alcohol Company and president of the United States Industrial Chemical Company. He resigned from both positions in 1927. In 1923 he received the Perkin Medal of the American section of the Society of Chemical Industry for his original work on the chemistry and production of alcohol and its derivatives. From 1911 to 1916 he was editor of the *Journal of Industrial and Engineering Chemistry.*

WHITBY, a seaport and watering place in the North Riding of Yorkshire, England, 40 miles N.E. of York. The old town, anciently called Streoneshalh, contains many picturesque houses and rises in terraces on a cliff. Its summit is crowned by the noble ruins of the Benedictine abbey, founded by St. Hilda about 657, where Cædmon lived and died. In 867 the abbey was burned by the Danes, who renamed the town Whitby (White town). In 1078 it was rebuilt by William de Percy as a monastery. There are shipbuilding and ship-repairing docks, rope and sail-making works, an active import and export trade, and important herring fisheries, and a specialty is the manufacture of jet ornaments from a variety of petrified wood found in the vicinity. Pop., about 12,500.

WHITE, ANDREW DICKSON (1832-1918), American educator, diplomat, and scholar, born in Homer, N.Y. In 1857 he became professor of history and English literature at the University of Michigan. From 1863 to 1867 he served as a member of the New York senate. He became president of Cornell University, which he had helped to found, in 1867, and occupied that position, together with the professorship of history, until 1885. Two years after his resignation he gave to a newly organized Cornell department, called in his honor the President White School of History and Political Science, his historical library, consisting of about 30,000 volumes and 10,000 pamphlets and manuscripts. The university, which received from him grants totaling $300,000, owns a bronze statue of White, done by Karl Bitter. White was minister to Germany (1879-81) and to Russia (1892-94). He served on the commission to investigate the Venezuela-Guiana boundary line (1896). From 1897 until 1902 he was ambassador to Germany, and in 1899 was made chairman of the American delegation to The Hague Peace Conference. He was the first president (1884) of the American Historical Association. His writings include *Autobiography* (1905) and *The Work of Benjamin Hale* (1911).

WHITE, CHARLES ABIATHAR (1826-1910), American geologist, born in North Dighton,

Elwyn Brooks White — Harper & Bros.

Mass. He was State geologist of Iowa from 1866 to 1870, and professor of natural history at the State University of Iowa from 1867 to 1873. From 1873 to 1875 he was professor of natural history at Bowdoin College. He was geologist and paleontologist of the United States Geological Survey between 1874 and 1892, and after 1895 was an associate in paleontology at the United States National Museum. Among his works are *Report on Invertebrate Fossils and Surveys West of the 100th Meridian* (1875) and *The Relation of Biology to Geological Investigation* (1894).

WHITE, EDWARD DOUGLASS (1845–1921), American jurist, born in Lafourche Parish, La., and educated at Mount St. Mary's College, Emmitsburg, Md., Georgetown College (now Georgetown University), and the Jesuit College in New Orleans. He left college to enlist in the Confederate Army, and served as a private during the latter part of the Civil War. At its close he began the study of law in the office of an attorney, and in 1868 was admitted to the Louisiana bar. His rise to distinction in his profession was rapid. Entering politics as a Democrat, he was elected State senator for the term 1874–78. Under appointment of Governor Nichols, he was an associate justice of the Louisiana supreme court from 1878 to 1891. In 1891 he was elected to the United States Senate, but in 1894, after three years' service, he was appointed by President Cleveland an associate justice of the United States Supreme Court. He soon became known as one of the ablest members of the court, and many of his opinions, some of which were delivered without manuscript, were of fundamental importance. In 1910 President Taft appointed him to the chief justiceship. Some of White's important opinions were on the Standard Oil Company and American Tobacco Company cases of 1911. In the latter cases he expounded the famous "rule of reason", a doctrine to be used in interpreting the antitrust laws. Important dissenting opinions were delivered in the Income Tax case of 1894, the Northern Securities case of 1904, and the Bakeshop cases.

WHITE, EDWIN (1817–77), American artist, born in South Hadley, Mass. He became well known as a painter of historical pictures, dealing chiefly with subjects of American history. Among his most celebrated works are "Washington Resigning His Commission" (State House, Annapolis), "The Antiquary" (Metropolitan Museum of Art, New York City), "The Death-bed of Luther", and "The Old Age of Milton".

WHITE, ELWYN BROOKS (1899–   ), American author, born in Mount Vernon, N.Y., and educated at Cornell University. He served in the U.S. Army during World War I, and in 1925 joined the staff of the *New Yorker* magazine, serving successively as writer, contributing editor, and editorial writer. From 1938 to 1943 he was also associated with *Harper's* magazine, for which he conducted a widely read department known as "One Man's Meat". White's work consists mainly of humorous essays and sketches satirizing the complexities and difficulties of modern civilization, and of light verse notable for its wit and perfection of form. After World War II, he became an outspoken and effective advocate for the doctrine of a unified world government and for organizations such as the United Nations which furthered this goal. Among his books are (verse) *The Lady Is Cold* (1929) and *The Fox of Peapack* (1938); (essays) *Quo Vadimus* (1939), *One Man's Meat* (1942, revised 1944), *The Wild Flag* (1946), and *This Is New York* (1949); and (fiction) *Stuart Little* (1945).

WHITE, FRANK (1856–1940), American public official, born in Stillman Valley, Ill. He was elected to the house of representatives of

North Dakota (1891–93) and to the State senate (1893–99). From 1901 to 1905 he was governor of North Dakota. During World War I he was a colonel of infantry (41st Division), serving fourteen months in France. From 1921 to 1928 he was treasurer of the United States.

WHITE, SIR GEORGE STUART (1835–1912), British soldier, born in County Antrim, Ireland. He enlisted in the army in 1853, and was made a captain in 1863 and major in 1873. In 1881 he became lieutenant colonel of the Gordon Highlanders and military secretary to the viceroy of India. During 1884 and 1885 he participated in the Nile expedition. He also took part in Lord Roberts' famous march to Kandahar. From 1893 to 1898 he was commander in chief of the forces in India. Participating in the Boer War, he conducted the defense of Ladysmith, a battle that made him famous. He was promoted to lieutenant general in 1895 and later to general and to field marshal.

WHITE, GILBERT (1720–93), English naturalist, born in Selborne in the county of Hampshire, and educated at Oriel College, Oxford University. He was appointed to a fellowship of his college in 1744, and in 1747 he entered holy orders and was appointed curate of Swarraton in Hampshire. In 1751 he received the curacy of the parish of Selborne and, after several other academic and ecclesiastical appointments, he returned to Selborne as curate in 1784. As a naturalist White was a keen and accurate observer of the various phenomena of nature, rather than a scientific biologist. In 1771 he began work on his book *Natural History and Antiquities of Selborne* (1789), which has become one of the classics of English literature.

WHITE, GLEESON JOSEPH WILLIAM (1851–98), English writer on art, born in Christ Church, Hampshire, and educated at Christ Church School. In 1890 he visited New York City, where he managed the *Art Amateur* (1891–92). Returning to England in 1893, he founded the *Studio,* which he edited for about a year, and to which he contributed up to the time of his death. Among his works are *Practical Designing* (1893), *Salisbury Cathedral* (1896), *English Illustrations in the Sixties* (1897), and *Master Painters of Great Britain* (4 vols., 1897–98). He edited during his last years the "Ex Libris Series"; the "Connoisseur Series"; the "Pageant"; and, with E.T. Strange, Bell's "Cathedral Series". White was also a designer of repute.

WHITE, HENRY (1850–1921), American diplomat, born in Baltimore, Md. He became secretary to the United States legation in Vienna (1883–84), and in London (1884–93). He was secretary to the United States embassy, London (1897–1905). After serving as ambassador to Italy, White was appointed ambassador to France by President Theodore Roosevelt in 1907. He remained in that position until 1909, when his resignation was accepted by President Taft. In 1918 he was appointed by President Wilson to serve on the American Peace Commission, and was one of the signers of the Treaty of Versailles.

WHITE, HORACE (1834–1916), American journalist and financial expert, born in Colebrook, N.H. As a reporter for the Chicago *Tribune,* he accompanied Abraham Lincoln in 1858 on his campaign against Stephen A. Douglas. White's account was later published in Herndon's *Life of Lincoln.* From 1864 to 1874 he was editor in chief and one of the owners of the Chicago *Tribune.* In 1883 he bought an interest in the New York *Evening Post,* in conjunction with Carl Schurz and Edwin L. Godkin, editor in chief. He succeeded Godkin as editor in chief in 1899 and held that position until his retirement in 1903. Widely known for his able discussions of currency and banking problems, he was the author of *Money and Banking* (1895) and *Life of Lyman Trumbull* (1913).

WHITE, HORATIO STEVENS (1852–1934), American educator and editor, born in Syracuse, N.Y. He taught at Cornell University (1876–1902), and then at Harvard University (1902–19), becoming professor emeritus, and in 1926 curator of the Germanic Museum at the latter institution. White was the editor of a number of German textbooks, including *Twentieth Century Series of German Classics*; he also wrote *Fiske's Chess Tales and Miscellanies* (1912) and *Willard Fiske—A Biographical Study* (1925).

WHITE, HUGH LAWSON (1773–1840), American political leader, born in Iredell County, N.C. He was a State senator in 1807, was United States district attorney (1808–09), judge of the Tennessee supreme court (1809–15), president of the Bank of Tennessee (1812–27), and United States senator (1825–40). For a time he was a supporter of President Andrew Jackson, but refused to vote in favor of expunging the resolutions of the Senate censuring the President. In 1838 he was nominated as an independent candidate for the Presidency against Van Buren, but received only 26 electoral votes.

WHITE, ISRAEL C(HARLES) (1848–1927), American geologist, born in Monongalia Co.,

W.Va., and educated at West Virginia University. He was professor of geology at that institution from 1877 to 1892. He resigned to take charge of a large petroleum business. In 1897 he was appointed State geologist of West Virginia. White became recognized as an authority on coal, petroleum, and natural gas. With Edward Orton (q.v.), he developed the anticlinal theory of gas accumulation.

WHITE, JAMES WILLIAM (1850–1916), American surgeon, born in Philadelphia, Pa., and educated at the University of Pennsylvania. He was a member of Louis Agassiz's staff in the Hassler expedition to the West Indies, the Straits of Magellan, and both coasts of South America (1871–72). Settling in Philadelphia, he held several hospital positions in that city, and also was connected with his alma mater successively, until his retirement, as professor of genitourinary surgery, of clinical surgery, and as John Rhea Barton professor of surgery. During the early part of World War I he was connected with the American Ambulance Hospital in Paris. He wrote, with W.W. Keen, *American Textbook of Surgery* (1896) and, with Edward Martin, *Genito-Urinary Surgery* (1897), both standard works.

WHITE, JOSEPH BLANCO (1775–1841), British writer, born in Seville, Spain. He was ordained a priest in 1799, but lost his faith, and in 1810 made his way to England, where he lived the rest of his life. His most important work is the posthumous autobiography, edited by J. Hamilton Thom (3 vols., 1845). He is chiefly remembered, however, for his sonnet *Night and Death,* which first appeared, with a dedication to Coleridge, in the *Bijou* for 1828.

WHITE, PEREGRINE (1620–1704), the first white child born in New England, delivered on the *Mayflower* (q.v.), as it lay at anchor in the harbor of present-day Provincetown, Mass. His mother, who was widowed soon after the birth of her son, shortly remarried and thus gained the distinction of being the first mother and first bride in Plymouth Colony. "In consideration of his birth", White was given 200 acres in Marshfield, Mass.

WHITE, RICHARD GRANT (1821–85), American Shakespearean scholar and linguistic critic, born in New York, and educated at New York University. He was admitted to the bar (1845), became a journalist, and during the Civil War wrote a remarkable series of letters for the London *Spectator,* signed "A Yankee". He was for many years chief of the United States Revenue Marine Bureau in the district of New York. His chief wr··· ..gs are a critical edition of *Shakespeare's Works* (1857–65), *Memoirs of William Shakespeare* (1865), *Studies in Shakespeare* (1885), *Words and Their Uses* (1870), and *Every-Day English* (1881).

WHITE, STANFORD (1853–1906), American architect, son of Richard Grant White, born in New York City. He studied architecture under Charles D. Gambrill and Henry H. Richardson and was chief assistant to the latter in the construction of Trinity Church, Boston. In 1881 he united with Charles F. McKim and William R. Mead to form the architectural firm of McKim, Mead & White. In association with this firm he designed, either wholly or in part, Madison Square Garden, the Washington Arch, the Tiffany Apartments, the library of Columbia University, buildings for New York University, and the Madison Square Presbyterian Church (1906) in New York City; buildings for the University of Virginia; pedestals for a number of statues, including Saint Gaudens' statue of Admiral Farragut, in Madison Square, New York; and numerous private residences. He was murdered in the Madison Square Roof Garden by Harry K. Thaw.

WHITE, STEWART EDWARD (1873–1946), American author, born in Grand Rapids, Mich., and educated at the University of Michigan and at Columbia Law School. His works include *The Westerners* (1901), *The Claim Jumpers* (1901), *Conjurer's House* (1903), *The Forest* (1903), *Blazed Trail Stories* (1904), *The Silent Places* (1904), *The Riverman* (1908), *Gold* (1913), *Gray Dawn* (1915), *The Forty Niners* (1918), *Daniel Boone* (1922), *Back of Beyond* (1927), *Dog Days* (1930), *The Shepper-Newfounder* (1931), *The Long Rifle* (1932), *Ranchero* (1933), and *Wild Geese Calling* (1940).

WHITE, TRUMBULL (1868–1941), American author and editor, born in Winterset, Iowa. After a varied newspaper career with the Decatur (Ill.) *Review,* Evansville (Ind.) *Call,* Chicago *Morning News,* Chicago *Times,* and Chicago *Record,* he undertook a number of investigations of gold fields, industrial conditions in Mexico and Alaska, and similar ventures. He was editor of *The Red Book* (1903–06), *Appleton's Magazine* (1906–09), *Adventure* (1910–11), and *Everybody's* (1911–15). He was also vice-president of Leo L. Redding & Co. from 1919 to 1929. Among his writings are *The Wizard of Wall Street* (1892), *Our War with Spain* (1898), and *Round the World Tours* (1902).

WHITE, WILLIAM ALANSON (1870–1937), American neurologist and alienist, born in Brooklyn, N.Y. For nine years he was an assistant physician at the Binghamton (N.Y.) State Hospital, and after 1903 superintendent of the Government Hospital for the Insane in Washington. In the same year he accepted the post of professor of nervous and mental diseases at Georgetown University, and in 1904 a similar chair at George Washington University. He also lectured at the Army Medical School. He wrote *Mental Mechanisms* (1911) and *Outlines of Psychiatry* (9th ed., rev., 1923), and also did important work in collaboration with Smith Ely Jelliffe (see JELLIFFE, SMITH ELY) on *Diseases of the Nervous System* (1915). Among his many monographs are *Mechanisms of Character Formation* (1916), *The Mental Hygiene of Childhood* (1919), *Insanity and the Criminal Law* (1923), *Essays in Psychopathology* (1925), *The Meaning of Disease* (1926), *The Major Psychoses* (1928), and *William Alanson White; the Autobiography of a Purpose* (1938).

WHITE, WILLIAM ALLEN (1868–1944), American journalist and author, born in Emporia, Kans. After working as a journalist on various newspapers, he became, in 1895, proprietor and editor of the Emporia *Gazette*. Under his guidance, the Gazette won a national reputation for its distinguished editorials and its progressive policy. He was the author of *The Court of Boyville* (1899), *Stratagems and Spoils* (1901), *In Our Town* (1906), *A Certain Rich Man* (1909), *In the Heart of a Fool* (1918), *Life of Woodrow Wilson* (1924), *Life of Calvin Coolidge* (1925), *A Puritan in Babylon* (1938), and *The Changing West* (1939). His writings, for the most part collected stories or sketches, picture life in a midwestern town with penetrating vision and broadly human outlook. During World War I, the American Red Cross sent him to Russia as an observer. In 1940 he founded the Committee to Defend America by Aiding the Allies, which greatly influenced the preparedness measures of the government prior to the Japanese attack on Pearl Harbor.

WHITE, SIR WILLIAM ARTHUR (1824–91), English diplomat, born in Pulawy, Poland. In 1857 he entered the British consular service as clerk to the consul general in Warsaw. In 1864 he was appointed consul in Danzig, and in 1875 was transferred to Belgrade as British agent and consul general. In this capacity he displayed wide knowledge of the Eastern question, and in 1879 was appointed envoy extraordinary and minister plenipotentiary in Bucharest, Romania. In 1886 he was confirmed as envoy extraordinary in Constantinople (now Istanbul). White exerted himself greatly to obtain the acceptance by the Great Powers of the annexation of eastern Rumelia to Bulgaria.

WHITE, WILLIAM HALE (about 1830–1913), English journalist and miscellaneous writer, born in Bedford. He owned his literary eminence to the powerful studies of domestic, social, moral, and theological problems contained in the remarkable trilogy of novels, *The Autobiography of Mark Rutherford* (1881), *Mark Rutherford's Deliverance* (1885), and *The Revolution in Tanner's Lane* (1887).

WHITE, SIR WILLIAM HENRY (1845–1913), English naval constructor, born in Devonport. In 1867 he entered the construction department of the Admiralty, rising to the rank of chief constructor in 1881. From 1870 to 1881 he was professor at the Royal School of Naval Architecture. In 1883 he organized the shipbuilding department of Sir W. Armstrong, Mitchell, and Company, remaining in charge of it for two years, during which time he designed, among other vessels, the warships *Takachiho* (Japanese) and *Charleston* (United States). These vessels were regarded as most important developments in cruiser design and attracted wide attention. In 1885 White returned to the Admiralty as director of naval construction and continued at the head of that department for seventeen years, during which he developed the battleship type which for two decades was adopted in nearly all navies. He retired because of ill-health in 1902, and Parliament made him a special grant in recognition of his services. During his later years he was largely responsible for the adoption of turbine engines in large passenger steamers and fast cruisers. His writings include *A Manual of Naval Architecture* (5th ed., 1900), *Architecture and Public Buildings* (1884), and *A Treatise on Shipbuilding.*

WHITE ANTS, a name often given to termites (q.v.).

WHITEBAIT, the young of the common herring, *Clupea harengus*, and the sprat, *C. sprattus*. It is in great demand in Great Britain as a delicacy, and is also sold in considerable quantity in the United States. The term is also applied to numerous other small food fishes, including young troutlike fishes of New Zealand, and gobies, silversides, and anchovies of fresh and salt waters in the United States.

WHITE BASS, or WHITE PERCH, a striped bass, *Lepibema chrysops,* common in the Great Lakes and upper Mississippi watershed. In color it is silvery, tinged with gold below, and marked with narrow, dusky lines on the sides. It is an excellent food fish. See BASS.

WHITEBOYS, the name given to peasant associations in Ireland, formed after 1760, for the purpose of visiting revenge on landlords, tax collectors, and the clergy. The members committed many outrages on the property and persons of those against whom they entertained grievances. Their depredations took place at night and those engaged in them were disguised by blackened faces and white garments.

WHITE BRETHREN, a sect of the 15th century, that sprang up in the Italian Alps. Their leader claimed to be Elias the prophet. They were clad in white and carried crucifixes from which blood appeared to come. The leader, who appears to have left no name, prophesied the destruction of the world and for a time had great success; but Pope Boniface IX seized the prophet and burned him at the stake, and within a year the sect passed out of existence.

WHITE CAPS, a general name derived from their disguise, for bodies of men in the United States who assume the function of administering punishment for real or fancied offenses against the community. See VIGILANCE COMMITTEE.

WHITECHAPEL, an eastern parliamentary district of metropolitan London, England, originally named from a certain chapel within its limits. In early times all distances east of London were measured from this chapel. It is one of the poorest and most congested districts of the city. It is traversed by Whitechapel Road, and London Hospital and the Tower of London are within its limits.

WHITE COMPANY, THE, a name assumed by various bands of 13th- and 14th-century freebooters. The first was organized and led by Folquet, Bishop of Toulouse, for the purpose of slaughtering heretics in France. A second, commanded by Bertrand Du Guesclin (q.v.), Constable of France, received its name from the white cross worn upon each member's shoulder. In 1366 Du Guesclin led his marauding company into Spain to support Henry of Trastamara against Pedro the Cruel. A third band crossed from France into Italy, and under the banners of Milan and Florence, or as independent freebooters under the command of Sir John Hawkwood, plundered the country until disbanded in 1391.

WHITE ELEPHANT, an infrequent albino type of Asiatic elephant which from its rarity is held to be sacred. Owing to the costly honors paid to such an animal, the term has become proverbial with the meaning of an expensive or unwelcome possession. The "Land of the White Elephant" is Siam.

WHITE ESKIMOS, or BLOND ESKIMOS, the popular name for a group of Eskimos residing on both sides of Coronation Gulf between Canada and Victoria Island, discovered by Stefansson in 1910. The peculiarity giving rise to the name is the frequent occurrence of light hair and gray or blue eyes in contrast to the universal black hair and dark eyes of all New World races. According to Stefansson's data the form of head and face among these blondlike Eskimos inclined toward the European type, upon the basis of which he proposed the theory that the phenomenon was due to early mixture with Norse colonists from Greenland.

WHITE EYE, or SILVER EYE, a large group of small, plainly dressed, titmouselike birds of the genus *Zosterops,* the many species of which are scattered over the tropics of the Old World, especially in the East, where several species are confined to single islands. Nearly all are yellow on the under surface. They are somewhat doubtfully classified with the honey eaters (Meliphagidae), and take their English name from the ring of white glistening feathers around the eye in most species.

WHITEFIELD, GEORGE (1714–70), English evangelist (see EVANGELICAL; EVANGELIST) and organizer of the Calvinistic (see CALVINISM) Methodists (q.v.), born in Gloucester, and educated at Pembroke College, Oxford University. During his undergraduate days Whitefield met John Wesley (q.v.) and his brother Charles, and with them established at Oxford the first Methodist society. In 1736 Whitefield was ordained deacon in the Church of England, and two years later followed the Wesley brothers to the American colony of Georgia. He received the post of minister at Savannah, and performed missionary work among the colonists and the Indians. After four months he returned to England to be ordained as a priest and to raise funds for an orphanage he had founded in Georgia. He began open-air preaching to large crowds, notably at Moorfields, Kensington, and Blackheath. In 1739, having collected over a thousand pounds for his orphanage, he returned to America. The cornerstone of the orphan asylum was laid in March, 1740, the institution being given the name of Bethesda. In the same year, Whitefield preached to large audiences in Savannah, Philadelphia, and Boston.

Because of his association with dissenters (q.v.) and his unconventional manner of preaching and conducting devotional services, Whitefield's relations with the Church of England became strained; about this time, moreover, doctrinal differences caused him to break with the Wesleys. In 1741 Whitefield went to England, where he preached with his customary zeal and eloquence, making excursions into Wales and Scotland. He presided at the first conference of Calvinistic Methodists held at Watford in 1743, and at the second conference a few months later was chosen perpetual moderator in England. From 1744 to 1748 he was once more in America, touring the colonies and drawing enthusiastic crowds with his vigorous eloquence. In 1748 he visited the Bermudas (Bermuda) for his health, and during his stay preached twice each day on the principal islands of the group. On his return to England in the same year he found his congregation scattered. He was then in pecuniary difficulties, having sold most of his property to support the Georgia orphanage. With the aid of friends, however, he gradually discharged his debts. About this time, Selina Hastings (see HASTINGS), Countess of Huntingdon, made Whitefield her chaplain and gave him the opportunity of preaching to various members of the English nobility in her home. She also built and endowed chapels to maintain his doctrines.

In 1751 Whitefield visited Ireland and Scotland and made a fourth voyage to America. On his return to London, he devoted himself to the establishment of a new tabernacle, which was opened on June 10, 1753. Soon thereafter, he undertook another evangelistic tour of England, traveling twelve hundred miles and preaching in many towns and hamlets. In 1754-55 he was again in America; in September, 1756, he opened a new chapel at Tottenham Court Road, London; and from 1763 to 1765 he visited America for the sixth time. By this time his health was failing and his power of preaching seriously impaired. Nevertheless, he dedicated the Countess of Huntingdon's chapel at Bath in October, 1765, opened her college at Trevecca, Wales, in August, 1768, and dedicated the chapel at Tunbridge Wells in July, 1769. Several months later, Whitefield sailed for the seventh time to America. On September 29, 1770, after preaching a two-hour sermon at Exeter, New Hampshire, he proceeded to Newburyport, Massachusetts, where he died the following morning.

Whitefield is said to have preached more than 18,000 sermons. It is believed that the extraordinary influence he exercised during his lifetime was due to the manner of his delivery rather than to the matter of his discourses, since his writings do not sustain the impression derived from contemporary accounts of his preaching. A number of his sermons and journals were collected and published in six volumes (London, 1771-72).

WHITEFISH, one of the many important fishes of the genus *Coregonus,* of the Salmon family, of which about fifteen species inhabit the lakes and streams of northern Europe, Asia, and America. The most familiar species is the common whitefish, *C. clupeiformis,* which exists throughout the Great Lakes and adjacent waters, and is the most important fresh-water fish in America. Whitefish reach a weight of 20 pounds in rare cases, the average weight being about 4 pounds. They remain in deep water for the most part, but during the spawning season, which is in autumn, and at certain other times, for purposes which are not yet clear, they migrate to shallower water in great shoals. They live mainly on small crustaceans, mollusks, insects, and larvae.

WHITE-FOOTED MOUSE, or DEER MOUSE, common name applied to a wild mouse, *Peromyscus leucopus,* native to wooded areas of E. United States; see MOUSE.

WHITEFRIARS, a region in London, near Fleet Street, in which a monastery of the Carmelites dating from the 13th century formerly stood. Until the end of the 17th century it formed a place of sanctuary for debtors and criminals. See ALSATIA.

WHITEHALL, a building, formerly a palace in London, once the residence of the Norman noble Hubert de Burgh; it was later the residence (13th century) of the archbishops of York, and was known as York Palace. After the death of Archbishop Thomas Wolsey (q.v.), it became crown property, and was called Whitehall. After a fire in 1615, King James I planned to replace it from designs by the English architect and stage designer Inigo Jones, who conceived an enormous structure with seven courts. Only the banqueting hall was built, the earliest specimen of Palladian architecture in England. The hall proper has ceiling paintings by the Flemish

Alfred North Whitehead — Macmillan

painter Peter Paul Rubens representing the apotheosis of James I and scenes from the career of King Charles I. The older parts of the palace were burned in 1691 and 1697. Whitehall was the scene of Wolsey's disgrace, Henry VIII's death, the execution of Charles I, and the deaths of Oliver Cromwell and Charles II. The hall now serves as a military and naval museum. The street leading from Trafalgar Square to Westminster is also known as Whitehall. It contains a number of public buildings, including the Horse Guards, Treasury, and public offices.

WHITE HALL, a city in Greene Co., Ill., situated 66 miles N.N.W. of St. Louis, Mo. It contains flour mills, machine shops, a milk-condensing plant, and manufactories of sewer pipe, drain, tile, and stoneware. Pop. (1940) 3025.

WHITEHALL, a village in Washington Co., N.Y., situated 78 miles N. of Albany, at the head of Lake Champlain. It has large lumber interests, and is engaged in the manufacture of silk. There are also boat and engine shops and several smaller industrial establishments. Pop. (1940) 4851.

An American garrison was stationed in Whitehall from 1776 until the approach of a British army under General John Burgoyne (q.v.), when the fort was blown up and the houses and mills were burned to prevent their falling into the hands of the enemy. In the War of 1812 the fort and blockhouse were rebuilt. The Champlain Canal was built from Whitehall to Fort Edward in 1819 and completed to Troy in 1824.

WHITEHAVEN, a municipal borough and seaport of Cumberland, England, situated 38 miles s.w. of Carlisle. In the neighborhood are extensive collieries, iron and brass foundries, iron-smelting works, and manufactures of cordage, sail cloth, and earthenware. The town was founded in 1633. Pop., about 21,000.

WHITEHEAD, ALFRED NORTH (1861–1947), English philosopher and mathematician, born at Ramsgate on the Isle of Thanet, Kent, and educated at Trinity College, Cambridge University. In 1885 he was awarded a fellowship at Trinity College, and from 1914 to 1924 he was professor and dean of the faculty at the Imperial College of Science and Technology in Kensington. In 1924, he became professor of philosophy at Harvard University, becoming professor emeritus in 1936. During his stay at Trinity he met Bertrand Russell, a pupil of his who later became a collaborator. After the publication of Whitehead's *Treatise of Universal Algebra* (1898) and Russell's *Principles of Mathematics* (1903), the two men combined their efforts, and over a period of eight or nine years wrote the famous *Principia Mathematica* (3 vols., 1910–13), a revolutionary treatise on mathematical theory, which established the foundations of mathematics in symbolic logic.

Whitehead, in addition to being noted as coauthor of *Principia Mathematica*, is well known for his philosophical interpretations of the discoveries of modern science, including an alternative rendering of the theory of relativity. He was fellow of the Royal Society, president of the Mathematical Association, and fellow of the British Academy. Among his works are *Principles of Natural Knowledge* (1919), *The Concept of Nature* (1920), *Science and the Modern World* (1925), *Religion in the Making* (1926), *The Aims of Education* (1929), *Adventures of Ideas* (1933), *Modes of Thought* (1938), and *Essays in Science and Philosophy* (1947).

WHITEHEAD, JOHN (1740?–1804), English Wesleyan clergyman and physician, born in London, and educated as a physician. He became a Methodist preacher in 1764, was chief physician to both John and Charles Wesley in their last illnesses, and preached

The White House, residence of the President of the United States, in Washington, D.C.

the funeral sermon of John Wesley. With Bishop Coke and Henry More, he was John Wesley's literary executor. A long dispute with the other executors as to the possession of the Wesley papers led to his expulsion from membership in the church. He retained the papers, however, and published the *Lives of John and Charles Wesley* (1793). In 1797 he returned the papers and was reinstated in his position in the church.

WHITEHEAD, JOHN BOSWELL (1872–   ), American electrical engineer, born in Norfolk, Virginia, and educated at Johns Hopkins University. From 1893 to 1897 he was associated with electric manufacturing and power companies. In 1897 he was appointed instructor in applied electricity at Johns Hopkins, becoming professor in 1910 and serving as dean from 1919 to 1938. He was appointed director of the school of engineering in 1938 and served until 1942, when he became professor emeritus. He is noted for his original research on such subjects as the magnetic effect of electric displacement, the operation of a single-phase railway system, submarine detection, and high voltage insulation. He was member of the National Academy of Sciences, and in 1933–34 he was president of the American Institute of Electrical Engineers. His works include *Electric Operation of Steam Railways* (1909), *Dielectric Theory and Insulation* (1927), and *Electricity and Magnetism* (1939).

WHITEHEAD, WILLIAM (1715–85), English poet laureate, born in Cambridge. For many years he lived in the households of the Earl of Jersey and the Earl of Harcourt, with whose sons he made a Continental tour (1754–56). He was appointed secretary and registrar of the Order of the Bath, and in 1758 he succeeded the English poet Colley Cibber in the poet-laureateship. He died in London. Whitehead's best work is to be found in his verse tales after the manner of the French writer of fables Jean de La Fontaine. He also composed two tragedies, *The Roman Father* (1750) and *Creusa, Queen of Athens* (1754); a comedy, *The School for Lovers* (1762); and a farce, *The Trip to Scotland* (1770).

WHITEHILL, CLARENCE EUGENE (1871–1932), American baritone, born in Marengo, Iowa, and trained in Paris. He made his operatic debut in Brussels (1900). After several years in Paris and Cologne, he joined the Metropolitan Opera Company in New York, and appeared with that company from 1909 to 1932. Whitehill was one of the leading singers in the German opera at the Metropolitan, having studied roles in the operas of the German composer Richard Wagner under Cosima Wagner, widow of the composer.

WHITE HOUSE, the official residence of the President of the United States, situated in Washington, D.C. The building is a two-story white freestone edifice, painted white, 170 by 86 feet, of dignified appearance, with an Ionic portico. It contains the private apartments of the President on the second floor and reception rooms on the first floor. Among the latter are the famous East Room, 80 by 40 feet, used for public receptions; the Blue Room, used for diplomatic and social functions; and the Red and Green rooms. The original executive mansion was begun in 1792 and first occupied by President John Adams in 1800. It was burned by the British in 1814, and rebuilt in 1818. In 1903 the pressure of space was relieved by the erection of executive offices on the grounds, connected with the main building. The White House is surrounded by an attractive park, in which the Marine Band plays during the summer. On occasions such as this, parts of the grounds are open to the public.

WHITE ISLAND, island to the E. of Northeast Land, Spitsbergen, in lat. 80°10′ N., long. 30°32′ E. It was discovered in 1707 by a Dutch whaler, Cornelis Giles, or Gillis. Occasionally seen, it was never visited until its exploration in 1898 by A.G. Nothorst. Its name is derived from the fact that it is almost entirely ice-capped.

WHITE LEG, or MILK LEG, technically *phlegmasia dolens,* an ailment of women, usually soon after parturition. It involves swelling of the leg, hardness, whiteness of the skin, caused by an accumulation of serum in the subcutaneous tissues, from thrombosis of the large veins.

WHITELOCKE, BULSTRODE (1605–75), English lawyer and statesman, born in London, and educated at St. John's College, Oxford. He read law in the temple, and in 1626 was called to the bar and elected member of Parliament for Stafford. In 1640 he was elected to the Long Parliament from Marlow, and, as chairman of the Impeachment Committee, conducted the prosecution of the Earl of Strafford. He was also one of the Oxford commissioners appointed to negotiate with Charles I, Commissioner of the Great Seal (1649), and ambassador to Sweden (1653). He refused to take part in the trial of Charles I. In 1656 he was speaker of the House of Commons; was one of Cromwell's lords, and after Cromwell's death Commissioner of the Great Seal to Richard Cromwell. His works include *Memorials of the English Affairs from the Beginning of the Reign of King Charles I to the Happy Restoration of King Charles II* (1682), *Journal of the Swedish Embassy in 1653 and 1654* (1772), and *Memorials of the English Affairs from the Supposed Expedition of Brute to this Island to the End of the Reign of James I.*

WHITEMAN, PAUL (1891–), American conductor, born in Denver, Colo. He was one of the first to organize and develop jazz (q.v.) music by systematic orchestration, and was well known as a conductor of large orchestras of that type. He made transcontinental and European tours with his own "symphonic jazz orchestra". Whiteman wrote *Jazz* (1926).

WHITE MOUNTAIN BUTTERFLY, a delicate, brownish, satyrine butterfly, *Oeneis semidea,* which occupies a very restricted range above 5000 feet elevation in the White Mountains of New Hampshire, most abundantly about half a mile from the summit of Mount Washington. It also occurs in the Rocky Mountains of Colorado, and some of its varieties or close relatives in Alaska and on Mount Katahdin, Me. A closely allied butterfly, *O. aello,* occurs in the Alps in Switzerland.

WHITE MOUNTAINS, a rugged group of monadnocks occupying the north central part of New Hampshire, where they cover an area of about 1300 sq.m. They belong to the older or crystalline belt of the Appalachian system. The group is divided into two main portions by a defile known as the Crawford Notch, the valley of the Saco River. West of this notch the principal group is called the Franconia Mountains, the highest point of which, Mount Lafayette, has an altitude of 5269 ft. above sea level. The highest peaks rise to the east of the notch in the Presidential Range, so called because its chief summits are named after Presidents of the United States. The culminating peak is Mount Washington, 6293 feet high. Other summits with their altitudes are Mount Adams, 5805 feet; Mount Jefferson, 5725 feet; Mount Clay, 5554 feet; Boot Spur, 5520 feet; Mount Monroe, 5390 feet; and Mount Madison, 5380 feet. The White Mountains are composed largely of igneous rocks and are bordered on the eastern side by Carboniferous sediments.

WHITE NILE. See NILE.

WHITE PLAINS, county seat of Westchester Co., N.Y., situated on the Bronx R., 23 miles N.N.E. of the heart of New York City, between the Hudson R. and Long Island Sound. It is a residential suburb of New York City and an important retail shopping center. Transportation facilities include a railroad and three major parkways. White Plains is the site of Good Counsel College (Roman Catholic), a college for women established in

1923. Among the notable buildings in the city are the Elijah Miller House, headquarters of General George Washington after the Battle of White Plains (see WHITE PLAINS, BATTLE OF); the County Courthouse; the County Office Building; the Westchester County Center, an auditorium seating 5000 persons; and the buildings of the White Plains Medical Center, constructed at a cost of $1,200,000. In the vicinity of the city is the Kensico Dam, a part of New York City's water-supply system. White Plains is of considerable historic interest. It was founded by a group of Connecticut Puritans in 1683. It became the county seat in 1759, and was incorporated as a village in 1866 and as a city in 1916. A Provincial Congress met at White Plains on July 10, 1776, declared New York a State, and began the drafting of its first constitution. Pop. (1950) 43,501.

WHITE PLAINS, BATTLE OF, a battle fought on October 28, 1776, during the American Revolution. As a result of the battle, General George Washington retrieved to some extent the defeat of his forces in the Long Island campaign. The British attack was directed on Chatterton Hill, an outlying American post, the defenders of which retreated in good order on the main body. Washington thereafter took post in an unassailable position at North Castle, thus depriving the British general, Sir William Howe, of the fruits of victory. In the battle the British lost 229 men, and the Americans 140.

WHITE RIVER, a river of Arkansas. It rises about 50 miles s. of the Arkansas-Missouri line, flows N. into Missouri, then turns S.E. and continues to the S.E. corner of Arkansas County, Ark., where the channel divides, one stream entering the Arkansas River and the other the Mississippi. The river is about 400 miles long.

WHITE RIVER, the chief tributary of the Wabash River in Indiana. It is formed by the confluence of the east and west branches and has a total length of 350 miles. The river is navigable only to Martinsville, some distance below Indianapolis, and on the east fork to Rockford.

WHITE RIVER, a tributary of the Missouri River. It rises in N.W. Nebraska, and after a course through South Dakota, empties into the Missouri near Oacoma. It flows through the Bad Lands. The length of the river is 325 miles.

WHITE RUSSIA, one of the sixteen constituent republics of the Union of Socialist Soviet Republics (q.v.). White Russia has an area of 49,022 sq.m. and a population of about 5,568,000. Following the Russo-German attack on Poland (see WORLD WAR II) in September, 1939, the White Russian provinces of Poland, comprising an area of 34,749 sq.m. and a population of over 4,000,000, were added to the republic. The capital is Minsk.

WHITE SEA, a large arm of the Arctic Ocean extending southwestward into N. U.S.S.R. The principal rivers entering the White Sea are the Dvina, the Mezen, and the Onega. The volume of trade and navigation is considerable. By means of canals connecting the Dvina with the Volga River and the latter with the Dnieper River, a continuous waterway is established between the White Sea and the Caspian and Black Seas.

WHITESIDE, JAMES (1804–76), Irish judge, born in Delgany, County Wicklow. He distinguished himself in the defense of the Irish revolutionists Daniel O'Connell (q.v.) in 1843 and William Smith O'Brien (q.v.) in 1848, and in the Yelverton case in 1861. Elected a Conservative member of Parliament in 1851, Whiteside represented Dublin University, 1859–66; he became solicitor general for Ireland in 1852, and held the attorney generalship, 1858–66. In the latter year he was appointed chief justice of the Queen's Bench in Ireland. Whiteside was author of *Italy in the Nineteenth Century* (3 vols., 1848) and *Early Sketches of Eminent Persons* (1870).

WHITESIDE, WALKER (1869–1942), American actor, born in Logansport, Ind. He attained prominence on the American stage through his portrayal of Shakespearean and classical roles. He also appeared in such plays as *The Melting Pot, Mr. Wu, The Master of Ballantrae,* and *The Hindu.*

WHITE SLAVERY, in law, a term used to designate the procurement (see PROCURER) of women for immoral purposes and the enforced service of the prostitute (see PROSTITUTION) for the profit of her procurer. In the United States, foreign and interstate traffic in women is punishable under the provisions of the White Slave Traffic Act of 1910, popularly known as the Mann Act; under the provisions of the Mann Act interstate transportation of women and girls for immoral purposes is a criminal offense. Investigation of violations of the Mann Act is under the jurisdiction of the Federal Bureau of Investigation; in a recent year violations of the Mann Act resulted in nearly 400 convictions, with sentences totaling over 1000 years, and fines amounting to nearly $25,000.

Various attempts have been made to eradicate international traffic in women. In 1875 the English social reformer Josephine Butler called a meeting of social workers and social scientists in Geneva, Switzerland, to consider the international aspects of the white-slave traffic and the feasibility of state regulation; as a result of this meeting the International Federation for the Abolition of State Regulation of Vice, devoted to complete suppression as opposed to governmental regulation of prostitution, was formed. A more important agency, the Congress for the Suppression of the White Slave Traffic, was organized in London in 1899, and included representatives of all the major European powers. The Congress maintains an International Bureau and various national committees; it held congresses in Frankfort in 1902, in Paris in 1906, in Madrid in 1910, and in London in 1913. The first congress formulated an international treaty designed for the suppression of the commerce in women, which was signed in 1904 by France, Germany, Great Britain, Italy, Russia, Sweden, Denmark, Belgium, Holland, Spain, Portugal, Norway, and Switzerland. In 1908 the United States signed this treaty. All the signatory states agreed to police ports and railway stations in order to identify and trace participants in the white-slave traffic; to protect and provide for the support of identified victims of the traffic; to arrange for their repatriation; and, if repatriation was impossible or undesirable, to maintain or supervise registry offices and employment agencies to place these women and girls in legitimate occupations.

In subsequent international agreements, the earliest of which were contained in an international convention signed in Paris in 1910, the same powers pledged themselves to more stringent measures. One of the most important of these agreements provided for the punishment of procurers of women and girls in whatever country their illegal acts had been committed, and for the enactment of legislation facilitating extradition proceedings in such cases.

In 1921 the League of Nations, which had been given authority to supervise execution of all existing agreements respecting the white-slave traffic, held an international conference in Geneva attended by representatives of thirty-four nations. Among the results of this conference was the conclusion of additional agreements designed to further effective control of the traffic. Extradition agreements were extended to provide for rapid voluntary extradition between any two countries which had not made a compulsory extradition agreement. The minimum age below which a woman was considered illegally procured even with her consent was fixed at twenty-one years. Punishment was provided for persons associated with or attempting to engage in the traffic as well as for actual procurers. Agreements relating to girls were broadened to apply to children of either sex. The conference also established an advisory committee which subsequently made extensive investigations of white-slave traffic; a report prepared by its committee of experts was published in 1927. The report recommended international co-operation to eradicate the traffic, more severe penalties for procurers, and the elimination of licensed brothels. The supervisory authority of the League was renewed and broadened in 1933.

With the dissolution in 1946 of the League of Nations, the powers vested in it with respect to the white-slave traffic were transferred to the United Nations. In 1946 the Economic and Social Council of the United Nations began a survey of existing conditions in the traffic throughout the world. Plans for carrying on the work of the League of Nations were considered, and the transfer of functions was approved by the U.N. General Assembly in 1947. In the same year a new advisory group of experts was formed to revise and co-ordinate international agreements and conventions for the suppression of the white-slave traffic. The recommendations of this committee were incorporated in a document unifying all the existing agreements mentioned above; this document was approved and adopted as a binding international agreement by the General Assembly in December, 1949.

WHITE SLAVE TRAFFIC. See WHITE SLAVERY.

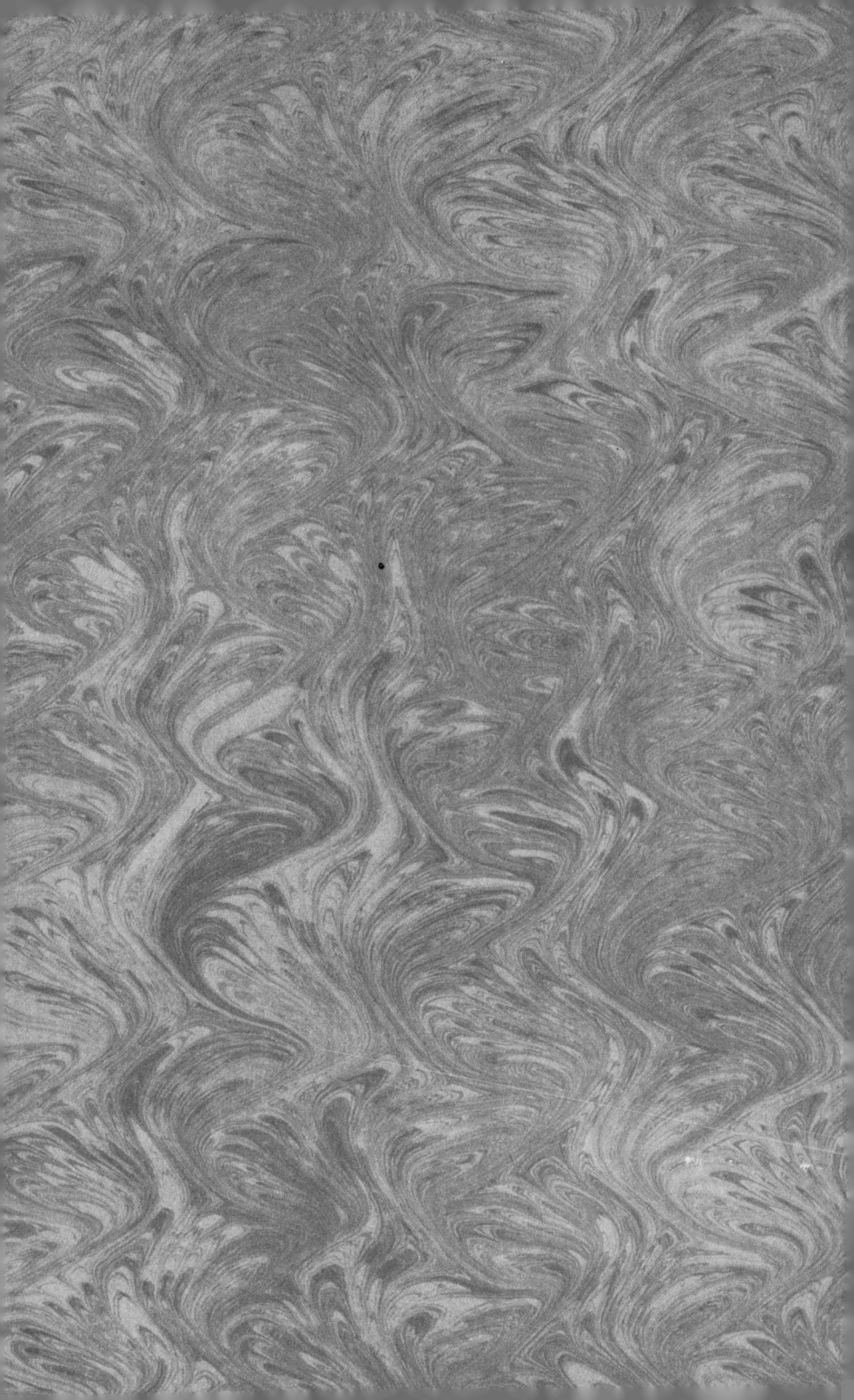